Scripts
Kurt Busiek
w/ Peter David

Pencils
Mark Bagley,
Mike Deodato Jr. &
Sal Buscema
w/ Bob McLeod, Tom Grummet, Ron Randall, Gene Colan, Darick Robertson, George Perez & Chris Marrinan

Inks
Vince Russell,
Tom Wegryzyn & Dick Giordano
w/ Al Milgrom, Will Blyberg, Scott Koblish, Jim Sanders, Tom Palmer, Bruce Patterson, Karl Kesel & Andrew Pepoy

Lettering
Dave Lanphear **w/ Janice Chiang**

Coloring
Joe Rosas, Tom Smith
& Glynis Oliver

Original Editors
Tom Brevoort
& Bobbie Chase

JUSTICE, LIKE LIGHTNING...

THUNDERB⚡LTS

chapter 1
Justice...Like Lightning!

chapter 2
Introducing the Thunderbolts!

chapter 3
The Dawn of a New Age of Heroes!

chapter 4
Deceiving Appearances

chapter 5
Old Scores

chapter 6
Too Many Masters!

chapter 7
A Shock to the System!

chapter 8
The Origin of the Thunderbolts

Mikhail Bortnik
Book Design

Jessica Schwartz
Production Assistant

Matty Ryan
Assistant Editor

Ben Abernathy
Collections Editor

Bernadette Thomas
Manufacturing Manager

Bob Greenberger
Director: Publishing Operations

Joe Quesada
Editor in Chief

Bill Jemas
President

Special thanks to "Intern Extraordinaire" Cory Sedlmeier

THUNDERBOLTS®: JUSTICE LIKE LIGHTNING Contains material originally published in magazine form as THUNDERBOLTS: Vol. 1, #'s 1-4, THUNDERBOLTS 1997 ANNUAL, INCREDIBLE HULK #449, TALES OF THE MARVEL UNIVERSE and SPIDER-MAN TEAM-UP FEATURING...#7. Published by MARVEL COMICS, a division of MARVEL ENTERPRISES, INC. Lou Gioia, Executive Vice-President, Publishing; Bob Greenberger, Director Publishing Operations; Stan Lee, Chairman Emeritus. OFFICE OF PUBLICATION: 10 EAST 40TH STREET, NEW YORK, N.Y. 10016. Copyright © 1996, 1997 and 2001 Marvel Characters, Inc. All rights reserved. No similarity between any of the names, characters, persons, and/or institutions in this magazine with those of any living or dead person or institution is intended, and any such similarity which may exist is purely coincidental. THUNDERBOLTS: JUSTICE LIKE LIGHTNING (including all prominent characters featured in this issue and the distinctive likenesses thereof) is a trademark of MARVEL CHARACTERS, INC. No part of this book may be printed or reproduced in any manner without the written permission of the publisher. Printed in Hong Kong. First Printing, December, 2001. ISBN: 0-7851-0817-3. GST #R127032852. MARVEL COMICS is a division of MARVEL ENTERPRISES, INC. Peter Cuneo, Chief Executive Officer; Avi Arad, Chief Creative Officer.

10 9 8 7 6 5 4 3 2 1

"The trickiest part of the whole thing was maintaining the surprise."

Not that we're doing so any more. The cover of this trade paperback, plus the text on the back, the catalog descriptions and most of the stories within, blab the secret right out there for any to see, so if you weren't around when *Thunderbolts* launched, you probably missed out on it being a surprise. But it wasn't easy, I'll tell you that.

At this point, let me drop back a little and explain how this series came to be. I went into it in more detail in the intro to the *Thunderbolts: Marvel's Most Wanted* trade paperback, but just to go over the basics:

It was just before *Onslaught*, which wiped out the Fantastic Four and (many of) the Avengers, and sent them off to another dimension for a year. Marvel was having a creators' summit, gathering together a mess of writers and artists to talk about what might happen in the main Marvel Universe, with so many heroes gone.

I noted that the missing heroes, for the most part, were the daylight heroes, the well-loved heroes, the heroes that made Marvel's citizens feel safe. Much of what was left included shadowy heroes like Spider-Man and Daredevil, feared outsiders like the X-Men, troubling creatures like the Ghost Rider and a more-savage-than-usual Hulk. The ordinary people of the Marvel Universe would be terrified, it seemed to me, and desperate for some sign of hope.

So what would happen, I asked editor Tom Brevoort, if a new group of heroes emerged – a group of bold, noble, reassuring heroes that made people feel safe in their beds? What would happen if they were embraced by the public, lionized as the successors to the much-mourned Avengers and Fantastic Four – but, as it turned out, they weren't heroes at all, but longtime Avengers enemies, the Masters of Evil in disguise, pulling the wool over the public's eyes as part of a scheme to take over the world?

And that question, I added, wouldn't just be about what happened to the world. What would it do to the villains themselves, many of them frustrated by years of defeat and humiliation, to suddenly be loved, to be celebrities, trusted and respected by the people who used to despise them? What would happen when it came time to unveil their plans, and revert to their criminal personas – would they want to do it? Or would they want to stay heroes, and keep their new-found fame?

By the time the summit ended, we had a green light from editor in chief Bob Harras for a new ongoing series. We lined up an artist – the versatile and inventive Mark Bagley – assembled a cast, supplied them with cover identities, and got rolling.

Now all we had to do was keep it a surprise.

After all, we had to be able to promote the new book – heck, we had to be able to *describe* it – and the single most distinctive thing about the series was something we couldn't tell anyone, not if we wanted the first-issue finale to work as a revelation. So we decided to just sell the cover story – these were new heroes who stepped up to the plate in the wake of Onslaught – and merely hint that they might have a "dark secret."

It wasn't easy, though. The people in promotion naturally wanted to sell the most copies, and being told they couldn't tell people what the book was about didn't sit well with them. And editors who weren't involved with the book, but who liked the idea, described it in interviews, not knowing that it was supposed to remain a secret. Luckily, the reporters involved immediately called us for confirmation, and we bribed them with exclusive interviews to shut up – the free press in action. We even had a near-disaster when the catalog was written, since the T-Bolts first appeared in *Incredible Hulk* #449, edited out of an office that didn't know it was supposed to be a secret – so the initial solicitation read something like, "The Hulk runs afoul of the Thunderbolts, a group of super-villains pretending to be superheroes." Luckily, Peter David, writer of *Hulk* at that point, caught it and squelched it for us.

And as we got closer to the series debut, the sales folks got more and more worried about making sure people actually bought the book, since they were essentially promoting a generic super-team made up of characters no one had ever heard of. So they started leaking out clues, and people here and there started figuring it out...

And Tom, Mark and I were getting worried ourselves – were we killing the long-term sales of the book in hopes of maintaining the first-issue surprise? Should we tell people? Did it matter? Were we getting too paranoid about nothing?

Luckily, it all worked out. The leaks came too late to reach many people. The first issue came out, and hit an audience that had no idea what was coming.

And the surprise worked like a charm.

After #1 came out, all we heard were astonished reactions, amazement from people who'd picked up *T-Bolts* #1, expecting another super-team, some worthy but undistinguished temporary replacements for the *real* Marvel heroes – and they'd been completely suckered by the ending. And any disadvantage we might have had in promoting the book ahead of time was more than made up for in word-of-mouth recommendations from delighted readers. Comics fans were telling their friends to get the comic, and to get it *now* – and refusing to tell them why.

The book sold out, and we had to go back to press with an extra printing of #1. Then that *second* printing sold out, and we did a quickie collection of #1 and #2 to keep up with the demand.

And I must admit to an ongoing satisfaction, on two fronts:

First, more and more comics creators, publishers and promotion folks have begun to see the value in keeping secrets – in letting readers discover the surprises by *reading* the comics, rather than telling them about it beforehand in the name of boosting sales.

And second, *Thunderbolts*, a book that launched during a very difficult period for comics, when new books rarely survived – and indeed, all the books it launched with are gone now – is still around, and still doing healthily. We heard from people who figured it wouldn't last more than a year when they thought it was just about replacement heroes, before the secret was out. And then we heard from the people who thought the secret was an interesting twist – but it wouldn't last eight issues, because there just wasn't enough material to be had from the concept.

And then they started saying it wouldn't last past 12 issues. And then that it wouldn't last past 18 issues. And then 25 issues. And once we passed #30, they stopped predicting our doom.

And now *T-Bolts* has passed #50, and has spawned a *Captain America/Citizen V* special, a *T-Bolts: Life Sentences* one-shot, and a *Citizen V and the V-Battalion* limited series — and a second *Citizen V* limited series is presently in the works.

And that, I have to attribute to there being more to Thunderbolts than that first surprise. The characters, created originally by Stan Lee, Jack Kirby, Don Heck, Carl Burgos, Roy Thomas, Tony Isabella, Sal Buscema, Roger Stern, Ralph Macchio, Mark Gruenwald and John Byrne, had what it took to be interesting and involving as we delved into their motivations and how they'd react to their new situation. The paces Tom, Mark and I put them through got readers hooked, and kept them reading, even after the T-Bolts set off in new directions. Fabian Nicieza and Patrick Zircher took over from Mark and me, and brought their own surprises and insights to the book. And most of all, the audience never stopped supporting us, never decided they'd had enough.

That's the best kind of reaction comics creators can get.

So with my thanks to Tom, Mark, Peter, Sal and everyone else whose hard work went into making these stories what they are, and to everyone who's read and appreciated them so far, here it is – the dawn of the Thunderbolts. If you're a T-Bolts fan filling in your collection, you probably already like the team. If you're a newcomer, you at least know their "dark secret." Either way, you'll have to take our word for it that the end of #1 made a big splash, and provided this book with a better kickoff than we could have hoped for. But don't worry too much about it. After all ... there's plenty more in here to make it worth your while.

Enjoy.

Kurt Busiek
August 2001

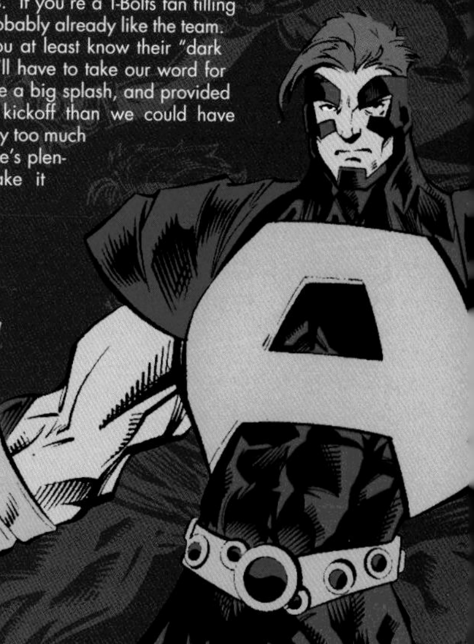

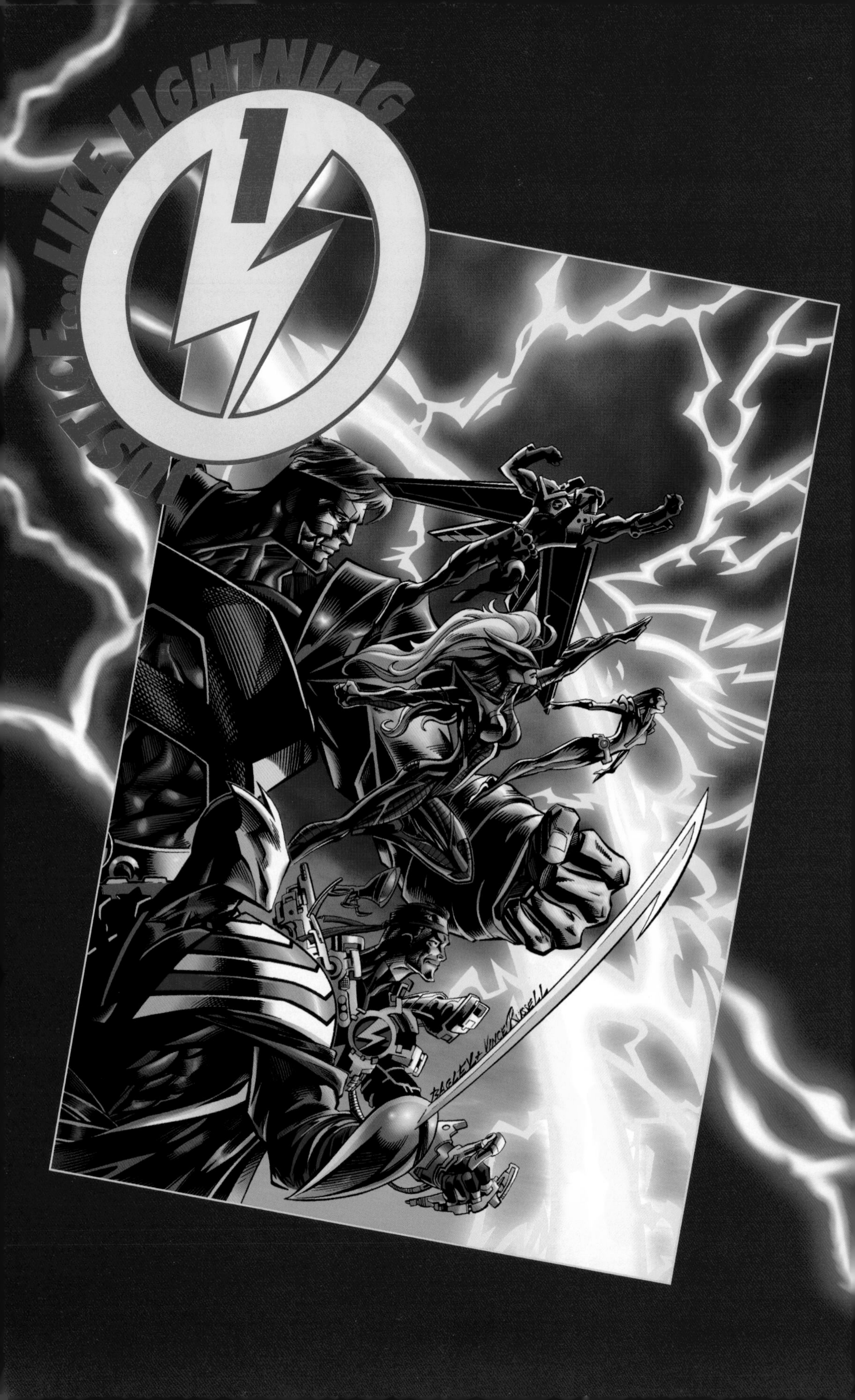
JUSTICE...LIKE LIGHTNING
BAGLEY + VINCE RUSSELL

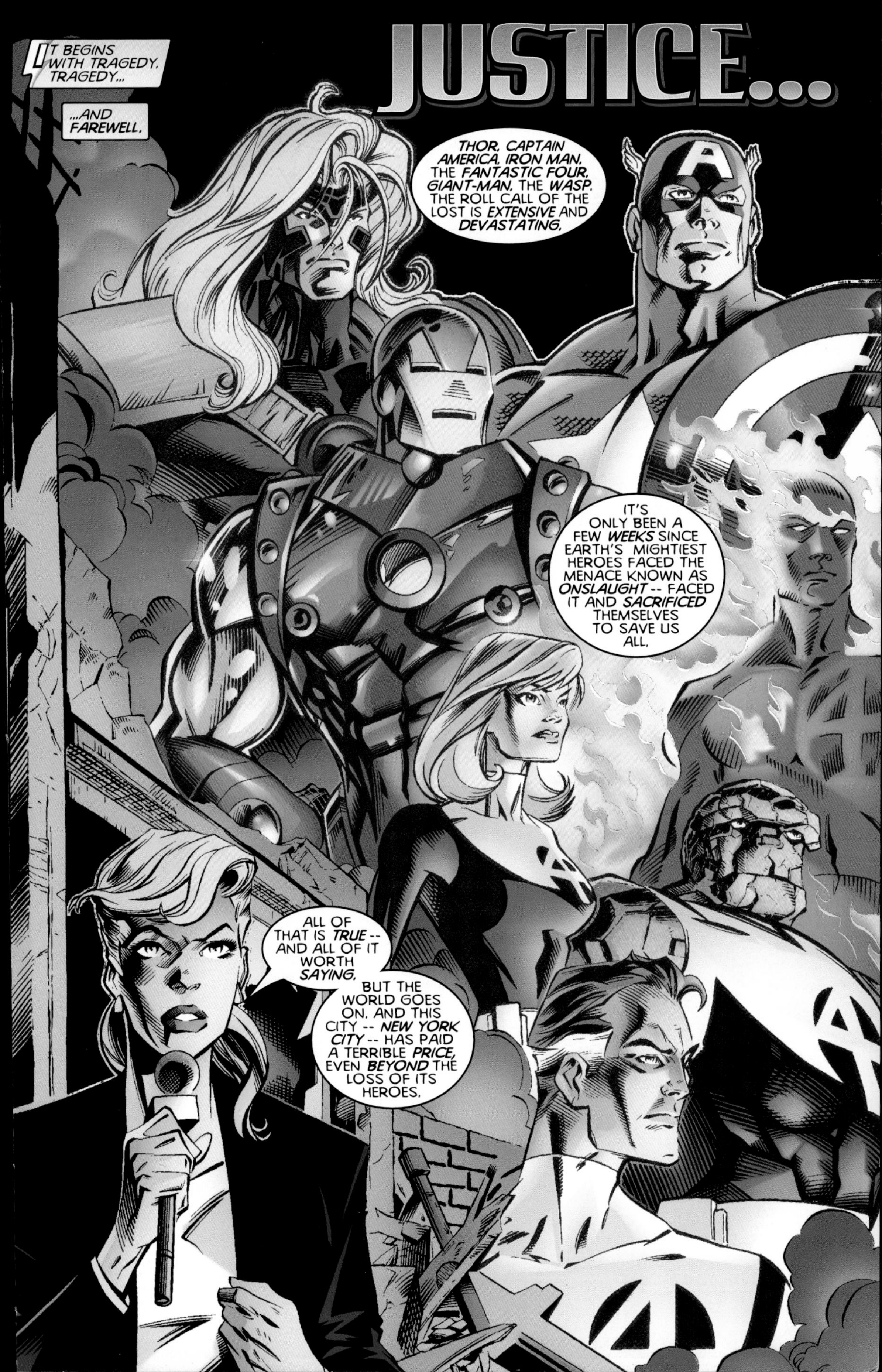

JUSTICE...
IT BEGINS WITH TRAGEDY. TRAGEDY...
...AND FAREWELL.
THOR, CAPTAIN AMERICA, IRON MAN, THE FANTASTIC FOUR, GIANT-MAN, THE WASP. THE ROLL CALL OF THE LOST IS EXTENSIVE AND DEVASTATING.
IT'S ONLY BEEN A FEW WEEKS SINCE EARTH'S MIGHTIEST HEROES FACED THE MENACE KNOWN AS ONSLAUGHT -- FACED IT AND SACRIFICED THEMSELVES TO SAVE US ALL.
ALL OF THAT IS TRUE -- AND ALL OF IT WORTH SAYING.
BUT THE WORLD GOES ON. AND THIS CITY -- NEW YORK CITY -- HAS PAID A TERRIBLE PRICE, EVEN BEYOND THE LOSS OF ITS HEROES.

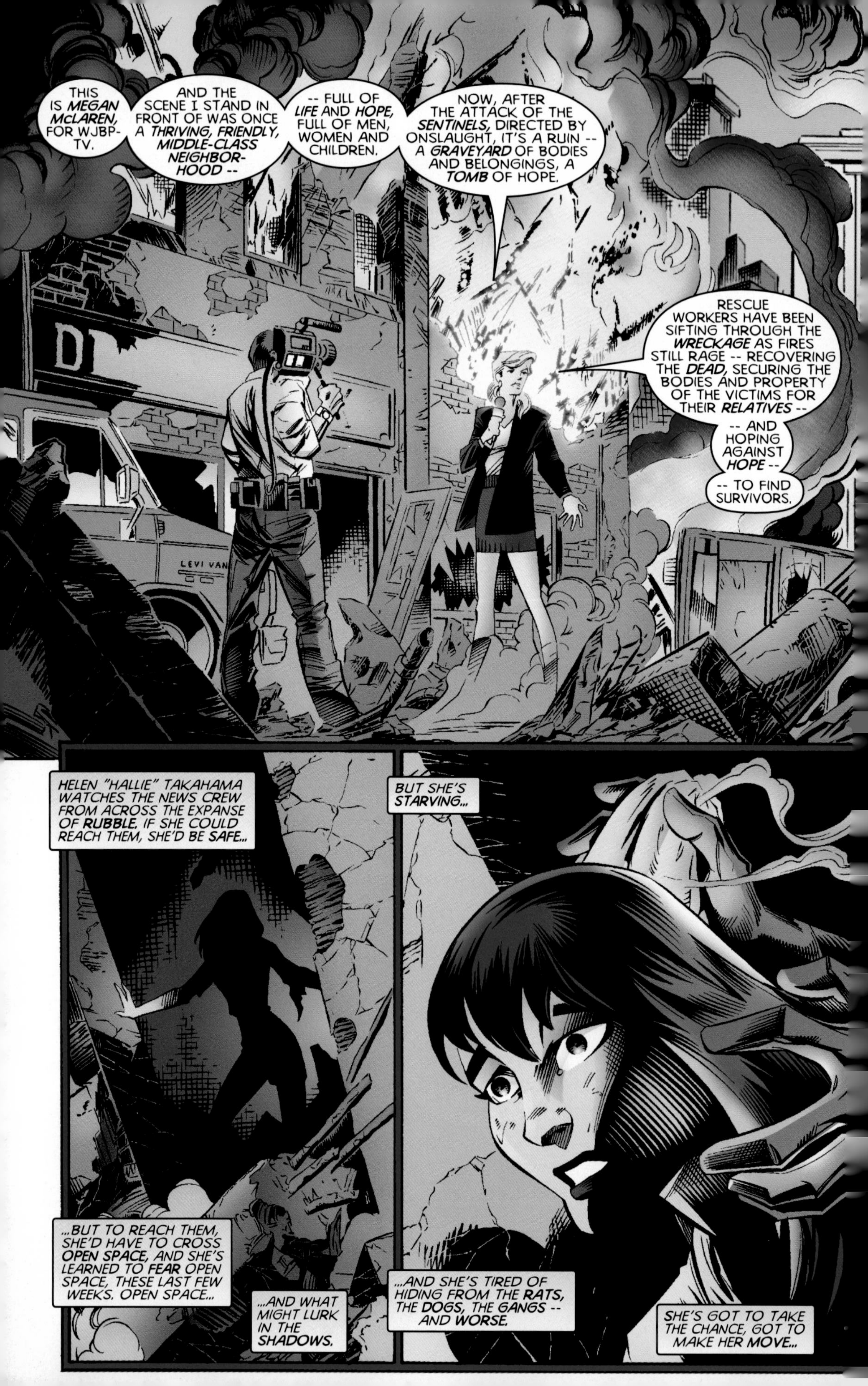
THIS IS MEGAN McLAREN, FOR WJBP-TV.
AND THE SCENE I STAND IN FRONT OF WAS ONCE A THRIVING, FRIENDLY, MIDDLE-CLASS NEIGHBOR-HOOD --
-- FULL OF LIFE AND HOPE, FULL OF MEN, WOMEN AND CHILDREN.
NOW, AFTER THE ATTACK OF THE SENTINELS, DIRECTED BY ONSLAUGHT, IT'S A RUIN -- A GRAVEYARD OF BODIES AND BELONGINGS, A TOMB OF HOPE.
RESCUE WORKERS HAVE BEEN SIFTING THROUGH THE WRECKAGE AS FIRES STILL RAGE -- RECOVERING THE DEAD, SECURING THE BODIES AND PROPERTY OF THE VICTIMS FOR THEIR RELATIVES --
-- AND HOPING AGAINST HOPE --
-- TO FIND SURVIVORS.
LEVI VAN
HELEN "HALLIE" TAKAHAMA WATCHES THE NEWS CREW FROM ACROSS THE EXPANSE OF RUBBLE. IF SHE COULD REACH THEM, SHE'D BE SAFE...
...BUT TO REACH THEM, SHE'D HAVE TO CROSS OPEN SPACE, AND SHE'S LEARNED TO FEAR OPEN SPACE, THESE LAST FEW WEEKS. OPEN SPACE...
...AND WHAT MIGHT LURK IN THE SHADOWS.
BUT SHE'S STARVING...
...AND SHE'S TIRED OF HIDING FROM THE RATS, THE DOGS, THE GANGS -- AND WORSE.
SHE'S GOT TO TAKE THE CHANCE, GOT TO MAKE HER MOVE...

...LIKE LIGHTNING!

KURT BUSIEK *Writer* **MARK BAGLEY** *Penciler* **VINCE RUSSELL** *Inker*
COMICRAFT'S DAVE'N'OSCAR *Lettering* JOE ROSAS *Colors* TOM BREVOORT *Editor* BOB HARRAS *Editor in Chief*

BUT THE WORK GOES *SLOWLY*, HERE AND IN OTHER *RAVAGED* NEIGHBORHOODS -- AND CLEANUP ISN'T EXPECTED TO BE COMPLETED FOR *MONTHS*.

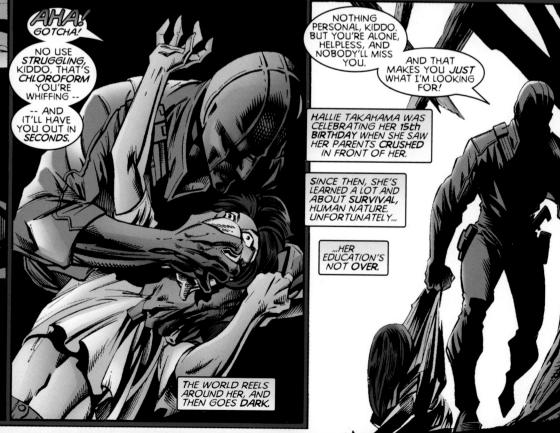

AHA! GOTCHA!

NO USE *STRUGGLING*, KIDDO, THAT'S *CHLOROFORM* YOU'RE WHIFFING --

-- AND IT'LL HAVE YOU OUT IN *SECONDS*.

THE WORLD REELS AROUND HER, AND THEN GOES *DARK*.

NOTHING PERSONAL, KIDDO, BUT YOU'RE ALONE, *HELPLESS*, AND NOBODY'LL MISS YOU.

AND THAT MAKES YOU *JUST* WHAT I'M LOOKING FOR!

HALLIE TAKAHAMA WAS CELEBRATING HER *15th* BIRTHDAY WHEN SHE SAW HER PARENTS *CRUSHED* IN FRONT OF HER.

SINCE THEN, SHE'S LEARNED A LOT AND ABOUT *SURVIVAL*, *HUMAN NATURE*, UNFORTUNATELY...

...HER EDUCATION'S NOT *OVER*.

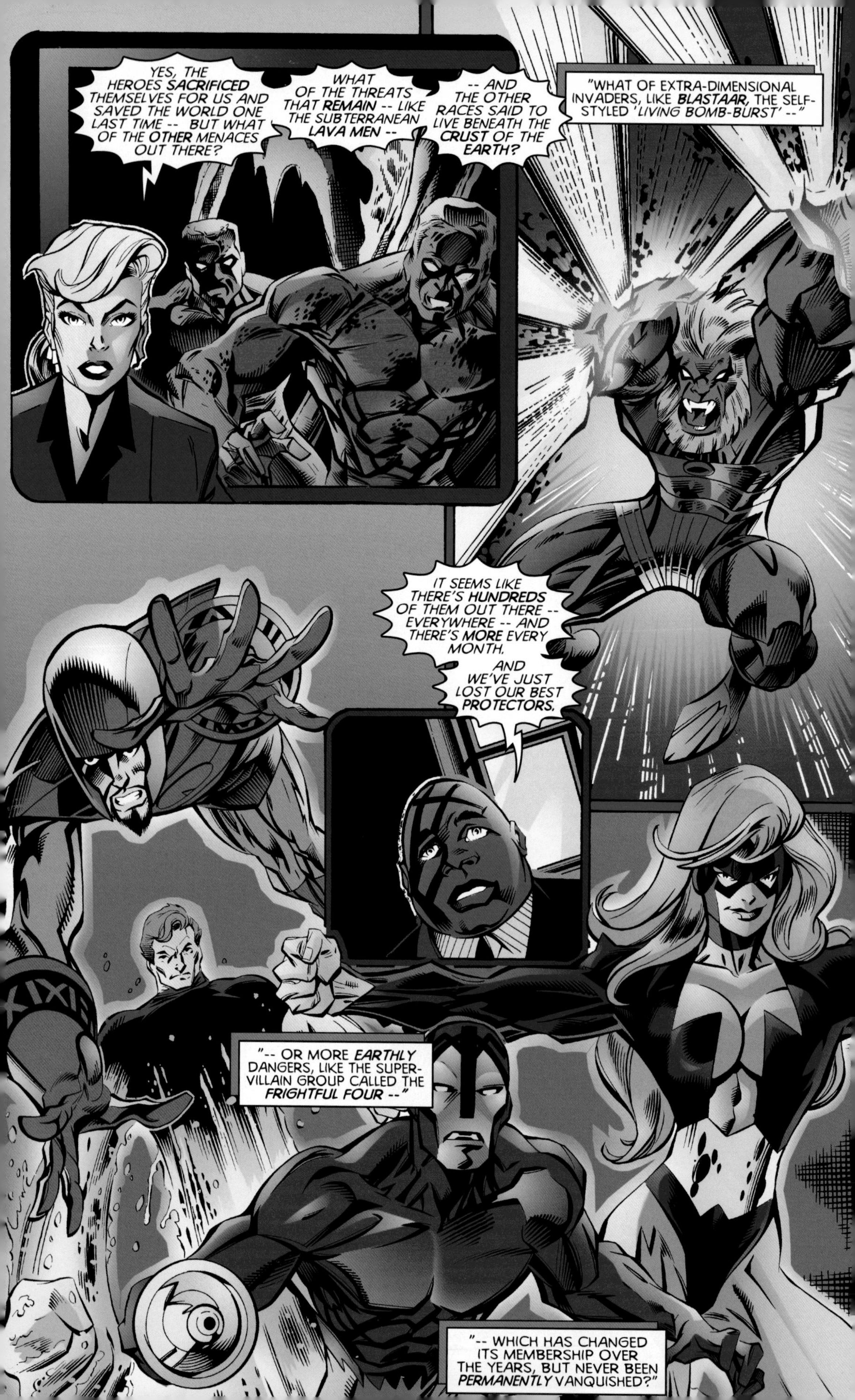
YES, THE HEROES SACRIFICED THEMSELVES FOR US AND SAVED THE WORLD ONE LAST TIME -- BUT WHAT OF THE OTHER MENACES OUT THERE?
WHAT OF THE THREATS THAT REMAIN -- LIKE THE SUBTERRANEAN LAVA MEN --
-- AND THE OTHER RACES SAID TO LIVE BENEATH THE CRUST OF THE EARTH?
"WHAT OF EXTRA-DIMENSIONAL INVADERS, LIKE BLASTAAR, THE SELF-STYLED 'LIVING BOMB-BURST' --"
IT SEEMS LIKE THERE'S HUNDREDS OF THEM OUT THERE -- EVERYWHERE -- AND THERE'S MORE EVERY MONTH.
AND WE'VE JUST LOST OUR BEST PROTECTORS.
"-- OR MORE EARTHLY DANGERS, LIKE THE SUPER-VILLAIN GROUP CALLED THE FRIGHTFUL FOUR --"
"-- WHICH HAS CHANGED ITS MEMBERSHIP OVER THE YEARS, BUT NEVER BEEN PERMANENTLY VANQUISHED?"

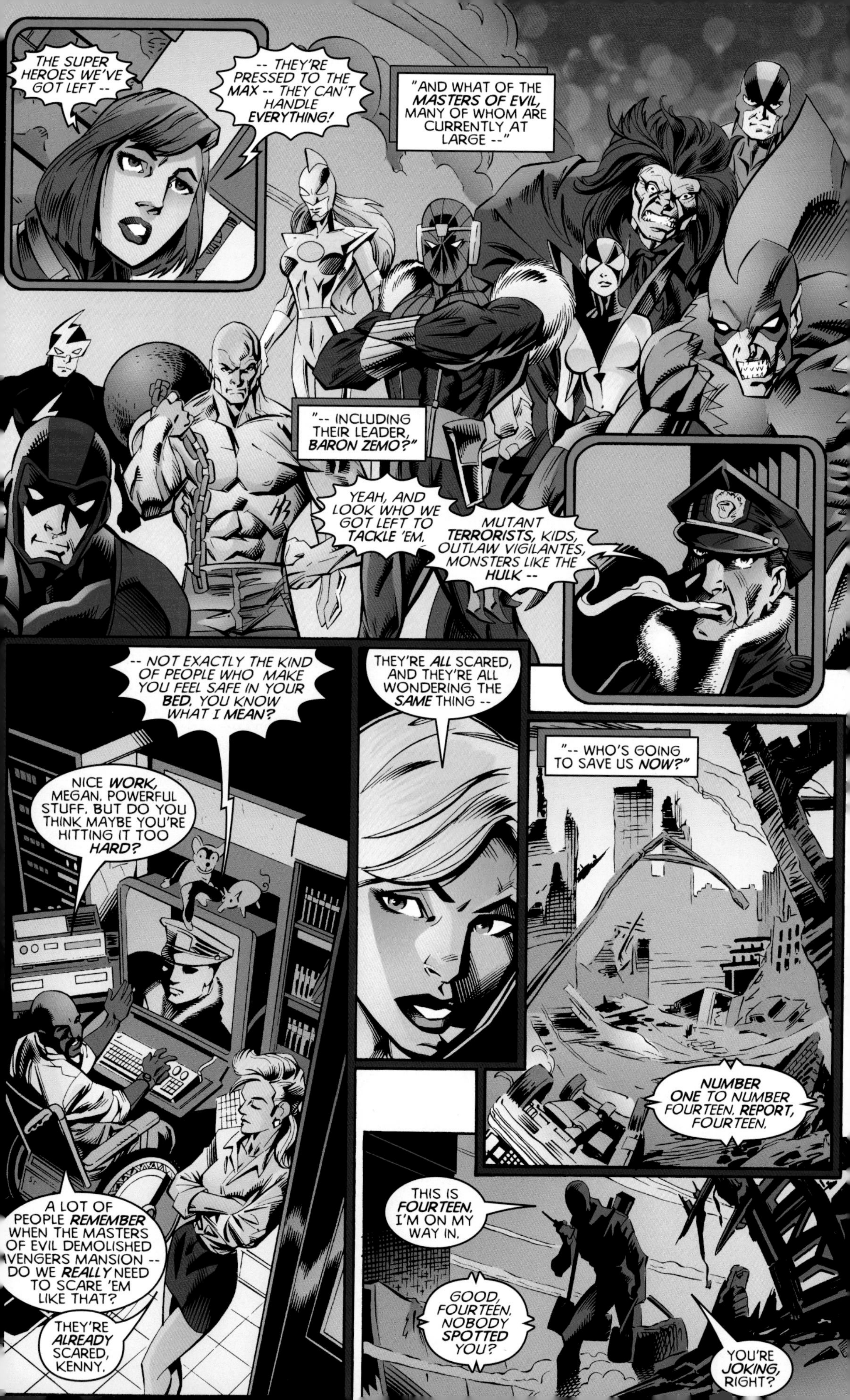
THE SUPER HEROES WE'VE GOT LEFT --
-- THEY'RE PRESSED TO THE MAX -- THEY CAN'T HANDLE EVERYTHING!
"AND WHAT OF THE MASTERS OF EVIL, MANY OF WHOM ARE CURRENTLY AT LARGE --"
"-- INCLUDING THEIR LEADER, BARON ZEMO?"
YEAH, AND LOOK WHO WE GOT LEFT TO TACKLE 'EM.
MUTANT TERRORISTS, KIDS, OUTLAW VIGILANTES, MONSTERS LIKE THE HULK --
-- NOT EXACTLY THE KIND OF PEOPLE WHO MAKE YOU FEEL SAFE IN YOUR BED, YOU KNOW WHAT I MEAN?
NICE WORK, MEGAN. POWERFUL STUFF. BUT DO YOU THINK MAYBE YOU'RE HITTING IT TOO HARD?
A LOT OF PEOPLE REMEMBER WHEN THE MASTERS OF EVIL DEMOLISHED AVENGERS MANSION -- DO WE REALLY NEED TO SCARE 'EM LIKE THAT?
THEY'RE ALREADY SCARED, KENNY.
THEY'RE ALL SCARED, AND THEY'RE ALL WONDERING THE SAME THING --
"-- WHO'S GOING TO SAVE US NOW?"
NUMBER ONE TO NUMBER FOURTEEN. REPORT, FOURTEEN.
THIS IS FOURTEEN, I'M ON MY WAY IN.
GOOD, FOURTEEN, NOBODY SPOTTED YOU?
YOU'RE JOKING, RIGHT?

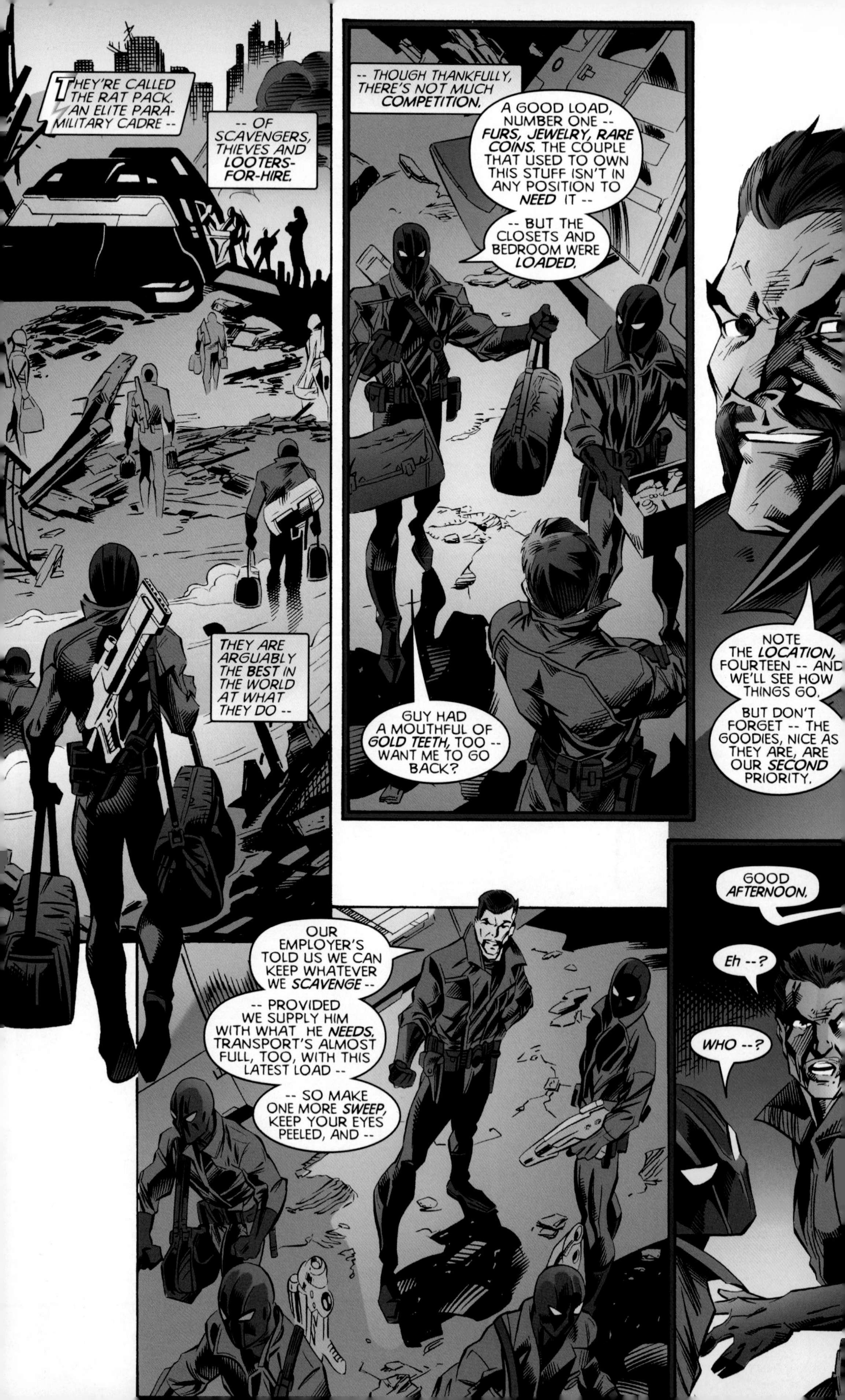

THEY'RE CALLED THE RAT PACK. AN ELITE PARA-MILITARY CADRE --
-- OF SCAVENGERS, THIEVES AND LOOTERS-FOR-HIRE.
THEY ARE ARGUABLY THE BEST IN THE WORLD AT WHAT THEY DO --
-- THOUGH THANKFULLY, THERE'S NOT MUCH COMPETITION.
A GOOD LOAD, NUMBER ONE -- FURS, JEWELRY, RARE COINS. THE COUPLE THAT USED TO OWN THIS STUFF ISN'T IN ANY POSITION TO NEED IT --
-- BUT THE CLOSETS AND BEDROOM WERE LOADED.
GUY HAD A MOUTHFUL OF GOLD TEETH, TOO -- WANT ME TO GO BACK?
NOTE THE LOCATION, FOURTEEN -- AND WE'LL SEE HOW THINGS GO.
BUT DON'T FORGET -- THE GOODIES, NICE AS THEY ARE, ARE OUR SECOND PRIORITY.
OUR EMPLOYER'S TOLD US WE CAN KEEP WHATEVER WE SCAVENGE --
-- PROVIDED WE SUPPLY HIM WITH WHAT HE NEEDS. TRANSPORT'S ALMOST FULL, TOO, WITH THIS LATEST LOAD --
-- SO MAKE ONE MORE SWEEP, KEEP YOUR EYES PEELED, AND --
GOOD AFTERNOON.
Eh --?
WHO --?

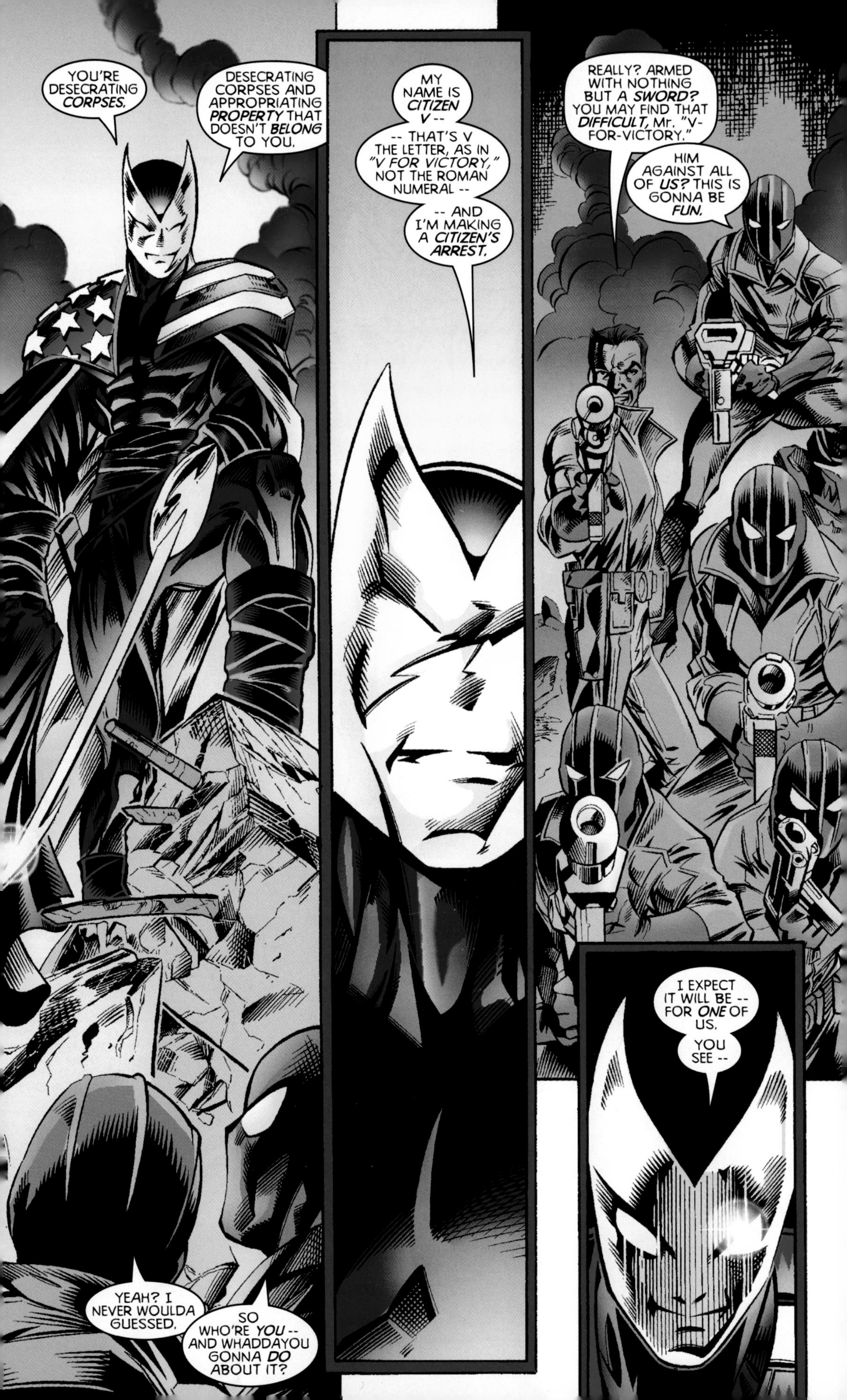
YOU'RE DESECRATING CORPSES.
DESECRATING CORPSES AND APPROPRIATING PROPERTY THAT DOESN'T BELONG TO YOU.
YEAH? I NEVER WOULDA GUESSED.
SO WHO'RE YOU -- AND WHADDAYOU GONNA DO ABOUT IT?
MY NAME IS CITIZEN V --
-- THAT'S V THE LETTER, AS IN "V FOR VICTORY," NOT THE ROMAN NUMERAL --
-- AND I'M MAKING A CITIZEN'S ARREST.
REALLY? ARMED WITH NOTHING BUT A SWORD? YOU MAY FIND THAT DIFFICULT, Mr. "V-FOR-VICTORY."
HIM AGAINST ALL OF US? THIS IS GONNA BE FUN.
I EXPECT IT WILL BE -- FOR ONE OF US.
YOU SEE --

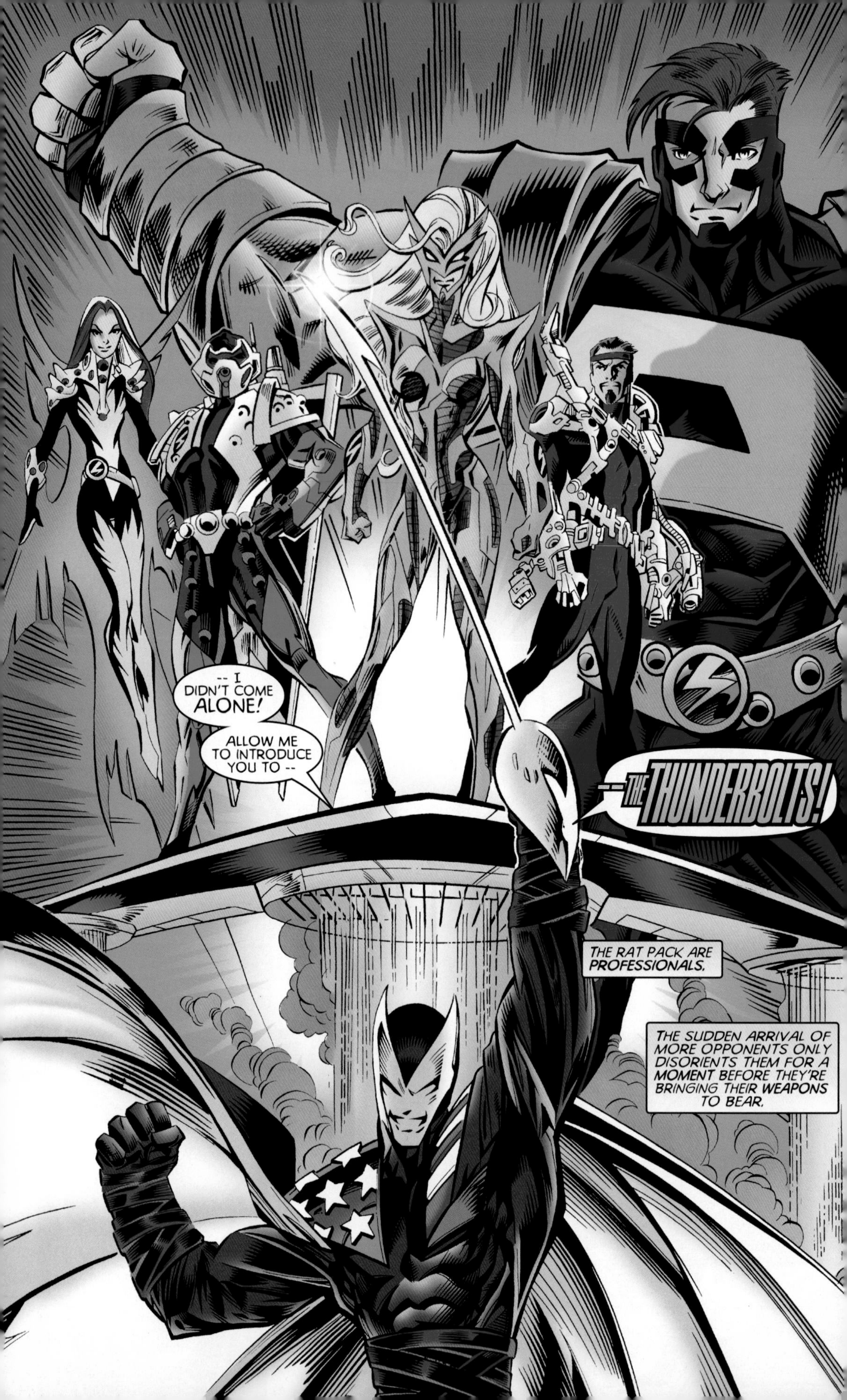
-- I DIDN'T COME ALONE!
ALLOW ME TO INTRODUCE YOU TO --
-- THE THUNDERBOLTS!
THE RAT PACK ARE PROFESSIONALS.
THE SUDDEN ARRIVAL OF MORE OPPONENTS ONLY DISORIENTS THEM FOR A MOMENT BEFORE THEY'RE BRINGING THEIR WEAPONS TO BEAR.

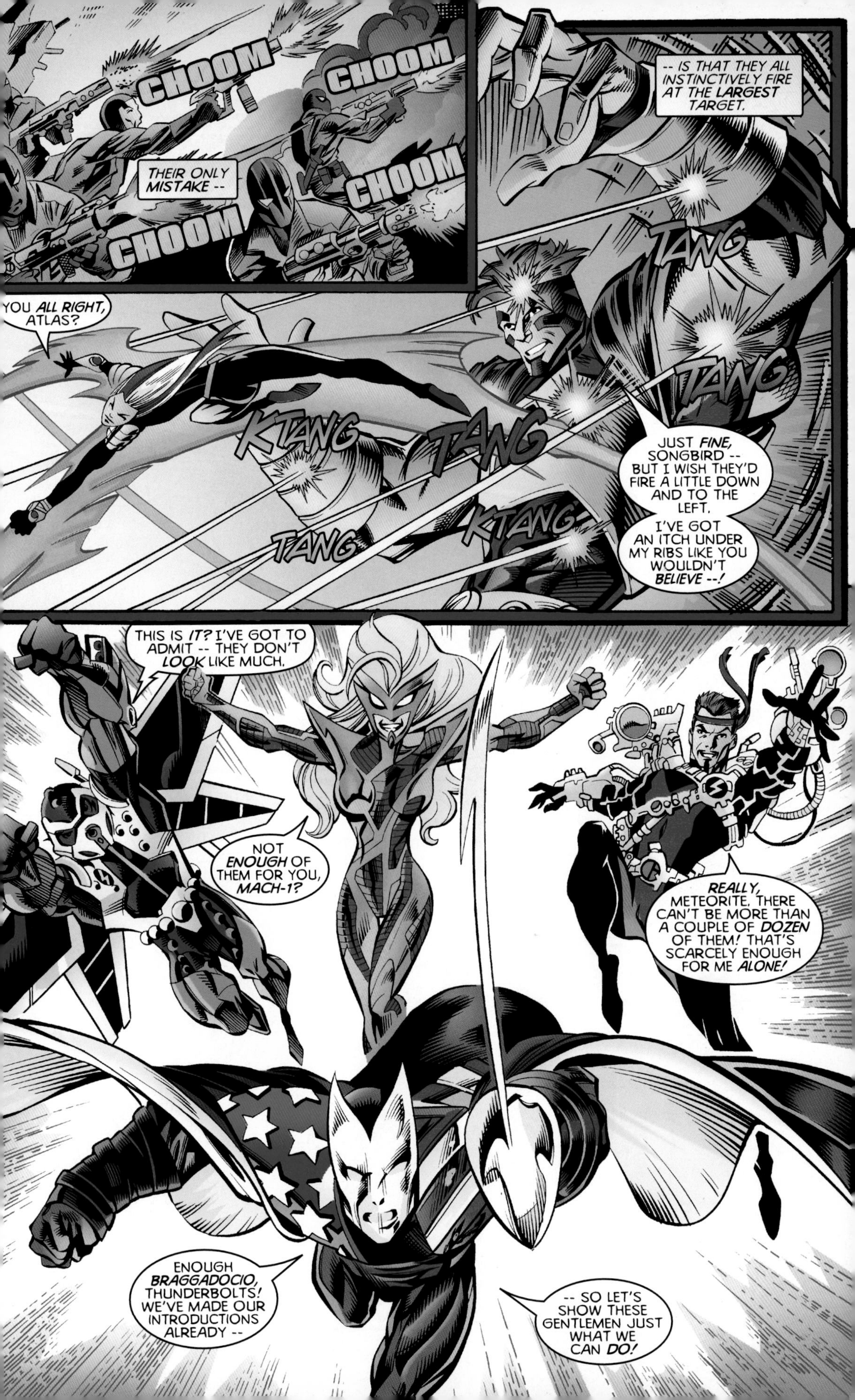
CHOOM
CHOOM
THEIR ONLY MISTAKE --
CHOOM
CHOOM
-- IS THAT THEY ALL INSTINCTIVELY FIRE AT THE LARGEST TARGET.
TANG
YOU ALL RIGHT, ATLAS?
TANG
KTANG
TANG
TANG
KTANG
JUST FINE, SONGBIRD -- BUT I WISH THEY'D FIRE A LITTLE DOWN AND TO THE LEFT.
I'VE GOT AN ITCH UNDER MY RIBS LIKE YOU WOULDN'T BELIEVE --!
THIS IS IT? I'VE GOT TO ADMIT -- THEY DON'T LOOK LIKE MUCH.
NOT ENOUGH OF THEM FOR YOU, MACH-1?
REALLY, METEORITE, THERE CAN'T BE MORE THAN A COUPLE OF DOZEN OF THEM! THAT'S SCARCELY ENOUGH FOR ME ALONE!
ENOUGH BRAGGADOCIO, THUNDERBOLTS! WE'VE MADE OUR INTRODUCTIONS ALREADY --
-- SO LET'S SHOW THESE GENTLEMEN JUST WHAT WE CAN DO!

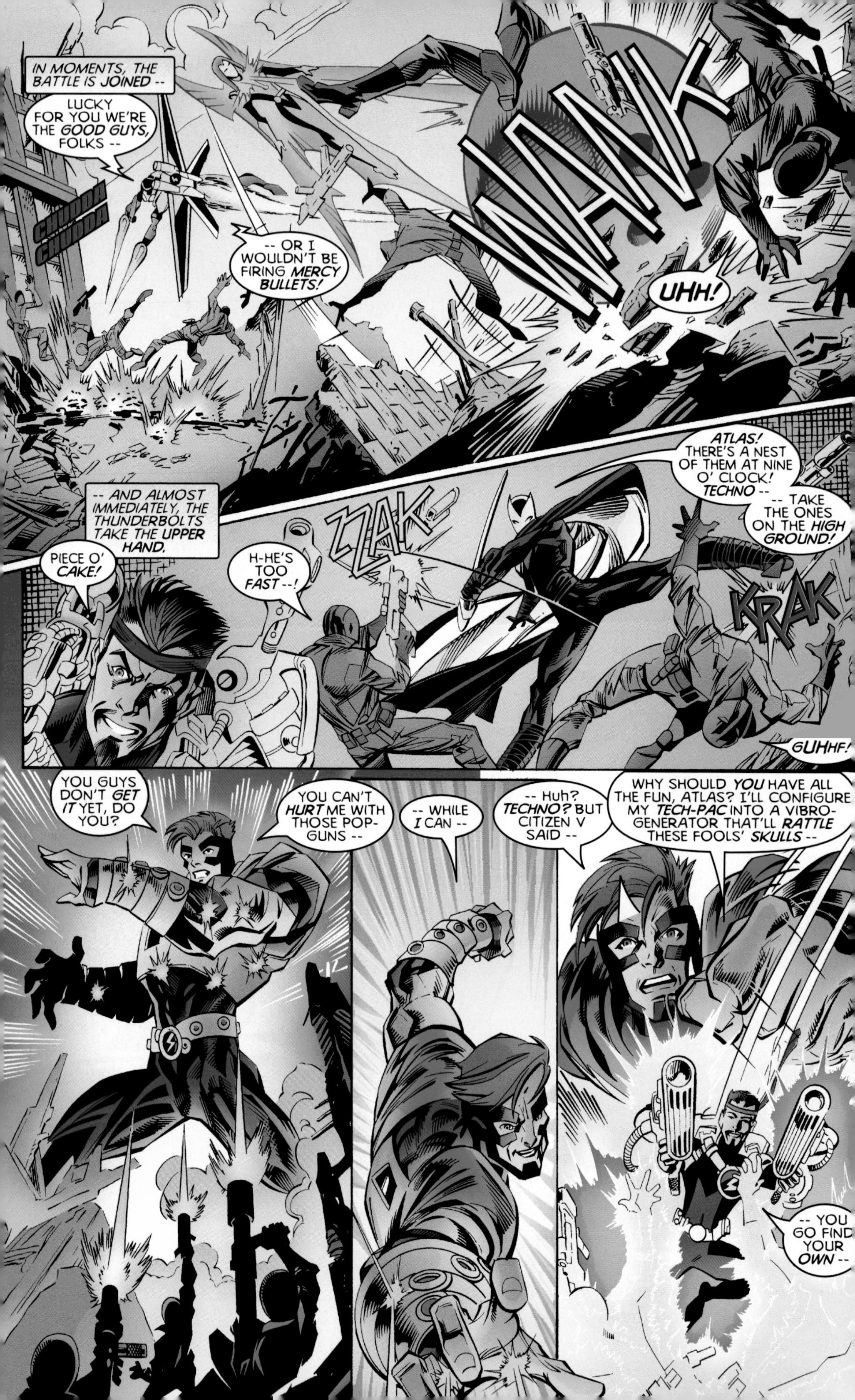
IN MOMENTS, THE BATTLE IS JOINED --
LUCKY FOR YOU WE'RE THE GOOD GUYS, FOLKS --
-- OR I WOULDN'T BE FIRING MERCY BULLETS!
CHUDDA CHUDDA
WANK
UHH!
-- AND ALMOST IMMEDIATELY, THE THUNDERBOLTS TAKE THE UPPER HAND.
ATLAS! THERE'S A NEST OF THEM AT NINE O' CLOCK! TECHNO --
-- TAKE THE ONES ON THE HIGH GROUND!
ZZAK
PIECE O' CAKE!
H-HE'S TOO FAST --!
KRAK
GUHHF!
YOU GUYS DON'T GET IT YET, DO YOU?
YOU CAN'T HURT ME WITH THOSE POP-GUNS --
-- WHILE I CAN --
-- Huh? TECHNO? BUT CITIZEN V SAID --
WHY SHOULD YOU HAVE ALL THE FUN, ATLAS? I'LL CONFIGURE MY TECH-PAC INTO A VIBRO-GENERATOR THAT'LL RATTLE THESE FOOLS' SKULLS --
-- YOU GO FIND YOUR OWN --

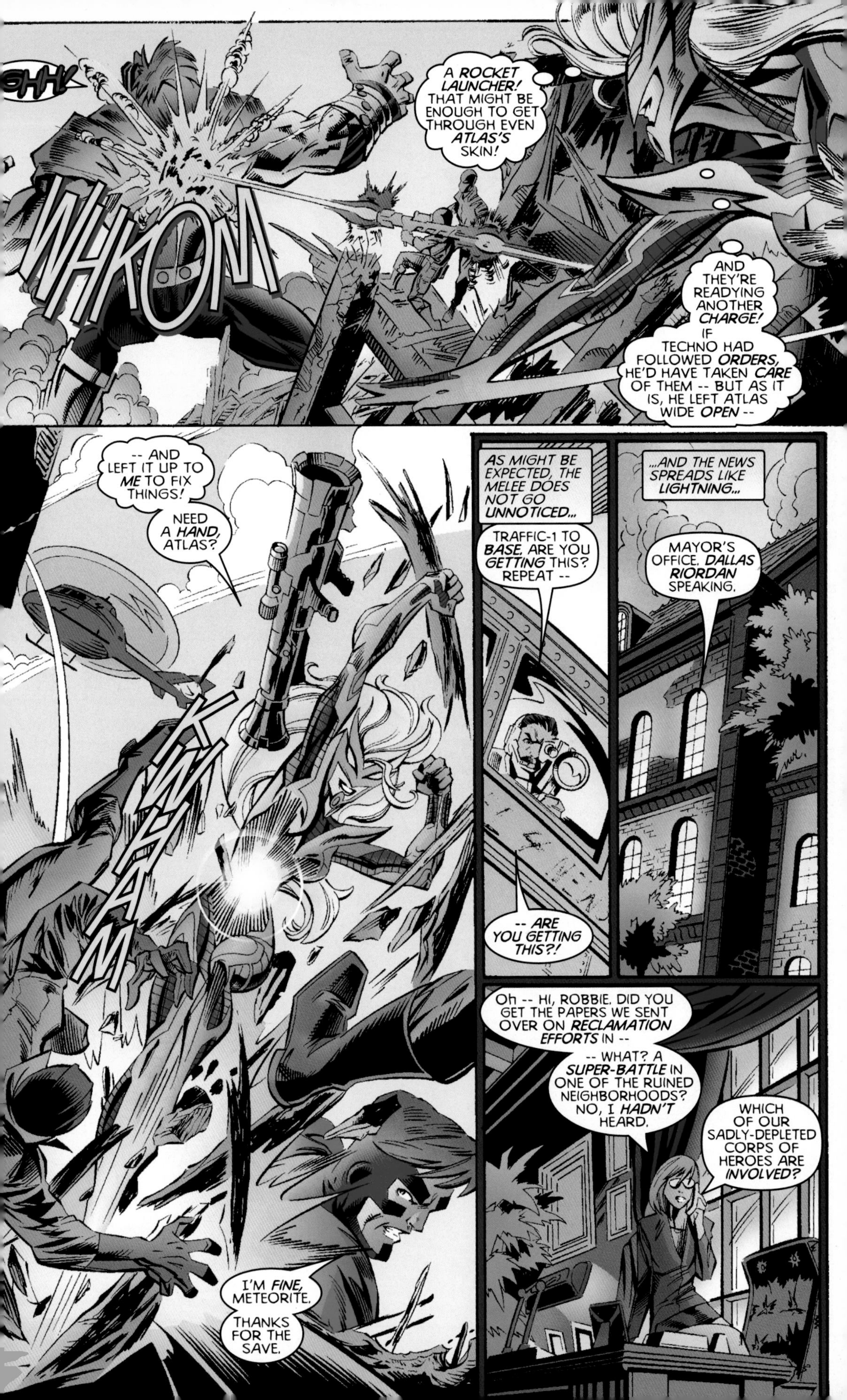
GHH!
A ROCKET LAUNCHER! THAT MIGHT BE ENOUGH TO GET THROUGH EVEN ATLAS'S SKIN!
WHKOM
AND THEY'RE READYING ANOTHER CHARGE! IF TECHNO HAD FOLLOWED ORDERS, HE'D HAVE TAKEN CARE OF THEM -- BUT AS IT IS, HE LEFT ATLAS WIDE OPEN --
-- AND LEFT IT UP TO ME TO FIX THINGS!
NEED A HAND, ATLAS?
KWHAM
I'M FINE, METEORITE.
THANKS FOR THE SAVE.
AS MIGHT BE EXPECTED, THE MELEE DOES NOT GO UNNOTICED...
TRAFFIC-1 TO BASE. ARE YOU GETTING THIS? REPEAT --
-- ARE YOU GETTING THIS?!
...AND THE NEWS SPREADS LIKE LIGHTNING...
MAYOR'S OFFICE. DALLAS RIORDAN SPEAKING.
Oh -- HI, ROBBIE. DID YOU GET THE PAPERS WE SENT OVER ON RECLAMATION EFFORTS IN --
-- WHAT? A SUPER-BATTLE IN ONE OF THE RUINED NEIGHBORHOODS? NO, I HADN'T HEARD.
WHICH OF OUR SADLY-DEPLETED CORPS OF HEROES ARE INVOLVED?

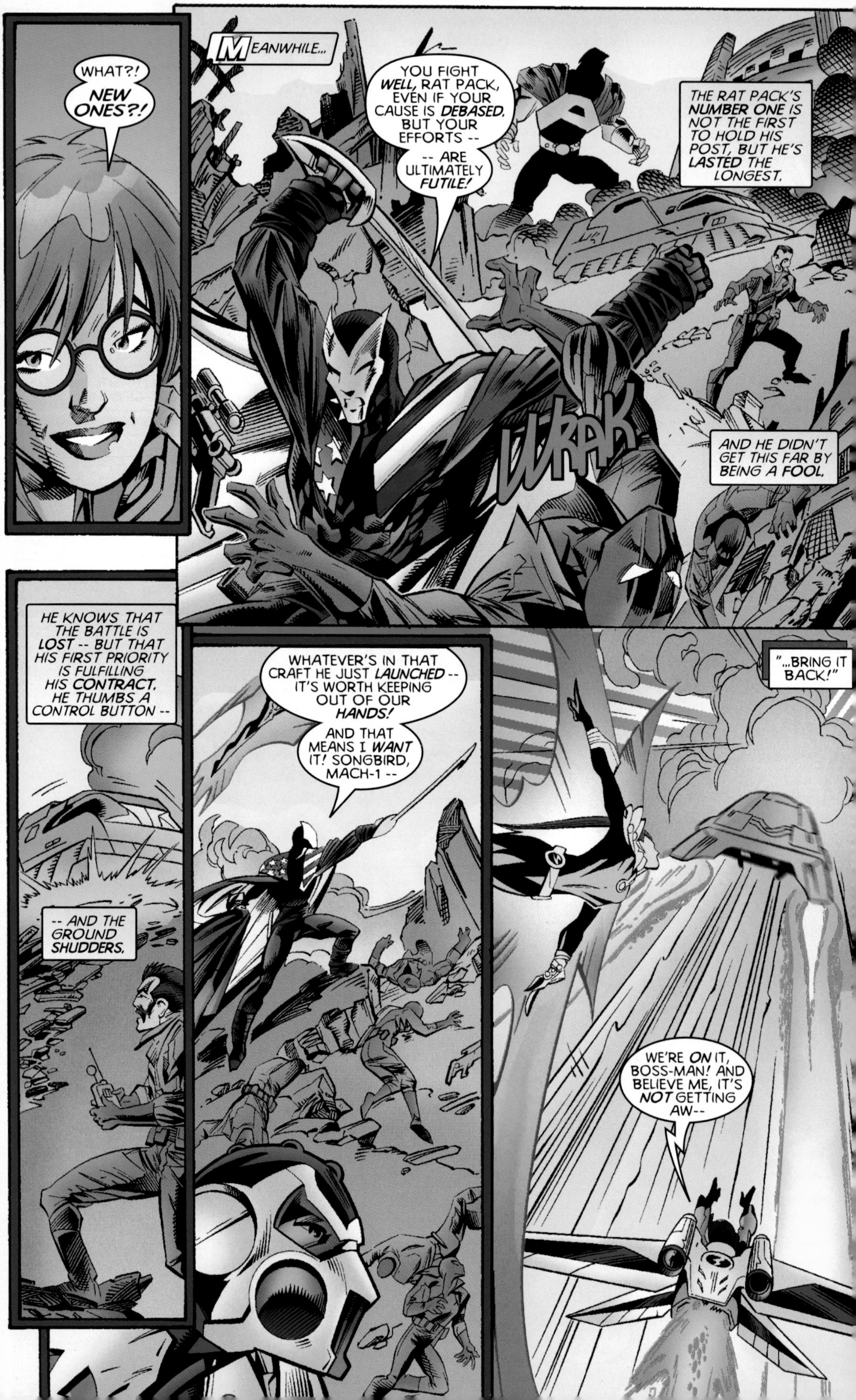
WHAT?! NEW ONES?!
MEANWHILE...
YOU FIGHT WELL, RAT PACK, EVEN IF YOUR CAUSE IS DEBASED, BUT YOUR EFFORTS --
-- ARE ULTIMATELY FUTILE!
THE RAT PACK'S NUMBER ONE IS NOT THE FIRST TO HOLD HIS POST, BUT HE'S LASTED THE LONGEST.
WRAK
AND HE DIDN'T GET THIS FAR BY BEING A FOOL.
HE KNOWS THAT THE BATTLE IS LOST -- BUT THAT HIS FIRST PRIORITY IS FULFILLING HIS CONTRACT. HE THUMBS A CONTROL BUTTON --
-- AND THE GROUND SHUDDERS.
WHATEVER'S IN THAT CRAFT HE JUST LAUNCHED -- IT'S WORTH KEEPING OUT OF OUR HANDS!
AND THAT MEANS I WANT IT! SONGBIRD, MACH-1 --
"...BRING IT BACK!"
WE'RE ON IT, BOSS-MAN! AND BELIEVE ME, IT'S NOT GETTING AW--

AAIIRGKH!

E-ELECTRICAL D-DIS-RUP-TORS!

THE WOMAN CALLED SONGBIRD *SCREAMS*. IN FACT, SHE'S BEEN SCREAMING ALL *ALONG*.

BUT IT'S NOT A SCREAM OF *TERROR*, OR EVEN RAGE. IT'S A LOW-LEVEL *SUBSONIC TRILL* -- AND AS SHE *MODIFIES* IT --

-- IT INTERACTS WITH THE CIRCUITRY OF THE SOPHISTICATED MANTLE SHE WEARS --

-- TO PRODUCE A SPHERE OF *SOLID SOUND* THAT SHIELDS MACH-1 AS EFFECTIVELY AS HER SOUND-GENERATED *WINGS* KEEP HER ALOFT.

Oh, *MAN!* I *OWE* YOU, SONG-BIRD!

ARE -- ARE YOU *OKAY?*

I'M FINE -- *NOW*, MY SYSTEMS ARE ALREADY *REBOOTING*.

NOW TURN ME *LOOSE*, WILLYA --

-- SO I CAN GIVE THOSE SLIMY S.O.B.'S A LITTLE SOMETHING IN *RETURN!*

WHAT --? NO!

WHROOM! WHROOM!

THE MISSILES EXPLODE IN A CLOUD OF *ANESTHETIC GAS* --

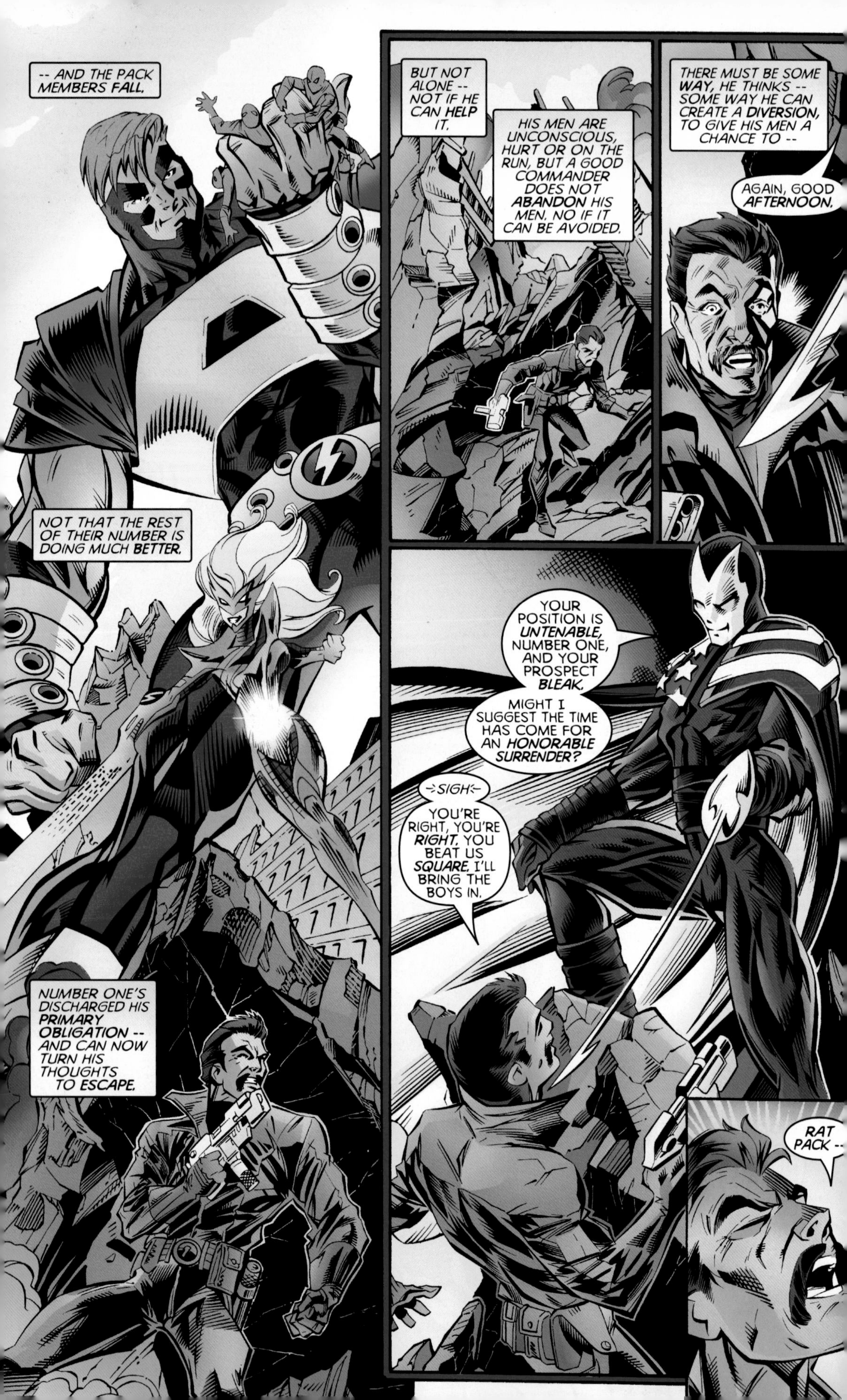

-- AND THE PACK MEMBERS FALL.
NOT THAT THE REST OF THEIR NUMBER IS DOING MUCH BETTER.
NUMBER ONE'S DISCHARGED HIS PRIMARY OBLIGATION -- AND CAN NOW TURN HIS THOUGHTS TO ESCAPE.
BUT NOT ALONE -- NOT IF HE CAN HELP IT.
HIS MEN ARE UNCONSCIOUS, HURT OR ON THE RUN, BUT A GOOD COMMANDER DOES NOT ABANDON HIS MEN. NO IF IT CAN BE AVOIDED.
THERE MUST BE SOME WAY, HE THINKS -- SOME WAY HE CAN CREATE A DIVERSION, TO GIVE HIS MEN A CHANCE TO --
AGAIN, GOOD AFTERNOON.
YOUR POSITION IS UNTENABLE, NUMBER ONE, AND YOUR PROSPECT BLEAK.
MIGHT I SUGGEST THE TIME HAS COME FOR AN HONORABLE SURRENDER?
SIGH
YOU'RE RIGHT, YOU'RE RIGHT, YOU BEAT US SQUARE. I'LL BRING THE BOYS IN.
RAT PACK --

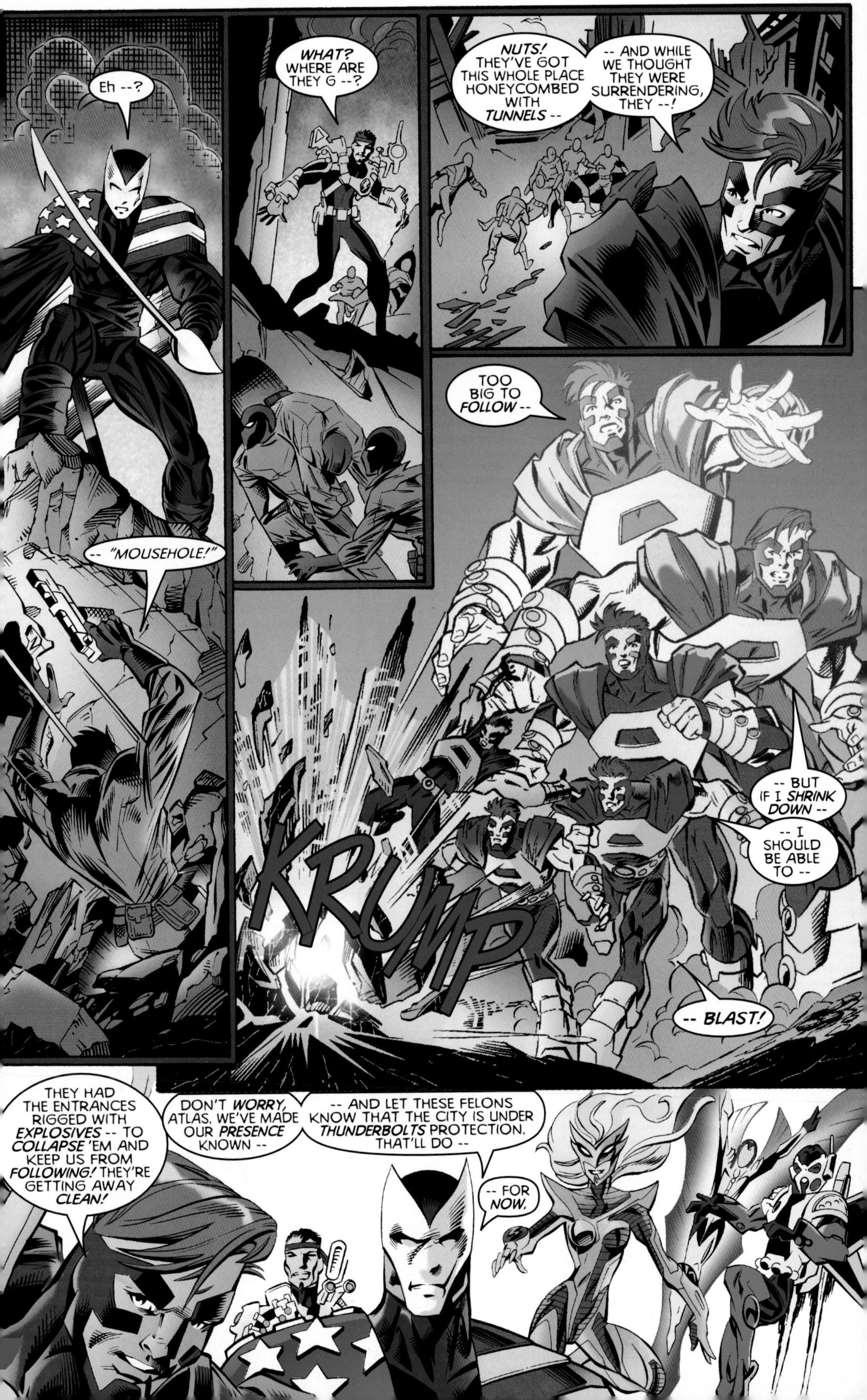
Eh --?
WHAT? WHERE ARE THEY G --?
NUTS! THEY'VE GOT THIS WHOLE PLACE HONEYCOMBED WITH TUNNELS --
-- AND WHILE WE THOUGHT THEY WERE SURRENDERING, THEY --!
-- "MOUSEHOLE!"
TOO BIG TO FOLLOW --
-- BUT IF I SHRINK DOWN --
-- I SHOULD BE ABLE TO --
KRUMP
-- BLAST!
THEY HAD THE ENTRANCES RIGGED WITH EXPLOSIVES -- TO COLLAPSE 'EM AND KEEP US FROM FOLLOWING! THEY'RE GETTING AWAY CLEAN!
DON'T WORRY, ATLAS, WE'VE MADE OUR PRESENCE KNOWN --
-- AND LET THESE FELONS KNOW THAT THE CITY IS UNDER THUNDERBOLTS PROTECTION. THAT'LL DO --
-- FOR NOW.

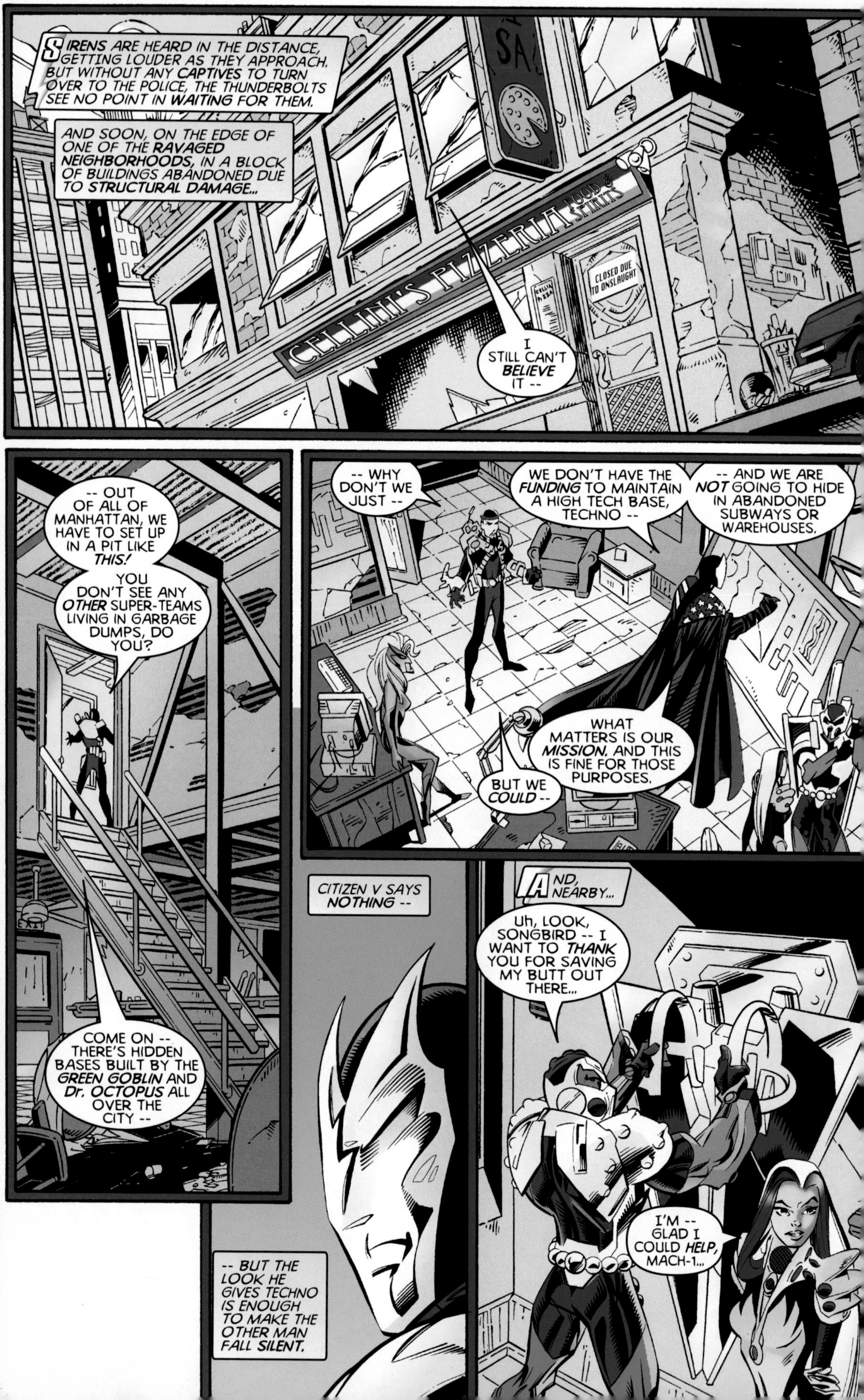
SIRENS ARE HEARD IN THE DISTANCE, GETTING LOUDER AS THEY APPROACH. BUT WITHOUT ANY CAPTIVES TO TURN OVER TO THE POLICE, THE THUNDERBOLTS SEE NO POINT IN WAITING FOR THEM.
AND SOON, ON THE EDGE OF ONE OF THE RAVAGED NEIGHBORHOODS, IN A BLOCK OF BUILDINGS ABANDONED DUE TO STRUCTURAL DAMAGE...
CELLINI'S PIZZERIA FOOD & SPIRITS
CLOSED DUE TO ONSLAUGHT
I STILL CAN'T BELIEVE IT --
-- OUT OF ALL OF MANHATTAN, WE HAVE TO SET UP IN A PIT LIKE THIS!
YOU DON'T SEE ANY OTHER SUPER-TEAMS LIVING IN GARBAGE DUMPS, DO YOU?
COME ON -- THERE'S HIDDEN BASES BUILT BY THE GREEN GOBLIN AND Dr. OCTOPUS ALL OVER THE CITY --
-- WHY DON'T WE JUST --
WE DON'T HAVE THE FUNDING TO MAINTAIN A HIGH TECH BASE, TECHNO --
-- AND WE ARE NOT GOING TO HIDE IN ABANDONED SUBWAYS OR WAREHOUSES.
WHAT MATTERS IS OUR MISSION, AND THIS IS FINE FOR THOSE PURPOSES.
BUT WE COULD --
CITIZEN V SAYS NOTHING --
-- BUT THE LOOK HE GIVES TECHNO IS ENOUGH TO MAKE THE OTHER MAN FALL SILENT.
AND, NEARBY...
Uh, LOOK, SONGBIRD -- I WANT TO THANK YOU FOR SAVING MY BUTT OUT THERE...
I'M -- GLAD I COULD HELP, MACH-1...

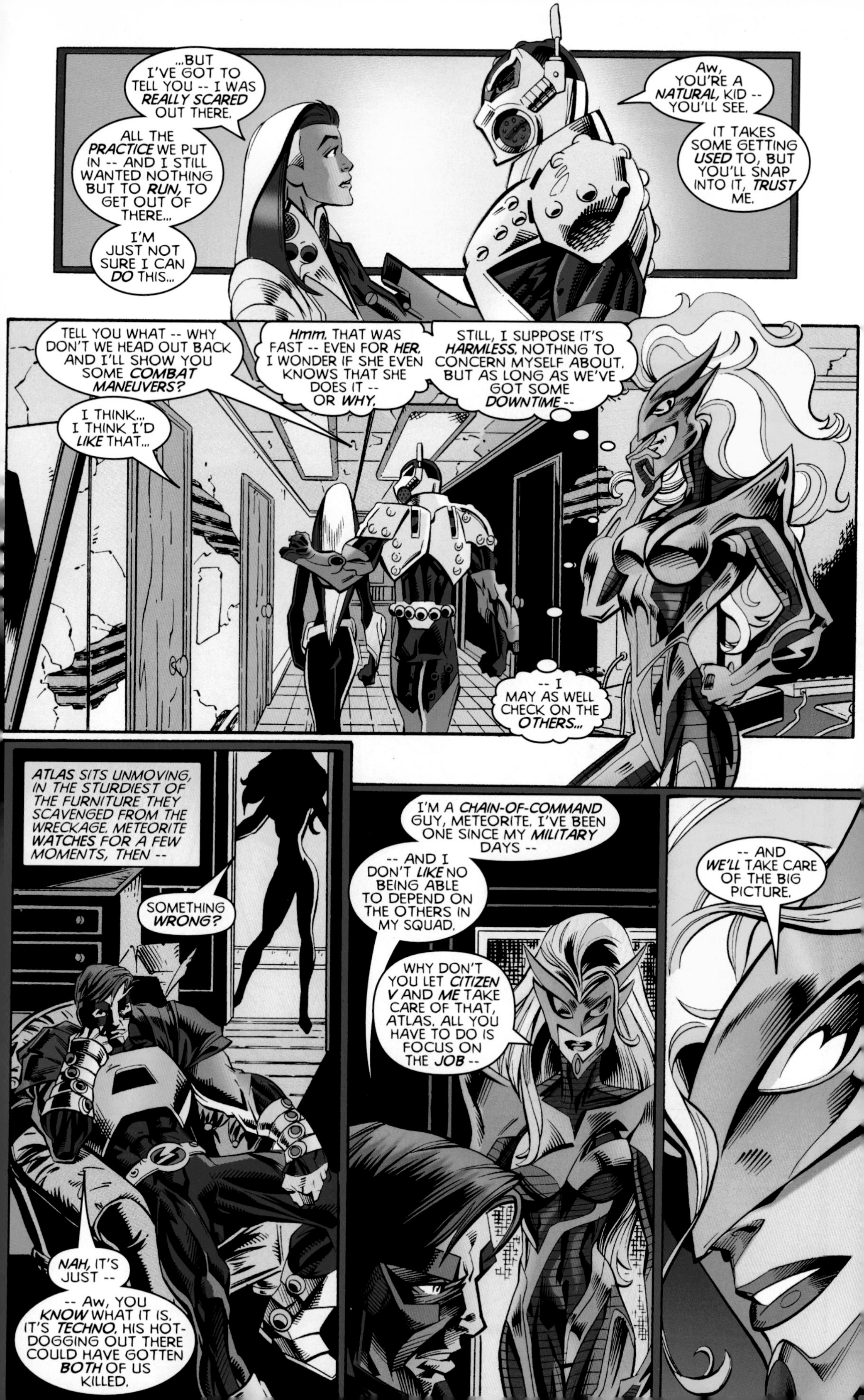

...BUT I'VE GOT TO TELL YOU -- I WAS REALLY SCARED OUT THERE.
ALL THE PRACTICE WE PUT IN -- AND I STILL WANTED NOTHING BUT TO RUN, TO GET OUT OF THERE...
I'M JUST NOT SURE I CAN DO THIS...
Aw, YOU'RE A NATURAL, KID -- YOU'LL SEE.
IT TAKES SOME GETTING USED TO, BUT YOU'LL SNAP INTO IT, TRUST ME.
TELL YOU WHAT -- WHY DON'T WE HEAD OUT BACK AND I'LL SHOW YOU SOME COMBAT MANEUVERS?
I THINK... I THINK I'D LIKE THAT...
Hmm. THAT WAS FAST -- EVEN FOR HER. I WONDER IF SHE EVEN KNOWS THAT SHE DOES IT -- OR WHY.
STILL, I SUPPOSE IT'S HARMLESS, NOTHING TO CONCERN MYSELF ABOUT. BUT AS LONG AS WE'VE GOT SOME DOWNTIME --
-- I MAY AS WELL CHECK ON THE OTHERS...
ATLAS SITS UNMOVING, IN THE STURDIEST OF THE FURNITURE THEY SCAVENGED FROM THE WRECKAGE. METEORITE WATCHES FOR A FEW MOMENTS, THEN --
SOMETHING WRONG?
NAH, IT'S JUST --
-- Aw, YOU KNOW WHAT IT IS. IT'S TECHNO. HIS HOT-DOGGING OUT THERE COULD HAVE GOTTEN BOTH OF US KILLED.
I'M A CHAIN-OF-COMMAND GUY, METEORITE. I'VE BEEN ONE SINCE MY MILITARY DAYS --
-- AND I DON'T LIKE NO BEING ABLE TO DEPEND ON THE OTHERS IN MY SQUAD.
WHY DON'T YOU LET CITIZEN V AND ME TAKE CARE OF THAT, ATLAS. ALL YOU HAVE TO DO IS FOCUS ON THE JOB --
-- AND WE'LL TAKE CARE OF THE BIG PICTURE.

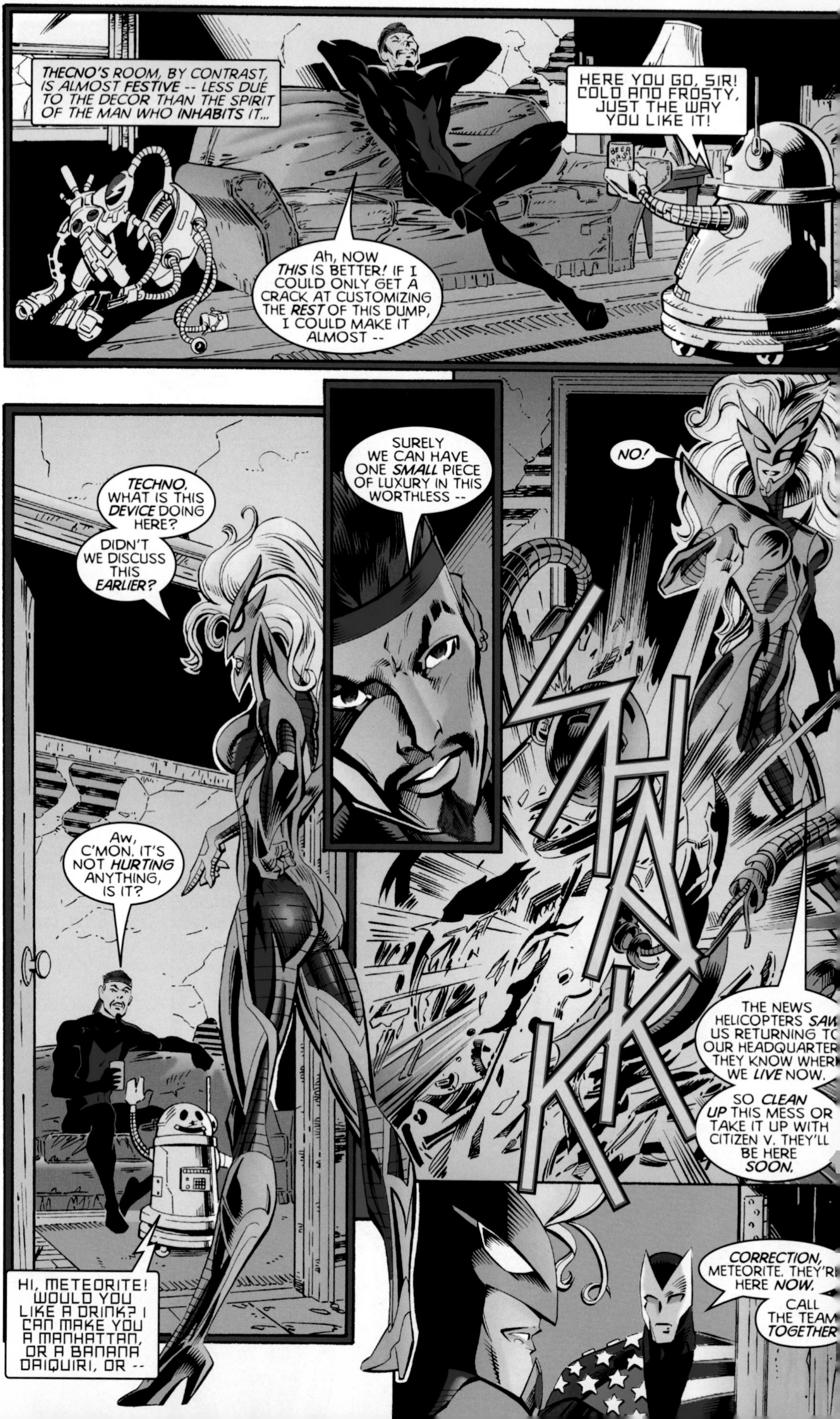
THECNO'S ROOM, BY CONTRAST, IS ALMOST FESTIVE -- LESS DUE TO THE DECOR THAN THE SPIRIT OF THE MAN WHO INHABITS IT...
HERE YOU GO, SIR! COLD AND FROSTY, JUST THE WAY YOU LIKE IT!
Ah, NOW THIS IS BETTER! IF I COULD ONLY GET A CRACK AT CUSTOMIZING THE REST OF THIS DUMP, I COULD MAKE IT ALMOST --
TECHNO, WHAT IS THIS DEVICE DOING HERE?
DIDN'T WE DISCUSS THIS EARLIER?
Aw, C'MON, IT'S NOT HURTING ANYTHING, IS IT?
HI, METEORITE! WOULD YOU LIKE A DRINK? I CAN MAKE YOU A MANHATTAN, OR A BANANA DAIQUIRI, OR --
SURELY WE CAN HAVE ONE SMALL PIECE OF LUXURY IN THIS WORTHLESS --
NO!
SHANKK
THE NEWS HELICOPTERS SAW US RETURNING TO OUR HEADQUARTERS. THEY KNOW WHERE WE LIVE NOW.
SO CLEAN UP THIS MESS OR TAKE IT UP WITH CITIZEN V. THEY'LL BE HERE SOON.
CORRECTION, METEORITE. THEY'RE HERE NOW.
CALL THE TEAM TOGETHER.

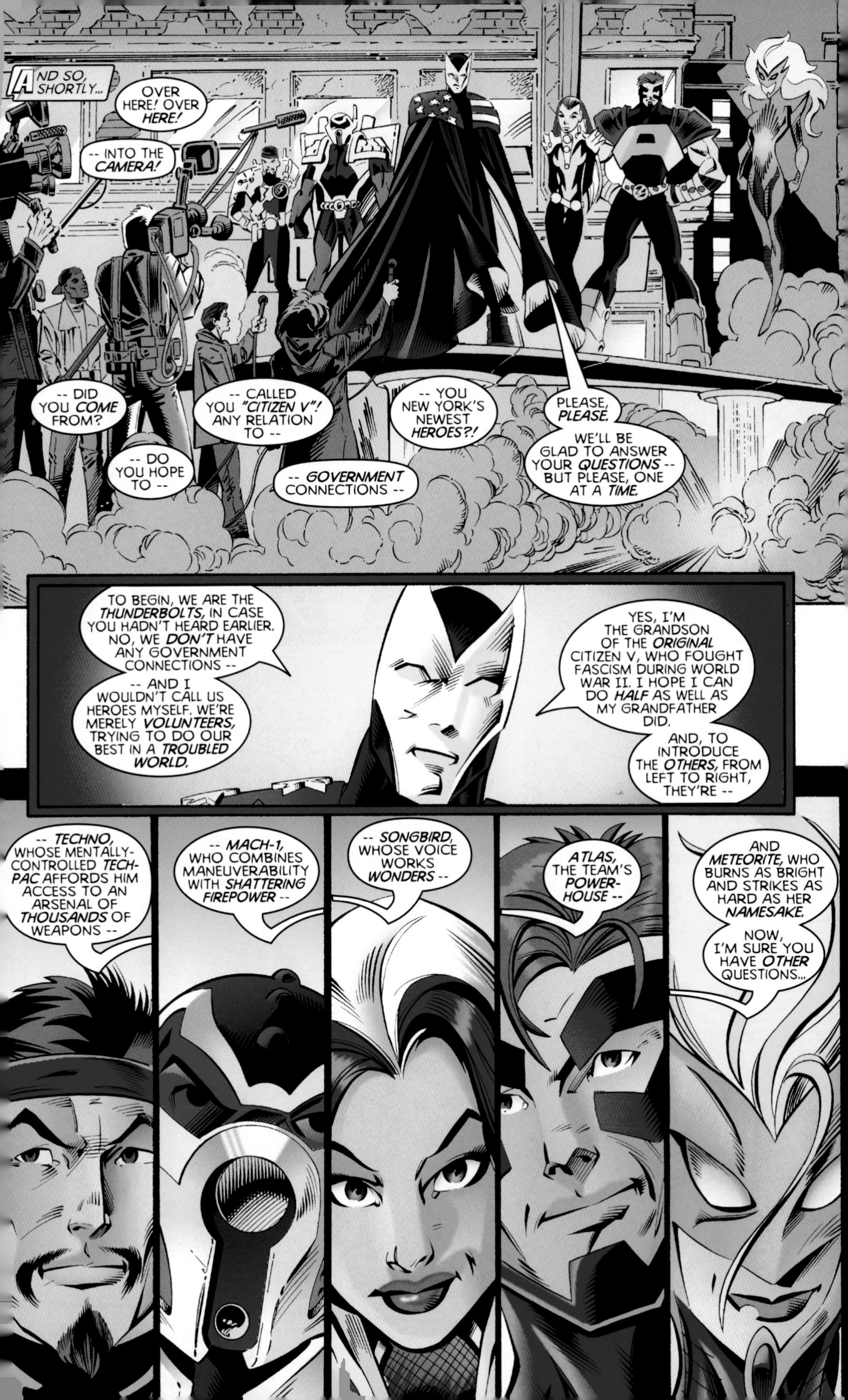
AND SO, SHORTLY...
OVER HERE! OVER HERE!
-- INTO THE CAMERA!
-- DID YOU COME FROM?
-- DO YOU HOPE TO --
-- CALLED YOU "CITIZEN V"! ANY RELATION TO --
-- GOVERNMENT CONNECTIONS --
-- YOU NEW YORK'S NEWEST HEROES?!
PLEASE, PLEASE.
WE'LL BE GLAD TO ANSWER YOUR QUESTIONS -- BUT PLEASE, ONE AT A TIME.
TO BEGIN, WE ARE THE THUNDERBOLTS, IN CASE YOU HADN'T HEARD EARLIER. NO, WE DON'T HAVE ANY GOVERNMENT CONNECTIONS --
-- AND I WOULDN'T CALL US HEROES MYSELF. WE'RE MERELY VOLUNTEERS, TRYING TO DO OUR BEST IN A TROUBLED WORLD.
YES, I'M THE GRANDSON OF THE ORIGINAL CITIZEN V, WHO FOUGHT FASCISM DURING WORLD WAR II. I HOPE I CAN DO HALF AS WELL AS MY GRANDFATHER DID.
AND, TO INTRODUCE THE OTHERS, FROM LEFT TO RIGHT, THEY'RE --
-- TECHNO, WHOSE MENTALLY-CONTROLLED TECH-PAC AFFORDS HIM ACCESS TO AN ARSENAL OF THOUSANDS OF WEAPONS --
-- MACH-1, WHO COMBINES MANEUVERABILITY WITH SHATTERING FIREPOWER --
-- SONGBIRD, WHOSE VOICE WORKS WONDERS --
ATLAS, THE TEAM'S POWER-HOUSE --
AND METEORITE, WHO BURNS AS BRIGHT AND STRIKES AS HARD AS HER NAMESAKE.
NOW, I'M SURE YOU HAVE OTHER QUESTIONS...

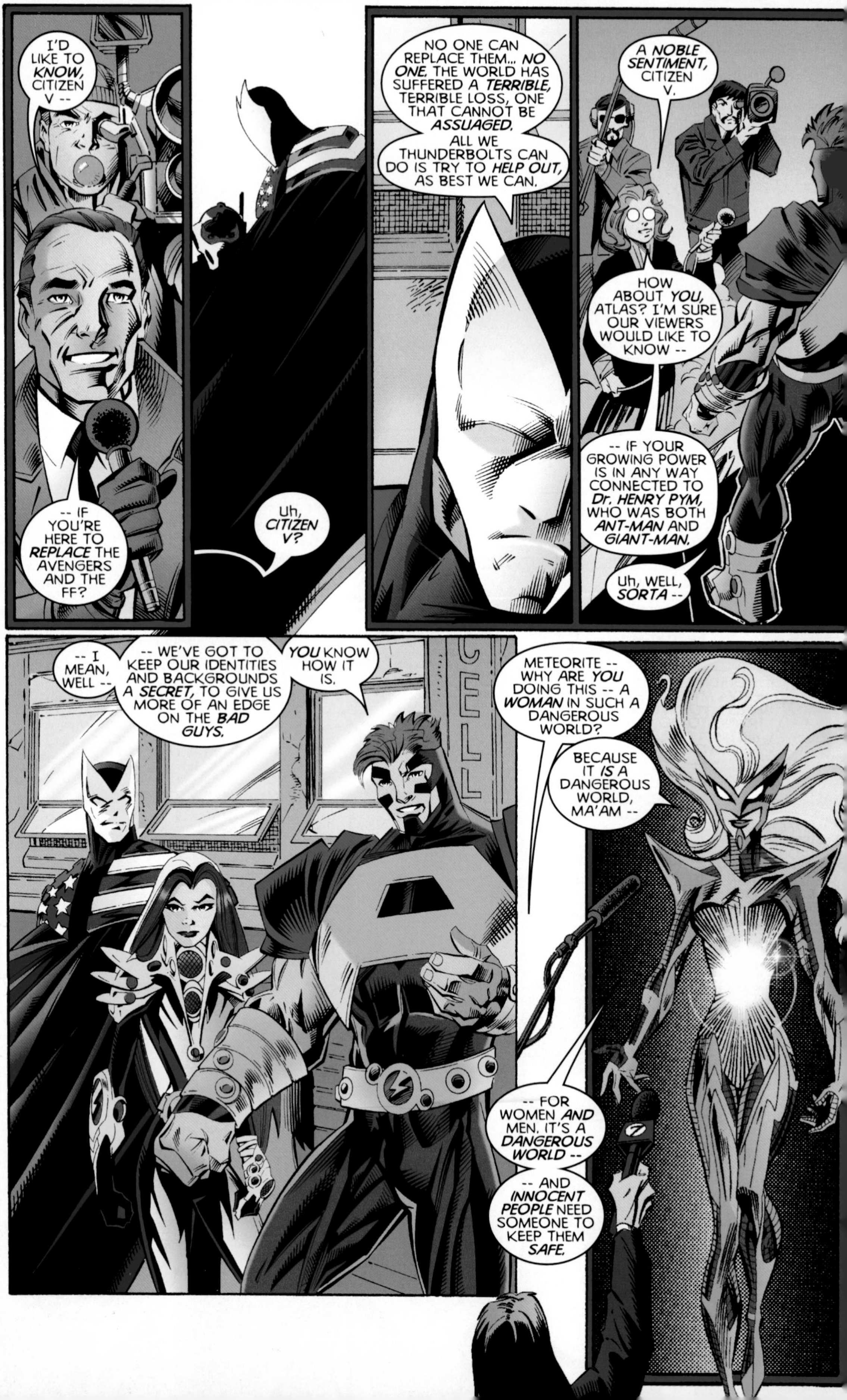
I'D LIKE TO KNOW, CITIZEN V --
-- IF YOU'RE HERE TO REPLACE THE AVENGERS AND THE FF?
Uh, CITIZEN V?
NO ONE CAN REPLACE THEM... NO ONE. THE WORLD HAS SUFFERED A TERRIBLE, TERRIBLE LOSS, ONE THAT CANNOT BE ASSUAGED.
ALL WE THUNDERBOLTS CAN DO IS TRY TO HELP OUT, AS BEST WE CAN.
A NOBLE SENTIMENT, CITIZEN V.
HOW ABOUT YOU, ATLAS? I'M SURE OUR VIEWERS WOULD LIKE TO KNOW --
-- IF YOUR GROWING POWER IS IN ANY WAY CONNECTED TO Dr. HENRY PYM, WHO WAS BOTH ANT-MAN AND GIANT-MAN.
Uh, WELL, SORTA --
-- I MEAN, WELL --
-- WE'VE GOT TO KEEP OUR IDENTITIES AND BACKGROUNDS A SECRET, TO GIVE US MORE OF AN EDGE ON THE BAD GUYS.
YOU KNOW HOW IT IS.
METEORITE -- WHY ARE YOU DOING THIS -- A WOMAN IN SUCH A DANGEROUS WORLD?
BECAUSE IT IS A DANGEROUS WORLD, MA'AM --
-- FOR WOMEN AND MEN, IT'S A DANGEROUS WORLD --
-- AND INNOCENT PEOPLE NEED SOMEONE TO KEEP THEM SAFE.

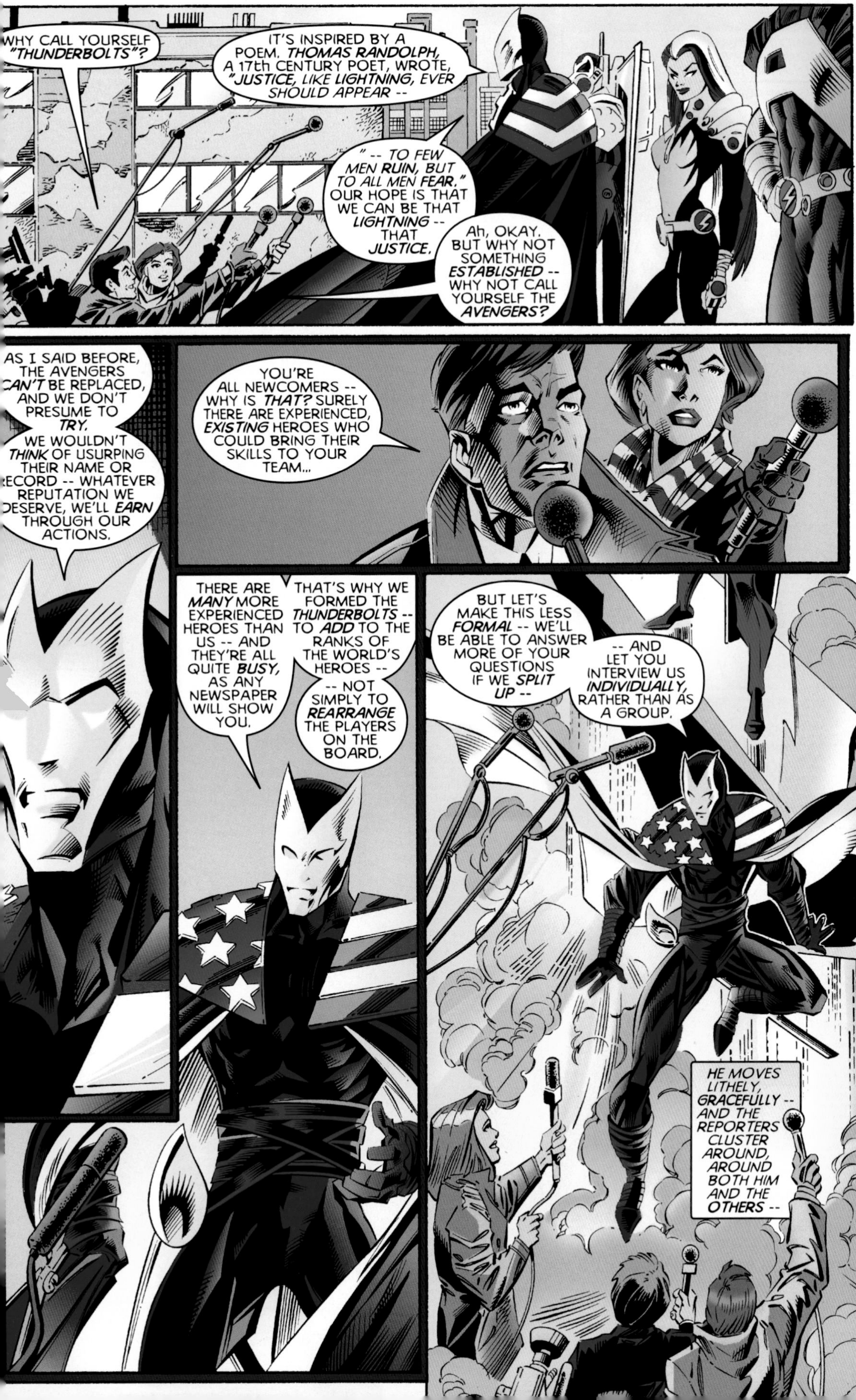

WHY CALL YOURSELF "THUNDERBOLTS"?
IT'S INSPIRED BY A POEM. THOMAS RANDOLPH, A 17th CENTURY POET, WROTE, "JUSTICE, LIKE LIGHTNING, EVER SHOULD APPEAR --
" -- TO FEW MEN RUIN, BUT TO ALL MEN FEAR." OUR HOPE IS THAT WE CAN BE THAT LIGHTNING -- THAT JUSTICE.
Ah, OKAY. BUT WHY NOT SOMETHING ESTABLISHED -- WHY NOT CALL YOURSELF THE AVENGERS?
AS I SAID BEFORE, THE AVENGERS CAN'T BE REPLACED, AND WE DON'T PRESUME TO TRY. WE WOULDN'T THINK OF USURPING THEIR NAME OR RECORD -- WHATEVER REPUTATION WE DESERVE, WE'LL EARN THROUGH OUR ACTIONS.
YOU'RE ALL NEWCOMERS -- WHY IS THAT? SURELY THERE ARE EXPERIENCED, EXISTING HEROES WHO COULD BRING THEIR SKILLS TO YOUR TEAM...
THERE ARE MANY MORE EXPERIENCED HEROES THAN US -- AND THEY'RE ALL QUITE BUSY, AS ANY NEWSPAPER WILL SHOW YOU.
THAT'S WHY WE FORMED THE THUNDERBOLTS -- TO ADD TO THE RANKS OF THE WORLD'S HEROES --
-- NOT SIMPLY TO REARRANGE THE PLAYERS ON THE BOARD.
BUT LET'S MAKE THIS LESS FORMAL -- WE'LL BE ABLE TO ANSWER MORE OF YOUR QUESTIONS IF WE SPLIT UP --
-- AND LET YOU INTERVIEW US INDIVIDUALLY, RATHER THAN AS A GROUP.
HE MOVES LITHELY, GRACEFULLY -- AND THE REPORTERS CLUSTER AROUND, AROUND BOTH HIM AND THE OTHERS --

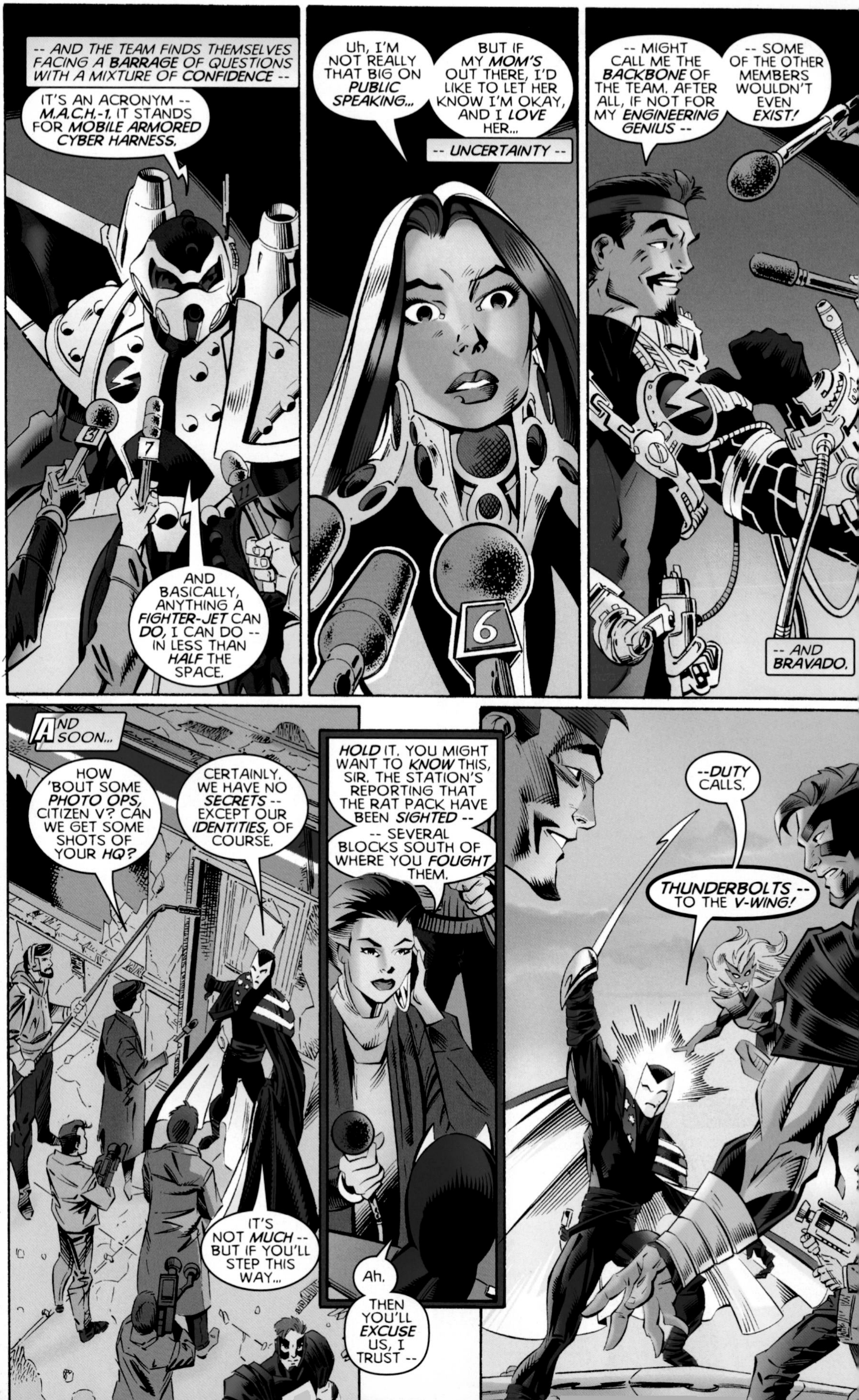
-- AND THE TEAM FINDS THEMSELVES FACING A BARRAGE OF QUESTIONS WITH A MIXTURE OF CONFIDENCE --
IT'S AN ACRONYM -- M.A.C.H.-1, IT STANDS FOR MOBILE ARMORED CYBER HARNESS.
AND BASICALLY, ANYTHING A FIGHTER-JET CAN DO, I CAN DO -- IN LESS THAN HALF THE SPACE.
Uh, I'M NOT REALLY THAT BIG ON PUBLIC SPEAKING...
BUT IF MY MOM'S OUT THERE, I'D LIKE TO LET HER KNOW I'M OKAY, AND I LOVE HER...
-- UNCERTAINTY --
-- MIGHT CALL ME THE BACKBONE OF THE TEAM. AFTER ALL, IF NOT FOR MY ENGINEERING GENIUS --
-- SOME OF THE OTHER MEMBERS WOULDN'T EVEN EXIST!
-- AND BRAVADO.
AND SOON...
HOW 'BOUT SOME PHOTO OPS, CITIZEN V? CAN WE GET SOME SHOTS OF YOUR HQ?
CERTAINLY. WE HAVE NO SECRETS -- EXCEPT OUR IDENTITIES, OF COURSE.
IT'S NOT MUCH -- BUT IF YOU'LL STEP THIS WAY...
HOLD IT. YOU MIGHT WANT TO KNOW THIS, SIR. THE STATION'S REPORTING THAT THE RAT PACK HAVE BEEN SIGHTED --
-- SEVERAL BLOCKS SOUTH OF WHERE YOU FOUGHT THEM.
Ah.
THEN YOU'LL EXCUSE US, I TRUST --
--DUTY CALLS.
THUNDERBOLTS -- TO THE V-WING!

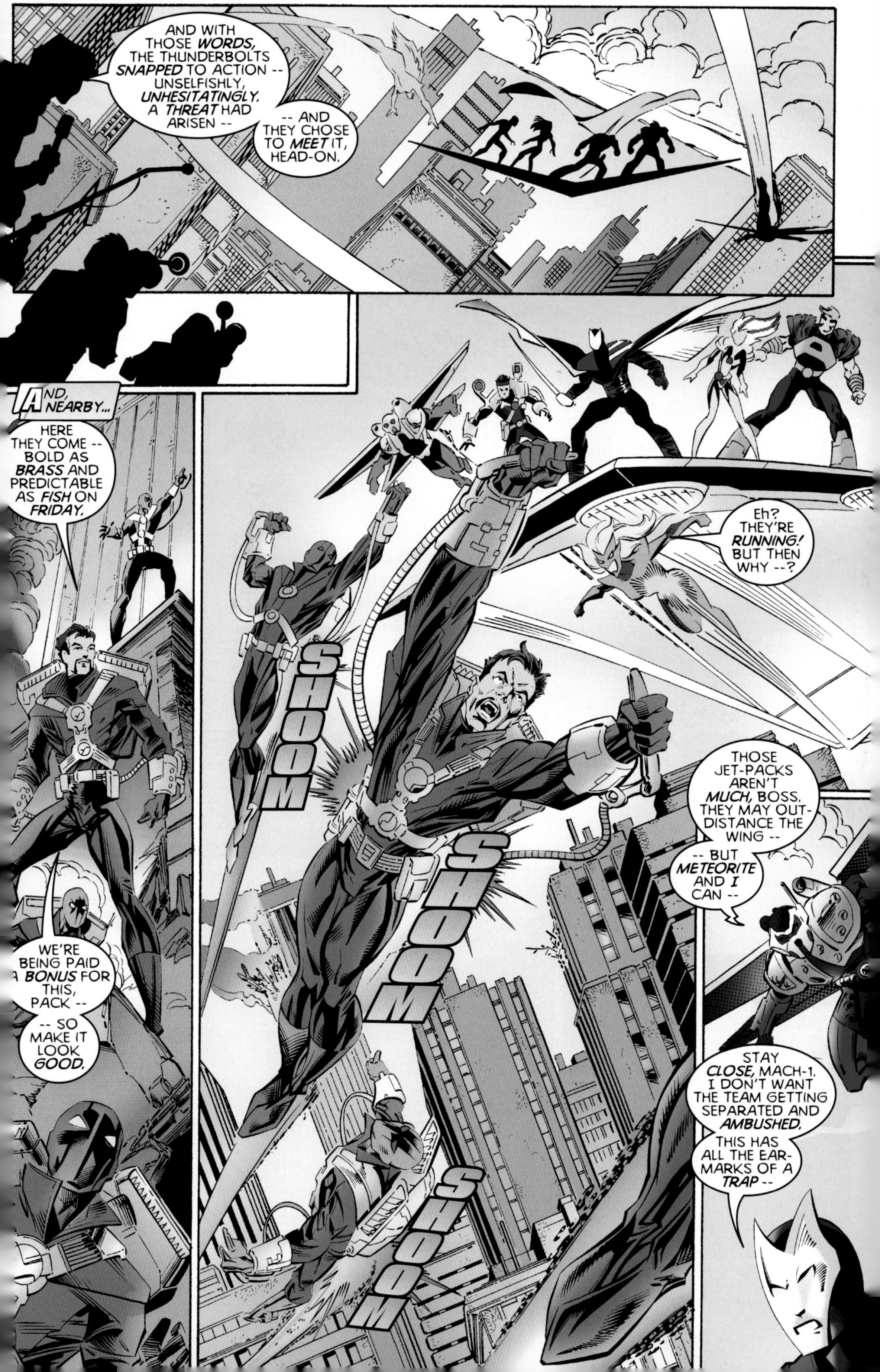
AND WITH THOSE WORDS, THE THUNDERBOLTS SNAPPED TO ACTION -- UNSELFISHLY, UNHESITATINGLY. A THREAT HAD ARISEN --
-- AND THEY CHOSE TO MEET IT, HEAD-ON.
AND, NEARBY...
HERE THEY COME -- BOLD AS BRASS AND PREDICTABLE AS FISH ON FRIDAY.
WE'RE BEING PAID A BONUS FOR THIS, PACK --
-- SO MAKE IT LOOK GOOD.
SHOOM
SHOOM
SHOOM
Eh? THEY'RE RUNNING! BUT THEN WHY --?
THOSE JET-PACKS AREN'T MUCH, BOSS. THEY MAY OUT-DISTANCE THE WING --
-- BUT METEORITE AND I CAN --
STAY CLOSE, MACH-1. I DON'T WANT THE TEAM GETTING SEPARATED AND AMBUSHED.
THIS HAS ALL THE EAR-MARKS OF A TRAP --

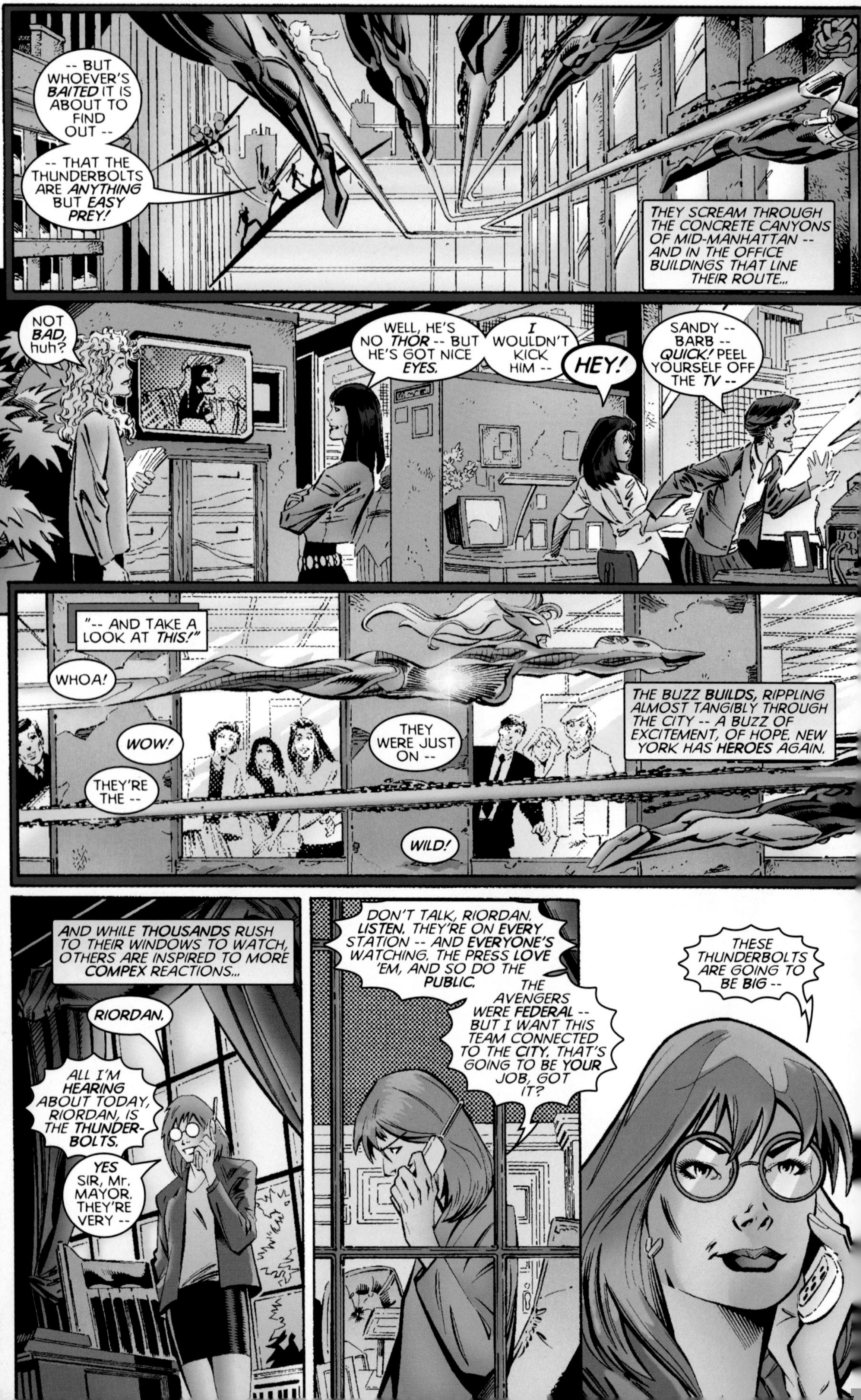
-- BUT WHOEVER'S BAITED IT IS ABOUT TO FIND OUT --
-- THAT THE THUNDERBOLTS ARE ANYTHING BUT EASY PREY!
THEY SCREAM THROUGH THE CONCRETE CANYONS OF MID-MANHATTAN -- AND IN THE OFFICE BUILDINGS THAT LINE THEIR ROUTE...
NOT BAD, huh?
WELL, HE'S NO THOR -- BUT HE'S GOT NICE EYES.
I WOULDN'T KICK HIM --
HEY!
SANDY -- BARB -- QUICK! PEEL YOURSELF OFF THE TV --
"-- AND TAKE A LOOK AT THIS!"
WHOA!
WOW!
THEY'RE THE --
THEY WERE JUST ON --
WILD!
THE BUZZ BUILDS, RIPPLING ALMOST TANGIBLY THROUGH THE CITY -- A BUZZ OF EXCITEMENT, OF HOPE. NEW YORK HAS HEROES AGAIN.
AND WHILE THOUSANDS RUSH TO THEIR WINDOWS TO WATCH, OTHERS ARE INSPIRED TO MORE COMPEX REACTIONS...
RIORDAN.
ALL I'M HEARING ABOUT TODAY, RIORDAN, IS THE THUNDER-BOLTS.
YES SIR, Mr. MAYOR. THEY'RE VERY --
DON'T TALK, RIORDAN. LISTEN. THEY'RE ON EVERY STATION -- AND EVERYONE'S WATCHING. THE PRESS LOVE 'EM, AND SO DO THE PUBLIC.
THE AVENGERS WERE FEDERAL -- BUT I WANT THIS TEAM CONNECTED TO THE CITY. THAT'S GOING TO BE YOUR JOB, GOT IT?
THESE THUNDERBOLTS ARE GOING TO BE BIG --

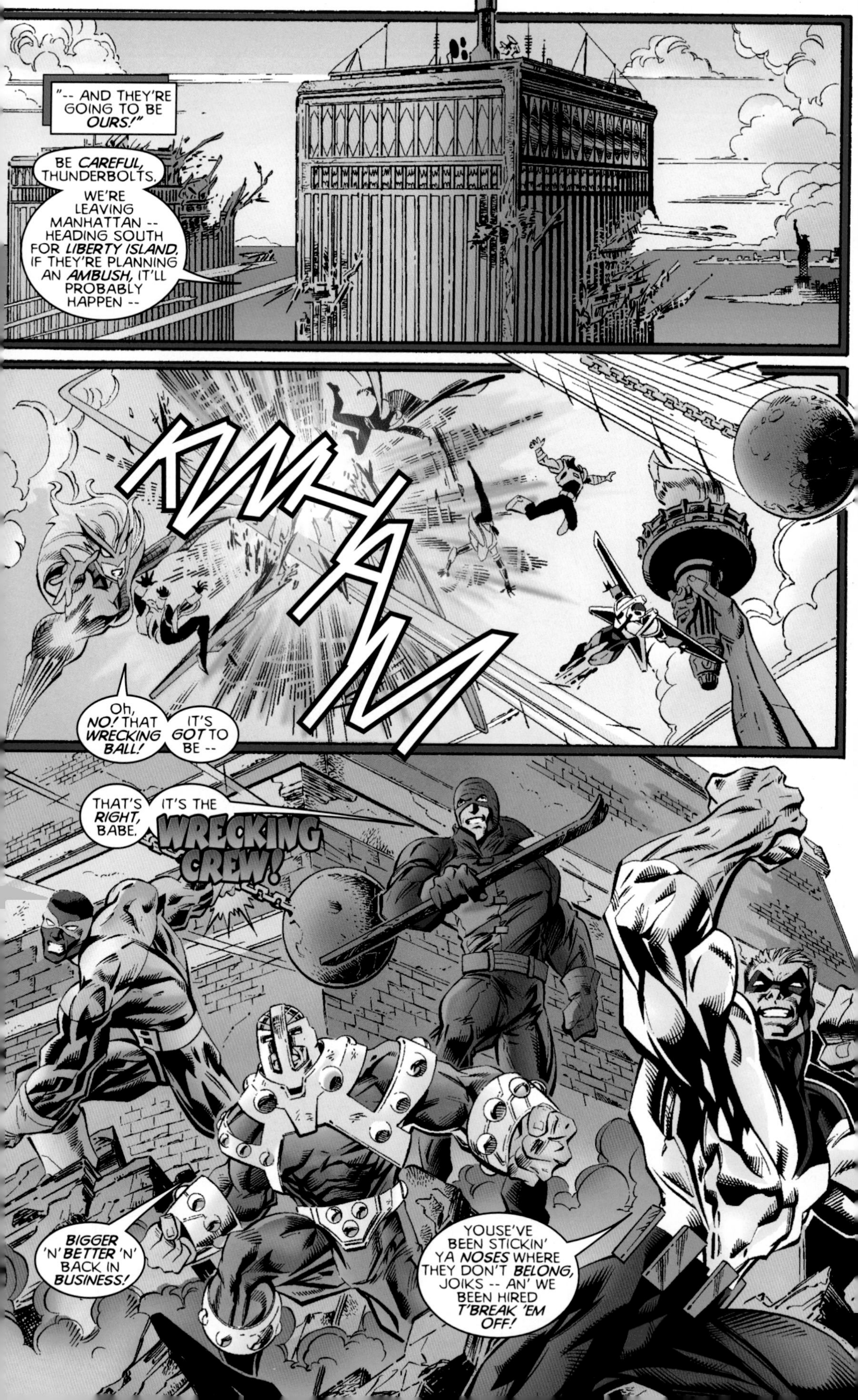
"-- AND THEY'RE GOING TO BE OURS!"
BE CAREFUL, THUNDERBOLTS.
WE'RE LEAVING MANHATTAN -- HEADING SOUTH FOR LIBERTY ISLAND. IF THEY'RE PLANNING AN AMBUSH, IT'LL PROBABLY HAPPEN --
KWHAM
Oh, NO! THAT WRECKING BALL!
IT'S GOT TO BE --
THAT'S RIGHT, BABE.
IT'S THE WRECKING CREW!
BIGGER 'N' BETTER 'N' BACK IN BUSINESS!
YOUSE'VE BEEN STICKIN' YA NOSES WHERE THEY DON'T BELONG, JOIKS -- AN' WE BEEN HIRED T'BREAK 'EM OFF!

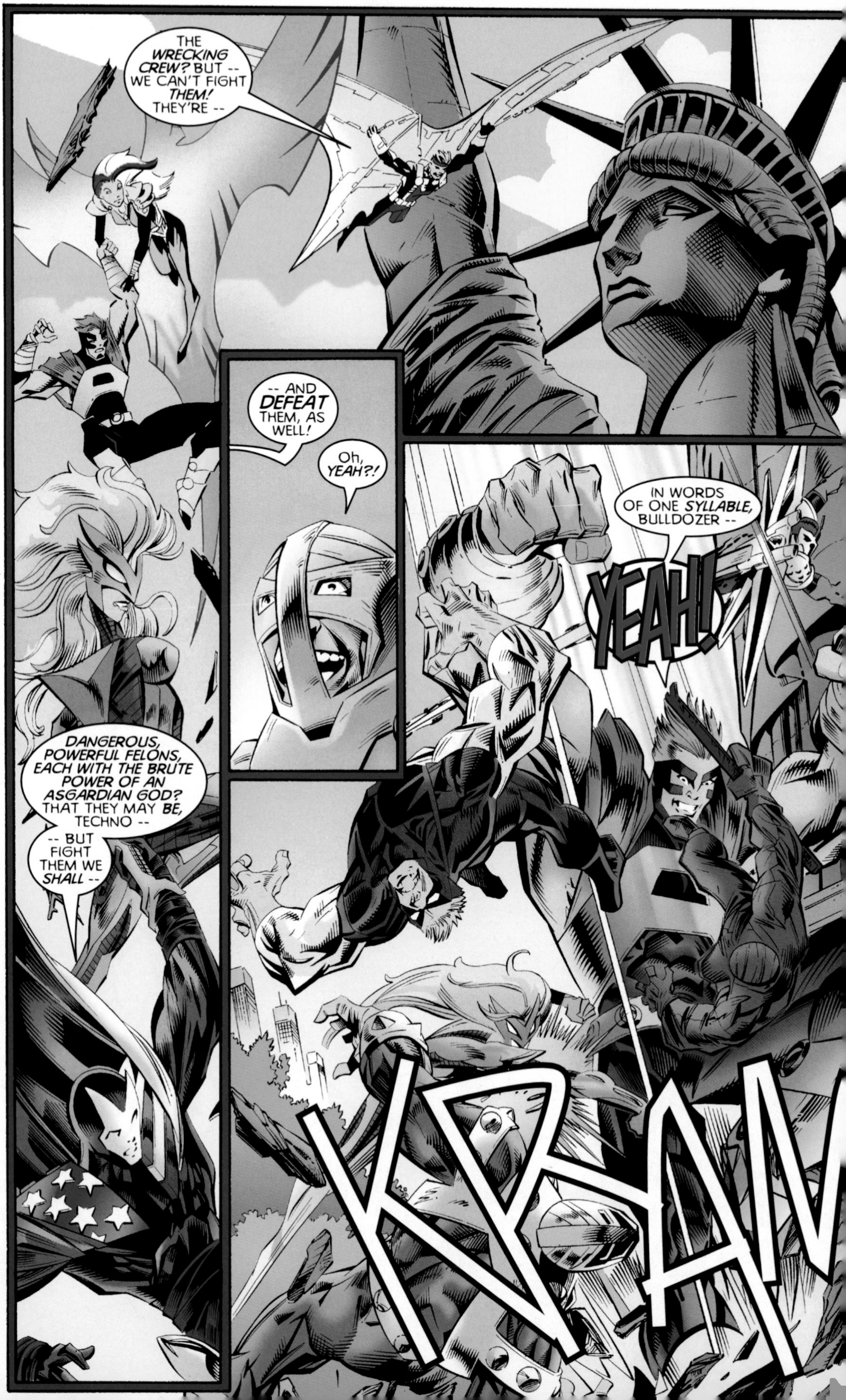
THE WRECKING CREW? BUT -- WE CAN'T FIGHT THEM! THEY'RE --
-- AND DEFEAT THEM, AS WELL!
Oh, YEAH?!
DANGEROUS, POWERFUL FELONS, EACH WITH THE BRUTE POWER OF AN ASGARDIAN GOD? THAT THEY MAY BE, TECHNO --
-- BUT FIGHT THEM WE SHALL --
IN WORDS OF ONE SYLLABLE, BULLDOZER --
YEAH!
KRAN

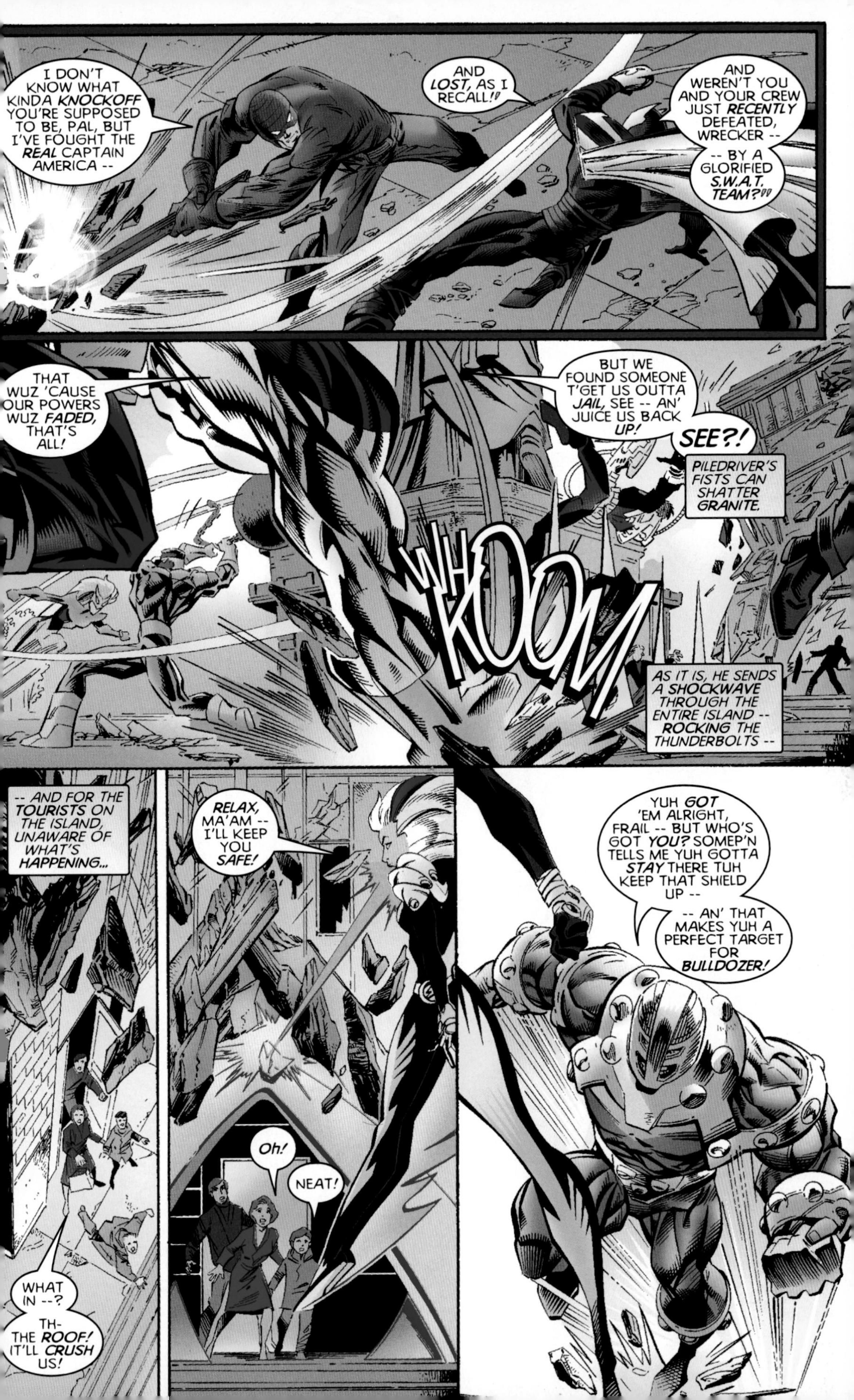
I DON'T KNOW WHAT KINDA KNOCKOFF YOU'RE SUPPOSED TO BE, PAL, BUT I'VE FOUGHT THE REAL CAPTAIN AMERICA --
AND LOST, AS I RECALL!?
AND WEREN'T YOU AND YOUR CREW JUST RECENTLY DEFEATED, WRECKER --
-- BY A GLORIFIED S.W.A.T. TEAM?!
THAT WUZ 'CAUSE OUR POWERS WUZ FADED, THAT'S ALL!
BUT WE FOUND SOMEONE T'GET US OUTTA JAIL, SEE -- AN' JUICE US BACK UP!
SEE?!
PILEDRIVER'S FISTS CAN SHATTER GRANITE.
WHKOOM
AS IT IS, HE SENDS A SHOCKWAVE THROUGH THE ENTIRE ISLAND -- ROCKING THE THUNDERBOLTS --
-- AND FOR THE TOURISTS ON THE ISLAND, UNAWARE OF WHAT'S HAPPENING...
WHAT IN --?
TH- THE ROOF! IT'LL CRUSH US!
RELAX, MA'AM -- I'LL KEEP YOU SAFE!
Oh!
NEAT!
YUH GOT 'EM ALRIGHT, FRAIL -- BUT WHO'S GOT YOU? SOMEP'N TELLS ME YUH GOTTA STAY THERE TUH KEEP THAT SHIELD UP --
-- AN' THAT MAKES YUH A PERFECT TARGET FOR BULLDOZER!

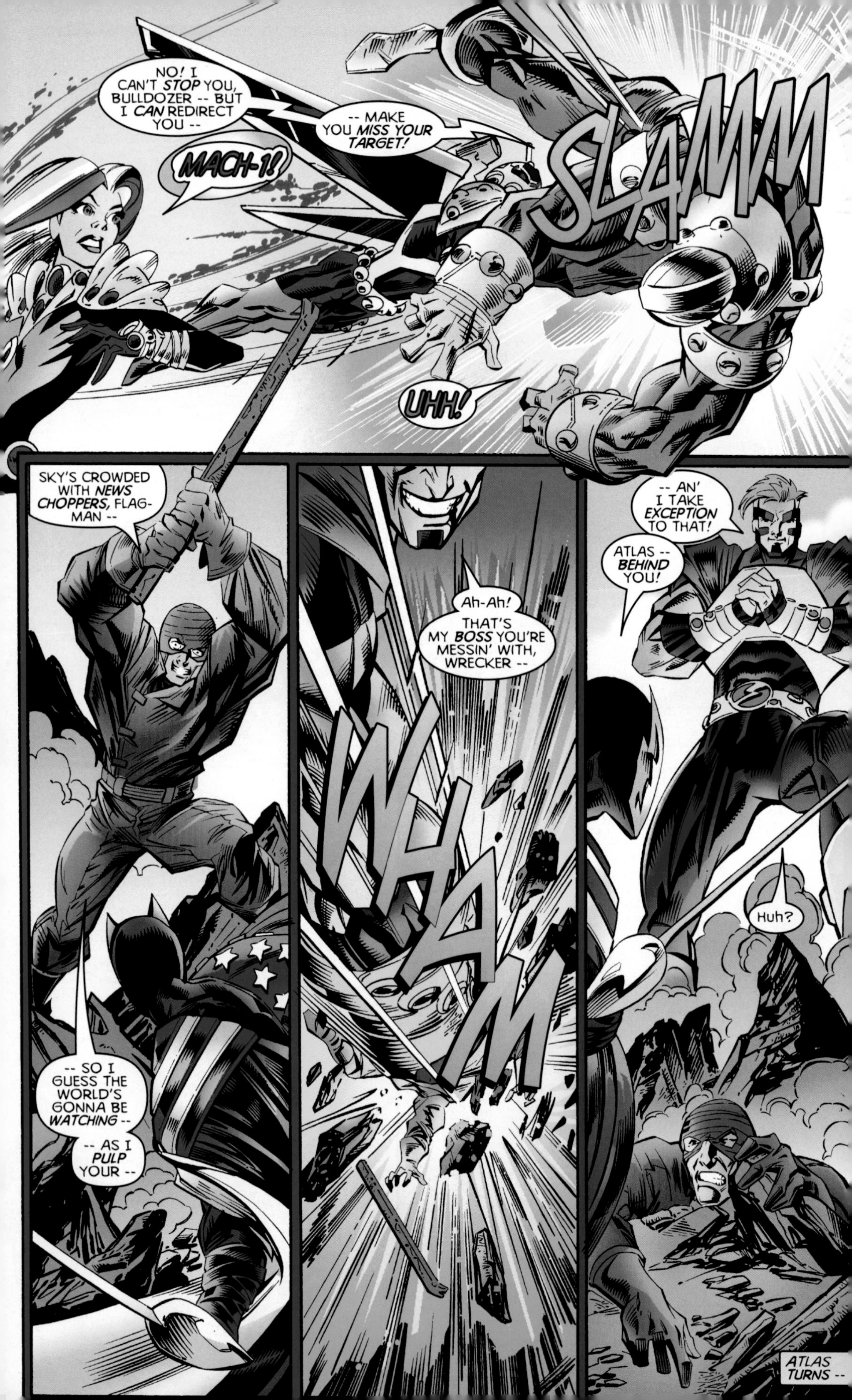
NO! I CAN'T STOP YOU, BULLDOZER -- BUT I CAN REDIRECT YOU --
-- MAKE YOU MISS YOUR TARGET!
MACH-1!
SLAMM
UHH!
SKY'S CROWDED WITH NEWS CHOPPERS, FLAG-MAN --
-- SO I GUESS THE WORLD'S GONNA BE WATCHING --
-- AS I PULP YOUR --
Ah-Ah!
THAT'S MY BOSS YOU'RE MESSIN' WITH, WRECKER --
WHAM
-- AN' I TAKE EXCEPTION TO THAT!
ATLAS -- BEHIND YOU!
Huh?
ATLAS TURNS --

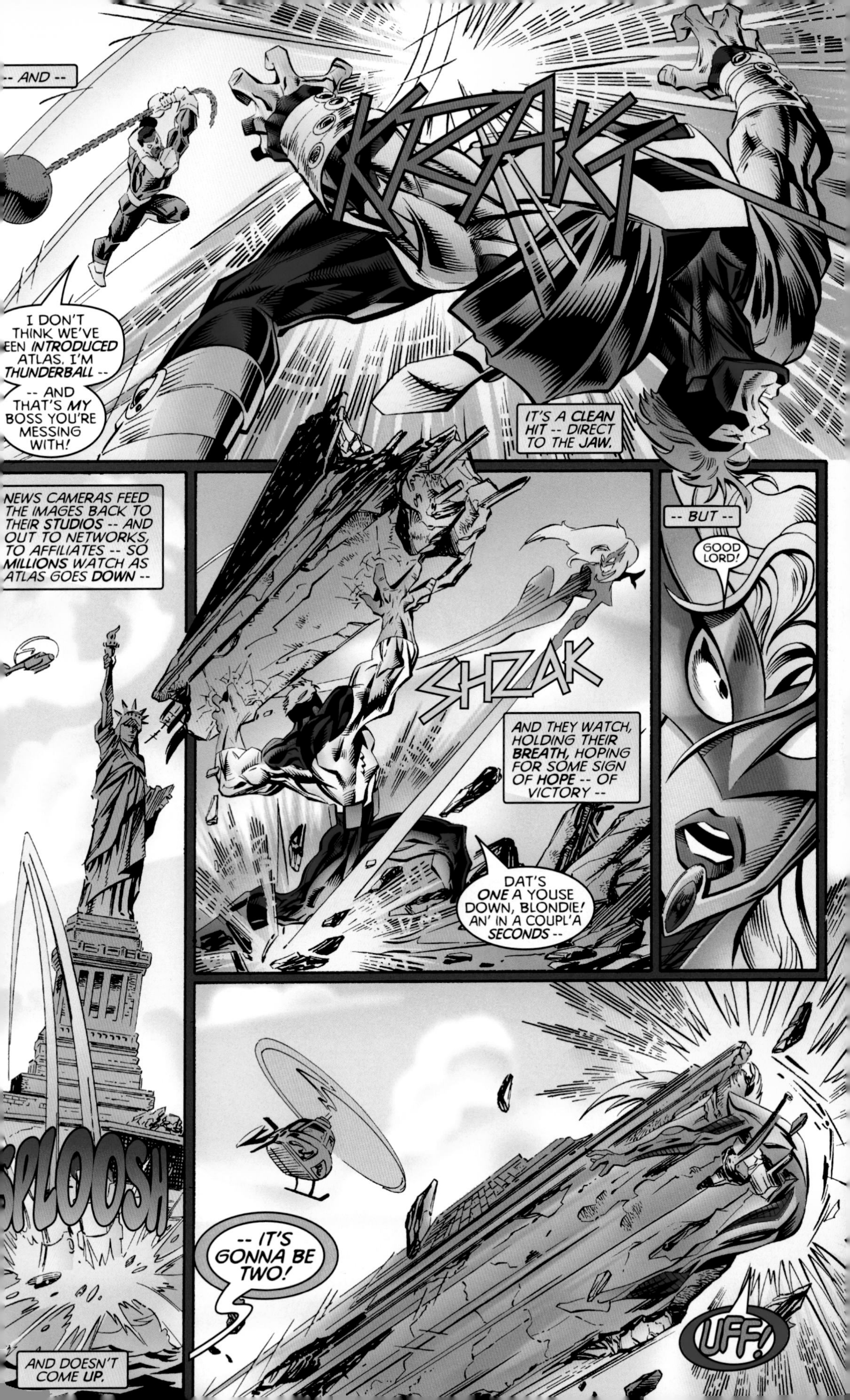
-- AND --
KRAKT
I DON'T THINK WE'VE BEEN INTRODUCED ATLAS, I'M THUNDERBALL --
-- AND THAT'S MY BOSS YOU'RE MESSING WITH!
IT'S A CLEAN HIT -- DIRECT TO THE JAW.
NEWS CAMERAS FEED THE IMAGES BACK TO THEIR STUDIOS -- AND OUT TO NETWORKS, TO AFFILIATES -- SO MILLIONS WATCH AS ATLAS GOES DOWN --
SPLOOSH
AND DOESN'T COME UP.
SHZAK
AND THEY WATCH, HOLDING THEIR BREATH, HOPING FOR SOME SIGN OF HOPE -- OF VICTORY --
DAT'S ONE A YOUSE DOWN, BLONDIE! AN' IN A COUPL'A SECONDS --
-- BUT --
GOOD LORD!
-- IT'S GONNA BE TWO!
UFF!

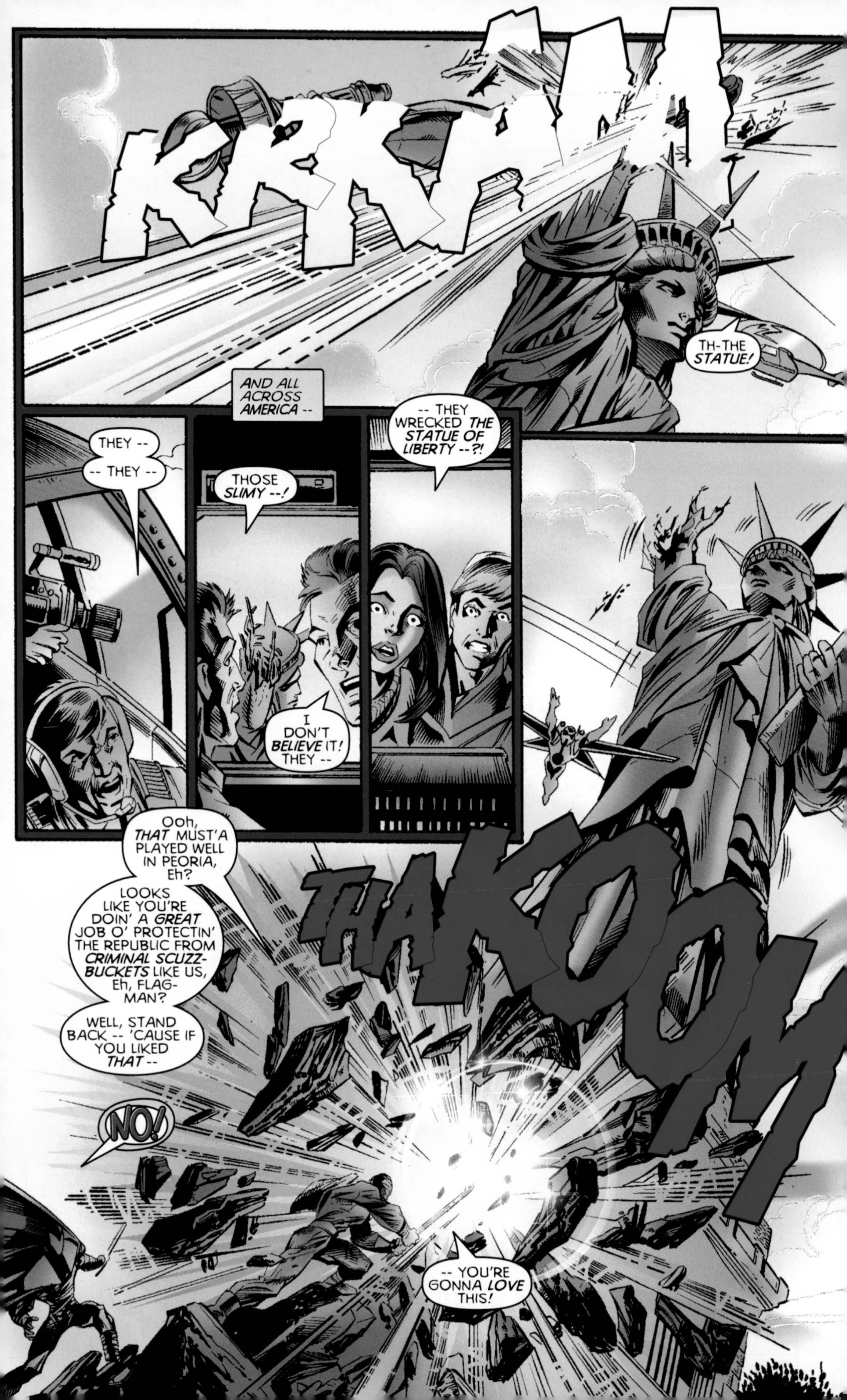
KRRKAAM
TH-THE STATUE!
AND ALL ACROSS AMERICA --
THEY --
-- THEY --
THOSE SLIMY --!
I DON'T BELIEVE IT! THEY --
-- THEY WRECKED THE STATUE OF LIBERTY --?!
Ooh, THAT MUST'A PLAYED WELL IN PEORIA, Eh?
LOOKS LIKE YOU'RE DOIN' A GREAT JOB O' PROTECTIN' THE REPUBLIC FROM CRIMINAL SCUZZ-BUCKETS LIKE US, Eh, FLAG-MAN?
WELL, STAND BACK -- 'CAUSE IF YOU LIKED THAT --
THAKOOM
NO!
-- YOU'RE GONNA LOVE THIS!

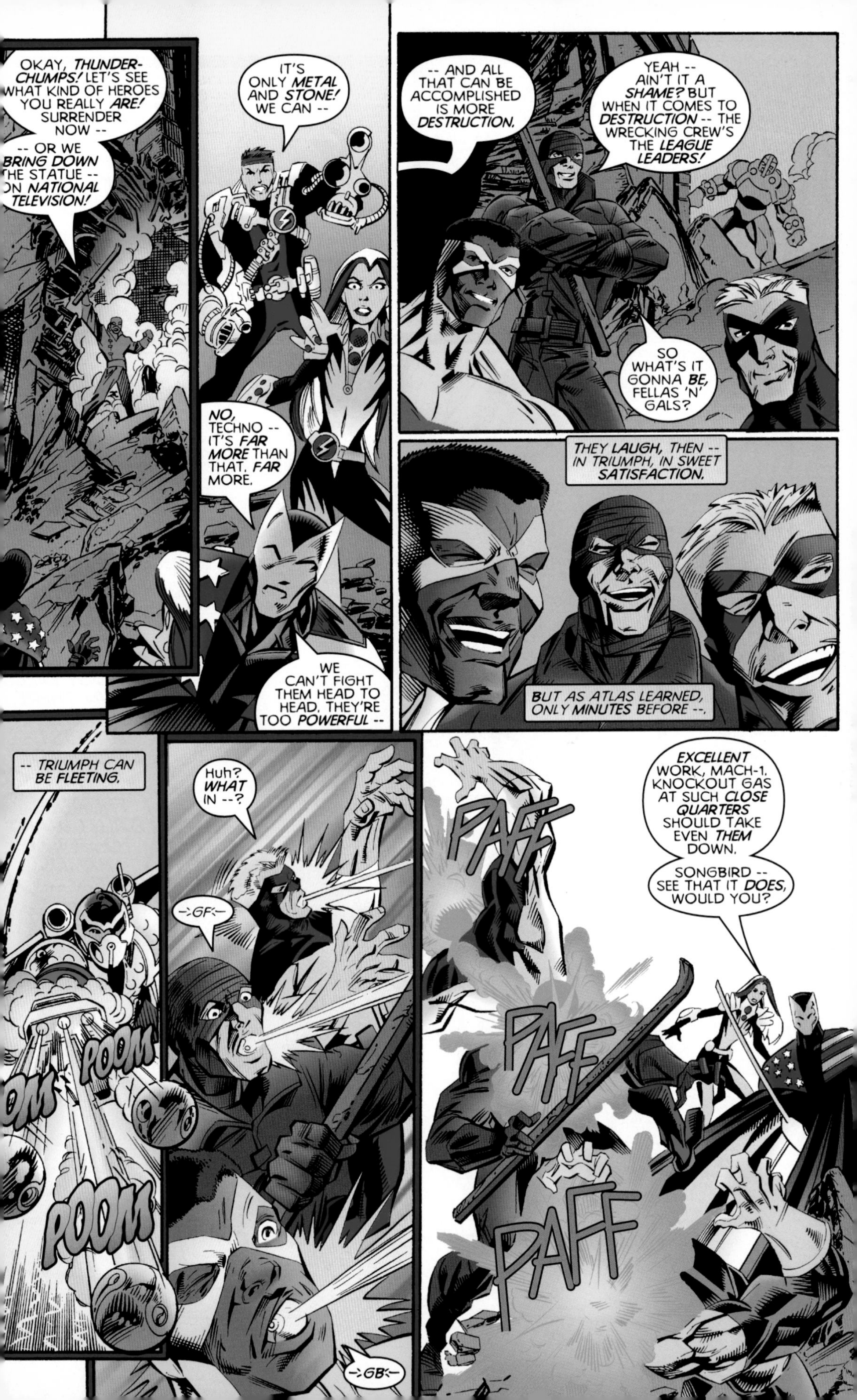

OKAY, THUNDER-CHUMPS! LET'S SEE WHAT KIND OF HEROES YOU REALLY ARE! SURRENDER NOW --
-- OR WE BRING DOWN THE STATUE -- ON NATIONAL TELEVISION!
IT'S ONLY METAL AND STONE! WE CAN --
NO, TECHNO -- IT'S FAR MORE THAN THAT. FAR MORE.
WE CAN'T FIGHT THEM HEAD TO HEAD. THEY'RE TOO POWERFUL --
-- AND ALL THAT CAN BE ACCOMPLISHED IS MORE DESTRUCTION.
YEAH -- AIN'T IT A SHAME? BUT WHEN IT COMES TO DESTRUCTION -- THE WRECKING CREW'S THE LEAGUE LEADERS!
SO WHAT'S IT GONNA BE, FELLAS 'N' GALS?
THEY LAUGH, THEN -- IN TRIUMPH, IN SWEET SATISFACTION.
BUT AS ATLAS LEARNED, ONLY MINUTES BEFORE --.
-- TRIUMPH CAN BE FLEETING.
POOM
POOM
POOM
Huh? WHAT IN --?
-GF-
-GB-
PAFF
PAFF
PAFF
EXCELLENT WORK, MACH-1. KNOCKOUT GAS AT SUCH CLOSE QUARTERS SHOULD TAKE EVEN THEM DOWN.
SONGBIRD -- SEE THAT IT DOES, WOULD YOU?

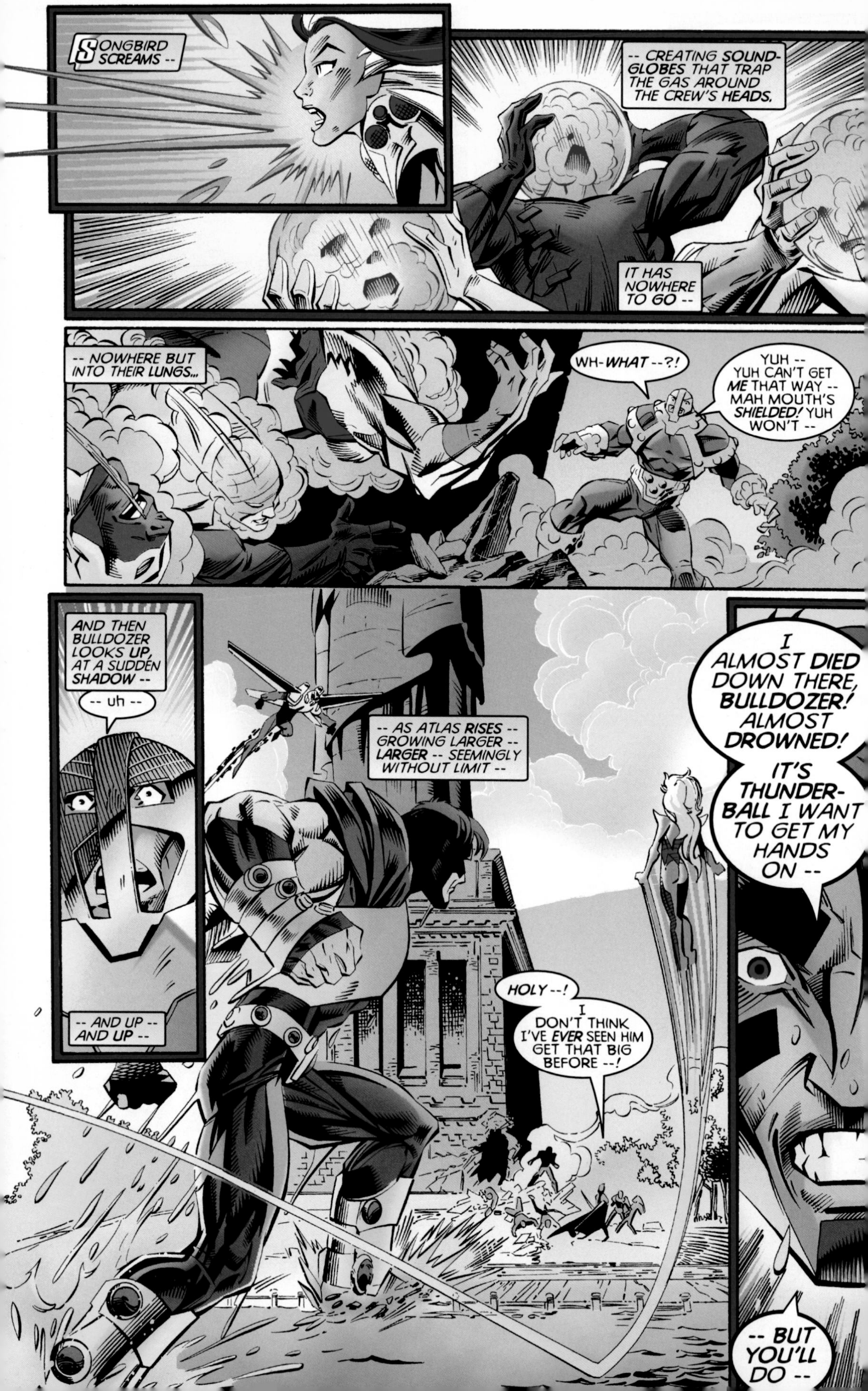
SONGBIRD SCREAMS --
-- CREATING SOUND-GLOBES THAT TRAP THE GAS AROUND THE CREW'S HEADS.
IT HAS NOWHERE TO GO --
-- NOWHERE BUT INTO THEIR LUNGS...
WH-WHAT --?!
YUH -- YUH CAN'T GET ME THAT WAY -- MAH MOUTH'S SHIELDED! YUH WON'T --
AND THEN BULLDOZER LOOKS UP, AT A SUDDEN SHADOW --
-- uh --
-- AND UP -- AND UP --
-- AS ATLAS RISES -- GROWING LARGER -- LARGER -- SEEMINGLY WITHOUT LIMIT --
HOLY --!
I DON'T THINK I'VE EVER SEEN HIM GET THAT BIG BEFORE --!
I ALMOST DIED DOWN THERE, BULLDOZER! ALMOST DROWNED!
IT'S THUNDERBALL I WANT TO GET MY HANDS ON --
-- BUT YOU'LL DO --

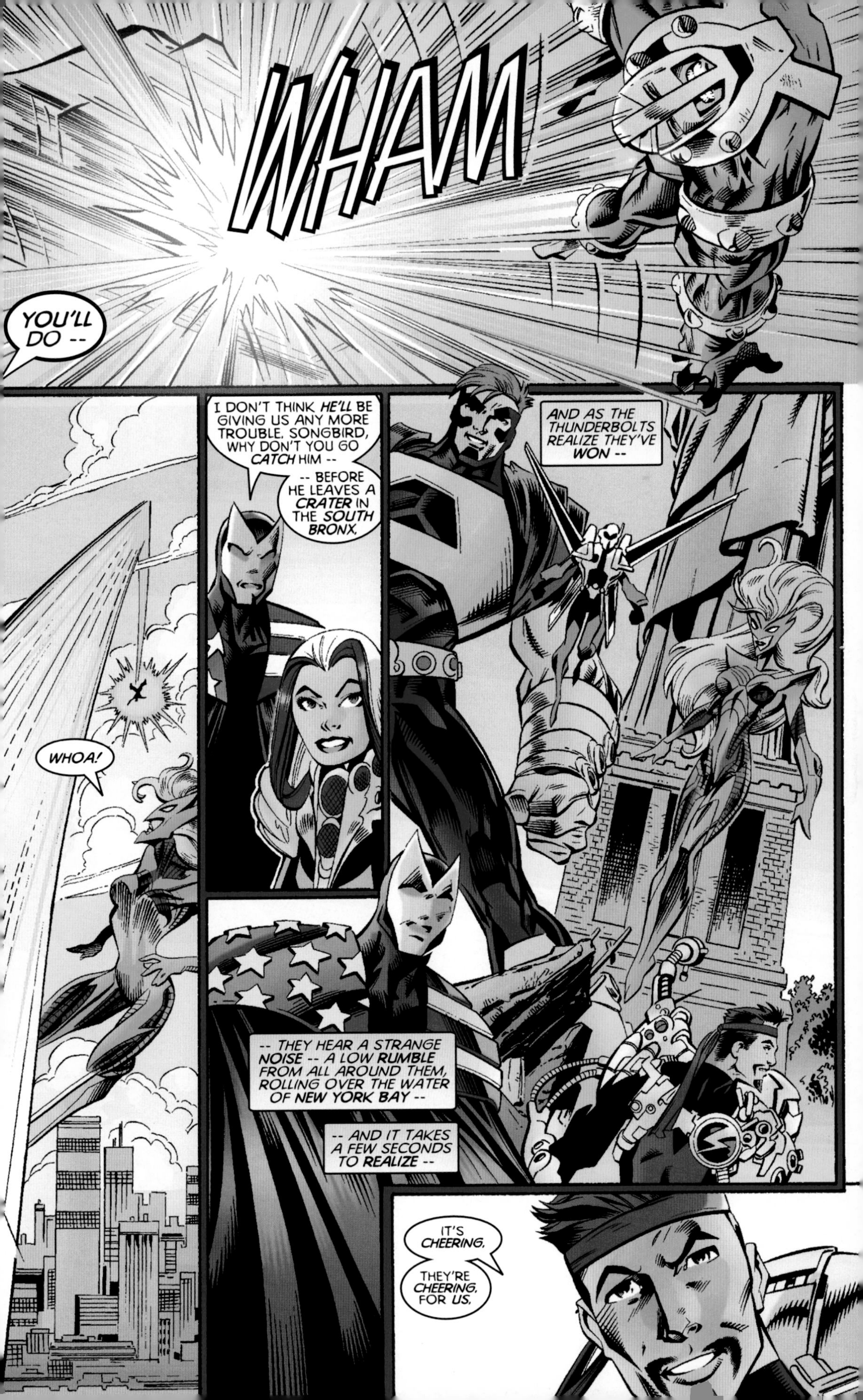
WHAM
YOU'LL DO --
WHOA!
I DON'T THINK HE'LL BE GIVING US ANY MORE TROUBLE, SONGBIRD, WHY DON'T YOU GO CATCH HIM --
-- BEFORE HE LEAVES A CRATER IN THE SOUTH BRONX.
AND AS THE THUNDERBOLTS REALIZE THEY'VE WON --
-- THEY HEAR A STRANGE NOISE -- A LOW RUMBLE FROM ALL AROUND THEM, ROLLING OVER THE WATER OF NEW YORK BAY --
-- AND IT TAKES A FEW SECONDS TO REALIZE --
IT'S CHEERING.
THEY'RE CHEERING. FOR US.

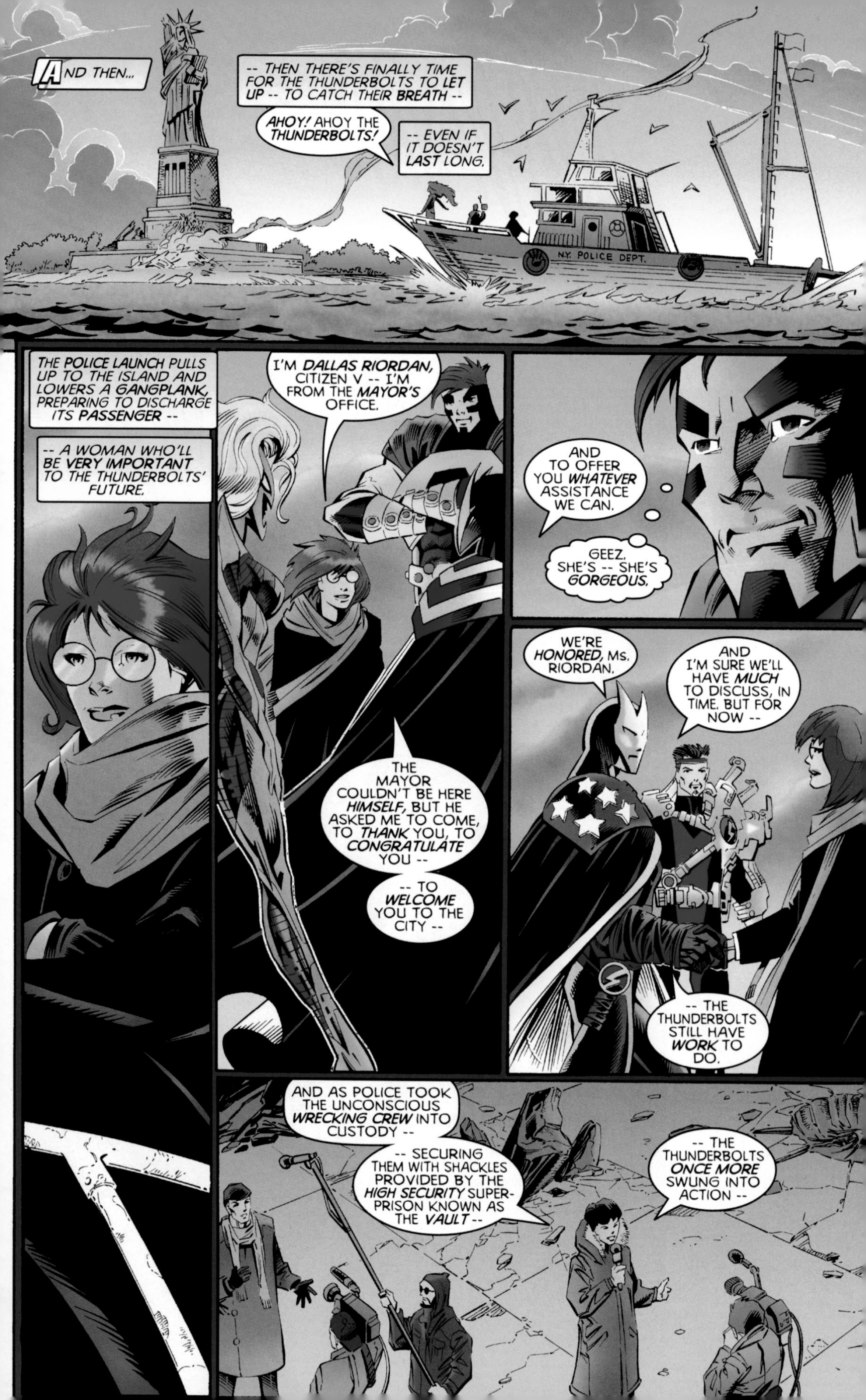
AND THEN...
-- THEN THERE'S FINALLY TIME FOR THE THUNDERBOLTS TO LET UP -- TO CATCH THEIR BREATH --
AHOY! AHOY THE THUNDERBOLTS!
-- EVEN IF IT DOESN'T LAST LONG.
N.Y. POLICE DEPT.
THE POLICE LAUNCH PULLS UP TO THE ISLAND AND LOWERS A GANGPLANK, PREPARING TO DISCHARGE ITS PASSENGER --
-- A WOMAN WHO'LL BE VERY IMPORTANT TO THE THUNDERBOLTS' FUTURE.
I'M DALLAS RIORDAN, CITIZEN V -- I'M FROM THE MAYOR'S OFFICE.
THE MAYOR COULDN'T BE HERE HIMSELF, BUT HE ASKED ME TO COME, TO THANK YOU, TO CONGRATULATE YOU --
-- TO WELCOME YOU TO THE CITY --
AND TO OFFER YOU WHATEVER ASSISTANCE WE CAN.
GEEZ. SHE'S -- SHE'S GORGEOUS.
WE'RE HONORED, Ms. RIORDAN.
AND I'M SURE WE'LL HAVE MUCH TO DISCUSS, IN TIME. BUT FOR NOW --
-- THE THUNDERBOLTS STILL HAVE WORK TO DO.
AND AS POLICE TOOK THE UNCONSCIOUS WRECKING CREW INTO CUSTODY --
-- SECURING THEM WITH SHACKLES PROVIDED BY THE HIGH SECURITY SUPER-PRISON KNOWN AS THE VAULT --
-- THE THUNDERBOLTS ONCE MORE SWUNG INTO ACTION --

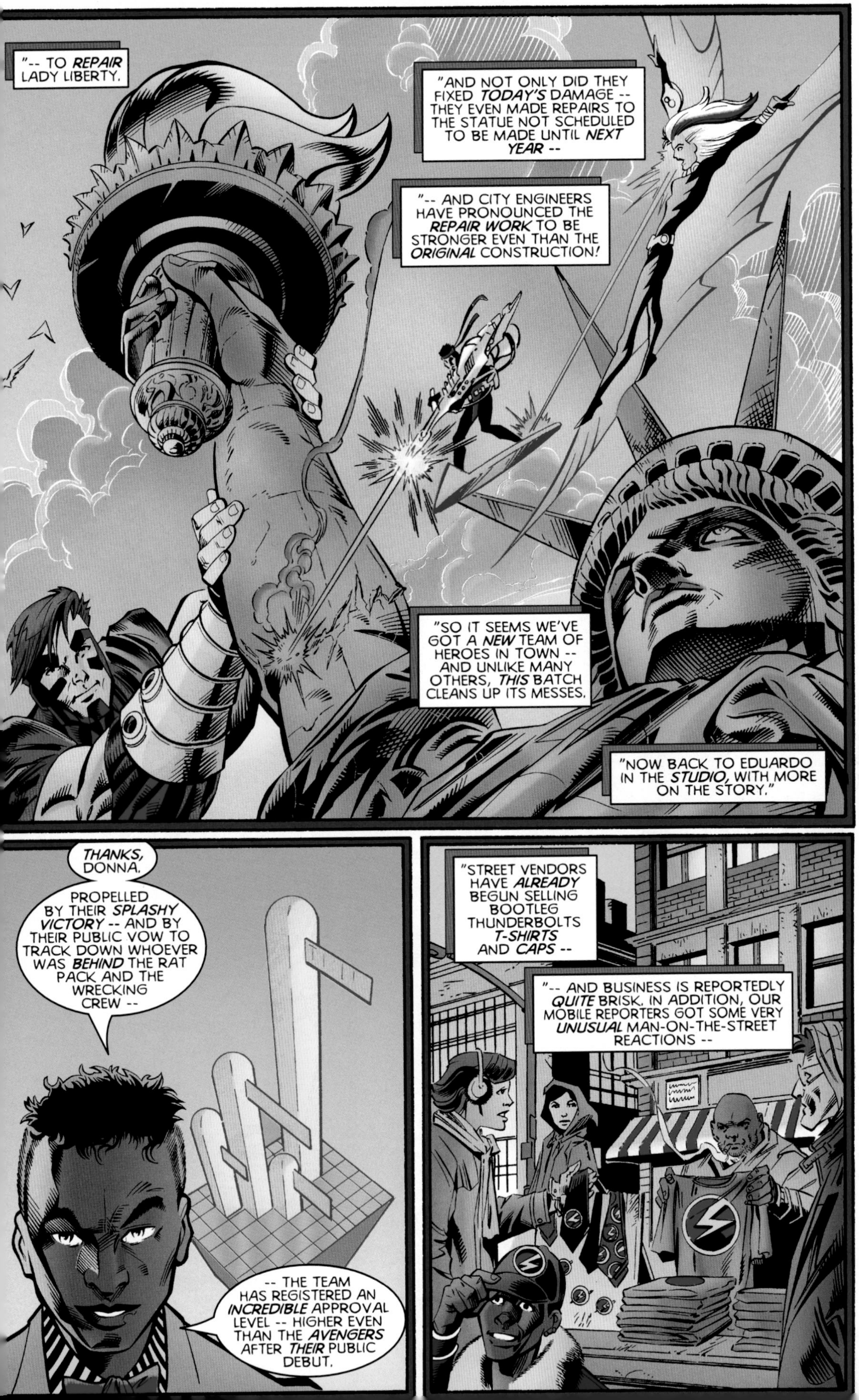
"-- TO REPAIR LADY LIBERTY.
"AND NOT ONLY DID THEY FIXED TODAY'S DAMAGE -- THEY EVEN MADE REPAIRS TO THE STATUE NOT SCHEDULED TO BE MADE UNTIL NEXT YEAR --
"-- AND CITY ENGINEERS HAVE PRONOUNCED THE REPAIR WORK TO BE STRONGER EVEN THAN THE ORIGINAL CONSTRUCTION!
"SO IT SEEMS WE'VE GOT A NEW TEAM OF HEROES IN TOWN -- AND UNLIKE MANY OTHERS, THIS BATCH CLEANS UP ITS MESSES.
"NOW BACK TO EDUARDO IN THE STUDIO, WITH MORE ON THE STORY."
THANKS, DONNA.
PROPELLED BY THEIR SPLASHY VICTORY -- AND BY THEIR PUBLIC VOW TO TRACK DOWN WHOEVER WAS BEHIND THE RAT PACK AND THE WRECKING CREW --
-- THE TEAM HAS REGISTERED AN INCREDIBLE APPROVAL LEVEL -- HIGHER EVEN THAN THE AVENGERS AFTER THEIR PUBLIC DEBUT.
"STREET VENDORS HAVE ALREADY BEGUN SELLING BOOTLEG THUNDERBOLTS T-SHIRTS AND CAPS --
"-- AND BUSINESS IS REPORTEDLY QUITE BRISK. IN ADDITION, OUR MOBILE REPORTERS GOT SOME VERY UNUSUAL MAN-ON-THE-STREET REACTIONS --

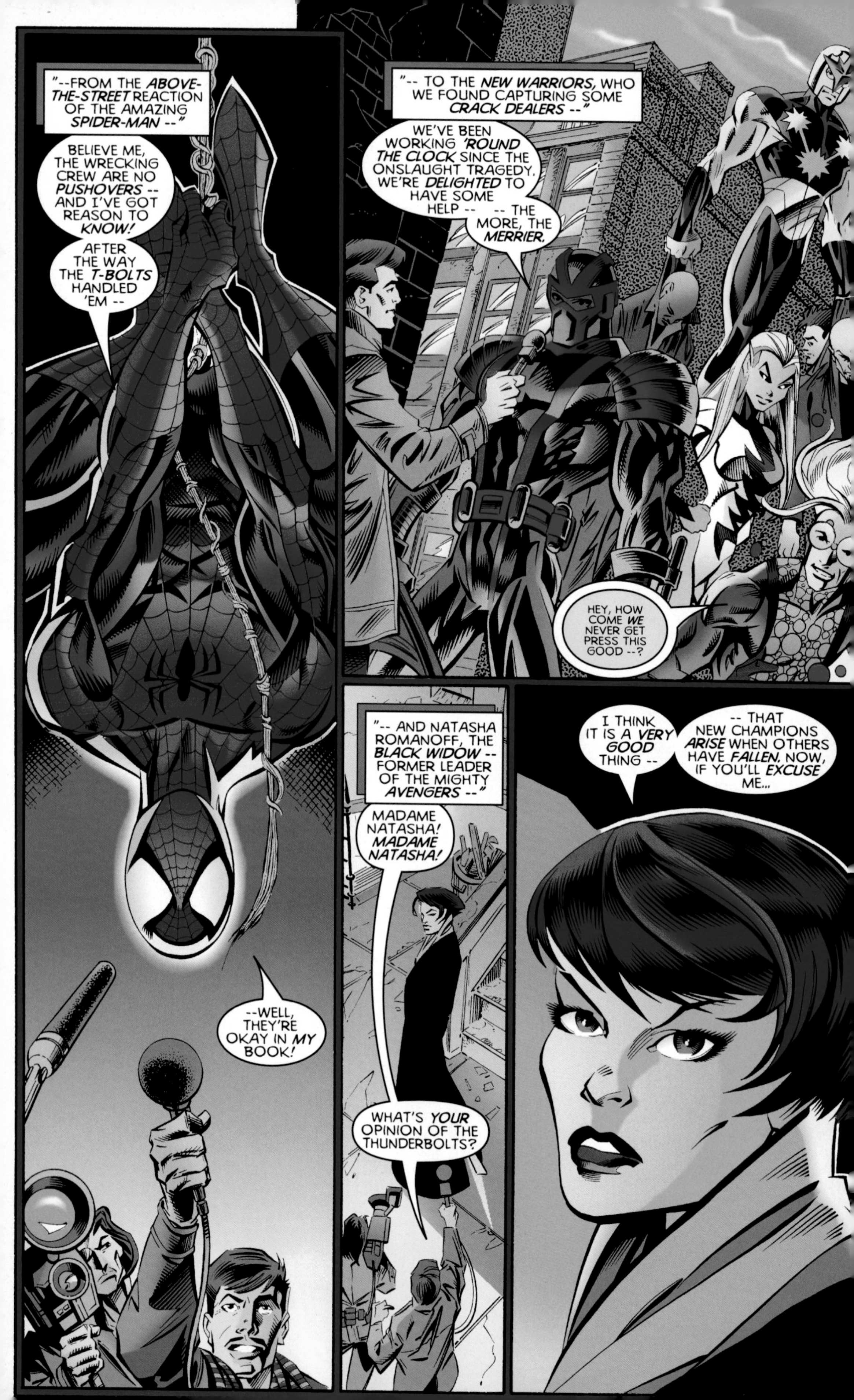
"--FROM THE ABOVE-THE-STREET REACTION OF THE AMAZING SPIDER-MAN --"
BELIEVE ME, THE WRECKING CREW ARE NO PUSHOVERS -- AND I'VE GOT REASON TO KNOW!
AFTER THE WAY THE T-BOLTS HANDLED 'EM --
--WELL, THEY'RE OKAY IN MY BOOK!
"-- TO THE NEW WARRIORS, WHO WE FOUND CAPTURING SOME CRACK DEALERS --"
WE'VE BEEN WORKING 'ROUND THE CLOCK SINCE THE ONSLAUGHT TRAGEDY. WE'RE DELIGHTED TO HAVE SOME HELP --
-- THE MORE, THE MERRIER.
HEY, HOW COME WE NEVER GET PRESS THIS GOOD --?
"-- AND NATASHA ROMANOFF, THE BLACK WIDOW -- FORMER LEADER OF THE MIGHTY AVENGERS --"
MADAME NATASHA! MADAME NATASHA!
WHAT'S YOUR OPINION OF THE THUNDERBOLTS?
I THINK IT IS A VERY GOOD THING --
-- THAT NEW CHAMPIONS ARISE WHEN OTHERS HAVE FALLEN. NOW, IF YOU'LL EXCUSE ME...

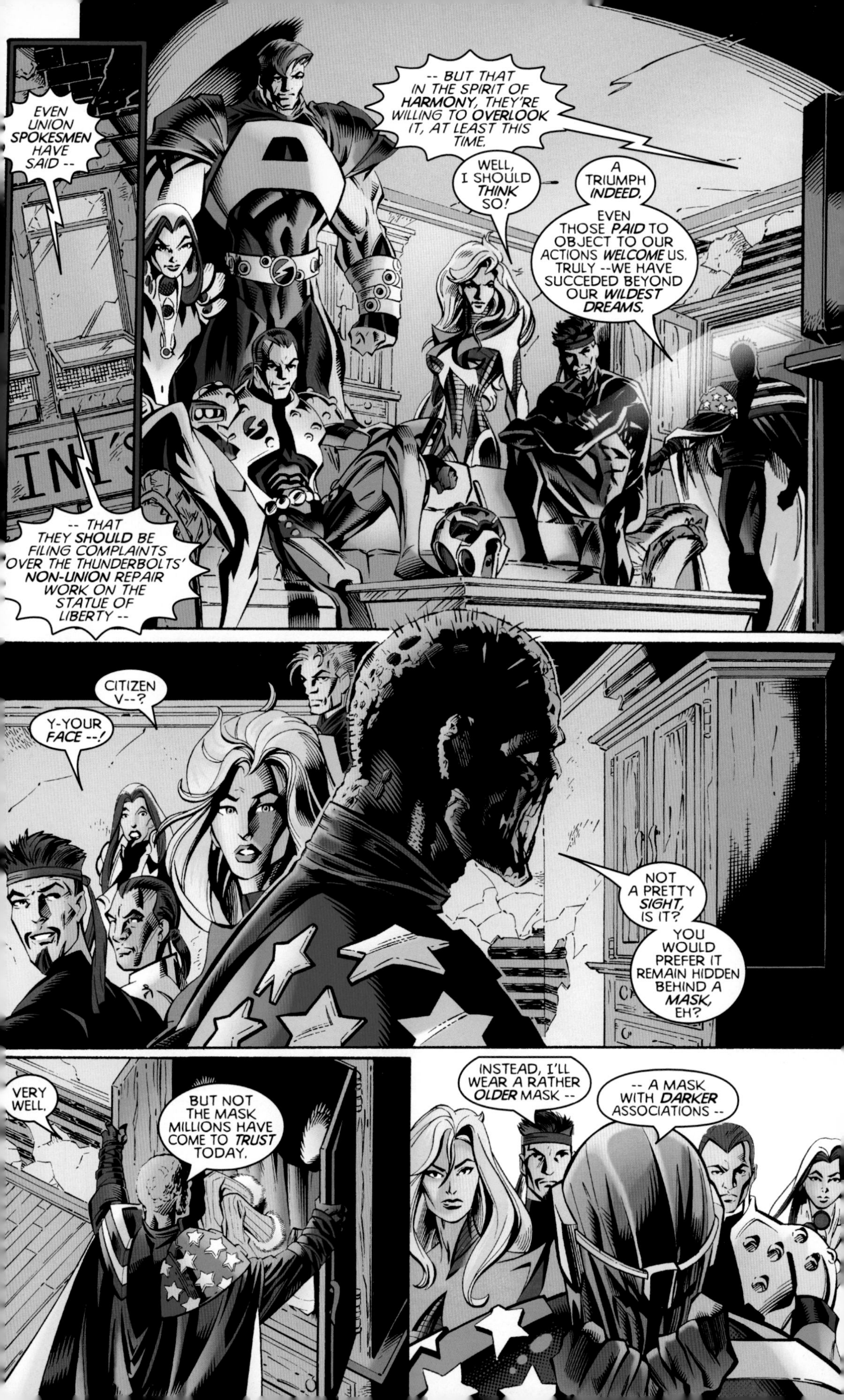
EVEN UNION SPOKESMEN HAVE SAID --
-- THAT THEY SHOULD BE FILING COMPLAINTS OVER THE THUNDERBOLTS' NON-UNION REPAIR WORK ON THE STATUE OF LIBERTY --
-- BUT THAT IN THE SPIRIT OF HARMONY, THEY'RE WILLING TO OVERLOOK IT, AT LEAST THIS TIME.
WELL, I SHOULD THINK SO!
A TRIUMPH INDEED.
EVEN THOSE PAID TO OBJECT TO OUR ACTIONS WELCOME US. TRULY --WE HAVE SUCCEDED BEYOND OUR WILDEST DREAMS.
INI'S
CITIZEN V--?
Y-YOUR FACE --!
NOT A PRETTY SIGHT, IS IT?
YOU WOULD PREFER IT REMAIN HIDDEN BEHIND A MASK, EH?
VERY WELL.
BUT NOT THE MASK MILLIONS HAVE COME TO TRUST TODAY.
INSTEAD, I'LL WEAR A RATHER OLDER MASK --
-- A MASK WITH DARKER ASSOCIATIONS --

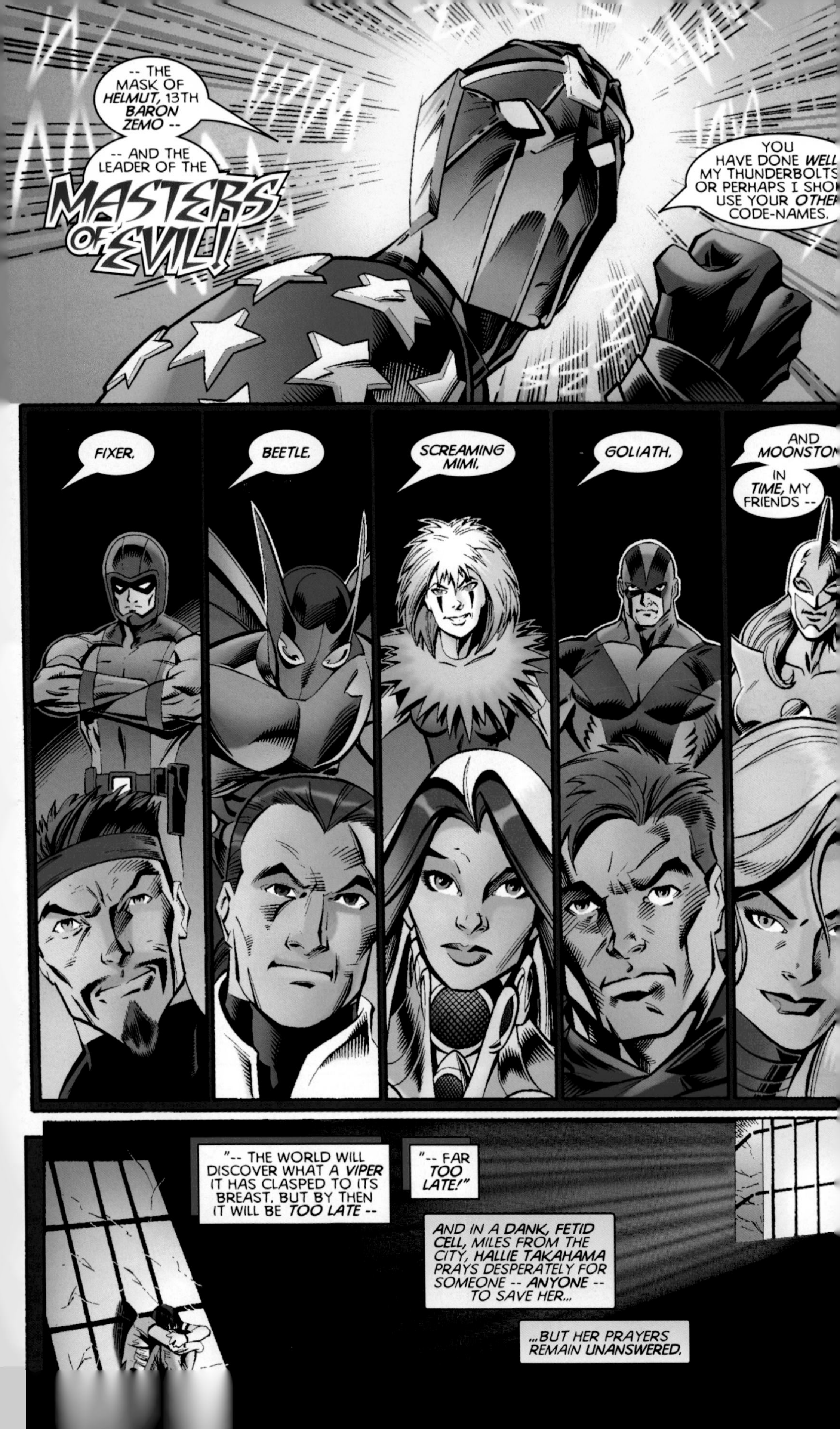
-- THE MASK OF HELMUT, 13TH BARON ZEMO --
-- AND THE LEADER OF THE
MASTERS OF EVIL!
YOU HAVE DONE WELL MY THUNDERBOLTS OR PERHAPS I SHO USE YOUR OTHER CODE-NAMES.
FIXER.
BEETLE.
SCREAMING MIMI.
GOLIATH.
AND MOONSTON
IN TIME, MY FRIENDS --
"-- THE WORLD WILL DISCOVER WHAT A VIPER IT HAS CLASPED TO ITS BREAST. BUT BY THEN IT WILL BE TOO LATE --
"-- FAR TOO LATE!"
AND IN A DANK, FETID CELL, MILES FROM THE CITY, HALLIE TAKAHAMA PRAYS DESPERATELY FOR SOMEONE -- ANYONE -- TO SAVE HER...
...BUT HER PRAYERS REMAIN UNANSWERED.

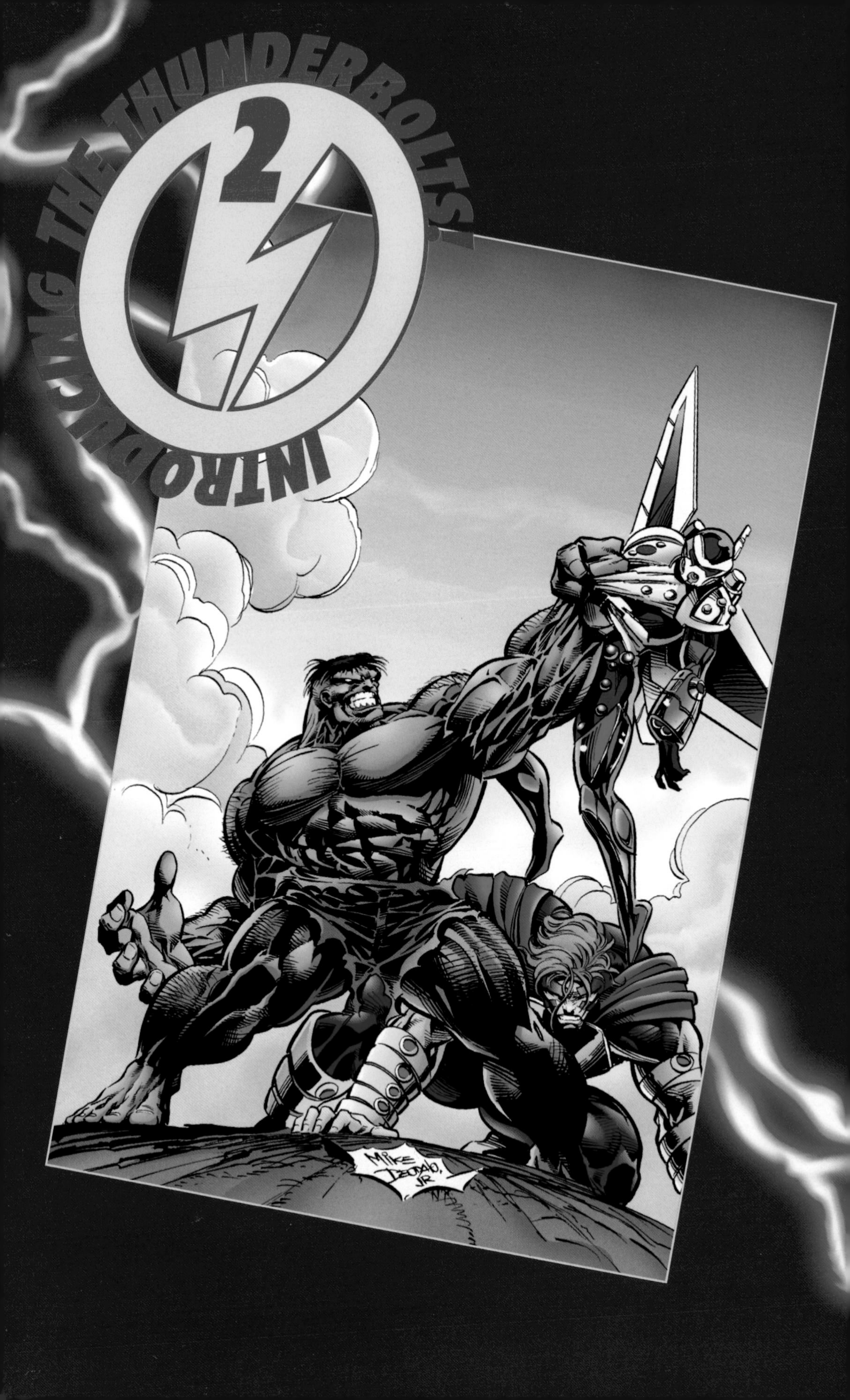
INTRODUCING THE THUNDERBOLTS!

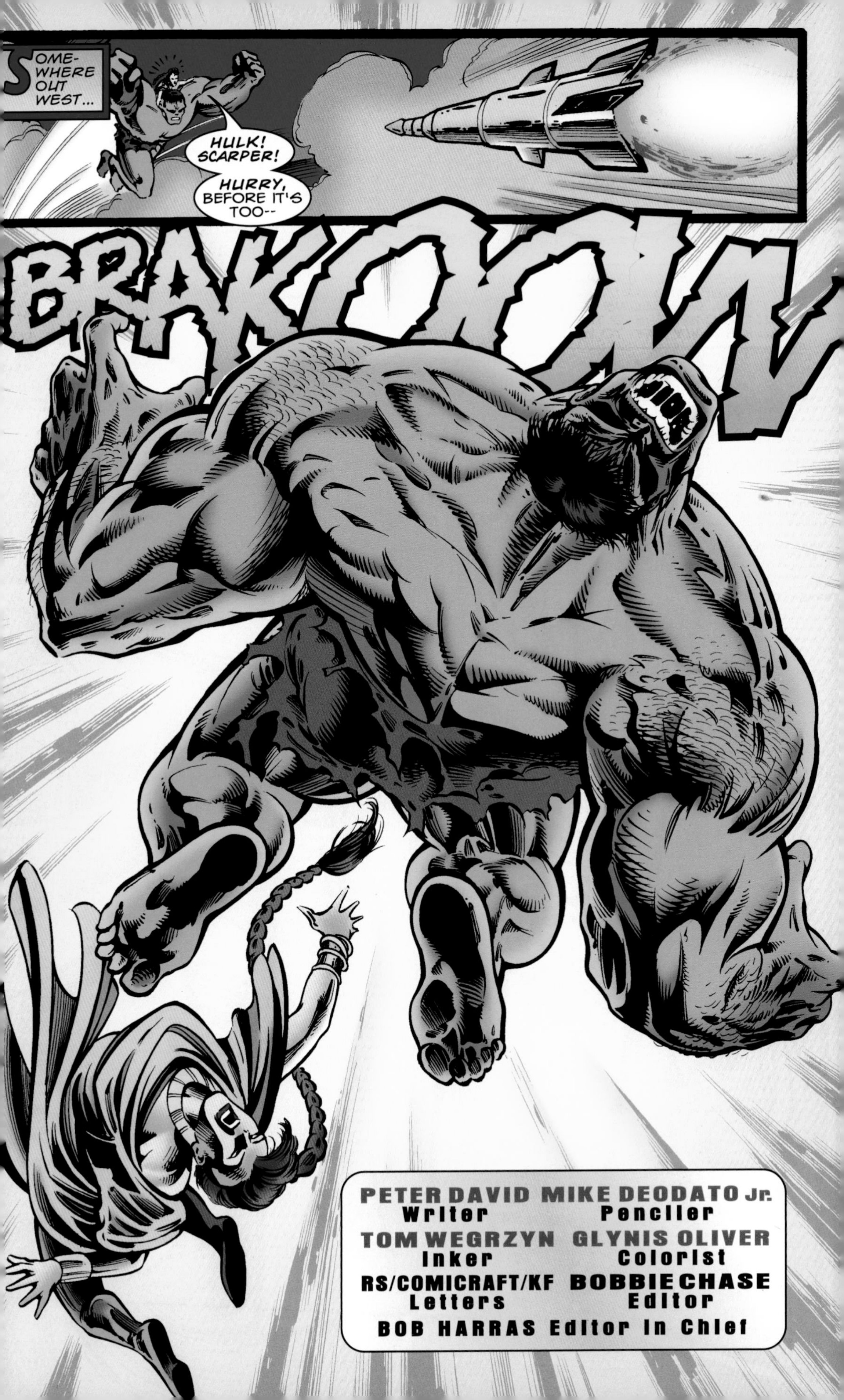

SOMEWHERE OUT WEST...
HULK! SCARPER!
HURRY, BEFORE IT'S TOO--
BRAKOOM
PETER DAVID Writer
MIKE DEODATO Jr. Penciler
TOM WEGRZYN Inker
GLYNIS OLIVER Colorist
RS/COMICRAFT/KF Letters
BOBBIE CHASE Editor
BOB HARRAS Editor in Chief

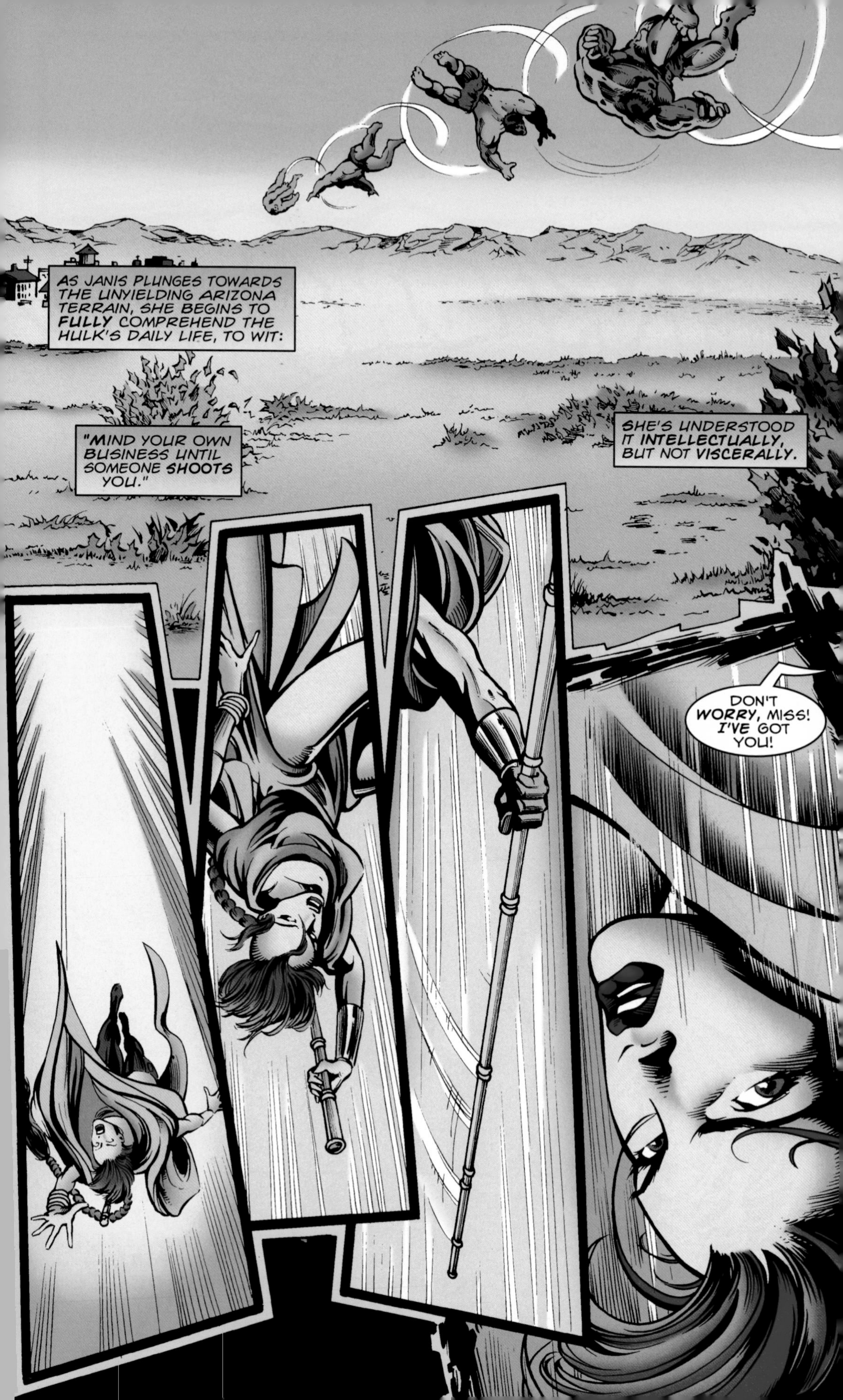
AS JANIS PLUNGES TOWARDS THE UNYIELDING ARIZONA TERRAIN, SHE BEGINS TO FULLY COMPREHEND THE HULK'S DAILY LIFE, TO WIT:
"MIND YOUR OWN BUSINESS UNTIL SOMEONE SHOOTS YOU."
SHE'S UNDERSTOOD IT INTELLECTUALLY, BUT NOT VISCERALLY.
DON'T WORRY, MISS! I'VE GOT YOU!

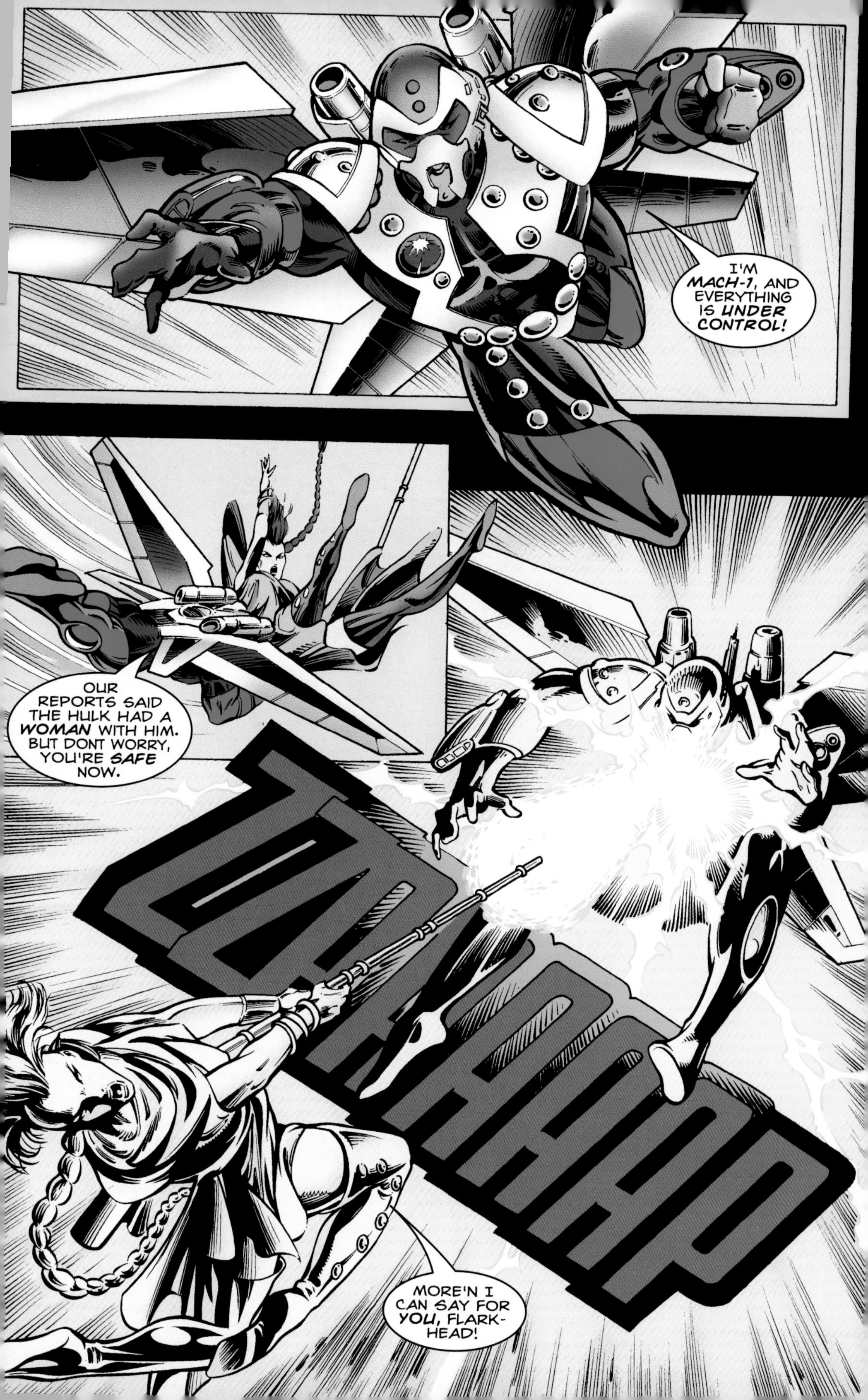
I'M MACH-1, AND EVERYTHING IS UNDER CONTROL!
OUR REPORTS SAID THE HULK HAD A WOMAN WITH HIM. BUT DONT WORRY, YOU'RE SAFE NOW.
MORE'N I CAN SAY FOR YOU, FLARK-HEAD!

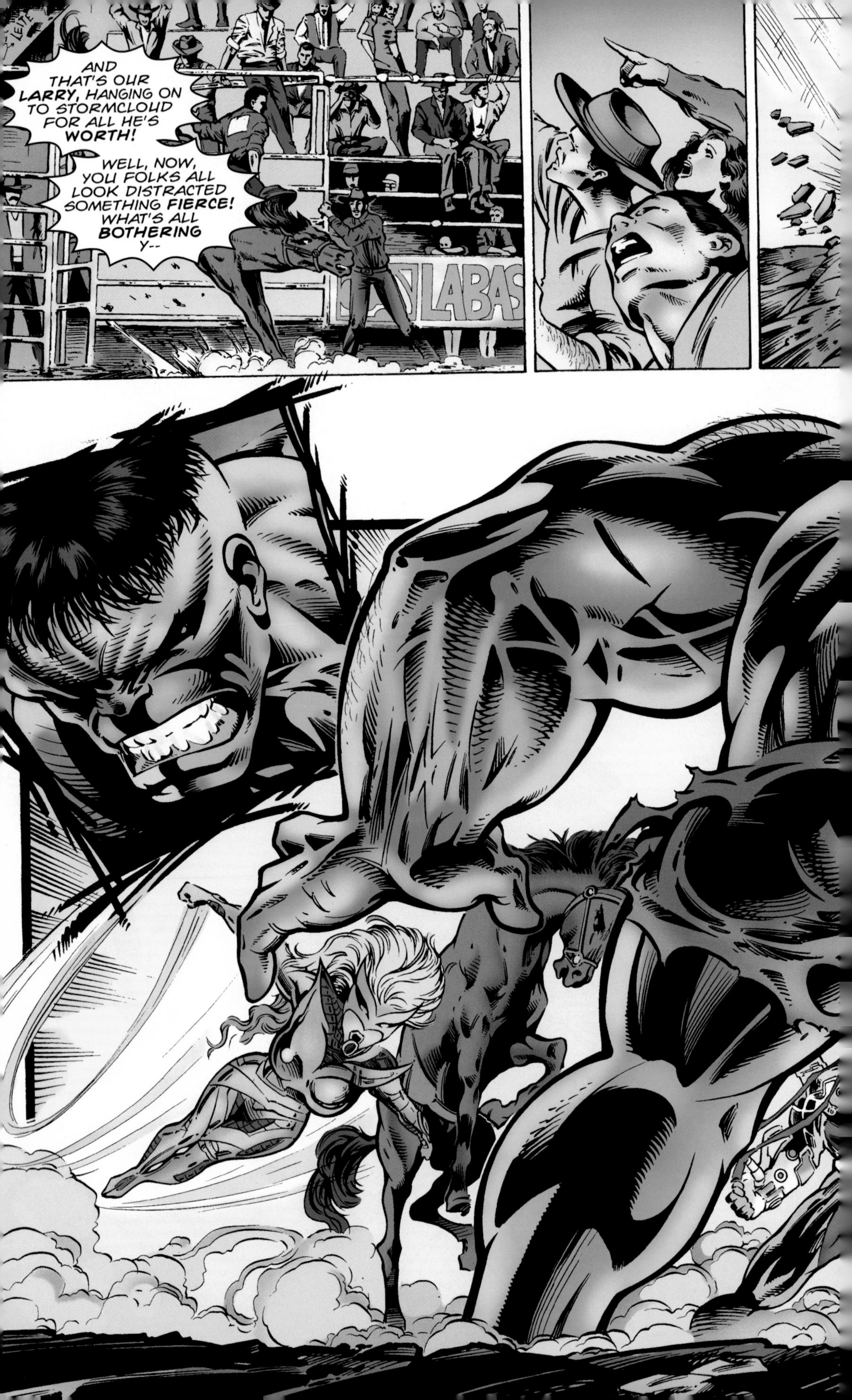
AND THAT'S OUR LARRY, HANGING ON TO STORMCLOUD FOR ALL HE'S WORTH!
WELL, NOW, YOU FOLKS ALL LOOK DISTRACTED SOMETHING FIERCE! WHAT'S ALL BOTHERING Y--
LABAS

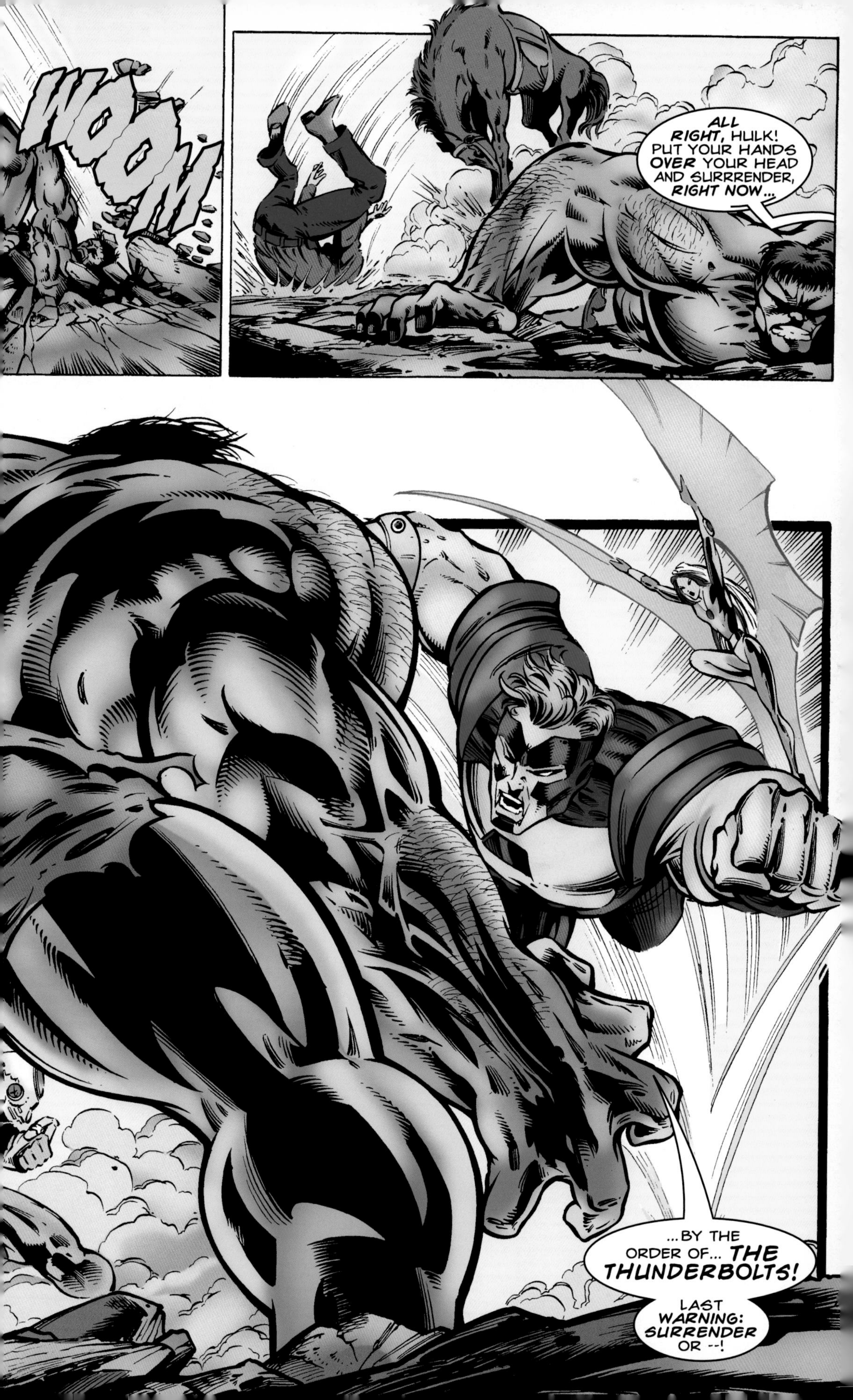
WOOM
ALL RIGHT, HULK! PUT YOUR HANDS OVER YOUR HEAD AND SURRRENDER, RIGHT NOW...
...BY THE ORDER OF... THE THUNDERBOLTS!
LAST WARNING: SURRENDER OR --!

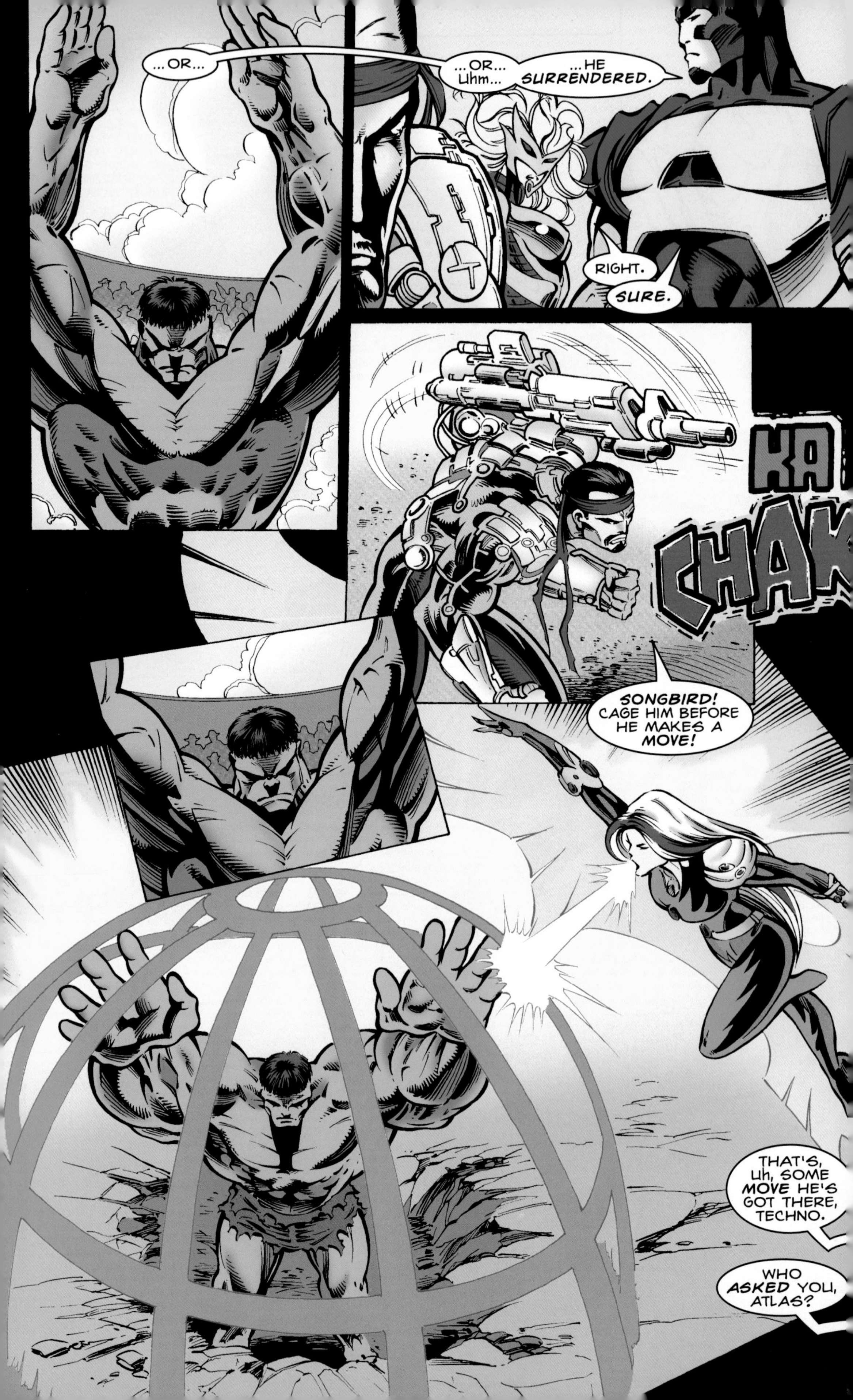
...OR...
...OR... Uhm...
...HE SURRENDERED.
RIGHT.
SURE.
KA
CHAK
SONGBIRD! CAGE HIM BEFORE HE MAKES A MOVE!
THAT'S, Uh, SOME MOVE HE'S GOT THERE, TECHNO.
WHO ASKED YOU, ATLAS?

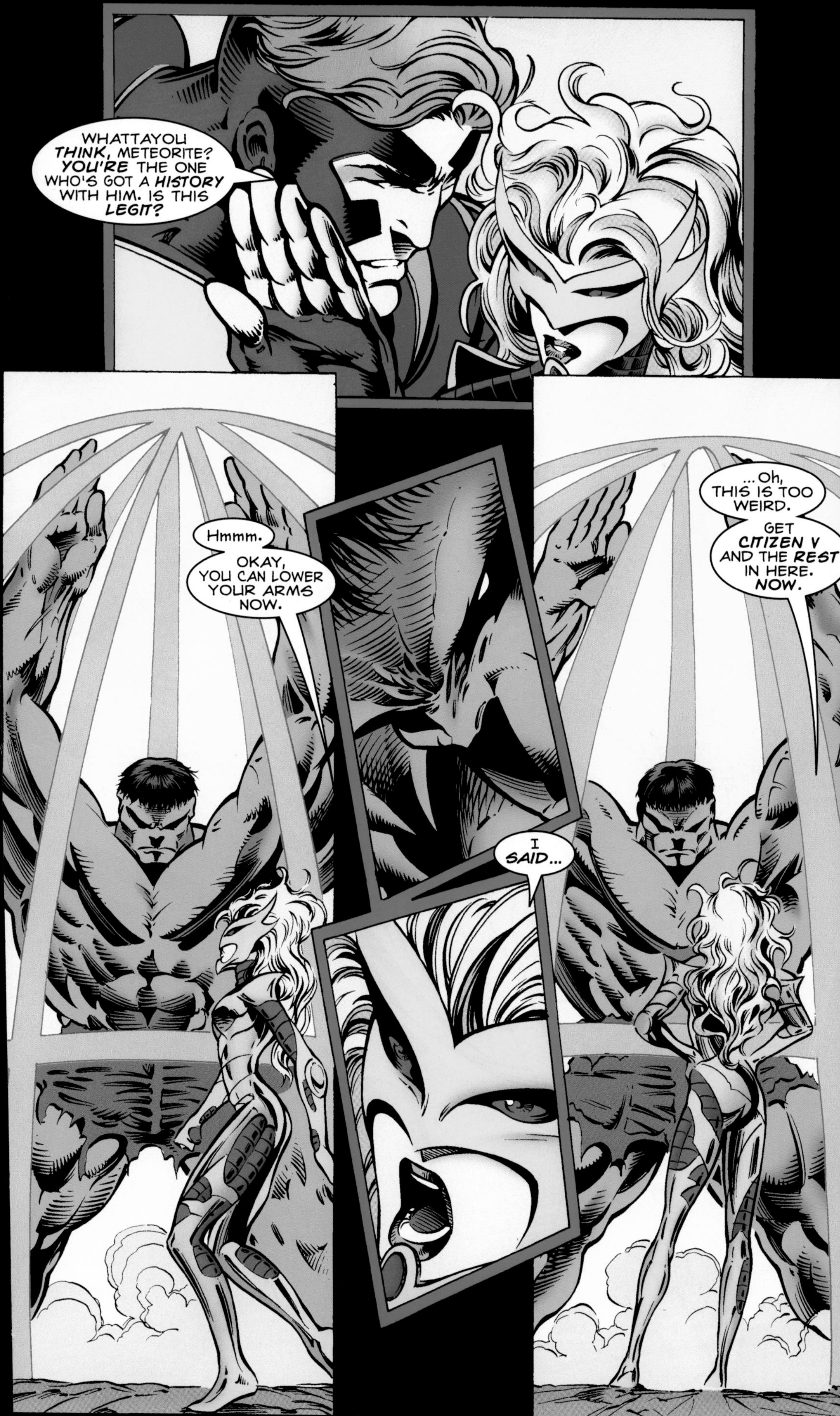
WHATTAYOU THINK, METEORITE? YOU'RE THE ONE WHO'S GOT A HISTORY WITH HIM. IS THIS LEGIT?
Hmmm.
OKAY, YOU CAN LOWER YOUR ARMS NOW.
I SAID...
...Oh, THIS IS TOO WEIRD.
GET CITIZEN V AND THE REST IN HERE. NOW.

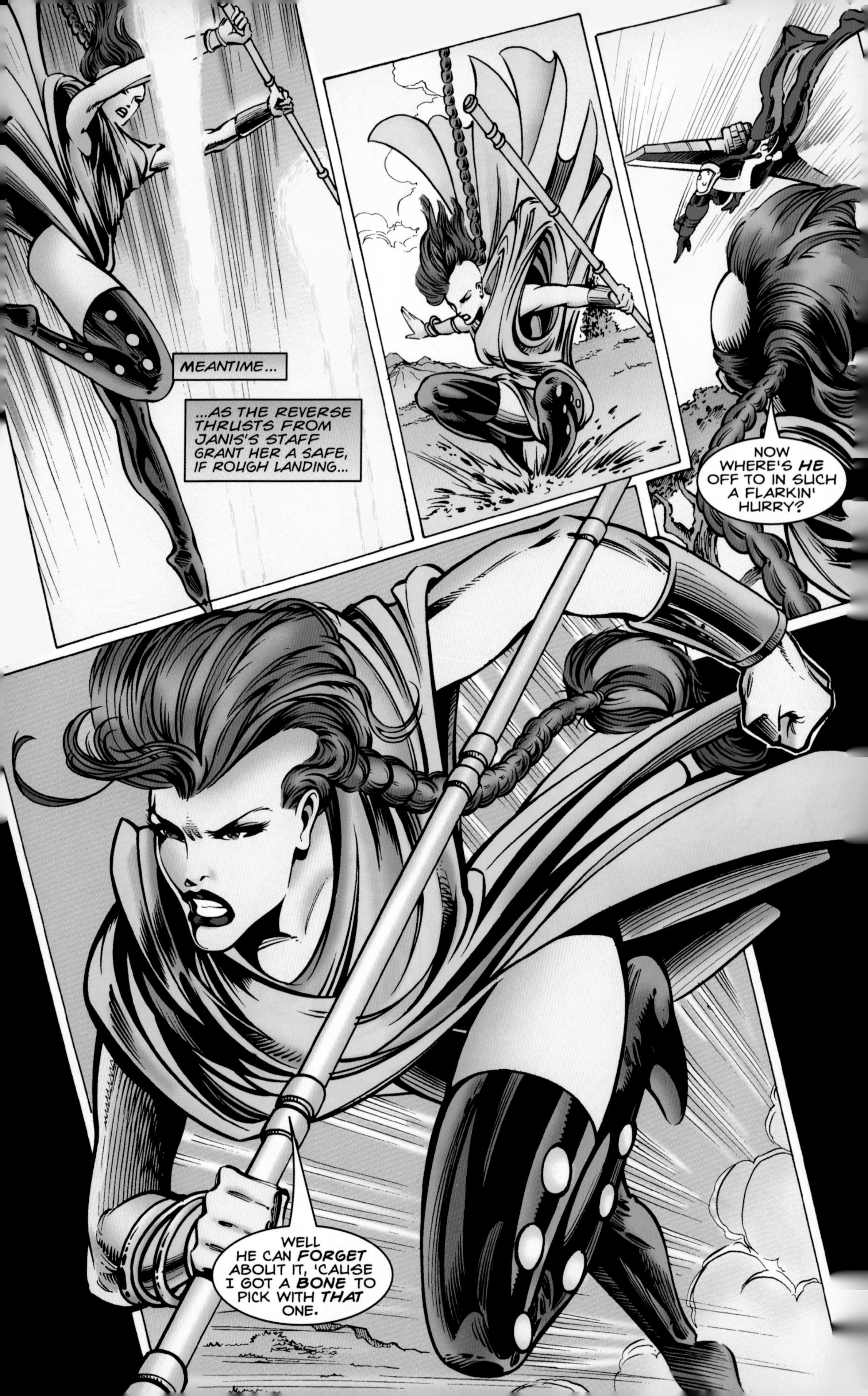

MEANTIME...
...AS THE REVERSE THRUSTS FROM JANIS'S STAFF GRANT HER A SAFE, IF ROUGH LANDING...
NOW WHERE'S **HE** OFF TO IN SUCH A FLARKIN' HURRY?
WELL HE CAN **FORGET** ABOUT IT, 'CAUSE I GOT A **BONE** TO PICK WITH **THAT** ONE.

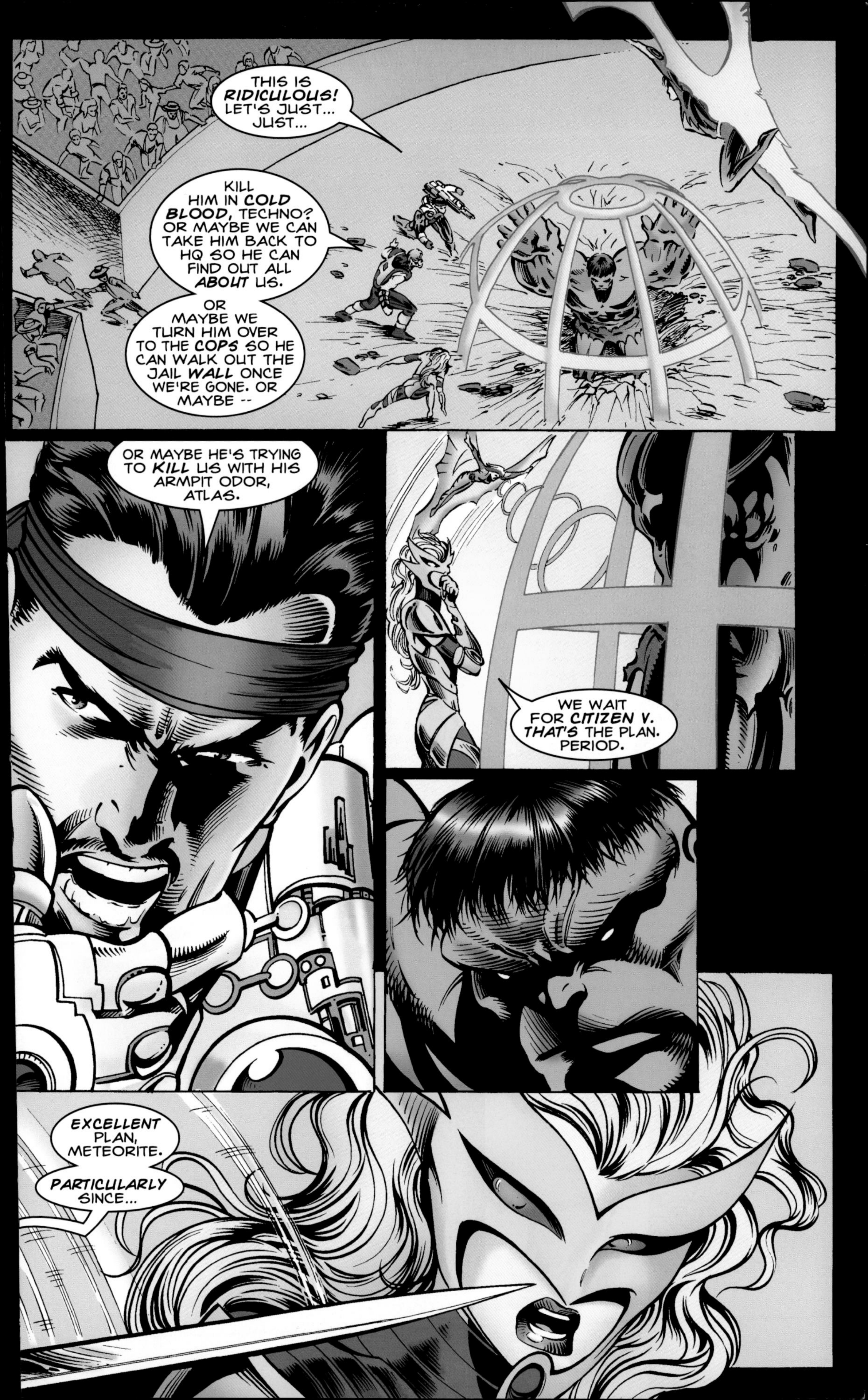
THIS IS RIDICULOUS! LET'S JUST... JUST...
KILL HIM IN COLD BLOOD, TECHNO? OR MAYBE WE CAN TAKE HIM BACK TO HQ SO HE CAN FIND OUT ALL ABOUT US.
OR MAYBE WE TURN HIM OVER TO THE COPS SO HE CAN WALK OUT THE JAIL WALL ONCE WE'RE GONE. OR MAYBE --
OR MAYBE HE'S TRYING TO KILL US WITH HIS ARMPIT ODOR, ATLAS.
WE WAIT FOR CITIZEN V. THAT'S THE PLAN. PERIOD.
EXCELLENT PLAN, METEORITE.
PARTICULARLY SINCE...

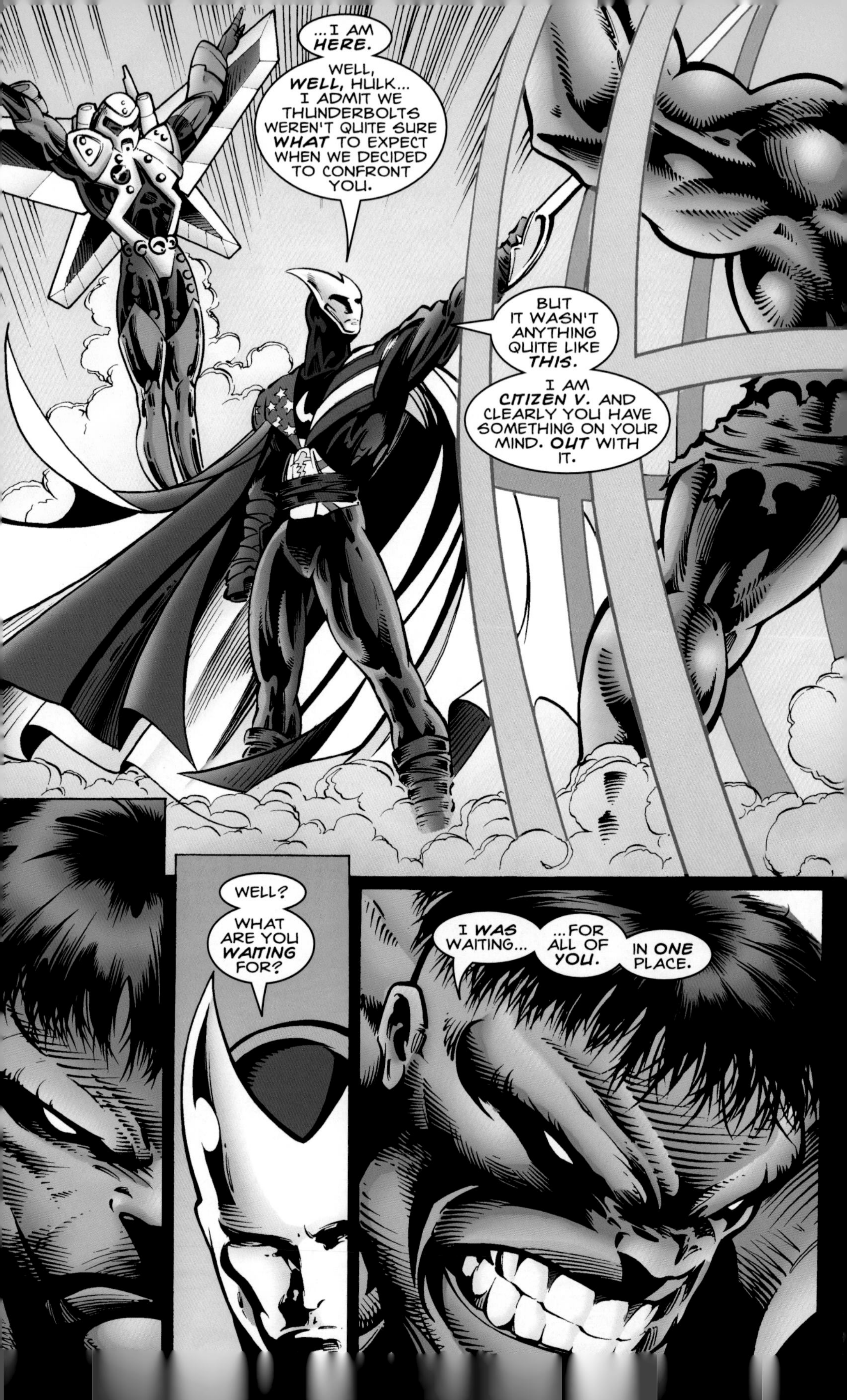
...I AM HERE.
WELL, WELL, HULK... I ADMIT WE THUNDERBOLTS WEREN'T QUITE SURE WHAT TO EXPECT WHEN WE DECIDED TO CONFRONT YOU.
BUT IT WASN'T ANYTHING QUITE LIKE THIS.
I AM CITIZEN V. AND CLEARLY YOU HAVE SOMETHING ON YOUR MIND. OUT WITH IT.
WELL?
WHAT ARE YOU WAITING FOR?
I WAS WAITING...
...FOR ALL OF YOU.
IN ONE PLACE.

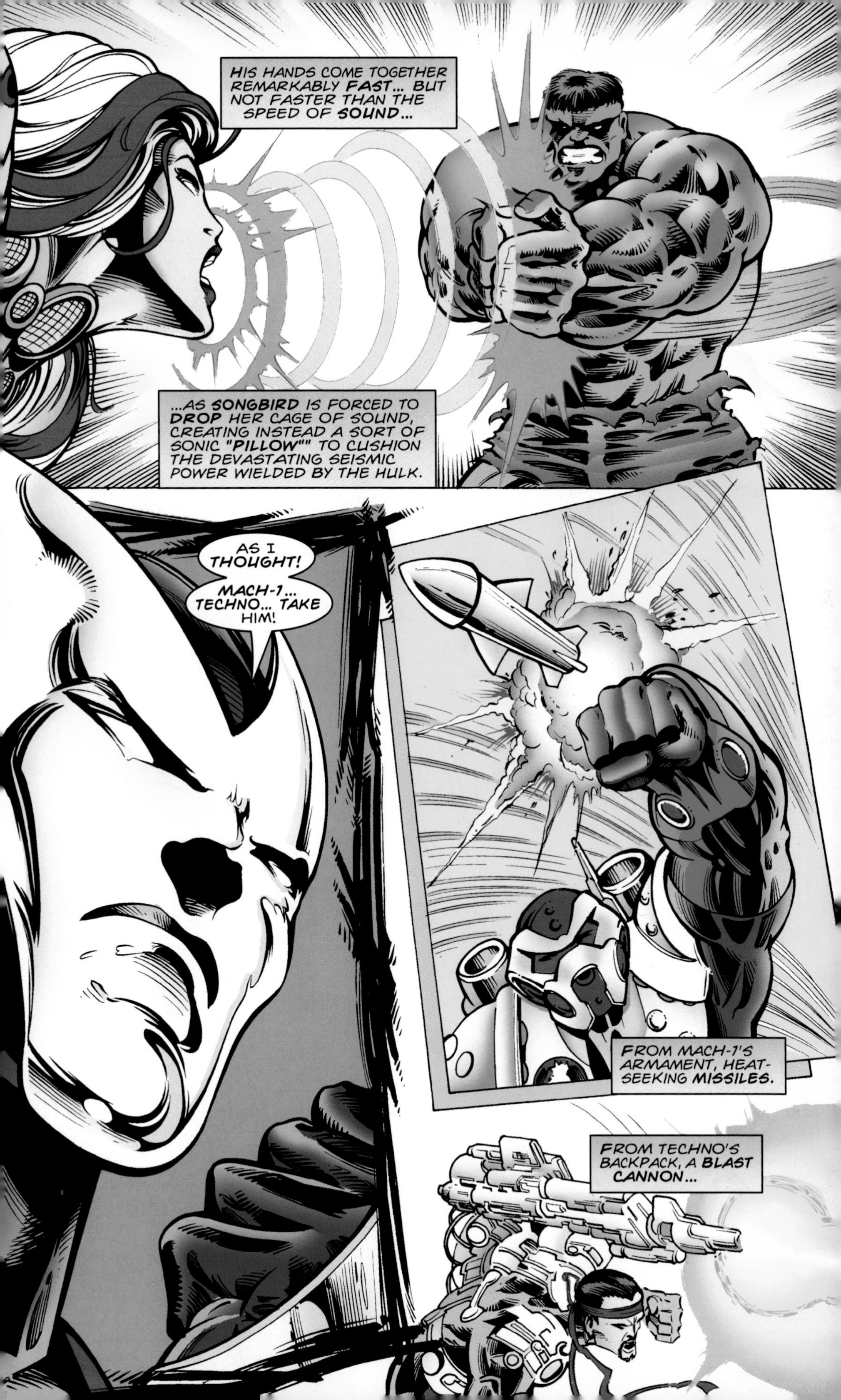
HIS HANDS COME TOGETHER REMARKABLY FAST... BUT NOT FASTER THAN THE SPEED OF SOUND...
...AS SONGBIRD IS FORCED TO DROP HER CAGE OF SOUND, CREATING INSTEAD A SORT OF SONIC "PILLOW"" TO CUSHION THE DEVASTATING SEISMIC POWER WIELDED BY THE HULK.
AS I THOUGHT!
MACH-1... TECHNO... TAKE HIM!
FROM MACH-1'S ARMAMENT, HEAT-SEEKING MISSILES.
FROM TECHNO'S BACKPACK, A BLAST CANNON...

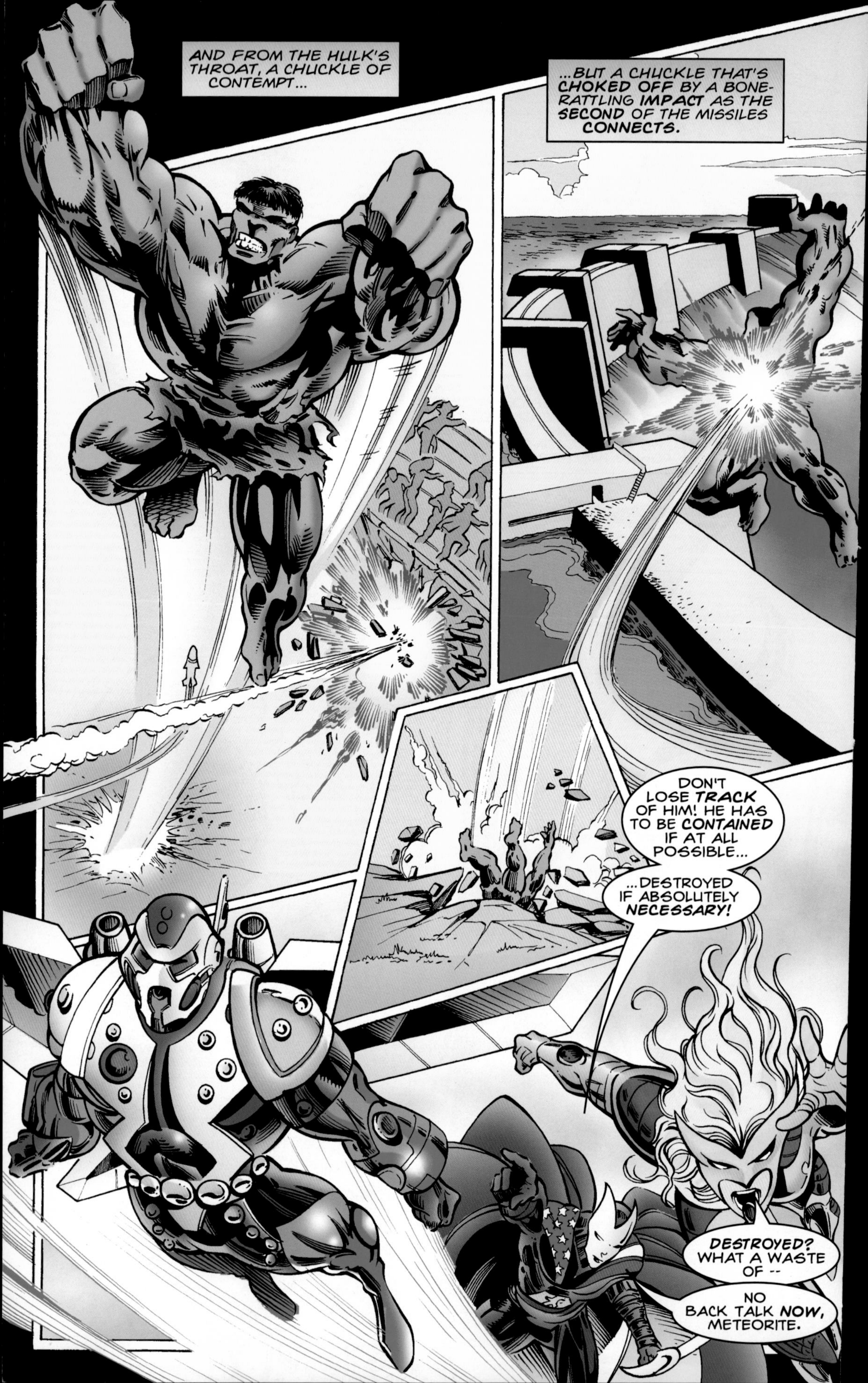
AND FROM THE HULK'S THROAT, A CHUCKLE OF CONTEMPT...
...BUT A CHUCKLE THAT'S CHOKED OFF BY A BONE-RATTLING IMPACT AS THE SECOND OF THE MISSILES CONNECTS.
DON'T LOSE TRACK OF HIM! HE HAS TO BE CONTAINED IF AT ALL POSSIBLE...
...DESTROYED IF ABSOLUTELY NECESSARY!
DESTROYED? WHAT A WASTE OF --
NO BACK TALK NOW, METEORITE.

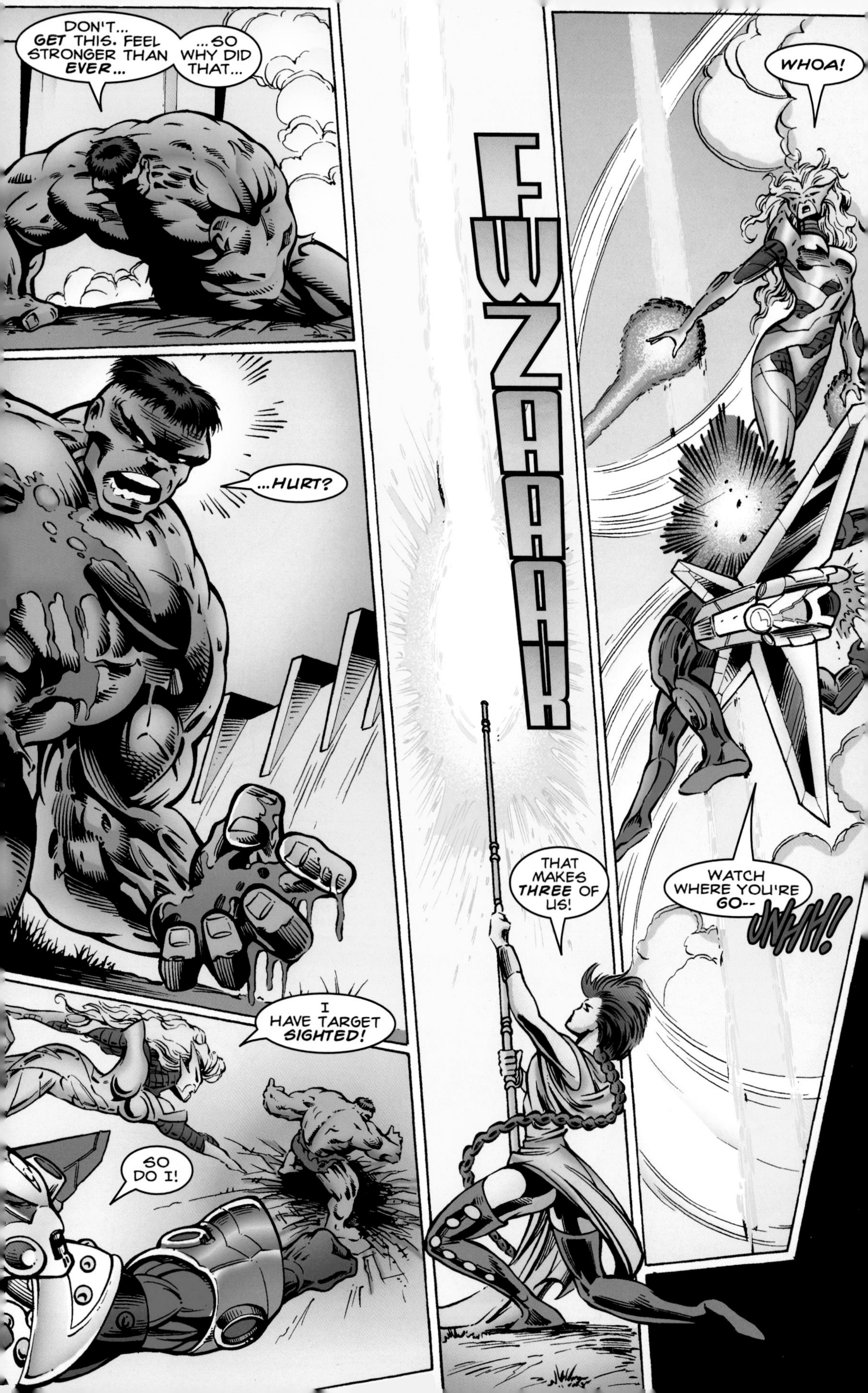
DON'T... GET THIS. FEEL STRONGER THAN EVER...
...SO WHY DID THAT...
...HURT?
I HAVE TARGET SIGHTED!
SO DO I!
FWZAAAAK
THAT MAKES THREE OF US!
WHOA!
WATCH WHERE YOU'RE GO--
UNHH!

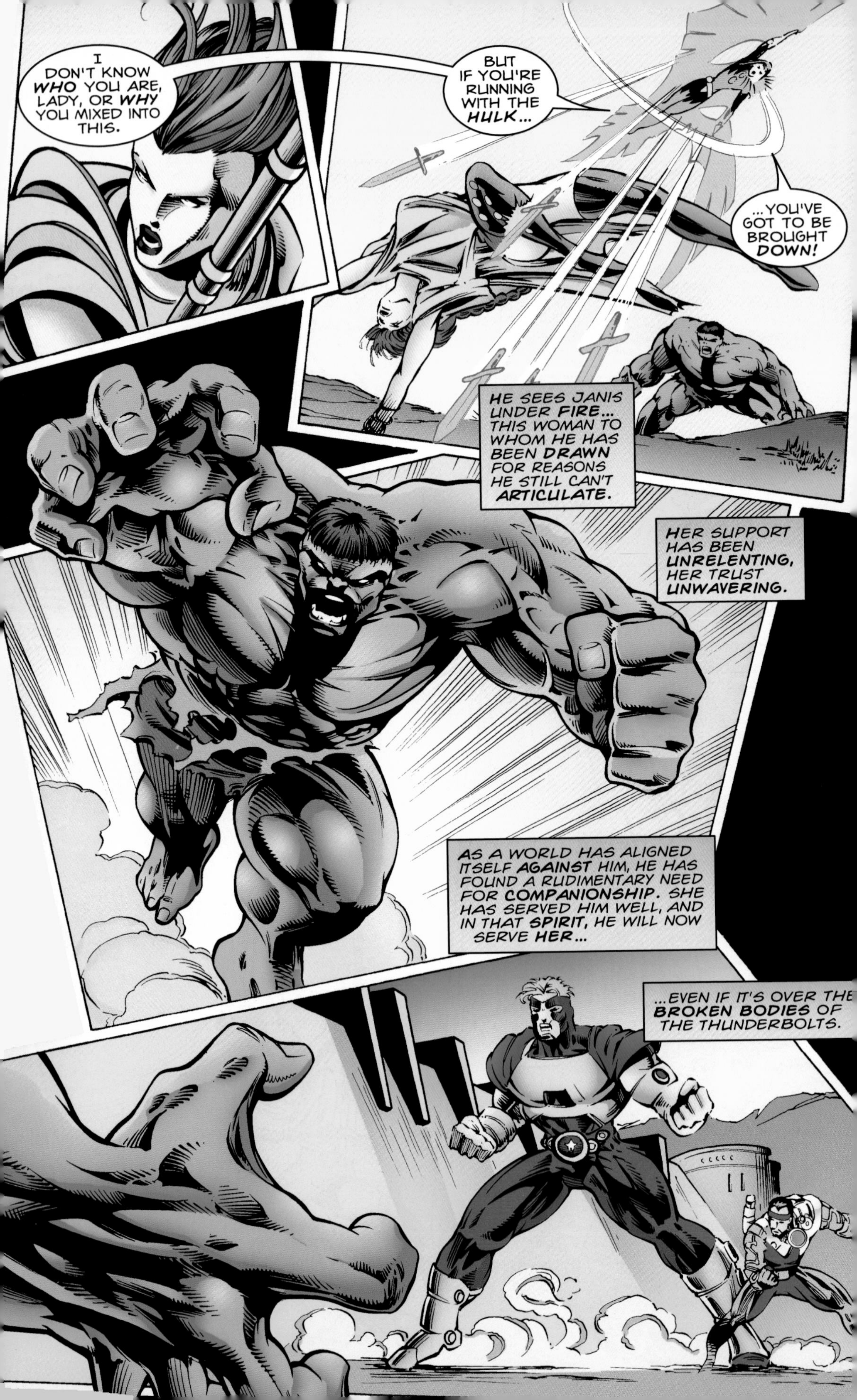
I DON'T KNOW WHO YOU ARE, LADY, OR WHY YOU MIXED INTO THIS.
BUT IF YOU'RE RUNNING WITH THE HULK...
...YOU'VE GOT TO BE BROUGHT DOWN!
HE SEES JANIS UNDER FIRE... THIS WOMAN TO WHOM HE HAS BEEN DRAWN FOR REASONS HE STILL CAN'T ARTICULATE.
HER SUPPORT HAS BEEN UNRELENTING, HER TRUST UNWAVERING.
AS A WORLD HAS ALIGNED ITSELF AGAINST HIM, HE HAS FOUND A RUDIMENTARY NEED FOR COMPANIONSHIP. SHE HAS SERVED HIM WELL, AND IN THAT SPIRIT, HE WILL NOW SERVE HER...
...EVEN IF IT'S OVER THE BROKEN BODIES OF THE THUNDERBOLTS.

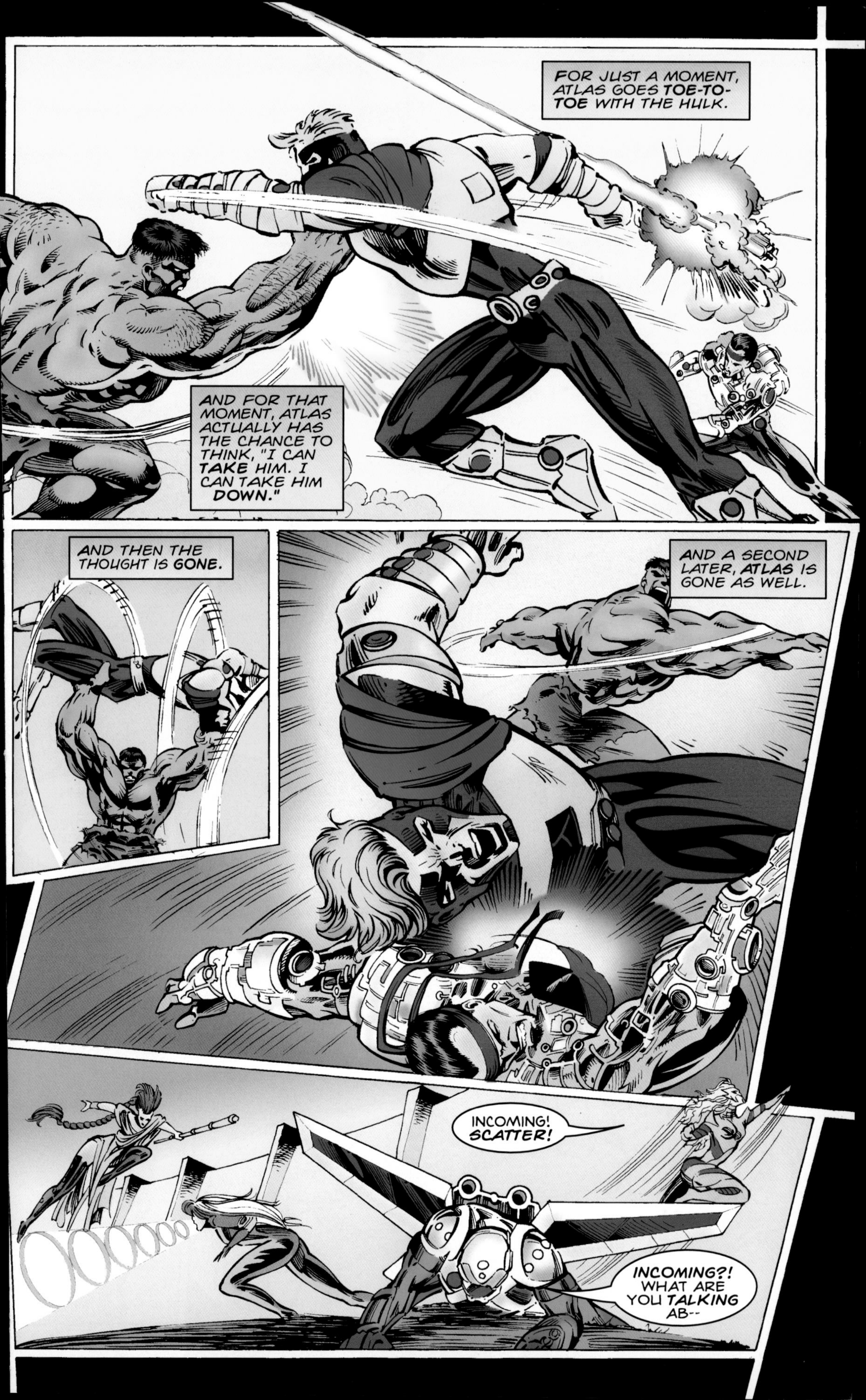
FOR JUST A MOMENT, ATLAS GOES TOE-TO-TOE WITH THE HULK.
AND FOR THAT MOMENT, ATLAS ACTUALLY HAS THE CHANCE TO THINK, "I CAN TAKE HIM. I CAN TAKE HIM DOWN."
AND THEN THE THOUGHT IS GONE.
AND A SECOND LATER, ATLAS IS GONE AS WELL.
INCOMING! SCATTER!
INCOMING?! WHAT ARE YOU TALKING AB--

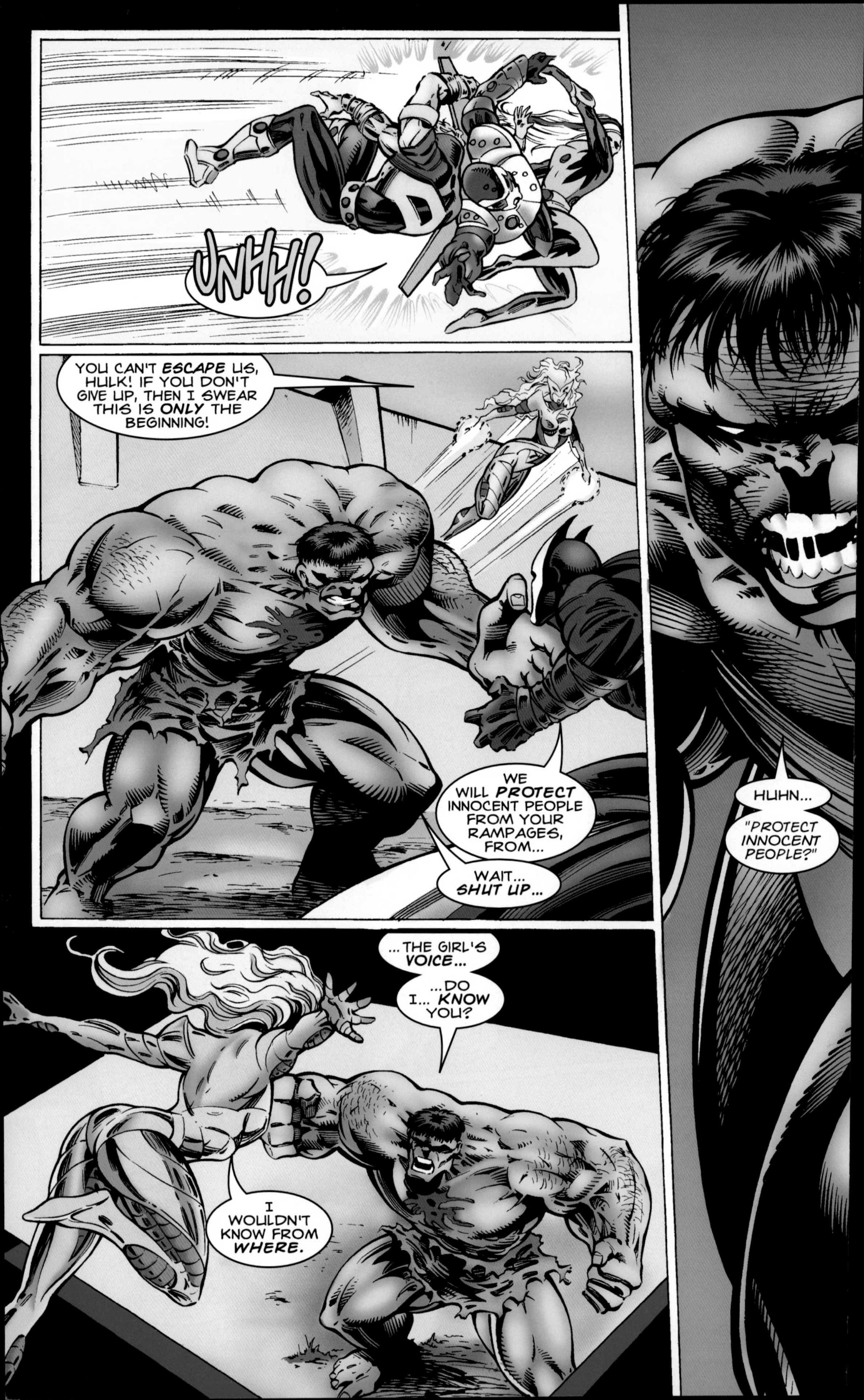
UNHH!
YOU CAN'T ESCAPE US, HULK! IF YOU DON'T GIVE UP, THEN I SWEAR THIS IS ONLY THE BEGINNING!
WE WILL PROTECT INNOCENT PEOPLE FROM YOUR RAMPAGES, FROM...
WAIT... SHUT UP...
HUHN...
"PROTECT INNOCENT PEOPLE?"
...THE GIRL'S VOICE...
...DO I... KNOW YOU?
I WOULDN'T KNOW FROM WHERE.

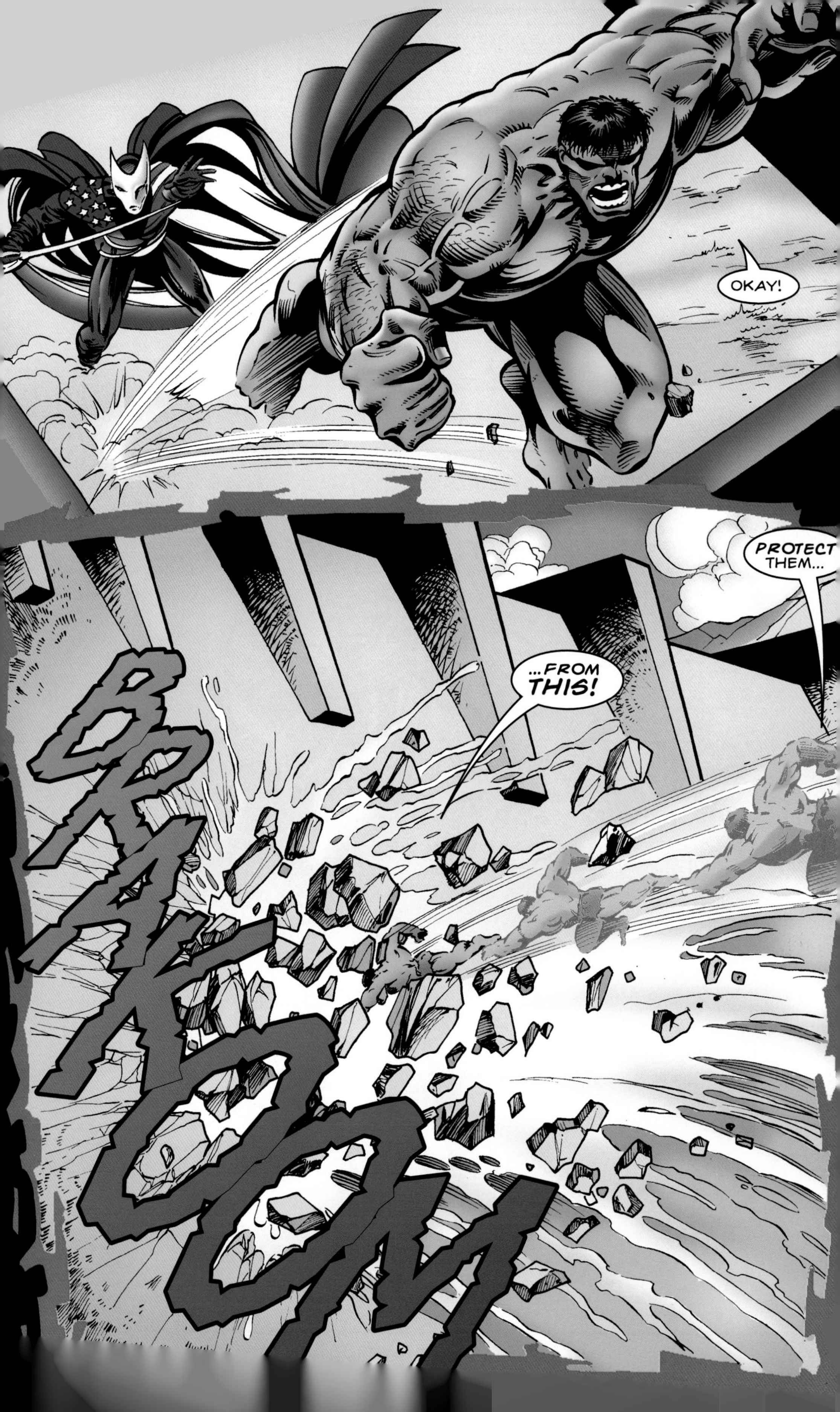
OKAY!
PROTECT THEM...
...FROM THIS!
BRAKOOM

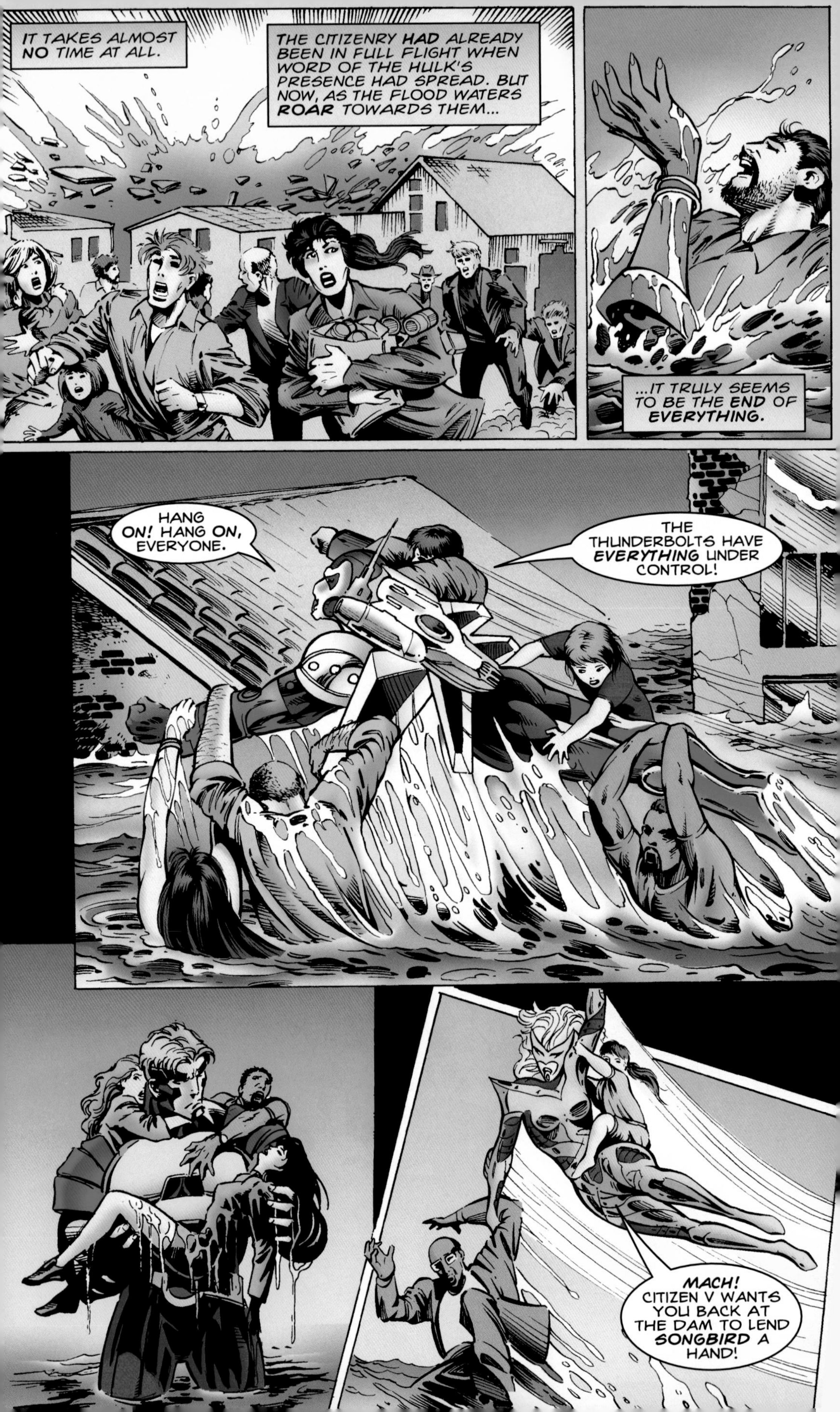
IT TAKES ALMOST NO TIME AT ALL.
THE CITIZENRY HAD ALREADY BEEN IN FULL FLIGHT WHEN WORD OF THE HULK'S PRESENCE HAD SPREAD. BUT NOW, AS THE FLOOD WATERS ROAR TOWARDS THEM...
...IT TRULY SEEMS TO BE THE END OF EVERYTHING.
HANG ON! HANG ON, EVERYONE.
THE THUNDERBOLTS HAVE EVERYTHING UNDER CONTROL!
MACH! CITIZEN V WANTS YOU BACK AT THE DAM TO LEND SONGBIRD A HAND!

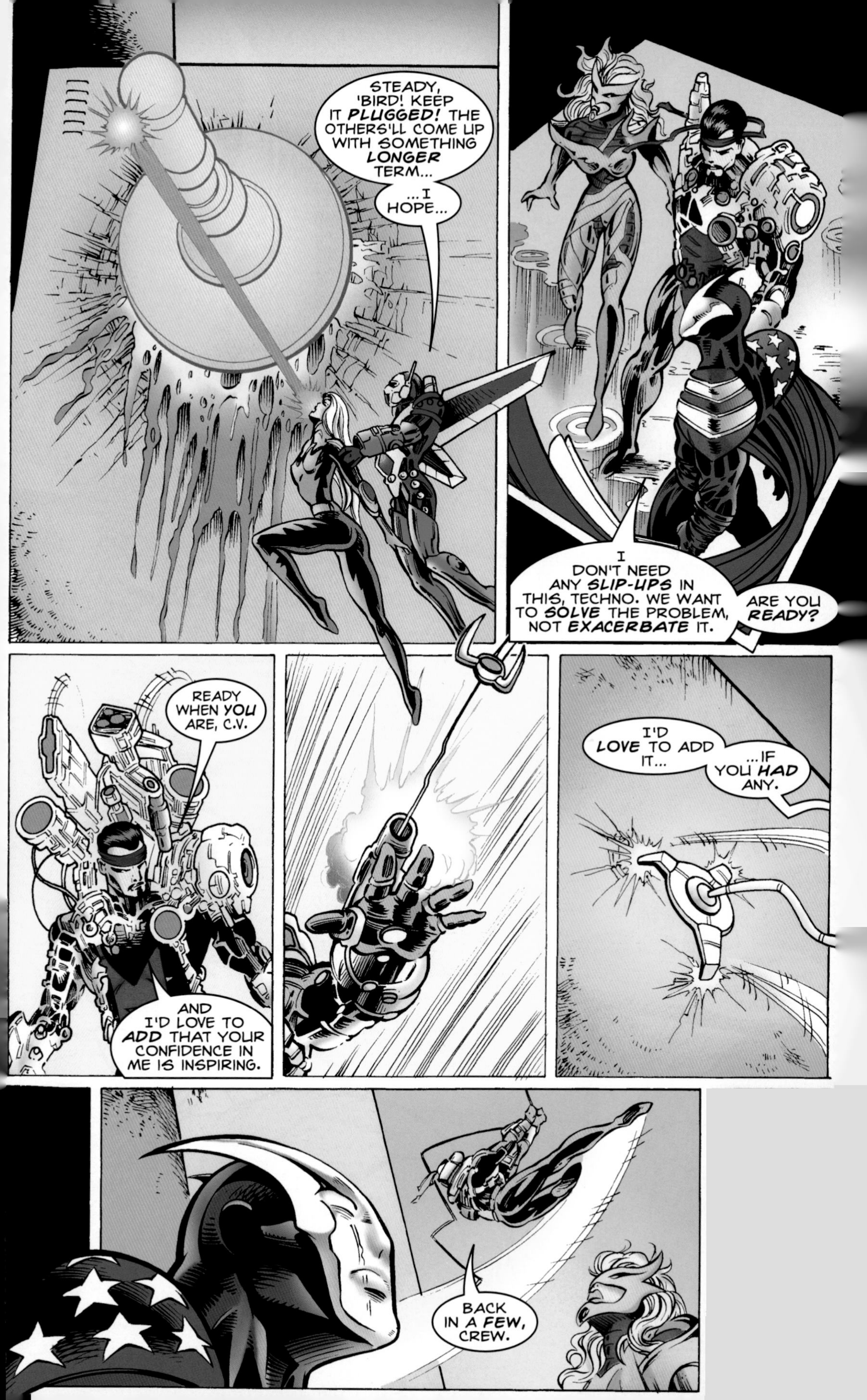
STEADY, 'BIRD! KEEP IT PLUGGED! THE OTHERS'LL COME UP WITH SOMETHING LONGER TERM...
...I HOPE...
I DON'T NEED ANY SLIP-UPS IN THIS, TECHNO. WE WANT TO SOLVE THE PROBLEM, NOT EXACERBATE IT.
ARE YOU READY?
READY WHEN YOU ARE, C.V.
AND I'D LOVE TO ADD THAT YOUR CONFIDENCE IN ME IS INSPIRING.
I'D LOVE TO ADD IT...
...IF YOU HAD ANY.
BACK IN A FEW, CREW.

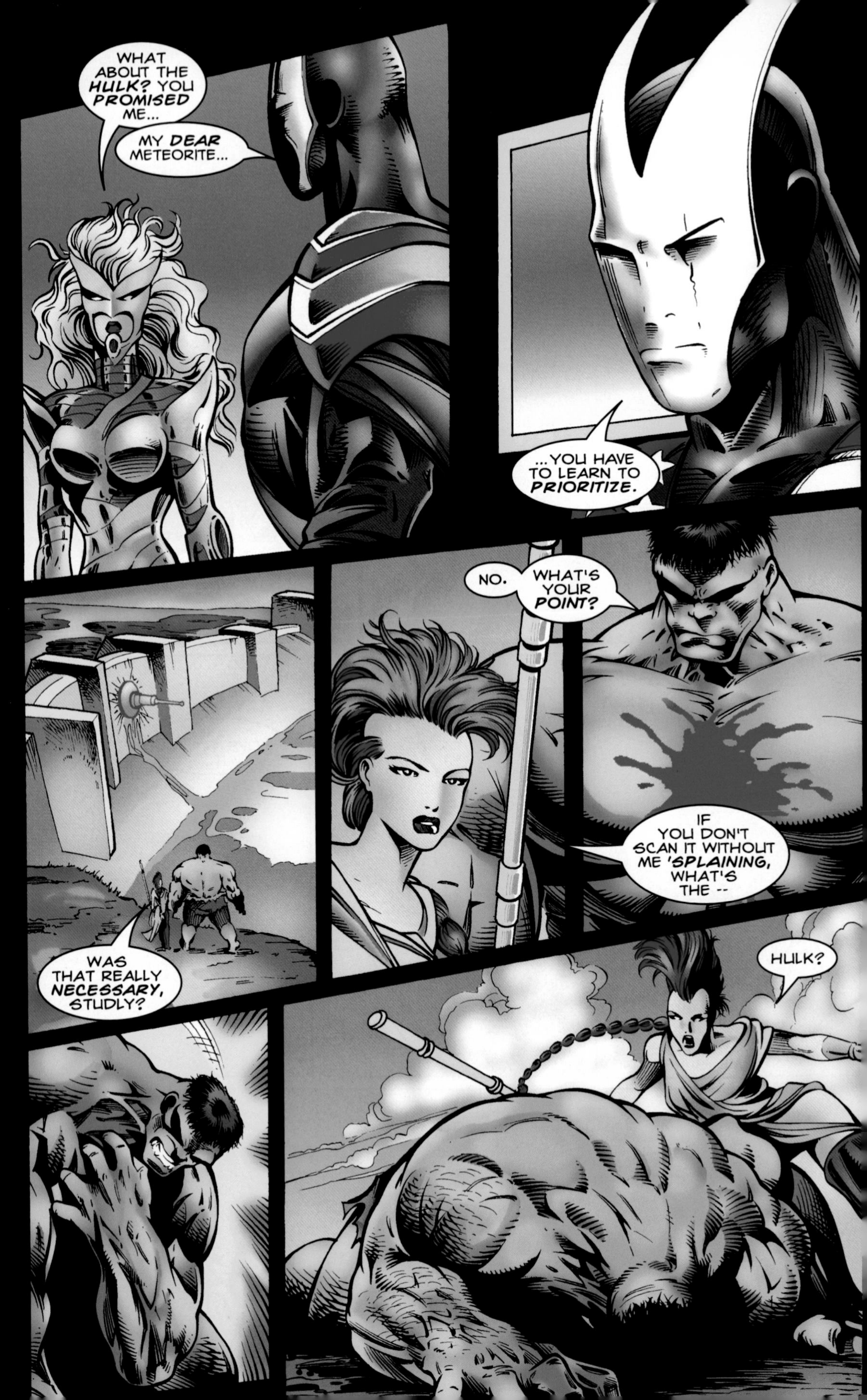
WHAT ABOUT THE HULK? YOU PROMISED ME...
MY DEAR METEORITE...
...YOU HAVE TO LEARN TO PRIORITIZE.
WAS THAT REALLY NECESSARY, STUDLY?
NO.
WHAT'S YOUR POINT?
IF YOU DON'T SCAN IT WITHOUT ME 'SPLAINING, WHAT'S THE --
HULK?

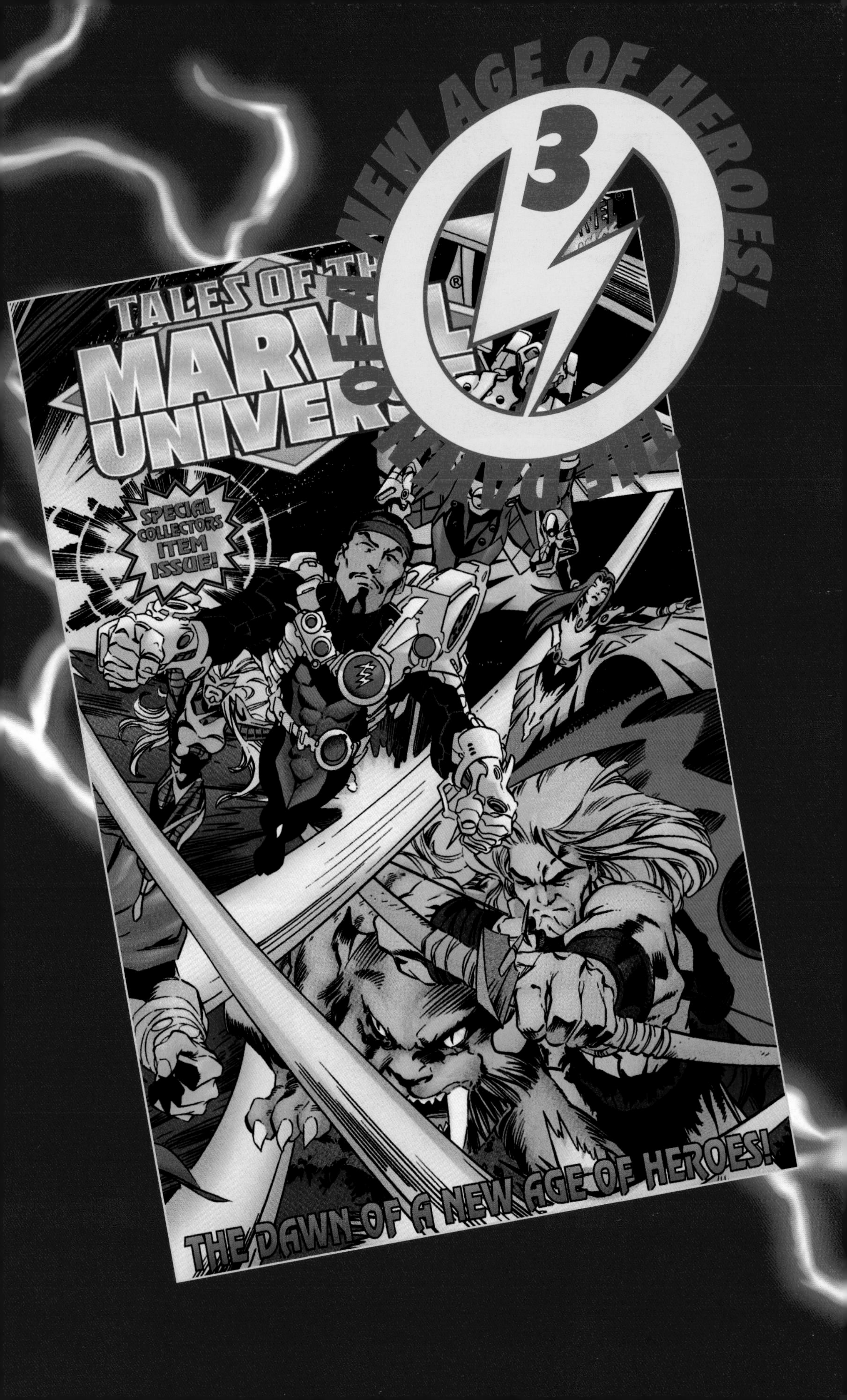

A NEW AGE OF HEROES!
3
THE DAWN OF
TALES OF THE
MARVEL UNIVERSE
SPECIAL COLLECTORS ITEM ISSUE!
THE DAWN OF A NEW AGE OF HEROES!

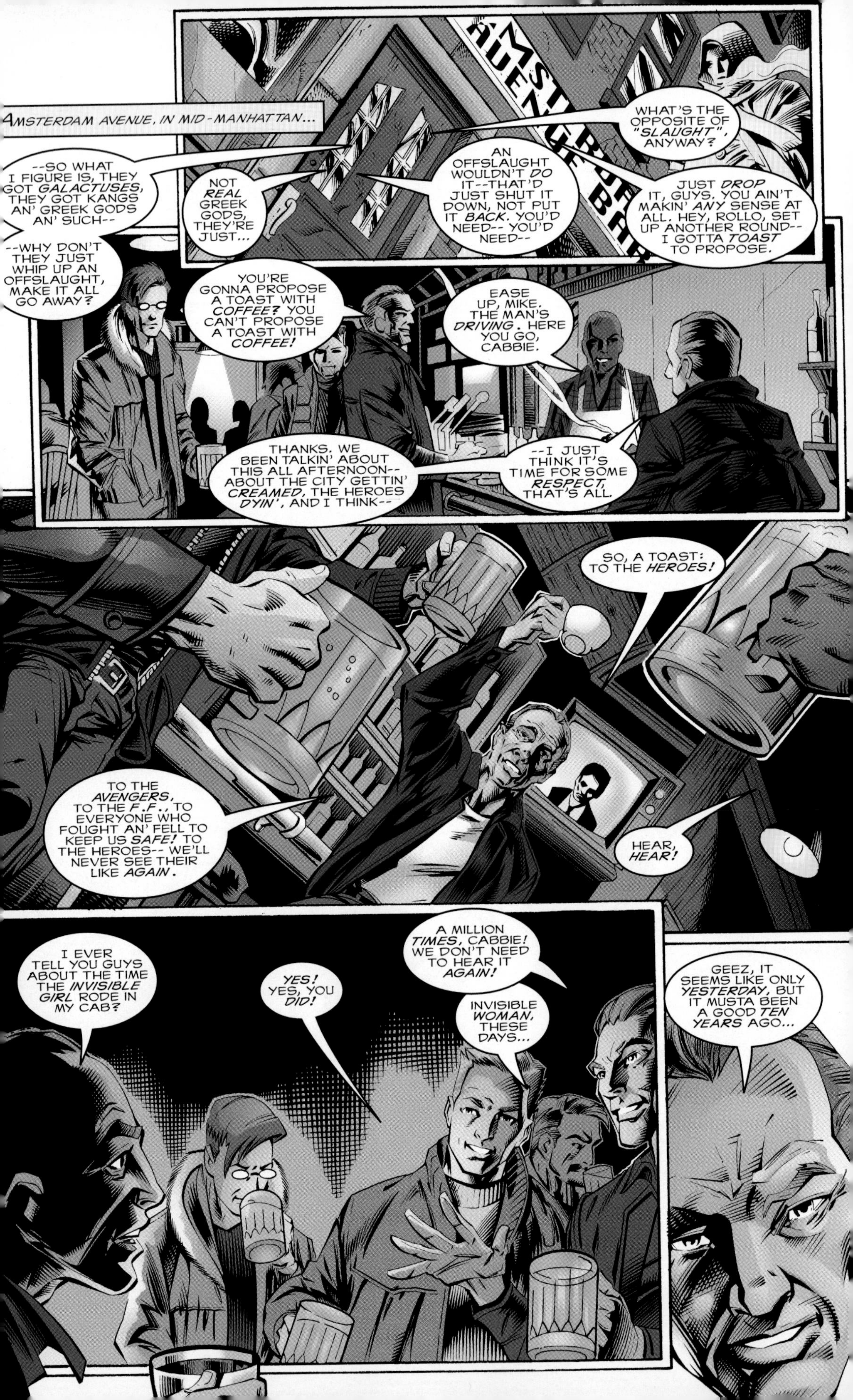
AMSTERDAM AVENUE, IN MID-MANHATTAN...
AMSTERDAM AVENUE BAR
--SO WHAT I FIGURE IS, THEY GOT GALACTUSES, THEY GOT KANGS AN' GREEK GODS AN' SUCH--
--WHY DON'T THEY JUST WHIP UP AN OFFSLAUGHT, MAKE IT ALL GO AWAY?
NOT REAL GREEK GODS, THEY'RE JUST...
AN OFFSLAUGHT WOULDN'T DO IT--THAT'D JUST SHUT IT DOWN, NOT PUT IT BACK. YOU'D NEED-- YOU'D NEED--
WHAT'S THE OPPOSITE OF "SLAUGHT", ANYWAY?
JUST DROP IT, GUYS. YOU AIN'T MAKIN' ANY SENSE AT ALL. HEY, ROLLO, SET UP ANOTHER ROUND-- I GOTTA TOAST TO PROPOSE.
YOU'RE GONNA PROPOSE A TOAST WITH COFFEE? YOU CAN'T PROPOSE A TOAST WITH COFFEE!
EASE UP, MIKE. THE MAN'S DRIVING. HERE YOU GO, CABBIE.
THANKS. WE BEEN TALKIN' ABOUT THIS ALL AFTERNOON-- ABOUT THE CITY GETTIN' CREAMED, THE HEROES DYIN', AND I THINK--
--I JUST THINK IT'S TIME FOR SOME RESPECT, THAT'S ALL.
SO, A TOAST: TO THE HEROES!
TO THE AVENGERS, TO THE F.F., TO EVERYONE WHO FOUGHT AN' FELL TO KEEP US SAFE! TO THE HEROES-- WE'LL NEVER SEE THEIR LIKE AGAIN.
HEAR, HEAR!
I EVER TELL YOU GUYS ABOUT THE TIME THE INVISIBLE GIRL RODE IN MY CAB?
YES! YES, YOU DID!
A MILLION TIMES, CABBIE! WE DON'T NEED TO HEAR IT AGAIN!
INVISIBLE WOMAN, THESE DAYS...
GEEZ, IT SEEMS LIKE ONLY YESTERDAY, BUT IT MUSTA BEEN A GOOD TEN YEARS AGO...

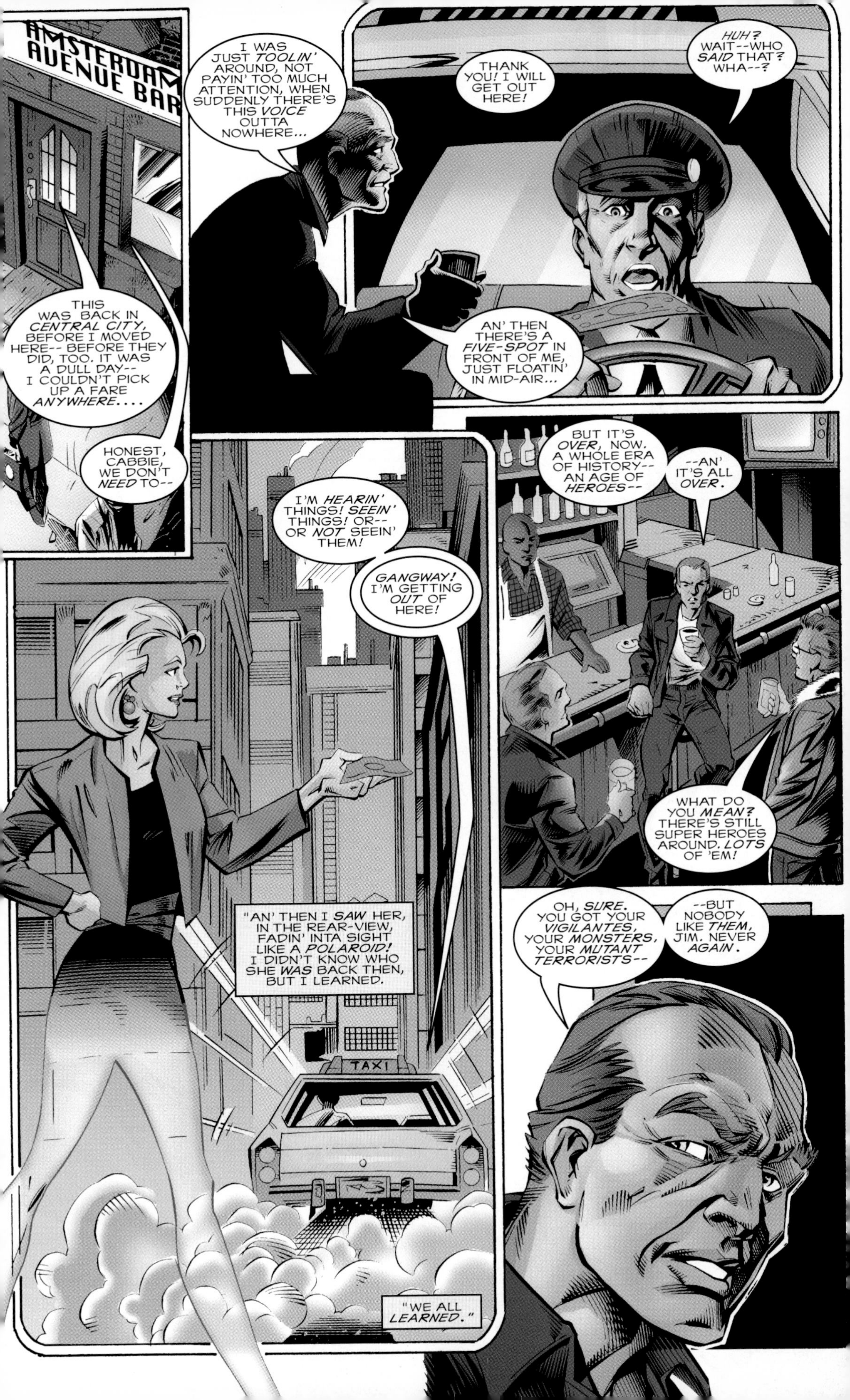

AMSTERDAM AVENUE BAR
I WAS JUST TOOLIN' AROUND, NOT PAYIN' TOO MUCH ATTENTION, WHEN SUDDENLY THERE'S THIS VOICE OUTTA NOWHERE...
THIS WAS BACK IN CENTRAL CITY, BEFORE I MOVED HERE-- BEFORE THEY DID, TOO. IT WAS A DULL DAY-- I COULDN'T PICK UP A FARE ANYWHERE....
THANK YOU! I WILL GET OUT HERE!
HUH? WAIT--WHO SAID THAT? WHA--?
AN' THEN THERE'S A FIVE-SPOT IN FRONT OF ME, JUST FLOATIN' IN MID-AIR...
HONEST, CABBIE, WE DON'T NEED TO--
I'M HEARIN' THINGS! SEEIN' THINGS! OR-- OR NOT SEEIN' THEM!
GANGWAY! I'M GETTING OUT OF HERE!
"AN' THEN I SAW HER, IN THE REAR-VIEW, FADIN' INTA SIGHT LIKE A POLAROID! I DIDN'T KNOW WHO SHE WAS BACK THEN, BUT I LEARNED.
TAXI
"WE ALL LEARNED."
BUT IT'S OVER, NOW. A WHOLE ERA OF HISTORY-- AN AGE OF HEROES--
--AN' IT'S ALL OVER.
WHAT DO YOU MEAN? THERE'S STILL SUPER HEROES AROUND. LOTS OF 'EM!
OH, SURE. YOU GOT YOUR VIGILANTES, YOUR MONSTERS, YOUR MUTANT TERRORISTS--
--BUT NOBODY LIKE THEM, JIM. NEVER AGAIN.

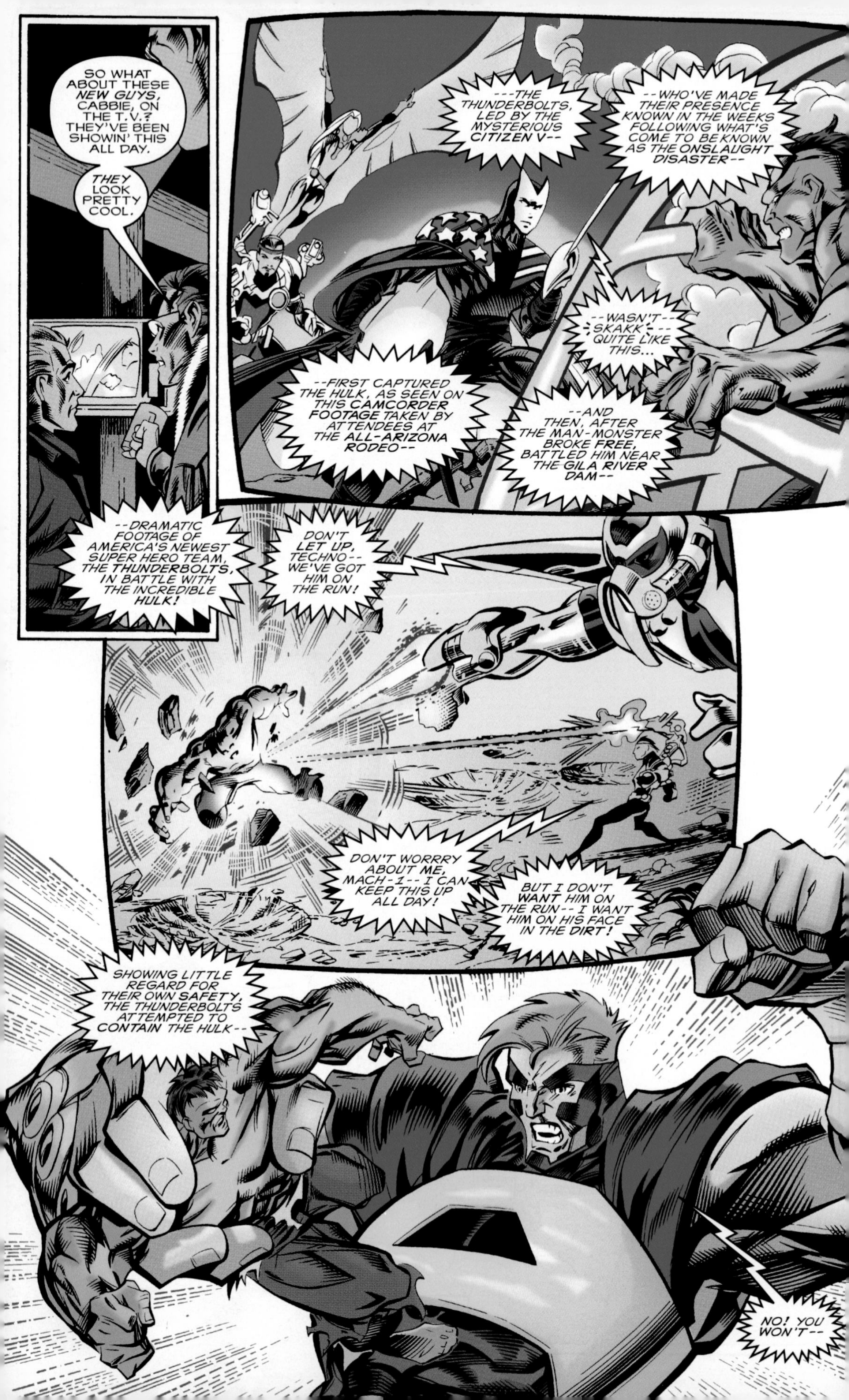
SO WHAT ABOUT THESE NEW GUYS, CABBIE, ON THE T.V.? THEY'VE BEEN SHOWIN' THIS ALL DAY.
THEY LOOK PRETTY COOL.
---THE THUNDERBOLTS, LED BY THE MYSTERIOUS CITIZEN V--
--WHO'VE MADE THEIR PRESENCE KNOWN IN THE WEEKS FOLLOWING WHAT'S COME TO BE KNOWN AS THE ONSLAUGHT DISASTER--
--WASN'T-- SKAKK-- QUITE LIKE THIS...
--FIRST CAPTURED THE HULK, AS SEEN ON THIS CAMCORDER FOOTAGE TAKEN BY ATTENDEES AT THE ALL-ARIZONA RODEO--
--AND THEN, AFTER THE MAN-MONSTER BROKE FREE, BATTLED HIM NEAR THE GILA RIVER DAM--
--DRAMATIC FOOTAGE OF AMERICA'S NEWEST SUPER HERO TEAM, THE THUNDERBOLTS, IN BATTLE WITH THE INCREDIBLE HULK!
DON'T LET UP, TECHNO-- WE'VE GOT HIM ON THE RUN!
DON'T WORRY ABOUT ME, MACH-1-- I CAN KEEP THIS UP ALL DAY!
BUT I DON'T WANT HIM ON THE RUN-- I WANT HIM ON HIS FACE IN THE DIRT!
SHOWING LITTLE REGARD FOR THEIR OWN SAFETY, THE THUNDERBOLTS ATTEMPTED TO CONTAIN THE HULK--
NO! YOU WON'T--

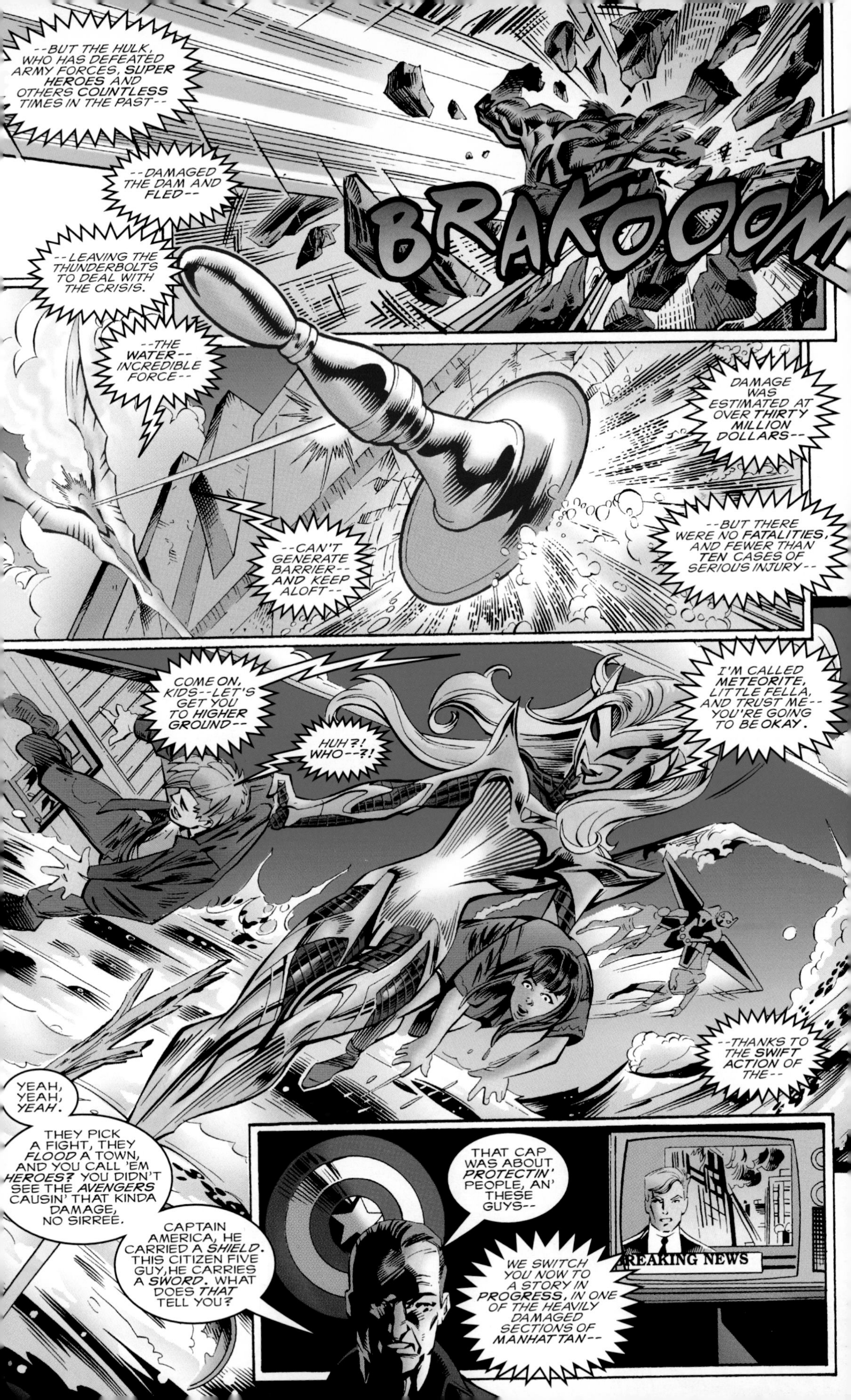
--BUT THE HULK, WHO HAS DEFEATED ARMY FORCES, SUPER HEROES AND OTHERS COUNTLESS TIMES IN THE PAST--
--DAMAGED THE DAM AND FLED--
BRAKOOOM
--LEAVING THE THUNDERBOLTS TO DEAL WITH THE CRISIS.
--THE WATER--INCREDIBLE FORCE--
DAMAGE WAS ESTIMATED AT OVER THIRTY MILLION DOLLARS--
--CAN'T GENERATE BARRIER--AND KEEP ALOFT--
--BUT THERE WERE NO FATALITIES, AND FEWER THAN TEN CASES OF SERIOUS INJURY--
COME ON, KIDS--LET'S GET YOU TO HIGHER GROUND--
HUH?! WHO--?!
I'M CALLED METEORITE, LITTLE FELLA, AND TRUST ME--YOU'RE GOING TO BE OKAY.
--THANKS TO THE SWIFT ACTION OF THE--
YEAH, YEAH, YEAH.
THEY PICK A FIGHT, THEY FLOOD A TOWN, AND YOU CALL 'EM HEROES? YOU DIDN'T SEE THE AVENGERS CAUSIN' THAT KINDA DAMAGE, NO SIRREE.
CAPTAIN AMERICA, HE CARRIED A SHIELD. THIS CITIZEN FIVE GUY, HE CARRIES A SWORD. WHAT DOES THAT TELL YOU?
THAT CAP WAS ABOUT PROTECTIN' PEOPLE, AN' THESE GUYS--
REAKING NEWS
WE SWITCH YOU NOW TO A STORY IN PROGRESS, IN ONE OF THE HEAVILY DAMAGED SECTIONS OF MANHATTAN--

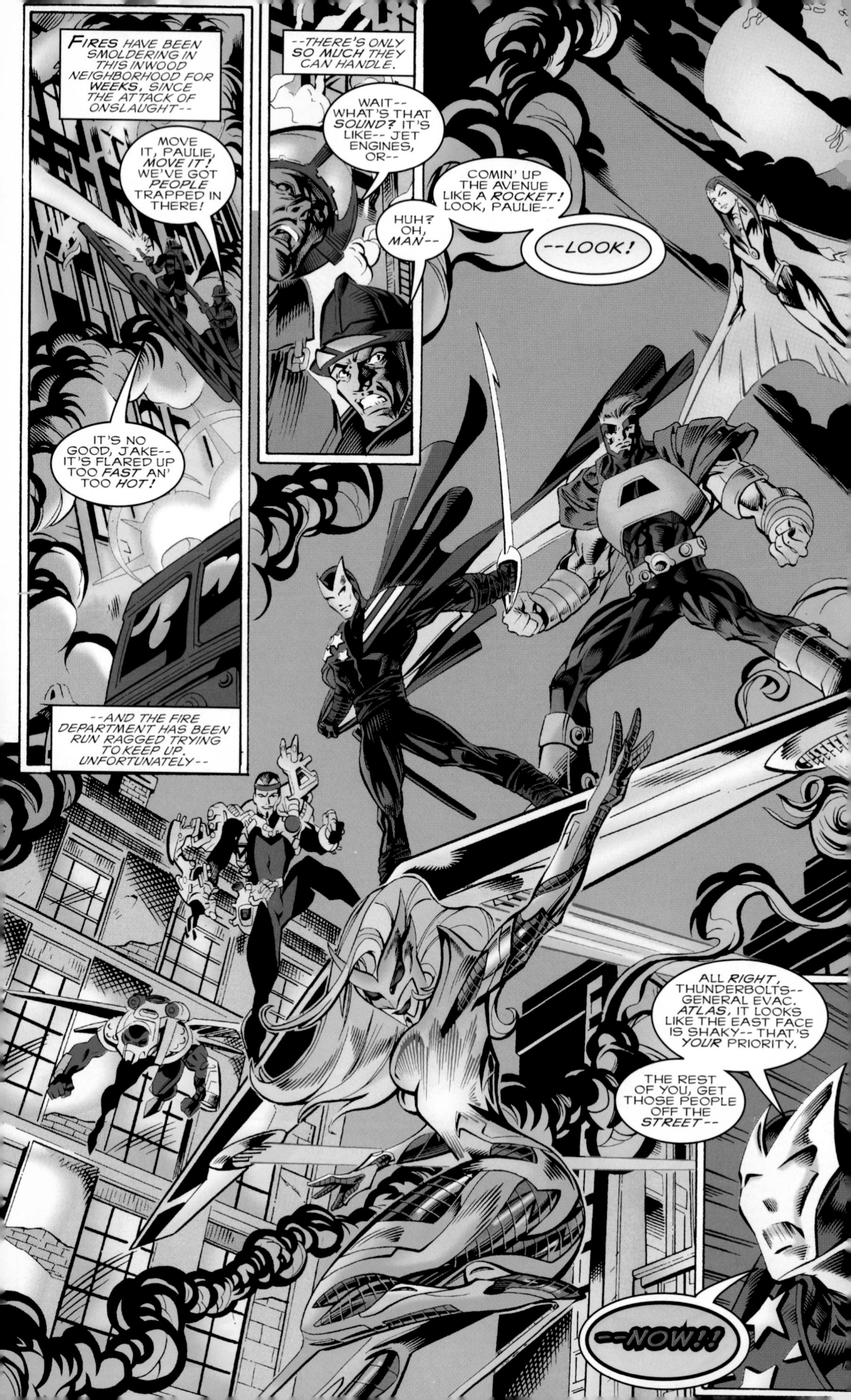
FIRES HAVE BEEN SMOLDERING IN THIS INWOOD NEIGHBORHOOD FOR WEEKS, SINCE THE ATTACK OF ONSLAUGHT--
MOVE IT, PAULIE, MOVE IT! WE'VE GOT PEOPLE TRAPPED IN THERE!
IT'S NO GOOD, JAKE-- IT'S FLARED UP TOO FAST AN' TOO HOT!
--AND THE FIRE DEPARTMENT HAS BEEN RUN RAGGED TRYING TO KEEP UP. UNFORTUNATELY--
--THERE'S ONLY SO MUCH THEY CAN HANDLE.
WAIT-- WHAT'S THAT SOUND? IT'S LIKE-- JET ENGINES, OR--
HUH? OH, MAN--
COMIN' UP THE AVENUE LIKE A ROCKET! LOOK, PAULIE--
--LOOK!
ALL RIGHT, THUNDERBOLTS-- GENERAL EVAC. ATLAS, IT LOOKS LIKE THE EAST FACE IS SHAKY-- THAT'S YOUR PRIORITY.
THE REST OF YOU, GET THOSE PEOPLE OFF THE STREET--
--NOW!!

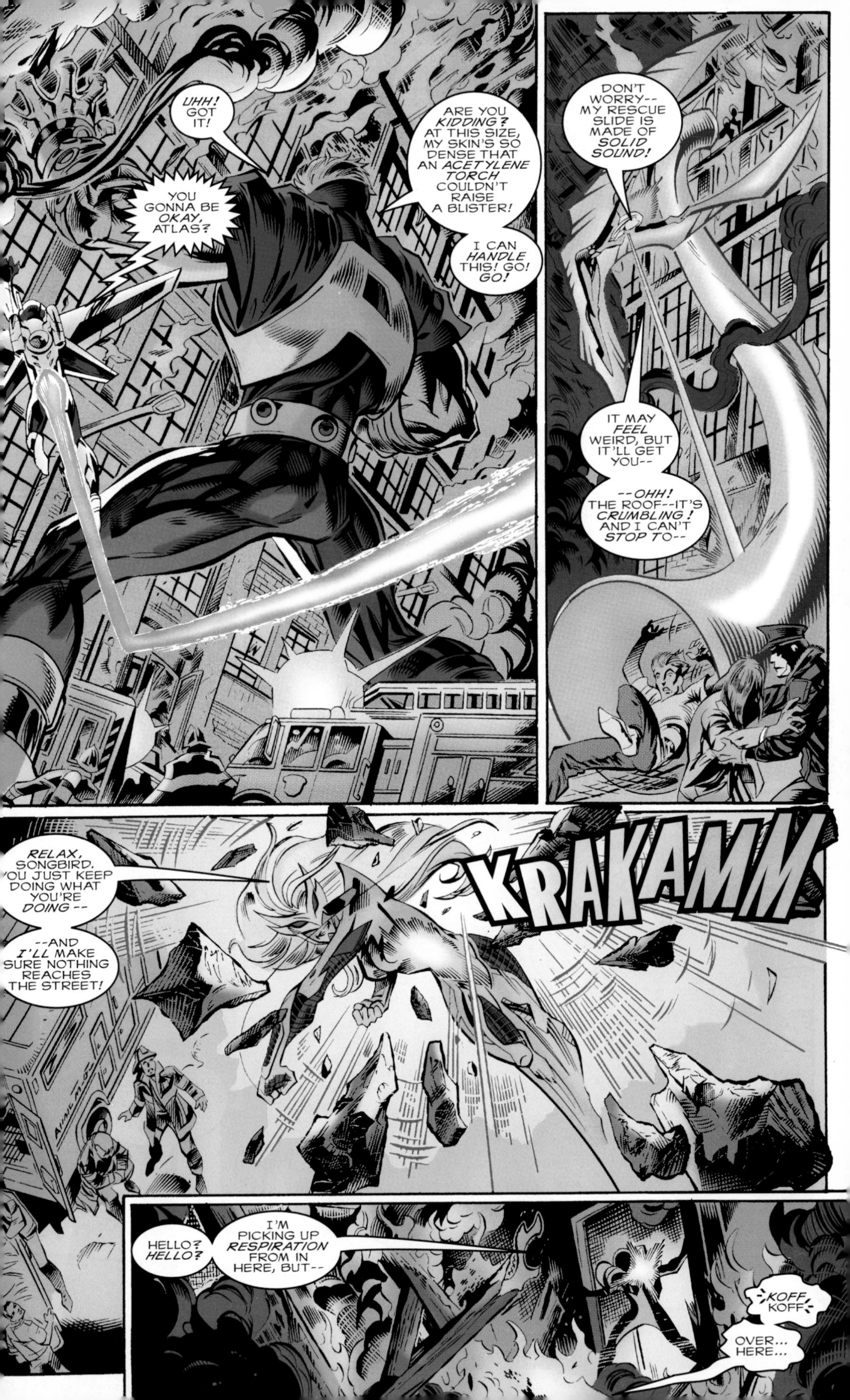
UHH! GOT IT!
YOU GONNA BE OKAY, ATLAS?
ARE YOU KIDDING? AT THIS SIZE, MY SKIN'S SO DENSE THAT AN ACETYLENE TORCH COULDN'T RAISE A BLISTER!
I CAN HANDLE THIS! GO! GO!
DON'T WORRY-- MY RESCUE SLIDE IS MADE OF SOLID SOUND!
IT MAY FEEL WEIRD, BUT IT'LL GET YOU--
--OHH! THE ROOF--IT'S CRUMBLING! AND I CAN'T STOP TO--
KRAKAMM
RELAX, SONGBIRD. YOU JUST KEEP DOING WHAT YOU'RE DOING--
--AND I'LL MAKE SURE NOTHING REACHES THE STREET!
HELLO? HELLO?
I'M PICKING UP RESPIRATION FROM IN HERE, BUT--
KOFF KOFF
OVER... HERE...

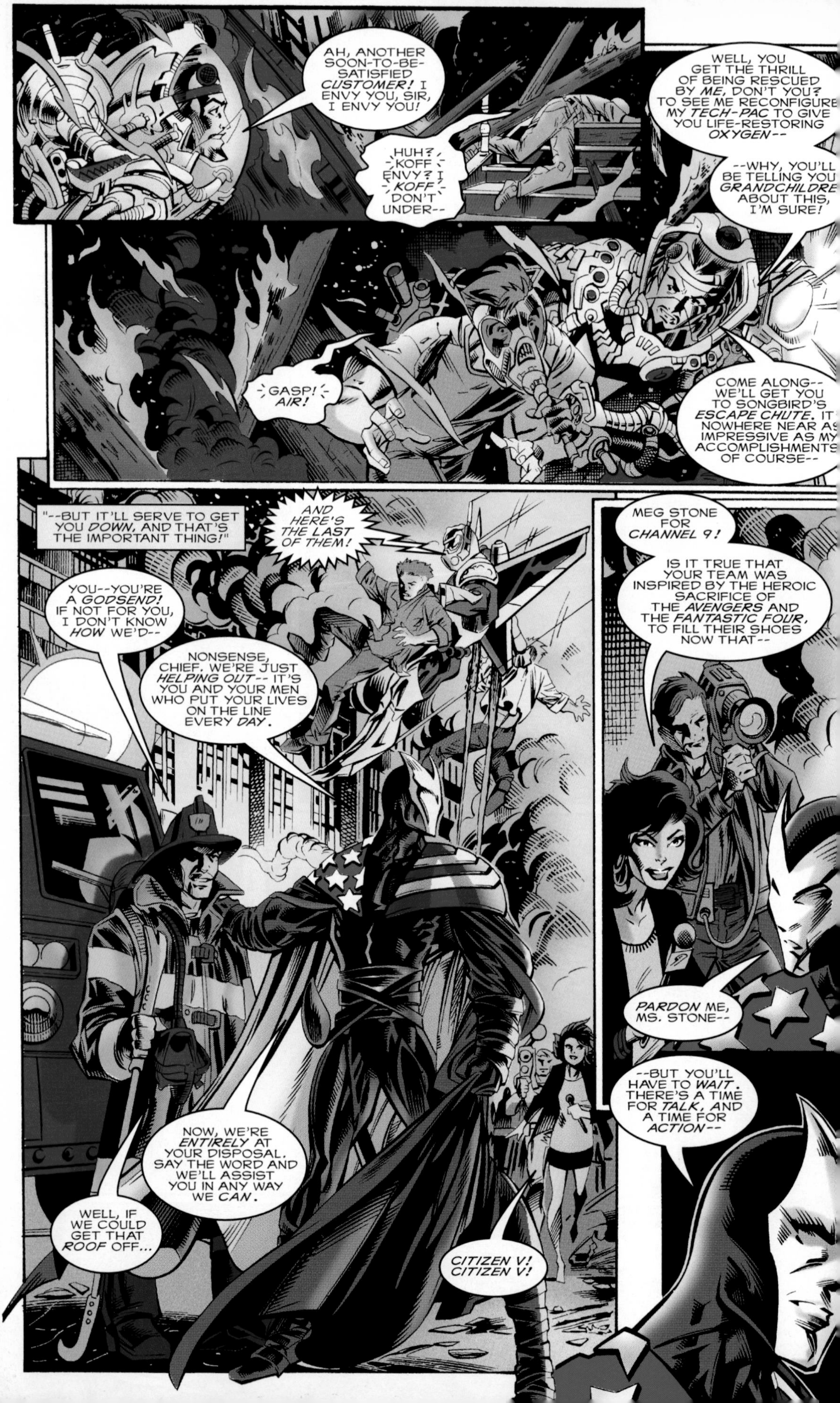
AH, ANOTHER SOON-TO-BE-SATISFIED CUSTOMER! I ENVY YOU, SIR, I ENVY YOU!
HUH? -KOFF- ENVY? I -KOFF- DON'T UNDER--
WELL, YOU GET THE THRILL OF BEING RESCUED BY ME, DON'T YOU? TO SEE ME RECONFIGURE MY TECH-PAC TO GIVE YOU LIFE-RESTORING OXYGEN--
--WHY, YOU'LL BE TELLING YOU GRANDCHILDRE ABOUT THIS, I'M SURE!
-GASP!- AIR!
COME ALONG-- WE'LL GET YOU TO SONGBIRD'S ESCAPE CHUTE. IT NOWHERE NEAR AS IMPRESSIVE AS MY ACCOMPLISHMENTS OF COURSE--
"--BUT IT'LL SERVE TO GET YOU DOWN, AND THAT'S THE IMPORTANT THING!"
AND HERE'S THE LAST OF THEM!
YOU--YOU'RE A GODSEND! IF NOT FOR YOU, I DON'T KNOW HOW WE'D--
NONSENSE, CHIEF. WE'RE JUST HELPING OUT-- IT'S YOU AND YOUR MEN WHO PUT YOUR LIVES ON THE LINE EVERY DAY.
NOW, WE'RE ENTIRELY AT YOUR DISPOSAL. SAY THE WORD AND WE'LL ASSIST YOU IN ANY WAY WE CAN.
WELL, IF WE COULD GET THAT ROOF OFF...
CITIZEN V! CITIZEN V!
MEG STONE FOR CHANNEL 9!
IS IT TRUE THAT YOUR TEAM WAS INSPIRED BY THE HEROIC SACRIFICE OF THE AVENGERS AND THE FANTASTIC FOUR, TO FILL THEIR SHOES NOW THAT--
PARDON ME, MS. STONE--
--BUT YOU'LL HAVE TO WAIT. THERE'S A TIME FOR TALK, AND A TIME FOR ACTION--

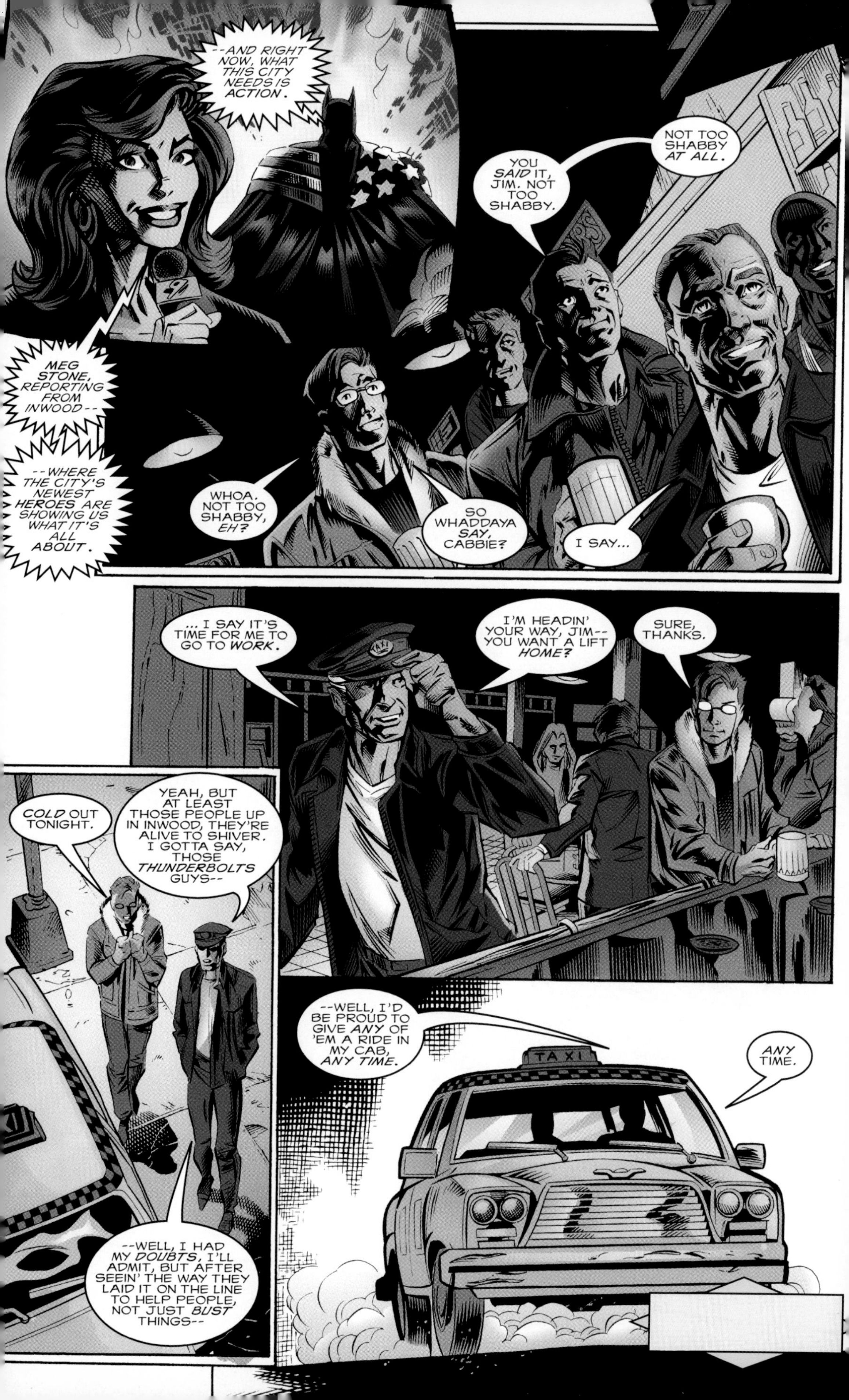
--AND RIGHT NOW, WHAT THIS CITY NEEDS IS ACTION.
MEG STONE, REPORTING FROM INWOOD--
--WHERE THE CITY'S NEWEST HEROES ARE SHOWING US WHAT IT'S ALL ABOUT.
NOT TOO SHABBY AT ALL.
YOU SAID IT, JIM. NOT TOO SHABBY.
WHOA. NOT TOO SHABBY, EH?
SO WHADDAYA SAY, CABBIE?
I SAY...
... I SAY IT'S TIME FOR ME TO GO TO WORK.
I'M HEADIN' YOUR WAY, JIM-- YOU WANT A LIFT HOME?
SURE, THANKS.
COLD OUT TONIGHT.
YEAH, BUT AT LEAST THOSE PEOPLE UP IN INWOOD, THEY'RE ALIVE TO SHIVER. I GOTTA SAY, THOSE THUNDERBOLTS GUYS--
--WELL, I HAD MY DOUBTS, I'LL ADMIT, BUT AFTER SEEIN' THE WAY THEY LAID IT ON THE LINE TO HELP PEOPLE, NOT JUST BUST THINGS--
--WELL, I'D BE PROUD TO GIVE ANY OF 'EM A RIDE IN MY CAB, ANY TIME.
TAXI
ANY TIME.

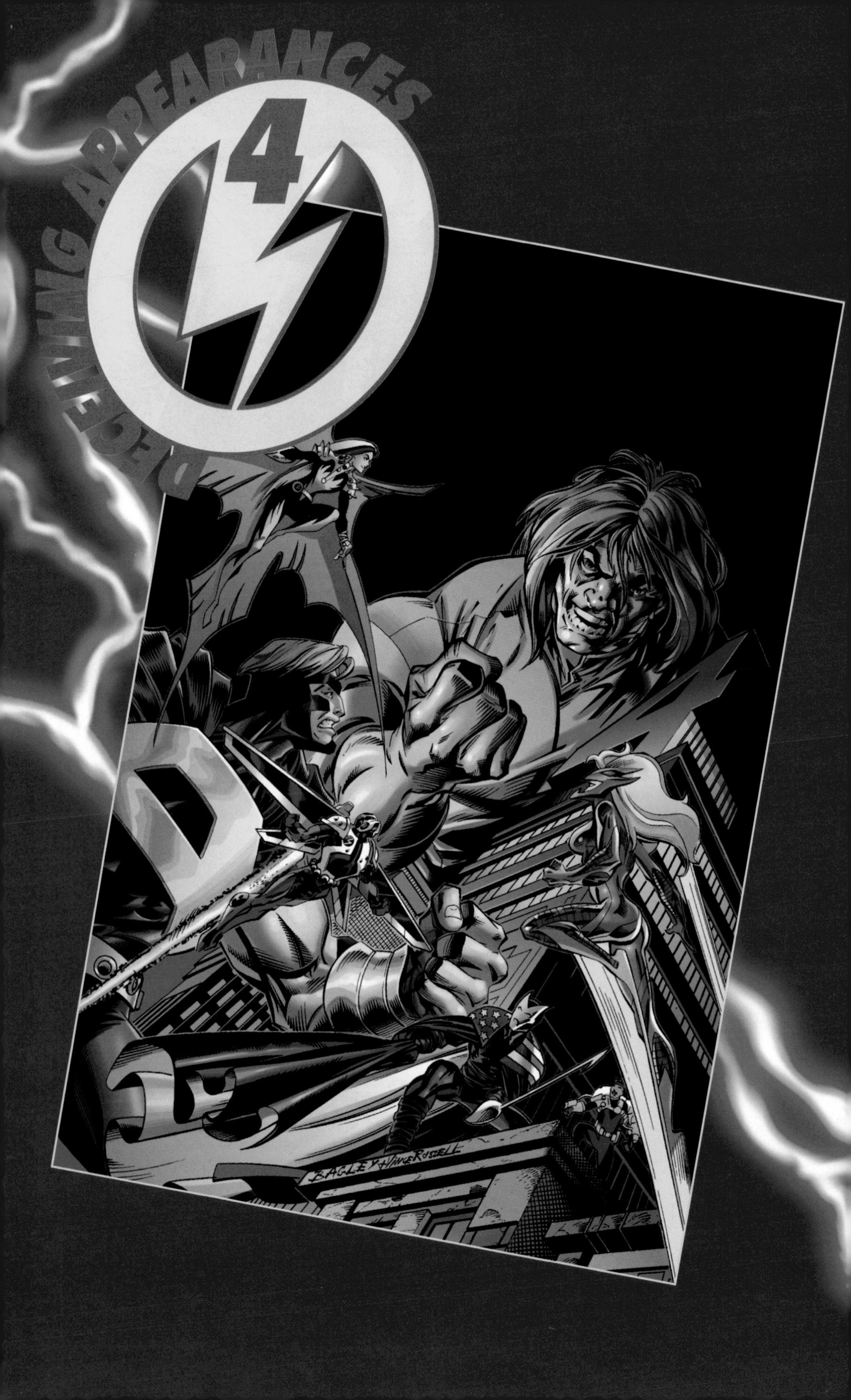
DECEIVING APPEARANCES
4
BAGLEY + VINCE RUSSELL

DECEIVING APPEARANCES

KURT BUSIEK Writer MARK BAGLEY Penciler VINCE RUSSELL Inker
COMICRAFT'S DAVE LANPHEAR/OG Lettering JOE ROSAS Colors TOM BREVOORT Editor BOB HARRAS Editor in Chief

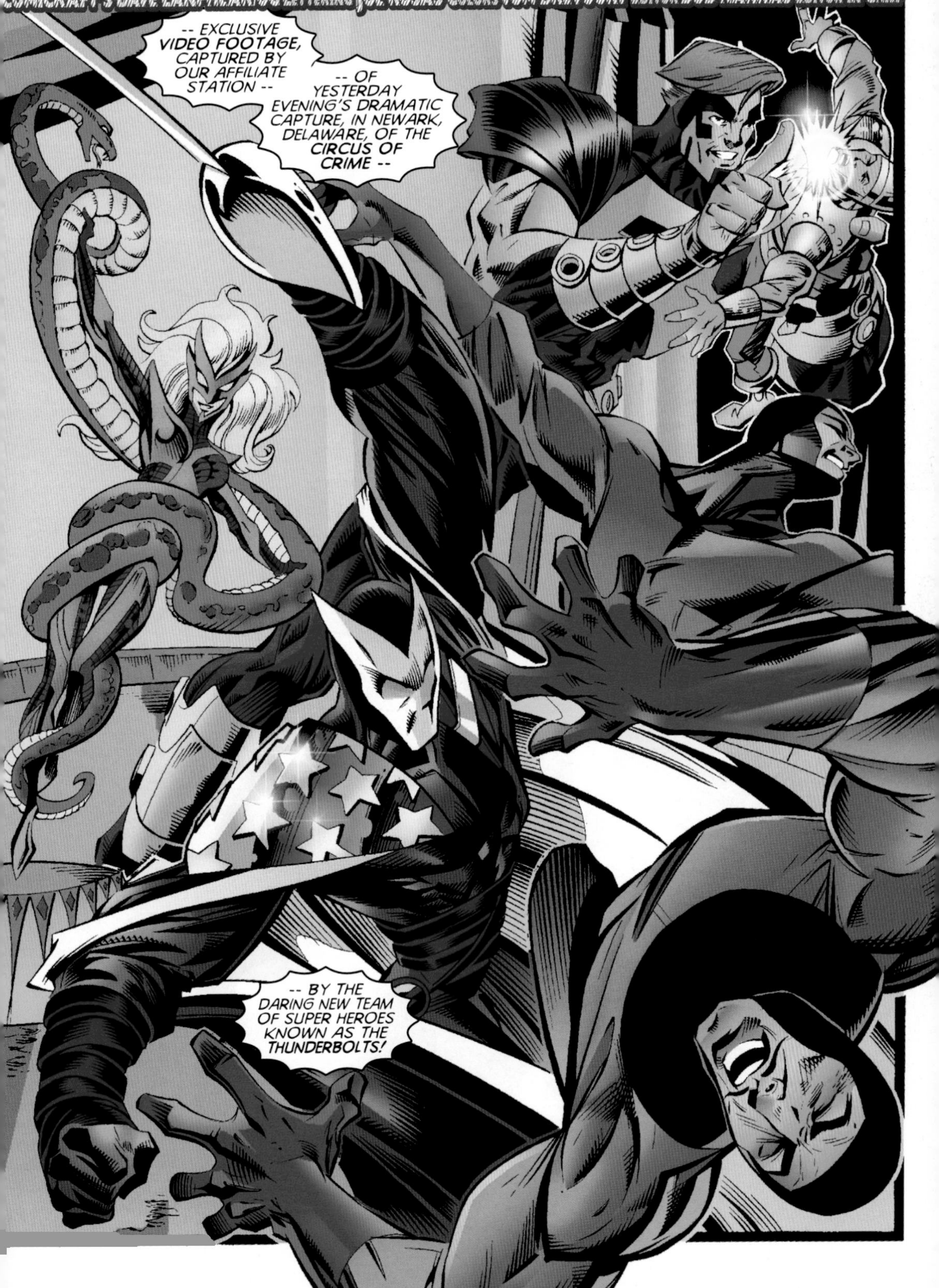
-- EXCLUSIVE VIDEO FOOTAGE, CAPTURED BY OUR AFFILIATE STATION --
-- OF YESTERDAY EVENING'S DRAMATIC CAPTURE, IN NEWARK, DELAWARE, OF THE CIRCUS OF CRIME --
-- BY THE DARING NEW TEAM OF SUPER HEROES KNOWN AS THE THUNDERBOLTS!

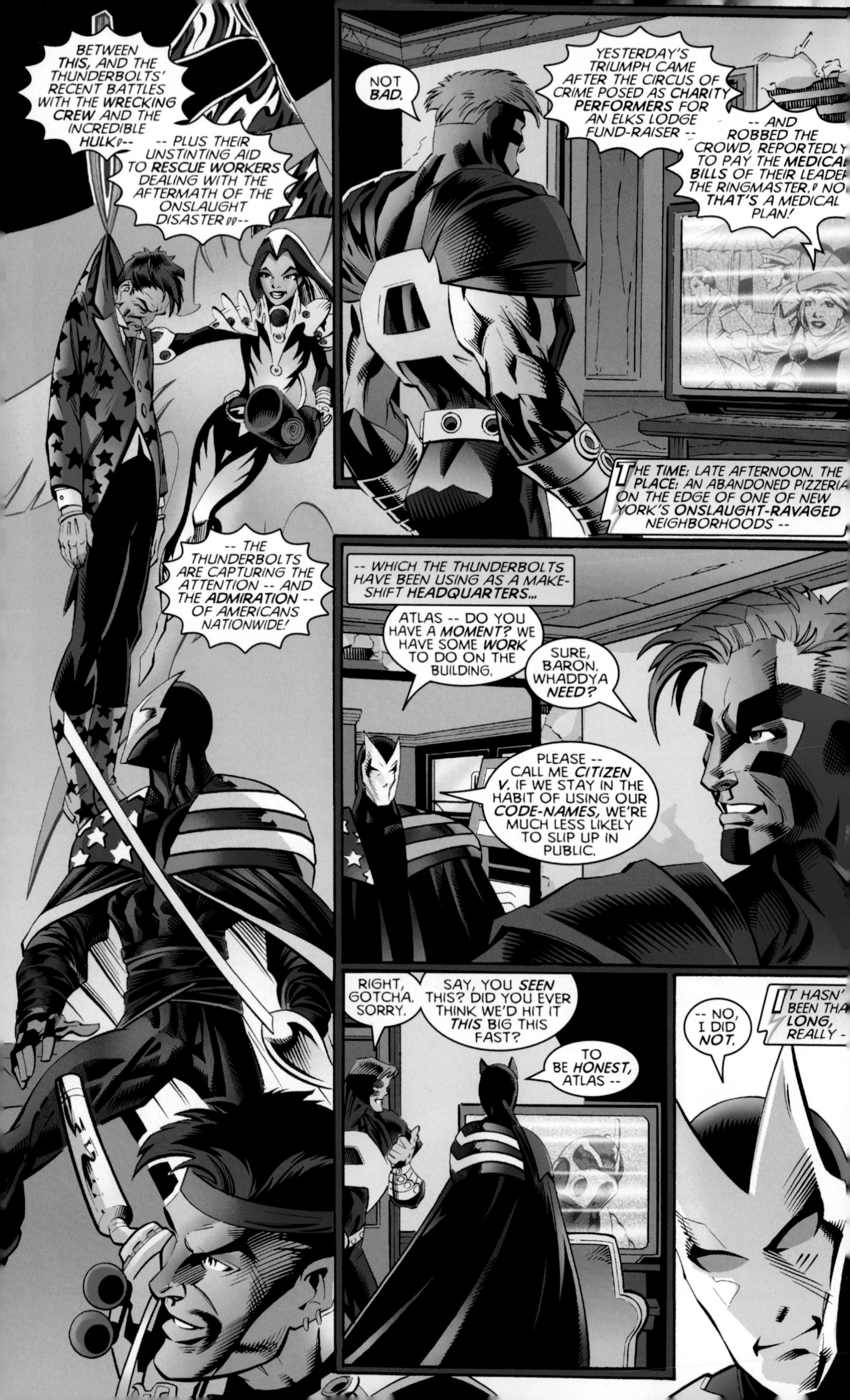
BETWEEN THIS, AND THE THUNDERBOLTS' RECENT BATTLES WITH THE WRECKING CREW AND THE INCREDIBLE HULK--
-- PLUS THEIR UNSTINTING AID TO RESCUE WORKERS DEALING WITH THE AFTERMATH OF THE ONSLAUGHT DISASTER--
-- THE THUNDERBOLTS ARE CAPTURING THE ATTENTION -- AND THE ADMIRATION -- OF AMERICANS NATIONWIDE!
NOT BAD.
YESTERDAY'S TRIUMPH CAME AFTER THE CIRCUS OF CRIME POSED AS CHARITY PERFORMERS FOR AN ELKS LODGE FUND-RAISER --
-- AND ROBBED THE CROWD, REPORTEDLY TO PAY THE MEDICAL BILLS OF THEIR LEADER THE RINGMASTER. NOW THAT'S A MEDICAL PLAN!
THE TIME: LATE AFTERNOON. THE PLACE: AN ABANDONED PIZZERIA ON THE EDGE OF ONE OF NEW YORK'S ONSLAUGHT-RAVAGED NEIGHBORHOODS --
-- WHICH THE THUNDERBOLTS HAVE BEEN USING AS A MAKE-SHIFT HEADQUARTERS...
ATLAS -- DO YOU HAVE A MOMENT? WE HAVE SOME WORK TO DO ON THE BUILDING.
SURE, BARON. WHADDYA NEED?
PLEASE -- CALL ME CITIZEN V. IF WE STAY IN THE HABIT OF USING OUR CODE-NAMES, WE'RE MUCH LESS LIKELY TO SLIP UP IN PUBLIC.
RIGHT, GOTCHA. SORRY.
SAY, YOU SEEN THIS? DID YOU EVER THINK WE'D HIT IT THIS BIG THIS FAST?
TO BE HONEST, ATLAS --
-- NO, I DID NOT.
IT HASN'T BEEN THAT LONG, REALLY --

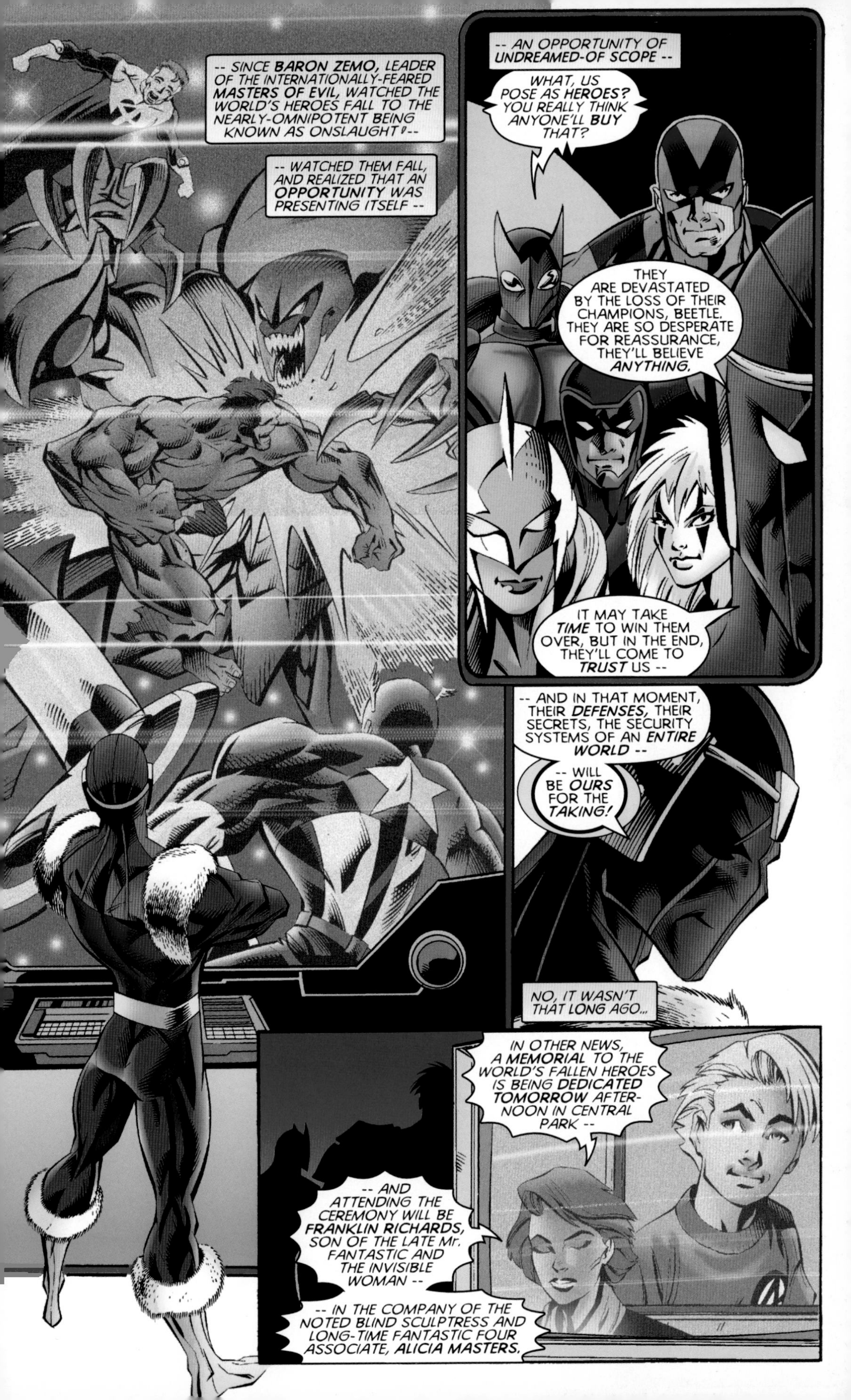
-- SINCE BARON ZEMO, LEADER OF THE INTERNATIONALLY-FEARED MASTERS OF EVIL, WATCHED THE WORLD'S HEROES FALL TO THE NEARLY-OMNIPOTENT BEING KNOWN AS ONSLAUGHT! --
-- WATCHED THEM FALL, AND REALIZED THAT AN OPPORTUNITY WAS PRESENTING ITSELF --
-- AN OPPORTUNITY OF UNDREAMED-OF SCOPE --
WHAT, US POSE AS HEROES? YOU REALLY THINK ANYONE'LL BUY THAT?
THEY ARE DEVASTATED BY THE LOSS OF THEIR CHAMPIONS, BEETLE. THEY ARE SO DESPERATE FOR REASSURANCE, THEY'LL BELIEVE ANYTHING.
IT MAY TAKE TIME TO WIN THEM OVER, BUT IN THE END, THEY'LL COME TO TRUST US --
-- AND IN THAT MOMENT, THEIR DEFENSES, THEIR SECRETS, THE SECURITY SYSTEMS OF AN ENTIRE WORLD --
-- WILL BE OURS FOR THE TAKING!
NO, IT WASN'T THAT LONG AGO...
IN OTHER NEWS, A MEMORIAL TO THE WORLD'S FALLEN HEROES IS BEING DEDICATED TOMORROW AFTER-NOON IN CENTRAL PARK --
-- AND ATTENDING THE CEREMONY WILL BE FRANKLIN RICHARDS, SON OF THE LATE Mr. FANTASTIC AND THE INVISIBLE WOMAN --
-- IN THE COMPANY OF THE NOTED BLIND SCULPTRESS AND LONG-TIME FANTASTIC FOUR ASSOCIATE, ALICIA MASTERS.

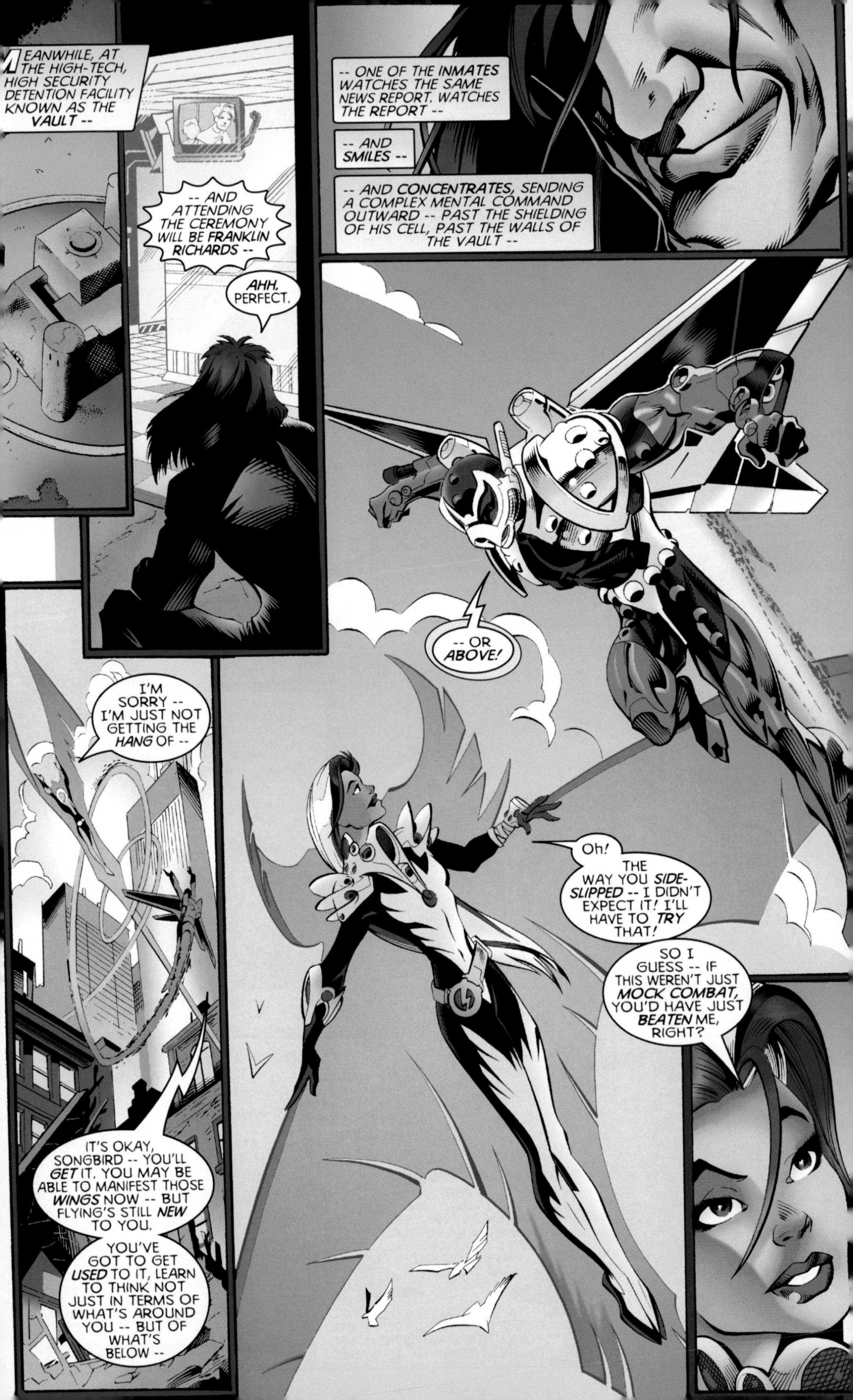
MEANWHILE, AT THE HIGH-TECH, HIGH SECURITY DETENTION FACILITY KNOWN AS THE VAULT --
-- AND ATTENDING THE CEREMONY WILL BE FRANKLIN RICHARDS --
AHH, PERFECT.
-- ONE OF THE INMATES WATCHES THE SAME NEWS REPORT. WATCHES THE REPORT --
-- AND SMILES --
-- AND CONCENTRATES, SENDING A COMPLEX MENTAL COMMAND OUTWARD -- PAST THE SHIELDING OF HIS CELL, PAST THE WALLS OF THE VAULT --
I'M SORRY -- I'M JUST NOT GETTING THE HANG OF --
IT'S OKAY, SONGBIRD -- YOU'LL GET IT. YOU MAY BE ABLE TO MANIFEST THOSE WINGS NOW -- BUT FLYING'S STILL NEW TO YOU.
YOU'VE GOT TO GET USED TO IT, LEARN TO THINK NOT JUST IN TERMS OF WHAT'S AROUND YOU -- BUT OF WHAT'S BELOW --
-- OR ABOVE!
Oh!
THE WAY YOU SIDE-SLIPPED -- I DIDN'T EXPECT IT! I'LL HAVE TO TRY THAT!
SO I GUESS -- IF THIS WEREN'T JUST MOCK COMBAT, YOU'D HAVE JUST BEATEN ME, RIGHT?

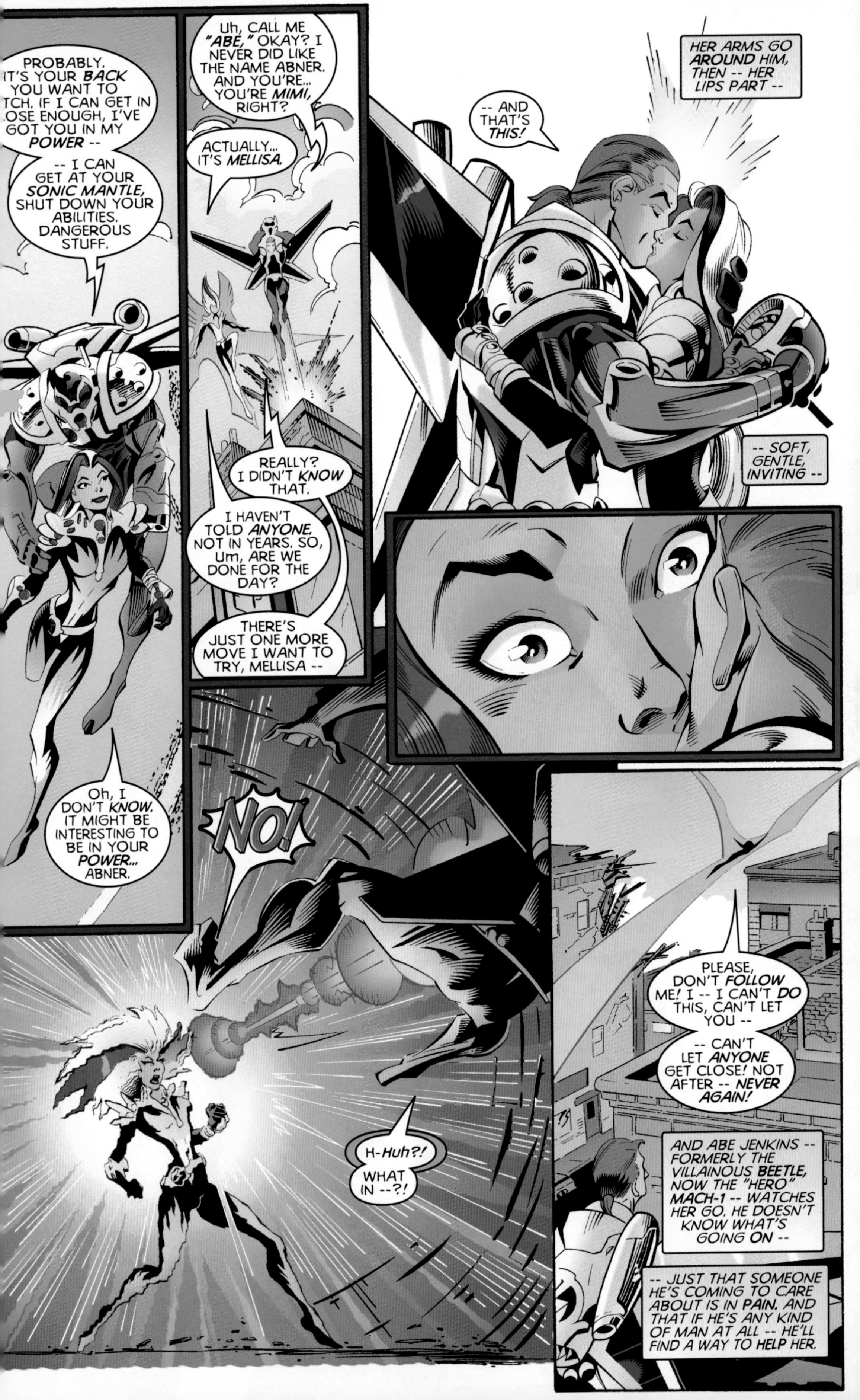

PROBABLY. IT'S YOUR BACK YOU WANT TO TCH. IF I CAN GET IN OSE ENOUGH, I'VE GOT YOU IN MY POWER --
-- I CAN GET AT YOUR SONIC MANTLE, SHUT DOWN YOUR ABILITIES. DANGEROUS STUFF.
Oh, I DON'T KNOW. IT MIGHT BE INTERESTING TO BE IN YOUR POWER... ABNER.
Uh, CALL ME "ABE," OKAY? I NEVER DID LIKE THE NAME ABNER. AND YOU'RE... YOU'RE MIMI, RIGHT?
ACTUALLY... IT'S MELLISA.
REALLY? I DIDN'T KNOW THAT.
I HAVEN'T TOLD ANYONE, NOT IN YEARS. SO, Um, ARE WE DONE FOR THE DAY?
THERE'S JUST ONE MORE MOVE I WANT TO TRY, MELLISA --
-- AND THAT'S THIS!
HER ARMS GO AROUND HIM, THEN -- HER LIPS PART --
-- SOFT, GENTLE, INVITING --
NO!
H-Huh?! WHAT IN --?!
PLEASE, DON'T FOLLOW ME! I -- I CAN'T DO THIS, CAN'T LET YOU --
-- CAN'T LET ANYONE GET CLOSE! NOT AFTER -- NEVER AGAIN!
AND ABE JENKINS -- FORMERLY THE VILLAINOUS BEETLE, NOW THE "HERO" MACH-1 -- WATCHES HER GO. HE DOESN'T KNOW WHAT'S GOING ON --
-- JUST THAT SOMEONE HE'S COMING TO CARE ABOUT IS IN PAIN. AND THAT IF HE'S ANY KIND OF MAN AT ALL -- HE'LL FIND A WAY TO HELP HER.

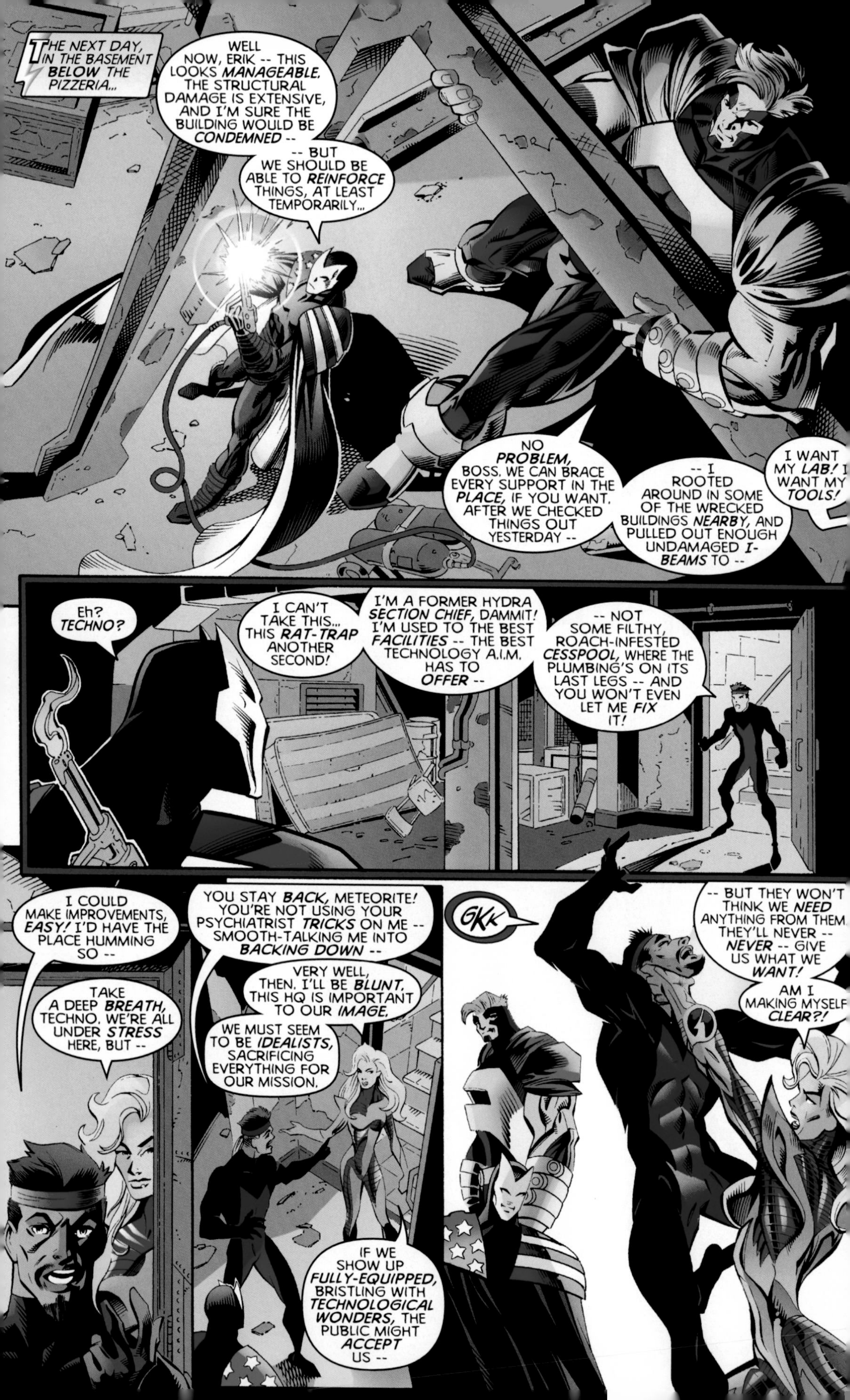
THE NEXT DAY, IN THE BASEMENT BELOW THE PIZZERIA...
WELL NOW, ERIK -- THIS LOOKS MANAGEABLE. THE STRUCTURAL DAMAGE IS EXTENSIVE, AND I'M SURE THE BUILDING WOULD BE CONDEMNED --
-- BUT WE SHOULD BE ABLE TO REINFORCE THINGS, AT LEAST TEMPORARILY...
NO PROBLEM, BOSS. WE CAN BRACE EVERY SUPPORT IN THE PLACE, IF YOU WANT. AFTER WE CHECKED THINGS OUT YESTERDAY --
-- I ROOTED AROUND IN SOME OF THE WRECKED BUILDINGS NEARBY, AND PULLED OUT ENOUGH UNDAMAGED I-BEAMS TO --
I WANT MY LAB! I WANT MY TOOLS!
Eh? TECHNO?
I CAN'T TAKE THIS... THIS RAT-TRAP ANOTHER SECOND!
I'M A FORMER HYDRA SECTION CHIEF, DAMMIT! I'M USED TO THE BEST FACILITIES -- THE BEST TECHNOLOGY A.I.M. HAS TO OFFER --
-- NOT SOME FILTHY, ROACH-INFESTED CESSPOOL, WHERE THE PLUMBING'S ON ITS LAST LEGS -- AND YOU WON'T EVEN LET ME FIX IT!
I COULD MAKE IMPROVEMENTS, EASY! I'D HAVE THE PLACE HUMMING SO --
TAKE A DEEP BREATH, TECHNO. WE'RE ALL UNDER STRESS HERE, BUT --
YOU STAY BACK, METEORITE! YOU'RE NOT USING YOUR PSYCHIATRIST TRICKS ON ME -- SMOOTH-TALKING ME INTO BACKING DOWN --
VERY WELL, THEN. I'LL BE BLUNT. THIS HQ IS IMPORTANT TO OUR IMAGE.
WE MUST SEEM TO BE IDEALISTS, SACRIFICING EVERYTHING FOR OUR MISSION.
IF WE SHOW UP FULLY-EQUIPPED, BRISTLING WITH TECHNOLOGICAL WONDERS, THE PUBLIC MIGHT ACCEPT US --
GKK
-- BUT THEY WON'T THINK WE NEED ANYTHING FROM THEM. THEY'LL NEVER -- NEVER -- GIVE US WHAT WE WANT!
AM I MAKING MYSELF CLEAR?!

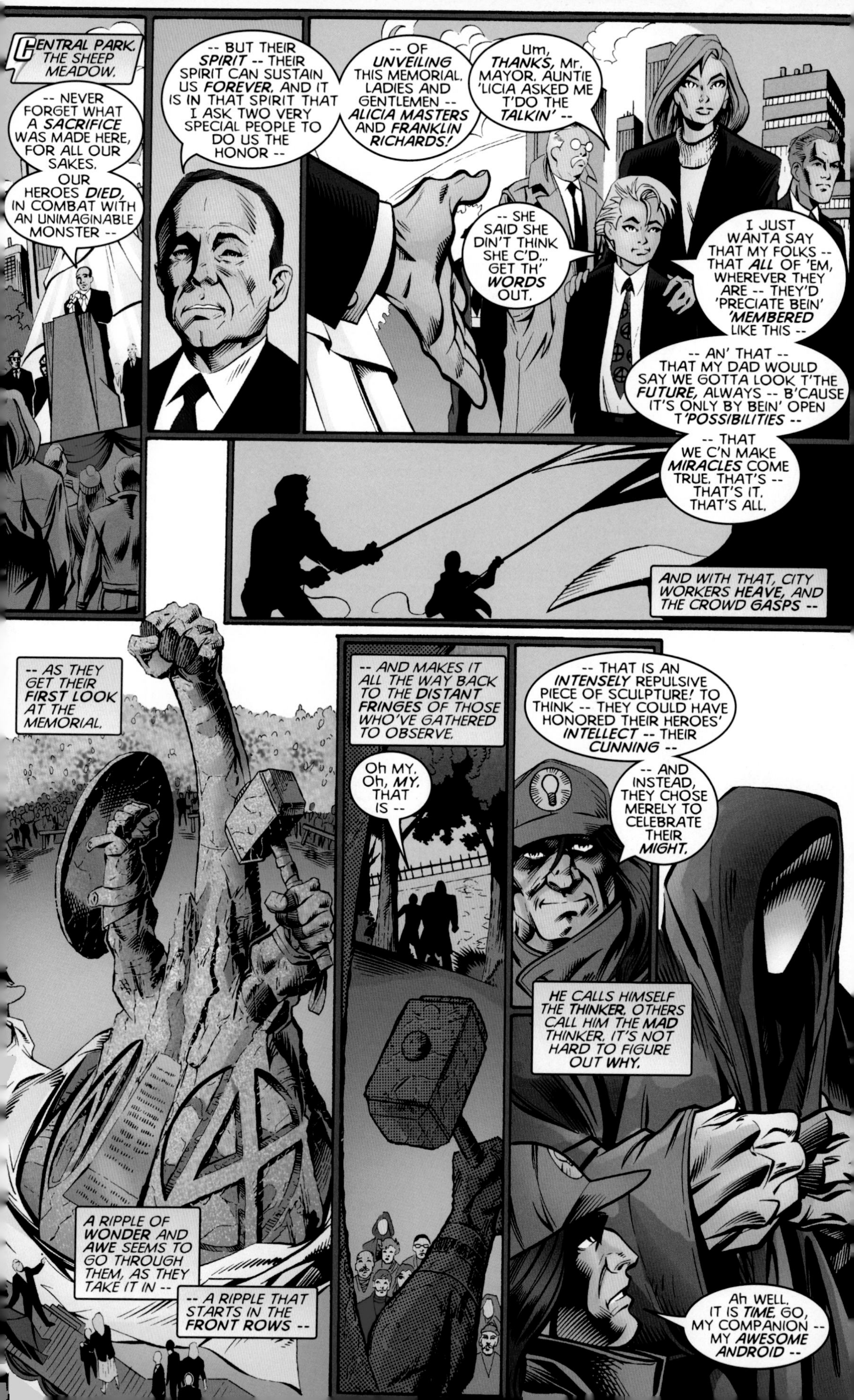
CENTRAL PARK. THE SHEEP MEADOW.
-- NEVER FORGET WHAT A SACRIFICE WAS MADE HERE, FOR ALL OUR SAKES.
OUR HEROES DIED, IN COMBAT WITH AN UNIMAGINABLE MONSTER --
-- BUT THEIR SPIRIT -- THEIR SPIRIT CAN SUSTAIN US FOREVER, AND IT IS IN THAT SPIRIT THAT I ASK TWO VERY SPECIAL PEOPLE TO DO US THE HONOR --
-- OF UNVEILING THIS MEMORIAL, LADIES AND GENTLEMEN -- ALICIA MASTERS AND FRANKLIN RICHARDS!
Um, THANKS, Mr. MAYOR. AUNTIE 'LICIA ASKED ME T'DO THE TALKIN' --
-- SHE SAID SHE DIN'T THINK SHE C'D... GET TH' WORDS OUT.
I JUST WANTA SAY THAT MY FOLKS -- THAT ALL OF 'EM, WHEREVER THEY ARE -- THEY'D 'PRECIATE BEIN' 'MEMBERED LIKE THIS --
-- AN' THAT -- THAT MY DAD WOULD SAY WE GOTTA LOOK T'THE FUTURE, ALWAYS -- B'CAUSE IT'S ONLY BY BEIN' OPEN T'POSSIBILITIES --
-- THAT WE C'N MAKE MIRACLES COME TRUE. THAT'S -- THAT'S IT. THAT'S ALL.
AND WITH THAT, CITY WORKERS HEAVE, AND THE CROWD GASPS --
-- AS THEY GET THEIR FIRST LOOK AT THE MEMORIAL.
A RIPPLE OF WONDER AND AWE SEEMS TO GO THROUGH THEM, AS THEY TAKE IT IN --
-- A RIPPLE THAT STARTS IN THE FRONT ROWS --
-- AND MAKES IT ALL THE WAY BACK TO THE DISTANT FRINGES OF THOSE WHO'VE GATHERED TO OBSERVE.
Oh MY. Oh, MY. THAT IS --
-- THAT IS AN INTENSELY REPULSIVE PIECE OF SCULPTURE! TO THINK -- THEY COULD HAVE HONORED THEIR HEROES' INTELLECT -- THEIR CUNNING --
-- AND INSTEAD, THEY CHOSE MERELY TO CELEBRATE THEIR MIGHT.
HE CALLS HIMSELF THE THINKER. OTHERS CALL HIM THE MAD THINKER. IT'S NOT HARD TO FIGURE OUT WHY.
Ah WELL. IT IS TIME. GO, MY COMPANION -- MY AWESOME ANDROID --

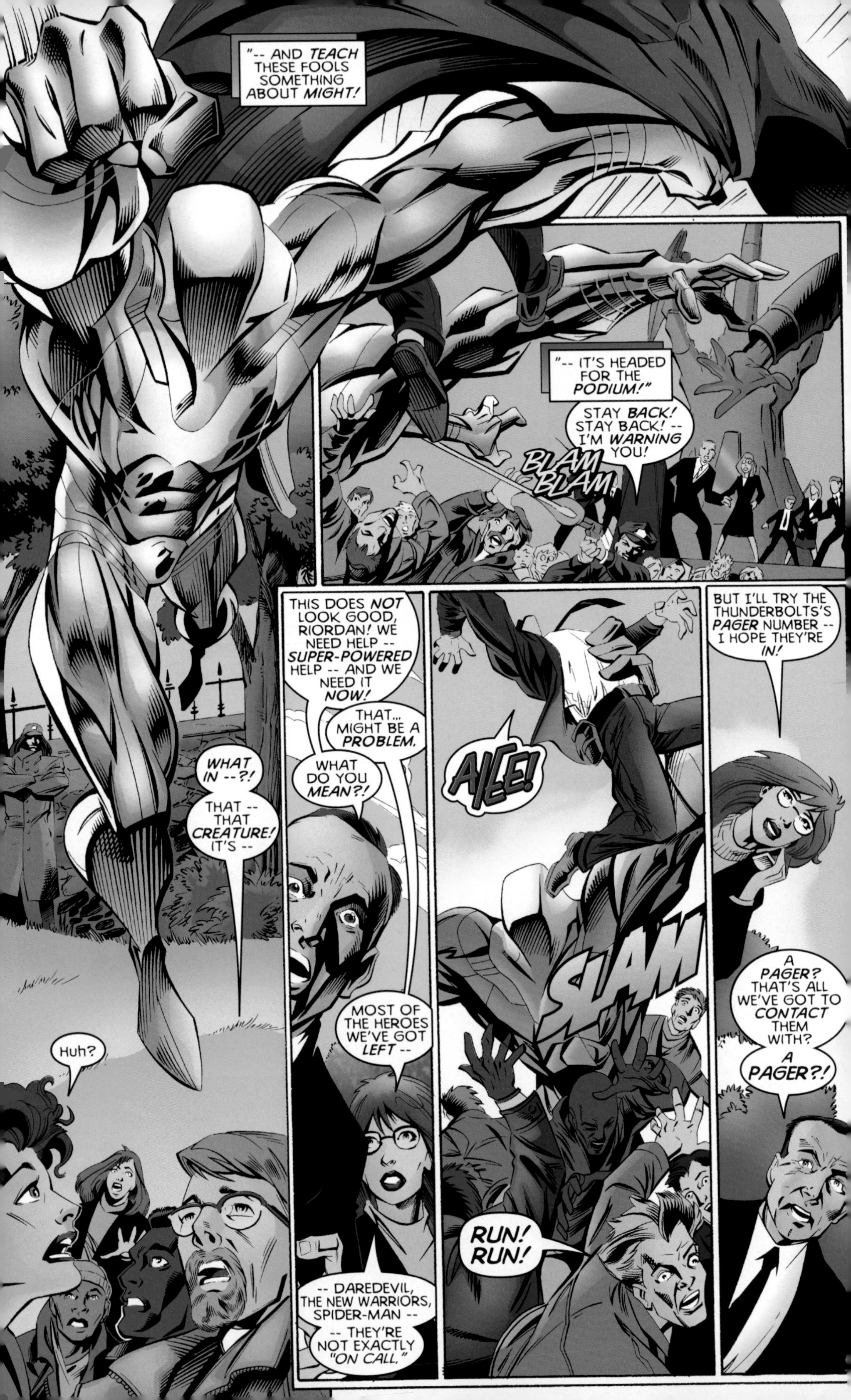
"-- AND TEACH THESE FOOLS SOMETHING ABOUT MIGHT!
"-- IT'S HEADED FOR THE PODIUM!"
STAY BACK! STAY BACK! -- I'M WARNING YOU!
BLAM BLAM
WHAT IN --?!
THAT -- THAT CREATURE! IT'S --
Huh?
THIS DOES NOT LOOK GOOD, RIORDAN! WE NEED HELP -- SUPER-POWERED HELP -- AND WE NEED IT NOW!
THAT... MIGHT BE A PROBLEM.
WHAT DO YOU MEAN?!
MOST OF THE HEROES WE'VE GOT LEFT --
-- DAREDEVIL, THE NEW WARRIORS, SPIDER-MAN --
-- THEY'RE NOT EXACTLY "ON CALL."
AIEEE!
SLAM
RUN! RUN!
BUT I'LL TRY THE THUNDERBOLTS'S PAGER NUMBER -- I HOPE THEY'RE IN!
A PAGER? THAT'S ALL WE'VE GOT TO CONTACT THEM WITH? A PAGER?!

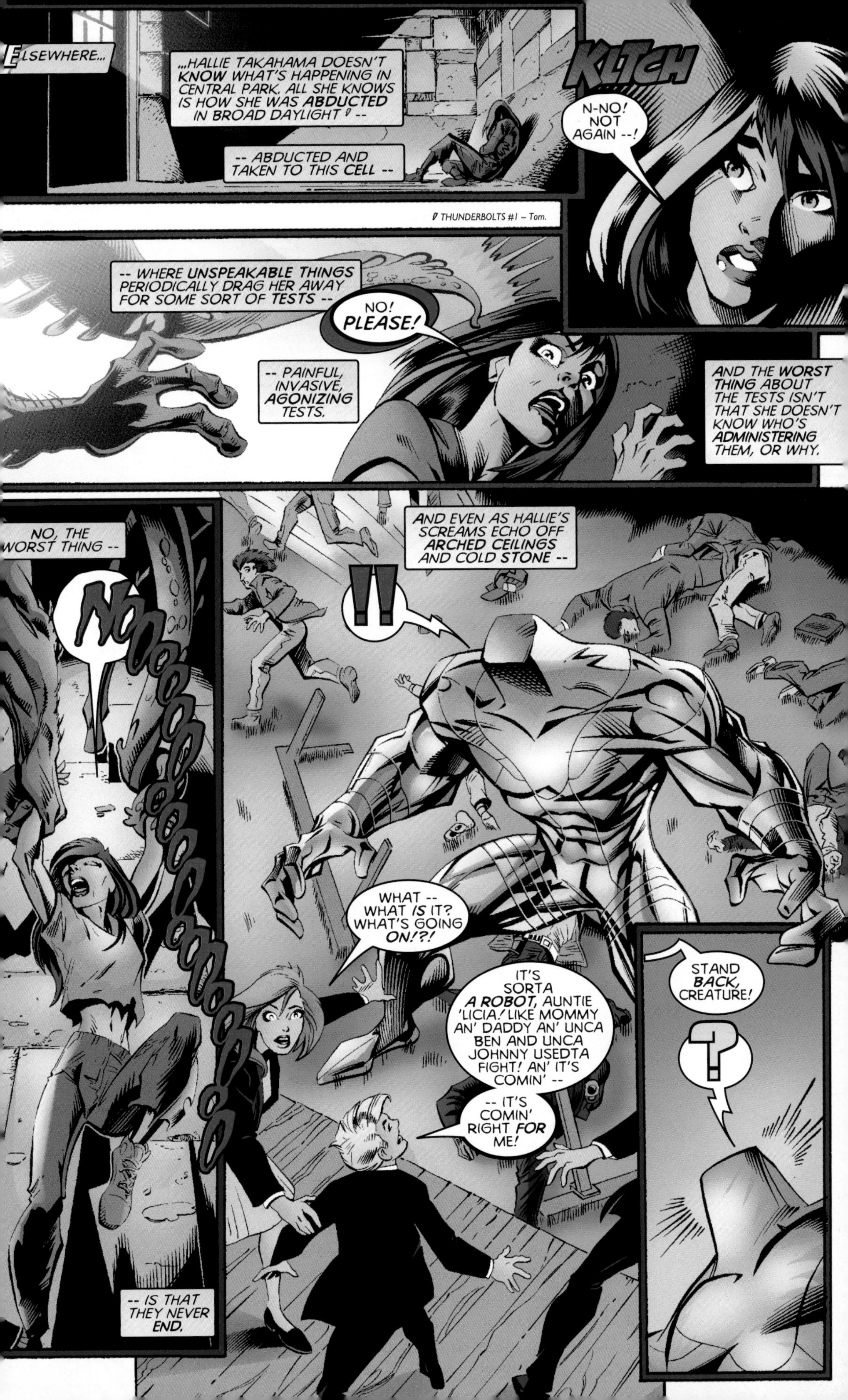
ELSEWHERE...
...HALLIE TAKAHAMA DOESN'T KNOW WHAT'S HAPPENING IN CENTRAL PARK. ALL SHE KNOWS IS HOW SHE WAS ABDUCTED IN BROAD DAYLIGHT --
-- ABDUCTED AND TAKEN TO THIS CELL --
THUNDERBOLTS #1 – Tom.
KLTCH
N-NO! NOT AGAIN --!
-- WHERE UNSPEAKABLE THINGS PERIODICALLY DRAG HER AWAY FOR SOME SORT OF TESTS --
NO! PLEASE!
-- PAINFUL, INVASIVE, AGONIZING TESTS.
AND THE WORST THING ABOUT THE TESTS ISN'T THAT SHE DOESN'T KNOW WHO'S ADMINISTERING THEM, OR WHY.
NO, THE WORST THING --
-- IS THAT THEY NEVER END.
AND EVEN AS HALLIE'S SCREAMS ECHO OFF ARCHED CEILINGS AND COLD STONE --
!!
WHAT -- WHAT IS IT? WHAT'S GOING ON!?!
IT'S SORTA A ROBOT, AUNTIE 'LICIA! LIKE MOMMY AN' DADDY AN' UNCA BEN AND UNCA JOHNNY USEDTA FIGHT! AN' IT'S COMIN' --
-- IT'S COMIN' RIGHT FOR ME!
STAND BACK, CREATURE!
?

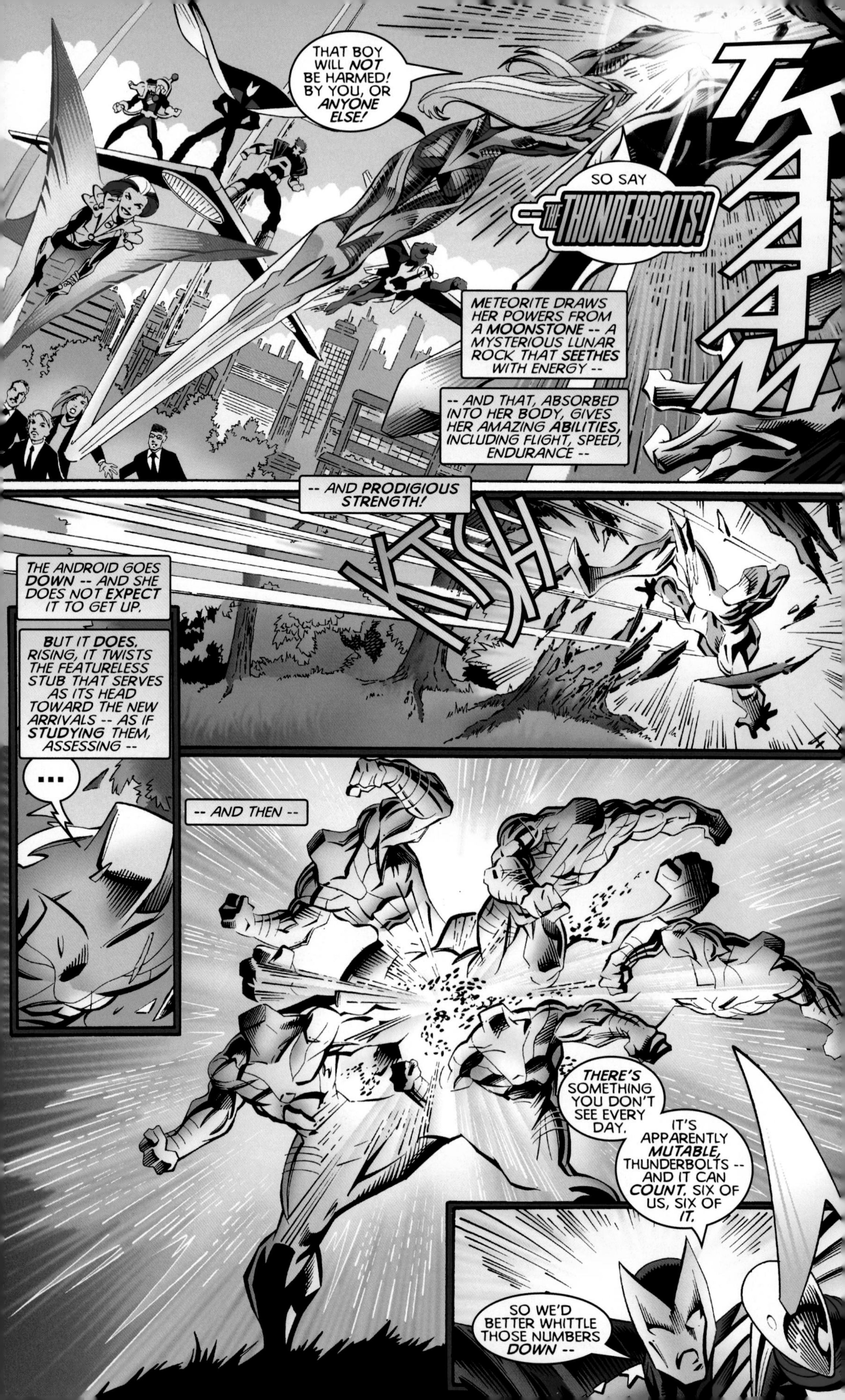

THAT BOY WILL NOT BE HARMED! BY YOU, OR ANYONE ELSE!
SO SAY THE THUNDERBOLTS!
THTAAAM
METEORITE DRAWS HER POWERS FROM A MOONSTONE -- A MYSTERIOUS LUNAR ROCK THAT SEETHES WITH ENERGY --
-- AND THAT, ABSORBED INTO HER BODY, GIVES HER AMAZING ABILITIES, INCLUDING FLIGHT, SPEED, ENDURANCE --
-- AND PRODIGIOUS STRENGTH!
KTSSH
THE ANDROID GOES DOWN -- AND SHE DOES NOT EXPECT IT TO GET UP.
BUT IT DOES. RISING, IT TWISTS THE FEATURELESS STUB THAT SERVES AS ITS HEAD TOWARD THE NEW ARRIVALS -- AS IF STUDYING THEM, ASSESSING --
...
-- AND THEN --
THERE'S SOMETHING YOU DON'T SEE EVERY DAY.
IT'S APPARENTLY MUTABLE, THUNDERBOLTS -- AND IT CAN COUNT. SIX OF US, SIX OF IT.
SO WE'D BETTER WHITTLE THOSE NUMBERS DOWN --

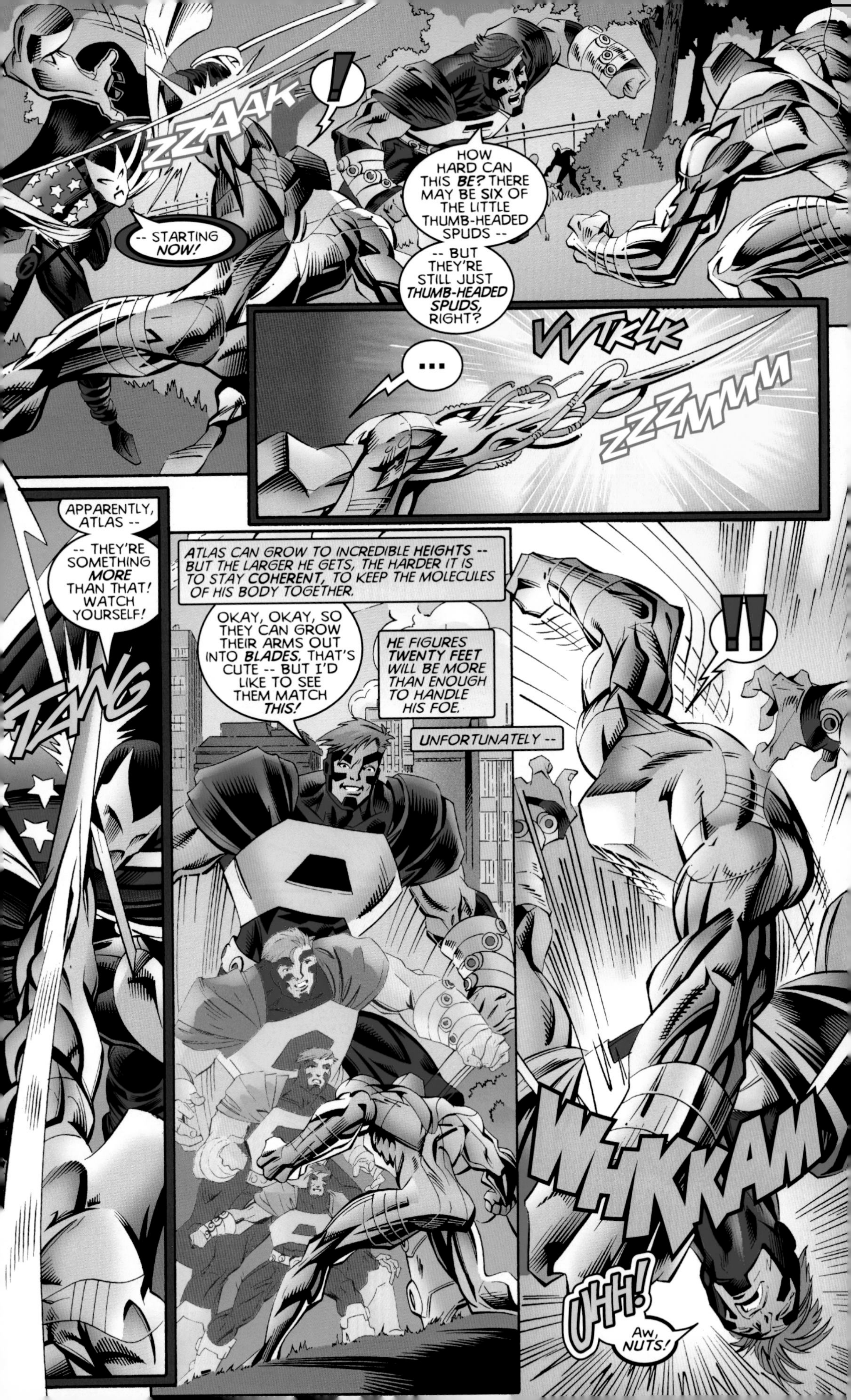
ZZAAK
!
-- STARTING NOW!
HOW HARD CAN THIS BE? THERE MAY BE SIX OF THE LITTLE THUMB-HEADED SPUDS --
-- BUT THEY'RE STILL JUST THUMB-HEADED SPUDS, RIGHT?
VVTKLK
...
ZZZMMM
APPARENTLY, ATLAS --
-- THEY'RE SOMETHING MORE THAN THAT! WATCH YOURSELF!
TANG
ATLAS CAN GROW TO INCREDIBLE HEIGHTS -- BUT THE LARGER HE GETS, THE HARDER IT IS TO STAY COHERENT, TO KEEP THE MOLECULES OF HIS BODY TOGETHER.
OKAY, OKAY, SO THEY CAN GROW THEIR ARMS OUT INTO BLADES. THAT'S CUTE -- BUT I'D LIKE TO SEE THEM MATCH THIS!
HE FIGURES TWENTY FEET WILL BE MORE THAN ENOUGH TO HANDLE HIS FOE.
UNFORTUNATELY --
!!
WHKKAM
UHH!
AW, NUTS!

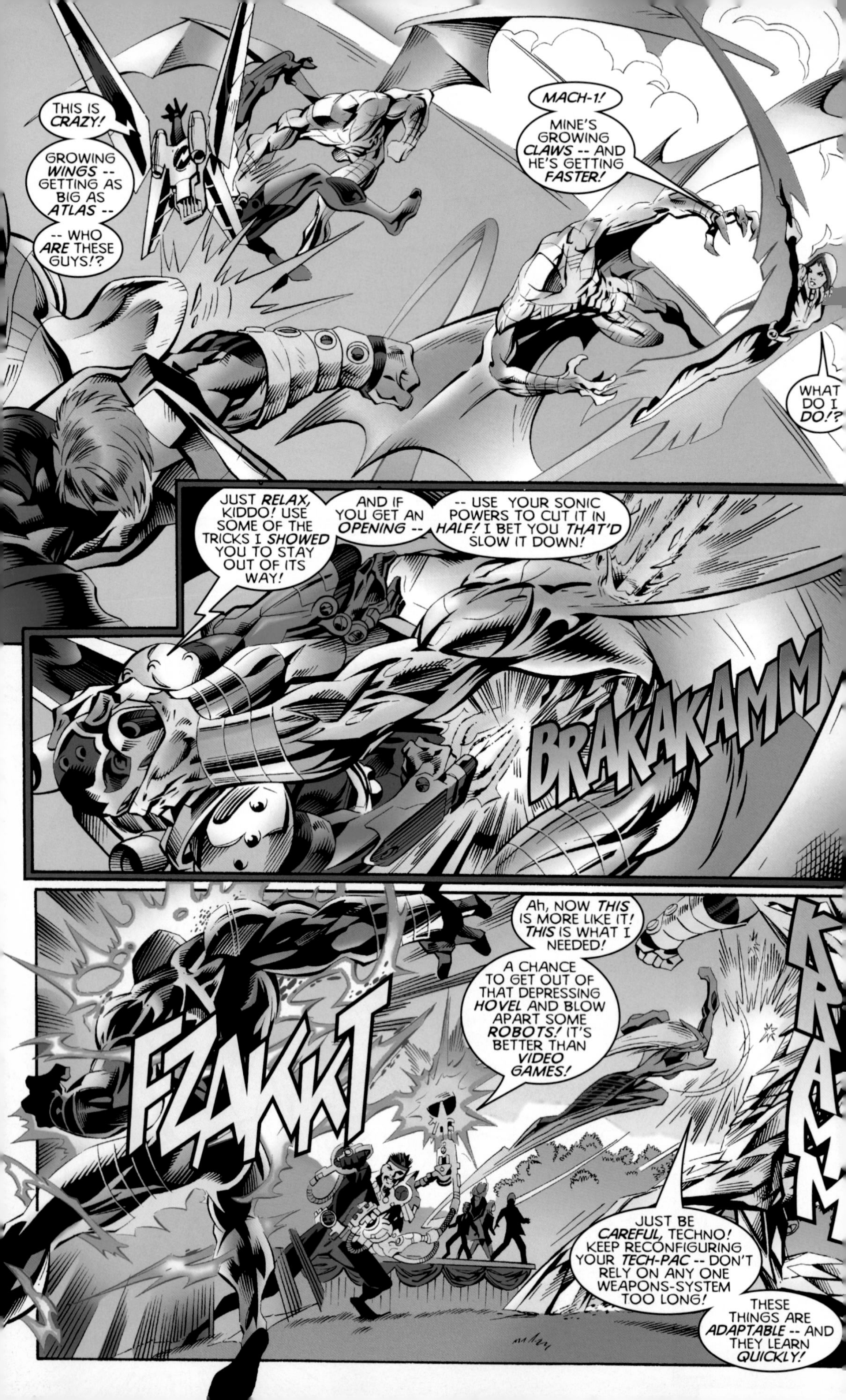
THIS IS CRAZY!
GROWING WINGS -- GETTING AS BIG AS ATLAS --
-- WHO ARE THESE GUYS!?
MACH-1!
MINE'S GROWING CLAWS -- AND HE'S GETTING FASTER!
WHAT DO I DO!?
JUST RELAX, KIDDO! USE SOME OF THE TRICKS I SHOWED YOU TO STAY OUT OF ITS WAY!
AND IF YOU GET AN OPENING --
-- USE YOUR SONIC POWERS TO CUT IT IN HALF! I BET YOU THAT'D SLOW IT DOWN!
BRAKAKAMM
FZAKKT
Ah, NOW THIS IS MORE LIKE IT! THIS IS WHAT I NEEDED!
A CHANCE TO GET OUT OF THAT DEPRESSING HOVEL AND BLOW APART SOME ROBOTS! IT'S BETTER THAN VIDEO GAMES!
KRAMM
JUST BE CAREFUL, TECHNO! KEEP RECONFIGURING YOUR TECH-PAC -- DON'T RELY ON ANY ONE WEAPONS-SYSTEM TOO LONG!
THESE THINGS ARE ADAPTABLE -- AND THEY LEARN QUICKLY!

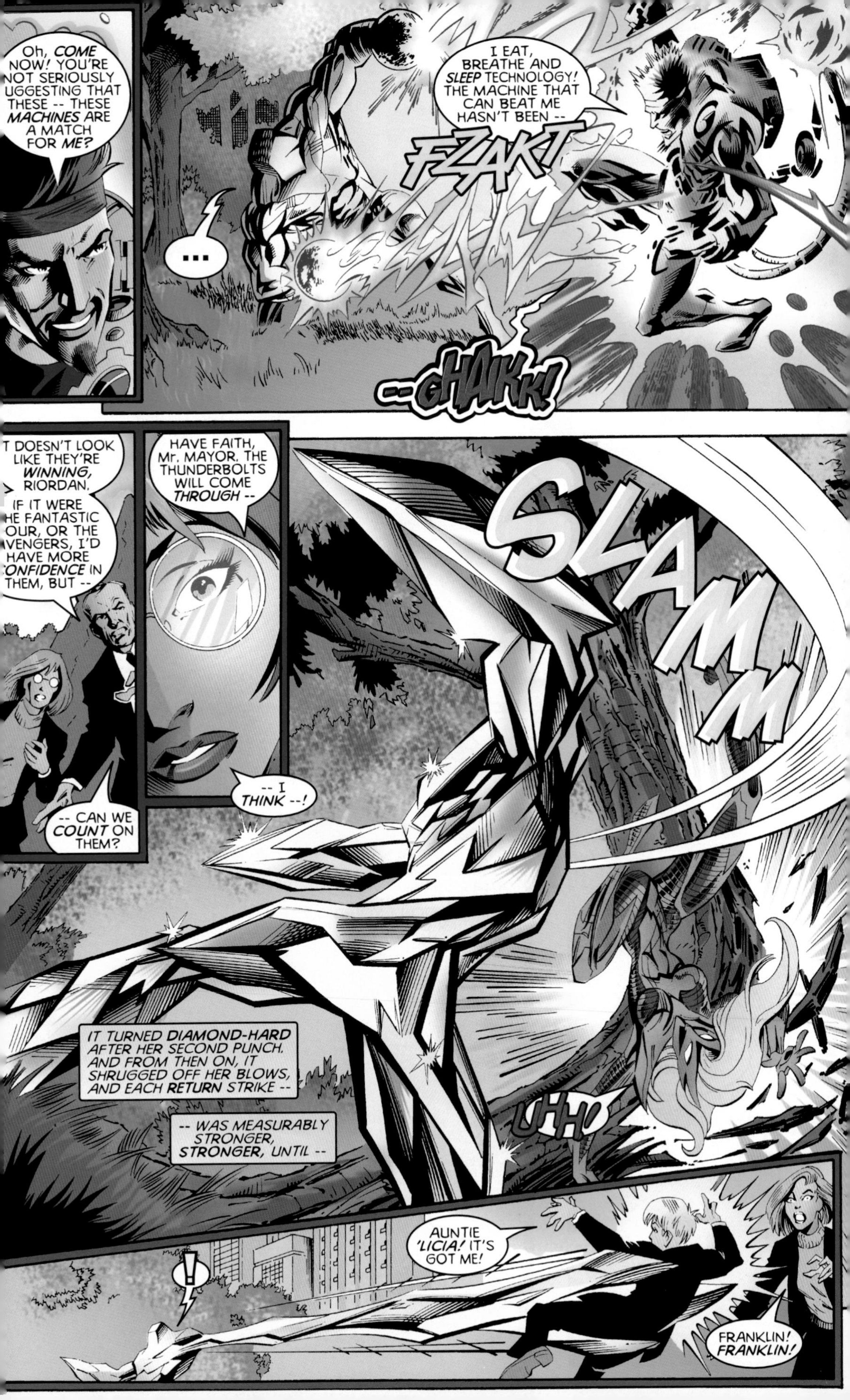

Oh, COME NOW! YOU'RE NOT SERIOUSLY UGGESTING THAT THESE -- THESE MACHINES ARE A MATCH FOR ME?
...
I EAT, BREATHE AND SLEEP TECHNOLOGY! THE MACHINE THAT CAN BEAT ME HASN'T BEEN --
FZAKT
--CHAIKK!
T DOESN'T LOOK LIKE THEY'RE WINNING, RIORDAN.
IF IT WERE HE FANTASTIC OUR, OR THE VENGERS, I'D HAVE MORE CONFIDENCE IN THEM, BUT --
-- CAN WE COUNT ON THEM?
HAVE FAITH, Mr. MAYOR. THE THUNDERBOLTS WILL COME THROUGH --
-- I THINK --!
SLAMM
IT TURNED DIAMOND-HARD AFTER HER SECOND PUNCH. AND FROM THEN ON, IT SHRUGGED OFF HER BLOWS, AND EACH RETURN STRIKE --
-- WAS MEASURABLY STRONGER, STRONGER, UNTIL --
UHH!
!
AUNTIE 'LICIA! IT'S GOT ME!
FRANKLIN! FRANKLIN!

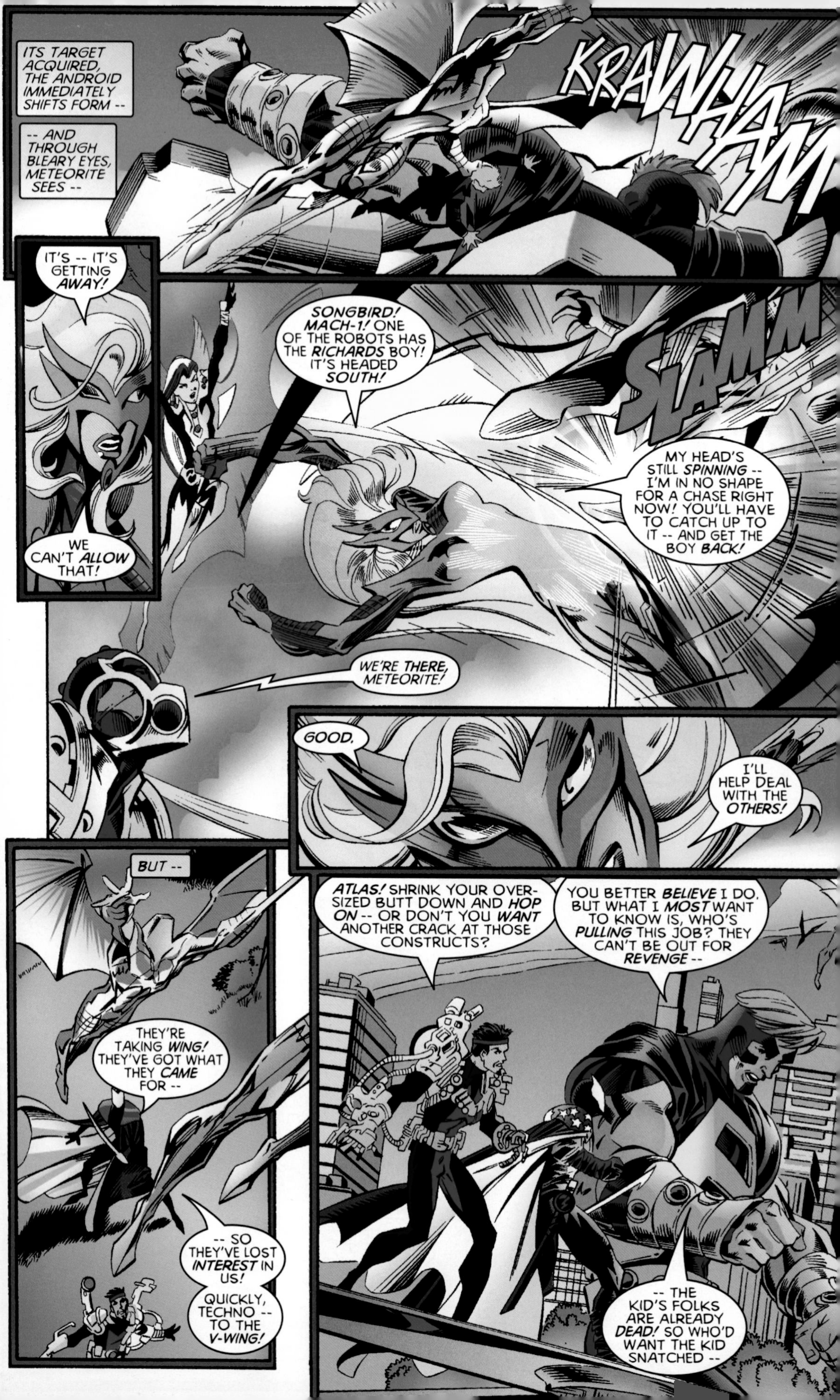
ITS TARGET ACQUIRED, THE ANDROID IMMEDIATELY SHIFTS FORM --
-- AND THROUGH BLEARY EYES, METEORITE SEES --
KRAWHAM
IT'S -- IT'S GETTING AWAY!
WE CAN'T ALLOW THAT!
SONGBIRD! MACH-1! ONE OF THE ROBOTS HAS THE RICHARDS BOY! IT'S HEADED SOUTH!
SLAMM
MY HEAD'S STILL SPINNING -- I'M IN NO SHAPE FOR A CHASE RIGHT NOW! YOU'LL HAVE TO CATCH UP TO IT -- AND GET THE BOY BACK!
WE'RE THERE, METEORITE!
GOOD.
I'LL HELP DEAL WITH THE OTHERS!
BUT --
THEY'RE TAKING WING! THEY'VE GOT WHAT THEY CAME FOR --
-- SO THEY'VE LOST INTEREST IN US!
QUICKLY, TECHNO -- TO THE V-WING!
ATLAS! SHRINK YOUR OVER-SIZED BUTT DOWN AND HOP ON -- OR DON'T YOU WANT ANOTHER CRACK AT THOSE CONSTRUCTS?
YOU BETTER BELIEVE I DO, BUT WHAT I MOST WANT TO KNOW IS, WHO'S PULLING THIS JOB? THEY CAN'T BE OUT FOR REVENGE --
-- THE KID'S FOLKS ARE ALREADY DEAD! SO WHO'D WANT THE KID SNATCHED --

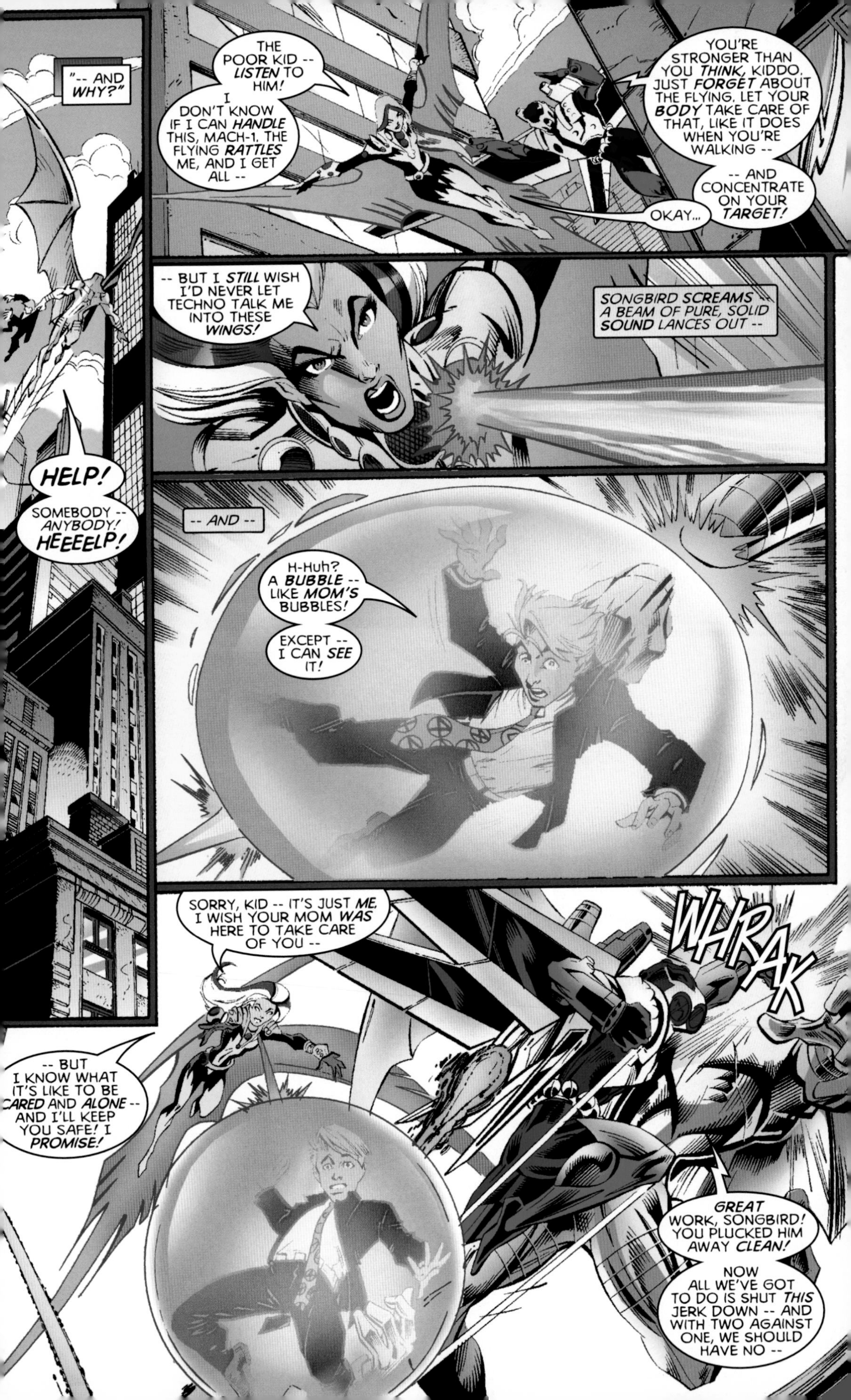
"-- AND WHY?"
THE POOR KID -- LISTEN TO HIM!
I DON'T KNOW IF I CAN HANDLE THIS, MACH-1. THE FLYING RATTLES ME, AND I GET ALL --
YOU'RE STRONGER THAN YOU THINK, KIDDO. JUST FORGET ABOUT THE FLYING. LET YOUR BODY TAKE CARE OF THAT, LIKE IT DOES WHEN YOU'RE WALKING --
-- AND CONCENTRATE ON YOUR TARGET!
OKAY...
-- BUT I STILL WISH I'D NEVER LET TECHNO TALK ME INTO THESE WINGS!
SONGBIRD SCREAMS -- A BEAM OF PURE, SOLID SOUND LANCES OUT --
HELP!
SOMEBODY -- ANYBODY! HEEEELP!
-- AND --
H-Huh? A BUBBLE -- LIKE MOM'S BUBBLES!
EXCEPT -- I CAN SEE IT!
SORRY, KID -- IT'S JUST ME. I WISH YOUR MOM WAS HERE TO TAKE CARE OF YOU --
-- BUT I KNOW WHAT IT'S LIKE TO BE SCARED AND ALONE -- AND I'LL KEEP YOU SAFE! I PROMISE!
WHRAK
GREAT WORK, SONGBIRD! YOU PLUCKED HIM AWAY CLEAN!
NOW ALL WE'VE GOT TO DO IS SHUT THIS JERK DOWN -- AND WITH TWO AGAINST ONE, WE SHOULD HAVE NO --

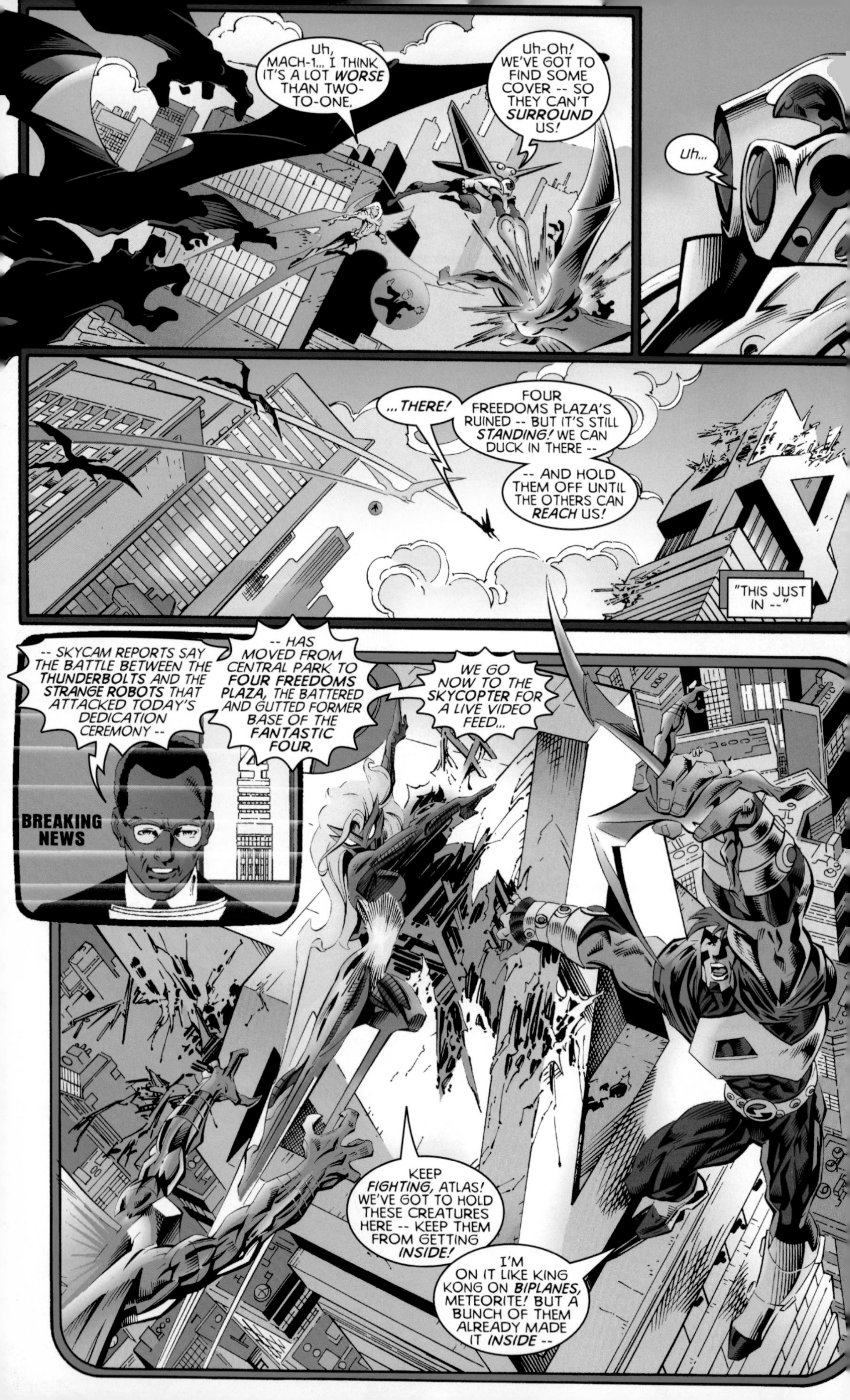

Uh, MACH-1... I THINK IT'S A LOT WORSE THAN TWO-TO-ONE.
Uh-Oh! WE'VE GOT TO FIND SOME COVER -- SO THEY CAN'T SURROUND US!
Uh...
...THERE!
FOUR FREEDOMS PLAZA'S RUINED -- BUT IT'S STILL STANDING! WE CAN DUCK IN THERE --
-- AND HOLD THEM OFF UNTIL THE OTHERS CAN REACH US!
"THIS JUST IN --"
-- SKYCAM REPORTS SAY THE BATTLE BETWEEN THE THUNDERBOLTS AND THE STRANGE ROBOTS THAT ATTACKED TODAY'S DEDICATION CEREMONY --
-- HAS MOVED FROM CENTRAL PARK TO FOUR FREEDOMS PLAZA, THE BATTERED AND GUTTED FORMER BASE OF THE FANTASTIC FOUR.
WE GO NOW TO THE SKYCOPTER FOR A LIVE VIDEO FEED...
BREAKING NEWS
KEEP FIGHTING, ATLAS! WE'VE GOT TO HOLD THESE CREATURES HERE -- KEEP THEM FROM GETTING INSIDE!
I'M ON IT LIKE KING KONG ON BIPLANES, METEORITE! BUT A BUNCH OF THEM ALREADY MADE IT INSIDE --

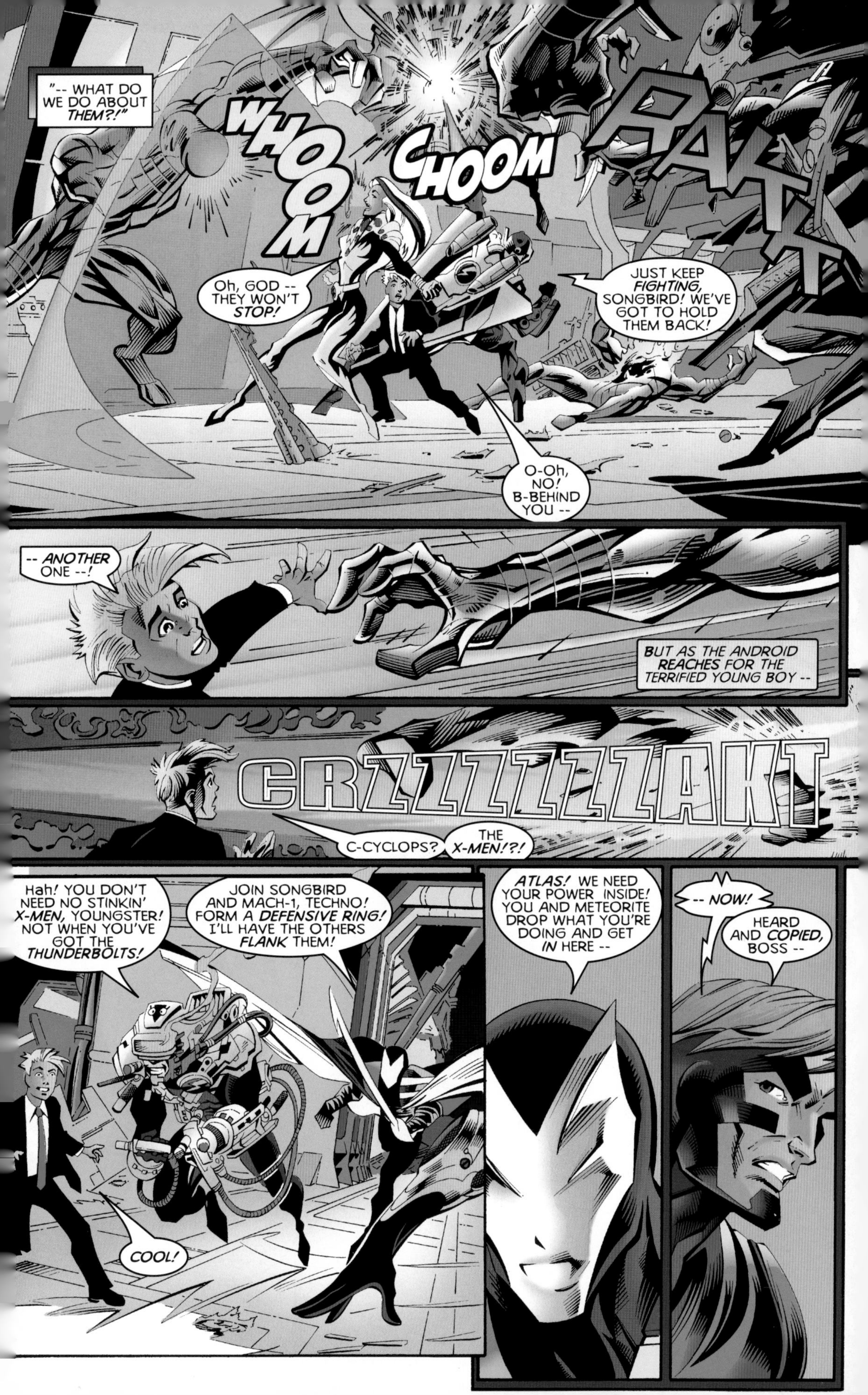
"-- WHAT DO WE DO ABOUT *THEM?!*"
WHOOOM
CHOOM
RAKKT
Oh, GOD -- THEY WON'T *STOP!*
JUST KEEP *FIGHTING,* SONGBIRD! WE'VE GOT TO HOLD THEM BACK!
O-Oh, NO! B-BEHIND YOU --
-- *ANOTHER* ONE --!
BUT AS THE ANDROID *REACHES* FOR THE TERRIFIED YOUNG BOY --
CRZZZZZZZAKT
C-CYCLOPS?
THE *X-MEN!?!*
Hah! YOU DON'T NEED NO STINKIN' *X-MEN,* YOUNGSTER! NOT WHEN YOU'VE GOT THE *THUNDERBOLTS!*
JOIN SONGBIRD AND MACH-1, TECHNO! FORM A *DEFENSIVE RING!* I'LL HAVE THE OTHERS *FLANK* THEM!
COOL!
ATLAS! WE NEED YOUR POWER INSIDE! YOU AND METEORITE DROP WHAT YOU'RE DOING AND GET *IN* HERE --
-- *NOW!*
HEARD AND *COPIED,* BOSS --

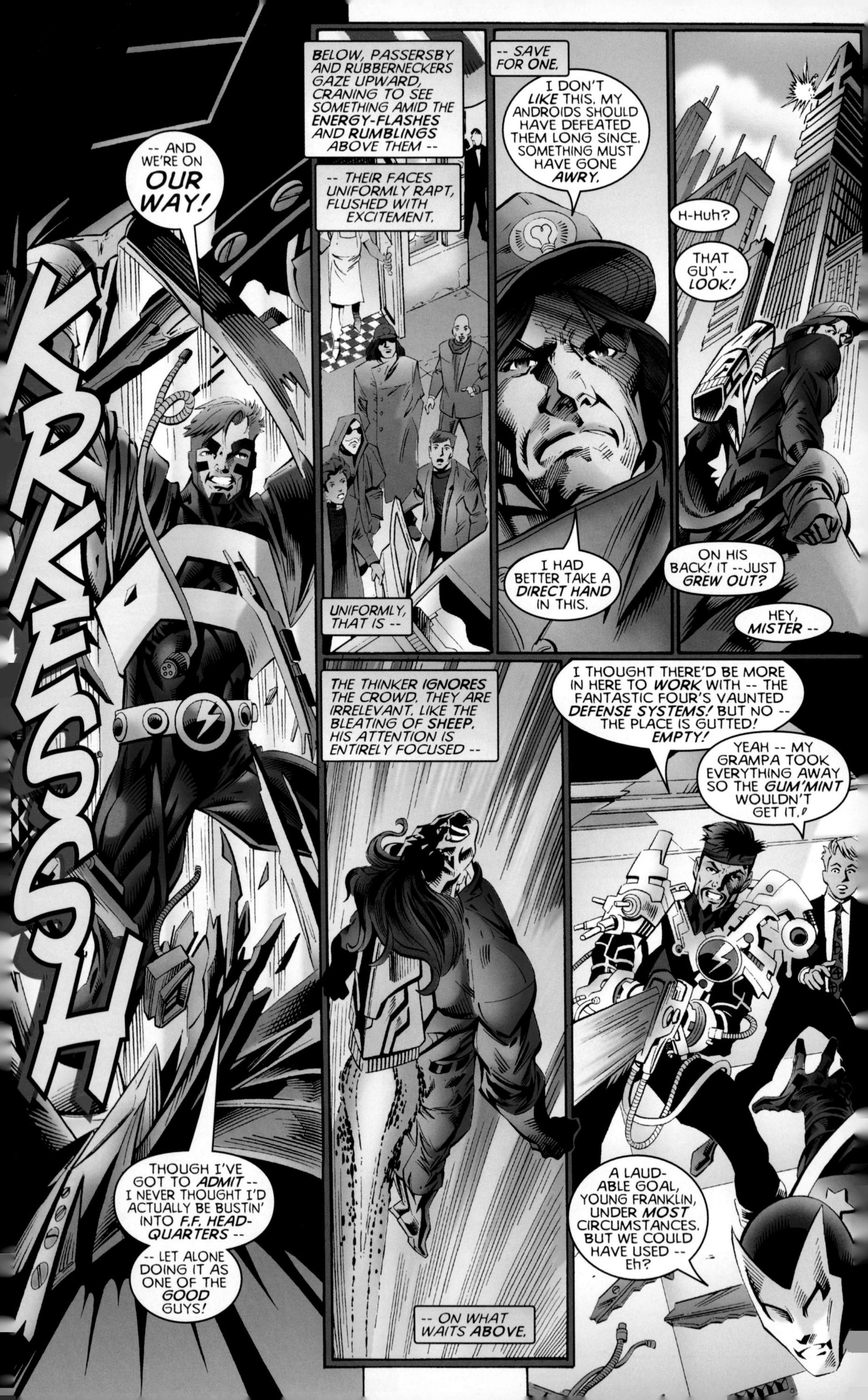
-- AND WE'RE ON OUR WAY!
KRAKASSH
THOUGH I'VE GOT TO ADMIT -- I NEVER THOUGHT I'D ACTUALLY BE BUSTIN' INTO F.F. HEAD-QUARTERS --
-- LET ALONE DOING IT AS ONE OF THE GOOD GUYS!
BELOW, PASSERSBY AND RUBBERNECKERS GAZE UPWARD, CRANING TO SEE SOMETHING AMID THE ENERGY-FLASHES AND RUMBLINGS ABOVE THEM --
-- THEIR FACES UNIFORMLY RAPT, FLUSHED WITH EXCITEMENT.
UNIFORMLY, THAT IS --
-- SAVE FOR ONE.
I DON'T LIKE THIS. MY ANDROIDS SHOULD HAVE DEFEATED THEM LONG SINCE. SOMETHING MUST HAVE GONE AWRY.
I HAD BETTER TAKE A DIRECT HAND IN THIS.
H-Huh?
THAT GUY -- LOOK!
ON HIS BACK! IT --JUST GREW OUT?
HEY, MISTER --
THE THINKER IGNORES THE CROWD. THEY ARE IRRELEVANT. LIKE THE BLEATING OF SHEEP. HIS ATTENTION IS ENTIRELY FOCUSED --
-- ON WHAT WAITS ABOVE.
I THOUGHT THERE'D BE MORE IN HERE TO WORK WITH -- THE FANTASTIC FOUR'S VAUNTED DEFENSE SYSTEMS! BUT NO -- THE PLACE IS GUTTED! EMPTY!
YEAH -- MY GRAMPA TOOK EVERYTHING AWAY SO THE GUM'MINT WOULDN'T GET IT.
A LAUD-ABLE GOAL, YOUNG FRANKLIN, UNDER MOST CIRCUMSTANCES, BUT WE COULD HAVE USED -- Eh?

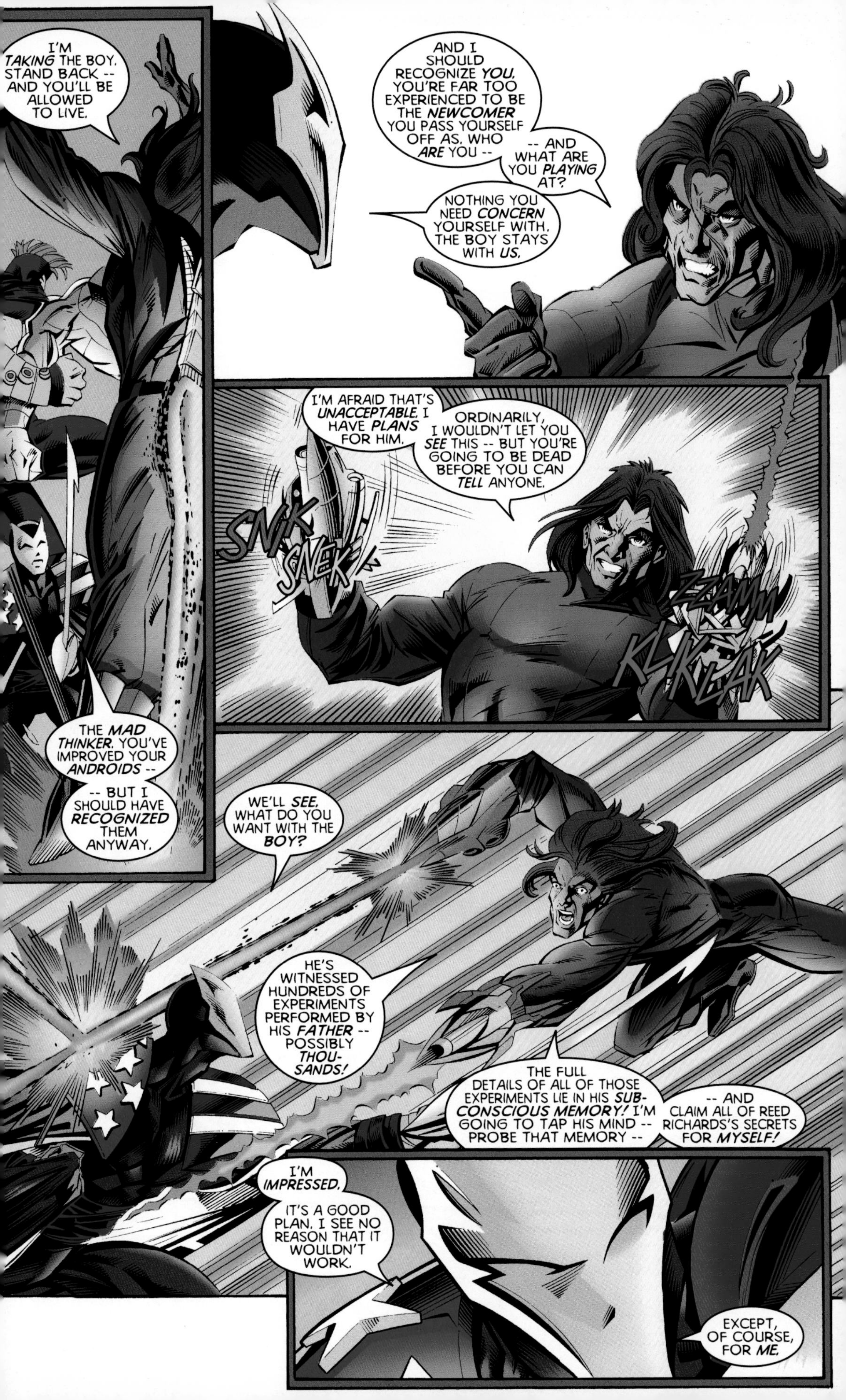

I'M TAKING THE BOY. STAND BACK -- AND YOU'LL BE ALLOWED TO LIVE.
AND I SHOULD RECOGNIZE YOU. YOU'RE FAR TOO EXPERIENCED TO BE THE NEWCOMER YOU PASS YOURSELF OFF AS. WHO ARE YOU --
-- AND WHAT ARE YOU PLAYING AT?
NOTHING YOU NEED CONCERN YOURSELF WITH. THE BOY STAYS WITH US.
I'M AFRAID THAT'S UNACCEPTABLE. I HAVE PLANS FOR HIM.
ORDINARILY, I WOULDN'T LET YOU SEE THIS -- BUT YOU'RE GOING TO BE DEAD BEFORE YOU CAN TELL ANYONE.
SNIK
SNEK
ZZAMM
KLIKLAK
THE MAD THINKER. YOU'VE IMPROVED YOUR ANDROIDS --
-- BUT I SHOULD HAVE RECOGNIZED THEM ANYWAY.
WE'LL SEE. WHAT DO YOU WANT WITH THE BOY?
HE'S WITNESSED HUNDREDS OF EXPERIMENTS PERFORMED BY HIS FATHER -- POSSIBLY THOU-SANDS!
THE FULL DETAILS OF ALL OF THOSE EXPERIMENTS LIE IN HIS SUB-CONSCIOUS MEMORY! I'M GOING TO TAP HIS MIND -- PROBE THAT MEMORY --
-- AND CLAIM ALL OF REED RICHARDS'S SECRETS FOR MYSELF!
I'M IMPRESSED.
IT'S A GOOD PLAN. I SEE NO REASON THAT IT WOULDN'T WORK.
EXCEPT, OF COURSE, FOR ME.

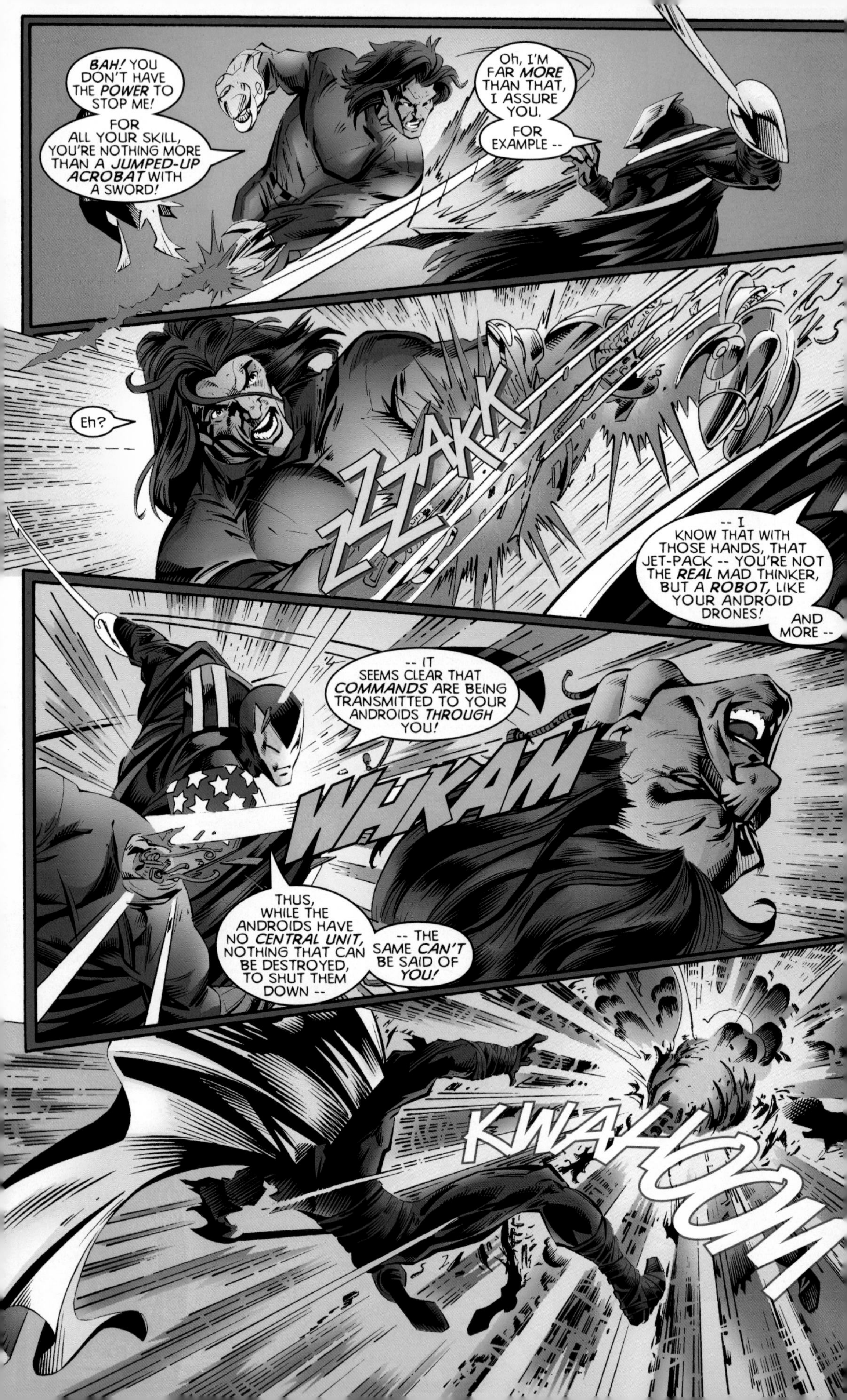
BAH! YOU DON'T HAVE THE POWER TO STOP ME!
FOR ALL YOUR SKILL, YOU'RE NOTHING MORE THAN A JUMPED-UP ACROBAT WITH A SWORD!
Oh, I'M FAR MORE THAN THAT, I ASSURE YOU.
FOR EXAMPLE --
Eh?
ZZZAKK
-- I KNOW THAT WITH THOSE HANDS, THAT JET-PACK -- YOU'RE NOT THE REAL MAD THINKER, BUT A ROBOT, LIKE YOUR ANDROID DRONES!
AND MORE --
-- IT SEEMS CLEAR THAT COMMANDS ARE BEING TRANSMITTED TO YOUR ANDROIDS THROUGH YOU!
WHKAM
THUS, WHILE THE ANDROIDS HAVE NO CENTRAL UNIT, NOTHING THAT CAN BE DESTROYED, TO SHUT THEM DOWN --
-- THE SAME CAN'T BE SAID OF YOU!
KWAKOOM

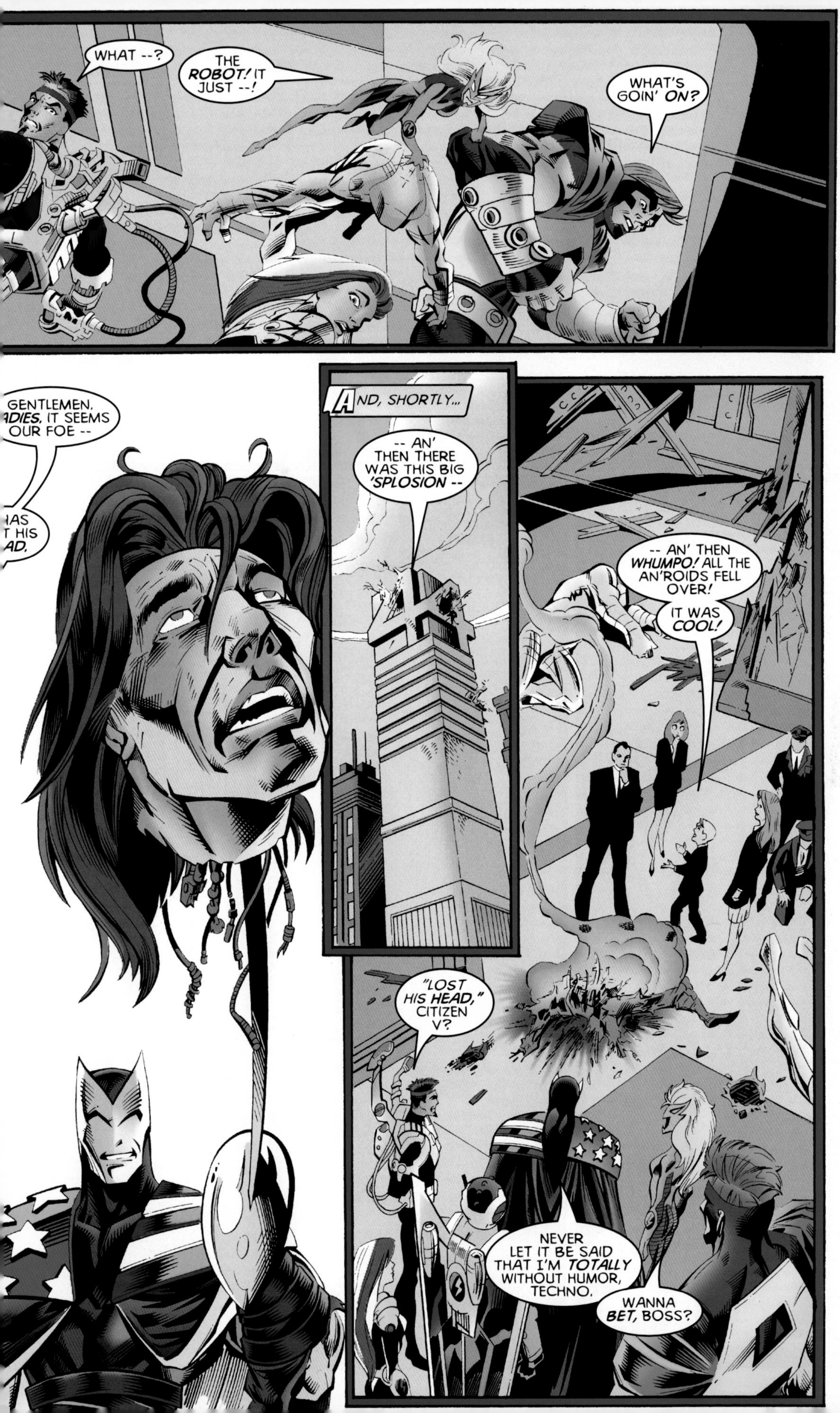

WHAT --?
THE ROBOT! IT JUST --!
WHAT'S GOIN' ON?
GENTLEMEN. ADIES. IT SEEMS OUR FOE --
HAS T HIS AD.
AND, SHORTLY...
-- AN' THEN THERE WAS THIS BIG 'SPLOSION --
-- AN' THEN WHUMPO! ALL THE AN'ROIDS FELL OVER!
IT WAS COOL!
"LOST HIS HEAD," CITIZEN V?
NEVER LET IT BE SAID THAT I'M TOTALLY WITHOUT HUMOR, TECHNO.
WANNA BET, BOSS?

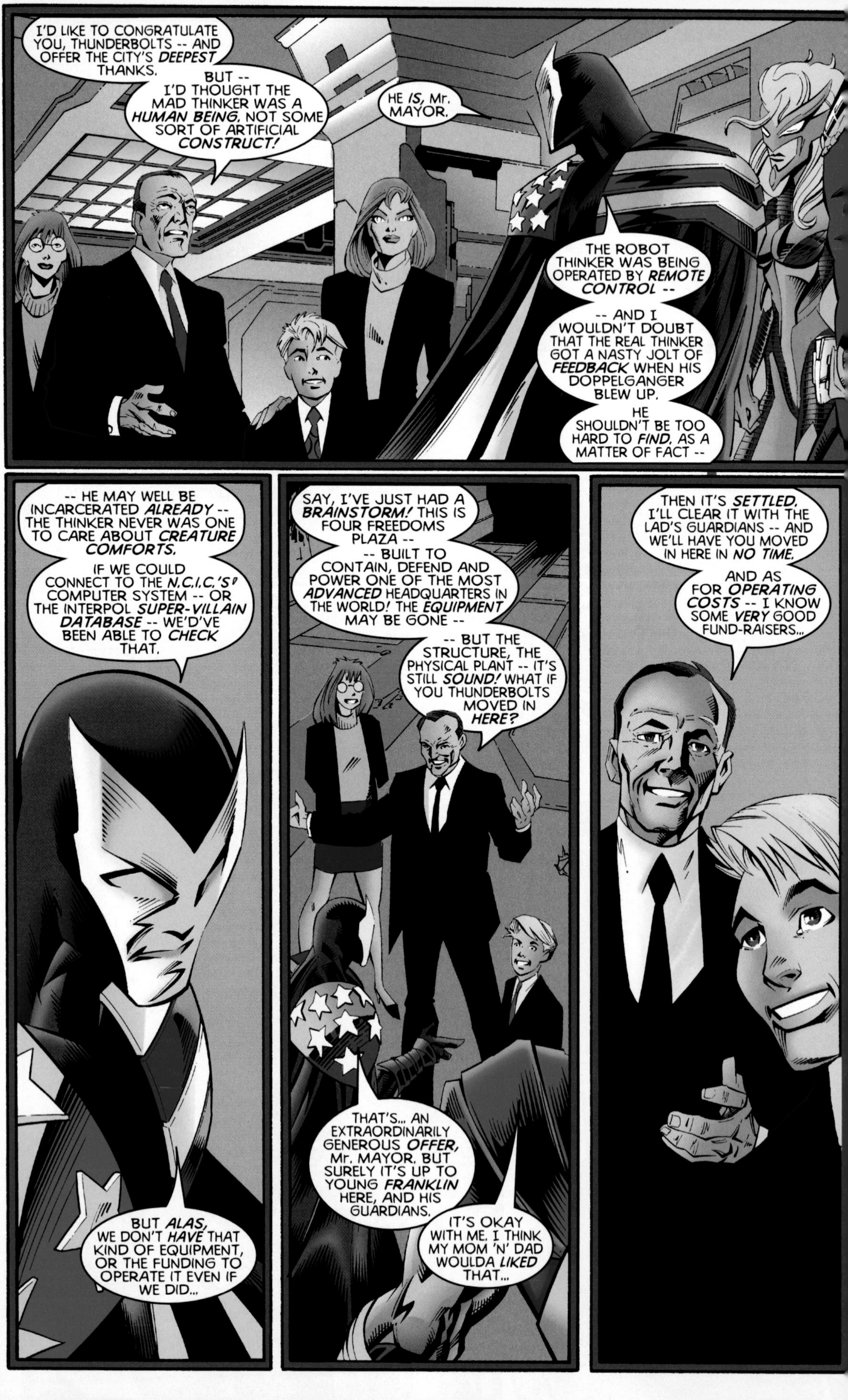
I'D LIKE TO CONGRATULATE YOU, THUNDERBOLTS -- AND OFFER THE CITY'S DEEPEST THANKS.
BUT -- I'D THOUGHT THE MAD THINKER WAS A HUMAN BEING, NOT SOME SORT OF ARTIFICIAL CONSTRUCT!
HE IS, Mr. MAYOR.
THE ROBOT THINKER WAS BEING OPERATED BY REMOTE CONTROL --
-- AND I WOULDN'T DOUBT THAT THE REAL THINKER GOT A NASTY JOLT OF FEEDBACK WHEN HIS DOPPELGANGER BLEW UP.
HE SHOULDN'T BE TOO HARD TO FIND, AS A MATTER OF FACT --
-- HE MAY WELL BE INCARCERATED ALREADY -- THE THINKER NEVER WAS ONE TO CARE ABOUT CREATURE COMFORTS.
IF WE COULD CONNECT TO THE N.C.I.C.'S COMPUTER SYSTEM -- OR THE INTERPOL SUPER-VILLAIN DATABASE -- WE'D'VE BEEN ABLE TO CHECK THAT.
BUT ALAS, WE DON'T HAVE THAT KIND OF EQUIPMENT, OR THE FUNDING TO OPERATE IT EVEN IF WE DID...
SAY, I'VE JUST HAD A BRAINSTORM! THIS IS FOUR FREEDOMS PLAZA --
-- BUILT TO CONTAIN, DEFEND AND POWER ONE OF THE MOST ADVANCED HEADQUARTERS IN THE WORLD! THE EQUIPMENT MAY BE GONE --
-- BUT THE STRUCTURE, THE PHYSICAL PLANT -- IT'S STILL SOUND! WHAT IF YOU THUNDERBOLTS MOVED IN HERE?
THAT'S... AN EXTRAORDINARILY GENEROUS OFFER, Mr. MAYOR. BUT SURELY IT'S UP TO YOUNG FRANKLIN HERE, AND HIS GUARDIANS.
IT'S OKAY WITH ME. I THINK MY MOM 'N' DAD WOULDA LIKED THAT...
THEN IT'S SETTLED. I'LL CLEAR IT WITH THE LAD'S GUARDIANS -- AND WE'LL HAVE YOU MOVED IN HERE IN NO TIME.
AND AS FOR OPERATING COSTS -- I KNOW SOME VERY GOOD FUND-RAISERS...

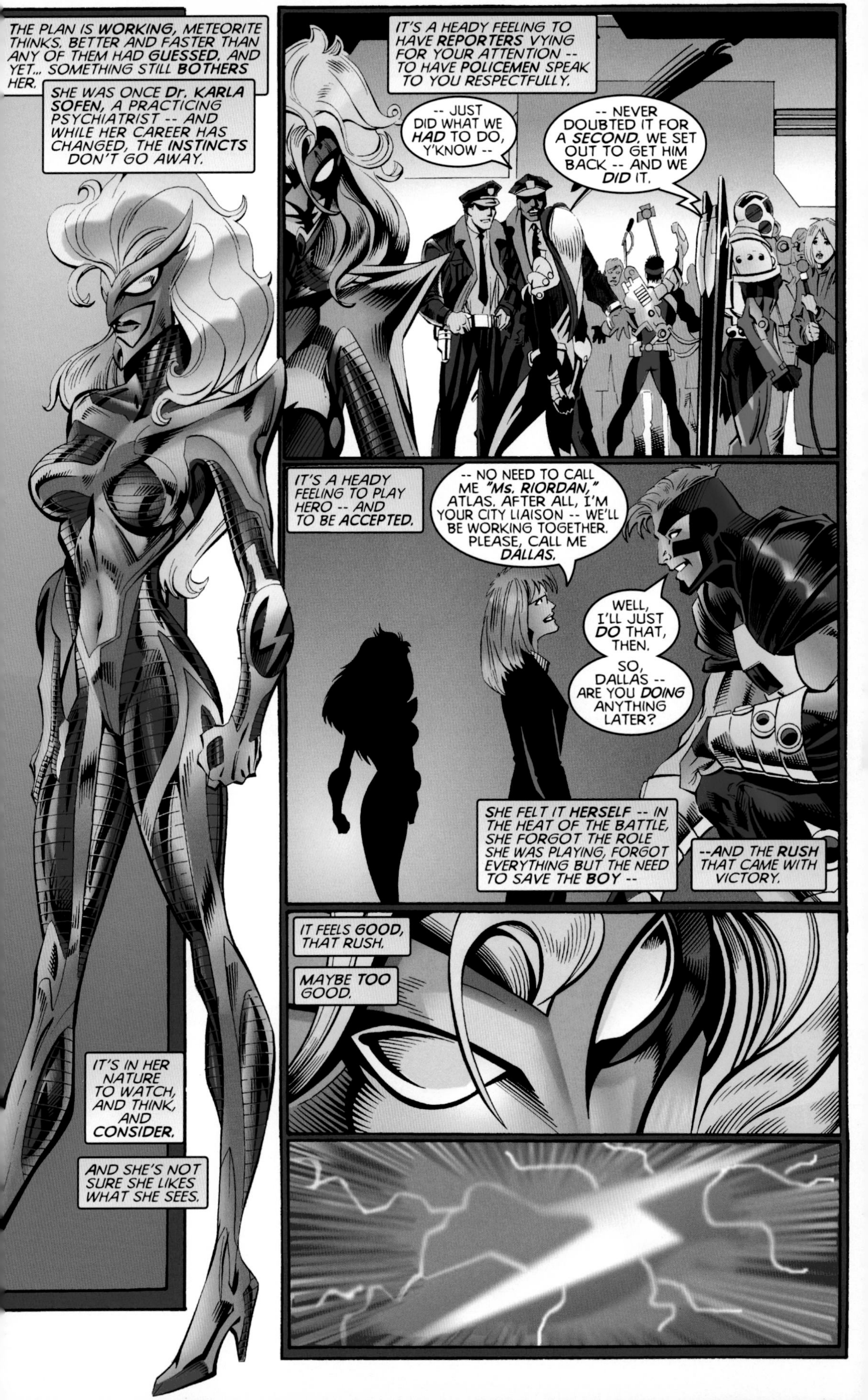
THE PLAN IS WORKING, METEORITE THINKS, BETTER AND FASTER THAN ANY OF THEM HAD GUESSED, AND YET... SOMETHING STILL BOTHERS HER.
SHE WAS ONCE Dr. KARLA SOFEN, A PRACTICING PSYCHIATRIST -- AND WHILE HER CAREER HAS CHANGED, THE INSTINCTS DON'T GO AWAY.
IT'S IN HER NATURE TO WATCH, AND THINK, AND CONSIDER.
AND SHE'S NOT SURE SHE LIKES WHAT SHE SEES.
IT'S A HEADY FEELING TO HAVE REPORTERS VYING FOR YOUR ATTENTION -- TO HAVE POLICEMEN SPEAK TO YOU RESPECTFULLY.
-- JUST DID WHAT WE HAD TO DO, Y'KNOW --
-- NEVER DOUBTED IT FOR A SECOND. WE SET OUT TO GET HIM BACK -- AND WE DID IT.
IT'S A HEADY FEELING TO PLAY HERO -- AND TO BE ACCEPTED.
-- NO NEED TO CALL ME "Ms. RIORDAN," ATLAS. AFTER ALL, I'M YOUR CITY LIAISON -- WE'LL BE WORKING TOGETHER. PLEASE, CALL ME DALLAS.
WELL, I'LL JUST DO THAT, THEN.
SO, DALLAS -- ARE YOU DOING ANYTHING LATER?
SHE FELT IT HERSELF -- IN THE HEAT OF THE BATTLE, SHE FORGOT THE ROLE SHE WAS PLAYING, FORGOT EVERYTHING BUT THE NEED TO SAVE THE BOY --
--AND THE RUSH THAT CAME WITH VICTORY.
IT FEELS GOOD, THAT RUSH.
MAYBE TOO GOOD.

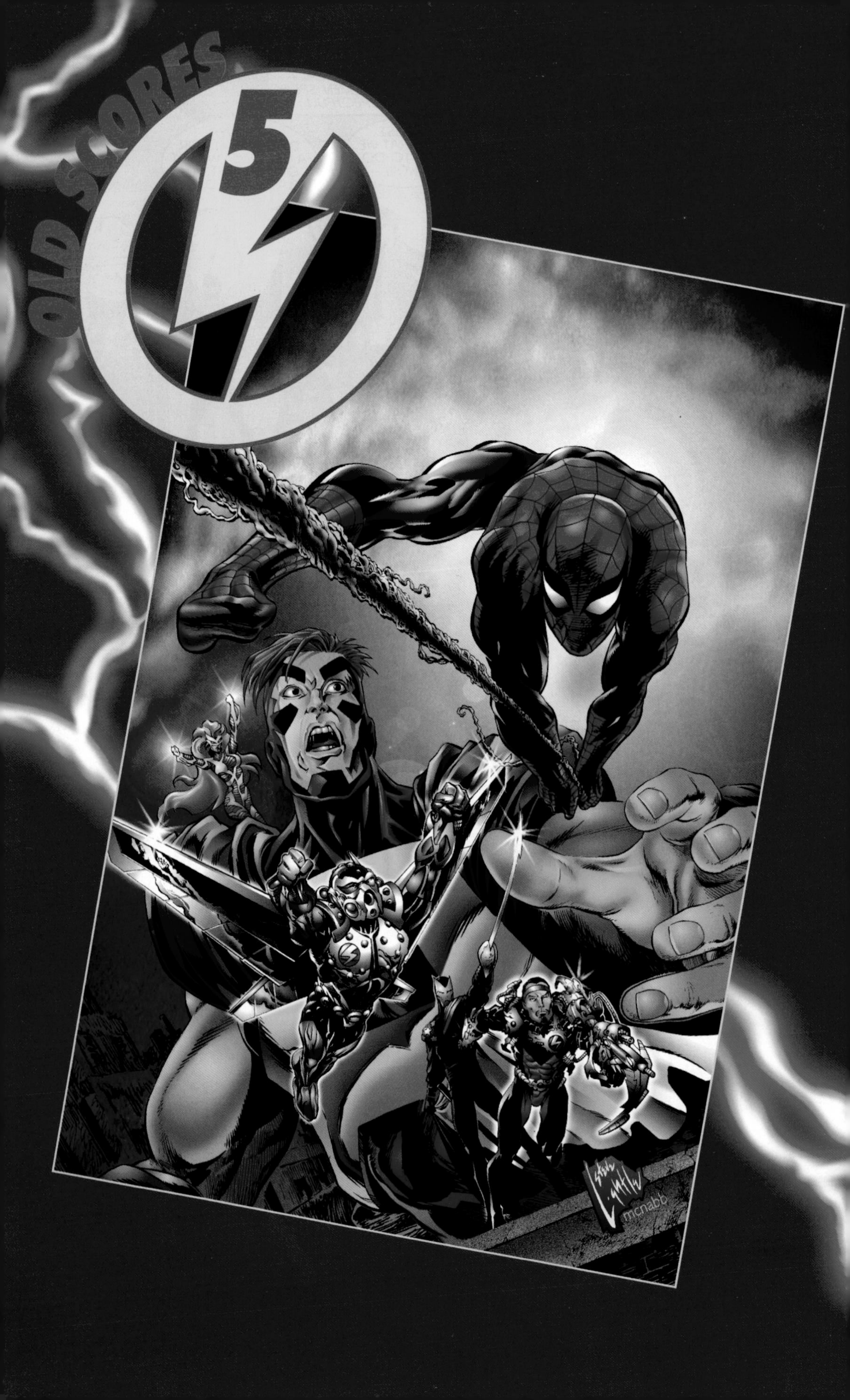
OLD SCORES
5
mcnabb

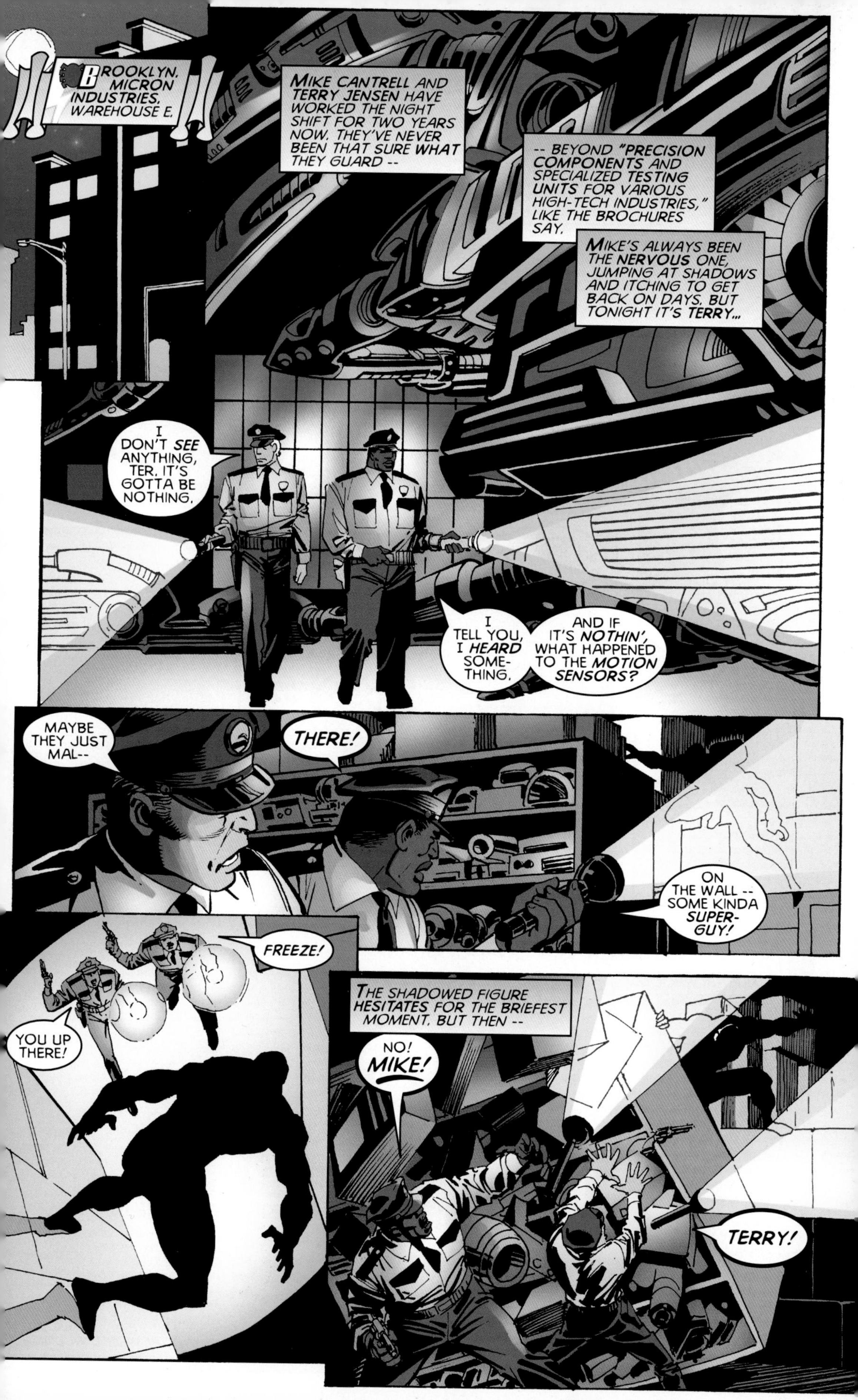
BROOKLYN. MICRON INDUSTRIES, WAREHOUSE E.
MIKE CANTRELL AND TERRY JENSEN HAVE WORKED THE NIGHT SHIFT FOR TWO YEARS NOW. THEY'VE NEVER BEEN THAT SURE WHAT THEY GUARD --
-- BEYOND "PRECISION COMPONENTS AND SPECIALIZED TESTING UNITS FOR VARIOUS HIGH-TECH INDUSTRIES," LIKE THE BROCHURES SAY.
MIKE'S ALWAYS BEEN THE NERVOUS ONE, JUMPING AT SHADOWS AND ITCHING TO GET BACK ON DAYS. BUT TONIGHT IT'S TERRY...
I DON'T SEE ANYTHING, TER. IT'S GOTTA BE NOTHING.
I TELL YOU, I HEARD SOME-THING.
AND IF IT'S NOTHIN', WHAT HAPPENED TO THE MOTION SENSORS?
MAYBE THEY JUST MAL--
THERE!
ON THE WALL -- SOME KINDA SUPER-GUY!
FREEZE!
YOU UP THERE!
THE SHADOWED FIGURE HESITATES FOR THE BRIEFEST MOMENT, BUT THEN --
NO! MIKE!
TERRY!

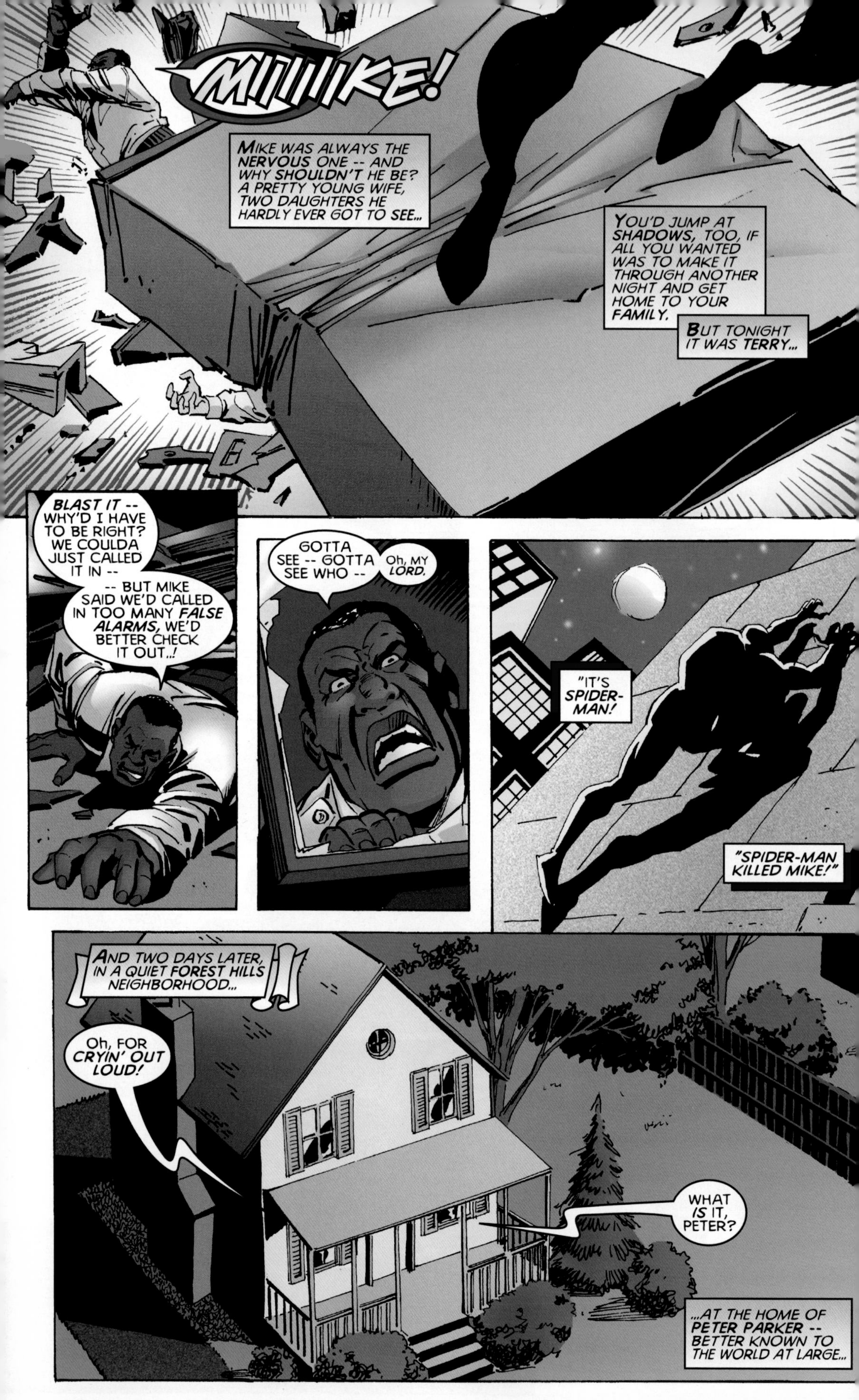
MIIIIKE!
MIKE WAS ALWAYS THE NERVOUS ONE -- AND WHY SHOULDN'T HE BE? A PRETTY YOUNG WIFE, TWO DAUGHTERS HE HARDLY EVER GOT TO SEE...
YOU'D JUMP AT SHADOWS, TOO, IF ALL YOU WANTED WAS TO MAKE IT THROUGH ANOTHER NIGHT AND GET HOME TO YOUR FAMILY.
BUT TONIGHT IT WAS TERRY...
BLAST IT -- WHY'D I HAVE TO BE RIGHT? WE COULDA JUST CALLED IT IN --
-- BUT MIKE SAID WE'D CALLED IN TOO MANY FALSE ALARMS, WE'D BETTER CHECK IT OUT..!
GOTTA SEE -- GOTTA SEE WHO --
Oh, MY LORD.
"IT'S SPIDER-MAN!
"SPIDER-MAN KILLED MIKE!"
AND TWO DAYS LATER, IN A QUIET FOREST HILLS NEIGHBORHOOD...
Oh, FOR CRYIN' OUT LOUD!
WHAT IS IT, PETER?
...AT THE HOME OF PETER PARKER -- BETTER KNOWN TO THE WORLD AT LARGE...

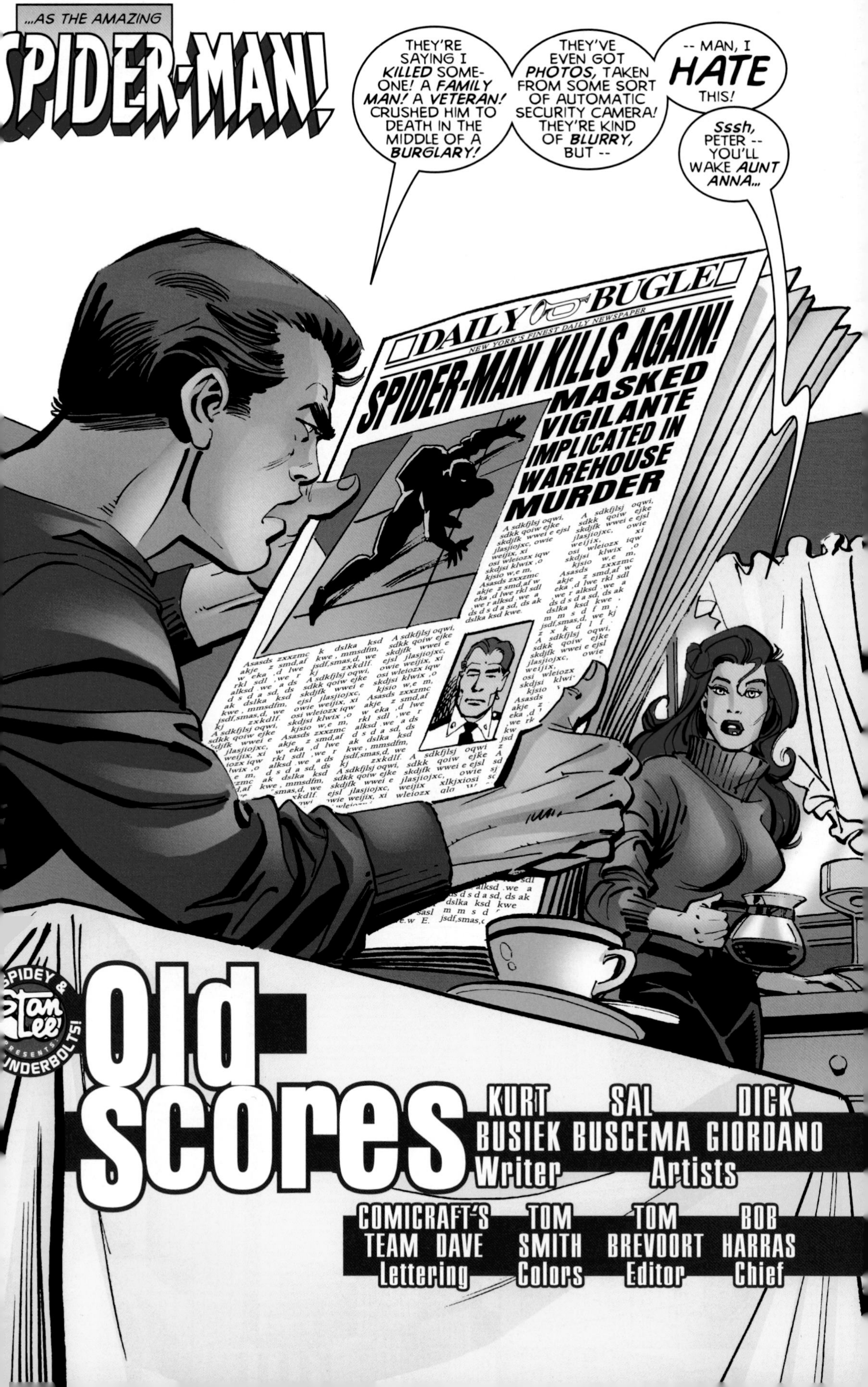
...AS THE AMAZING
SPIDER-MAN!
THEY'RE SAYING I KILLED SOMEONE! A FAMILY MAN! A VETERAN! CRUSHED HIM TO DEATH IN THE MIDDLE OF A BURGLARY!
THEY'VE EVEN GOT PHOTOS, TAKEN FROM SOME SORT OF AUTOMATIC SECURITY CAMERA! THEY'RE KIND OF BLURRY, BUT --
-- MAN, I HATE THIS!
Sssh, PETER -- YOU'LL WAKE AUNT ANNA...
DAILY BUGLE
NEW YORK'S FINEST DAILY NEWSPAPER
SPIDER-MAN KILLS AGAIN!
MASKED VIGILANTE IMPLICATED IN WAREHOUSE MURDER
SPIDEY & STAN LEE PRESENTS THUNDERBOLTS!
Old Scores
KURT BUSIEK Writer
SAL BUSCEMA DICK GIORDANO Artists
COMICRAFT'S TEAM DAVE Lettering
TOM SMITH Colors
TOM BREVOORT Editor
BOB HARRAS Chief

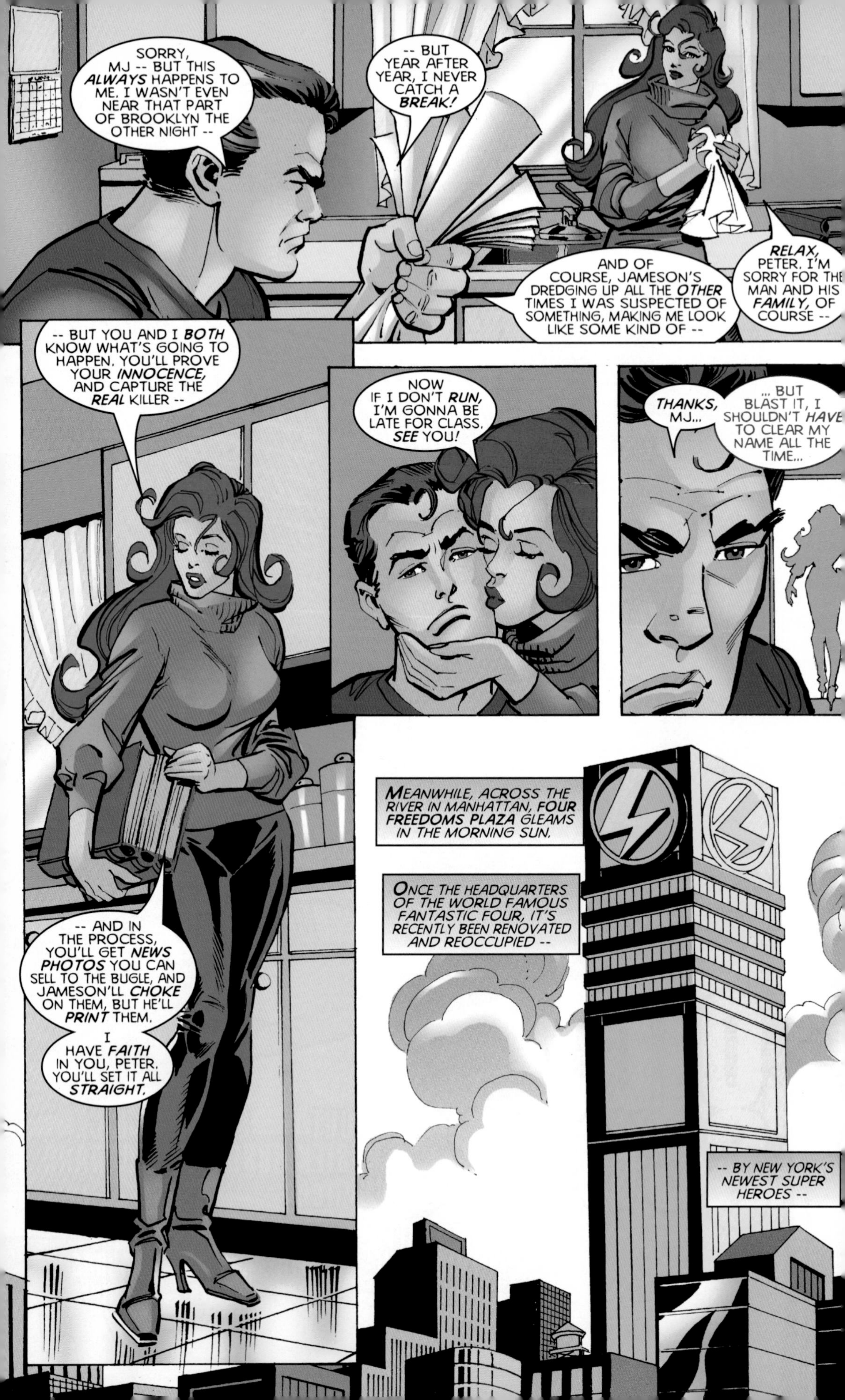

SORRY, MJ -- BUT THIS ALWAYS HAPPENS TO ME. I WASN'T EVEN NEAR THAT PART OF BROOKLYN THE OTHER NIGHT --
-- BUT YEAR AFTER YEAR, I NEVER CATCH A BREAK!
AND OF COURSE, JAMESON'S DREDGING UP ALL THE OTHER TIMES I WAS SUSPECTED OF SOMETHING, MAKING ME LOOK LIKE SOME KIND OF --
RELAX, PETER. I'M SORRY FOR THE MAN AND HIS FAMILY, OF COURSE --
-- BUT YOU AND I BOTH KNOW WHAT'S GOING TO HAPPEN. YOU'LL PROVE YOUR INNOCENCE, AND CAPTURE THE REAL KILLER --
-- AND IN THE PROCESS, YOU'LL GET NEWS PHOTOS YOU CAN SELL TO THE BUGLE, AND JAMESON'LL CHOKE ON THEM, BUT HE'LL PRINT THEM.
I HAVE FAITH IN YOU, PETER. YOU'LL SET IT ALL STRAIGHT.
NOW IF I DON'T RUN, I'M GONNA BE LATE FOR CLASS. SEE YOU!
THANKS, MJ...
... BUT BLAST IT, I SHOULDN'T HAVE TO CLEAR MY NAME ALL THE TIME...
MEANWHILE, ACROSS THE RIVER IN MANHATTAN, FOUR FREEDOMS PLAZA GLEAMS IN THE MORNING SUN.
ONCE THE HEADQUARTERS OF THE WORLD FAMOUS FANTASTIC FOUR, IT'S RECENTLY BEEN RENOVATED AND REOCCUPIED --
-- BY NEW YORK'S NEWEST SUPER HEROES --

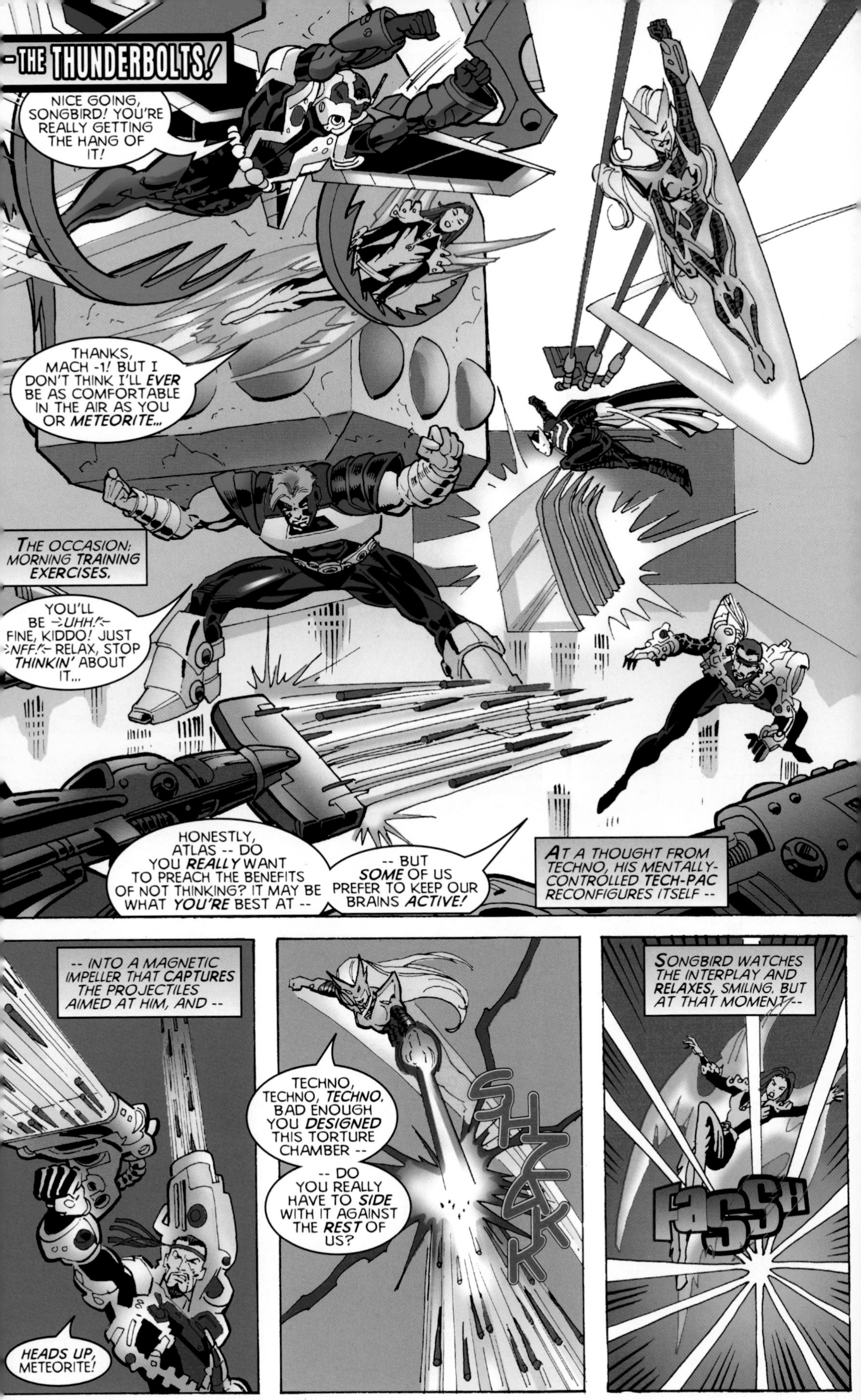

-THE THUNDERBOLTS!
NICE GOING, SONGBIRD! YOU'RE REALLY GETTING THE HANG OF IT!
THANKS, MACH -1! BUT I DON'T THINK I'LL EVER BE AS COMFORTABLE IN THE AIR AS YOU OR METEORITE...
THE OCCASION: MORNING TRAINING EXERCISES.
YOU'LL BE -UHH!- FINE, KIDDO! JUST -NFF!- RELAX, STOP THINKIN' ABOUT IT...
HONESTLY, ATLAS -- DO YOU REALLY WANT TO PREACH THE BENEFITS OF NOT THINKING? IT MAY BE WHAT YOU'RE BEST AT --
-- BUT SOME OF US PREFER TO KEEP OUR BRAINS ACTIVE!
AT A THOUGHT FROM TECHNO, HIS MENTALLY-CONTROLLED TECH-PAC RECONFIGURES ITSELF --
-- INTO A MAGNETIC IMPELLER THAT CAPTURES THE PROJECTILES AIMED AT HIM, AND --
HEADS UP, METEORITE!
TECHNO, TECHNO, TECHNO. BAD ENOUGH YOU DESIGNED THIS TORTURE CHAMBER --
-- DO YOU REALLY HAVE TO SIDE WITH IT AGAINST THE REST OF US?
SONGBIRD WATCHES THE INTERPLAY AND RELAXES, SMILING, BUT AT THAT MOMENT--

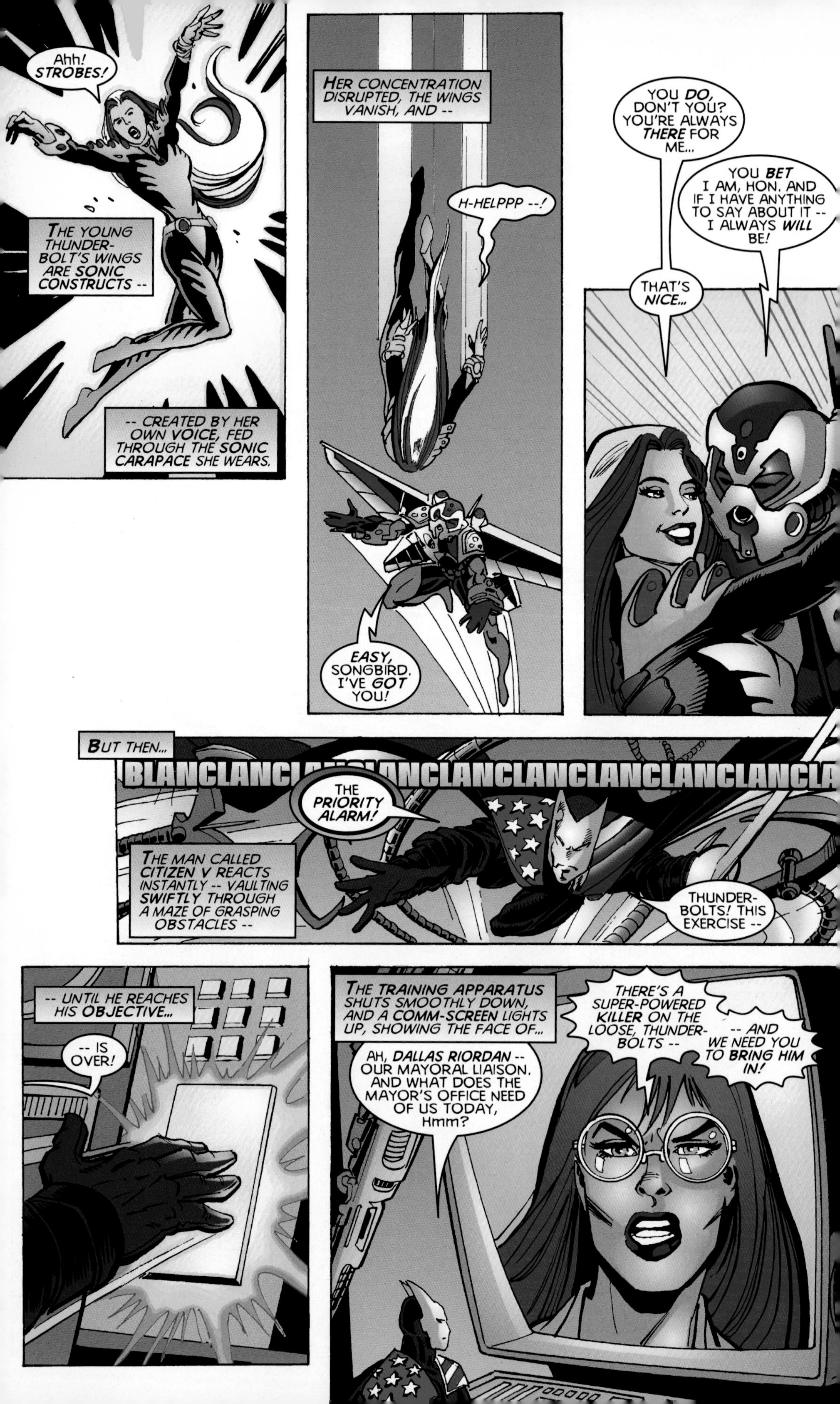

Ahh! STROBES!
THE YOUNG THUNDER-BOLT'S WINGS ARE SONIC CONSTRUCTS --
-- CREATED BY HER OWN VOICE, FED THROUGH THE SONIC CARAPACE SHE WEARS.
HER CONCENTRATION DISRUPTED, THE WINGS VANISH, AND --
H-HELPPP --!
EASY, SONGBIRD, I'VE GOT YOU!
YOU DO, DON'T YOU? YOU'RE ALWAYS THERE FOR ME...
YOU BET I AM, HON. AND IF I HAVE ANYTHING TO SAY ABOUT IT -- I ALWAYS WILL BE!
THAT'S NICE...
BUT THEN...
BLANCLANCLANCLANCLANCLANCLANCLANCLANCLA
THE PRIORITY ALARM!
THE MAN CALLED CITIZEN V REACTS INSTANTLY -- VAULTING SWIFTLY THROUGH A MAZE OF GRASPING OBSTACLES --
THUNDER-BOLTS! THIS EXERCISE --
-- UNTIL HE REACHES HIS OBJECTIVE...
-- IS OVER!
THE TRAINING APPARATUS SHUTS SMOOTHLY DOWN, AND A COMM-SCREEN LIGHTS UP, SHOWING THE FACE OF...
AH, DALLAS RIORDAN -- OUR MAYORAL LIAISON. AND WHAT DOES THE MAYOR'S OFFICE NEED OF US TODAY, Hmm?
THERE'S A SUPER-POWERED KILLER ON THE LOOSE, THUNDER-BOLTS --
-- AND WE NEED YOU TO BRING HIM IN!

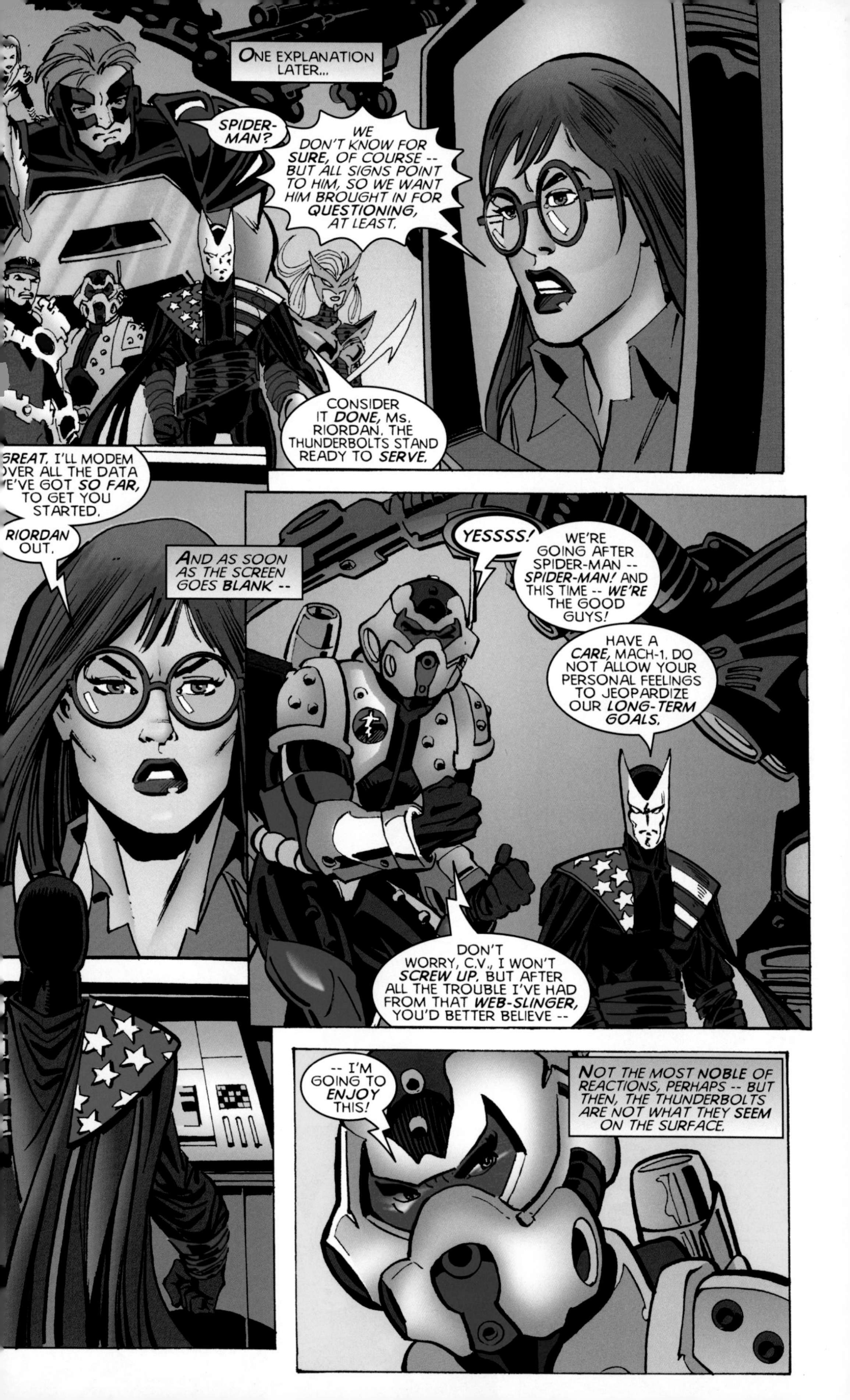
ONE EXPLANATION LATER...
SPIDER-MAN?
WE DON'T KNOW FOR SURE, OF COURSE -- BUT ALL SIGNS POINT TO HIM, SO WE WANT HIM BROUGHT IN FOR QUESTIONING, AT LEAST.
CONSIDER IT DONE, Ms. RIORDAN. THE THUNDERBOLTS STAND READY TO SERVE.
GREAT. I'LL MODEM OVER ALL THE DATA WE'VE GOT SO FAR, TO GET YOU STARTED.
RIORDAN OUT.
AND AS SOON AS THE SCREEN GOES BLANK --
YESSSS!
WE'RE GOING AFTER SPIDER-MAN -- SPIDER-MAN! AND THIS TIME -- WE'RE THE GOOD GUYS!
HAVE A CARE, MACH-1. DO NOT ALLOW YOUR PERSONAL FEELINGS TO JEOPARDIZE OUR LONG-TERM GOALS.
DON'T WORRY, C.V., I WON'T SCREW UP, BUT AFTER ALL THE TROUBLE I'VE HAD FROM THAT WEB-SLINGER, YOU'D BETTER BELIEVE --
-- I'M GOING TO ENJOY THIS!
NOT THE MOST NOBLE OF REACTIONS, PERHAPS -- BUT THEN, THE THUNDERBOLTS ARE NOT WHAT THEY SEEM ON THE SURFACE.

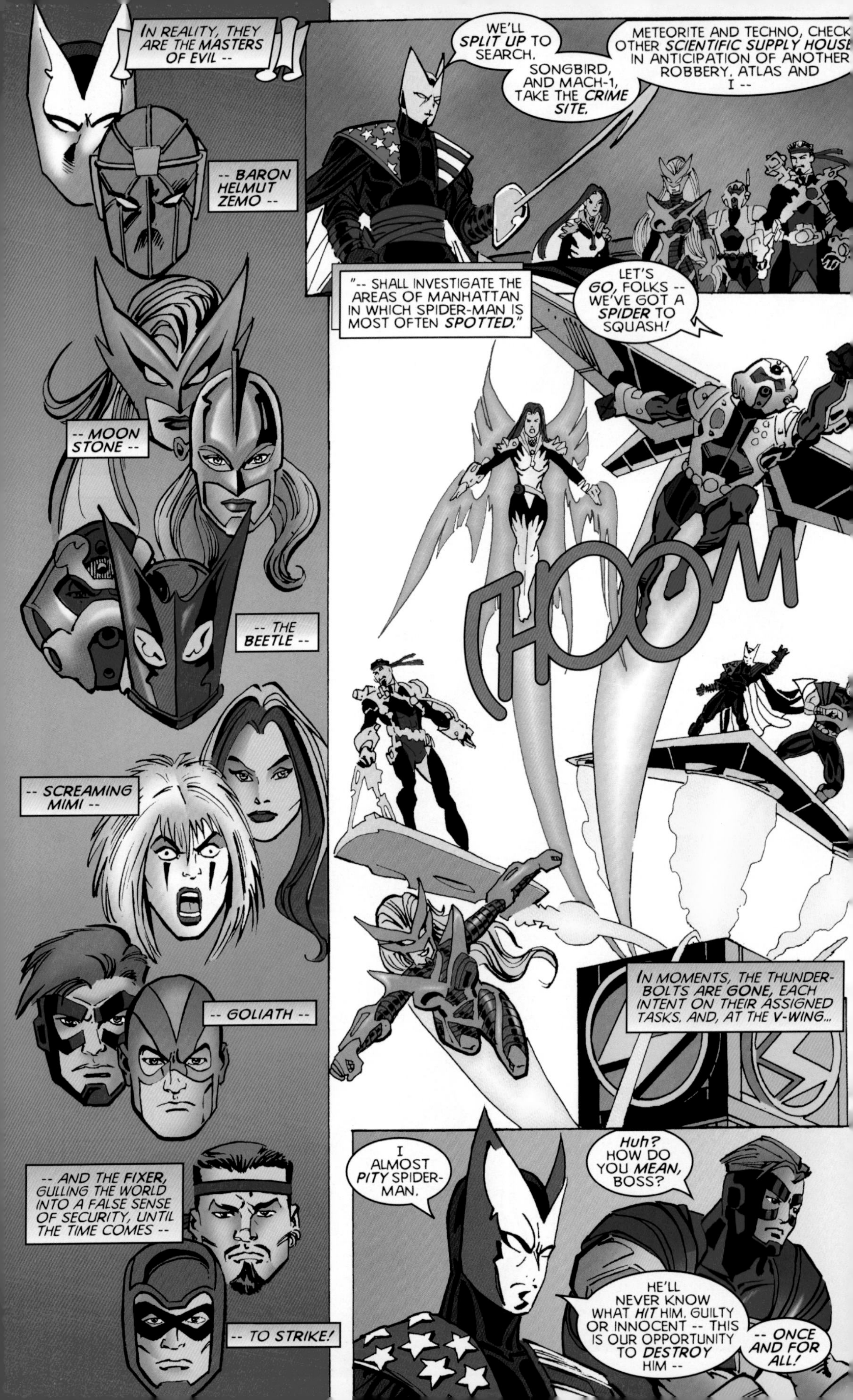
IN REALITY, THEY ARE THE MASTERS OF EVIL --
-- BARON HELMUT ZEMO --
-- MOON STONE --
-- THE BEETLE --
-- SCREAMING MIMI --
-- GOLIATH --
-- AND THE FIXER, GULLING THE WORLD INTO A FALSE SENSE OF SECURITY, UNTIL THE TIME COMES --
-- TO STRIKE!
WE'LL SPLIT UP TO SEARCH.
SONGBIRD, AND MACH-1, TAKE THE CRIME SITE.
METEORITE AND TECHNO, CHECK OTHER SCIENTIFIC SUPPLY HOUSE IN ANTICIPATION OF ANOTHER ROBBERY. ATLAS AND I --
"-- SHALL INVESTIGATE THE AREAS OF MANHATTAN IN WHICH SPIDER-MAN IS MOST OFTEN SPOTTED."
LET'S GO, FOLKS -- WE'VE GOT A SPIDER TO SQUASH!
CHOOM
IN MOMENTS, THE THUNDER-BOLTS ARE GONE, EACH INTENT ON THEIR ASSIGNED TASKS. AND, AT THE V-WING...
I ALMOST PITY SPIDER-MAN.
Huh? HOW DO YOU MEAN, BOSS?
HE'LL NEVER KNOW WHAT HIT HIM. GUILTY OR INNOCENT -- THIS IS OUR OPPORTUNITY TO DESTROY HIM --
-- ONCE AND FOR ALL!

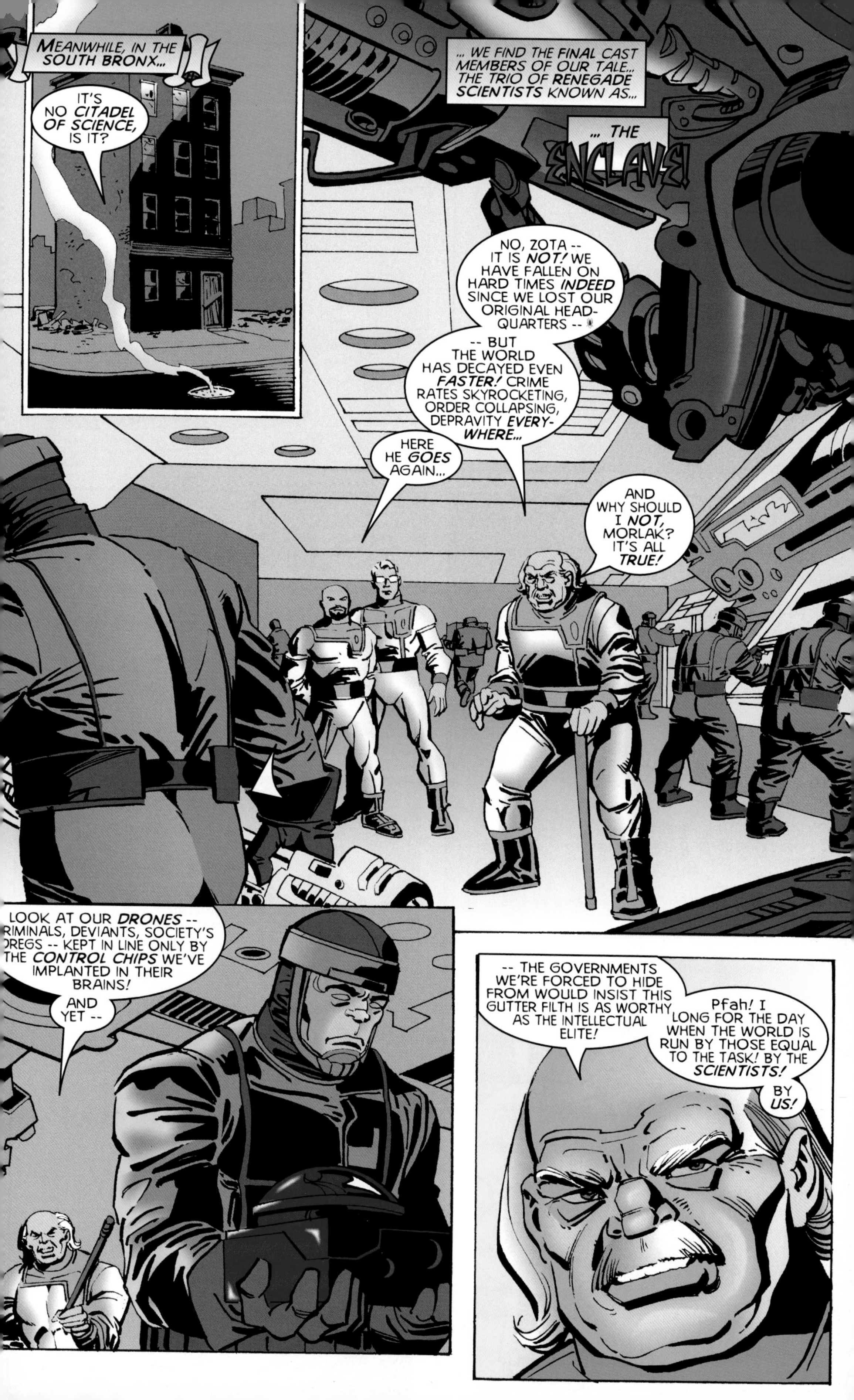
MEANWHILE, IN THE SOUTH BRONX...
IT'S NO CITADEL OF SCIENCE, IS IT?
... WE FIND THE FINAL CAST MEMBERS OF OUR TALE... THE TRIO OF RENEGADE SCIENTISTS KNOWN AS...
... THE ENCLAVE!
NO, ZOTA -- IT IS NOT! WE HAVE FALLEN ON HARD TIMES INDEED SINCE WE LOST OUR ORIGINAL HEAD-QUARTERS --
-- BUT THE WORLD HAS DECAYED EVEN FASTER! CRIME RATES SKYROCKETING, ORDER COLLAPSING, DEPRAVITY EVERY-WHERE...
HERE HE GOES AGAIN...
AND WHY SHOULD I NOT, MORLAK? IT'S ALL TRUE!
LOOK AT OUR DRONES -- RIMINALS, DEVIANTS, SOCIETY'S DREGS -- KEPT IN LINE ONLY BY THE CONTROL CHIPS WE'VE IMPLANTED IN THEIR BRAINS!
AND YET --
-- THE GOVERNMENTS WE'RE FORCED TO HIDE FROM WOULD INSIST THIS GUTTER FILTH IS AS WORTHY AS THE INTELLECTUAL ELITE!
Pfah! I LONG FOR THE DAY WHEN THE WORLD IS RUN BY THOSE EQUAL TO THE TASK! BY THE SCIENTISTS!
BY US!

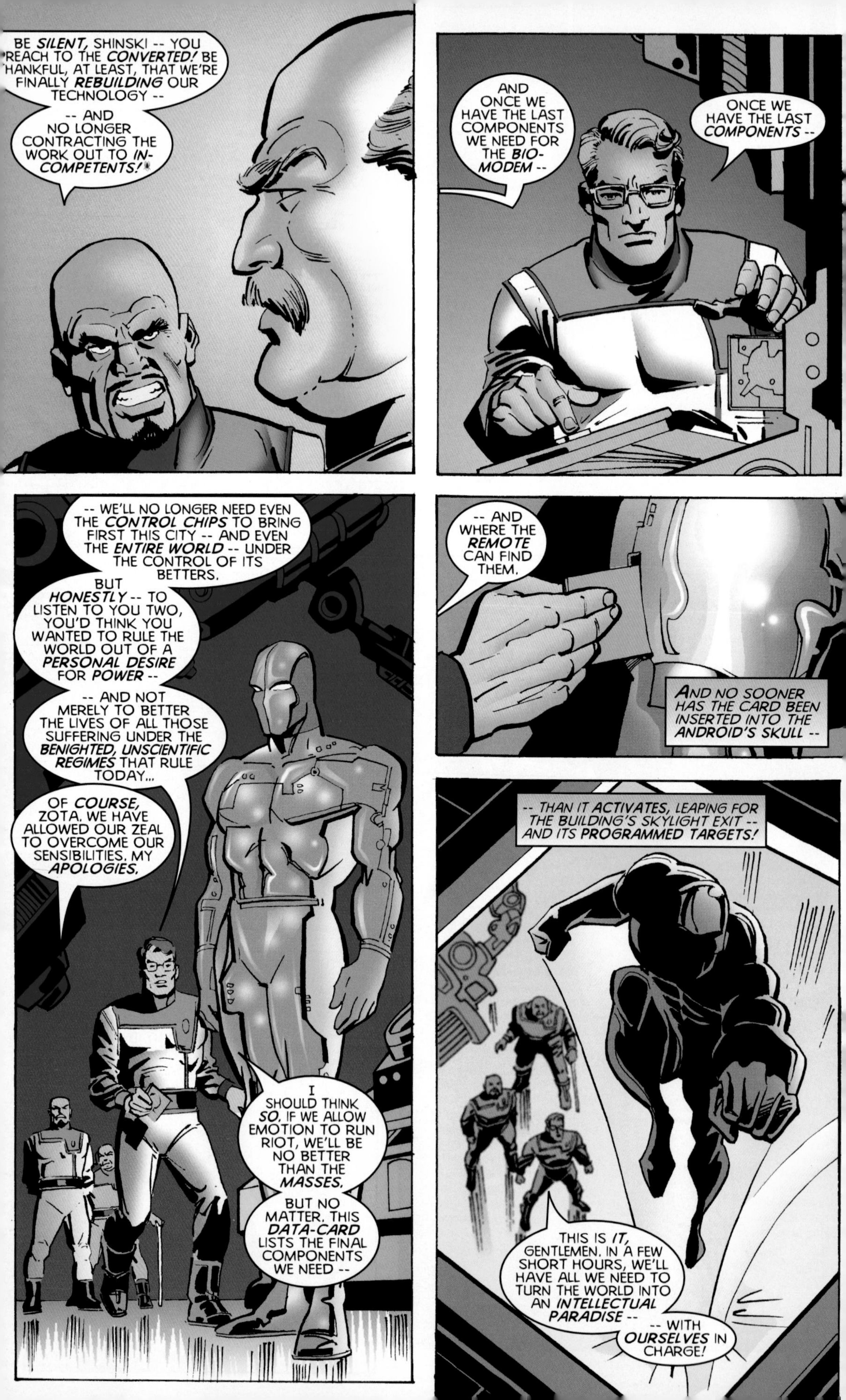
BE SILENT, SHINSKI -- YOU PREACH TO THE CONVERTED! BE THANKFUL, AT LEAST, THAT WE'RE FINALLY REBUILDING OUR TECHNOLOGY --
-- AND NO LONGER CONTRACTING THE WORK OUT TO IN-COMPETENTS!
AND ONCE WE HAVE THE LAST COMPONENTS WE NEED FOR THE BIO-MODEM --
ONCE WE HAVE THE LAST COMPONENTS --
-- WE'LL NO LONGER NEED EVEN THE CONTROL CHIPS TO BRING FIRST THIS CITY -- AND EVEN THE ENTIRE WORLD -- UNDER THE CONTROL OF ITS BETTERS.
BUT HONESTLY -- TO LISTEN TO YOU TWO, YOU'D THINK YOU WANTED TO RULE THE WORLD OUT OF A PERSONAL DESIRE FOR POWER --
-- AND NOT MERELY TO BETTER THE LIVES OF ALL THOSE SUFFERING UNDER THE BENIGHTED, UNSCIENTIFIC REGIMES THAT RULE TODAY...
OF COURSE, ZOTA. WE HAVE ALLOWED OUR ZEAL TO OVERCOME OUR SENSIBILITIES. MY APOLOGIES.
I SHOULD THINK SO. IF WE ALLOW EMOTION TO RUN RIOT, WE'LL BE NO BETTER THAN THE MASSES.
BUT NO MATTER. THIS DATA-CARD LISTS THE FINAL COMPONENTS WE NEED --
-- AND WHERE THE REMOTE CAN FIND THEM.
AND NO SOONER HAS THE CARD BEEN INSERTED INTO THE ANDROID'S SKULL --
-- THAN IT ACTIVATES, LEAPING FOR THE BUILDING'S SKYLIGHT EXIT -- AND ITS PROGRAMMED TARGETS!
THIS IS IT, GENTLEMEN. IN A FEW SHORT HOURS, WE'LL HAVE ALL WE NEED TO TURN THE WORLD INTO AN INTELLECTUAL PARADISE --
-- WITH OURSELVES IN CHARGE!

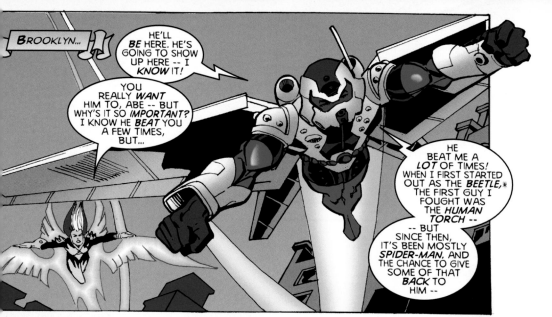

BROOKLYN...

HE'LL *BE* HERE. HE'S GOING TO SHOW UP HERE -- I *KNOW* IT!

YOU *REALLY WANT* HIM TO, ABE -- BUT WHY'S IT SO *IMPORTANT?* I KNOW HE *BEAT* YOU A FEW TIMES, BUT...

HE BEAT ME A *LOT* OF TIMES! WHEN I FIRST STARTED OUT AS THE *BEETLE,* THE FIRST GUY I FOUGHT WAS THE *HUMAN TORCH* --

-- BUT SINCE THEN, IT'S BEEN MOSTLY *SPIDER-MAN,* AND THE CHANCE TO GIVE SOME OF THAT *BACK* TO HIM --

-- TO BE THE *HERO* WHO BRINGS HIM IN -- I JUST WANT THAT SO BAD I CAN *TASTE* IT!

I GUESS I CAN *SEE* THAT. BUT... HOW DO YOU KNOW HE'LL *BE* HERE?

BECAUSE HE'S *INNOCENT.*

FUNNY, ISN'T IT -- I'M ONE OF SPIDER-MAN'S GREATEST *ENEMIES,* AND I'M ONE OF THE FEW PEOPLE ABSOLUTEY *SURE* HE'S INNOCENT.

HE'D NEVER DO ANYTHING LIKE *THIS,* SO HE'LL WANT TO CLEAR HIS *NAME,* AND HE'LL START INVESTIGATING *HERE...*

AND SURE ENOUGH...

THERE HE IS!

SURRENDER, SPIDER-MAN -- IN THE NAME OF THE *THUNDERBOLTS!*

WHAT? Oh, *MAN* --

-- THIS I *DON'T* NEED!

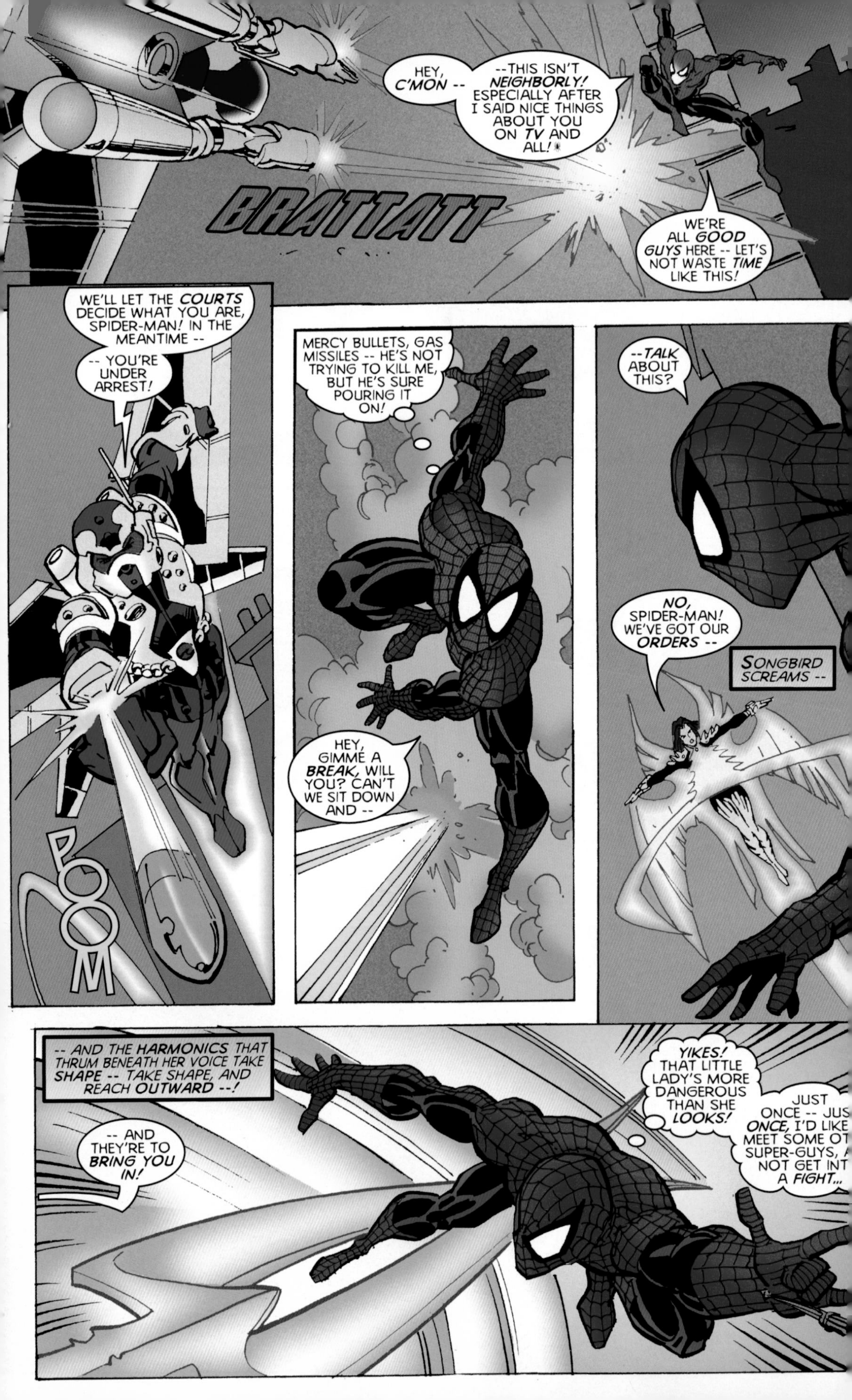
HEY, C'MON --
--THIS ISN'T NEIGHBORLY! ESPECIALLY AFTER I SAID NICE THINGS ABOUT YOU ON TV AND ALL!
BRATTATT
WE'RE ALL GOOD GUYS HERE -- LET'S NOT WASTE TIME LIKE THIS!
WE'LL LET THE COURTS DECIDE WHAT YOU ARE, SPIDER-MAN! IN THE MEANTIME --
-- YOU'RE UNDER ARREST!
POOM
MERCY BULLETS, GAS MISSILES -- HE'S NOT TRYING TO KILL ME, BUT HE'S SURE POURING IT ON!
HEY, GIMME A BREAK, WILL YOU? CAN'T WE SIT DOWN AND --
--TALK ABOUT THIS?
NO, SPIDER-MAN! WE'VE GOT OUR ORDERS --
SONGBIRD SCREAMS --
-- AND THE HARMONICS THAT THRUM BENEATH HER VOICE TAKE SHAPE -- TAKE SHAPE, AND REACH OUTWARD --!
-- AND THEY'RE TO BRING YOU IN!
YIKES! THAT LITTLE LADY'S MORE DANGEROUS THAN SHE LOOKS!
JUST ONCE -- JUS ONCE, I'D LIKE MEET SOME OT SUPER-GUYS, A NOT GET INT A FIGHT...

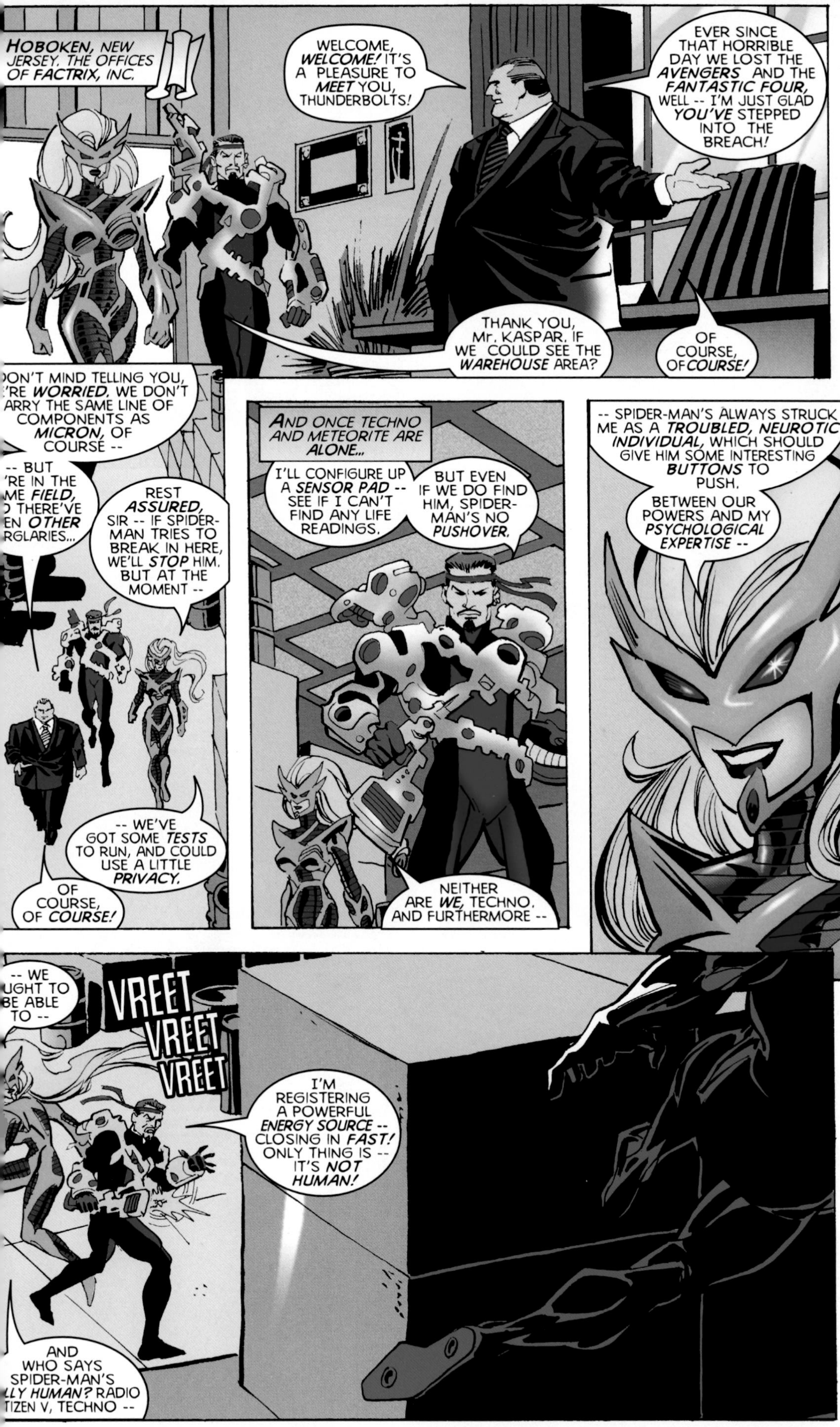
HOBOKEN, NEW JERSEY. THE OFFICES OF FACTRIX, INC.
WELCOME, WELCOME! IT'S A PLEASURE TO MEET YOU, THUNDERBOLTS!
EVER SINCE THAT HORRIBLE DAY WE LOST THE AVENGERS AND THE FANTASTIC FOUR, WELL -- I'M JUST GLAD YOU'VE STEPPED INTO THE BREACH!
THANK YOU, Mr. KASPAR. IF WE COULD SEE THE WAREHOUSE AREA?
OF COURSE, OF COURSE!
DON'T MIND TELLING YOU, 'RE WORRIED. WE DON'T ARRY THE SAME LINE OF COMPONENTS AS MICRON, OF COURSE --
-- BUT 'RE IN THE ME FIELD, D THERE'VE EN OTHER RGLARIES...
REST ASSURED, SIR -- IF SPIDER-MAN TRIES TO BREAK IN HERE, WE'LL STOP HIM. BUT AT THE MOMENT --
-- WE'VE GOT SOME TESTS TO RUN, AND COULD USE A LITTLE PRIVACY.
OF COURSE, OF COURSE!
AND ONCE TECHNO AND METEORITE ARE ALONE...
I'LL CONFIGURE UP A SENSOR PAD -- SEE IF I CAN'T FIND ANY LIFE READINGS.
BUT EVEN IF WE DO FIND HIM, SPIDER-MAN'S NO PUSHOVER.
NEITHER ARE WE, TECHNO. AND FURTHERMORE --
-- SPIDER-MAN'S ALWAYS STRUCK ME AS A TROUBLED, NEUROTIC INDIVIDUAL, WHICH SHOULD GIVE HIM SOME INTERESTING BUTTONS TO PUSH.
BETWEEN OUR POWERS AND MY PSYCHOLOGICAL EXPERTISE --
-- WE UGHT TO BE ABLE TO --
VREET VREET VREET
I'M REGISTERING A POWERFUL ENERGY SOURCE -- CLOSING IN FAST! ONLY THING IS -- IT'S NOT HUMAN!
AND WHO SAYS SPIDER-MAN'S LLY HUMAN? RADIO TIZEN V, TECHNO --

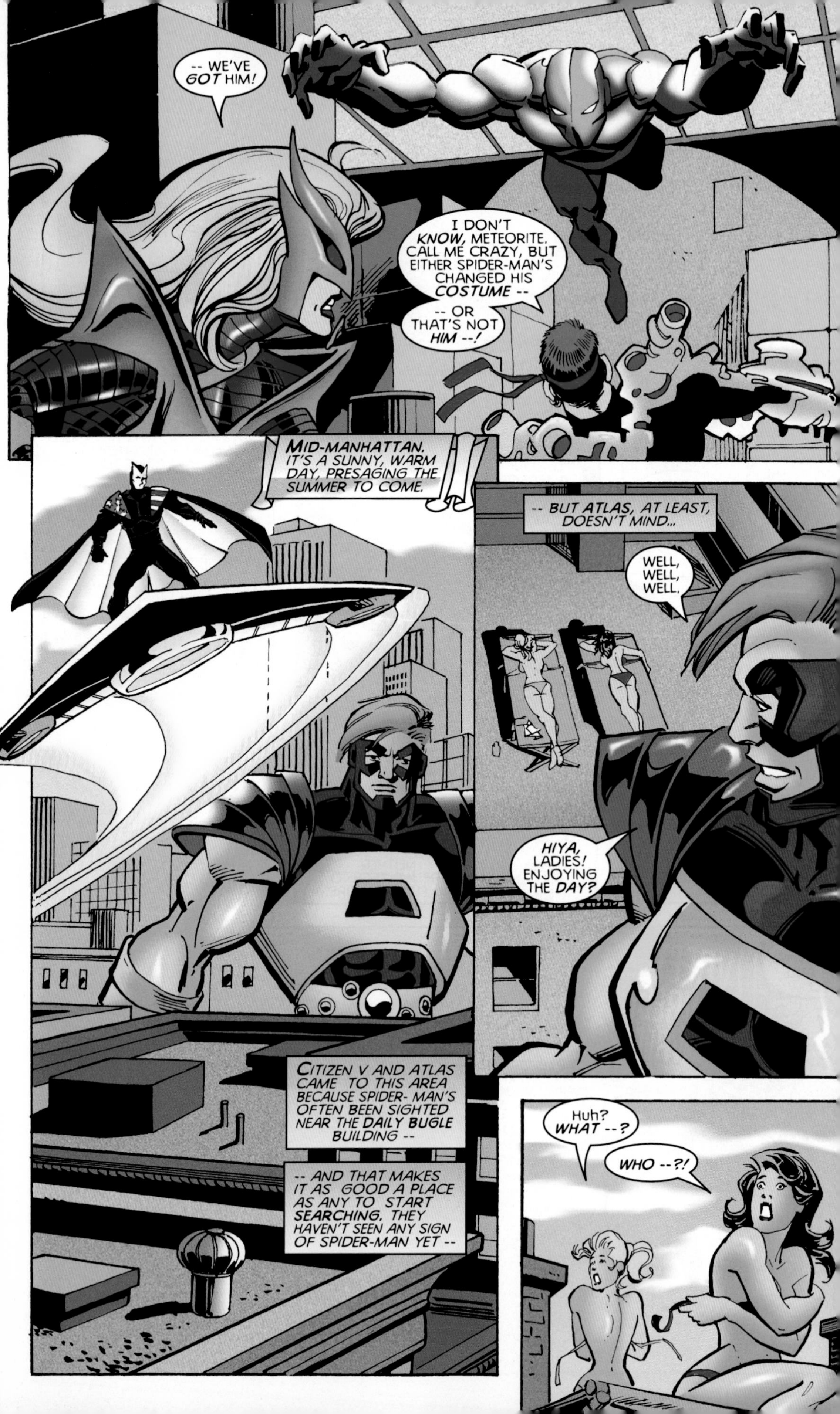
-- WE'VE GOT HIM!
I DON'T KNOW, METEORITE. CALL ME CRAZY, BUT EITHER SPIDER-MAN'S CHANGED HIS COSTUME --
-- OR THAT'S NOT HIM --!
MID-MANHATTAN. IT'S A SUNNY, WARM DAY, PRESAGING THE SUMMER TO COME.
CITIZEN V AND ATLAS CAME TO THIS AREA BECAUSE SPIDER-MAN'S OFTEN BEEN SIGHTED NEAR THE DAILY BUGLE BUILDING --
-- AND THAT MAKES IT AS GOOD A PLACE AS ANY TO START SEARCHING. THEY HAVEN'T SEEN ANY SIGN OF SPIDER-MAN YET --
-- BUT ATLAS, AT LEAST, DOESN'T MIND...
WELL, WELL, WELL.
HIYA, LADIES! ENJOYING THE DAY?
Huh? WHAT --?
WHO --?!

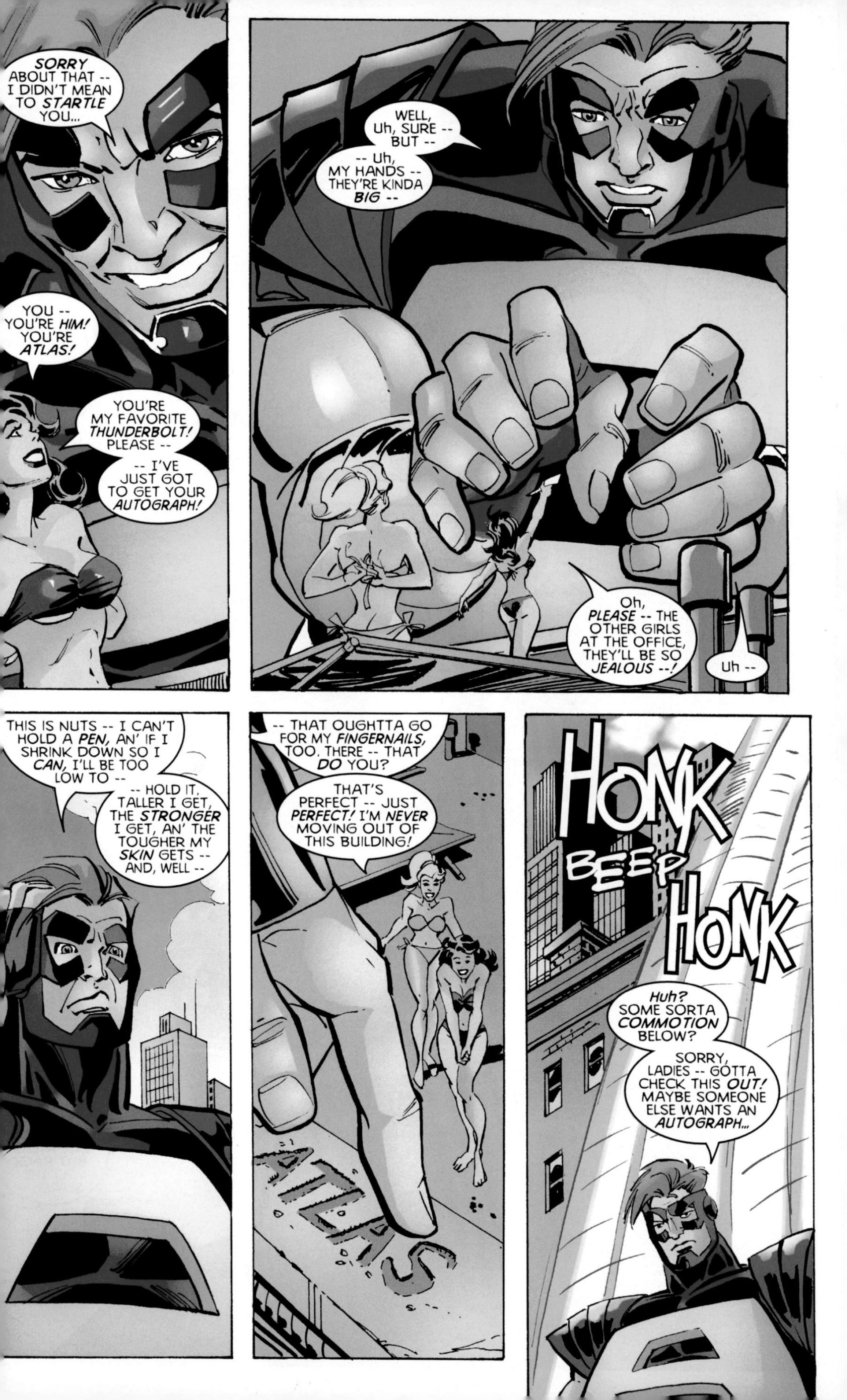
SORRY ABOUT THAT -- I DIDN'T MEAN TO STARTLE YOU...
YOU -- YOU'RE HIM! YOU'RE ATLAS!
YOU'RE MY FAVORITE THUNDERBOLT! PLEASE --
-- I'VE JUST GOT TO GET YOUR AUTOGRAPH!
WELL, Uh, SURE -- BUT --
-- Uh, MY HANDS -- THEY'RE KINDA BIG --
Oh, PLEASE -- THE OTHER GIRLS AT THE OFFICE, THEY'LL BE SO JEALOUS --!
Uh --
THIS IS NUTS -- I CAN'T HOLD A PEN, AN' IF I SHRINK DOWN SO I CAN, I'LL BE TOO LOW TO --
-- HOLD IT. TALLER I GET, THE STRONGER I GET, AN' THE TOUGHER MY SKIN GETS -- AND, WELL --
-- THAT OUGHTTA GO FOR MY FINGERNAILS, TOO. THERE -- THAT DO YOU?
THAT'S PERFECT -- JUST PERFECT! I'M NEVER MOVING OUT OF THIS BUILDING!
ATLAS
HONK
BEEP
HONK
Huh? SOME SORTA COMMOTION BELOW?
SORRY, LADIES -- GOTTA CHECK THIS OUT! MAYBE SOMEONE ELSE WANTS AN AUTOGRAPH...

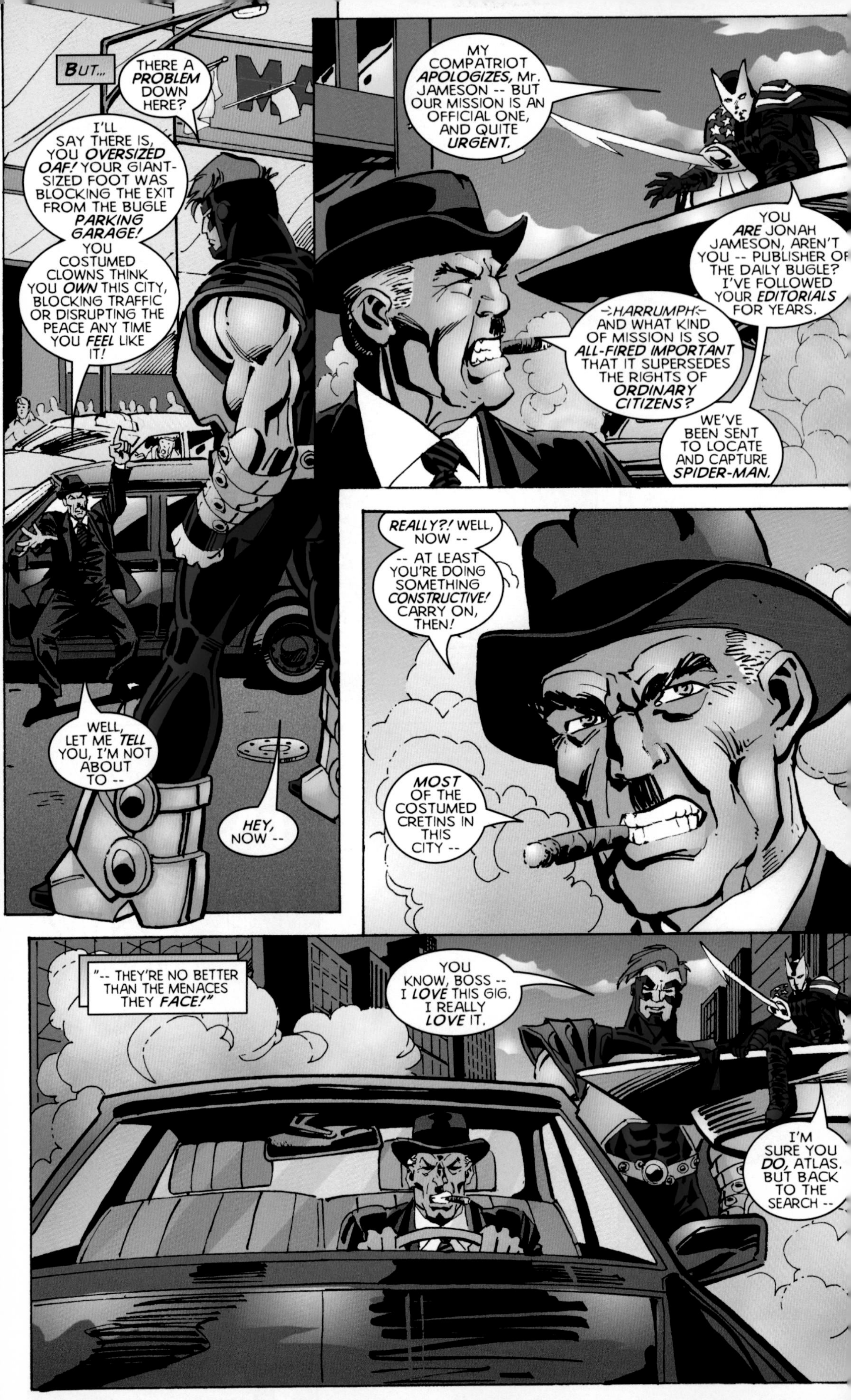
BUT...
THERE A PROBLEM DOWN HERE?
I'LL SAY THERE IS, YOU OVERSIZED OAF! YOUR GIANT-SIZED FOOT WAS BLOCKING THE EXIT FROM THE BUGLE PARKING GARAGE!
YOU COSTUMED CLOWNS THINK YOU OWN THIS CITY, BLOCKING TRAFFIC OR DISRUPTING THE PEACE ANY TIME YOU FEEL LIKE IT!
WELL, LET ME TELL YOU, I'M NOT ABOUT TO --
HEY, NOW --
MY COMPATRIOT APOLOGIZES, Mr. JAMESON -- BUT OUR MISSION IS AN OFFICIAL ONE, AND QUITE URGENT.
YOU ARE JONAH JAMESON, AREN'T YOU -- PUBLISHER OF THE DAILY BUGLE? I'VE FOLLOWED YOUR EDITORIALS FOR YEARS.
-HARRUMPH- AND WHAT KIND OF MISSION IS SO ALL-FIRED IMPORTANT THAT IT SUPERSEDES THE RIGHTS OF ORDINARY CITIZENS?
WE'VE BEEN SENT TO LOCATE AND CAPTURE SPIDER-MAN.
REALLY?! WELL, NOW --
-- AT LEAST YOU'RE DOING SOMETHING CONSTRUCTIVE! CARRY ON, THEN!
MOST OF THE COSTUMED CRETINS IN THIS CITY --
"-- THEY'RE NO BETTER THAN THE MENACES THEY FACE!"
YOU KNOW, BOSS -- I LOVE THIS GIG. I REALLY LOVE IT.
I'M SURE YOU DO, ATLAS. BUT BACK TO THE SEARCH --

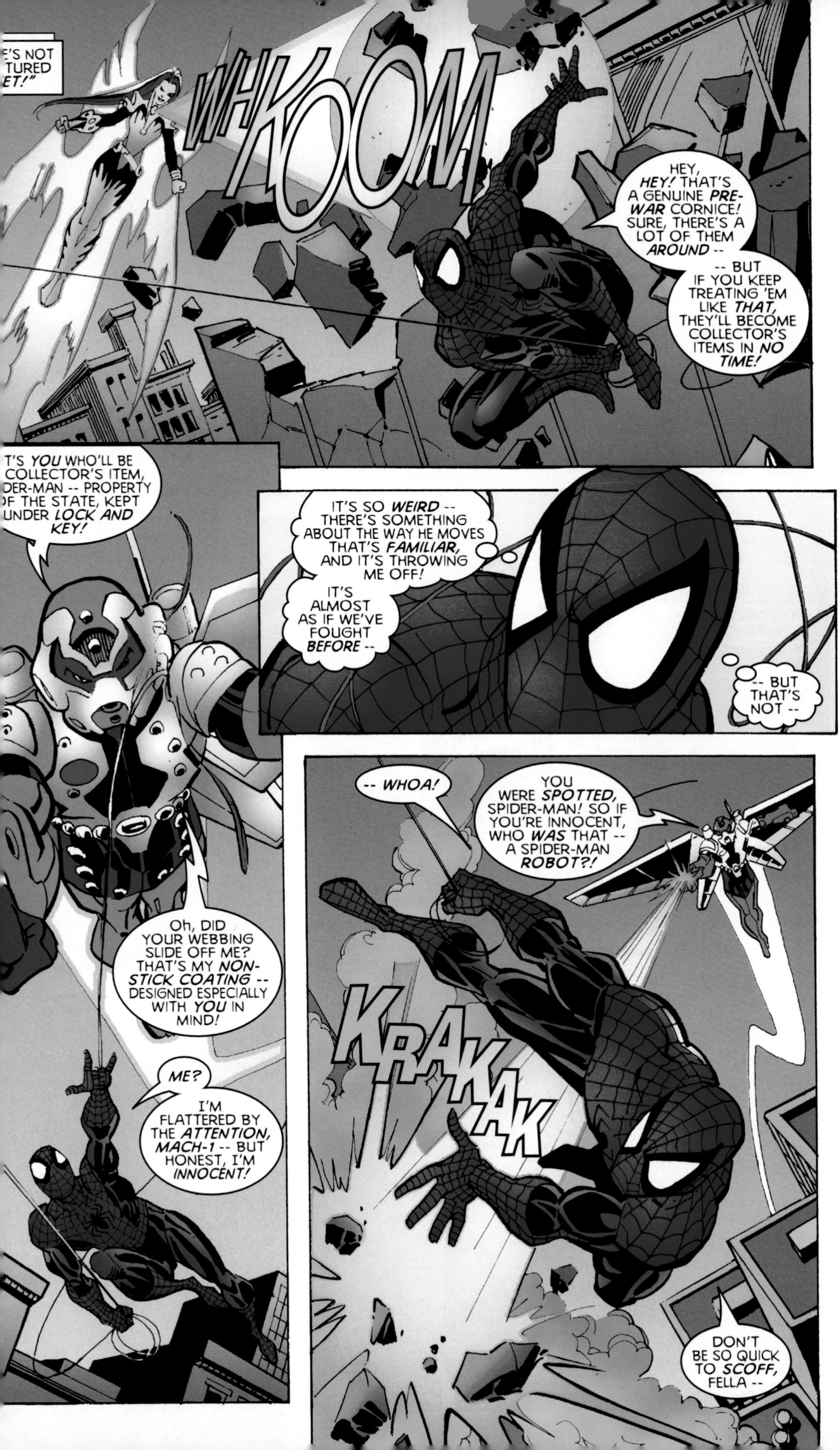

E'S NOT
TURED
ET!"
WHKOOM
HEY, HEY! THAT'S A GENUINE PRE-WAR CORNICE! SURE, THERE'S A LOT OF THEM AROUND --
-- BUT IF YOU KEEP TREATING 'EM LIKE THAT, THEY'LL BECOME COLLECTOR'S ITEMS IN NO TIME!
T'S YOU WHO'LL BE COLLECTOR'S ITEM, DER-MAN -- PROPERTY OF THE STATE, KEPT UNDER LOCK AND KEY!
IT'S SO WEIRD -- THERE'S SOMETHING ABOUT THE WAY HE MOVES THAT'S FAMILIAR, AND IT'S THROWING ME OFF!
IT'S ALMOST AS IF WE'VE FOUGHT BEFORE --
-- BUT THAT'S NOT --
Oh, DID YOUR WEBBING SLIDE OFF ME? THAT'S MY NON-STICK COATING -- DESIGNED ESPECIALLY WITH YOU IN MIND!
ME?
I'M FLATTERED BY THE ATTENTION, MACH-1 -- BUT HONEST, I'M INNOCENT!
-- WHOA!
YOU WERE SPOTTED, SPIDER-MAN! SO IF YOU'RE INNOCENT, WHO WAS THAT -- A SPIDER-MAN ROBOT?!
KRAKAKAK
DON'T BE SO QUICK TO SCOFF, FELLA --

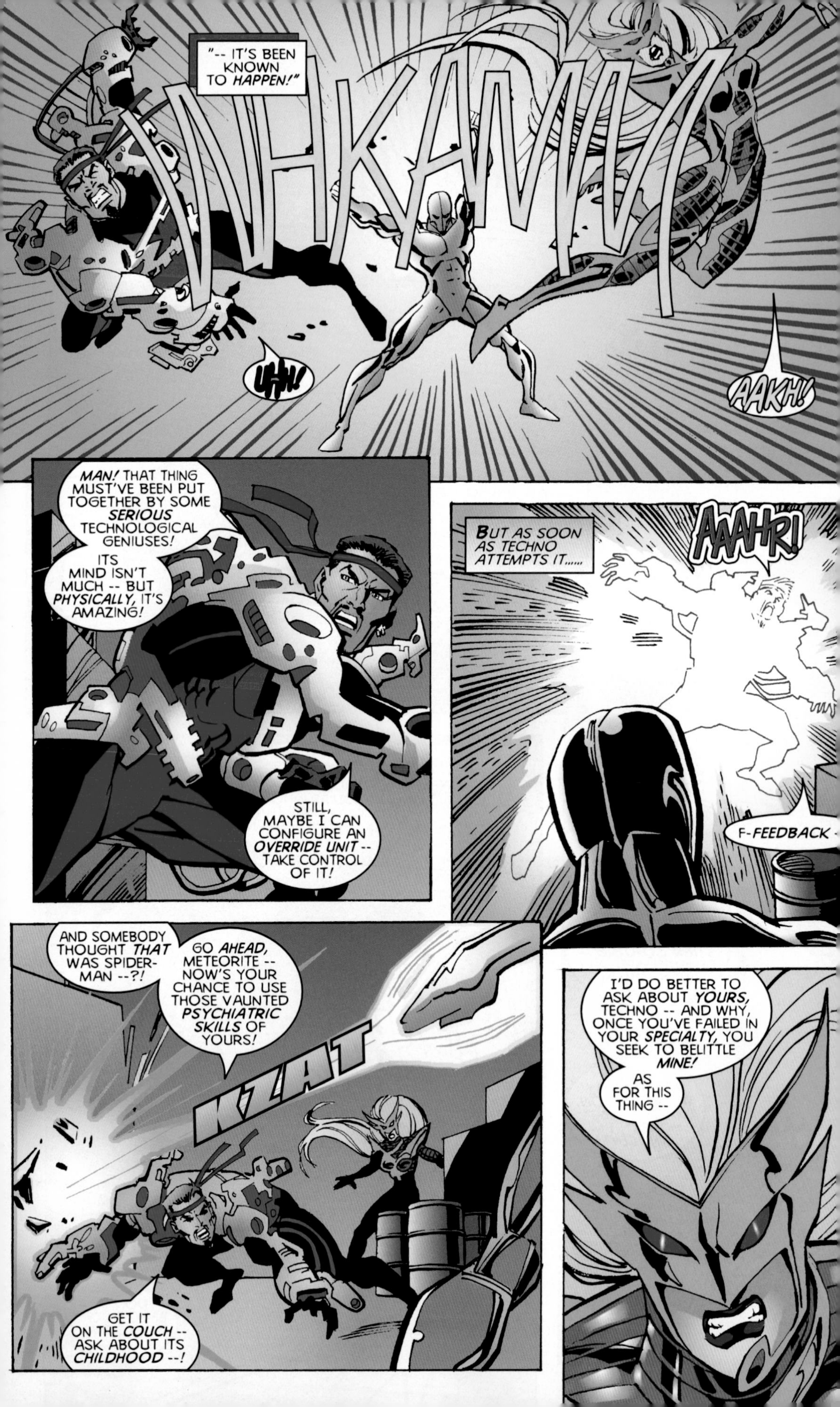
"-- IT'S BEEN KNOWN TO HAPPEN!"
WHKAMM
UHH!
AAKH!
MAN! THAT THING MUST'VE BEEN PUT TOGETHER BY SOME SERIOUS TECHNOLOGICAL GENIUSES!
ITS MIND ISN'T MUCH -- BUT PHYSICALLY, IT'S AMAZING!
STILL, MAYBE I CAN CONFIGURE AN OVERRIDE UNIT -- TAKE CONTROL OF IT!
BUT AS SOON AS TECHNO ATTEMPTS IT......
AAAHR!
F-FEEDBACK -
AND SOMEBODY THOUGHT THAT WAS SPIDER-MAN --?!
GO AHEAD, METEORITE -- NOW'S YOUR CHANCE TO USE THOSE VAUNTED PSYCHIATRIC SKILLS OF YOURS!
KZAT
GET IT ON THE COUCH -- ASK ABOUT ITS CHILDHOOD --!
I'D DO BETTER TO ASK ABOUT YOURS, TECHNO -- AND WHY, ONCE YOU'VE FAILED IN YOUR SPECIALTY, YOU SEEK TO BELITTLE MINE!
AS FOR THIS THING --

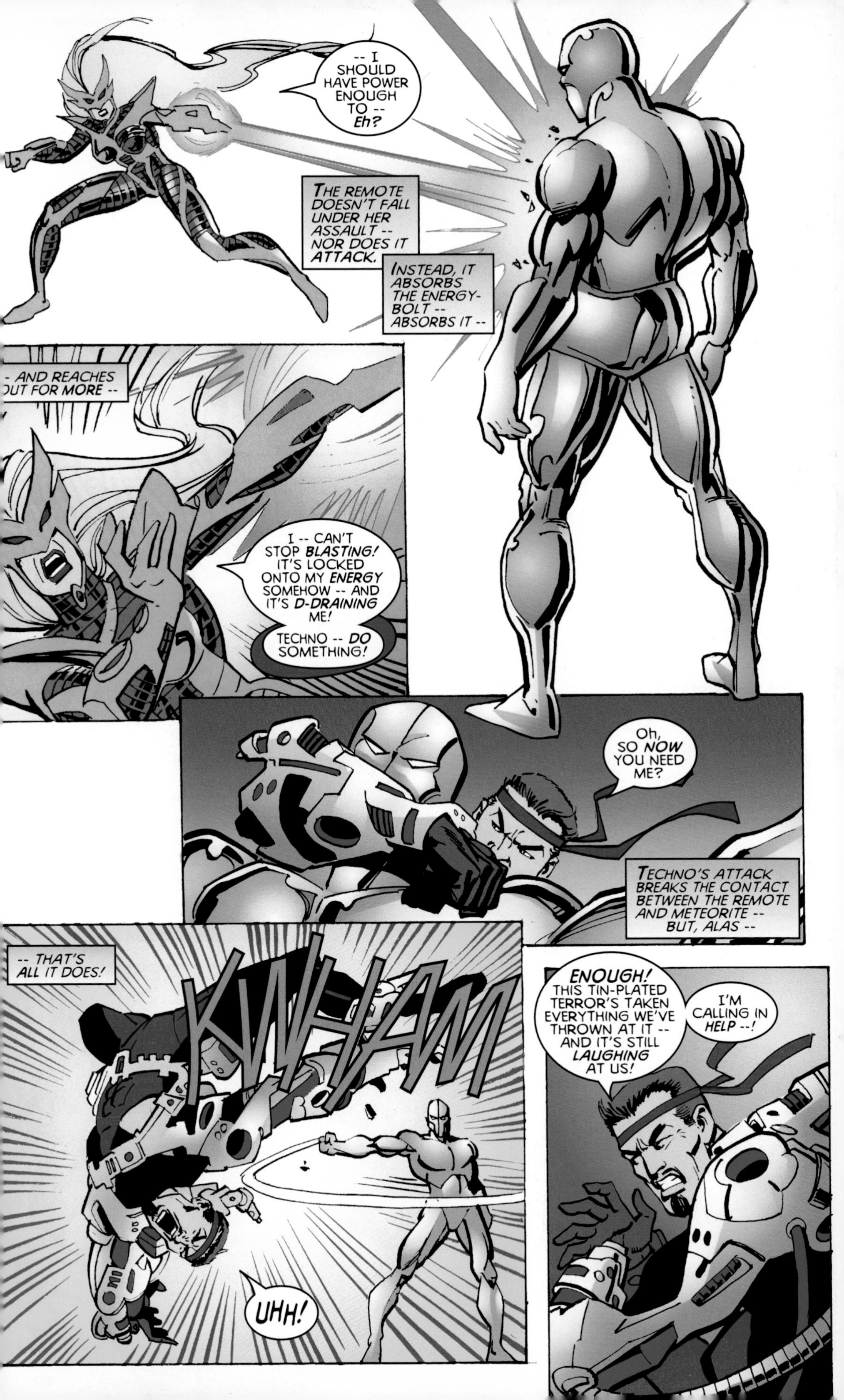
-- I SHOULD HAVE POWER ENOUGH TO -- Eh?
THE REMOTE DOESN'T FALL UNDER HER ASSAULT -- NOR DOES IT ATTACK.
INSTEAD, IT ABSORBS THE ENERGY-BOLT -- ABSORBS IT --
-- AND REACHES OUT FOR MORE --
I -- CAN'T STOP BLASTING! IT'S LOCKED ONTO MY ENERGY SOMEHOW -- AND IT'S D-DRAINING ME!
TECHNO -- DO SOMETHING!
Oh, SO NOW YOU NEED ME?
TECHNO'S ATTACK BREAKS THE CONTACT BETWEEN THE REMOTE AND METEORITE -- BUT, ALAS --
-- THAT'S ALL IT DOES!
KWHAM
UHH!
ENOUGH! THIS TIN-PLATED TERROR'S TAKEN EVERYTHING WE'VE THROWN AT IT -- AND IT'S STILL LAUGHING AT US!
I'M CALLING IN HELP --!

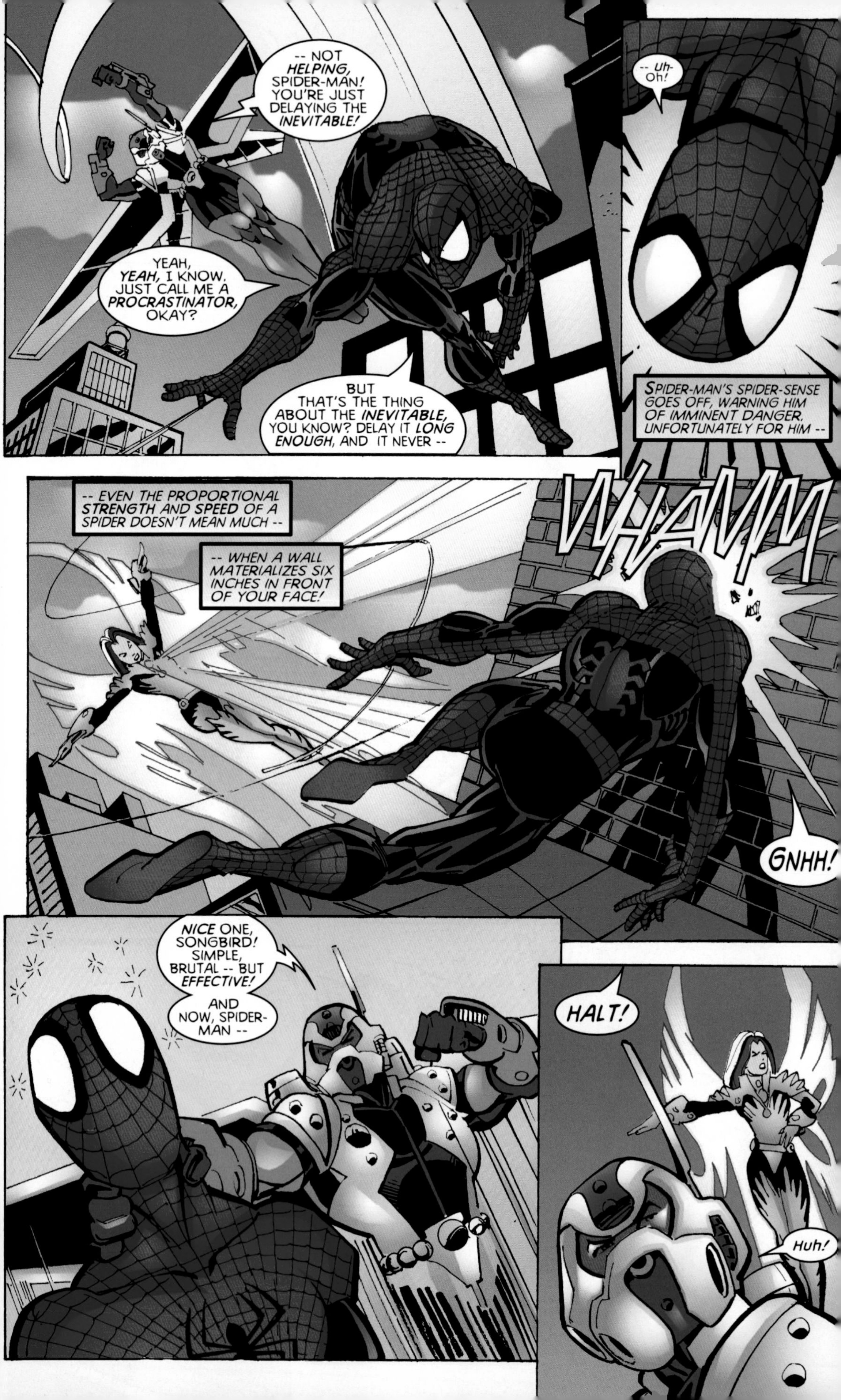
-- NOT HELPING, SPIDER-MAN! YOU'RE JUST DELAYING THE INEVITABLE!
YEAH, YEAH, I KNOW. JUST CALL ME A PROCRASTINATOR, OKAY?
BUT THAT'S THE THING ABOUT THE INEVITABLE, YOU KNOW? DELAY IT LONG ENOUGH, AND IT NEVER --
-- UH-OH!
SPIDER-MAN'S SPIDER-SENSE GOES OFF, WARNING HIM OF IMMINENT DANGER. UNFORTUNATELY FOR HIM --
-- EVEN THE PROPORTIONAL STRENGTH AND SPEED OF A SPIDER DOESN'T MEAN MUCH --
-- WHEN A WALL MATERIALIZES SIX INCHES IN FRONT OF YOUR FACE!
WHAMM
GNHH!
NICE ONE, SONGBIRD! SIMPLE, BRUTAL -- BUT EFFECTIVE!
AND NOW, SPIDER-MAN --
HALT!
HUH!

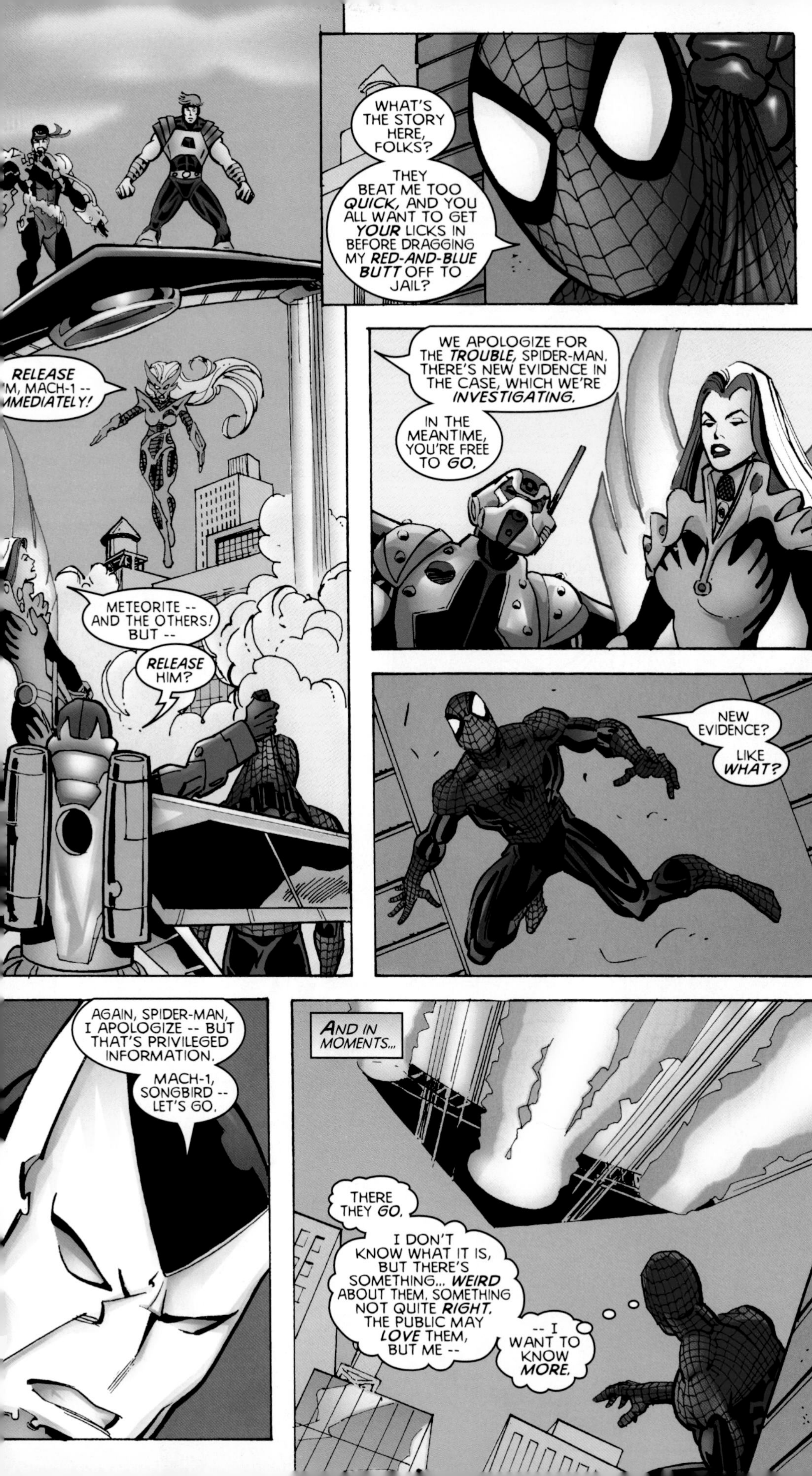
WHAT'S THE STORY HERE, FOLKS?
THEY BEAT ME TOO QUICK, AND YOU ALL WANT TO GET YOUR LICKS IN BEFORE DRAGGING MY RED-AND-BLUE BUTT OFF TO JAIL?
RELEASE M, MACH-1 -- MMEDIATELY!
METEORITE -- AND THE OTHERS! BUT --
RELEASE HIM?
WE APOLOGIZE FOR THE TROUBLE, SPIDER-MAN. THERE'S NEW EVIDENCE IN THE CASE, WHICH WE'RE INVESTIGATING.
IN THE MEANTIME, YOU'RE FREE TO GO.
NEW EVIDENCE?
LIKE WHAT?
AGAIN, SPIDER-MAN, I APOLOGIZE -- BUT THAT'S PRIVILEGED INFORMATION.
MACH-1, SONGBIRD -- LET'S GO.
AND IN MOMENTS...
THERE THEY GO.
I DON'T KNOW WHAT IT IS, BUT THERE'S SOMETHING... WEIRD ABOUT THEM. SOMETHING NOT QUITE RIGHT. THE PUBLIC MAY LOVE THEM, BUT ME --
-- I WANT TO KNOW MORE.

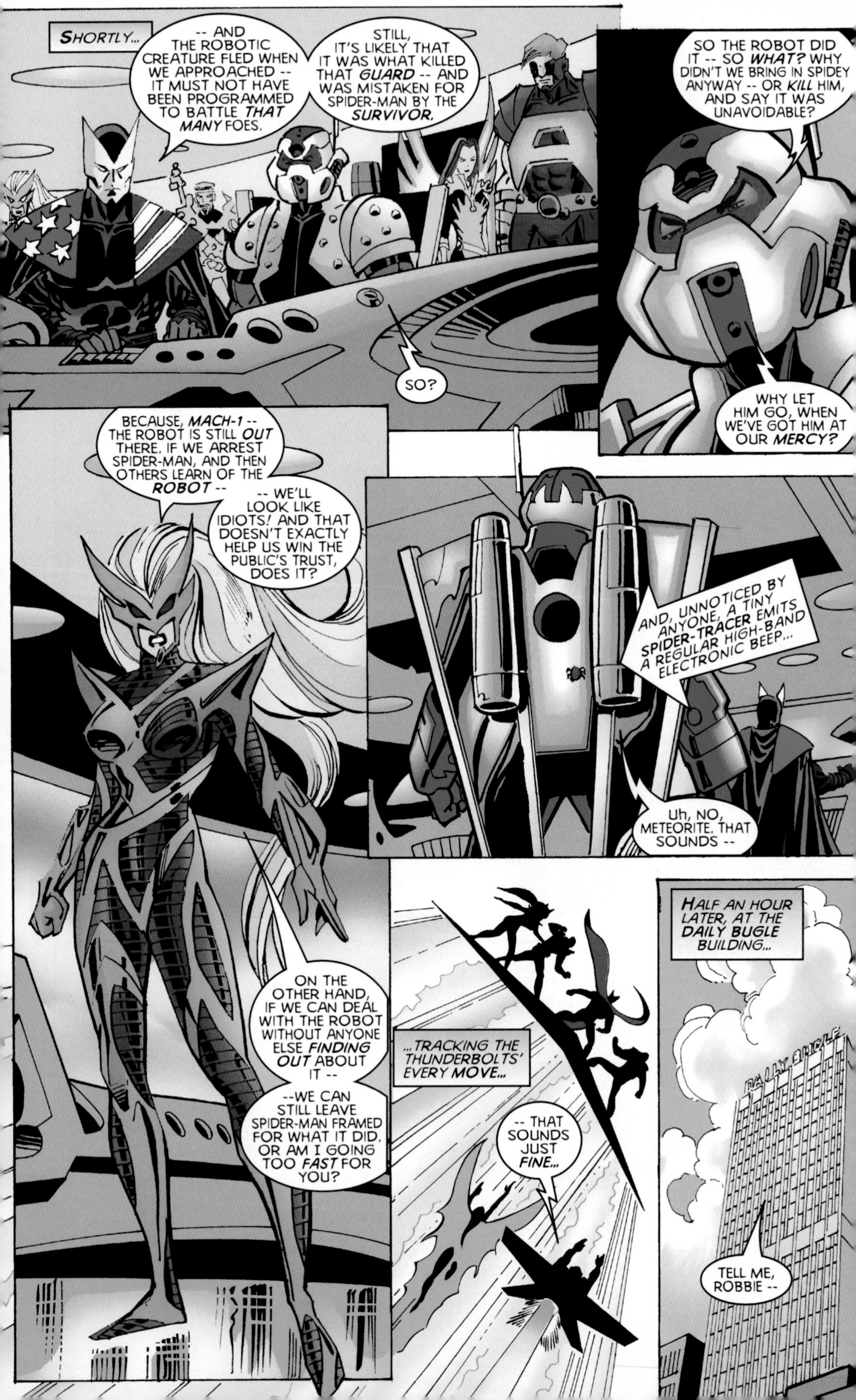
SHORTLY...
-- AND THE ROBOTIC CREATURE FLED WHEN WE APPROACHED -- IT MUST NOT HAVE BEEN PROGRAMMED TO BATTLE THAT MANY FOES.
STILL, IT'S LIKELY THAT IT WAS WHAT KILLED THAT GUARD -- AND WAS MISTAKEN FOR SPIDER-MAN BY THE SURVIVOR.
SO?
SO THE ROBOT DID IT -- SO WHAT? WHY DIDN'T WE BRING IN SPIDEY ANYWAY -- OR KILL HIM, AND SAY IT WAS UNAVOIDABLE?
WHY LET HIM GO, WHEN WE'VE GOT HIM AT OUR MERCY?
BECAUSE, MACH-1 -- THE ROBOT IS STILL OUT THERE. IF WE ARREST SPIDER-MAN, AND THEN OTHERS LEARN OF THE ROBOT --
-- WE'LL LOOK LIKE IDIOTS! AND THAT DOESN'T EXACTLY HELP US WIN THE PUBLIC'S TRUST, DOES IT?
ON THE OTHER HAND, IF WE CAN DEAL WITH THE ROBOT WITHOUT ANYONE ELSE FINDING OUT ABOUT IT --
--WE CAN STILL LEAVE SPIDER-MAN FRAMED FOR WHAT IT DID. OR AM I GOING TOO FAST FOR YOU?
AND, UNNOTICED BY ANYONE, A TINY SPIDER-TRACER EMITS A REGULAR HIGH-BAND ELECTRONIC BEEP...
Uh, NO, METEORITE. THAT SOUNDS --
...TRACKING THE THUNDERBOLTS' EVERY MOVE...
-- THAT SOUNDS JUST FINE...
HALF AN HOUR LATER, AT THE DAILY BUGLE BUILDING...
DAILY BUGLE
TELL ME, ROBBIE --

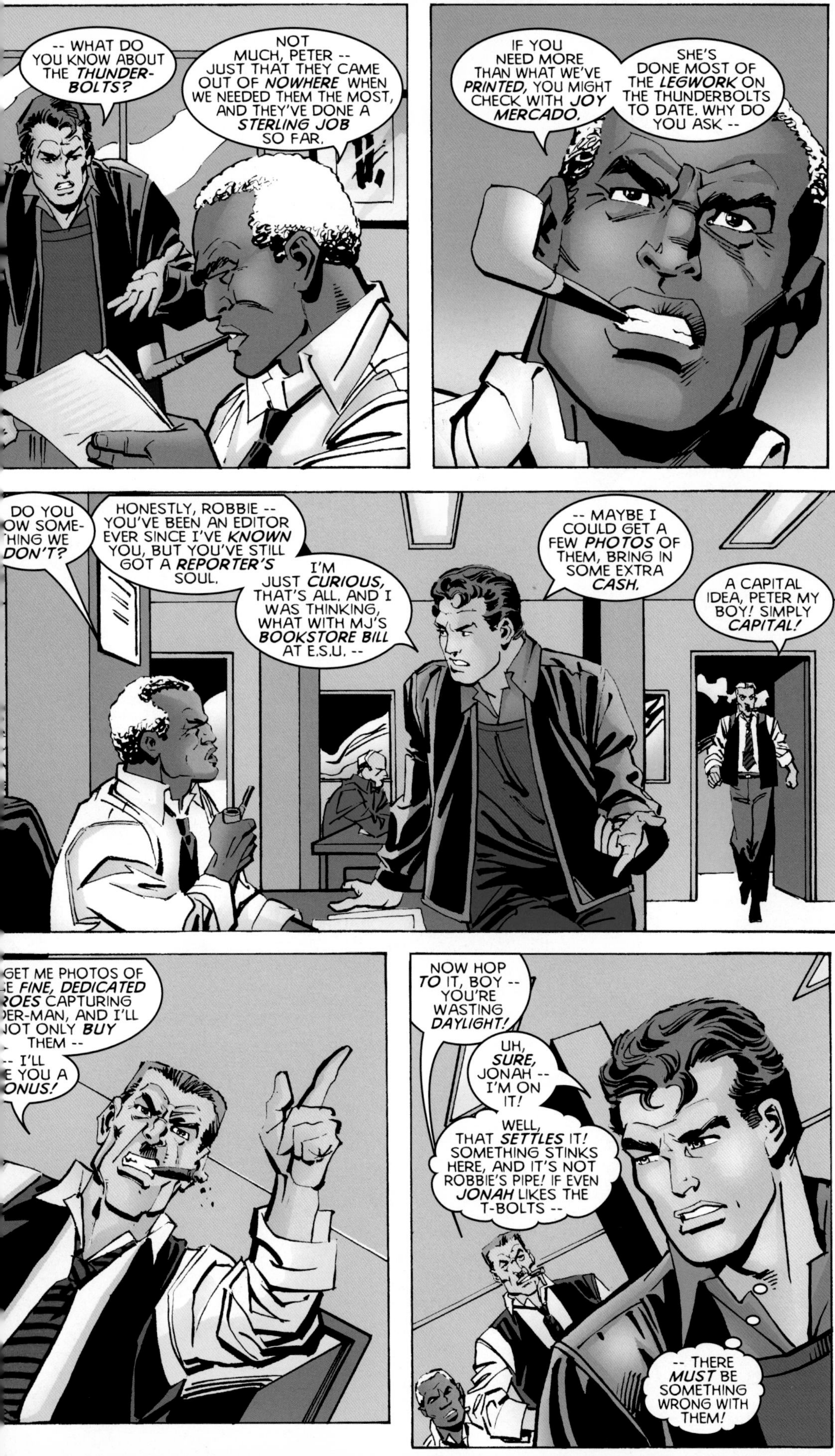
-- WHAT DO YOU KNOW ABOUT THE THUNDER-BOLTS?
NOT MUCH, PETER -- JUST THAT THEY CAME OUT OF NOWHERE WHEN WE NEEDED THEM THE MOST, AND THEY'VE DONE A STERLING JOB SO FAR.
IF YOU NEED MORE THAN WHAT WE'VE PRINTED, YOU MIGHT CHECK WITH JOY MERCADO.
SHE'S DONE MOST OF THE LEGWORK ON THE THUNDERBOLTS TO DATE. WHY DO YOU ASK --
DO YOU OW SOME-THING WE DON'T?
HONESTLY, ROBBIE -- YOU'VE BEEN AN EDITOR EVER SINCE I'VE KNOWN YOU, BUT YOU'VE STILL GOT A REPORTER'S SOUL.
I'M JUST CURIOUS, THAT'S ALL. AND I WAS THINKING, WHAT WITH MJ'S BOOKSTORE BILL AT E.S.U. --
-- MAYBE I COULD GET A FEW PHOTOS OF THEM, BRING IN SOME EXTRA CASH.
A CAPITAL IDEA, PETER MY BOY! SIMPLY CAPITAL!
GET ME PHOTOS OF E FINE, DEDICATED ROES CAPTURING DER-MAN, AND I'LL NOT ONLY BUY THEM --
-- I'LL E YOU A ONUS!
NOW HOP TO IT, BOY -- YOU'RE WASTING DAYLIGHT!
UH, SURE, JONAH -- I'M ON IT!
WELL, THAT SETTLES IT! SOMETHING STINKS HERE, AND IT'S NOT ROBBIE'S PIPE! IF EVEN JONAH LIKES THE T-BOLTS --
-- THERE MUST BE SOMETHING WRONG WITH THEM!

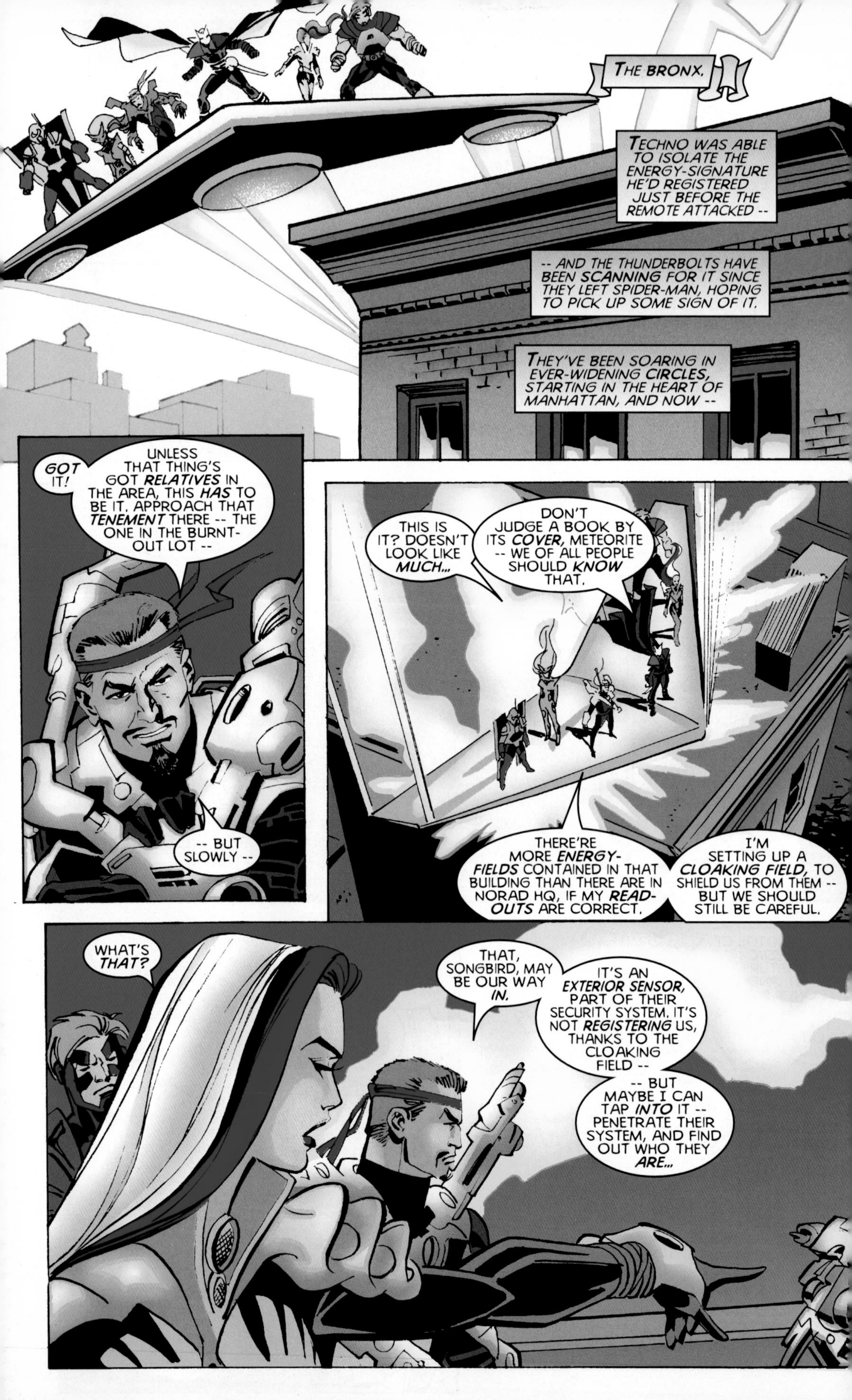
THE BRONX.
TECHNO WAS ABLE TO ISOLATE THE ENERGY-SIGNATURE HE'D REGISTERED JUST BEFORE THE REMOTE ATTACKED --
-- AND THE THUNDERBOLTS HAVE BEEN SCANNING FOR IT SINCE THEY LEFT SPIDER-MAN, HOPING TO PICK UP SOME SIGN OF IT.
THEY'VE BEEN SOARING IN EVER-WIDENING CIRCLES, STARTING IN THE HEART OF MANHATTAN, AND NOW --
GOT IT!
UNLESS THAT THING'S GOT RELATIVES IN THE AREA, THIS HAS TO BE IT. APPROACH THAT TENEMENT THERE -- THE ONE IN THE BURNT-OUT LOT --
-- BUT SLOWLY --
THIS IS IT? DOESN'T LOOK LIKE MUCH...
DON'T JUDGE A BOOK BY ITS COVER, METEORITE -- WE OF ALL PEOPLE SHOULD KNOW THAT.
THERE'RE MORE ENERGY-FIELDS CONTAINED IN THAT BUILDING THAN THERE ARE IN NORAD HQ, IF MY READ-OUTS ARE CORRECT.
I'M SETTING UP A CLOAKING FIELD, TO SHIELD US FROM THEM -- BUT WE SHOULD STILL BE CAREFUL.
WHAT'S THAT?
THAT, SONGBIRD, MAY BE OUR WAY IN.
IT'S AN EXTERIOR SENSOR, PART OF THEIR SECURITY SYSTEM. IT'S NOT REGISTERING US, THANKS TO THE CLOAKING FIELD --
-- BUT MAYBE I CAN TAP INTO IT -- PENETRATE THEIR SYSTEM, AND FIND OUT WHO THEY ARE...

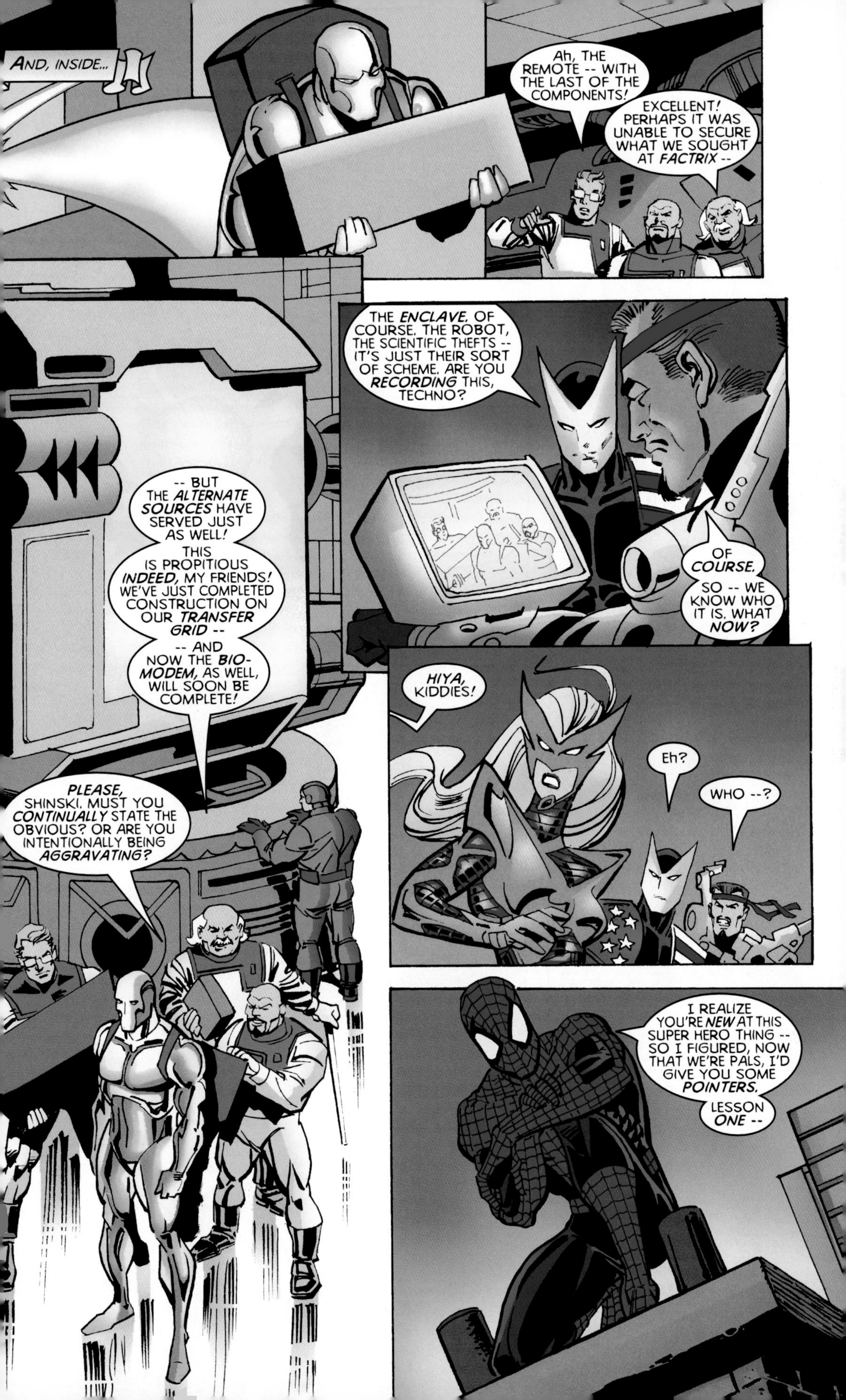
AND, INSIDE...
Ah, THE REMOTE -- WITH THE LAST OF THE COMPONENTS!
EXCELLENT! PERHAPS IT WAS UNABLE TO SECURE WHAT WE SOUGHT AT FACTRIX --
-- BUT THE ALTERNATE SOURCES HAVE SERVED JUST AS WELL!
THIS IS PROPITIOUS INDEED, MY FRIENDS! WE'VE JUST COMPLETED CONSTRUCTION ON OUR TRANSFER GRID --
-- AND NOW THE BIO-MODEM, AS WELL, WILL SOON BE COMPLETE!
PLEASE, SHINSKI, MUST YOU CONTINUALLY STATE THE OBVIOUS? OR ARE YOU INTENTIONALLY BEING AGGRAVATING?
THE ENCLAVE, OF COURSE. THE ROBOT, THE SCIENTIFIC THEFTS -- IT'S JUST THEIR SORT OF SCHEME. ARE YOU RECORDING THIS, TECHNO?
OF COURSE.
SO -- WE KNOW WHO IT IS. WHAT NOW?
HIYA, KIDDIES!
Eh?
WHO --?
I REALIZE YOU'RE NEW AT THIS SUPER HERO THING -- SO I FIGURED, NOW THAT WE'RE PALS, I'D GIVE YOU SOME POINTERS.
LESSON ONE --

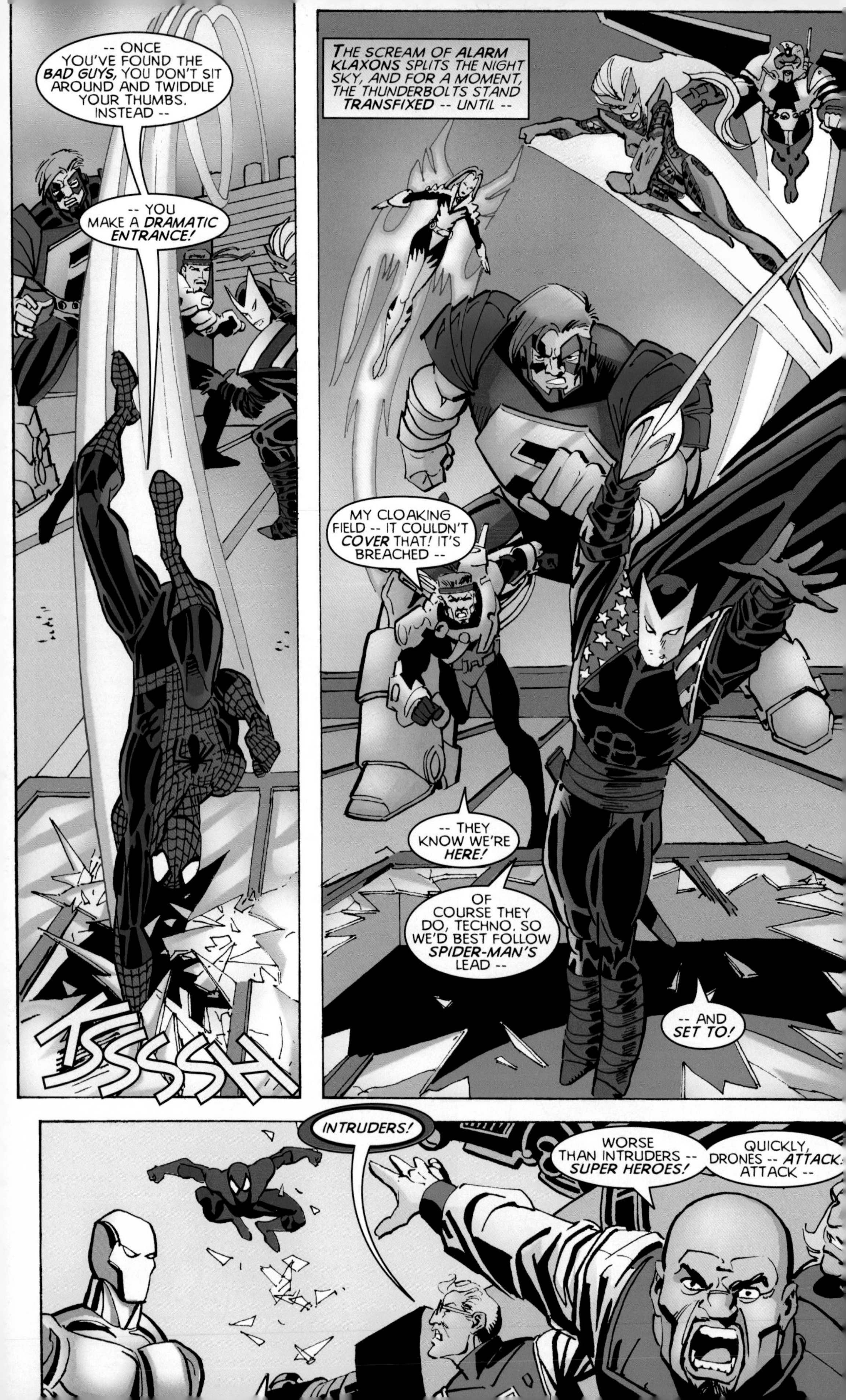
-- ONCE YOU'VE FOUND THE BAD GUYS, YOU DON'T SIT AROUND AND TWIDDLE YOUR THUMBS. INSTEAD --
-- YOU MAKE A DRAMATIC ENTRANCE!
KSSSSH
THE SCREAM OF ALARM KLAXONS SPLITS THE NIGHT SKY, AND FOR A MOMENT, THE THUNDERBOLTS STAND TRANSFIXED -- UNTIL --
MY CLOAKING FIELD -- IT COULDN'T COVER THAT! IT'S BREACHED --
-- THEY KNOW WE'RE HERE!
OF COURSE THEY DO, TECHNO. SO WE'D BEST FOLLOW SPIDER-MAN'S LEAD --
-- AND SET TO!
INTRUDERS!
WORSE THAN INTRUDERS -- SUPER HEROES!
QUICKLY, DRONES -- ATTACK! ATTACK --

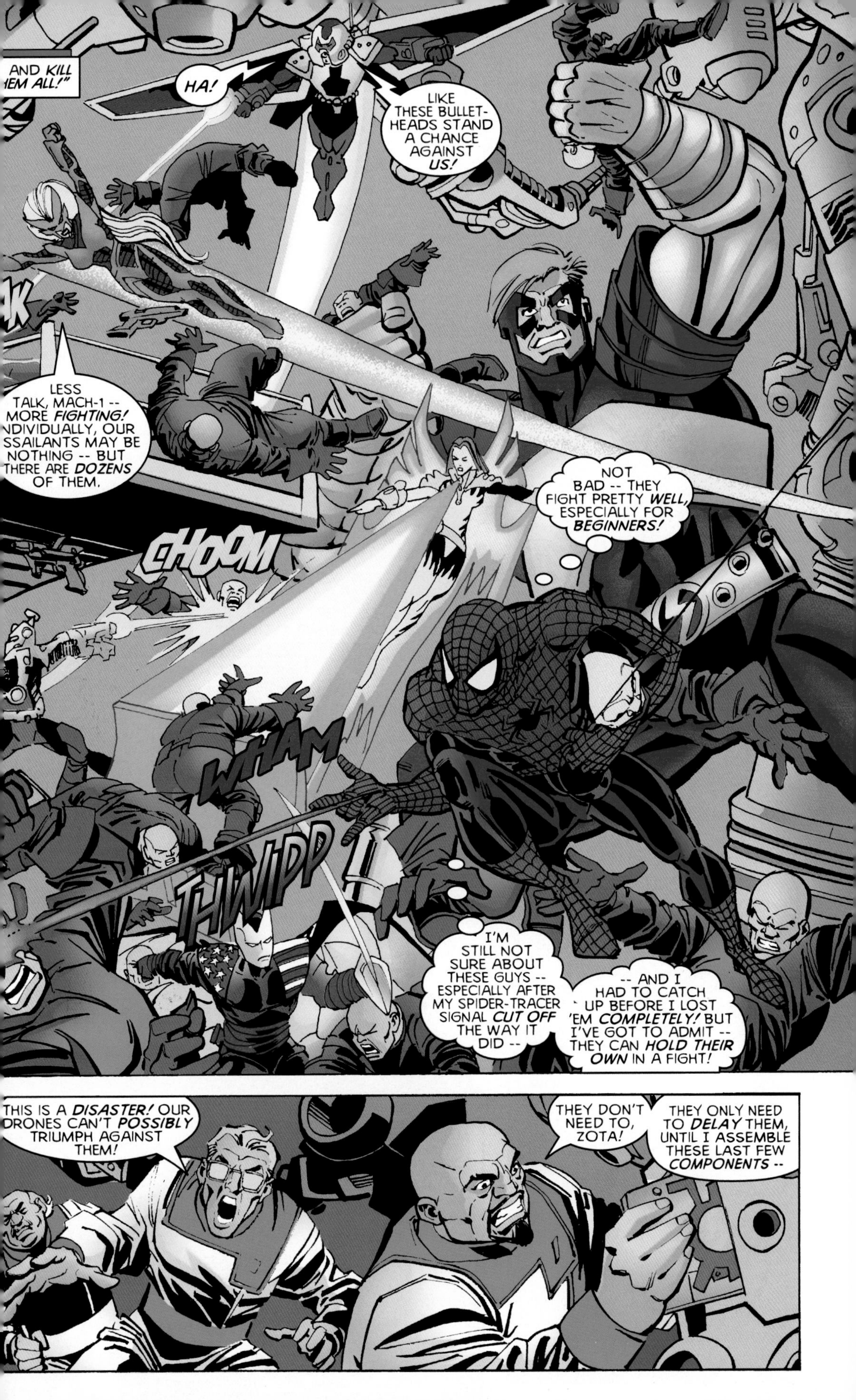
AND KILL
HEM ALL!"
HA!
LIKE THESE BULLET-HEADS STAND A CHANCE AGAINST US!
LESS TALK, MACH-1 -- MORE FIGHTING! NDIVIDUALLY, OUR SSAILANTS MAY BE NOTHING -- BUT THERE ARE DOZENS OF THEM.
NOT BAD -- THEY FIGHT PRETTY WELL, ESPECIALLY FOR BEGINNERS!
CHOOM
WHAM
THWIPP
I'M STILL NOT SURE ABOUT THESE GUYS -- ESPECIALLY AFTER MY SPIDER-TRACER SIGNAL CUT OFF THE WAY IT DID --
-- AND I HAD TO CATCH UP BEFORE I LOST 'EM COMPLETELY! BUT I'VE GOT TO ADMIT -- THEY CAN HOLD THEIR OWN IN A FIGHT!
THIS IS A DISASTER! OUR DRONES CAN'T POSSIBLY TRIUMPH AGAINST THEM!
THEY DON'T NEED TO, ZOTA!
THEY ONLY NEED TO DELAY THEM, UNTIL I ASSEMBLE THESE LAST FEW COMPONENTS --

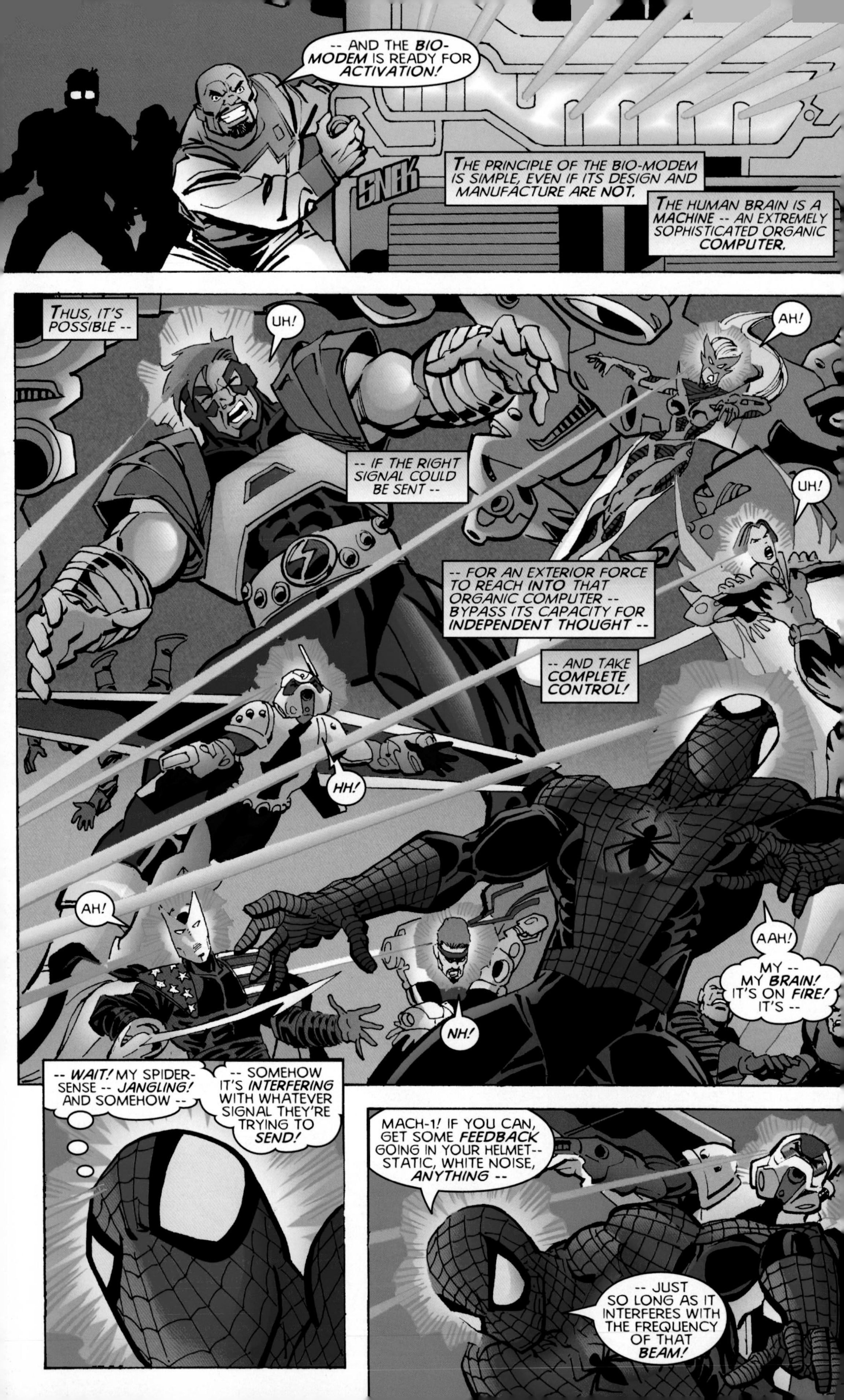
-- AND THE BIO-MODEM IS READY FOR ACTIVATION!
SNEK
THE PRINCIPLE OF THE BIO-MODEM IS SIMPLE, EVEN IF ITS DESIGN AND MANUFACTURE ARE NOT.
THE HUMAN BRAIN IS A MACHINE -- AN EXTREMELY SOPHISTICATED ORGANIC COMPUTER.
THUS, IT'S POSSIBLE --
UH!
AH!
-- IF THE RIGHT SIGNAL COULD BE SENT --
UH!
-- FOR AN EXTERIOR FORCE TO REACH INTO THAT ORGANIC COMPUTER -- BYPASS ITS CAPACITY FOR INDEPENDENT THOUGHT --
-- AND TAKE COMPLETE CONTROL!
HH!
AH!
AAH!
MY -- MY BRAIN! IT'S ON FIRE! IT'S --
NH!
-- WAIT! MY SPIDER-SENSE -- JANGLING! AND SOMEHOW --
-- SOMEHOW IT'S INTERFERING WITH WHATEVER SIGNAL THEY'RE TRYING TO SEND!
MACH-1! IF YOU CAN, GET SOME FEEDBACK GOING IN YOUR HELMET-- STATIC, WHITE NOISE, ANYTHING --
-- JUST SO LONG AS IT INTERFERES WITH THE FREQUENCY OF THAT BEAM!

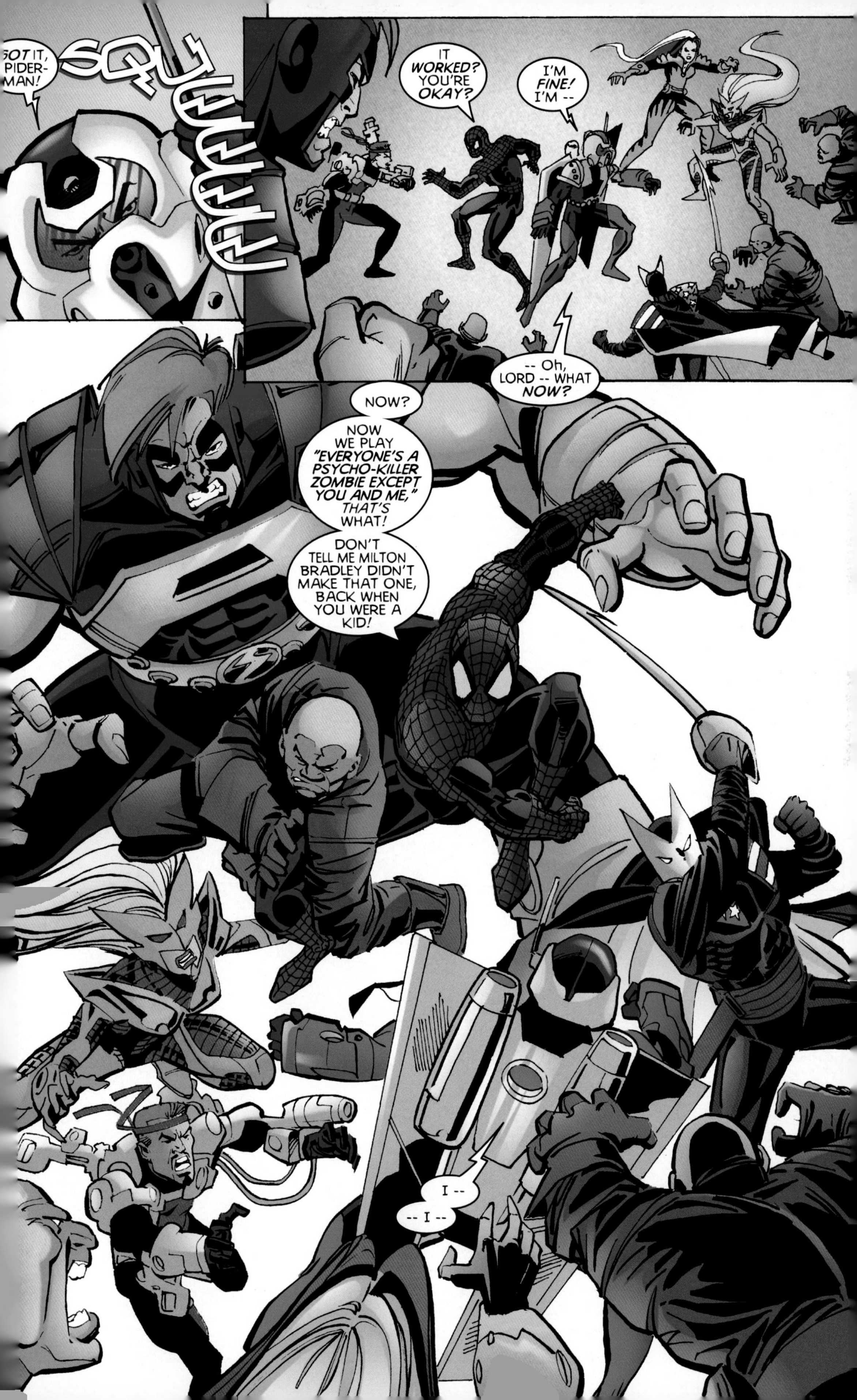

GOT IT, SPIDER-MAN!
SQUUNNN
IT WORKED? YOU'RE OKAY?
I'M FINE! I'M --
-- Oh, LORD -- WHAT NOW?
NOW?
NOW WE PLAY "EVERYONE'S A PSYCHO-KILLER ZOMBIE EXCEPT YOU AND ME," THAT'S WHAT!
DON'T TELL ME MILTON BRADLEY DIDN'T MAKE THAT ONE, BACK WHEN YOU WERE A KID!
I --
-- I --

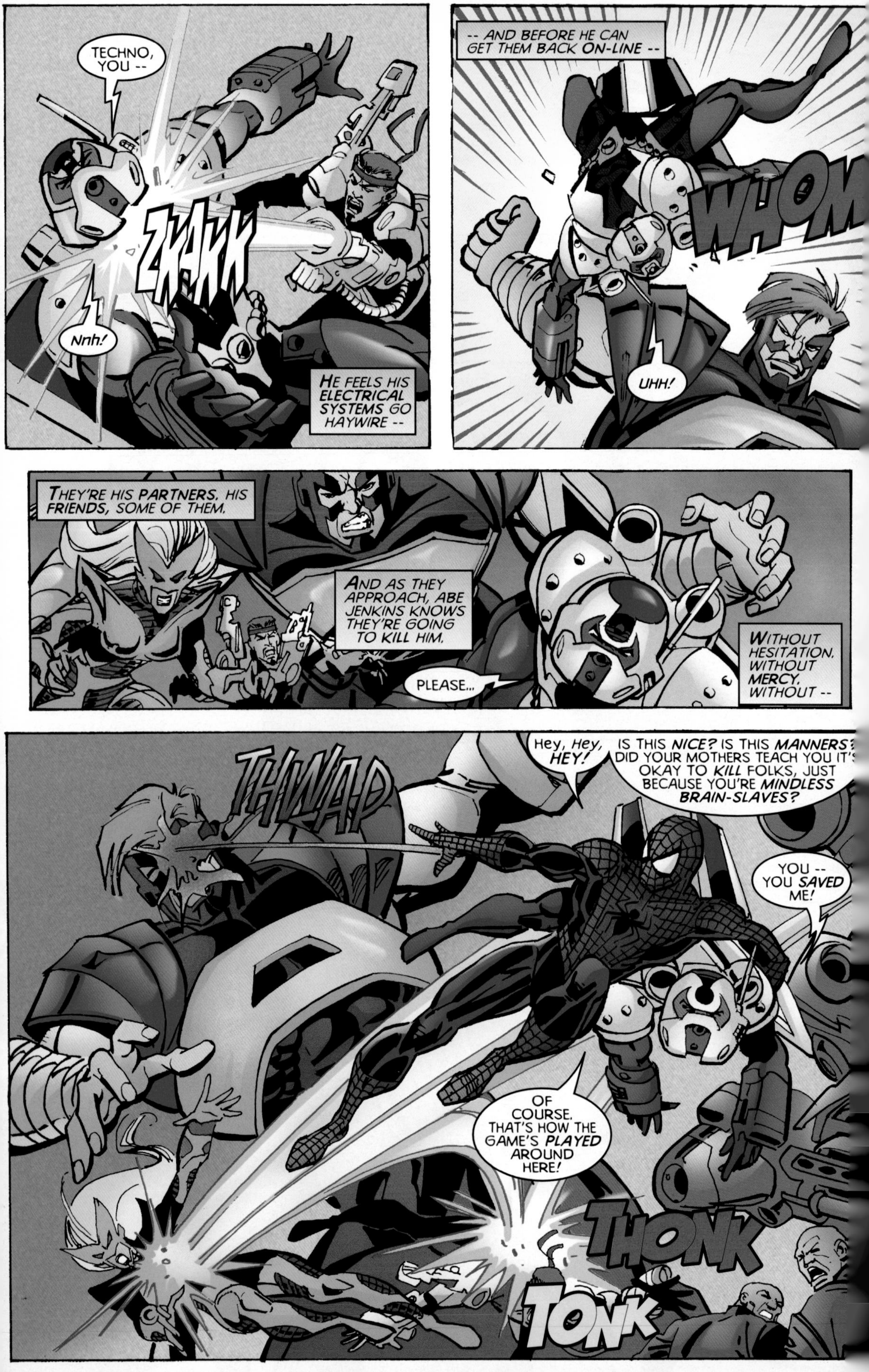
TECHNO, YOU --
ZKAKK
Nnh!
HE FEELS HIS ELECTRICAL SYSTEMS GO HAYWIRE --
-- AND BEFORE HE CAN GET THEM BACK ON-LINE --
WHOM
UHH!
THEY'RE HIS PARTNERS. HIS FRIENDS, SOME OF THEM.
AND AS THEY APPROACH, ABE JENKINS KNOWS THEY'RE GOING TO KILL HIM.
PLEASE...
WITHOUT HESITATION. WITHOUT MERCY. WITHOUT --
THWAP
Hey, Hey, HEY!
IS THIS NICE? IS THIS MANNERS? DID YOUR MOTHERS TEACH YOU IT'S OKAY TO KILL FOLKS, JUST BECAUSE YOU'RE MINDLESS BRAIN-SLAVES?
YOU -- YOU SAVED ME!
OF COURSE. THAT'S HOW THE GAME'S PLAYED AROUND HERE!
THONK
TONK

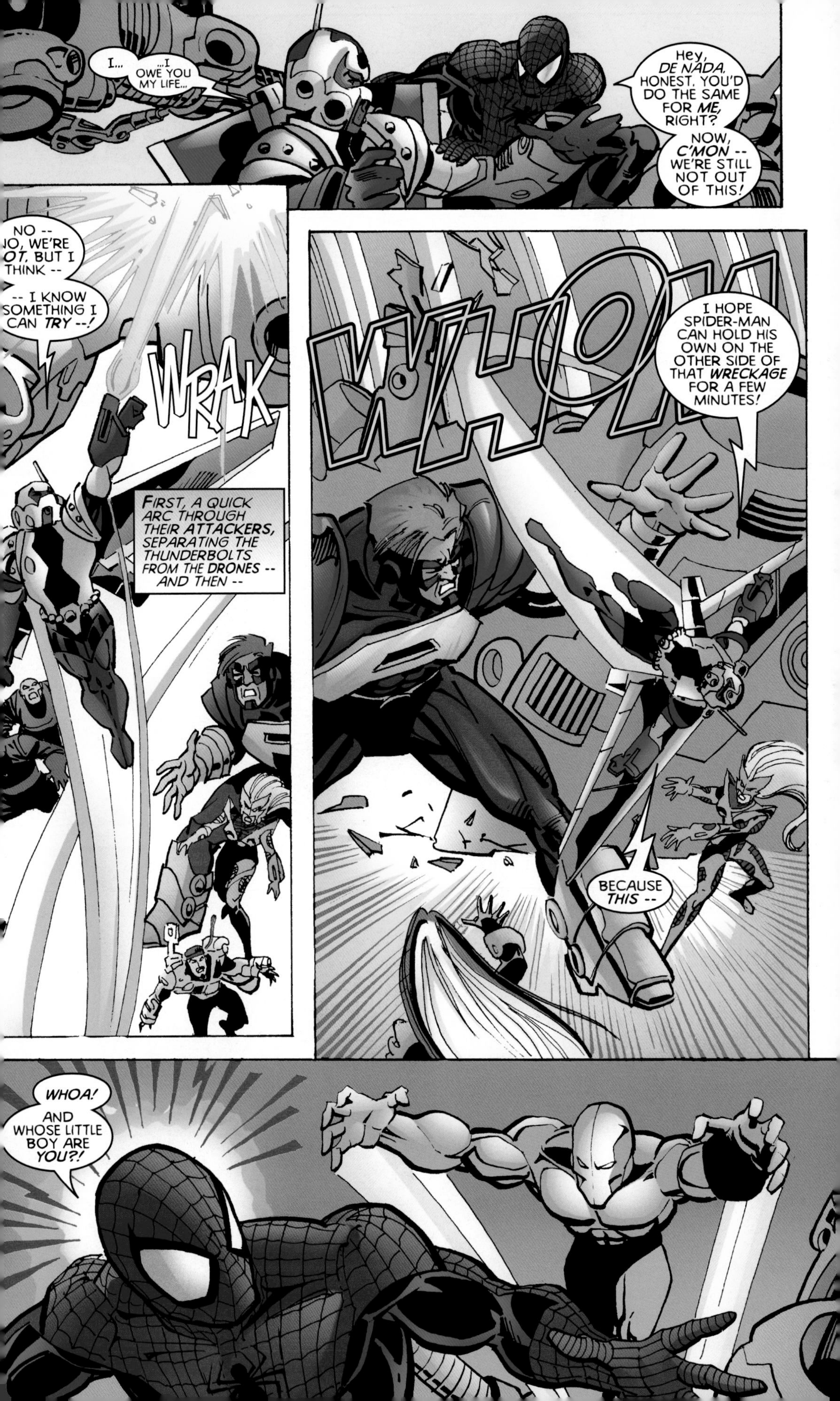
I...
...I OWE YOU MY LIFE...
Hey, DE NADA, HONEST. YOU'D DO THE SAME FOR ME, RIGHT?
NOW, C'MON -- WE'RE STILL NOT OUT OF THIS!
NO -- NO, WE'RE NOT, BUT I THINK --
-- I KNOW SOMETHING I CAN TRY --!
WRAK
FIRST, A QUICK ARC THROUGH THEIR ATTACKERS, SEPARATING THE THUNDERBOLTS FROM THE DRONES -- AND THEN --
WHOM
I HOPE SPIDER-MAN CAN HOLD HIS OWN ON THE OTHER SIDE OF THAT WRECKAGE FOR A FEW MINUTES!
BECAUSE THIS --
WHOA! AND WHOSE LITTLE BOY ARE YOU?!

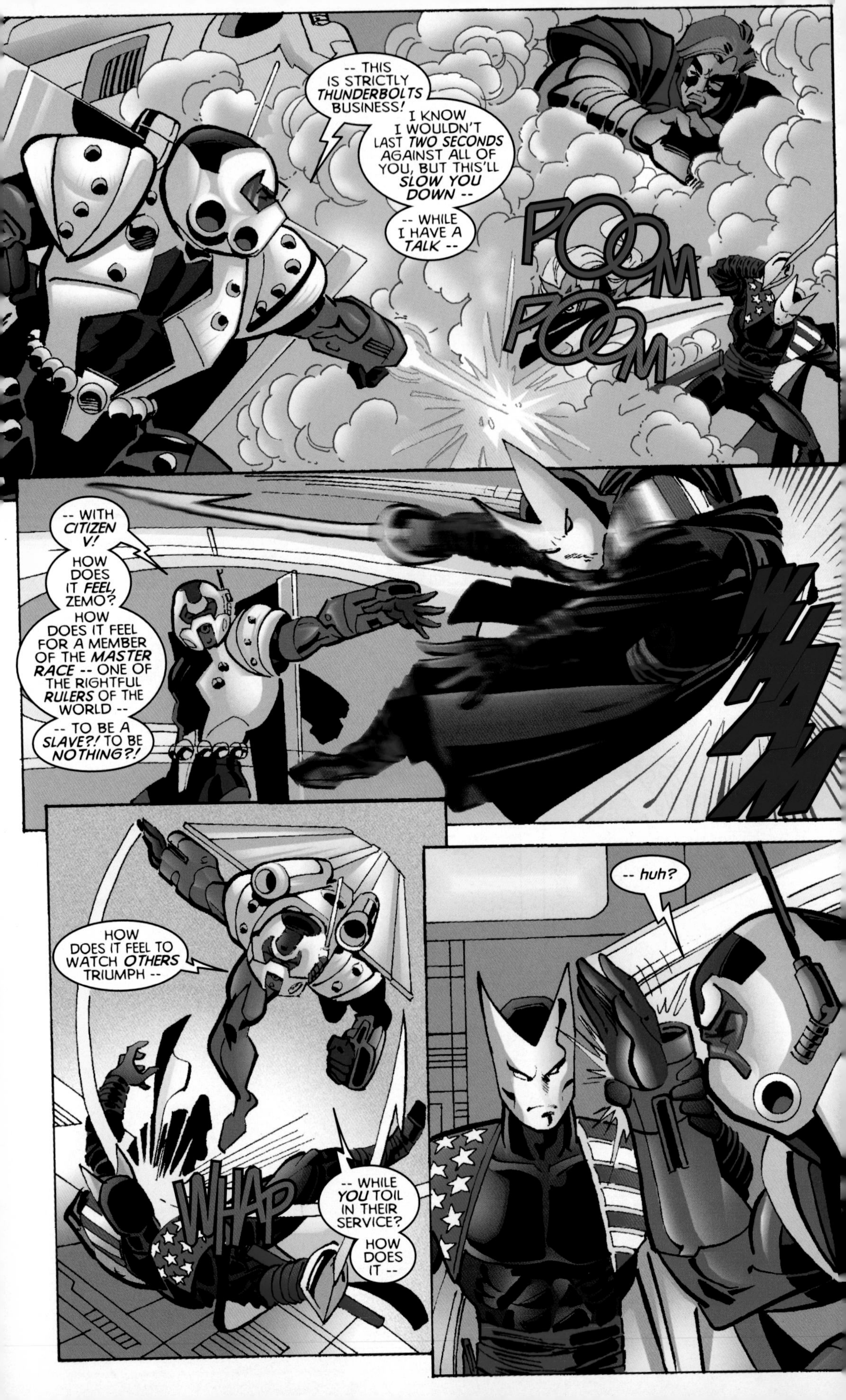
-- THIS IS STRICTLY THUNDERBOLTS BUSINESS!
I KNOW I WOULDN'T LAST TWO SECONDS AGAINST ALL OF YOU, BUT THIS'LL SLOW YOU DOWN --
-- WHILE I HAVE A TALK --
POOM
POOM
-- WITH CITIZEN V!
HOW DOES IT FEEL, ZEMO?
HOW DOES IT FEEL FOR A MEMBER OF THE MASTER RACE -- ONE OF THE RIGHTFUL RULERS OF THE WORLD --
-- TO BE A SLAVE?! TO BE NOTHING?!
WHAM
HOW DOES IT FEEL TO WATCH OTHERS TRIUMPH --
WHAP
-- WHILE YOU TOIL IN THEIR SERVICE?
HOW DOES IT --
-- huh?

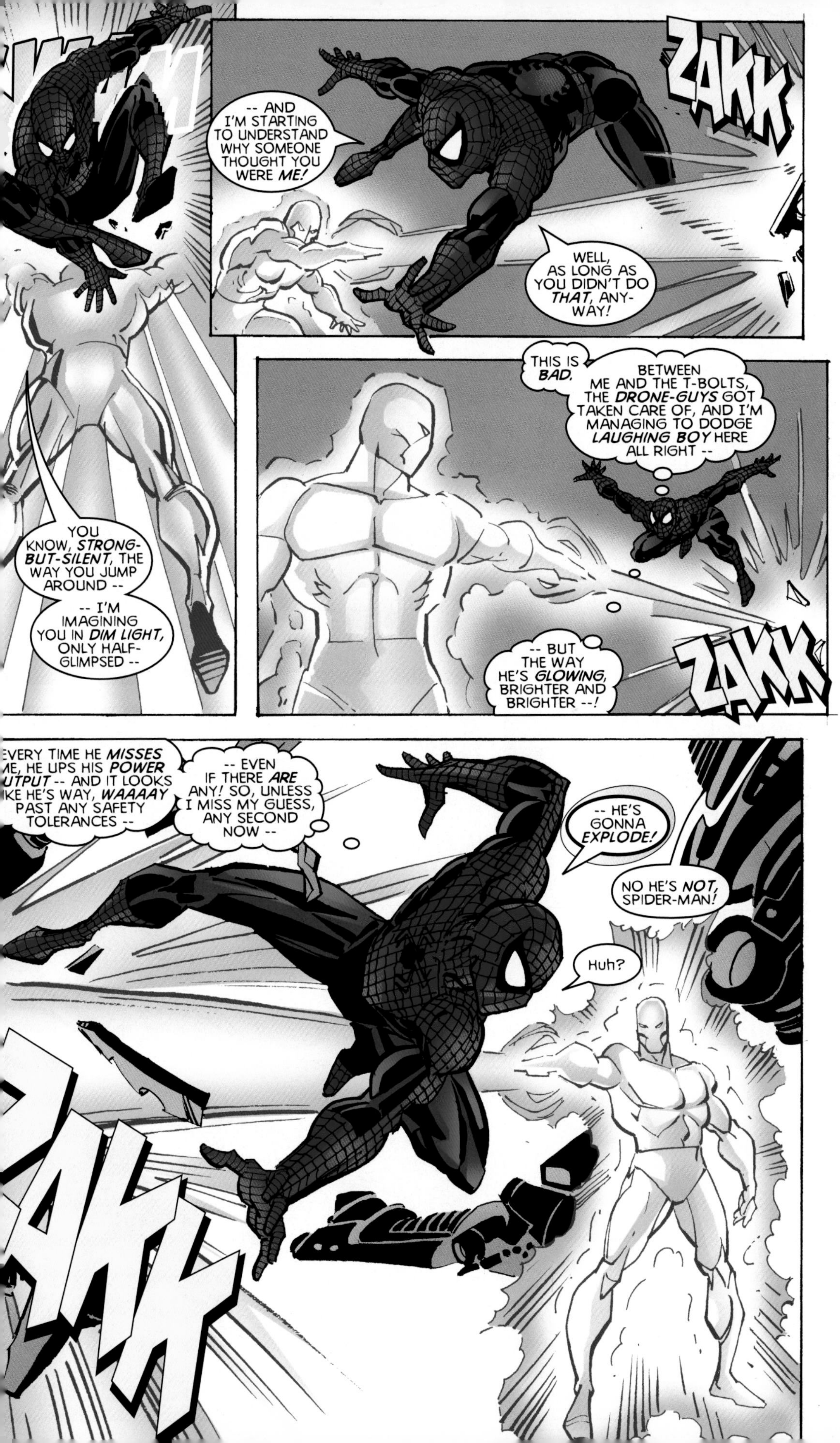

-- AND I'M STARTING TO UNDERSTAND WHY SOMEONE THOUGHT YOU WERE *ME!*
ZAKK
WELL, AS LONG AS YOU DIDN'T DO *THAT*, ANY-WAY!
YOU KNOW, *STRONG-BUT-SILENT*, THE WAY YOU JUMP AROUND --
-- I'M IMAGINING YOU IN *DIM LIGHT*, ONLY HALF-GLIMPSED --
THIS IS *BAD.*
BETWEEN ME AND THE T-BOLTS, THE *DRONE-GUYS* GOT TAKEN CARE OF, AND I'M MANAGING TO DODGE *LAUGHING BOY* HERE ALL RIGHT --
-- BUT THE WAY HE'S *GLOWING*, BRIGHTER AND BRIGHTER --!
ZAKK
EVERY TIME HE *MISSES* ME, HE UPS HIS *POWER* OUTPUT -- AND IT LOOKS LIKE HE'S WAY, *WAAAAY* PAST ANY SAFETY TOLERANCES --
-- EVEN IF THERE *ARE* ANY! SO, UNLESS I MISS MY GUESS, ANY SECOND NOW --
-- HE'S GONNA *EXPLODE!*
NO HE'S *NOT*, SPIDER-MAN!
Huh?

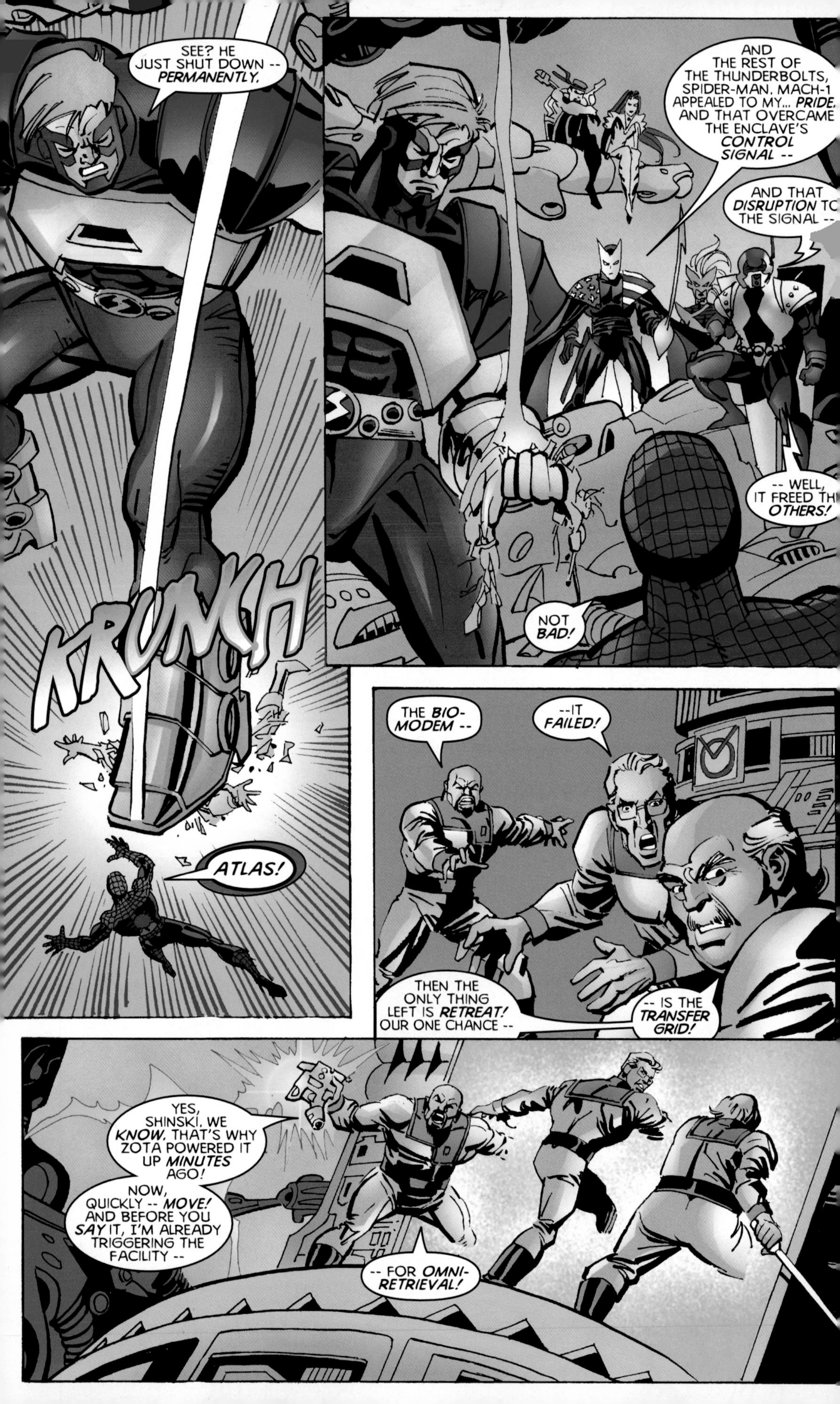
SEE? HE JUST SHUT DOWN -- PERMANENTLY.
KRUNCH
ATLAS!
AND THE REST OF THE THUNDERBOLTS, SPIDER-MAN. MACH-1 APPEALED TO MY... PRIDE, AND THAT OVERCAME THE ENCLAVE'S CONTROL SIGNAL --
AND THAT DISRUPTION TO THE SIGNAL --
-- WELL, IT FREED THE OTHERS!
NOT BAD!
THE BIO-MODEM --
--IT FAILED!
THEN THE ONLY THING LEFT IS RETREAT! OUR ONE CHANCE --
-- IS THE TRANSFER GRID!
YES, SHINSKI, WE KNOW. THAT'S WHY ZOTA POWERED IT UP MINUTES AGO!
NOW, QUICKLY -- MOVE! AND BEFORE YOU SAY IT, I'M ALREADY TRIGGERING THE FACILITY --
-- FOR OMNI-RETRIEVAL!

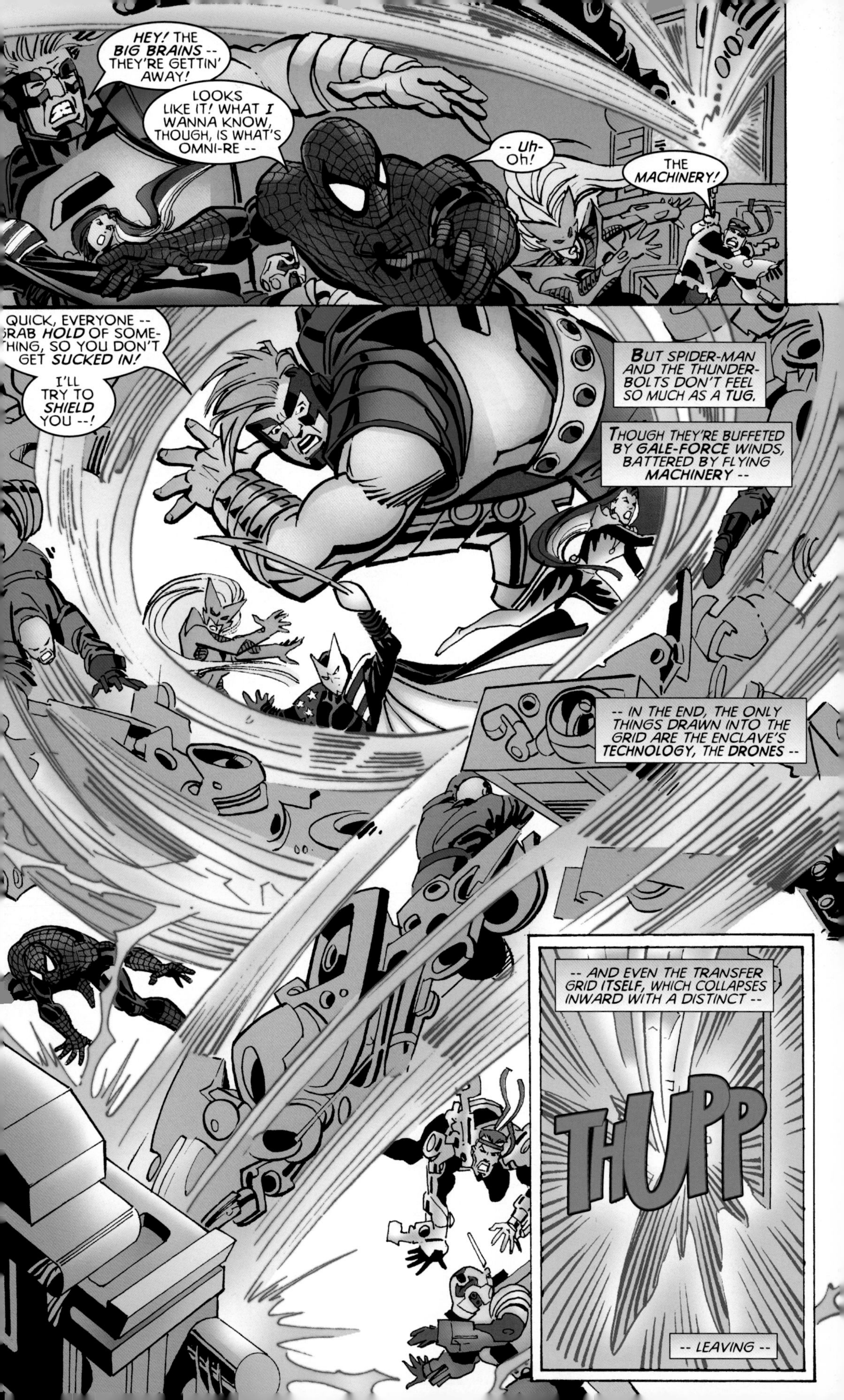
HEY! THE BIG BRAINS -- THEY'RE GETTIN' AWAY!
LOOKS LIKE IT! WHAT I WANNA KNOW, THOUGH, IS WHAT'S OMNI-RE --
-- Uh-Oh!
THE MACHINERY!
QUICK, EVERYONE -- GRAB HOLD OF SOMETHING, SO YOU DON'T GET SUCKED IN!
I'LL TRY TO SHIELD YOU --!
BUT SPIDER-MAN AND THE THUNDERBOLTS DON'T FEEL SO MUCH AS A TUG.
THOUGH THEY'RE BUFFETED BY GALE-FORCE WINDS, BATTERED BY FLYING MACHINERY --
-- IN THE END, THE ONLY THINGS DRAWN INTO THE GRID ARE THE ENCLAVE'S TECHNOLOGY, THE DRONES --
-- AND EVEN THE TRANSFER GRID ITSELF, WHICH COLLAPSES INWARD WITH A DISTINCT --
THUPP
-- LEAVING --

NOTHING! THEY CLEANED THE WHOLE PLACE OUT -- IN SECONDS!

SHEESH! THEY COULD MAKE A FORTUNE IN THE LONG-DISTANCE MOVING BUSINESS, THAT'S FOR SURE!

Oh, WELL, WE PUT THE KIBOSH ON THIS PARTICULAR SCHEME, ANY-WAY.

BUT THEY'RE STILL OUT THERE, SOMEWHERE, AND WORSE, AT LEAST FOR ME --

-- THEY'VE BUGGED OUT WITH EVERY SCRAP OF EVIDENCE I COULD USE TO CLEAR MYSELF!

BUT, UH -- YOU GUYS'LL BACK ME UP, RIGHT?

CITIZEN V? METEORITE?

Psst -- TECHNO! YOU RECORDED THE ENCLAVE BEFORE WE BUSTED IN, RIGHT?

DIGITAL DOLBY AND EVERYTHING -- WHY?

LET ME HAVE A COPY!

SURE, BUT WHAT DO YOU --

HERE YOU GO, SPIDER-MAN, THE DATA ON THIS DISK CLEARLY SHOWS THE ENCLAVE'S ROBOT DELIVERING STOLEN COMPONENTS.

IT SHOUL... ALL Y... NEE...

HEY, GREAT!

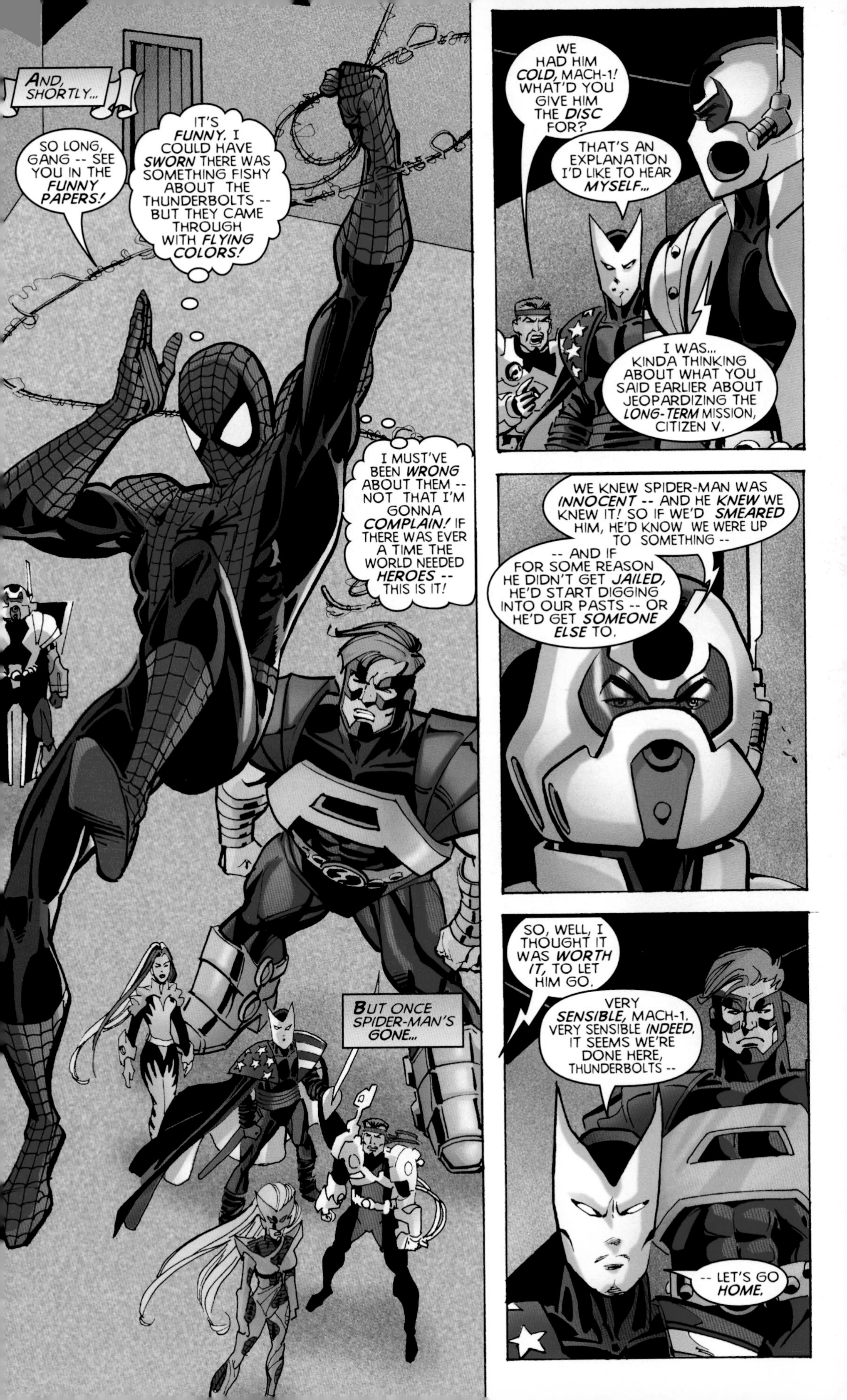
AND, SHORTLY...
SO LONG, GANG -- SEE YOU IN THE FUNNY PAPERS!
IT'S FUNNY. I COULD HAVE SWORN THERE WAS SOMETHING FISHY ABOUT THE THUNDERBOLTS -- BUT THEY CAME THROUGH WITH FLYING COLORS!
I MUST'VE BEEN WRONG ABOUT THEM -- NOT THAT I'M GONNA COMPLAIN! IF THERE WAS EVER A TIME THE WORLD NEEDED HEROES -- THIS IS IT!
BUT ONCE SPIDER-MAN'S GONE...
WE HAD HIM COLD, MACH-1! WHAT'D YOU GIVE HIM THE DISC FOR?
THAT'S AN EXPLANATION I'D LIKE TO HEAR MYSELF...
I WAS... KINDA THINKING ABOUT WHAT YOU SAID EARLIER ABOUT JEOPARDIZING THE LONG-TERM MISSION, CITIZEN V.
WE KNEW SPIDER-MAN WAS INNOCENT -- AND HE KNEW WE KNEW IT! SO IF WE'D SMEARED HIM, HE'D KNOW WE WERE UP TO SOMETHING --
-- AND IF FOR SOME REASON HE DIDN'T GET JAILED, HE'D START DIGGING INTO OUR PASTS -- OR HE'D GET SOMEONE ELSE TO.
SO, WELL, I THOUGHT IT WAS WORTH IT, TO LET HIM GO.
VERY SENSIBLE, MACH-1. VERY SENSIBLE INDEED. IT SEEMS WE'RE DONE HERE, THUNDERBOLTS --
-- LET'S GO HOME.

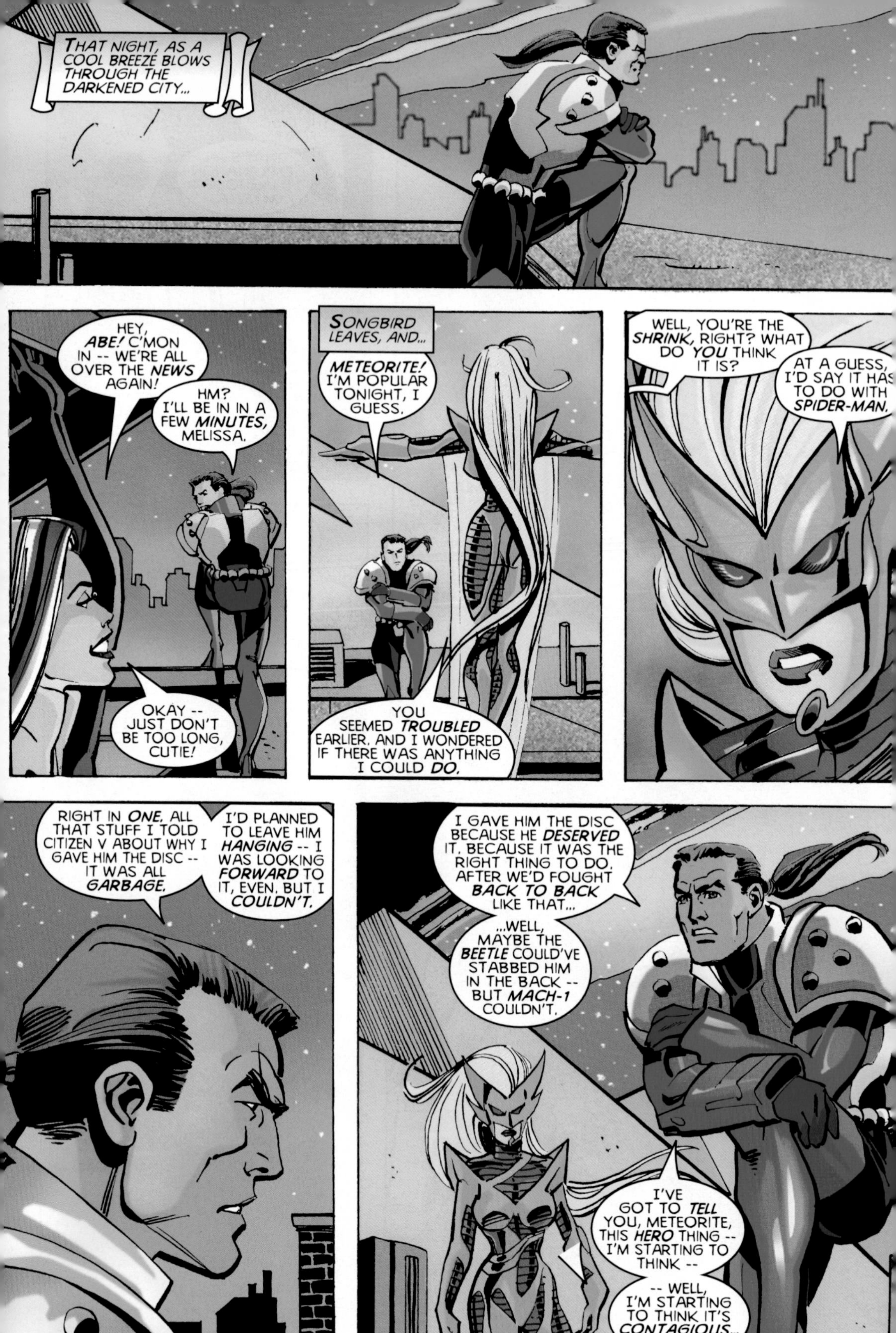
THAT NIGHT, AS A COOL BREEZE BLOWS THROUGH THE DARKENED CITY...
HEY, ABE! C'MON IN -- WE'RE ALL OVER THE NEWS AGAIN!
HM? I'LL BE IN IN A FEW MINUTES, MELISSA.
OKAY -- JUST DON'T BE TOO LONG, CUTIE!
SONGBIRD LEAVES, AND...
METEORITE! I'M POPULAR TONIGHT, I GUESS.
YOU SEEMED TROUBLED EARLIER, AND I WONDERED IF THERE WAS ANYTHING I COULD DO.
WELL, YOU'RE THE SHRINK, RIGHT? WHAT DO YOU THINK IT IS?
AT A GUESS, I'D SAY IT HAS TO DO WITH SPIDER-MAN.
RIGHT IN ONE. ALL THAT STUFF I TOLD CITIZEN V ABOUT WHY I GAVE HIM THE DISC -- IT WAS ALL GARBAGE.
I'D PLANNED TO LEAVE HIM HANGING -- I WAS LOOKING FORWARD TO IT, EVEN, BUT I COULDN'T.
I GAVE HIM THE DISC BECAUSE HE DESERVED IT. BECAUSE IT WAS THE RIGHT THING TO DO, AFTER WE'D FOUGHT BACK TO BACK LIKE THAT...
...WELL, MAYBE THE BEETLE COULD'VE STABBED HIM IN THE BACK -- BUT MACH-1 COULDN'T.
I'VE GOT TO TELL YOU, METEORITE, THIS HERO THING -- I'M STARTING TO THINK --
-- WELL, I'M STARTING TO THINK IT'S CONTAGIOUS...

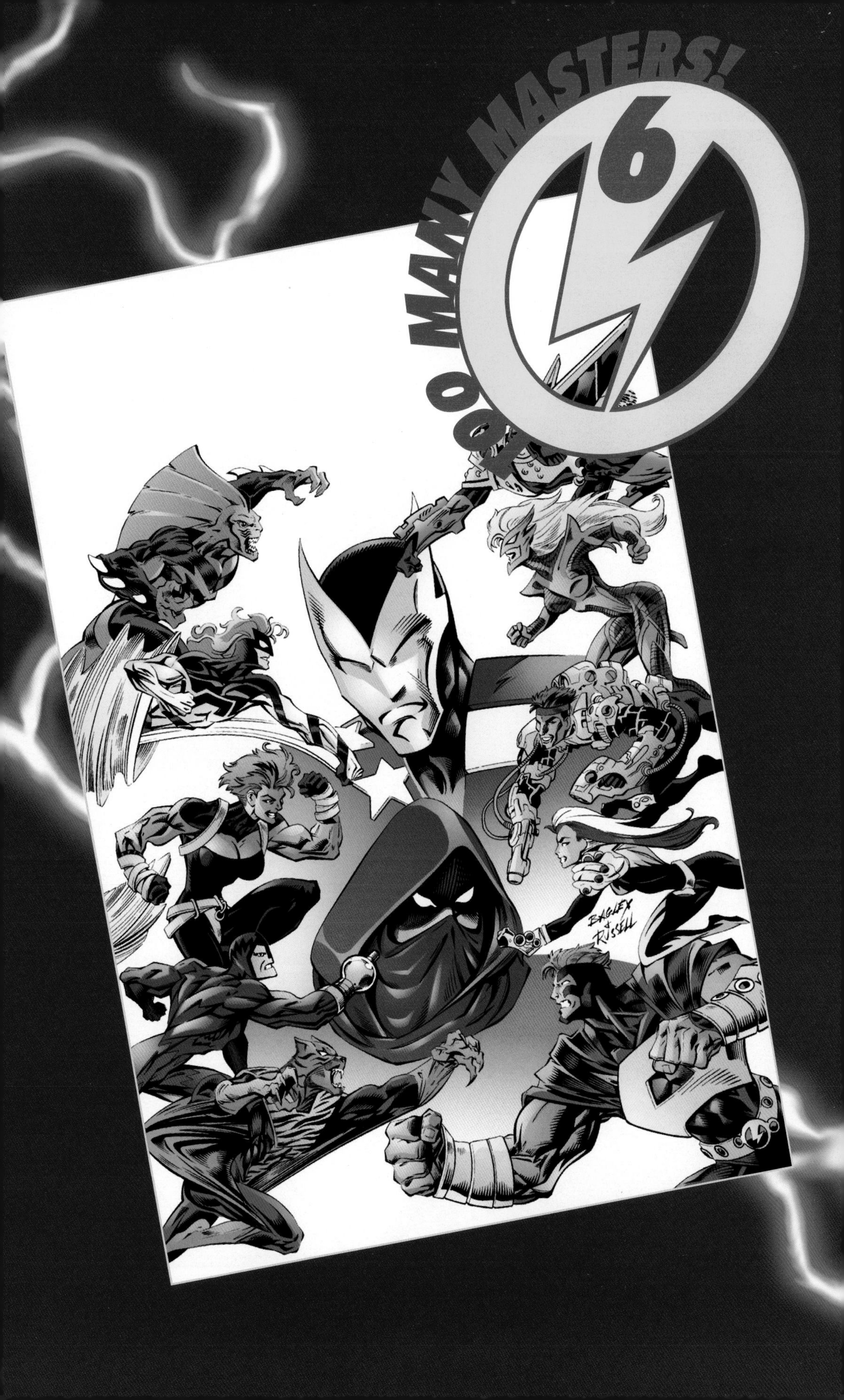
TOO MANY MASTERS!
6
BAGLEY
RUSSELL

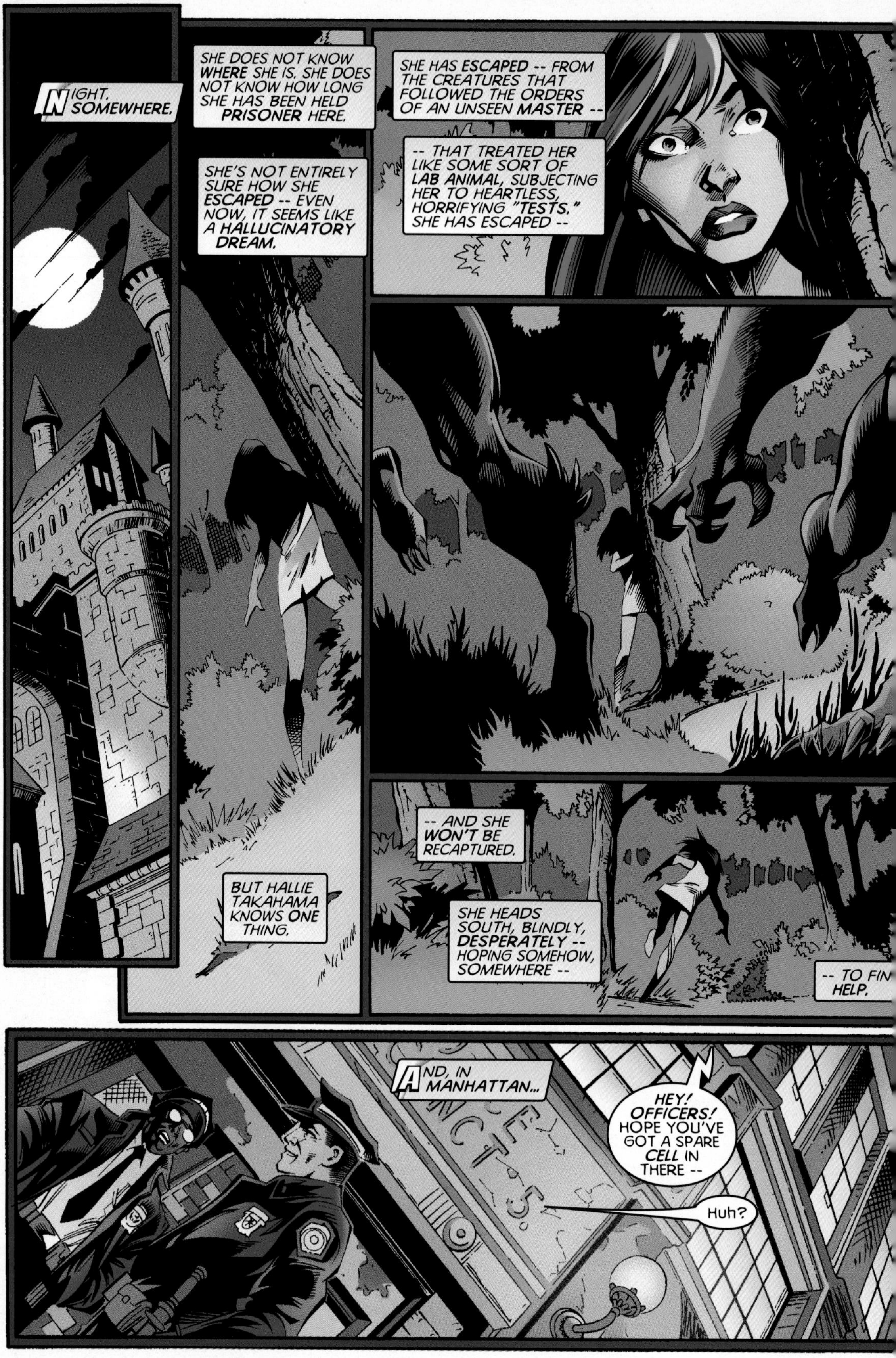
NIGHT, SOMEWHERE.
SHE DOES NOT KNOW WHERE SHE IS, SHE DOES NOT KNOW HOW LONG SHE HAS BEEN HELD PRISONER HERE.
SHE'S NOT ENTIRELY SURE HOW SHE ESCAPED -- EVEN NOW, IT SEEMS LIKE A HALLUCINATORY DREAM.
BUT HALLIE TAKAHAMA KNOWS ONE THING.
SHE HAS ESCAPED -- FROM THE CREATURES THAT FOLLOWED THE ORDERS OF AN UNSEEN MASTER --
-- THAT TREATED HER LIKE SOME SORT OF LAB ANIMAL, SUBJECTING HER TO HEARTLESS, HORRIFYING "TESTS." SHE HAS ESCAPED --
-- AND SHE WON'T BE RECAPTURED.
SHE HEADS SOUTH, BLINDLY, DESPERATELY -- HOPING SOMEHOW, SOMEWHERE --
-- TO FIN
HELP.
AND, IN MANHATTAN...
HEY! OFFICERS! HOPE YOU'VE GOT A SPARE CELL IN THERE --
Huh?

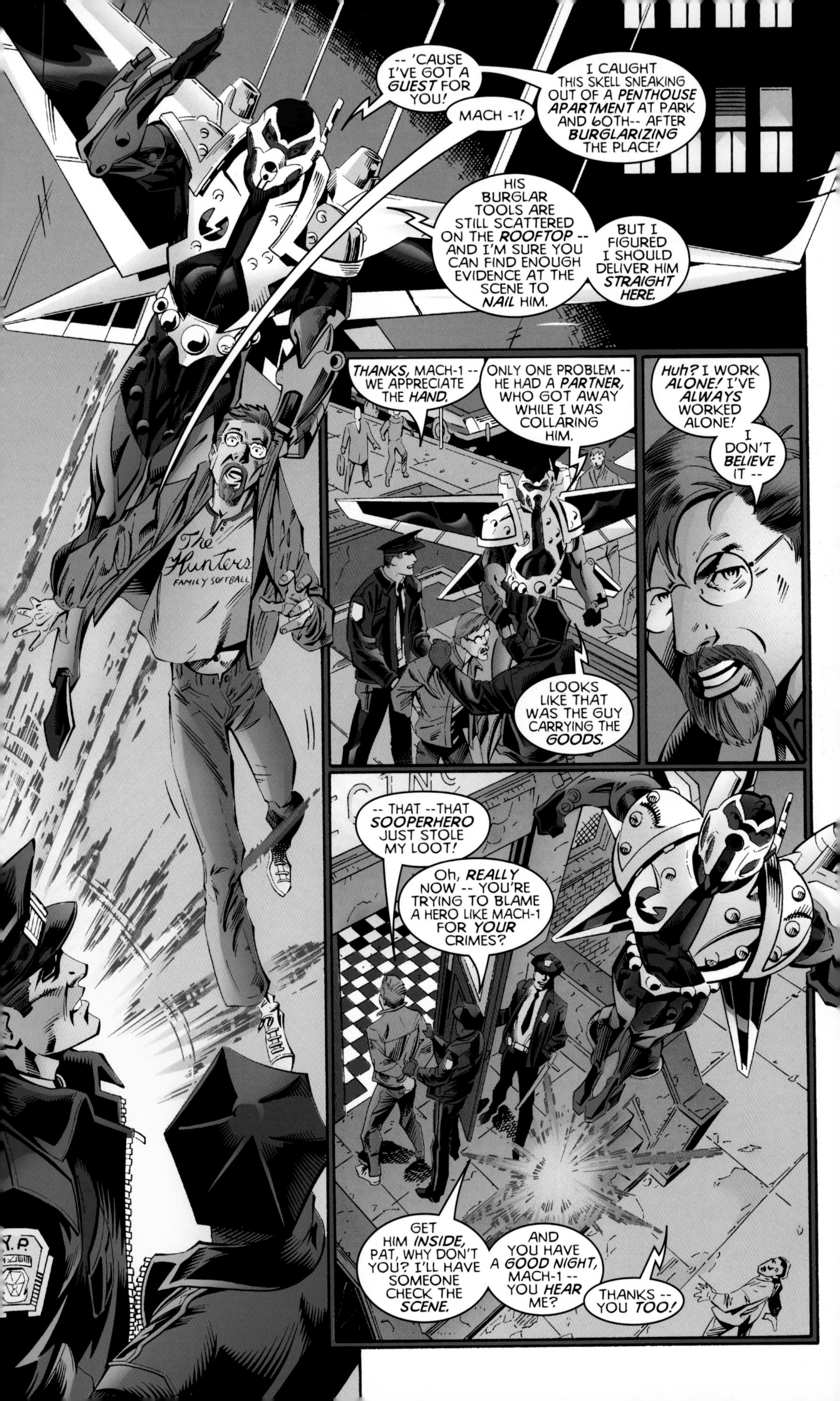
-- 'CAUSE I'VE GOT A GUEST FOR YOU!
MACH -1!
I CAUGHT THIS SKELL SNEAKING OUT OF A PENTHOUSE APARTMENT AT PARK AND 60TH-- AFTER BURGLARIZING THE PLACE!
HIS BURGLAR TOOLS ARE STILL SCATTERED ON THE ROOFTOP -- AND I'M SURE YOU CAN FIND ENOUGH EVIDENCE AT THE SCENE TO NAIL HIM.
BUT I FIGURED I SHOULD DELIVER HIM STRAIGHT HERE.
The Hunters FAMILY SOFTBALL
THANKS, MACH-1 -- WE APPRECIATE THE HAND.
ONLY ONE PROBLEM -- HE HAD A PARTNER, WHO GOT AWAY WHILE I WAS COLLARING HIM.
LOOKS LIKE THAT WAS THE GUY CARRYING THE GOODS.
Huh? I WORK ALONE! I'VE ALWAYS WORKED ALONE!
I DON'T BELIEVE IT --
-- THAT --THAT SOOPERHERO JUST STOLE MY LOOT!
Oh, REALLY NOW -- YOU'RE TRYING TO BLAME A HERO LIKE MACH-1 FOR YOUR CRIMES?
GET HIM INSIDE, PAT, WHY DON'T YOU? I'LL HAVE SOMEONE CHECK THE SCENE.
AND YOU HAVE A GOOD NIGHT, MACH-1 -- YOU HEAR ME?
THANKS -- YOU TOO!

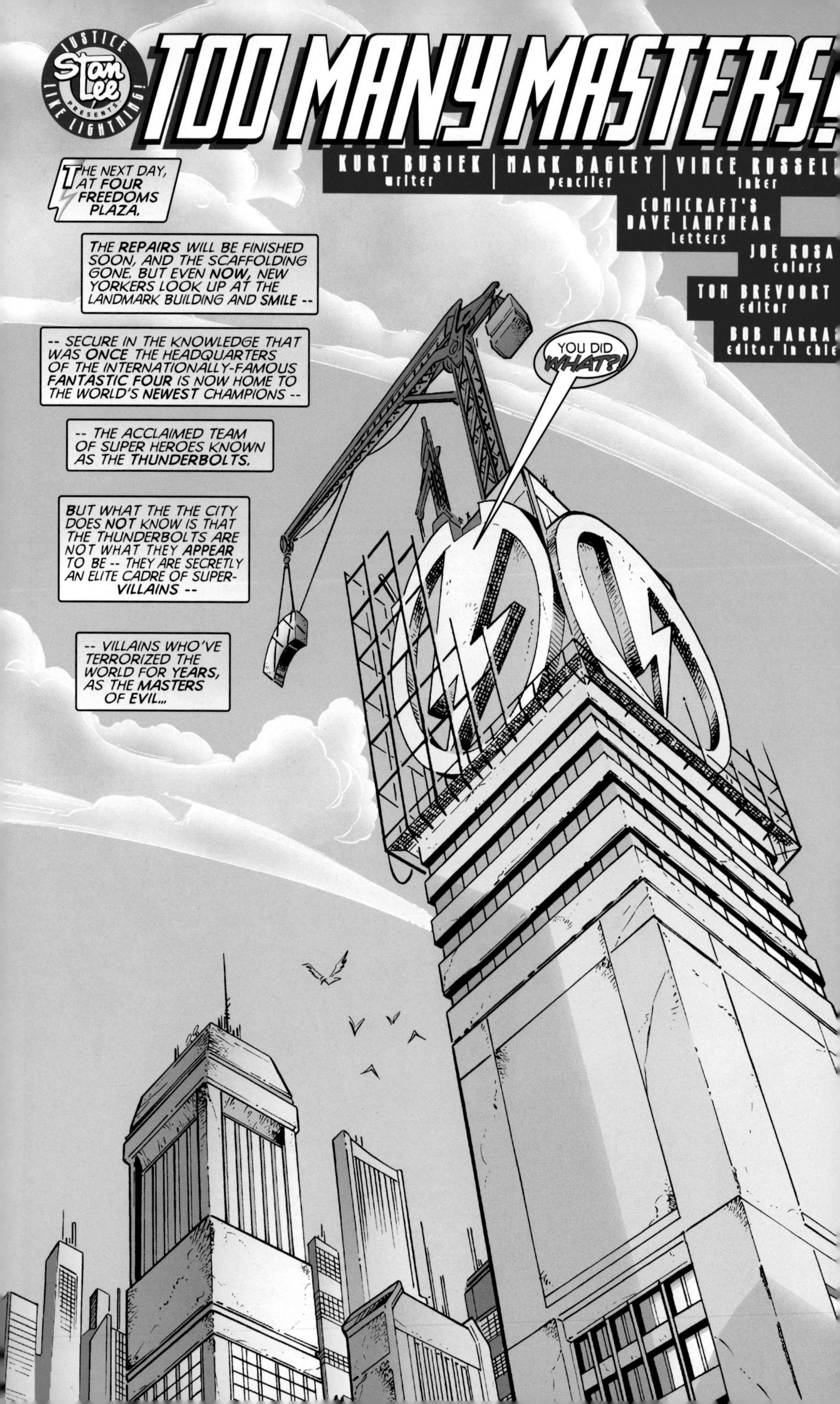

JUSTICE LIKE LIGHTNING! Stan Lee PRESENTS
TOO MANY MASTERS!
KURT BUSIEK writer | MARK BAGLEY penciler | VINCE RUSSELL inker
COMICRAFT'S DAVE LANPHEAR letters
JOE ROSA colors
TOM BREVOORT editor
BOB HARRAS editor in chief
THE NEXT DAY, AT FOUR FREEDOMS PLAZA.
THE REPAIRS WILL BE FINISHED SOON, AND THE SCAFFOLDING GONE. BUT EVEN NOW, NEW YORKERS LOOK UP AT THE LANDMARK BUILDING AND SMILE --
-- SECURE IN THE KNOWLEDGE THAT WAS ONCE THE HEADQUARTERS OF THE INTERNATIONALLY-FAMOUS FANTASTIC FOUR IS NOW HOME TO THE WORLD'S NEWEST CHAMPIONS --
-- THE ACCLAIMED TEAM OF SUPER HEROES KNOWN AS THE THUNDERBOLTS.
BUT WHAT THE THE CITY DOES NOT KNOW IS THAT THE THUNDERBOLTS ARE NOT WHAT THEY APPEAR TO BE -- THEY ARE SECRETLY AN ELITE CADRE OF SUPER-VILLAINS --
-- VILLAINS WHO'VE TERRORIZED THE WORLD FOR YEARS, AS THE MASTERS OF EVIL...
YOU DID WHAT?!

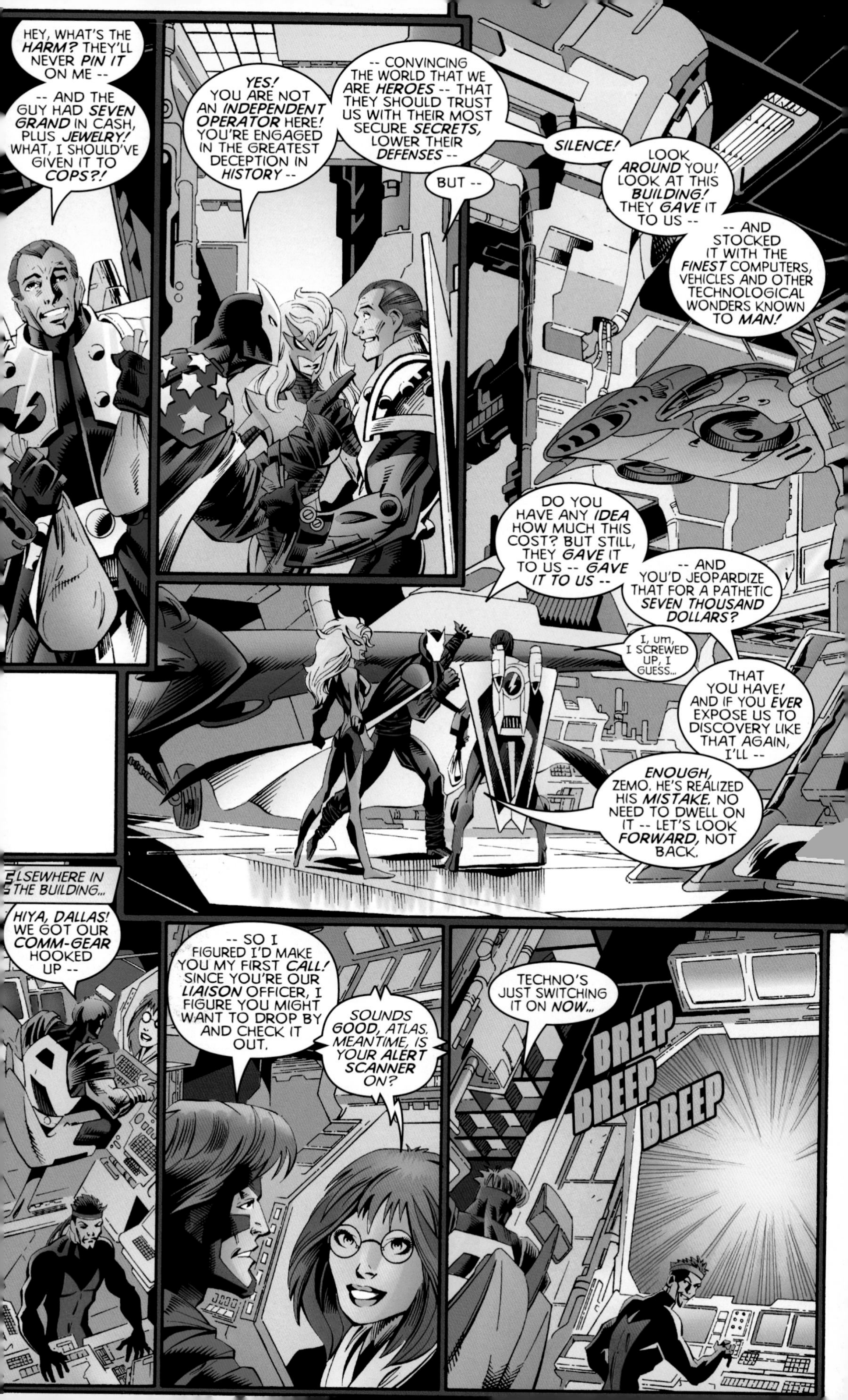
HEY, WHAT'S THE HARM? THEY'LL NEVER PIN IT ON ME --
-- AND THE GUY HAD SEVEN GRAND IN CASH, PLUS JEWELRY! WHAT, I SHOULD'VE GIVEN IT TO COPS?!
YES! YOU ARE NOT AN INDEPENDENT OPERATOR HERE! YOU'RE ENGAGED IN THE GREATEST DECEPTION IN HISTORY --
-- CONVINCING THE WORLD THAT WE ARE HEROES -- THAT THEY SHOULD TRUST US WITH THEIR MOST SECURE SECRETS, LOWER THEIR DEFENSES --
BUT --
SILENCE!
LOOK AROUND YOU! LOOK AT THIS BUILDING! THEY GAVE IT TO US --
-- AND STOCKED IT WITH THE FINEST COMPUTERS, VEHICLES AND OTHER TECHNOLOGICAL WONDERS KNOWN TO MAN!
DO YOU HAVE ANY IDEA HOW MUCH THIS COST? BUT STILL, THEY GAVE IT TO US -- GAVE IT TO US --
-- AND YOU'D JEOPARDIZE THAT FOR A PATHETIC SEVEN THOUSAND DOLLARS?
I, UM, I SCREWED UP, I GUESS...
THAT YOU HAVE! AND IF YOU EVER EXPOSE US TO DISCOVERY LIKE THAT AGAIN, I'LL --
ENOUGH, ZEMO. HE'S REALIZED HIS MISTAKE, NO NEED TO DWELL ON IT -- LET'S LOOK FORWARD, NOT BACK.
ELSEWHERE IN THE BUILDING...
HIYA, DALLAS! WE GOT OUR COMM-GEAR HOOKED UP --
-- SO I FIGURED I'D MAKE YOU MY FIRST CALL! SINCE YOU'RE OUR LIAISON OFFICER, I FIGURE YOU MIGHT WANT TO DROP BY AND CHECK IT OUT.
SOUNDS GOOD, ATLAS. MEANTIME, IS YOUR ALERT SCANNER ON?
TECHNO'S JUST SWITCHING IT ON NOW...
BREEP BREEP BREEP

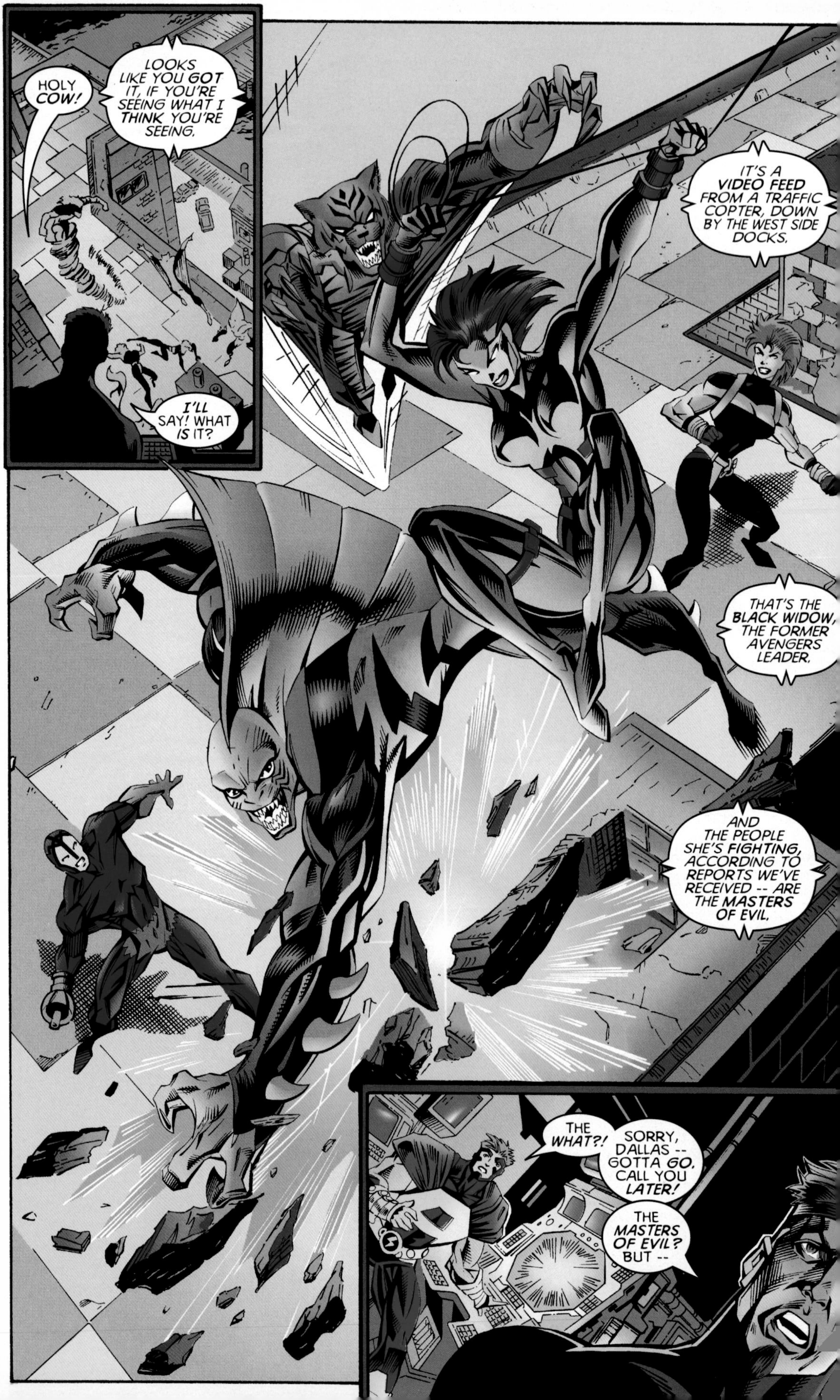
HOLY COW!
LOOKS LIKE YOU GOT IT, IF YOU'RE SEEING WHAT I THINK YOU'RE SEEING.
I'LL SAY! WHAT IS IT?
IT'S A VIDEO FEED FROM A TRAFFIC COPTER, DOWN BY THE WEST SIDE DOCKS.
THAT'S THE BLACK WIDOW, THE FORMER AVENGERS LEADER.
AND THE PEOPLE SHE'S FIGHTING, ACCORDING TO REPORTS WE'VE RECEIVED -- ARE THE MASTERS OF EVIL.
THE WHAT?!
SORRY, DALLAS -- GOTTA GO. CALL YOU LATER!
THE MASTERS OF EVIL? BUT --

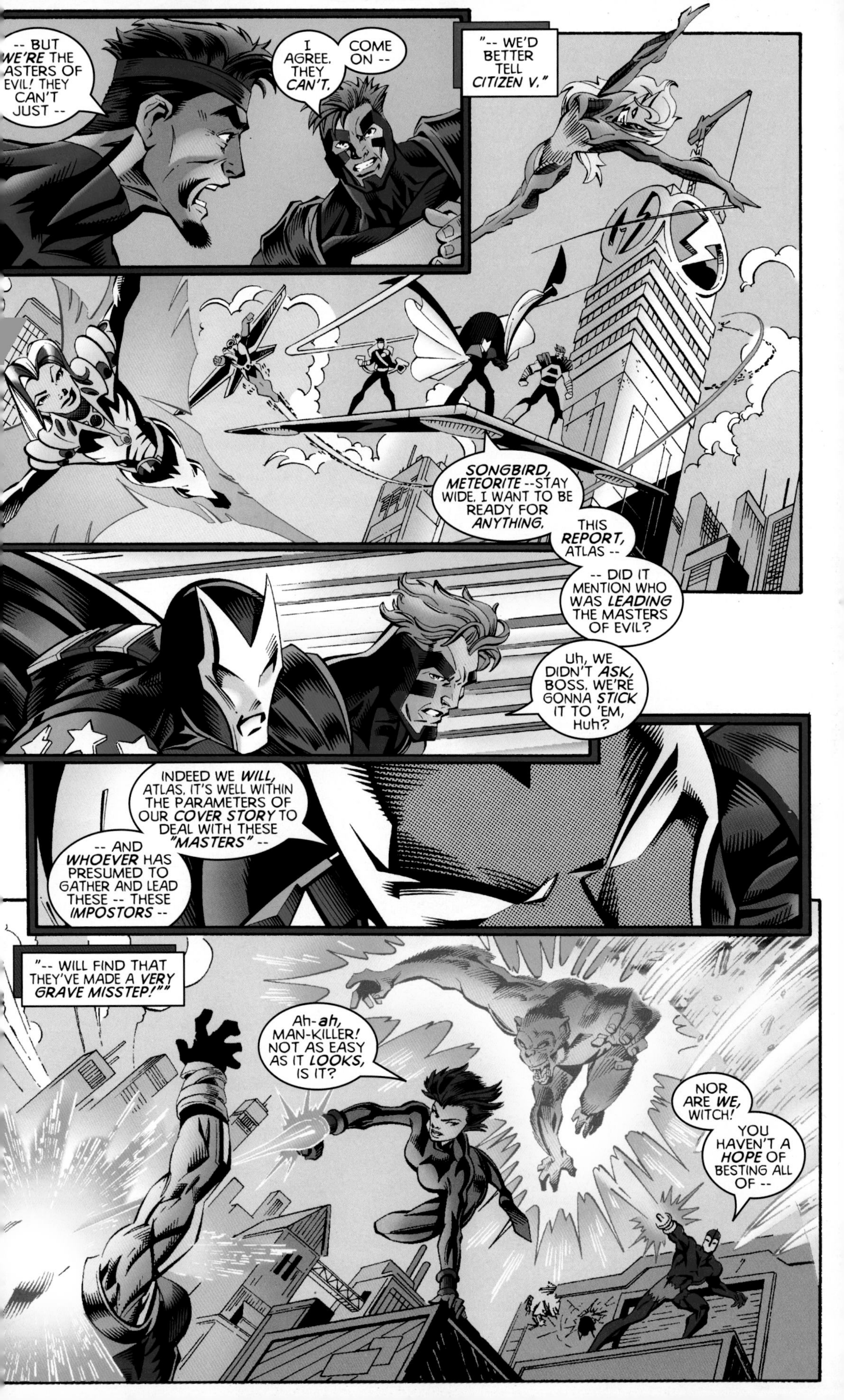
-- BUT WE'RE THE ASTERS OF EVIL! THEY CAN'T JUST --
I AGREE. THEY CAN'T.
COME ON --
"-- WE'D BETTER TELL CITIZEN V."
SONGBIRD, METEORITE --STAY WIDE. I WANT TO BE READY FOR ANYTHING.
THIS REPORT, ATLAS --
-- DID IT MENTION WHO WAS LEADING THE MASTERS OF EVIL?
Uh, WE DIDN'T ASK, BOSS. WE'RE GONNA STICK IT TO 'EM, Huh?
INDEED WE WILL, ATLAS. IT'S WELL WITHIN THE PARAMETERS OF OUR COVER STORY TO DEAL WITH THESE "MASTERS" --
-- AND WHOEVER HAS PRESUMED TO GATHER AND LEAD THESE -- THESE IMPOSTORS --
"-- WILL FIND THAT THEY'VE MADE A VERY GRAVE MISSTEP!""
Ah-ah, MAN-KILLER! NOT AS EASY AS IT LOOKS, IS IT?
NOR ARE WE, WITCH!
YOU HAVEN'T A HOPE OF BESTING ALL OF --

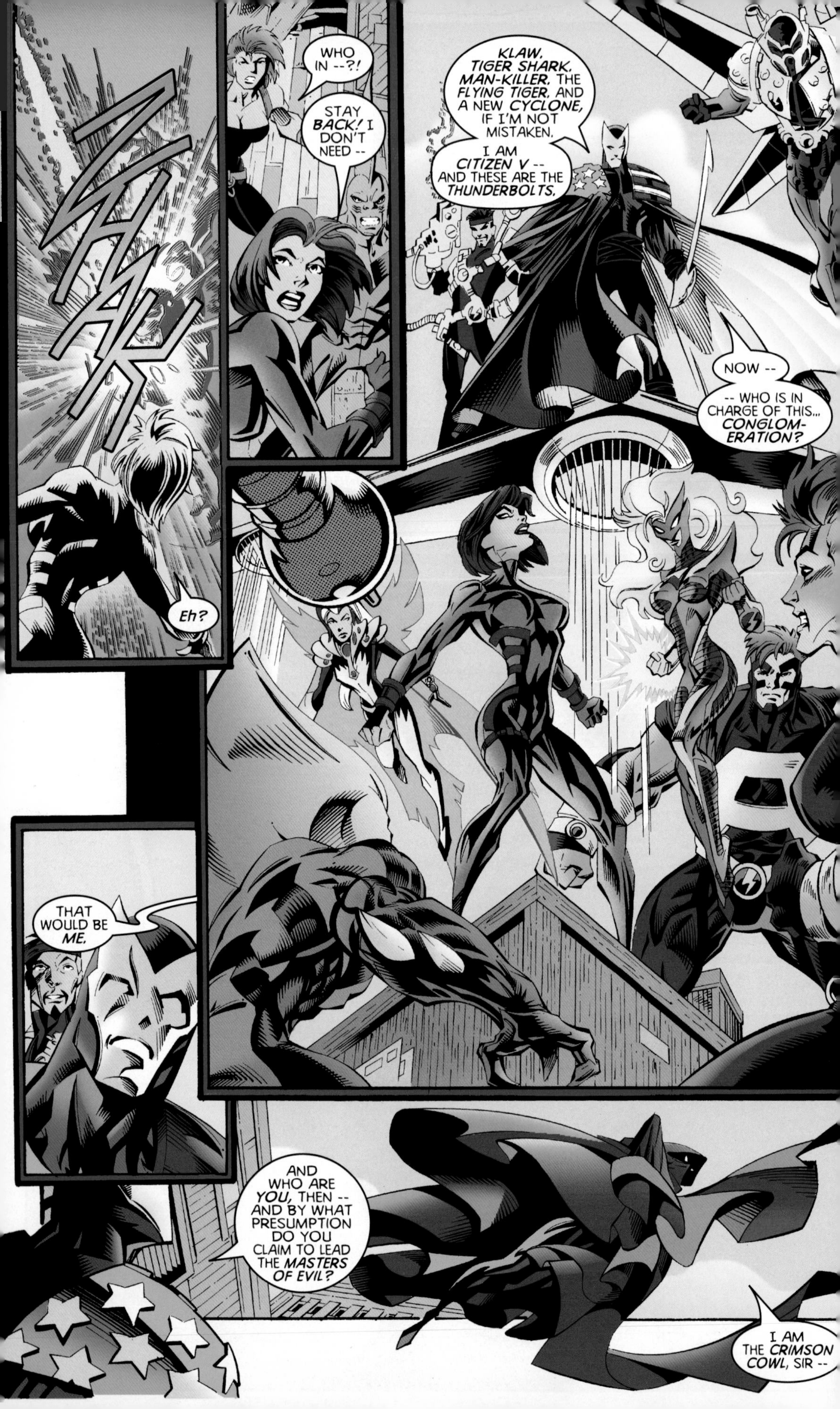

ZHAK!
WHO IN --?!
STAY BACK! I DON'T NEED --
Eh?
KLAW, TIGER SHARK, MAN-KILLER, THE FLYING TIGER, AND A NEW CYCLONE, IF I'M NOT MISTAKEN.
I AM CITIZEN V -- AND THESE ARE THE THUNDERBOLTS.
NOW --
-- WHO IS IN CHARGE OF THIS... CONGLOM-ERATION?
THAT WOULD BE ME.
AND WHO ARE YOU, THEN -- AND BY WHAT PRESUMPTION DO YOU CLAIM TO LEAD THE MASTERS OF EVIL?
I AM THE CRIMSON COWL, SIR --

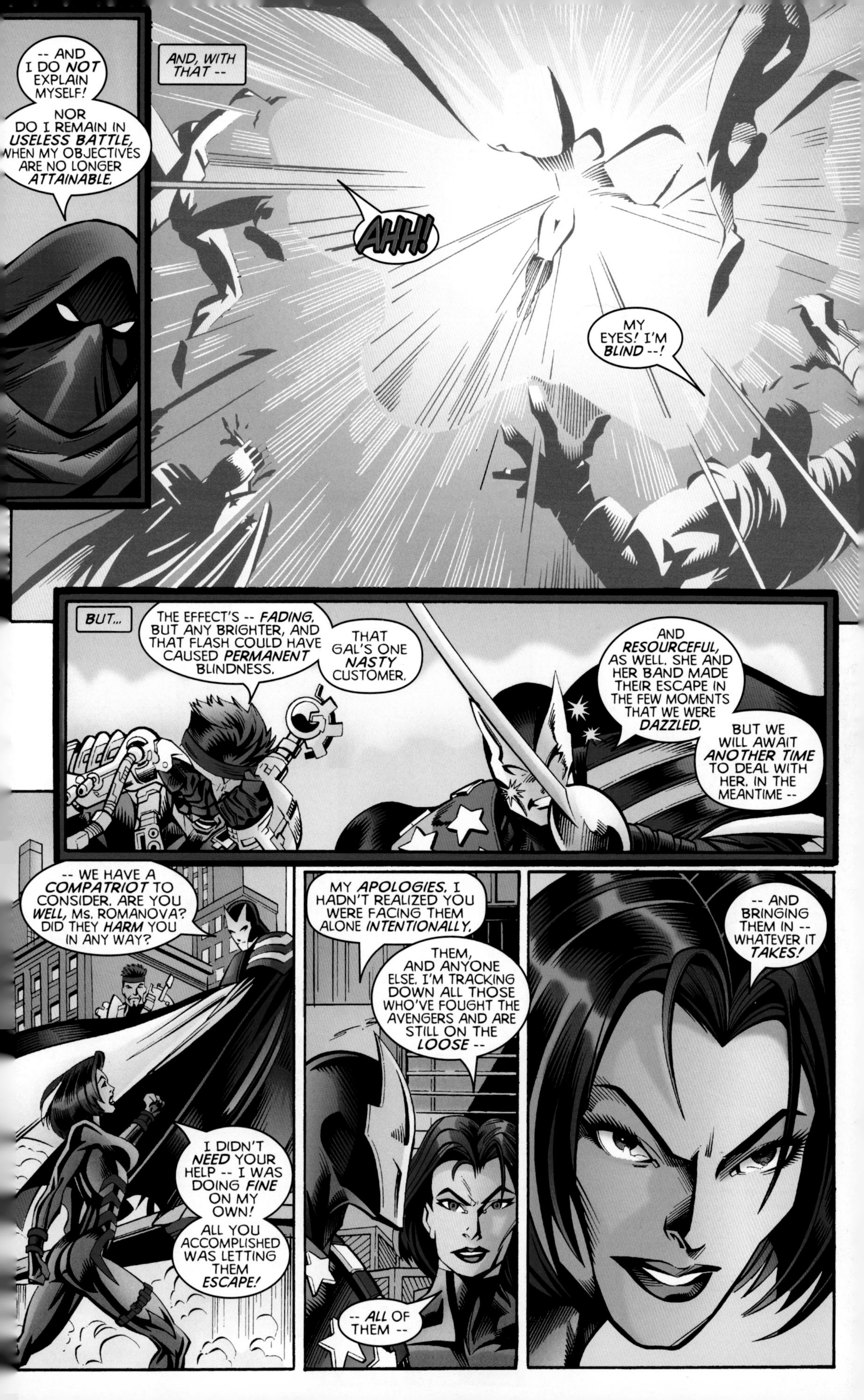
-- AND I DO NOT EXPLAIN MYSELF!
NOR DO I REMAIN IN USELESS BATTLE, WHEN MY OBJECTIVES ARE NO LONGER ATTAINABLE.
AND, WITH THAT --
AHH!
MY EYES! I'M BLIND --!
BUT...
THE EFFECT'S -- FADING, BUT ANY BRIGHTER, AND THAT FLASH COULD HAVE CAUSED PERMANENT BLINDNESS.
THAT GAL'S ONE NASTY CUSTOMER.
AND RESOURCEFUL, AS WELL. SHE AND HER BAND MADE THEIR ESCAPE IN THE FEW MOMENTS THAT WE WERE DAZZLED.
BUT WE WILL AWAIT ANOTHER TIME TO DEAL WITH HER. IN THE MEANTIME --
-- WE HAVE A COMPATRIOT TO CONSIDER. ARE YOU WELL, Ms. ROMANOVA? DID THEY HARM YOU IN ANY WAY?
I DIDN'T NEED YOUR HELP -- I WAS DOING FINE ON MY OWN!
ALL YOU ACCOMPLISHED WAS LETTING THEM ESCAPE!
MY APOLOGIES. I HADN'T REALIZED YOU WERE FACING THEM ALONE INTENTIONALLY.
THEM, AND ANYONE ELSE. I'M TRACKING DOWN ALL THOSE WHO'VE FOUGHT THE AVENGERS AND ARE STILL ON THE LOOSE --
-- ALL OF THEM --
-- AND BRINGING THEM IN -- WHATEVER IT TAKES!

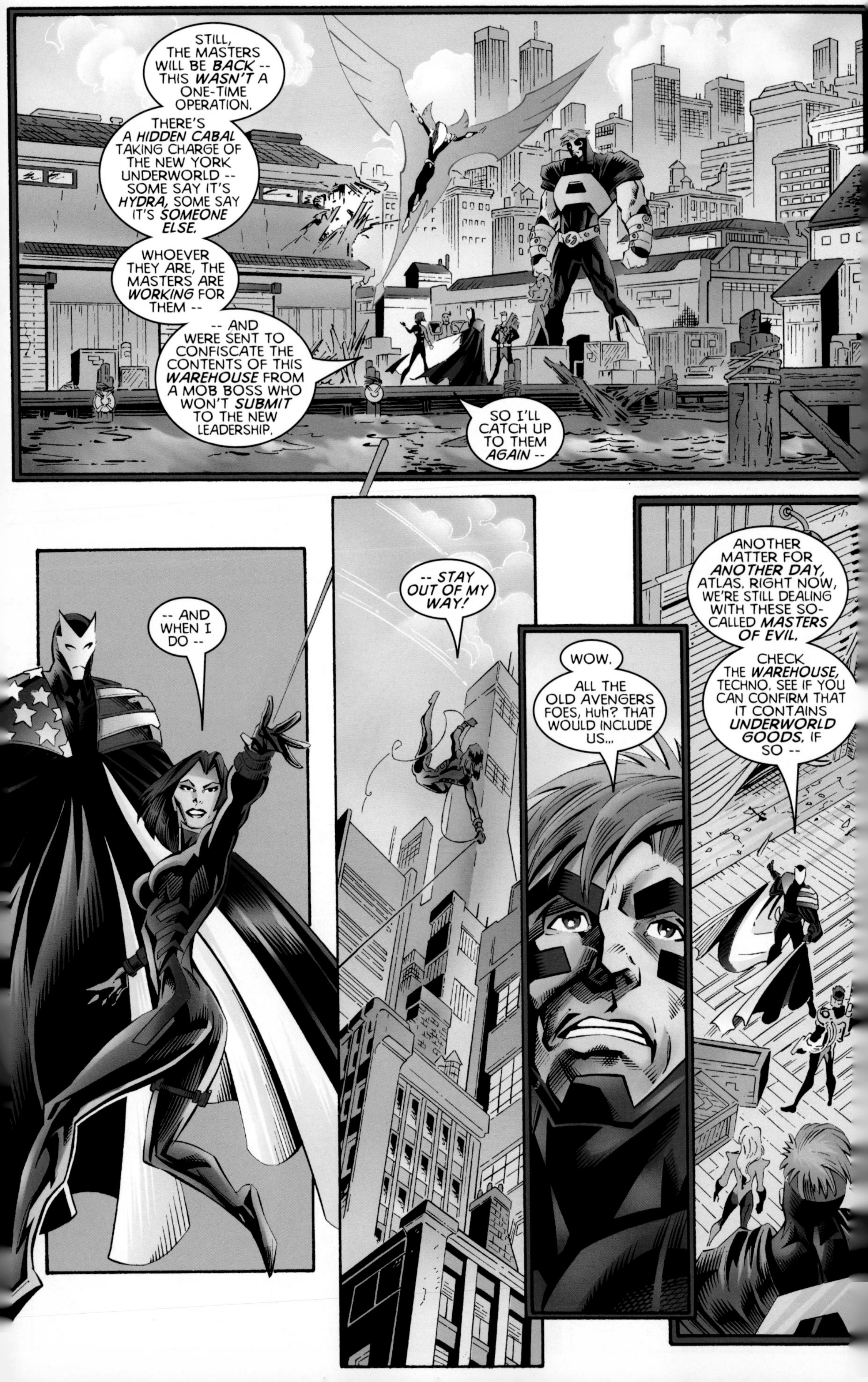
STILL, THE MASTERS WILL BE BACK -- THIS WASN'T A ONE-TIME OPERATION.
THERE'S A HIDDEN CABAL TAKING CHARGE OF THE NEW YORK UNDERWORLD -- SOME SAY IT'S HYDRA, SOME SAY IT'S SOMEONE ELSE.
WHOEVER THEY ARE, THE MASTERS ARE WORKING FOR THEM --
-- AND WERE SENT TO CONFISCATE THE CONTENTS OF THIS WAREHOUSE FROM A MOB BOSS WHO WON'T SUBMIT TO THE NEW LEADERSHIP.
SO I'LL CATCH UP TO THEM AGAIN --
-- AND WHEN I DO --
-- STAY OUT OF MY WAY!
WOW.
ALL THE OLD AVENGERS FOES, Huh? THAT WOULD INCLUDE US...
ANOTHER MATTER FOR ANOTHER DAY, ATLAS. RIGHT NOW, WE'RE STILL DEALING WITH THESE SO-CALLED MASTERS OF EVIL.
CHECK THE WAREHOUSE, TECHNO. SEE IF YOU CAN CONFIRM THAT IT CONTAINS UNDERWORLD GOODS. IF SO --

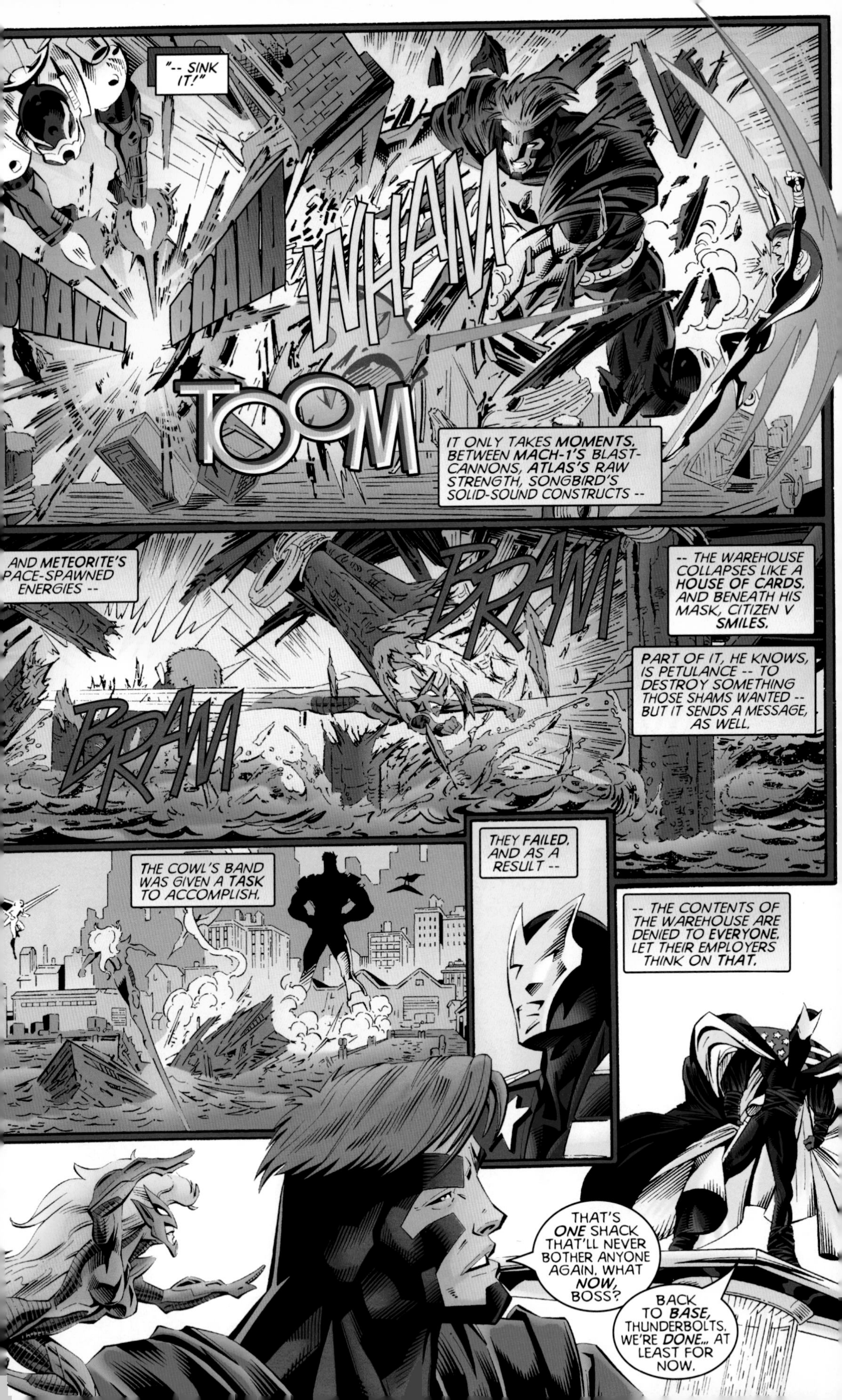
"-- SINK IT!"
BRAKA
BRAKA
WHAM
TOOM
IT ONLY TAKES MOMENTS. BETWEEN MACH-1'S BLAST-CANNONS, ATLAS'S RAW STRENGTH, SONGBIRD'S SOLID-SOUND CONSTRUCTS --
AND METEORITE'S SPACE-SPAWNED ENERGIES --
BRAM
BRAM
-- THE WAREHOUSE COLLAPSES LIKE A HOUSE OF CARDS, AND BENEATH HIS MASK, CITIZEN V SMILES.
PART OF IT, HE KNOWS, IS PETULANCE -- TO DESTROY SOMETHING THOSE SHAMS WANTED -- BUT IT SENDS A MESSAGE, AS WELL.
THE COWL'S BAND WAS GIVEN A TASK TO ACCOMPLISH.
THEY FAILED, AND AS A RESULT --
-- THE CONTENTS OF THE WAREHOUSE ARE DENIED TO EVERYONE. LET THEIR EMPLOYERS THINK ON THAT.
THAT'S ONE SHACK THAT'LL NEVER BOTHER ANYONE AGAIN. WHAT NOW, BOSS?
BACK TO BASE, THUNDERBOLTS. WE'RE DONE... AT LEAST FOR NOW.

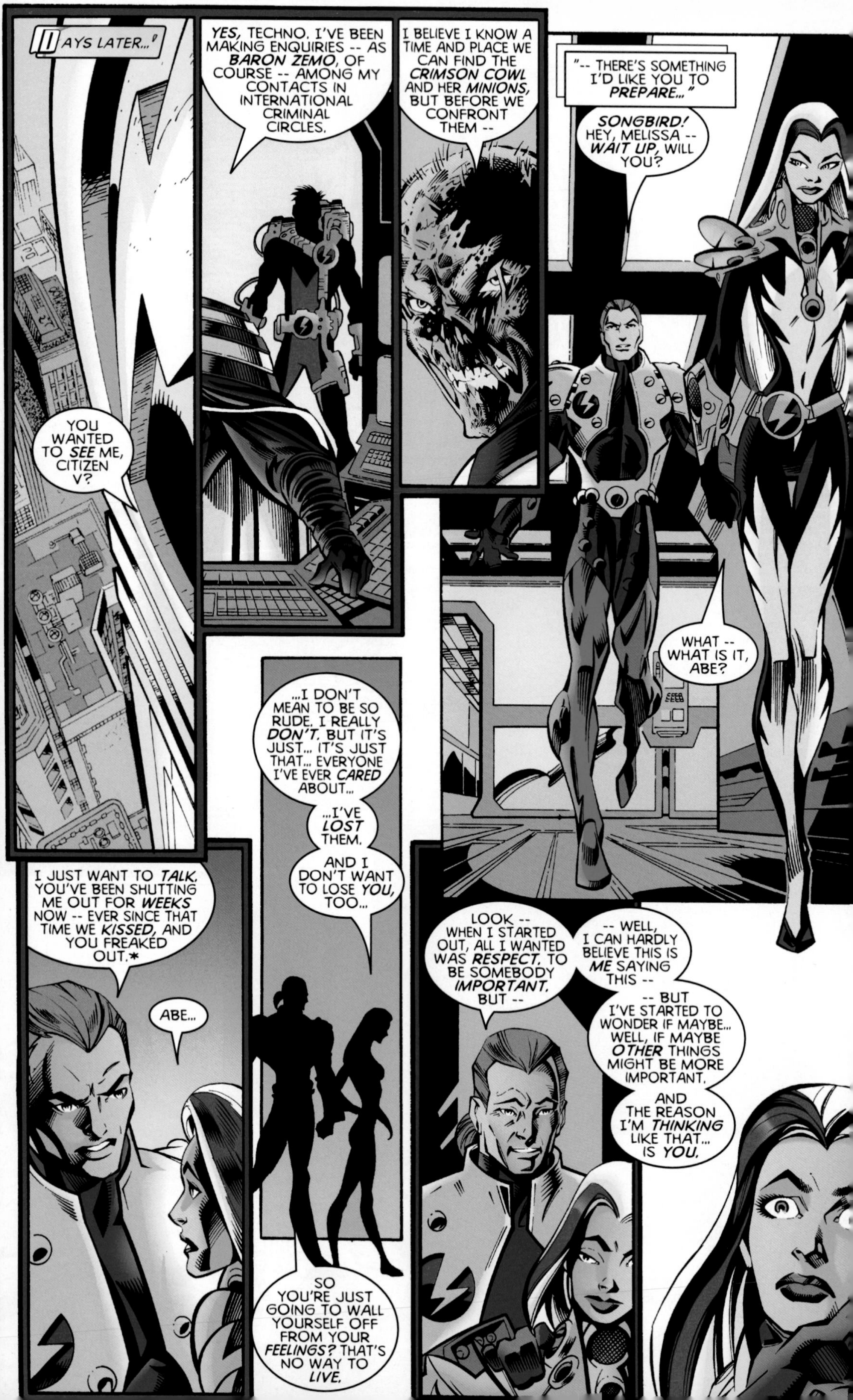
DAYS LATER...
YOU WANTED TO SEE ME, CITIZEN V?
YES, TECHNO. I'VE BEEN MAKING ENQUIRIES -- AS BARON ZEMO, OF COURSE -- AMONG MY CONTACTS IN INTERNATIONAL CRIMINAL CIRCLES.
I BELIEVE I KNOW A TIME AND PLACE WE CAN FIND THE CRIMSON COWL AND HER MINIONS, BUT BEFORE WE CONFRONT THEM --
"-- THERE'S SOMETHING I'D LIKE YOU TO PREPARE..."
SONGBIRD! HEY, MELISSA -- WAIT UP, WILL YOU?
WHAT -- WHAT IS IT, ABE?
I JUST WANT TO TALK. YOU'VE BEEN SHUTTING ME OUT FOR WEEKS NOW -- EVER SINCE THAT TIME WE KISSED, AND YOU FREAKED OUT.*
ABE...
...I DON'T MEAN TO BE SO RUDE. I REALLY DON'T. BUT IT'S JUST... IT'S JUST THAT... EVERYONE I'VE EVER CARED ABOUT...
...I'VE LOST THEM.
AND I DON'T WANT TO LOSE YOU, TOO...
SO YOU'RE JUST GOING TO WALL YOURSELF OFF FROM YOUR FEELINGS? THAT'S NO WAY TO LIVE.
LOOK -- WHEN I STARTED OUT, ALL I WANTED WAS RESPECT, TO BE SOMEBODY IMPORTANT. BUT --
-- WELL, I CAN HARDLY BELIEVE THIS IS ME SAYING THIS --
-- BUT I'VE STARTED TO WONDER IF MAYBE... WELL, IF MAYBE OTHER THINGS MIGHT BE MORE IMPORTANT.
AND THE REASON I'M THINKING LIKE THAT... IS YOU.

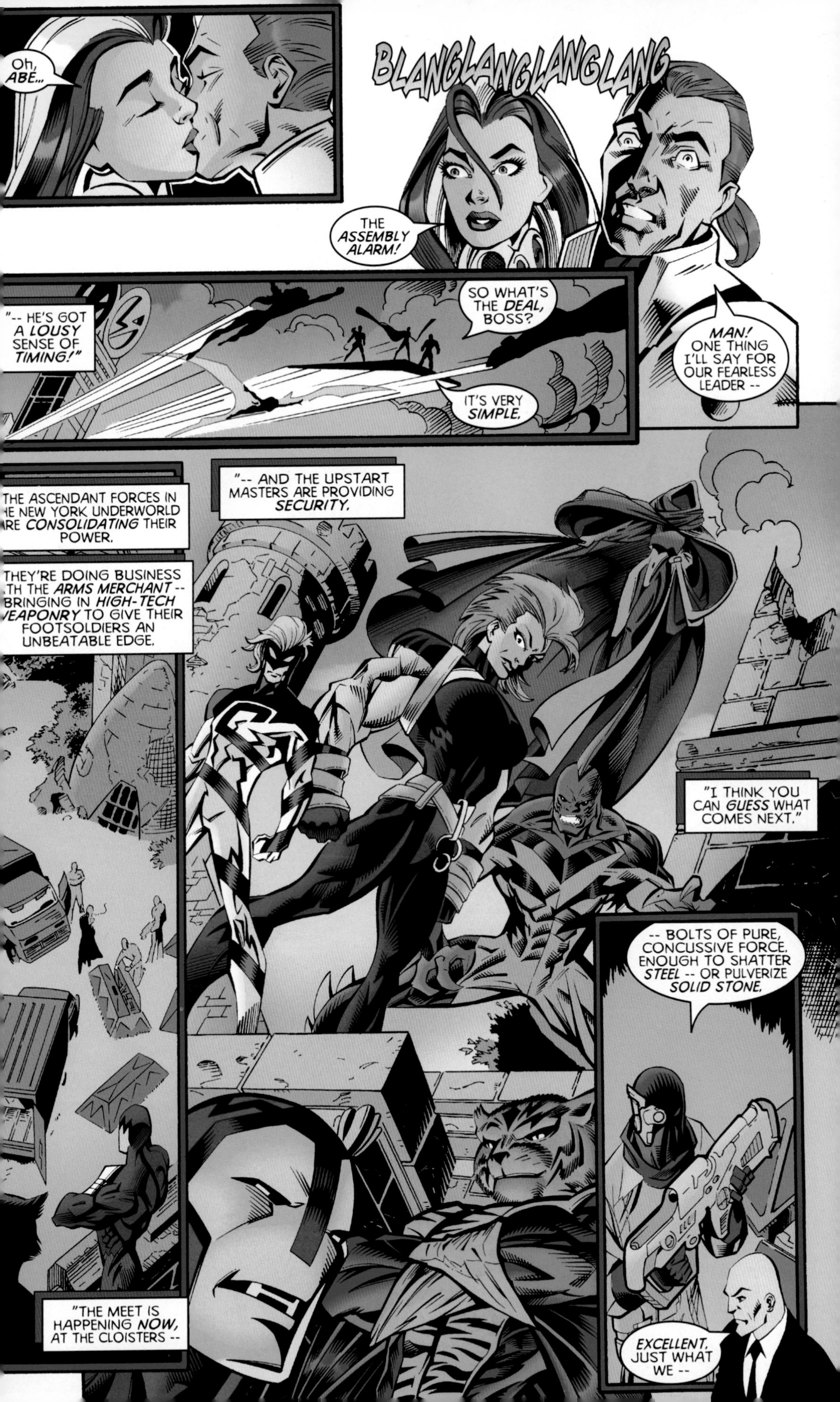

Oh, ABE...
BLANGLANGLANGLANG
THE ASSEMBLY ALARM!
MAN! ONE THING I'LL SAY FOR OUR FEARLESS LEADER --
"-- HE'S GOT A LOUSY SENSE OF TIMING!"
SO WHAT'S THE DEAL, BOSS?
IT'S VERY SIMPLE.
THE ASCENDANT FORCES IN HE NEW YORK UNDERWORLD RE CONSOLIDATING THEIR POWER.
THEY'RE DOING BUSINESS ..TH THE ARMS MERCHANT -- BRINGING IN HIGH-TECH VEAPONRY TO GIVE THEIR FOOTSOLDIERS AN UNBEATABLE EDGE.
"-- AND THE UPSTART MASTERS ARE PROVIDING SECURITY.
"I THINK YOU CAN GUESS WHAT COMES NEXT."
"THE MEET IS HAPPENING NOW, AT THE CLOISTERS --
-- BOLTS OF PURE, CONCUSSIVE FORCE. ENOUGH TO SHATTER STEEL -- OR PULVERIZE SOLID STONE.
EXCELLENT. JUST WHAT WE --

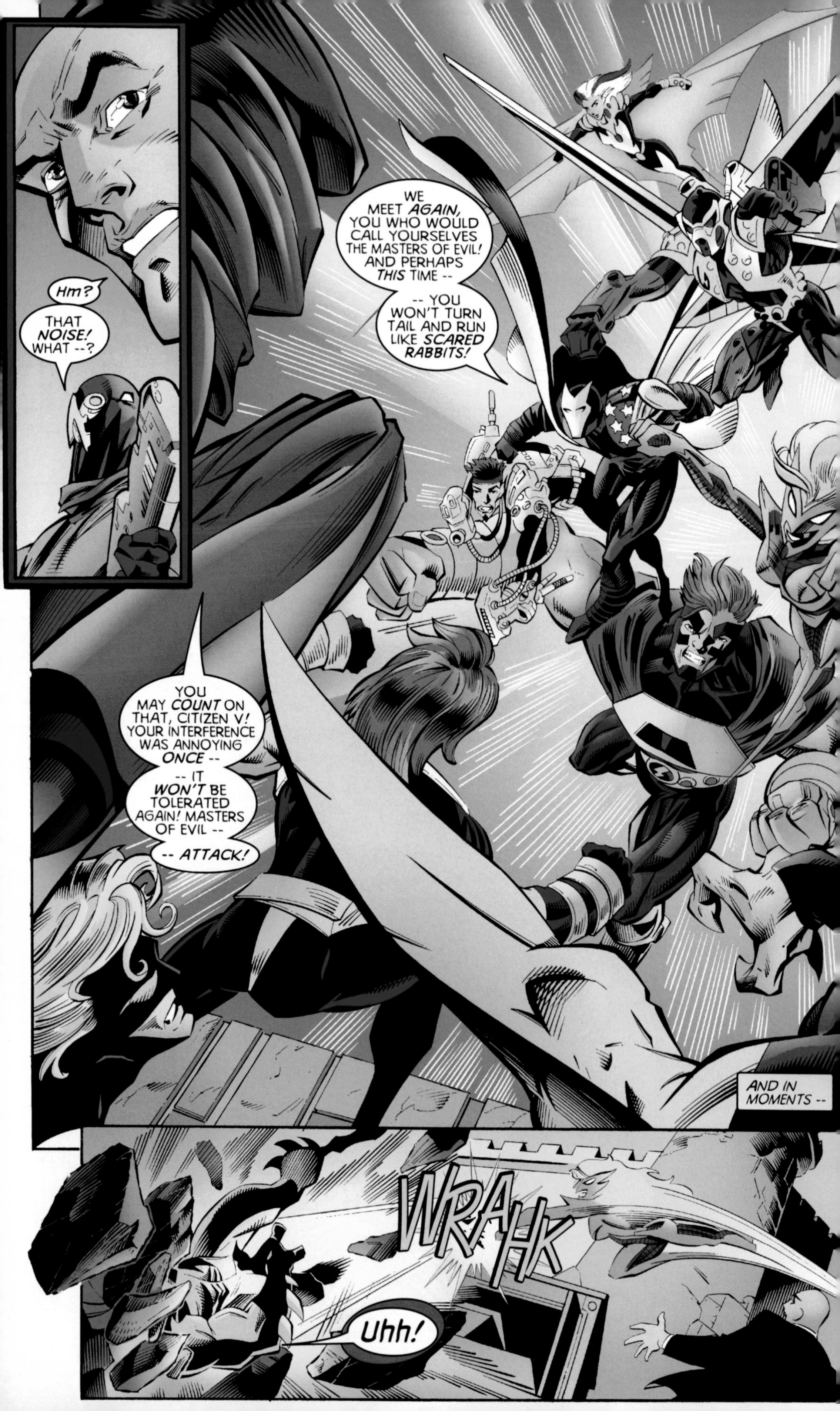
Hm?
THAT NOISE! WHAT --?
WE MEET AGAIN, YOU WHO WOULD CALL YOURSELVES THE MASTERS OF EVIL! AND PERHAPS THIS TIME --
-- YOU WON'T TURN TAIL AND RUN LIKE SCARED RABBITS!
YOU MAY COUNT ON THAT, CITIZEN V! YOUR INTERFERENCE WAS ANNOYING ONCE --
-- IT WON'T BE TOLERATED AGAIN! MASTERS OF EVIL --
-- ATTACK!
AND IN MOMENTS --
WRAHK
Uhh!

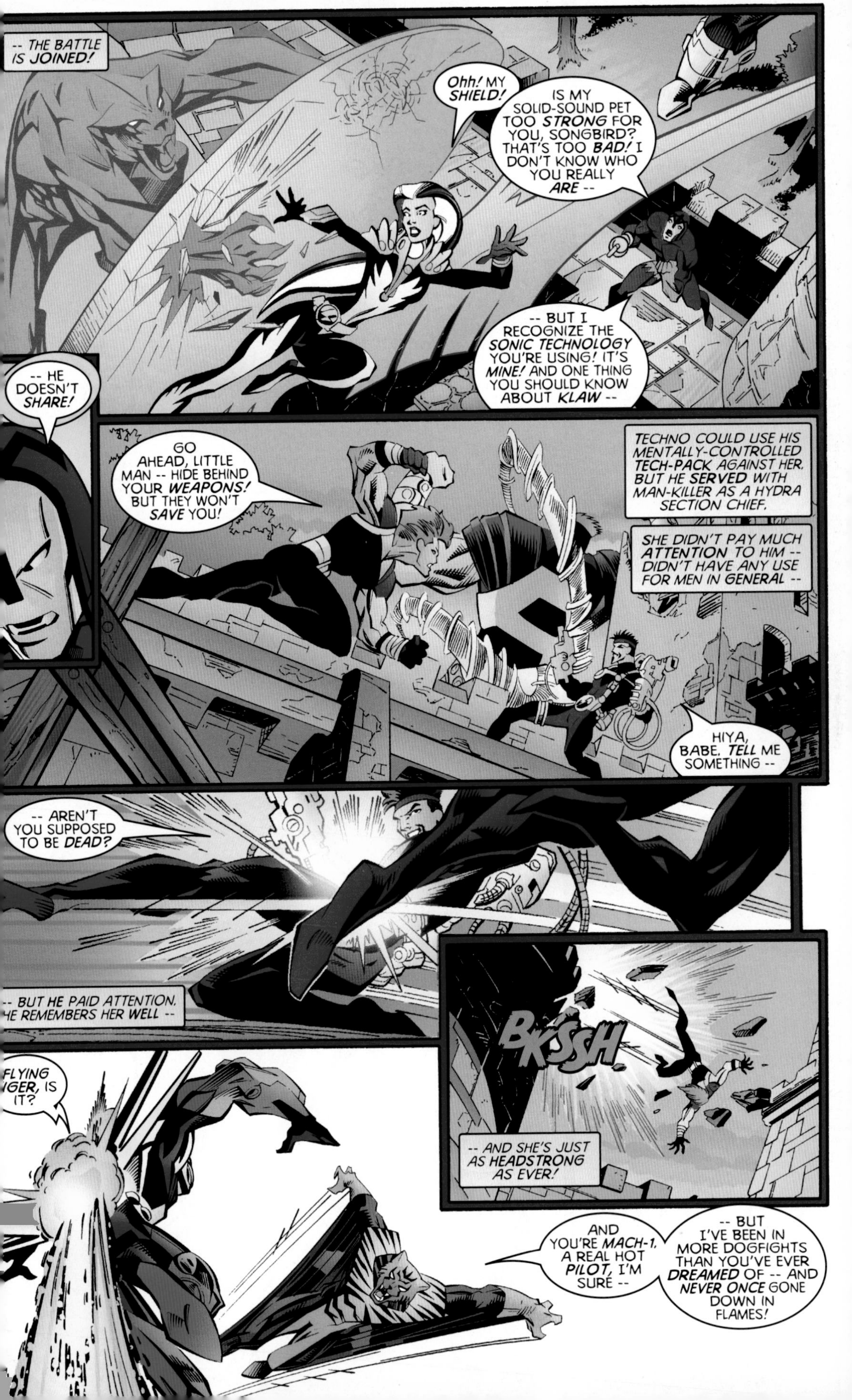

-- THE BATTLE IS JOINED!
Ohh! MY SHIELD!
IS MY SOLID-SOUND PET TOO STRONG FOR YOU, SONGBIRD? THAT'S TOO BAD! I DON'T KNOW WHO YOU REALLY ARE --
-- BUT I RECOGNIZE THE SONIC TECHNOLOGY YOU'RE USING! IT'S MINE! AND ONE THING YOU SHOULD KNOW ABOUT KLAW --
-- HE DOESN'T SHARE!
GO AHEAD, LITTLE MAN -- HIDE BEHIND YOUR WEAPONS! BUT THEY WON'T SAVE YOU!
TECHNO COULD USE HIS MENTALLY-CONTROLLED TECH-PACK AGAINST HER, BUT HE SERVED WITH MAN-KILLER AS A HYDRA SECTION CHIEF.
SHE DIDN'T PAY MUCH ATTENTION TO HIM -- DIDN'T HAVE ANY USE FOR MEN IN GENERAL --
HIYA, BABE, TELL ME SOMETHING --
-- AREN'T YOU SUPPOSED TO BE DEAD?
-- BUT HE PAID ATTENTION. HE REMEMBERS HER WELL --
BKSSH
-- AND SHE'S JUST AS HEADSTRONG AS EVER!
FLYING IGER, IS IT?
AND YOU'RE MACH-1, A REAL HOT PILOT, I'M SURE --
-- BUT I'VE BEEN IN MORE DOGFIGHTS THAN YOU'VE EVER DREAMED OF -- AND NEVER ONCE GONE DOWN IN FLAMES!

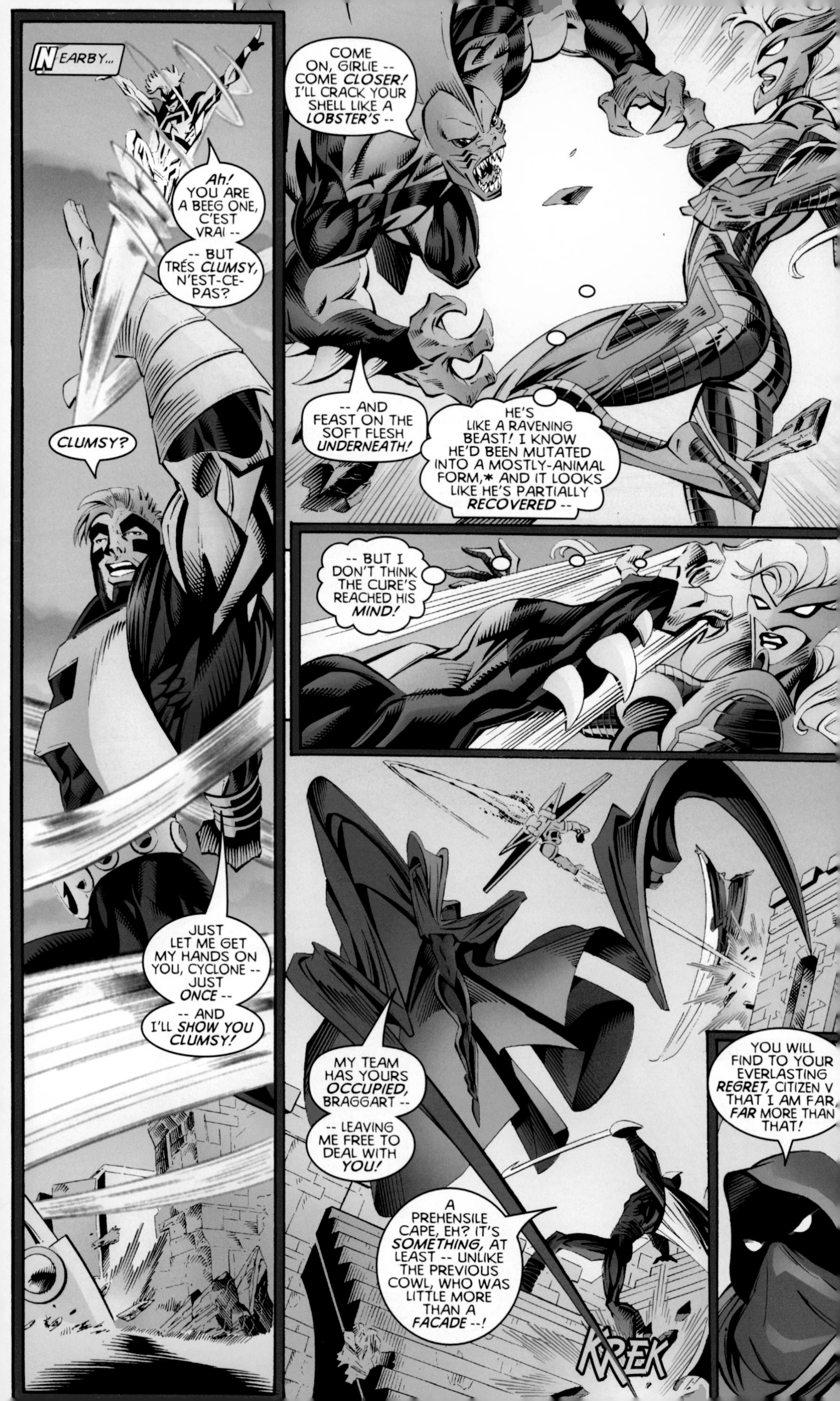
NEARBY...
Ah! YOU ARE A BEEG ONE, C'EST VRAI --
-- BUT TRÉS CLUMSY, N'EST-CE-PAS?
CLUMSY?
JUST LET ME GET MY HANDS ON YOU, CYCLONE -- JUST ONCE --
-- AND I'LL SHOW YOU CLUMSY!
COME ON, GIRLIE -- COME CLOSER! I'LL CRACK YOUR SHELL LIKE A LOBSTER'S --
-- AND FEAST ON THE SOFT FLESH UNDERNEATH!
HE'S LIKE A RAVENING BEAST! I KNOW HE'D BEEN MUTATED INTO A MOSTLY-ANIMAL FORM,* AND IT LOOKS LIKE HE'S PARTIALLY RECOVERED --
-- BUT I DON'T THINK THE CURE'S REACHED HIS MIND!
MY TEAM HAS YOURS OCCUPIED, BRAGGART --
-- LEAVING ME FREE TO DEAL WITH YOU!
YOU WILL FIND TO YOUR EVERLASTING REGRET, CITIZEN V THAT I AM FAR, FAR MORE THAN THAT!
A PREHENSILE CAPE, EH? IT'S SOMETHING, AT LEAST -- UNLIKE THE PREVIOUS COWL, WHO WAS LITTLE MORE THAN A FACADE --!
KREK

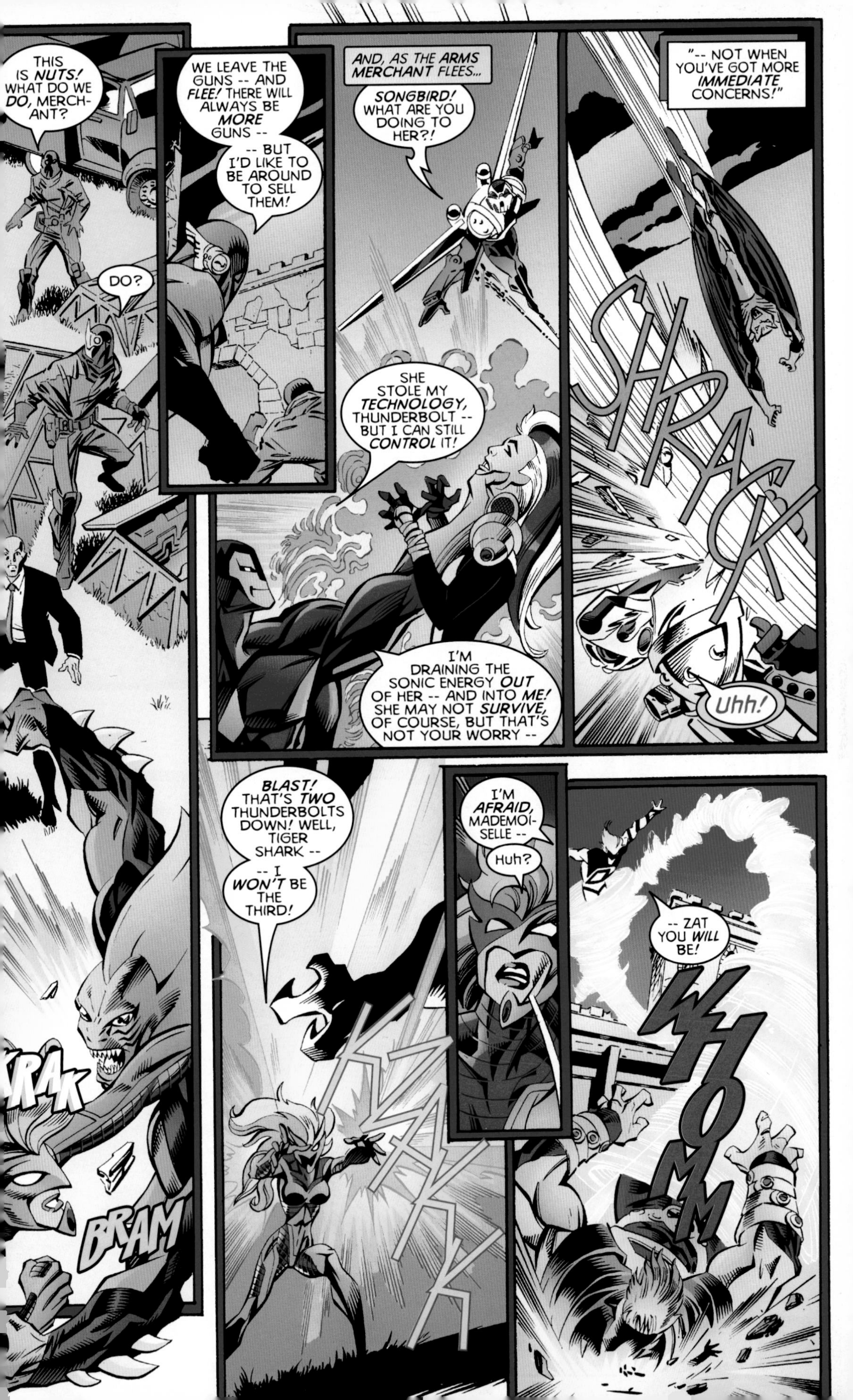
THIS IS NUTS! WHAT DO WE DO, MERCHANT?
DO?
WE LEAVE THE GUNS -- AND FLEE! THERE WILL ALWAYS BE MORE GUNS --
-- BUT I'D LIKE TO BE AROUND TO SELL THEM!
AND, AS THE ARMS MERCHANT FLEES...
SONGBIRD! WHAT ARE YOU DOING TO HER?!
SHE STOLE MY TECHNOLOGY, THUNDERBOLT -- BUT I CAN STILL CONTROL IT!
I'M DRAINING THE SONIC ENERGY OUT OF HER -- AND INTO ME! SHE MAY NOT SURVIVE, OF COURSE, BUT THAT'S NOT YOUR WORRY --
"-- NOT WHEN YOU'VE GOT MORE IMMEDIATE CONCERNS!"
SHRACK
Uhh!
KRAK
BRAM
BLAST! THAT'S TWO THUNDERBOLTS DOWN! WELL, TIGER SHARK --
-- I WON'T BE THE THIRD!
KRAKKK
I'M AFRAID, MADEMOISELLE --
Huh?
-- ZAT YOU WILL BE!
WHOMMM

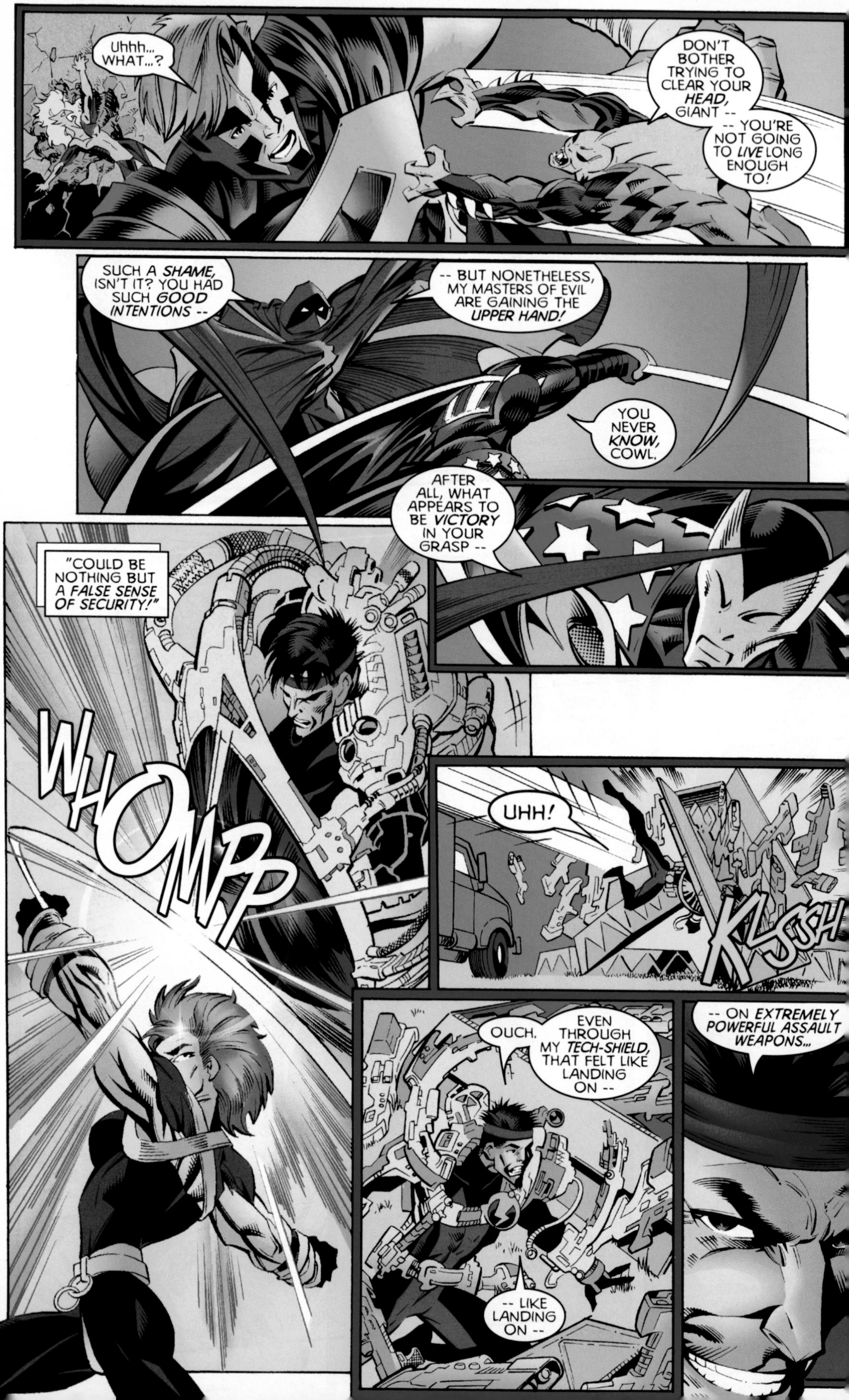

Uhhh... WHAT...?
DON'T BOTHER TRYING TO CLEAR YOUR HEAD, GIANT --
-- YOU'RE NOT GOING TO LIVE LONG ENOUGH TO!
SUCH A SHAME, ISN'T IT? YOU HAD SUCH GOOD INTENTIONS --
-- BUT NONETHELESS, MY MASTERS OF EVIL ARE GAINING THE UPPER HAND!
YOU NEVER KNOW, COWL.
AFTER ALL, WHAT APPEARS TO BE VICTORY IN YOUR GRASP --
"COULD BE NOTHING BUT A FALSE SENSE OF SECURITY!"
WHOMPP
UHH!
KLSSH
OUCH.
EVEN THROUGH MY TECH-SHIELD, THAT FELT LIKE LANDING ON --
-- LIKE LANDING ON --
-- ON EXTREMELY POWERFUL ASSAULT WEAPONS...

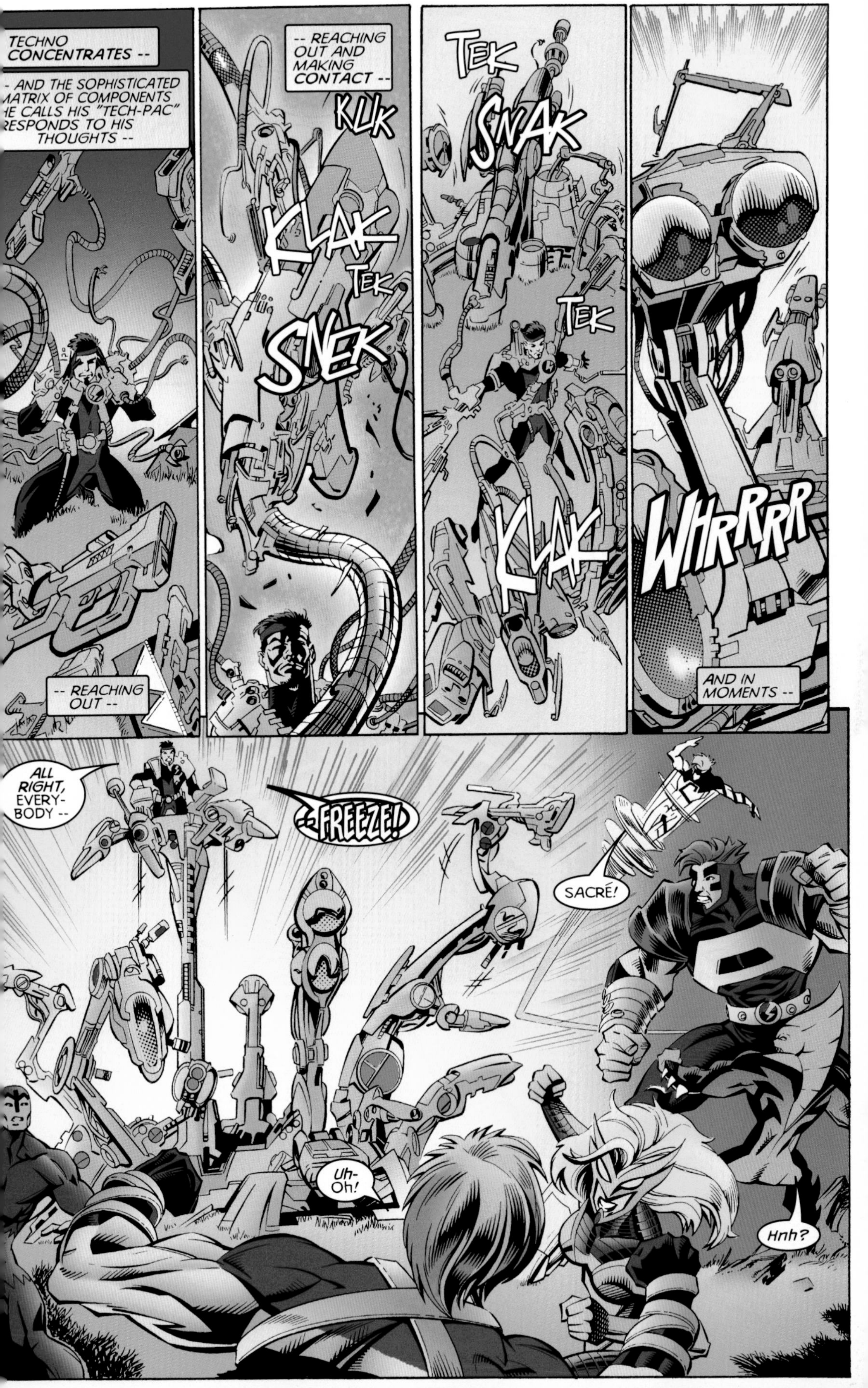
TECHNO CONCENTRATES --
-- AND THE SOPHISTICATED MATRIX OF COMPONENTS HE CALLS HIS "TECH-PAC" RESPONDS TO HIS THOUGHTS --
-- REACHING OUT --
-- REACHING OUT AND MAKING CONTACT --
KLIK
KLAK
TEK
SNEK
TEK
SNAK
TEK
KLAK
WHRRRR
AND IN MOMENTS --
ALL RIGHT, EVERY-BODY --
-- FREEZE!
SACRÉ!
Uh-Oh!
Hnh?

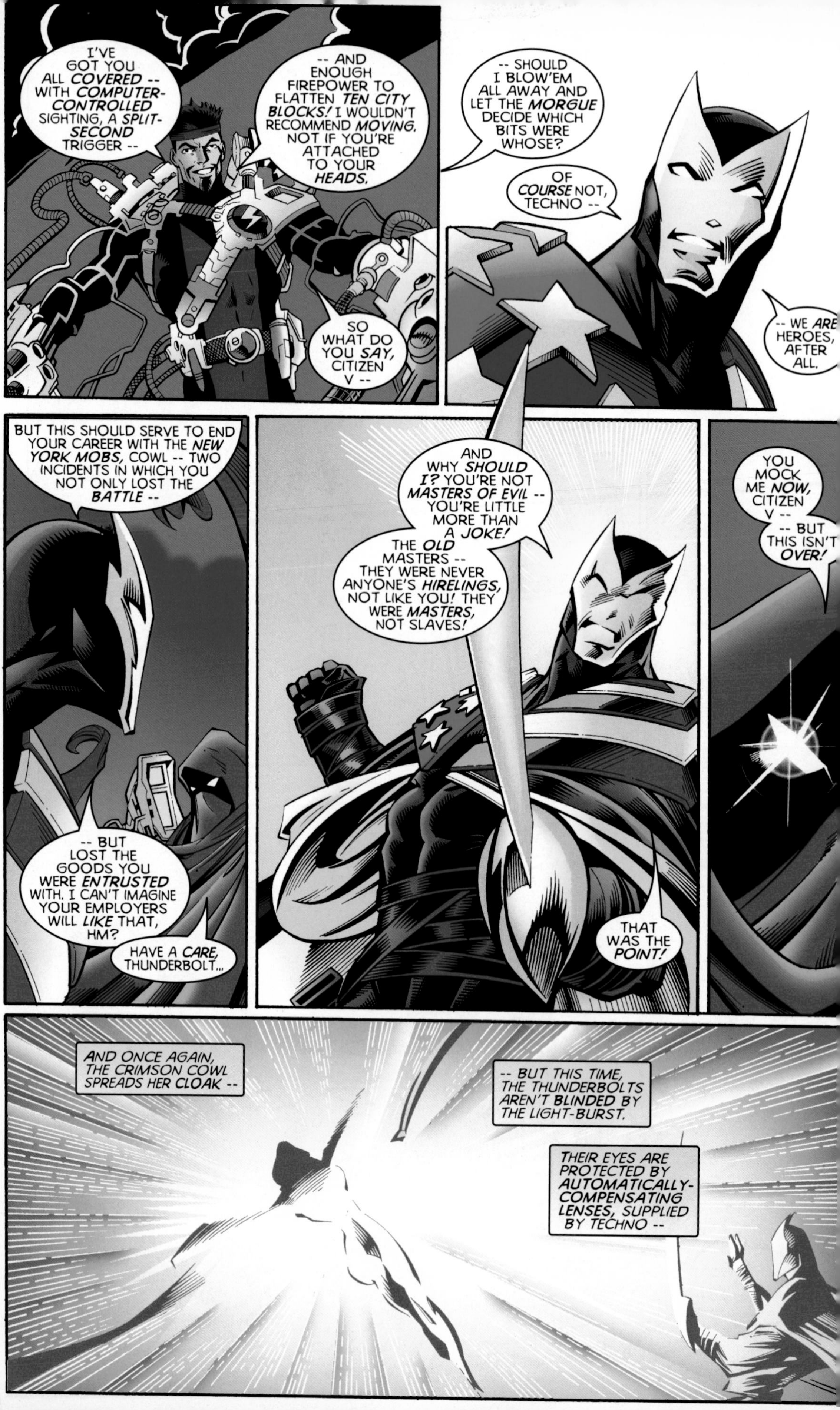
I'VE GOT YOU ALL COVERED -- WITH COMPUTER-CONTROLLED SIGHTING, A SPLIT-SECOND TRIGGER --
-- AND ENOUGH FIREPOWER TO FLATTEN TEN CITY BLOCKS! I WOULDN'T RECOMMEND MOVING, NOT IF YOU'RE ATTACHED TO YOUR HEADS.
SO WHAT DO YOU SAY, CITIZEN V --
-- SHOULD I BLOW'EM ALL AWAY AND LET THE MORGUE DECIDE WHICH BITS WERE WHOSE?
OF COURSE NOT, TECHNO --
-- WE ARE HEROES, AFTER ALL.
BUT THIS SHOULD SERVE TO END YOUR CAREER WITH THE NEW YORK MOBS, COWL -- TWO INCIDENTS IN WHICH YOU NOT ONLY LOST THE BATTLE --
-- BUT LOST THE GOODS YOU WERE ENTRUSTED WITH. I CAN'T IMAGINE YOUR EMPLOYERS WILL LIKE THAT, HM?
HAVE A CARE, THUNDERBOLT...
AND WHY SHOULD I? YOU'RE NOT MASTERS OF EVIL -- YOU'RE LITTLE MORE THAN A JOKE!
THE OLD MASTERS -- THEY WERE NEVER ANYONE'S HIRELINGS, NOT LIKE YOU! THEY WERE MASTERS, NOT SLAVES!
THAT WAS THE POINT!
YOU MOCK ME NOW, CITIZEN V --
-- BUT THIS ISN'T OVER!
AND ONCE AGAIN, THE CRIMSON COWL SPREADS HER CLOAK --
-- BUT THIS TIME, THE THUNDERBOLTS AREN'T BLINDED BY THE LIGHT-BURST.
THEIR EYES ARE PROTECTED BY AUTOMATICALLY-COMPENSATING LENSES, SUPPLIED BY TECHNO --

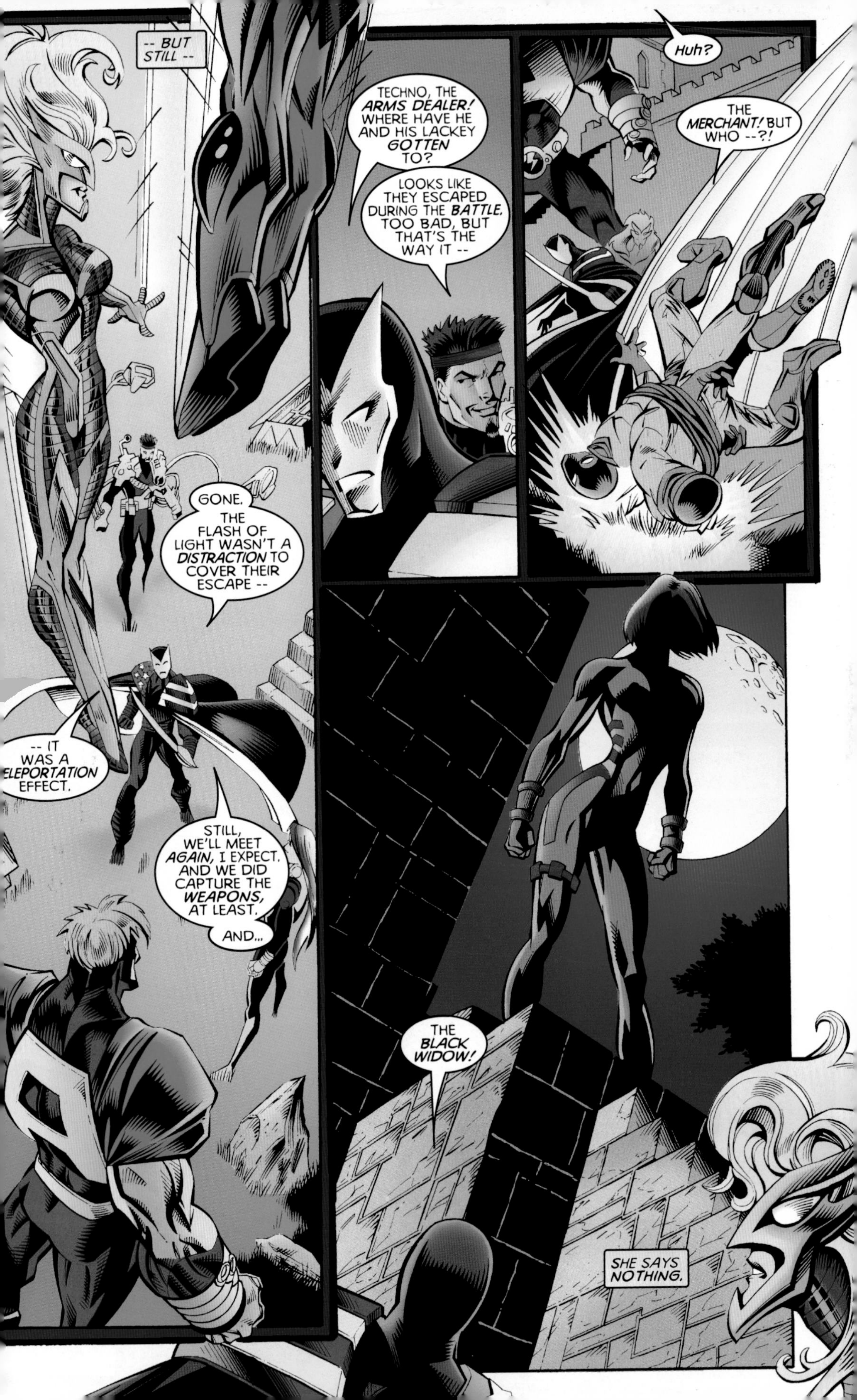
-- BUT STILL --
TECHNO, THE ARMS DEALER! WHERE HAVE HE AND HIS LACKEY GOTTEN TO?
LOOKS LIKE THEY ESCAPED DURING THE BATTLE. TOO BAD, BUT THAT'S THE WAY IT --
Huh?
THE MERCHANT! BUT WHO --?!
GONE. THE FLASH OF LIGHT WASN'T A DISTRACTION TO COVER THEIR ESCAPE --
-- IT WAS A ELEPORTATION EFFECT.
STILL, WE'LL MEET AGAIN, I EXPECT. AND WE DID CAPTURE THE WEAPONS, AT LEAST.
AND...
THE BLACK WIDOW!
SHE SAYS NOTHING.

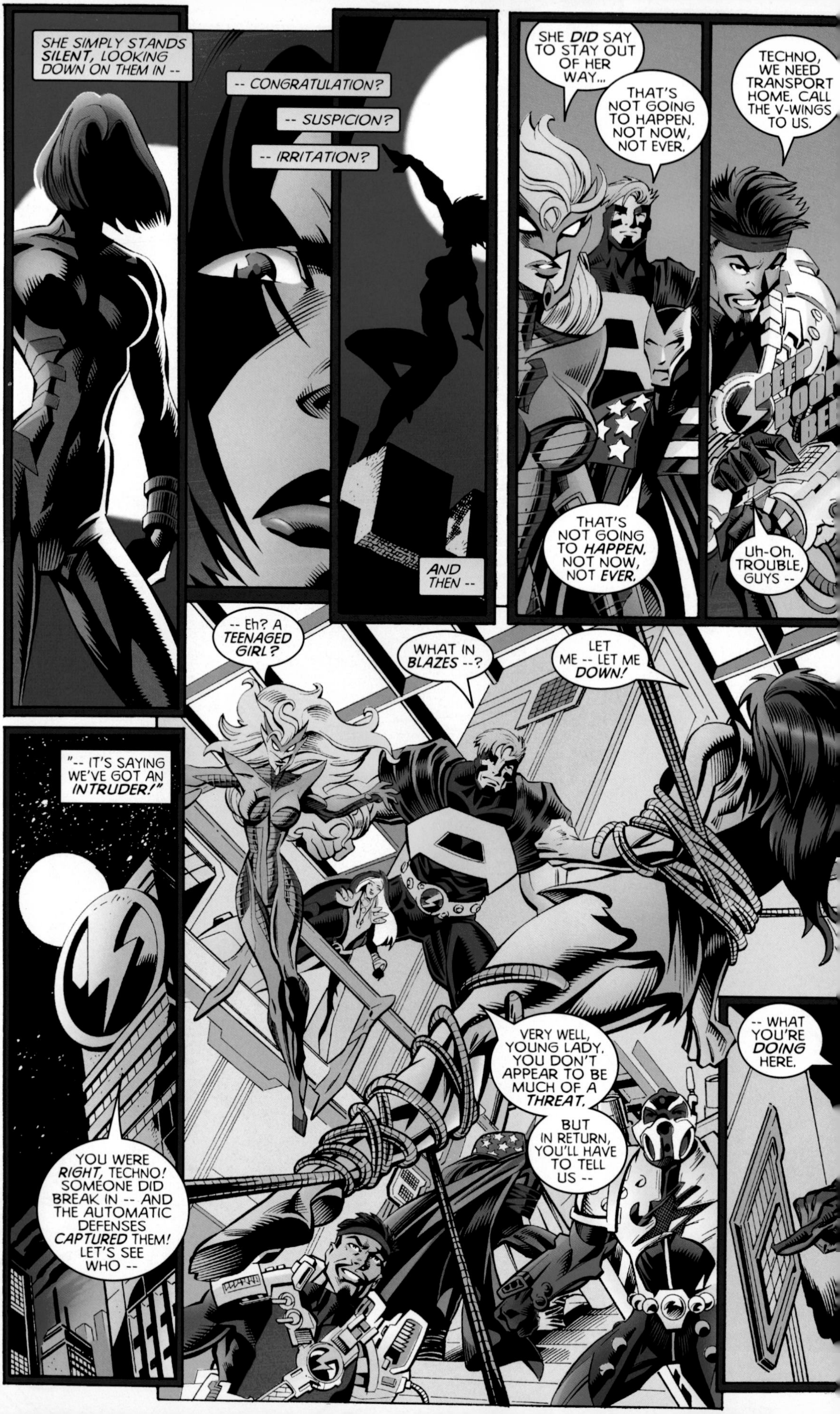
SHE SIMPLY STANDS SILENT, LOOKING DOWN ON THEM IN --
-- CONGRATULATION?
-- SUSPICION?
-- IRRITATION?
AND THEN --
SHE DID SAY TO STAY OUT OF HER WAY...
THAT'S NOT GOING TO HAPPEN. NOT NOW, NOT EVER.
THAT'S NOT GOING TO HAPPEN. NOT NOW, NOT EVER.
TECHNO, WE NEED TRANSPORT HOME. CALL THE V-WINGS TO US.
BEEP BOOP BEE
Uh-Oh. TROUBLE, GUYS --
"-- IT'S SAYING WE'VE GOT AN INTRUDER!"
YOU WERE RIGHT, TECHNO! SOMEONE DID BREAK IN -- AND THE AUTOMATIC DEFENSES CAPTURED THEM! LET'S SEE WHO --
-- Eh? A TEENAGED GIRL?
WHAT IN BLAZES --?
LET ME -- LET ME DOWN!
VERY WELL, YOUNG LADY. YOU DON'T APPEAR TO BE MUCH OF A THREAT.
BUT IN RETURN, YOU'LL HAVE TO TELL US --
-- WHAT YOU'RE DOING HERE.

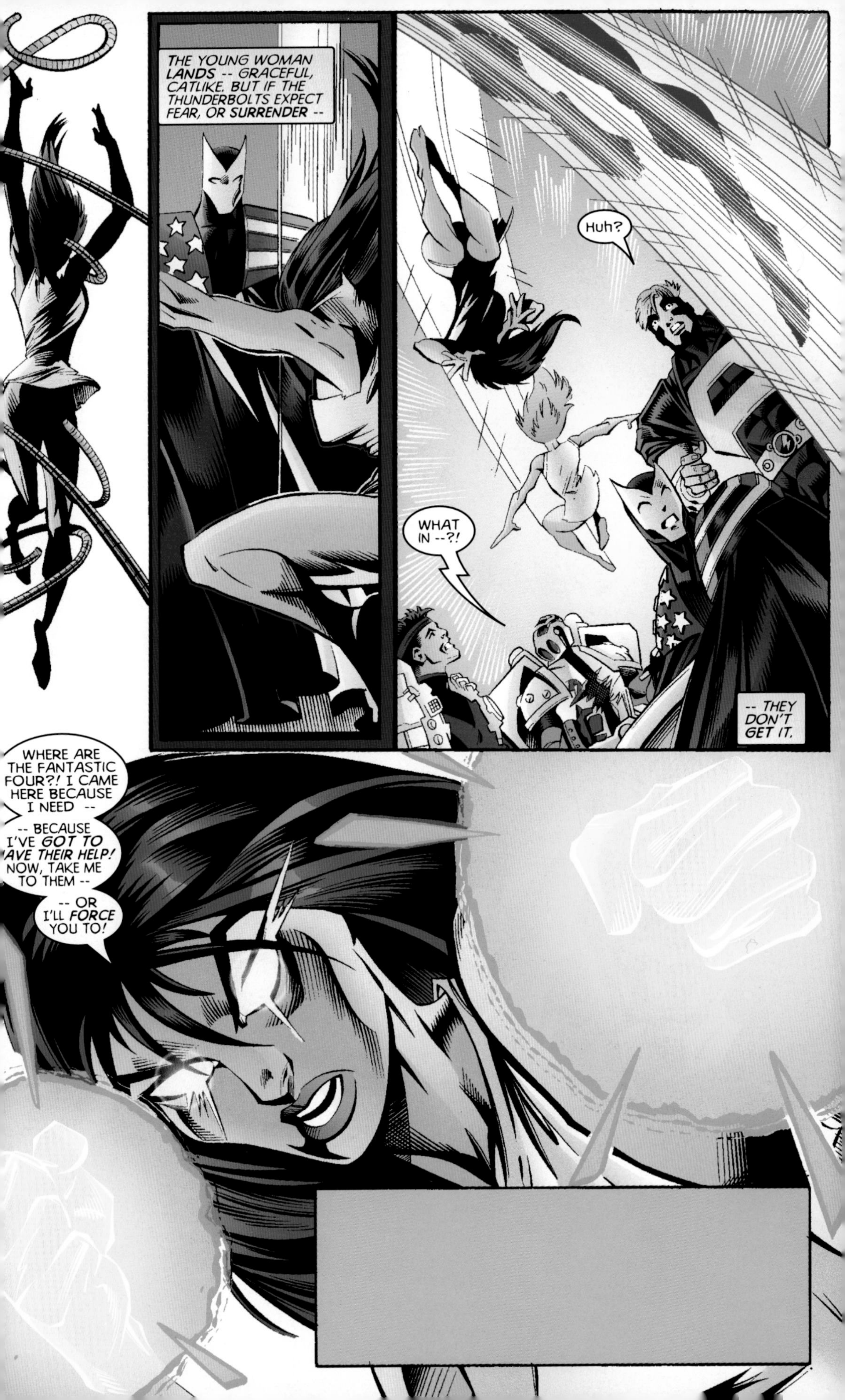
THE YOUNG WOMAN LANDS -- GRACEFUL, CATLIKE. BUT IF THE THUNDERBOLTS EXPECT FEAR, OR SURRENDER --
Huh?
WHAT IN --?!
-- THEY DON'T GET IT.
WHERE ARE THE FANTASTIC FOUR?! I CAME HERE BECAUSE I NEED --
-- BECAUSE I'VE GOT TO HAVE THEIR HELP! NOW, TAKE ME TO THEM --
-- OR I'LL FORCE YOU TO!

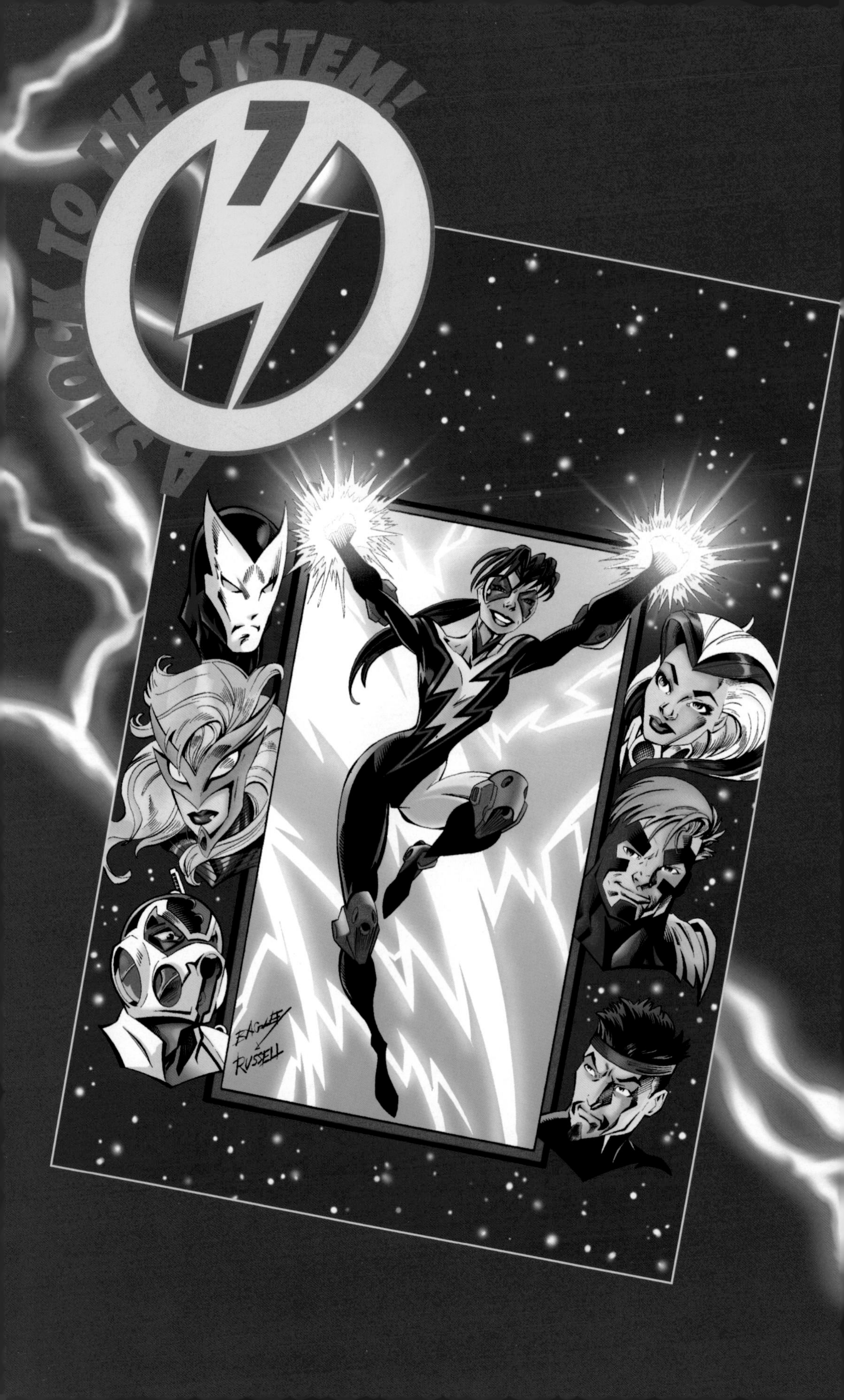
A SHOCK TO THE SYSTEM!
RUSSELL

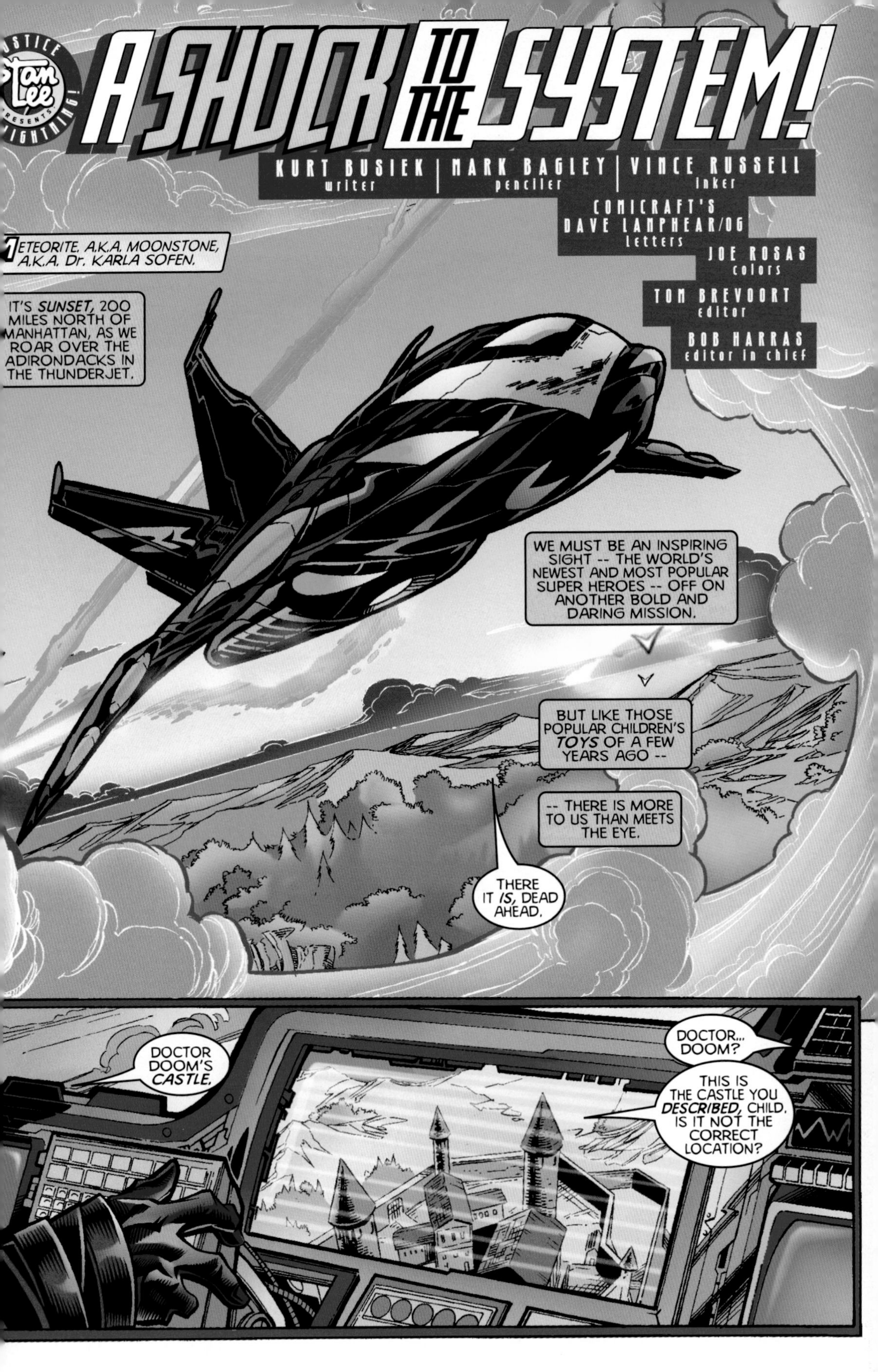
Stan Lee presents JUSTICE / LIGHTNING!
A SHOCK TO THE SYSTEM!
KURT BUSIEK writer | MARK BAGLEY penciler | VINCE RUSSELL inker
COMICRAFT'S DAVE LANPHEAR/OG letters
JOE ROSAS colors
TOM BREVOORT editor
BOB HARRAS editor in chief
METEORITE, A.K.A. MOONSTONE, A.K.A. Dr. KARLA SOFEN.
IT'S SUNSET, 200 MILES NORTH OF MANHATTAN, AS WE ROAR OVER THE ADIRONDACKS IN THE THUNDERJET.
WE MUST BE AN INSPIRING SIGHT -- THE WORLD'S NEWEST AND MOST POPULAR SUPER HEROES -- OFF ON ANOTHER BOLD AND DARING MISSION.
BUT LIKE THOSE POPULAR CHILDREN'S TOYS OF A FEW YEARS AGO --
-- THERE IS MORE TO US THAN MEETS THE EYE.
THERE IT IS, DEAD AHEAD.
DOCTOR DOOM'S CASTLE.
DOCTOR... DOOM?
THIS IS THE CASTLE YOU DESCRIBED, CHILD. IS IT NOT THE CORRECT LOCATION?

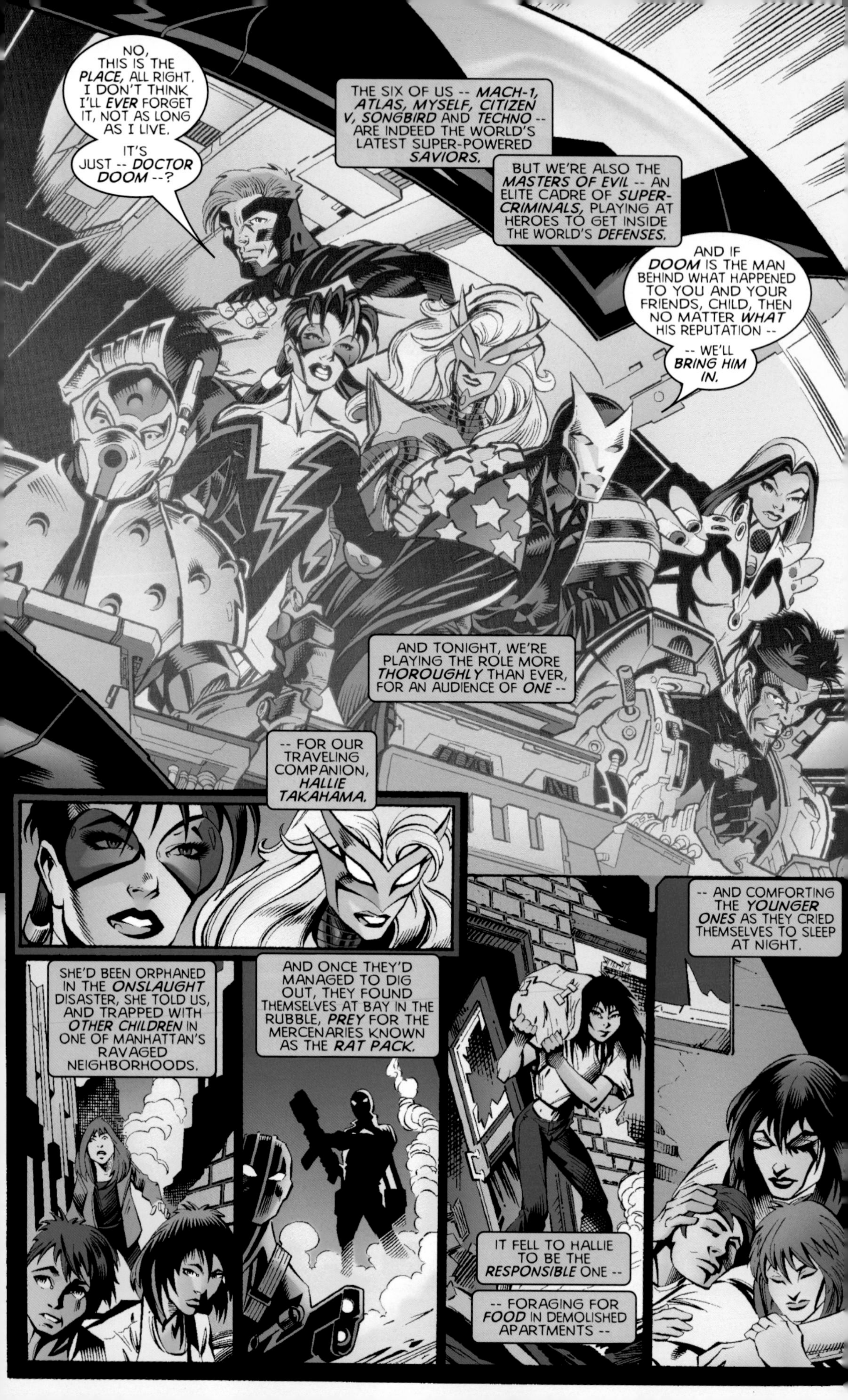
NO, THIS IS THE PLACE, ALL RIGHT. I DON'T THINK I'LL EVER FORGET IT, NOT AS LONG AS I LIVE.
IT'S JUST -- DOCTOR DOOM --?
THE SIX OF US -- MACH-1, ATLAS, MYSELF, CITIZEN V, SONGBIRD AND TECHNO -- ARE INDEED THE WORLD'S LATEST SUPER-POWERED SAVIORS.
BUT WE'RE ALSO THE MASTERS OF EVIL -- AN ELITE CADRE OF SUPER-CRIMINALS, PLAYING AT HEROES TO GET INSIDE THE WORLD'S DEFENSES.
AND IF DOOM IS THE MAN BEHIND WHAT HAPPENED TO YOU AND YOUR FRIENDS, CHILD, THEN NO MATTER WHAT HIS REPUTATION --
-- WE'LL BRING HIM IN.
AND TONIGHT, WE'RE PLAYING THE ROLE MORE THOROUGHLY THAN EVER, FOR AN AUDIENCE OF ONE --
-- FOR OUR TRAVELING COMPANION, HALLIE TAKAHAMA.
SHE'D BEEN ORPHANED IN THE ONSLAUGHT DISASTER, SHE TOLD US, AND TRAPPED WITH OTHER CHILDREN IN ONE OF MANHATTAN'S RAVAGED NEIGHBORHOODS.
AND ONCE THEY'D MANAGED TO DIG OUT, THEY FOUND THEMSELVES AT BAY IN THE RUBBLE, PREY FOR THE MERCENARIES KNOWN AS THE RAT PACK.
IT FELL TO HALLIE TO BE THE RESPONSIBLE ONE --
-- FORAGING FOR FOOD IN DEMOLISHED APARTMENTS --
-- AND COMFORTING THE YOUNGER ONES AS THEY CRIED THEMSELVES TO SLEEP AT NIGHT.

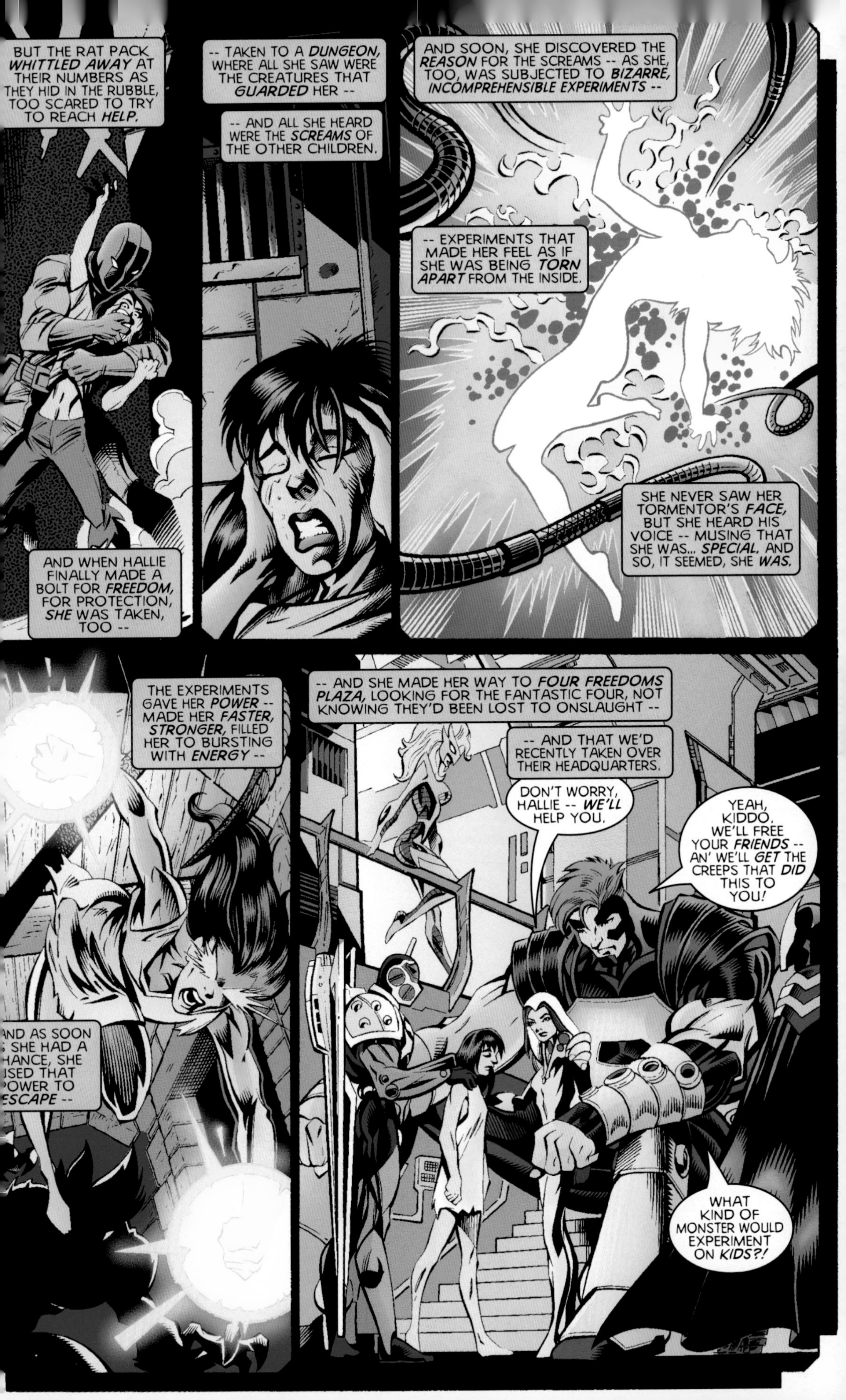
BUT THE RAT PACK WHITTLED AWAY AT THEIR NUMBERS AS THEY HID IN THE RUBBLE, TOO SCARED TO TRY TO REACH HELP.
AND WHEN HALLIE FINALLY MADE A BOLT FOR FREEDOM, FOR PROTECTION, SHE WAS TAKEN, TOO --
-- TAKEN TO A DUNGEON, WHERE ALL SHE SAW WERE THE CREATURES THAT GUARDED HER --
-- AND ALL SHE HEARD WERE THE SCREAMS OF THE OTHER CHILDREN.
AND SOON, SHE DISCOVERED THE REASON FOR THE SCREAMS -- AS SHE, TOO, WAS SUBJECTED TO BIZARRE, INCOMPREHENSIBLE EXPERIMENTS --
-- EXPERIMENTS THAT MADE HER FEEL AS IF SHE WAS BEING TORN APART FROM THE INSIDE.
SHE NEVER SAW HER TORMENTOR'S FACE, BUT SHE HEARD HIS VOICE -- MUSING THAT SHE WAS... SPECIAL. AND SO, IT SEEMED, SHE WAS.
THE EXPERIMENTS GAVE HER POWER -- MADE HER FASTER, STRONGER, FILLED HER TO BURSTING WITH ENERGY --
AND AS SOON S SHE HAD A HANCE, SHE USED THAT POWER TO ESCAPE --
-- AND SHE MADE HER WAY TO FOUR FREEDOMS PLAZA, LOOKING FOR THE FANTASTIC FOUR, NOT KNOWING THEY'D BEEN LOST TO ONSLAUGHT --
-- AND THAT WE'D RECENTLY TAKEN OVER THEIR HEADQUARTERS.
DON'T WORRY, HALLIE -- WE'LL HELP YOU.
YEAH, KIDDO. WE'LL FREE YOUR FRIENDS -- AN' WE'LL GET THE CREEPS THAT DID THIS TO YOU!
WHAT KIND OF MONSTER WOULD EXPERIMENT ON KIDS?!

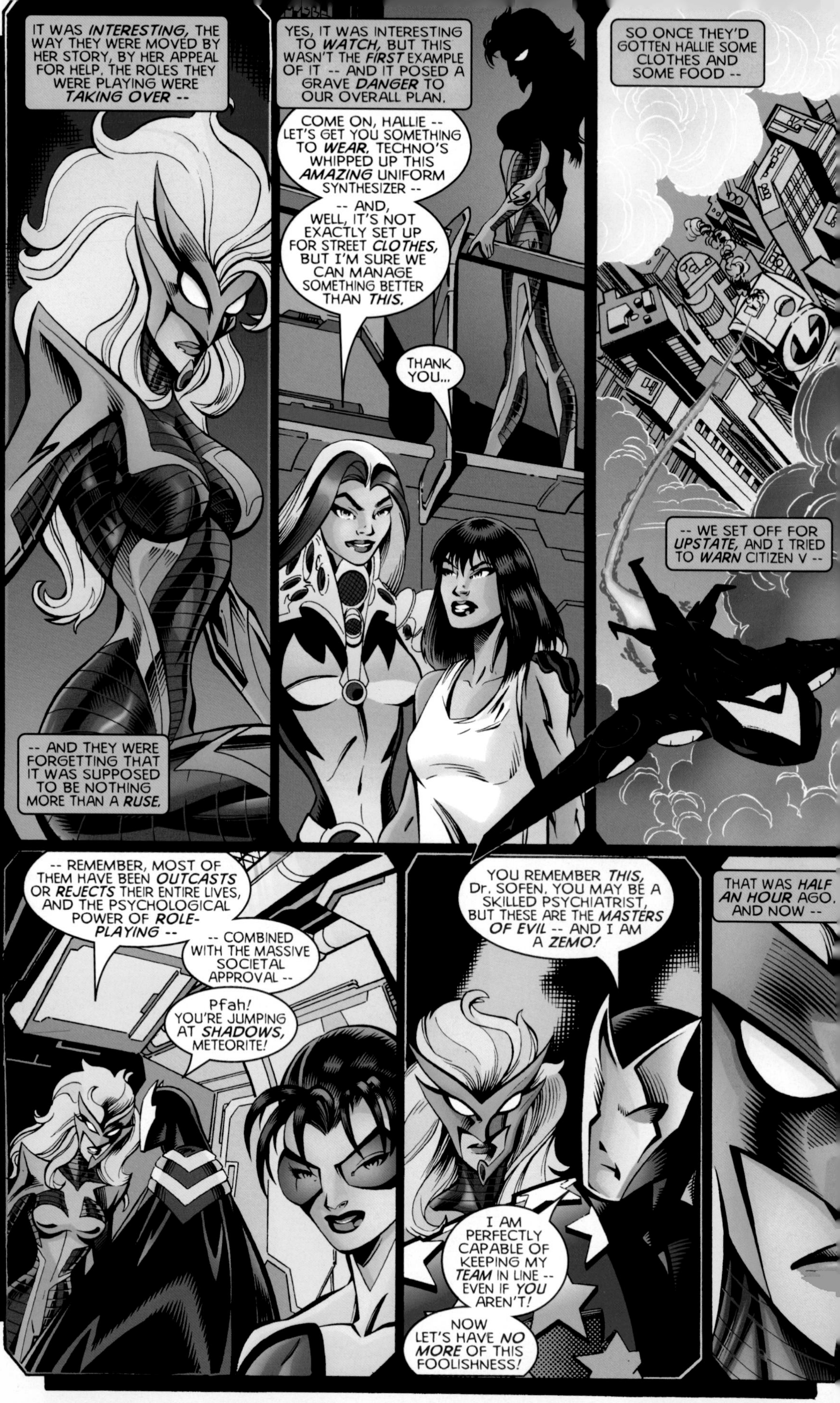
IT WAS *INTERESTING,* THE WAY THEY WERE MOVED BY HER STORY, BY HER APPEAL FOR HELP. THE ROLES THEY WERE PLAYING WERE *TAKING OVER* --
-- AND THEY WERE FORGETTING THAT IT WAS SUPPOSED TO BE NOTHING MORE THAN A *RUSE.*
YES, IT WAS INTERESTING TO *WATCH,* BUT THIS WASN'T THE *FIRST* EXAMPLE OF IT -- AND IT POSED A GRAVE *DANGER* TO OUR OVERALL PLAN.
COME ON, HALLIE -- LET'S GET YOU SOMETHING TO *WEAR.* TECHNO'S WHIPPED UP THIS *AMAZING* UNIFORM SYNTHESIZER --
-- AND, WELL, IT'S NOT EXACTLY SET UP FOR STREET *CLOTHES,* BUT I'M SURE WE CAN MANAGE SOMETHING BETTER THAN *THIS.*
THANK YOU...
SO ONCE THEY'D GOTTEN HALLIE SOME CLOTHES AND SOME FOOD --
-- WE SET OFF FOR *UPSTATE,* AND I TRIED TO *WARN* CITIZEN V --
-- REMEMBER, MOST OF THEM HAVE BEEN *OUTCASTS* OR *REJECTS* THEIR ENTIRE LIVES, AND THE PSYCHOLOGICAL POWER OF *ROLE-PLAYING* --
-- COMBINED WITH THE MASSIVE SOCIETAL APPROVAL --
Pfah! YOU'RE JUMPING AT *SHADOWS,* METEORITE!
YOU REMEMBER *THIS,* Dr. SOFEN. YOU MAY BE A SKILLED PSYCHIATRIST, BUT THESE ARE THE *MASTERS OF EVIL* -- AND I AM A *ZEMO!*
I AM PERFECTLY CAPABLE OF KEEPING MY *TEAM* IN LINE -- EVEN IF *YOU* AREN'T!
NOW LET'S HAVE *NO MORE* OF THIS FOOLISHNESS!
THAT WAS *HALF AN HOUR* AGO. AND NOW --

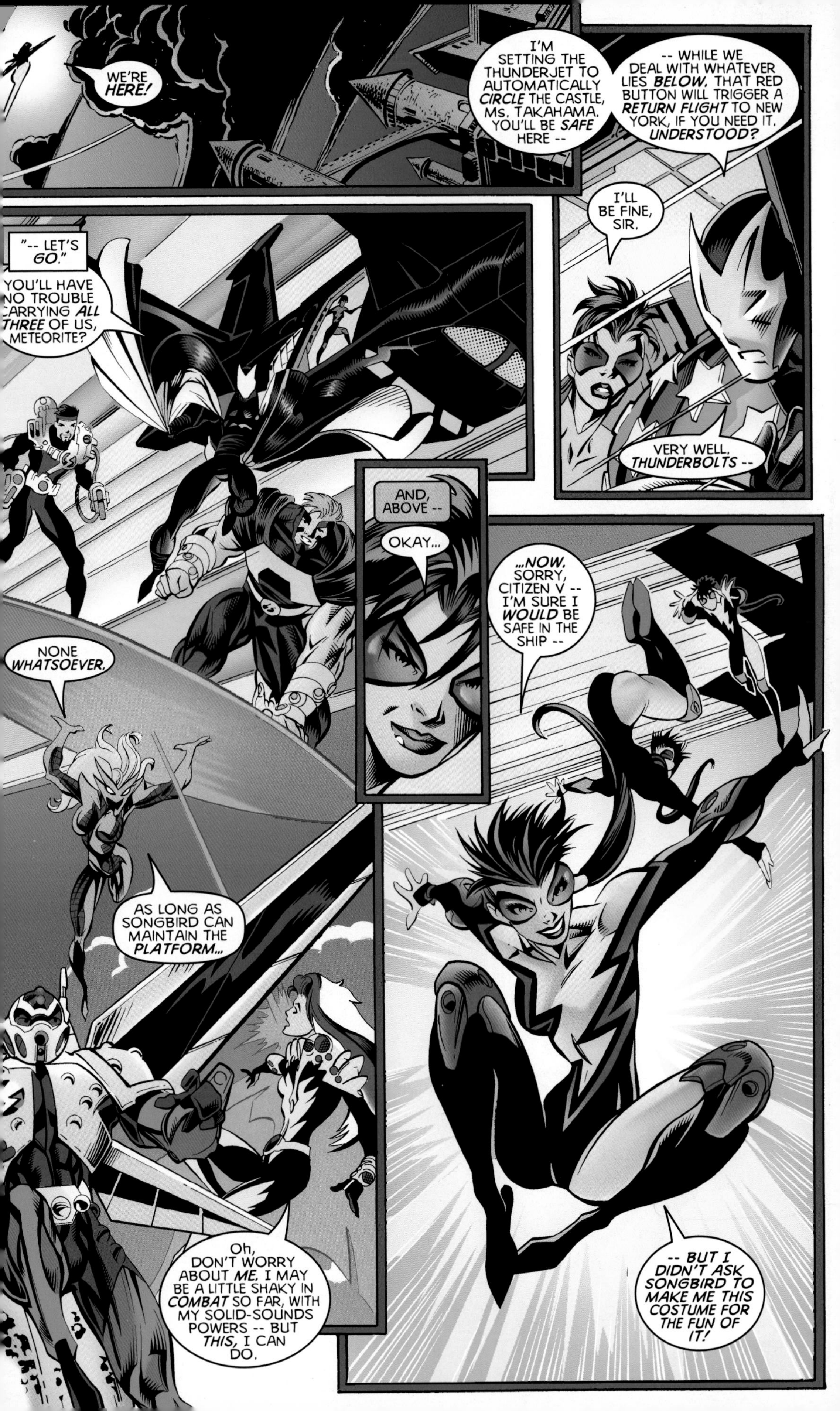
WE'RE HERE!
I'M SETTING THE THUNDERJET TO AUTOMATICALLY CIRCLE THE CASTLE, Ms. TAKAHAMA. YOU'LL BE SAFE HERE --
-- WHILE WE DEAL WITH WHATEVER LIES BELOW. THAT RED BUTTON WILL TRIGGER A RETURN FLIGHT TO NEW YORK, IF YOU NEED IT. UNDERSTOOD?
I'LL BE FINE, SIR.
VERY WELL, THUNDERBOLTS --
"-- LET'S GO."
YOU'LL HAVE NO TROUBLE CARRYING ALL THREE OF US, METEORITE?
NONE WHATSOEVER.
AS LONG AS SONGBIRD CAN MAINTAIN THE PLATFORM...
Oh, DON'T WORRY ABOUT ME. I MAY BE A LITTLE SHAKY IN COMBAT SO FAR, WITH MY SOLID-SOUNDS POWERS -- BUT THIS, I CAN DO.
AND, ABOVE --
OKAY...
...NOW, SORRY, CITIZEN V -- I'M SURE I WOULD BE SAFE IN THE SHIP --
-- BUT I DIDN'T ASK SONGBIRD TO MAKE ME THIS COSTUME FOR THE FUN OF IT!

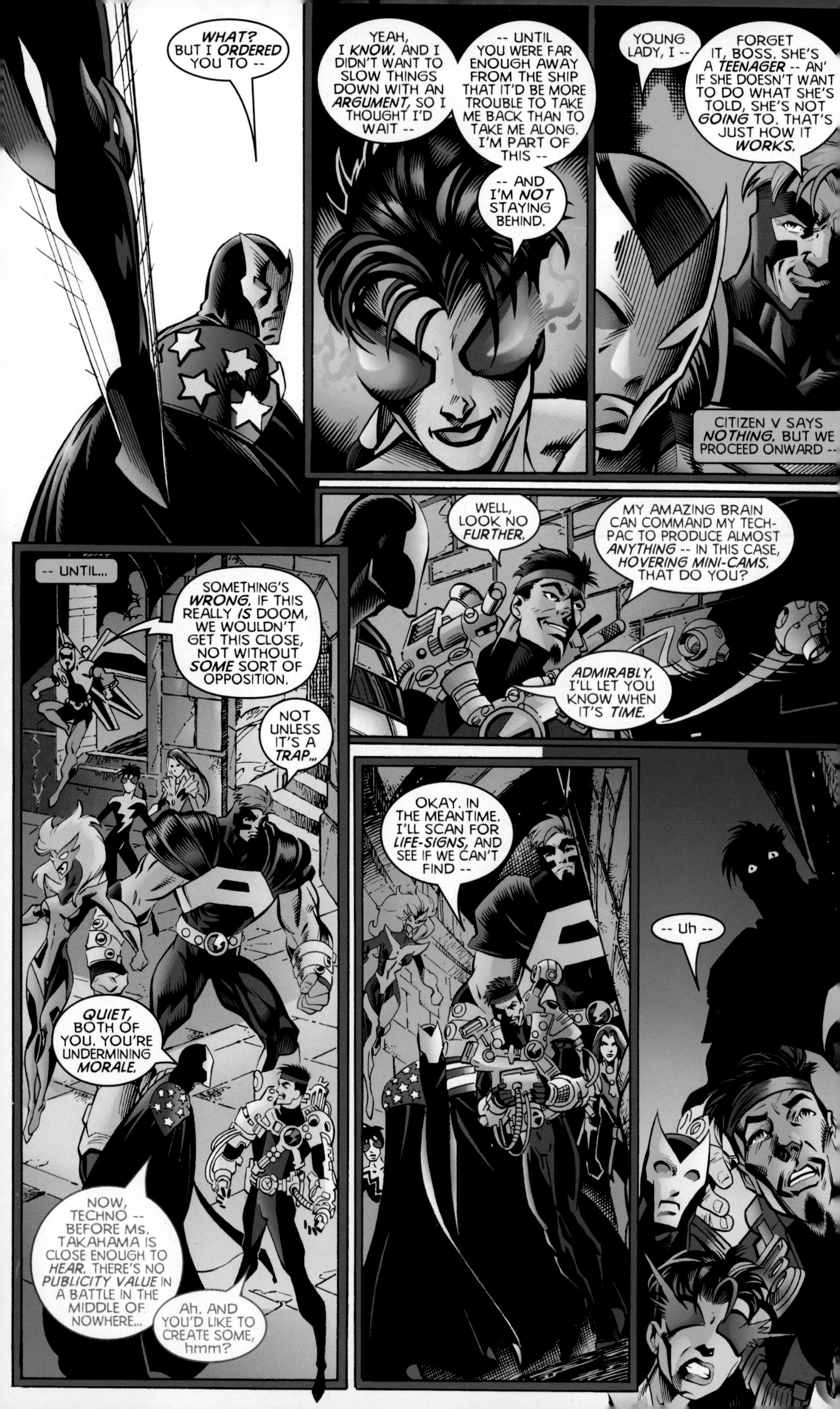

WHAT? BUT I ORDERED YOU TO --
YEAH, I KNOW. AND I DIDN'T WANT TO SLOW THINGS DOWN WITH AN ARGUMENT, SO I THOUGHT I'D WAIT --
-- UNTIL YOU WERE FAR ENOUGH AWAY FROM THE SHIP THAT IT'D BE MORE TROUBLE TO TAKE ME BACK THAN TO TAKE ME ALONG. I'M PART OF THIS --
-- AND I'M NOT STAYING BEHIND.
YOUNG LADY, I --
FORGET IT, BOSS. SHE'S A TEENAGER -- AN' IF SHE DOESN'T WANT TO DO WHAT SHE'S TOLD, SHE'S NOT GOING TO. THAT'S JUST HOW IT WORKS.
CITIZEN V SAYS NOTHING, BUT WE PROCEED ONWARD --
-- UNTIL...
SOMETHING'S WRONG. IF THIS REALLY IS DOOM, WE WOULDN'T GET THIS CLOSE, NOT WITHOUT SOME SORT OF OPPOSITION.
NOT UNLESS IT'S A TRAP...
QUIET, BOTH OF YOU. YOU'RE UNDERMINING MORALE.
NOW, TECHNO -- BEFORE Ms. TAKAHAMA IS CLOSE ENOUGH TO HEAR, THERE'S NO PUBLICITY VALUE IN A BATTLE IN THE MIDDLE OF NOWHERE...
Ah. AND YOU'D LIKE TO CREATE SOME, hmm?
WELL, LOOK NO FURTHER.
MY AMAZING BRAIN CAN COMMAND MY TECH-PAC TO PRODUCE ALMOST ANYTHING -- IN THIS CASE, HOVERING MINI-CAMS. THAT DO YOU?
ADMIRABLY. I'LL LET YOU KNOW WHEN IT'S TIME.
OKAY. IN THE MEANTIME, I'LL SCAN FOR LIFE-SIGNS, AND SEE IF WE CAN'T FIND --
-- Uh --

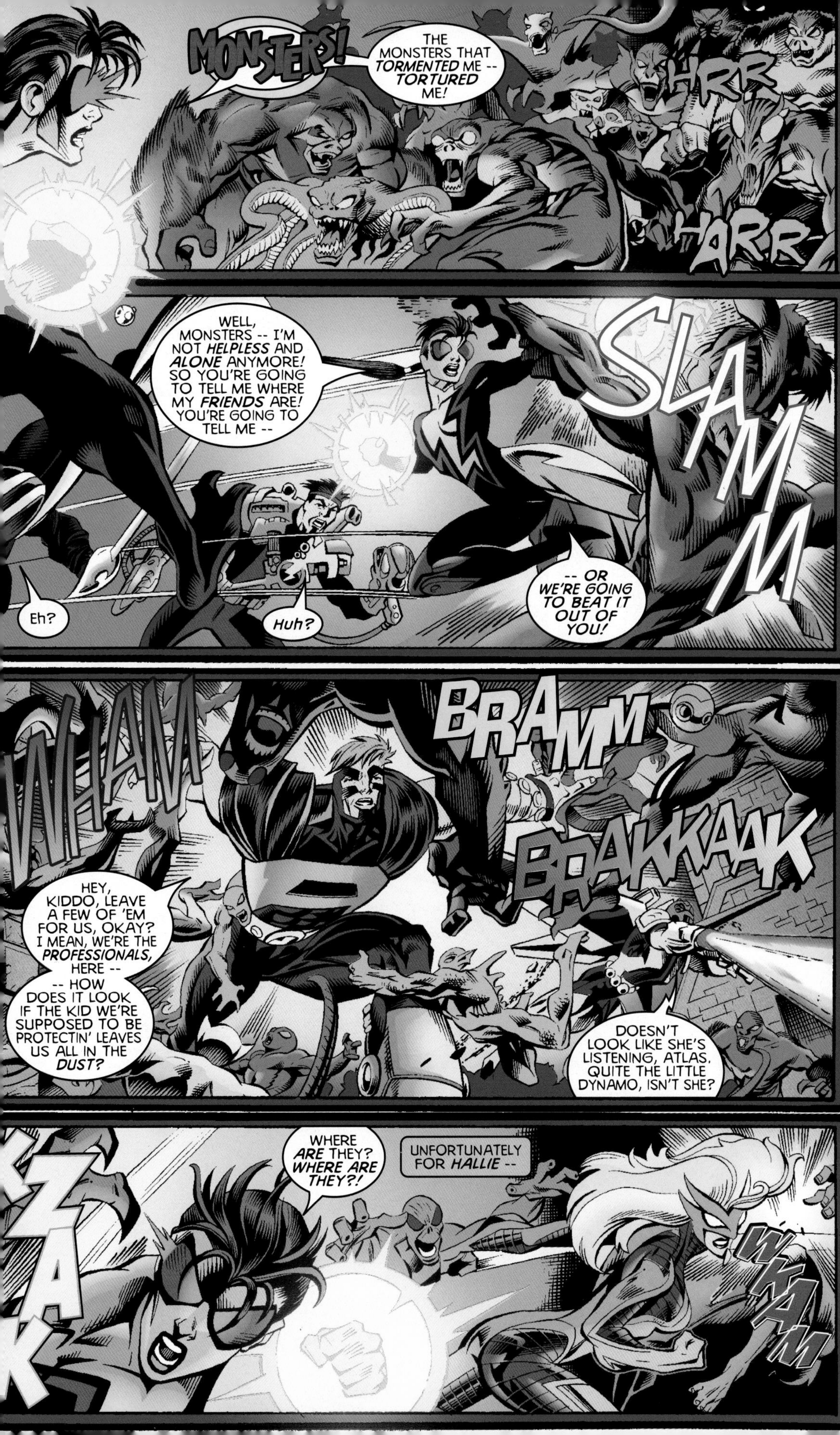
MONSTERS!
THE MONSTERS THAT TORMENTED ME -- TORTURED ME!
HRR
HARR
WELL, MONSTERS -- I'M NOT HELPLESS AND ALONE ANYMORE! SO YOU'RE GOING TO TELL ME WHERE MY FRIENDS ARE! YOU'RE GOING TO TELL ME --
SLAMMM
Eh?
Huh?
-- OR WE'RE GOING TO BEAT IT OUT OF YOU!
WHAM
BRAMM
BRAKKAAK
HEY, KIDDO, LEAVE A FEW OF 'EM FOR US, OKAY? I MEAN, WE'RE THE PROFESSIONALS, HERE --
-- HOW DOES IT LOOK IF THE KID WE'RE SUPPOSED TO BE PROTECTIN' LEAVES US ALL IN THE DUST?
DOESN'T LOOK LIKE SHE'S LISTENING, ATLAS. QUITE THE LITTLE DYNAMO, ISN'T SHE?
ZZAK
WHERE ARE THEY? WHERE ARE THEY?!
UNFORTUNATELY FOR HALLIE --
WKAM

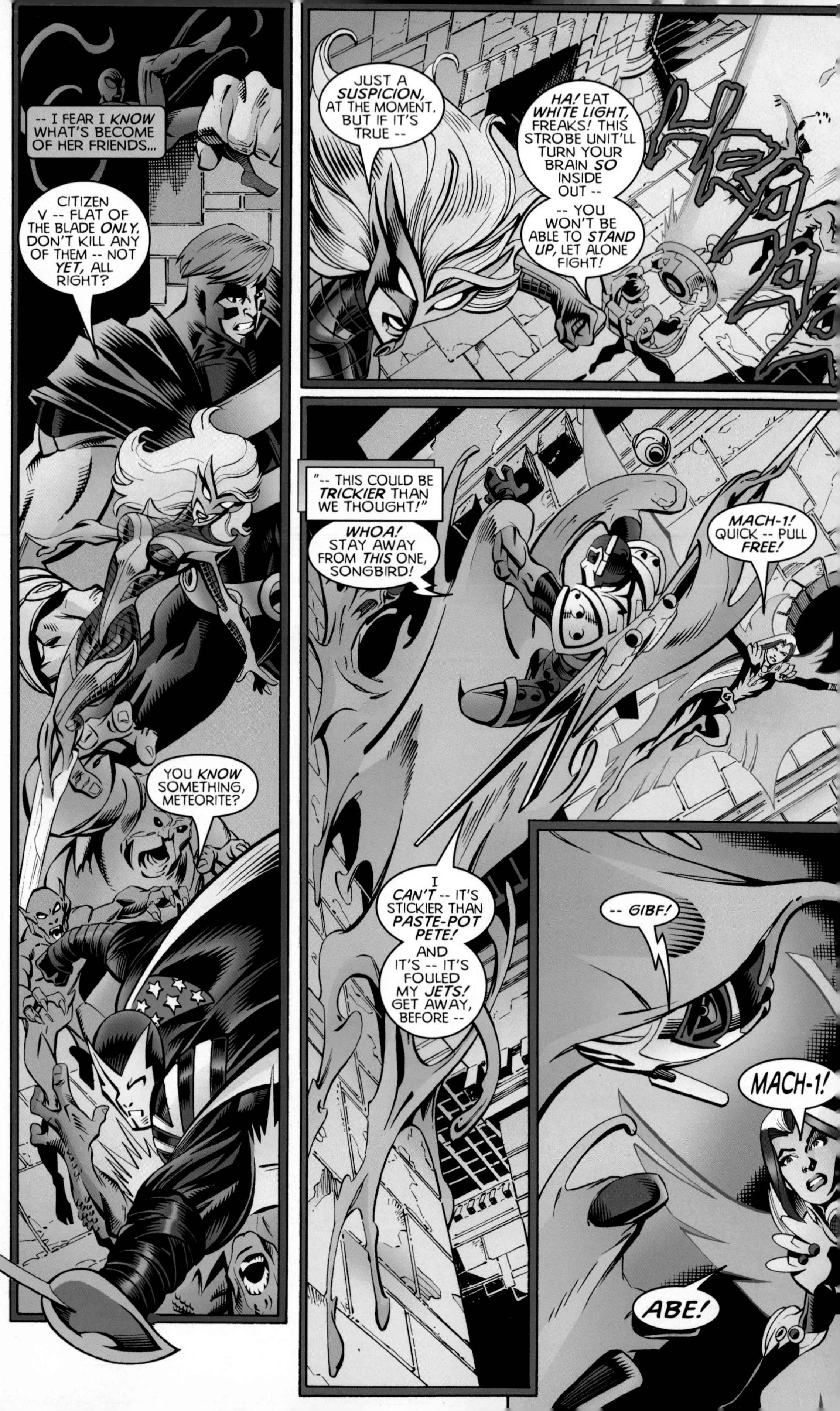
-- I FEAR I *KNOW* WHAT'S BECOME OF HER FRIENDS...
CITIZEN V -- FLAT OF THE BLADE *ONLY*, DON'T KILL ANY OF THEM -- NOT *YET*, ALL RIGHT?
YOU *KNOW* SOMETHING, METEORITE?
JUST A *SUSPICION*, AT THE MOMENT. BUT IF IT'S TRUE --
HA! EAT *WHITE LIGHT*, FREAKS! THIS STROBE UNIT'LL TURN YOUR BRAIN *SO* INSIDE OUT --
-- YOU WON'T BE ABLE TO *STAND UP*, LET ALONE FIGHT!
"-- THIS COULD BE *TRICKIER* THAN WE THOUGHT!"
WHOA! STAY AWAY FROM *THIS* ONE, SONGBIRD!
MACH-1! QUICK -- PULL *FREE!*
I *CAN'T* -- IT'S STICKIER THAN *PASTE-POT PETE!* AND IT'S -- IT'S FOULED MY *JETS!* GET AWAY, BEFORE --
-- *GIBF!*
MACH-1!
ABE!

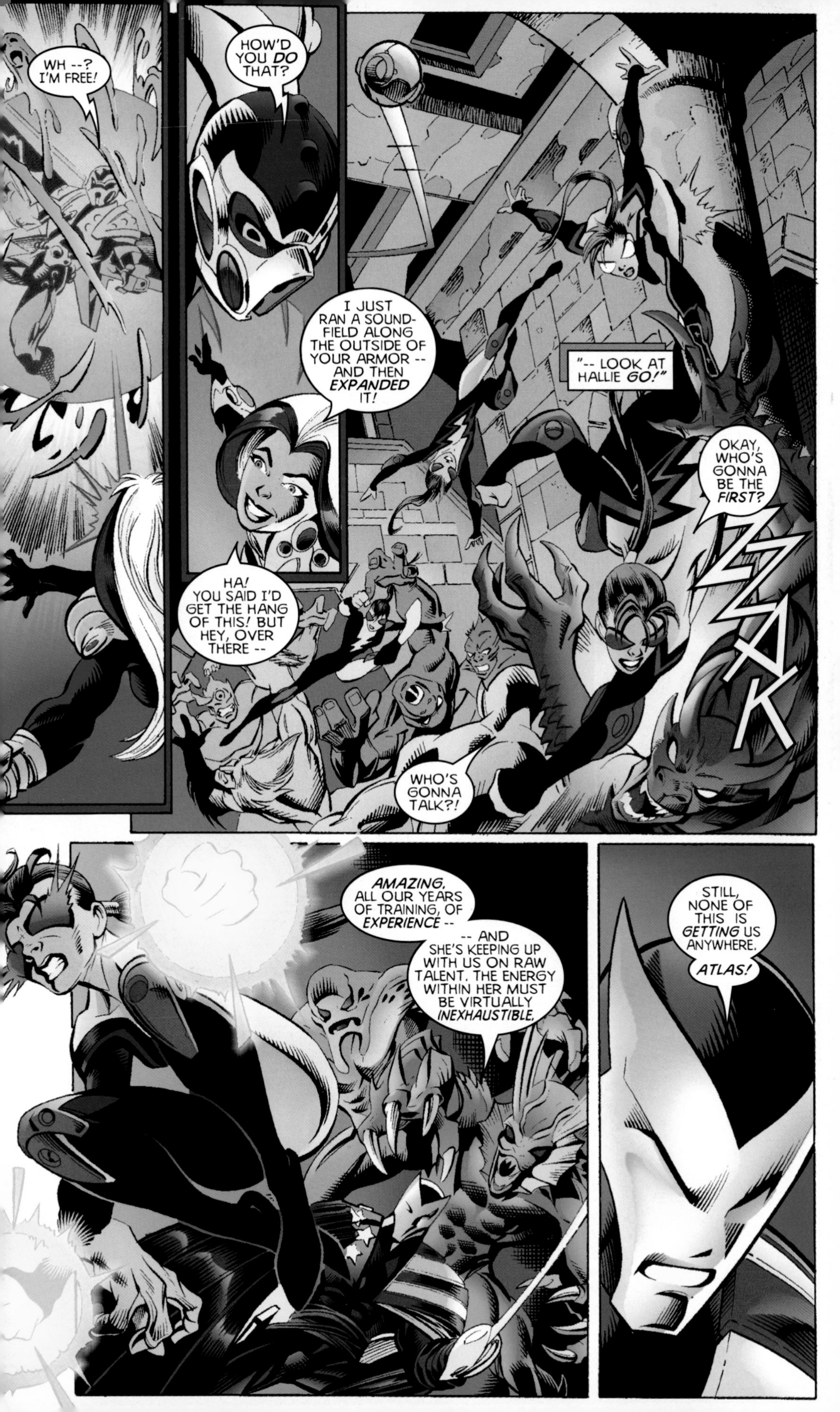
WH --? I'M FREE!
HOW'D YOU *DO* THAT?
I JUST RAN A SOUND-FIELD ALONG THE OUTSIDE OF YOUR ARMOR -- AND THEN *EXPANDED* IT!
HA! YOU SAID I'D GET THE HANG OF THIS! BUT HEY, OVER THERE --
"-- LOOK AT HALLIE *GO!*"
OKAY, WHO'S GONNA BE THE *FIRST?*
ZZAK
WHO'S GONNA TALK?!
AMAZING. ALL OUR YEARS OF TRAINING, OF *EXPERIENCE* --
-- AND SHE'S KEEPING UP WITH US ON RAW TALENT. THE ENERGY WITHIN HER MUST BE VIRTUALLY *INEXHAUSTIBLE.*
STILL, NONE OF THIS IS *GETTING* US ANYWHERE, *ATLAS!*

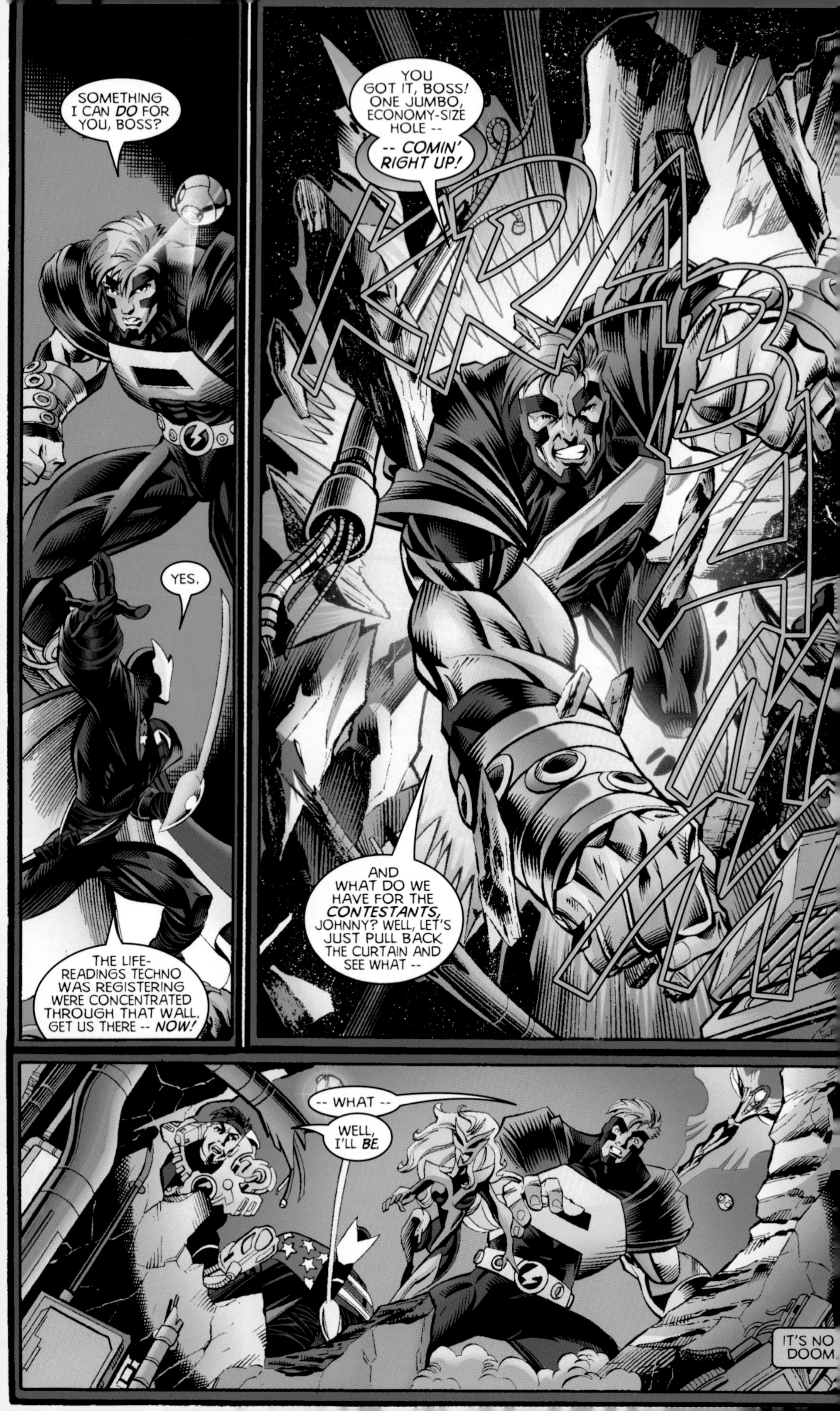
SOMETHING I CAN *DO* FOR YOU, BOSS?
YES.
THE LIFE-READINGS TECHNO WAS REGISTERING WERE CONCENTRATED THROUGH THAT WALL. GET US THERE -- *NOW!*
YOU GOT IT, BOSS! ONE JUMBO, ECONOMY-SIZE HOLE --
-- *COMIN' RIGHT UP!*
AND WHAT DO WE HAVE FOR THE *CONTESTANTS,* JOHNNY? WELL, LET'S JUST PULL BACK THE CURTAIN AND SEE WHAT --
-- WHAT --
WELL, I'LL *BE.*
IT'S NO
DOOM

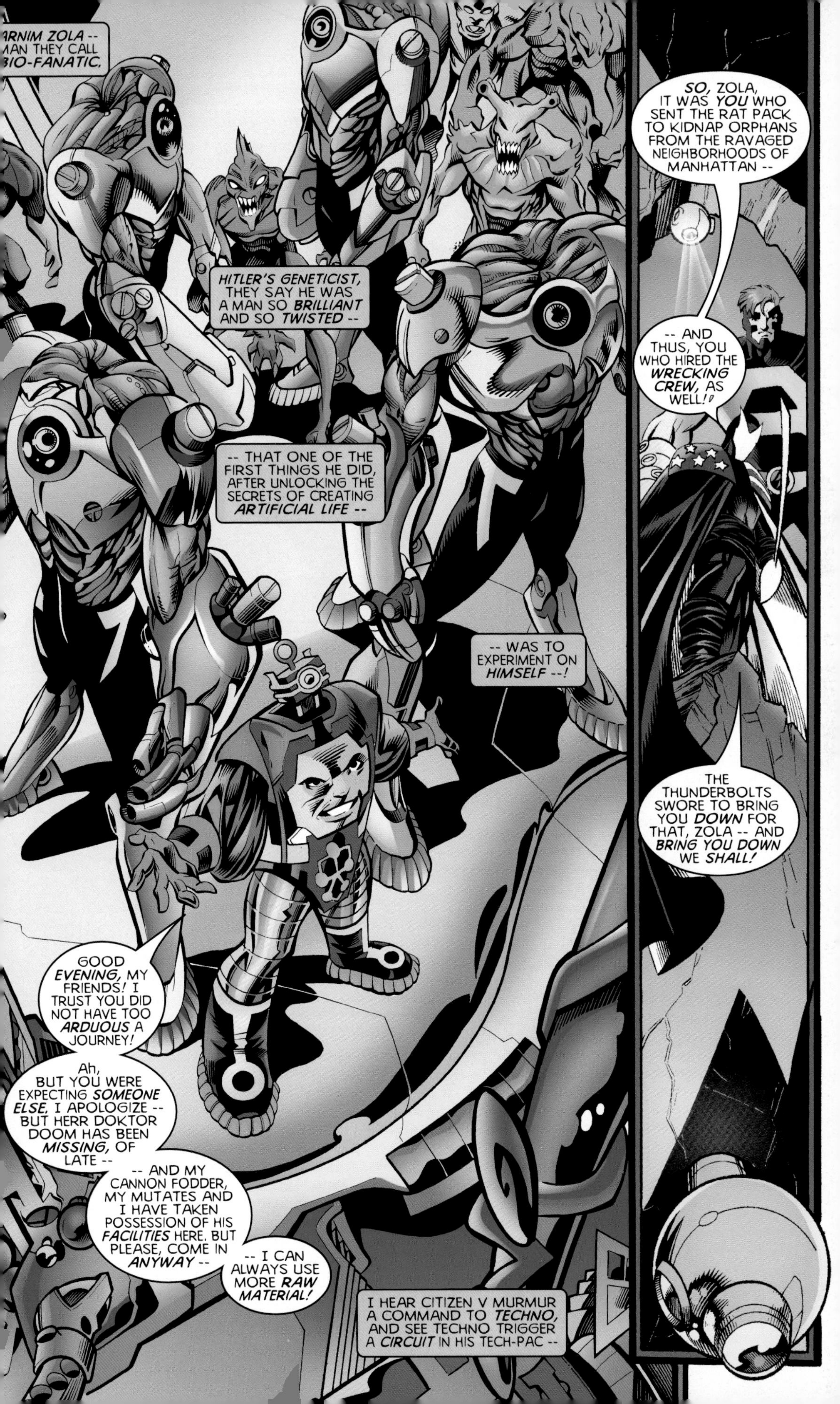

ARNIM ZOLA -- MAN THEY CALL BIO-FANATIC.
HITLER'S GENETICIST, THEY SAY HE WAS A MAN SO BRILLIANT AND SO TWISTED --
-- THAT ONE OF THE FIRST THINGS HE DID, AFTER UNLOCKING THE SECRETS OF CREATING ARTIFICIAL LIFE --
-- WAS TO EXPERIMENT ON HIMSELF --!
GOOD EVENING, MY FRIENDS! I TRUST YOU DID NOT HAVE TOO ARDUOUS A JOURNEY!
Ah, BUT YOU WERE EXPECTING SOMEONE ELSE, I APOLOGIZE -- BUT HERR DOKTOR DOOM HAS BEEN MISSING, OF LATE --
-- AND MY CANNON FODDER, MY MUTATES AND I HAVE TAKEN POSSESSION OF HIS FACILITIES HERE. BUT PLEASE, COME IN ANYWAY --
-- I CAN ALWAYS USE MORE RAW MATERIAL!
SO, ZOLA, IT WAS YOU WHO SENT THE RAT PACK TO KIDNAP ORPHANS FROM THE RAVAGED NEIGHBORHOODS OF MANHATTAN --
-- AND THUS, YOU WHO HIRED THE WRECKING CREW, AS WELL!
THE THUNDERBOLTS SWORE TO BRING YOU DOWN FOR THAT, ZOLA -- AND BRING YOU DOWN WE SHALL!
I HEAR CITIZEN V MURMUR A COMMAND TO TECHNO, AND SEE TECHNO TRIGGER A CIRCUIT IN HIS TECH-PAC --

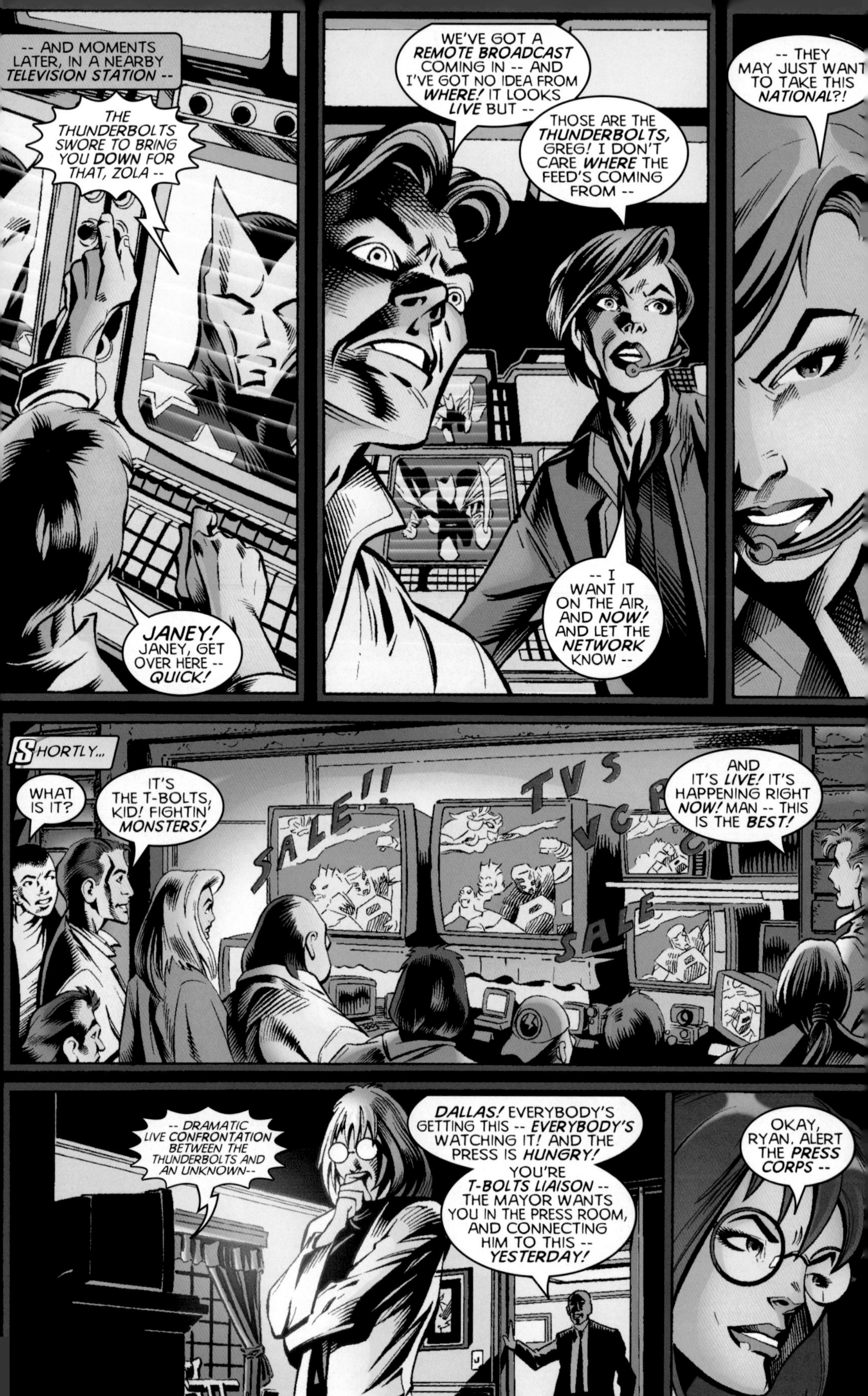

-- AND MOMENTS LATER, IN A NEARBY TELEVISION STATION --
THE THUNDERBOLTS SWORE TO BRING YOU DOWN FOR THAT, ZOLA --
JANEY! JANEY, GET OVER HERE -- QUICK!
WE'VE GOT A REMOTE BROADCAST COMING IN -- AND I'VE GOT NO IDEA FROM WHERE! IT LOOKS LIVE BUT --
THOSE ARE THE THUNDERBOLTS, GREG! I DON'T CARE WHERE THE FEED'S COMING FROM --
-- I WANT IT ON THE AIR, AND NOW! AND LET THE NETWORK KNOW --
-- THEY MAY JUST WANT TO TAKE THIS NATIONAL?!
SHORTLY...
WHAT IS IT?
IT'S THE T-BOLTS, KID! FIGHTIN' MONSTERS!
SALE!!
TVS
VCR
SALE
AND IT'S LIVE! IT'S HAPPENING RIGHT NOW! MAN -- THIS IS THE BEST!
-- DRAMATIC LIVE CONFRONTATION BETWEEN THE THUNDERBOLTS AND AN UNKNOWN--
DALLAS! EVERYBODY'S GETTING THIS -- EVERYBODY'S WATCHING IT! AND THE PRESS IS HUNGRY!
YOU'RE T-BOLTS LIAISON -- THE MAYOR WANTS YOU IN THE PRESS ROOM, AND CONNECTING HIM TO THIS -- YESTERDAY!
OKAY, RYAN. ALERT THE PRESS CORPS --

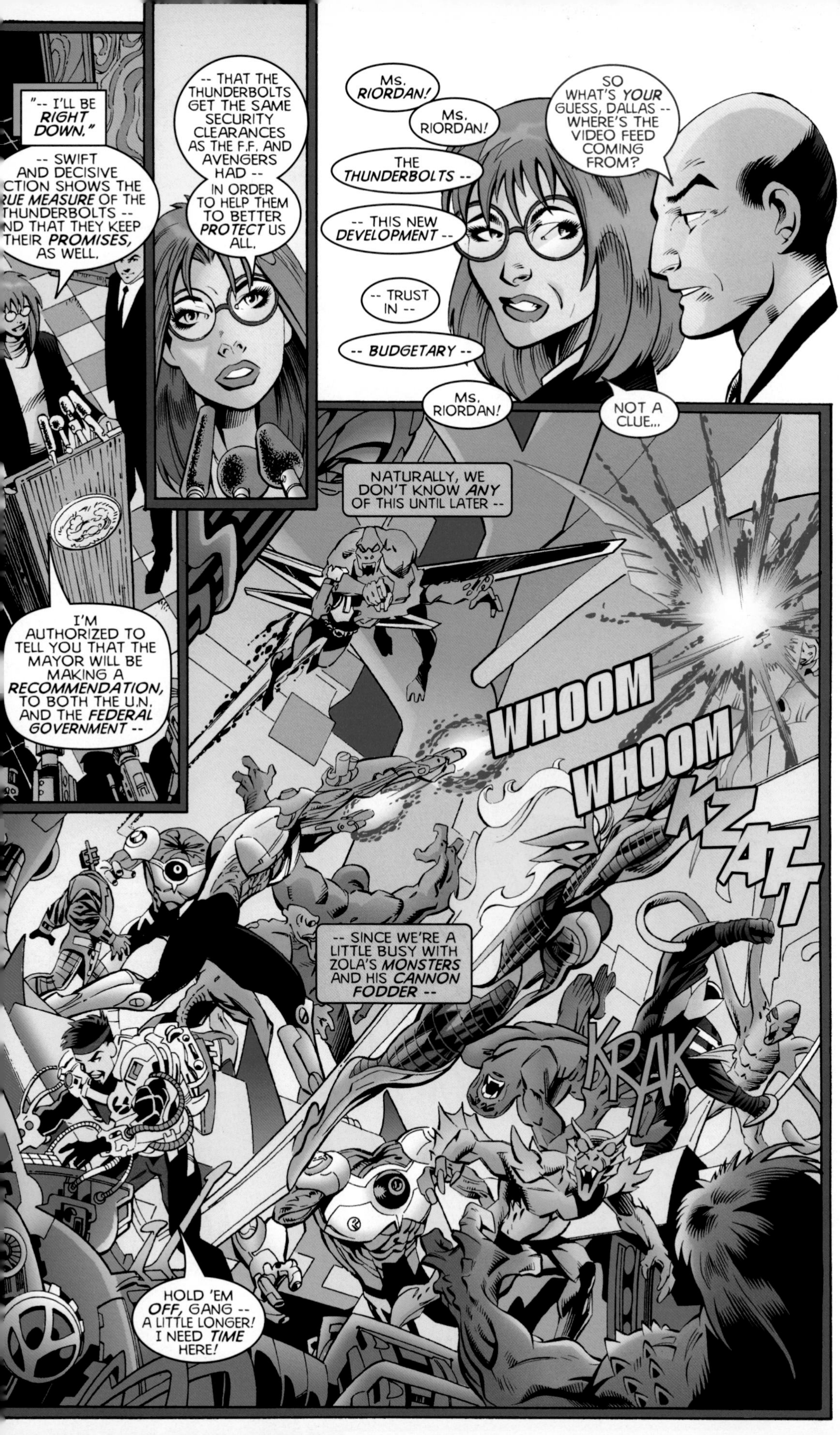
"-- I'LL BE RIGHT DOWN."
-- SWIFT AND DECISIVE ACTION SHOWS THE TRUE MEASURE OF THE THUNDERBOLTS -- AND THAT THEY KEEP THEIR PROMISES, AS WELL.
I'M AUTHORIZED TO TELL YOU THAT THE MAYOR WILL BE MAKING A RECOMMENDATION, TO BOTH THE U.N. AND THE FEDERAL GOVERNMENT --
-- THAT THE THUNDERBOLTS GET THE SAME SECURITY CLEARANCES AS THE F.F. AND AVENGERS HAD --
IN ORDER TO HELP THEM TO BETTER PROTECT US ALL.
Ms. RIORDAN!
Ms. RIORDAN!
THE THUNDERBOLTS --
-- THIS NEW DEVELOPMENT --
-- TRUST IN --
-- BUDGETARY --
Ms. RIORDAN!
SO WHAT'S YOUR GUESS, DALLAS -- WHERE'S THE VIDEO FEED COMING FROM?
NOT A CLUE...
NATURALLY, WE DON'T KNOW ANY OF THIS UNTIL LATER --
WHOOM
WHOOM
KZAT
-- SINCE WE'RE A LITTLE BUSY WITH ZOLA'S MONSTERS AND HIS CANNON FODDER --
KRAK
HOLD 'EM OFF, GANG -- A LITTLE LONGER! I NEED TIME HERE!

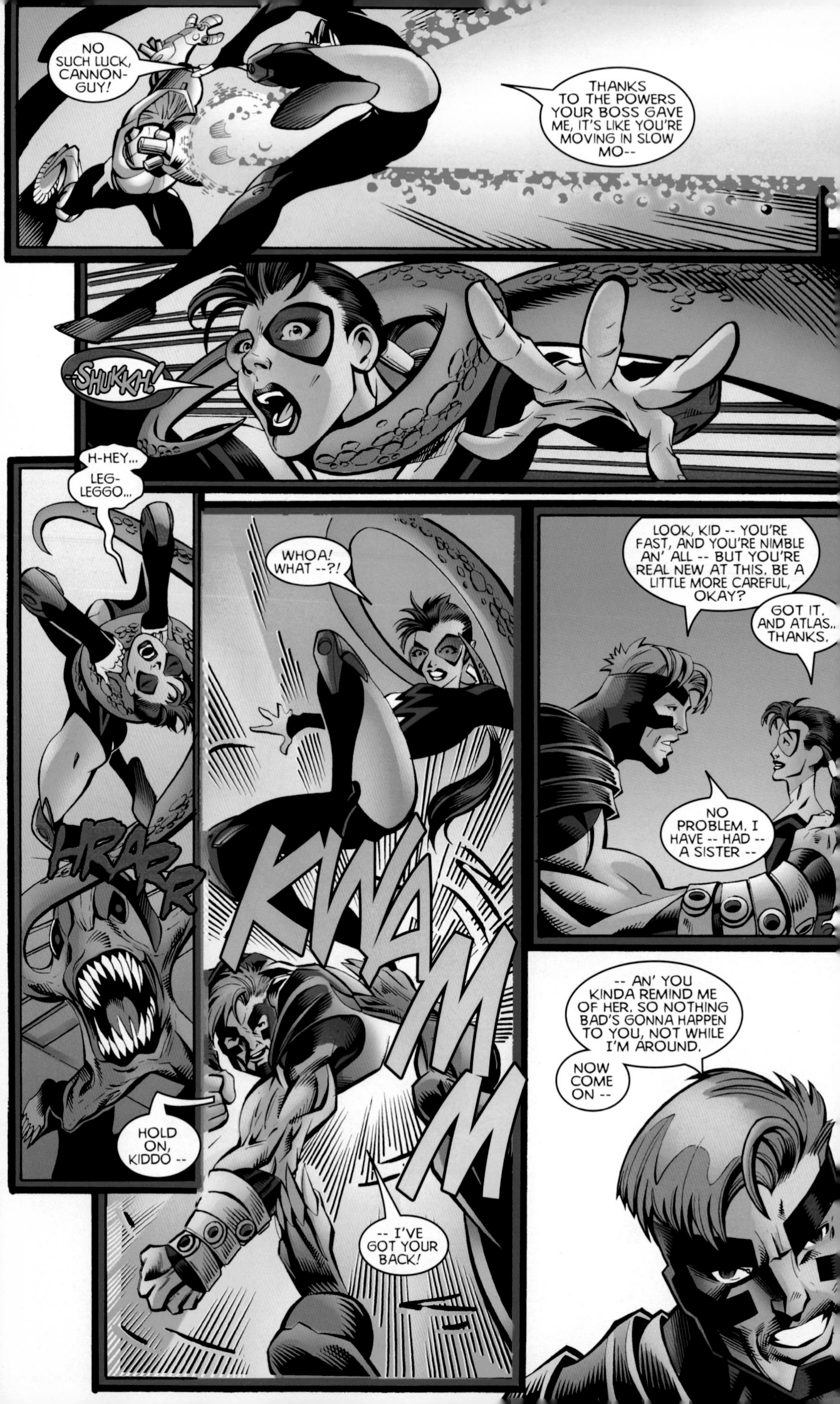
NO SUCH LUCK, CANNON-GUY!
THANKS TO THE POWERS YOUR BOSS GAVE ME, IT'S LIKE YOU'RE MOVING IN SLOW MO--
SHUKKH!
H-HEY... LEG-LEGGO...
HRARR
HOLD ON, KIDDO --
WHOA! WHAT --?!
KWAMM
-- I'VE GOT YOUR BACK!
LOOK, KID -- YOU'RE FAST, AND YOU'RE NIMBLE AN' ALL -- BUT YOU'RE REAL NEW AT THIS. BE A LITTLE MORE CAREFUL, OKAY?
GOT IT. AND ATLAS.. THANKS.
NO PROBLEM. I HAVE -- HAD -- A SISTER --
-- AN' YOU KINDA REMIND ME OF HER. SO NOTHING BAD'S GONNA HAPPEN TO YOU, NOT WHILE I'M AROUND.
NOW COME ON --

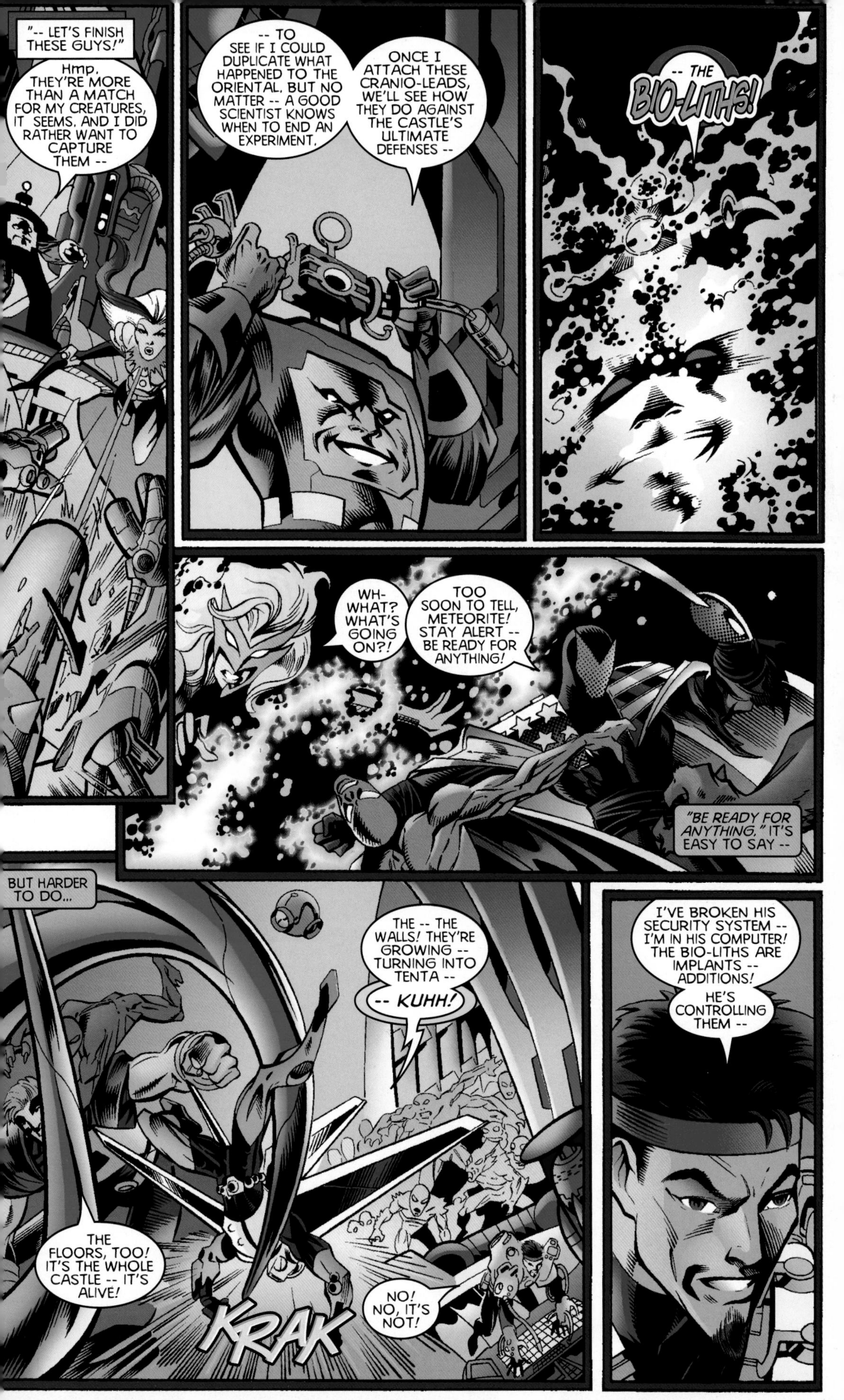
"-- LET'S FINISH THESE GUYS!"
Hmp, THEY'RE MORE THAN A MATCH FOR MY CREATURES, IT SEEMS, AND I DID RATHER WANT TO CAPTURE THEM --
-- TO SEE IF I COULD DUPLICATE WHAT HAPPENED TO THE ORIENTAL, BUT NO MATTER -- A GOOD SCIENTIST KNOWS WHEN TO END AN EXPERIMENT.
ONCE I ATTACH THESE CRANIO-LEADS, WE'LL SEE HOW THEY DO AGAINST THE CASTLE'S ULTIMATE DEFENSES --
-- THE BIO-LITHS!
WH-WHAT? WHAT'S GOING ON?!
TOO SOON TO TELL, METEORITE! STAY ALERT -- BE READY FOR ANYTHING!
"BE READY FOR ANYTHING," IT'S EASY TO SAY --
BUT HARDER TO DO...
THE -- THE WALLS! THEY'RE GROWING -- TURNING INTO TENTA --
-- KUHH!
THE FLOORS, TOO! IT'S THE WHOLE CASTLE -- IT'S ALIVE!
KRAK
NO! NO, IT'S NOT!
I'VE BROKEN HIS SECURITY SYSTEM -- I'M IN HIS COMPUTER! THE BIO-LITHS ARE IMPLANTS -- ADDITIONS!
HE'S CONTROLLING THEM --

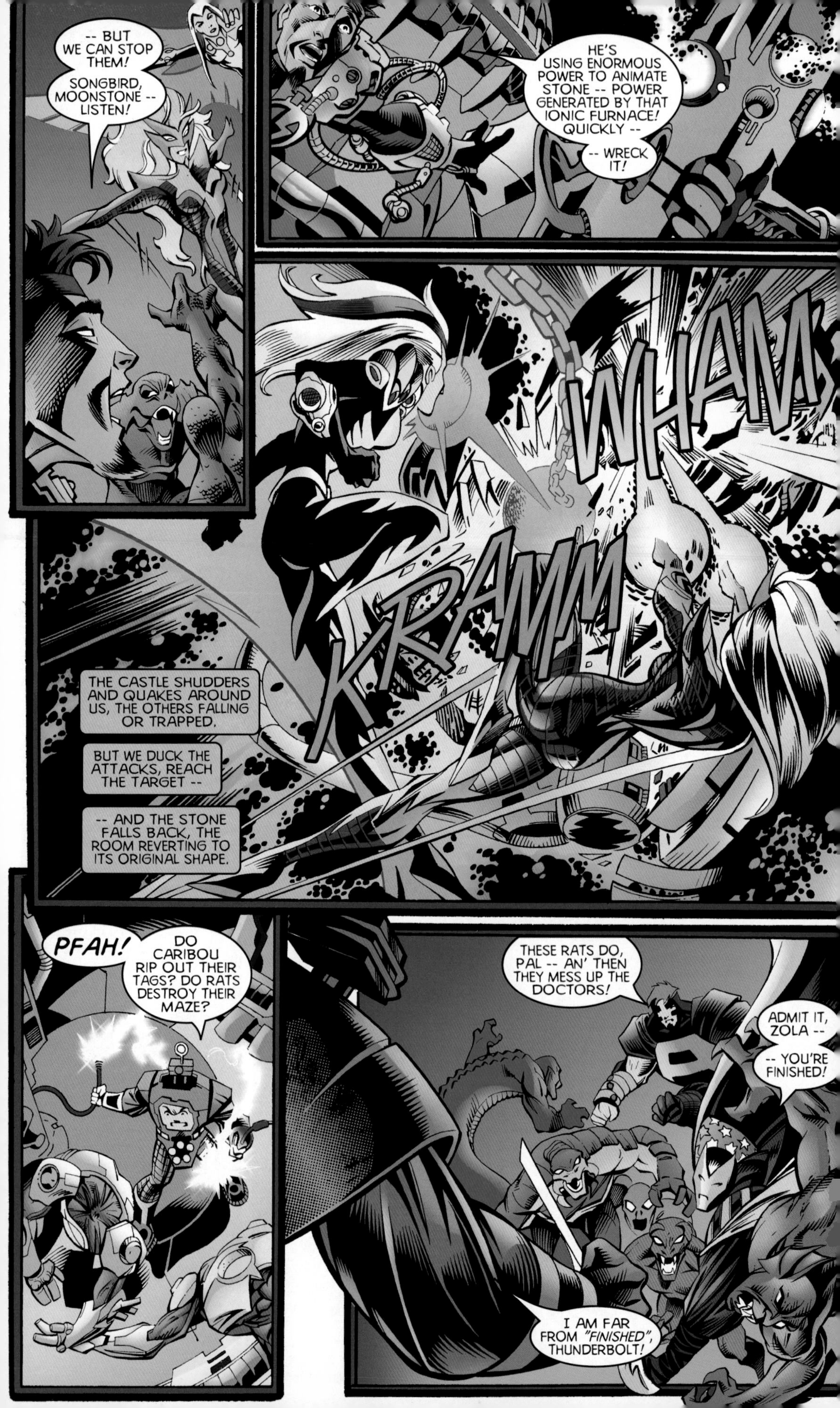
-- BUT WE CAN STOP THEM!
SONGBIRD, MOONSTONE -- LISTEN!
HE'S USING ENORMOUS POWER TO ANIMATE STONE -- POWER GENERATED BY THAT IONIC FURNACE! QUICKLY --
-- WRECK IT!
WHAM
KRAMM
THE CASTLE SHUDDERS AND QUAKES AROUND US, THE OTHERS FALLING OR TRAPPED.
BUT WE DUCK THE ATTACKS, REACH THE TARGET --
-- AND THE STONE FALLS BACK, THE ROOM REVERTING TO ITS ORIGINAL SHAPE.
PFAH!
DO CARIBOU RIP OUT THEIR TAGS? DO RATS DESTROY THEIR MAZE?
THESE RATS DO, PAL -- AN' THEN THEY MESS UP THE DOCTORS!
ADMIT IT, ZOLA --
-- YOU'RE FINISHED!
I AM FAR FROM "FINISHED", THUNDERBOLT!

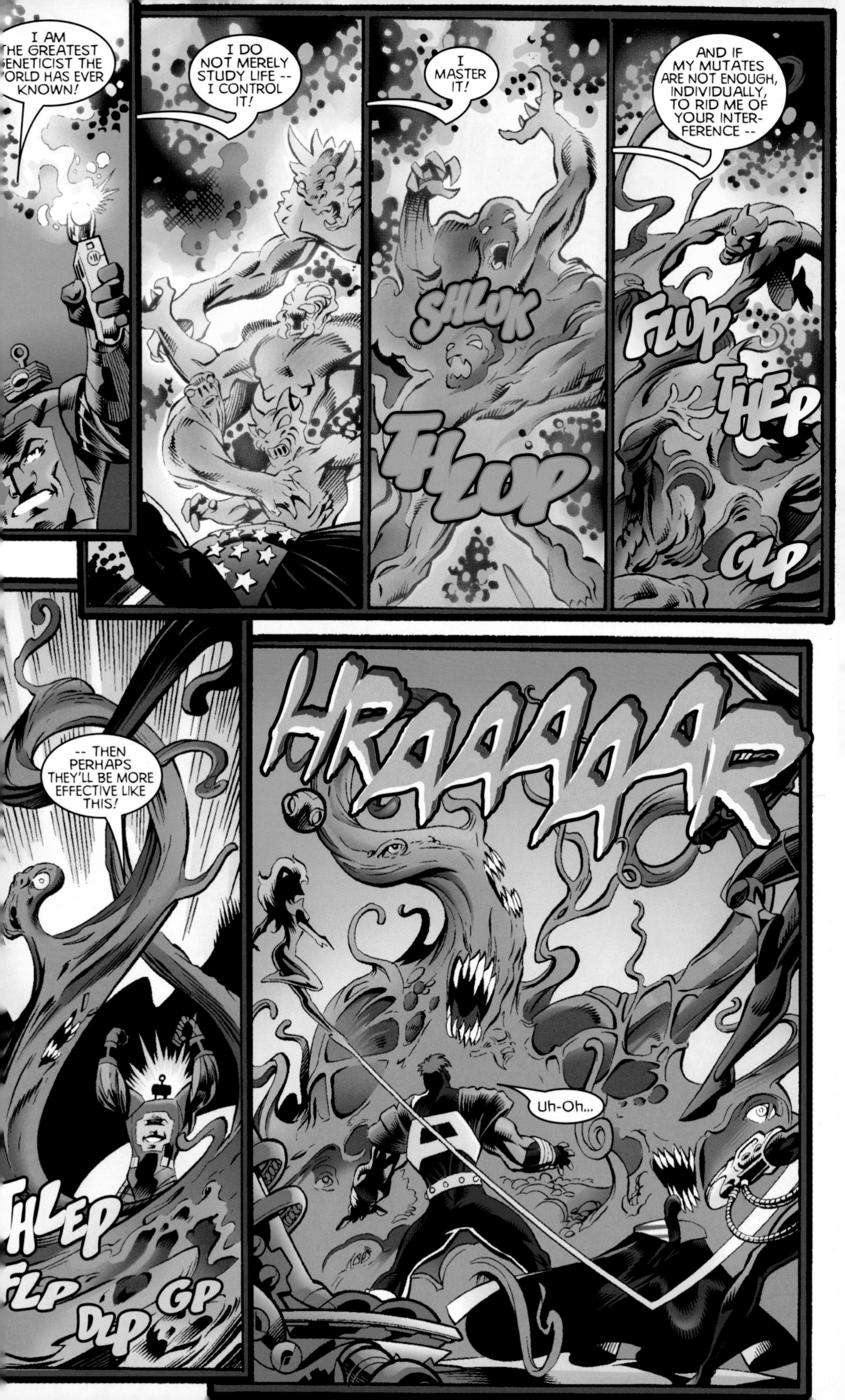
I AM THE GREATEST GENETICIST THE WORLD HAS EVER KNOWN!
I DO NOT MERELY STUDY LIFE -- I CONTROL IT!
I MASTER IT!
SHLUK
THLOP
AND IF MY MUTATES ARE NOT ENOUGH, INDIVIDUALLY, TO RID ME OF YOUR INTER-FERENCE --
FLUP
THEP
GLP
-- THEN PERHAPS THEY'LL BE MORE EFFECTIVE LIKE THIS!
THLEP
FLP
DLP
GP
HRAAAAAR
Uh-Oh...

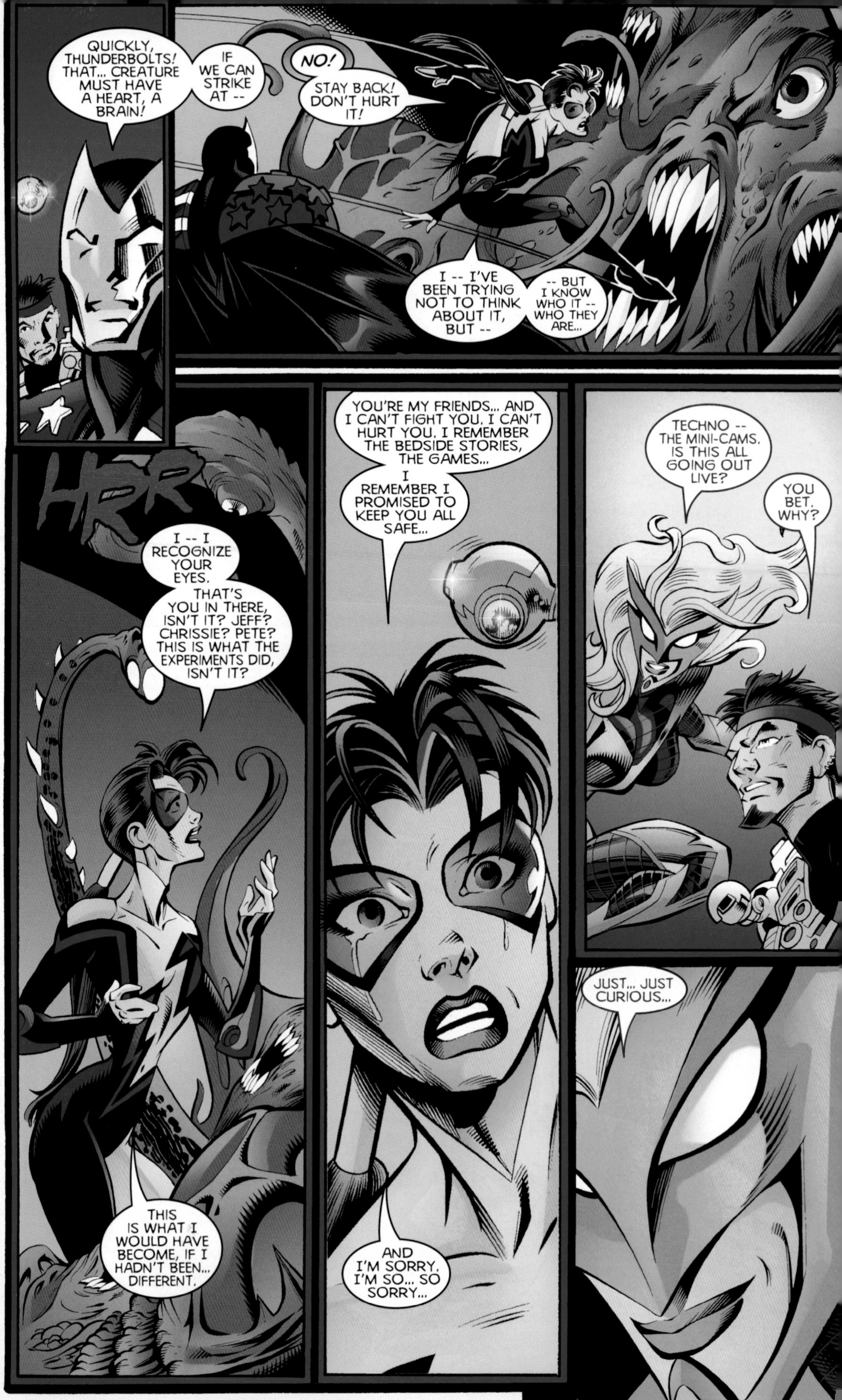
QUICKLY, THUNDERBOLTS! THAT... CREATURE MUST HAVE A HEART, A BRAIN!
IF WE CAN STRIKE AT --
NO!
STAY BACK! DON'T HURT IT!
I -- I'VE BEEN TRYING NOT TO THINK ABOUT IT, BUT --
-- BUT I KNOW WHO IT -- WHO THEY ARE...
HRR
I -- I RECOGNIZE YOUR EYES.
THAT'S YOU IN THERE, ISN'T IT? JEFF? CHRISSIE? PETE? THIS IS WHAT THE EXPERIMENTS DID, ISN'T IT?
THIS IS WHAT I WOULD HAVE BECOME, IF I HADN'T BEEN... DIFFERENT.
YOU'RE MY FRIENDS... AND I CAN'T FIGHT YOU. I CAN'T HURT YOU. I REMEMBER THE BEDSIDE STORIES, THE GAMES...
I REMEMBER I PROMISED TO KEEP YOU ALL SAFE...
AND I'M SORRY. I'M SO... SO SORRY...
TECHNO -- THE MINI-CAMS. IS THIS ALL GOING OUT LIVE?
YOU BET. WHY?
JUST... JUST CURIOUS...

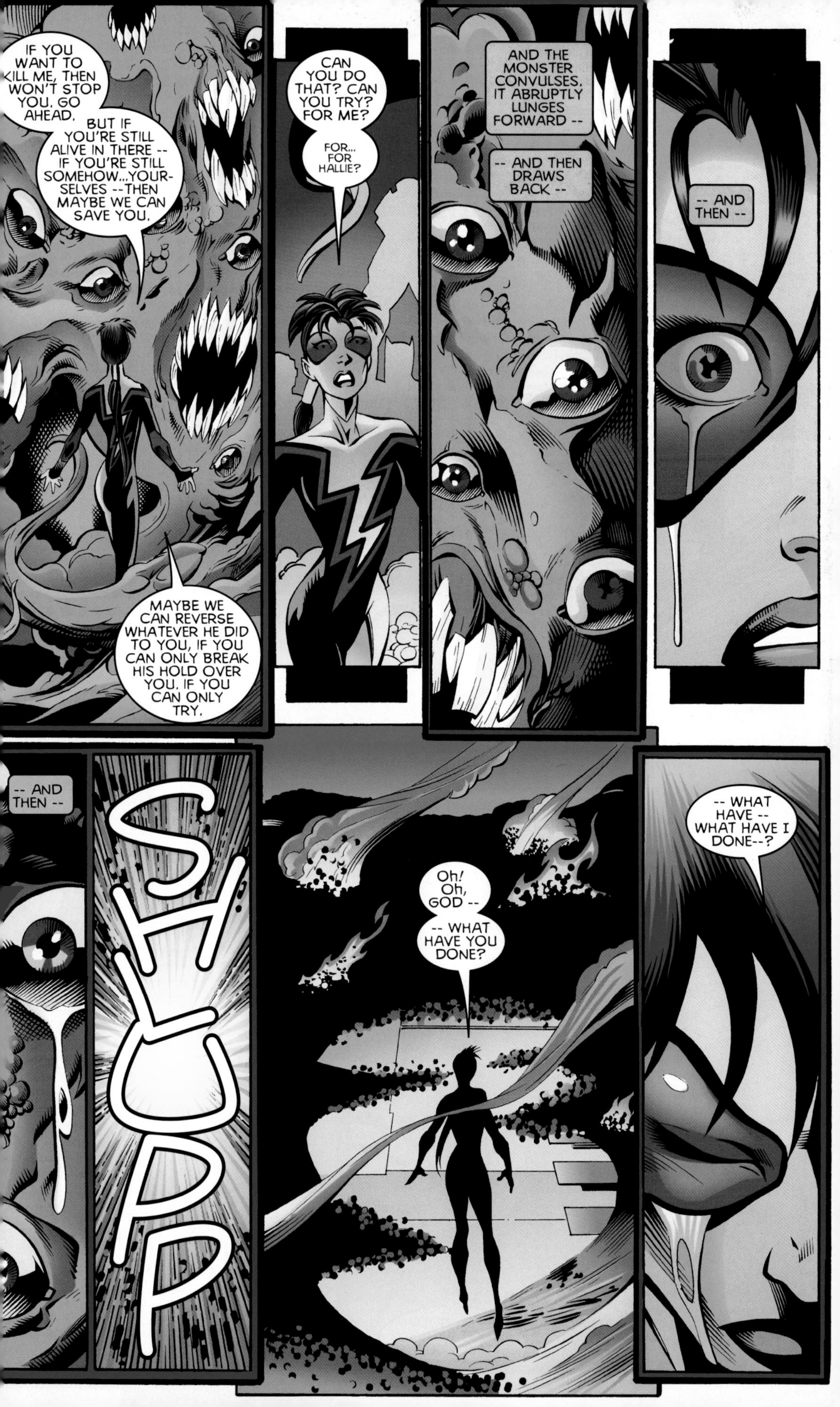
IF YOU WANT TO KILL ME, THEN WON'T STOP YOU. GO AHEAD.
BUT IF YOU'RE STILL ALIVE IN THERE -- IF YOU'RE STILL SOMEHOW...YOURSELVES --THEN MAYBE WE CAN SAVE YOU.
MAYBE WE CAN REVERSE WHATEVER HE DID TO YOU, IF YOU CAN ONLY BREAK HIS HOLD OVER YOU, IF YOU CAN ONLY TRY.
CAN YOU DO THAT? CAN YOU TRY? FOR ME?
FOR... FOR HALLIE?
AND THE MONSTER CONVULSES, IT ABRUPTLY LUNGES FORWARD --
-- AND THEN DRAWS BACK --
-- AND THEN --
-- AND THEN --
SHLUPP
Oh! Oh, GOD --
-- WHAT HAVE YOU DONE?
-- WHAT HAVE -- WHAT HAVE I DONE--?

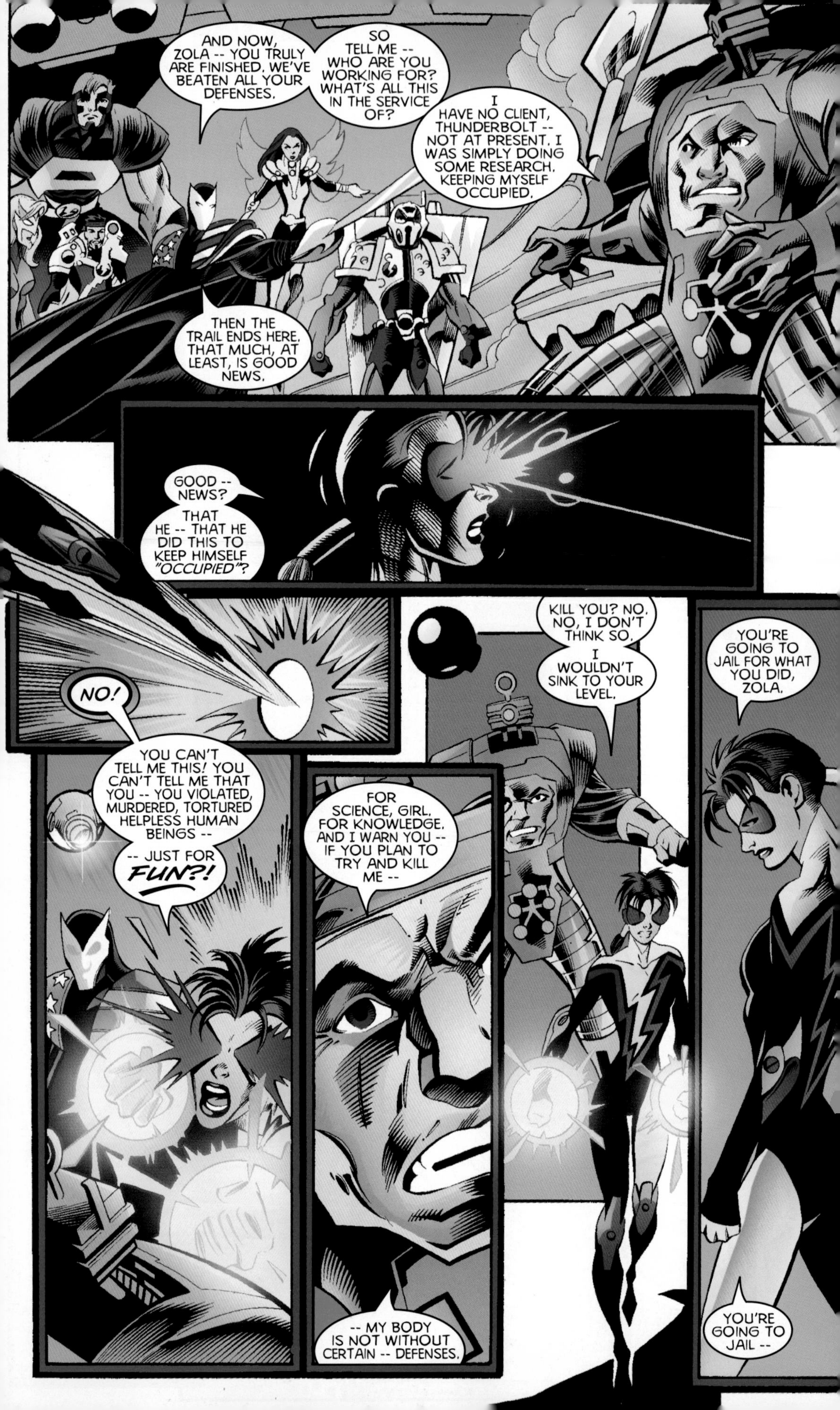
AND NOW, ZOLA -- YOU TRULY ARE FINISHED. WE'VE BEATEN ALL YOUR DEFENSES.
SO TELL ME -- WHO ARE YOU WORKING FOR? WHAT'S ALL THIS IN THE SERVICE OF?
I HAVE NO CLIENT, THUNDERBOLT -- NOT AT PRESENT. I WAS SIMPLY DOING SOME RESEARCH. KEEPING MYSELF OCCUPIED.
THEN THE TRAIL ENDS HERE. THAT MUCH, AT LEAST, IS GOOD NEWS.
GOOD -- NEWS?
THAT HE -- THAT HE DID THIS TO KEEP HIMSELF *"OCCUPIED"*?
NO!
YOU CAN'T TELL ME THIS! YOU CAN'T TELL ME THAT YOU -- YOU VIOLATED, MURDERED, TORTURED HELPLESS HUMAN BEINGS --
-- JUST FOR *FUN?!*
FOR SCIENCE, GIRL, FOR KNOWLEDGE. AND I WARN YOU -- IF YOU PLAN TO TRY AND KILL ME --
-- MY BODY IS NOT WITHOUT CERTAIN -- DEFENSES.
KILL YOU? NO. NO, I DON'T THINK SO.
I WOULDN'T SINK TO YOUR LEVEL.
YOU'RE GOING TO JAIL FOR WHAT YOU DID, ZOLA.
YOU'RE GOING TO JAIL --

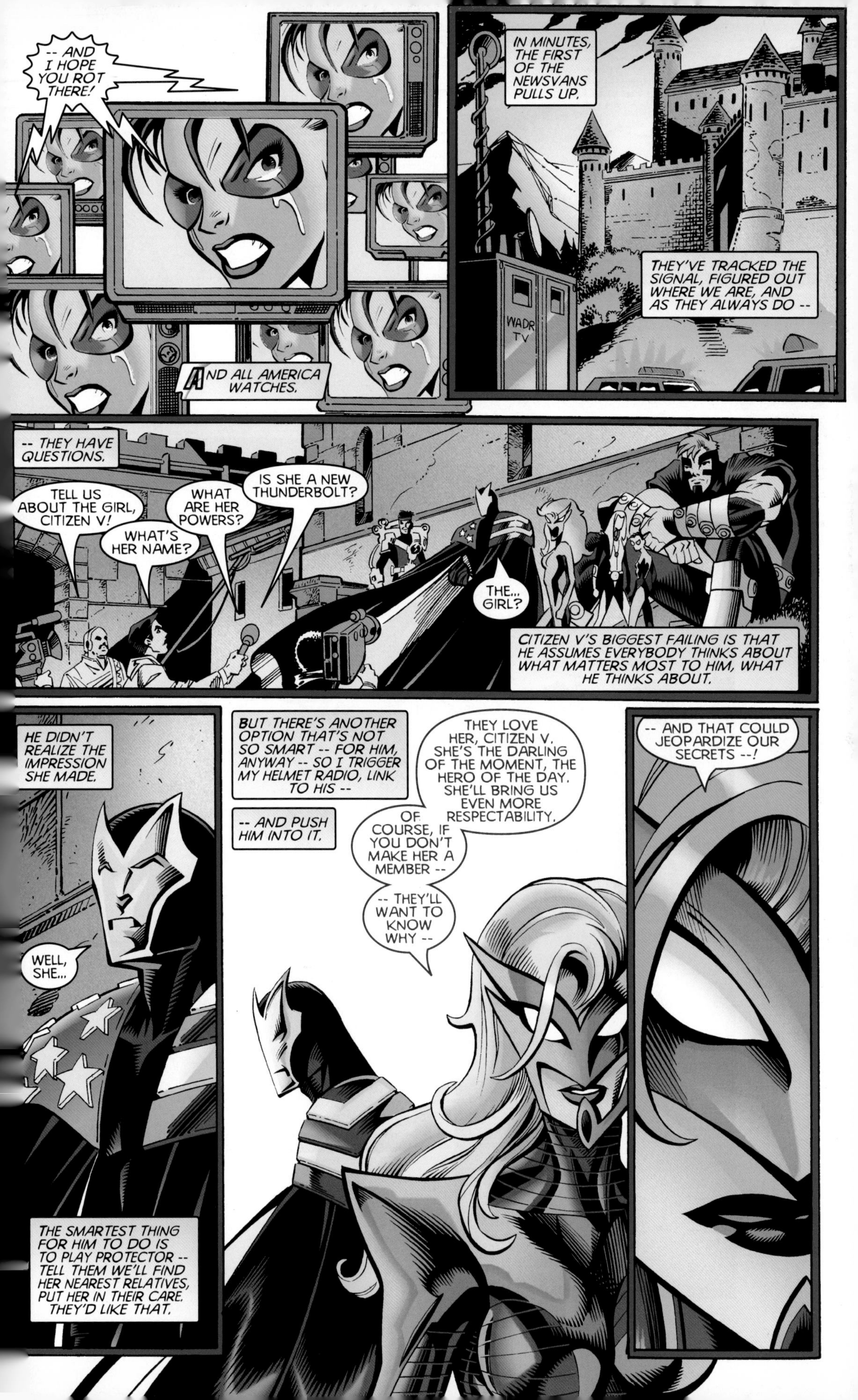
-- AND I HOPE YOU ROT THERE!
AND ALL AMERICA WATCHES.
IN MINUTES, THE FIRST OF THE NEWSVANS PULLS UP.
WADR TV
THEY'VE TRACKED THE SIGNAL, FIGURED OUT WHERE WE ARE, AND AS THEY ALWAYS DO --
-- THEY HAVE QUESTIONS.
TELL US ABOUT THE GIRL, CITIZEN V!
WHAT'S HER NAME?
WHAT ARE HER POWERS?
IS SHE A NEW THUNDERBOLT?
THE... GIRL?
CITIZEN V'S BIGGEST FAILING IS THAT HE ASSUMES EVERYBODY THINKS ABOUT WHAT MATTERS MOST TO HIM, WHAT HE THINKS ABOUT.
HE DIDN'T REALIZE THE IMPRESSION SHE MADE.
WELL, SHE...
THE SMARTEST THING FOR HIM TO DO IS TO PLAY PROTECTOR -- TELL THEM WE'LL FIND HER NEAREST RELATIVES, PUT HER IN THEIR CARE. THEY'D LIKE THAT.
BUT THERE'S ANOTHER OPTION THAT'S NOT SO SMART -- FOR HIM, ANYWAY -- SO I TRIGGER MY HELMET RADIO, LINK TO HIS --
-- AND PUSH HIM INTO IT.
THEY LOVE HER, CITIZEN V. SHE'S THE DARLING OF THE MOMENT, THE HERO OF THE DAY. SHE'LL BRING US EVEN MORE RESPECTABILITY.
OF COURSE, IF YOU DON'T MAKE HER A MEMBER --
-- THEY'LL WANT TO KNOW WHY --
-- AND THAT COULD JEOPARDIZE OUR SECRETS --!

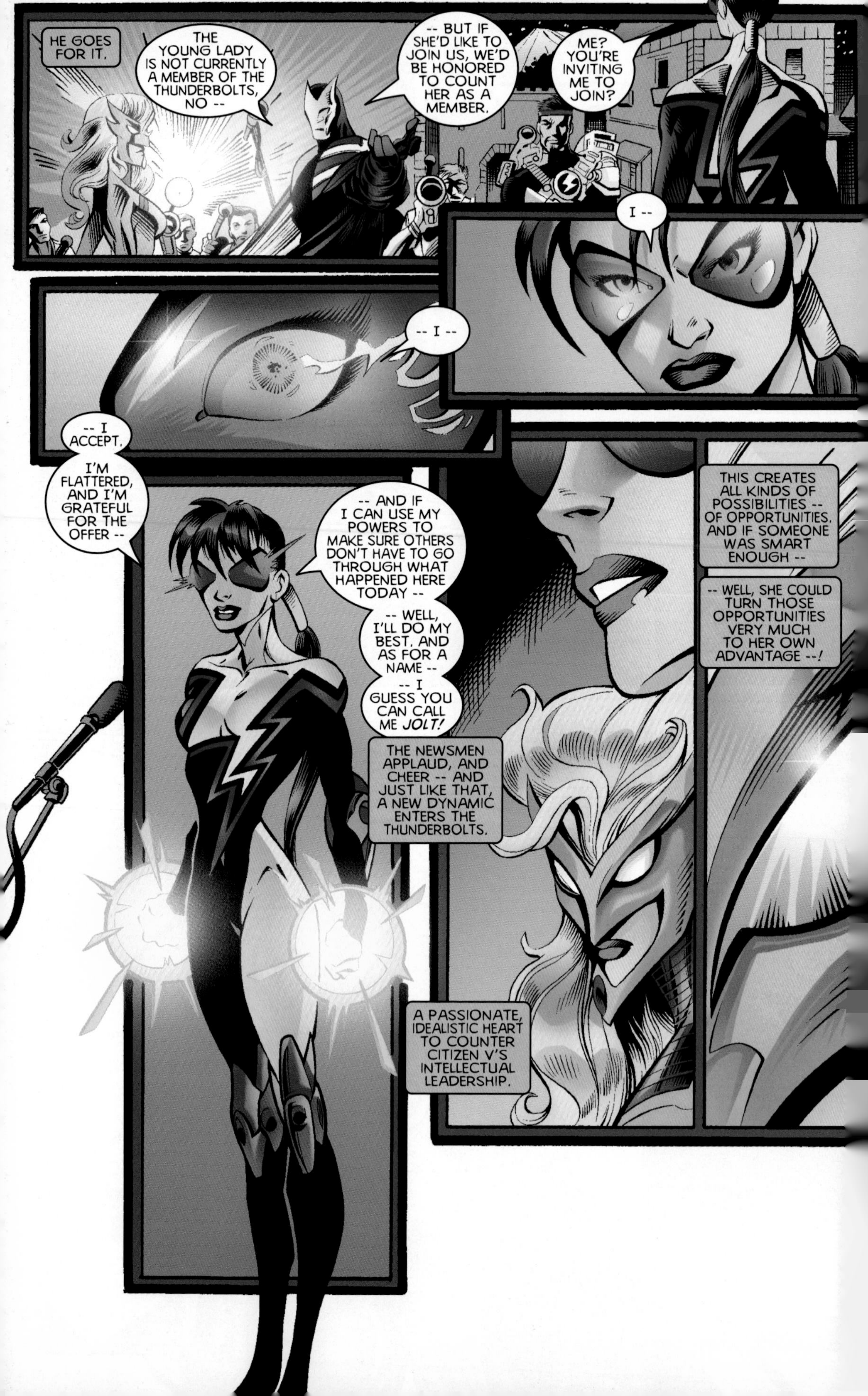
HE GOES FOR IT.
THE YOUNG LADY IS NOT CURRENTLY A MEMBER OF THE THUNDERBOLTS, NO --
-- BUT IF SHE'D LIKE TO JOIN US, WE'D BE HONORED TO COUNT HER AS A MEMBER.
ME? YOU'RE INVITING ME TO JOIN?
I --
-- I --
-- I ACCEPT.
I'M FLATTERED, AND I'M GRATEFUL FOR THE OFFER --
-- AND IF I CAN USE MY POWERS TO MAKE SURE OTHERS DON'T HAVE TO GO THROUGH WHAT HAPPENED HERE TODAY --
-- WELL, I'LL DO MY BEST, AND AS FOR A NAME --
-- I GUESS YOU CAN CALL ME *JOLT!*
THE NEWSMEN APPLAUD, AND CHEER -- AND JUST LIKE THAT, A NEW DYNAMIC ENTERS THE THUNDERBOLTS.
A PASSIONATE, IDEALISTIC HEART TO COUNTER CITIZEN V'S INTELLECTUAL LEADERSHIP.
THIS CREATES ALL KINDS OF POSSIBILITIES -- OF OPPORTUNITIES, AND IF SOMEONE WAS SMART ENOUGH --
-- WELL, SHE COULD TURN THOSE OPPORTUNITIES VERY MUCH TO HER OWN ADVANTAGE --!

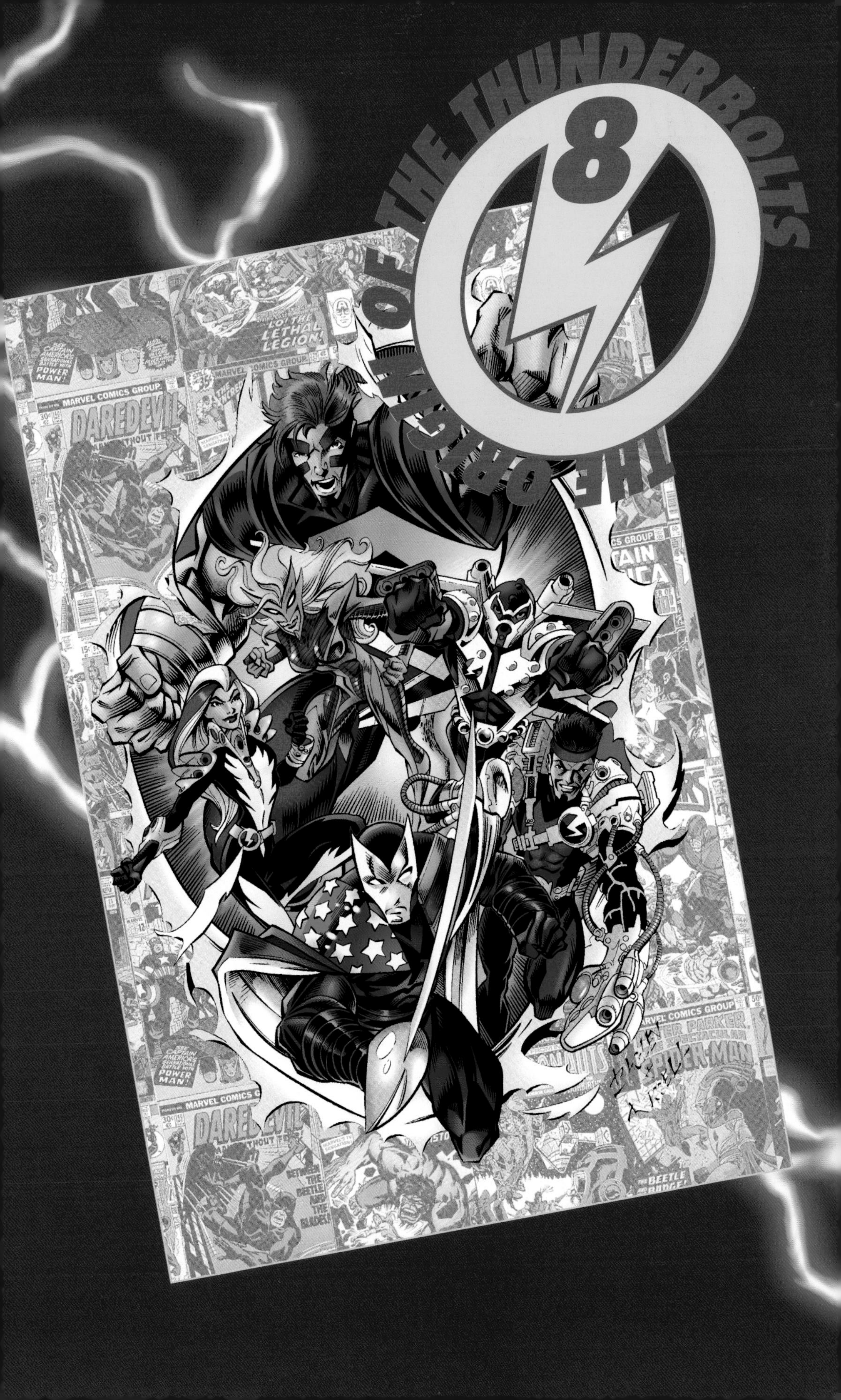
THE ORIGIN OF THE THUNDERBOLTS
8
MARVEL COMICS GROUP
DAREDEVIL
LO! THE LETHAL LEGION!
SEE CAPTAIN AMERICA'S SENSATIONAL BATTLE WITH POWER MAN!
BETWEEN THE BEETLE AND THE BLADES!
PETER PARKER, THE SPECTACULAR SPIDER-MAN

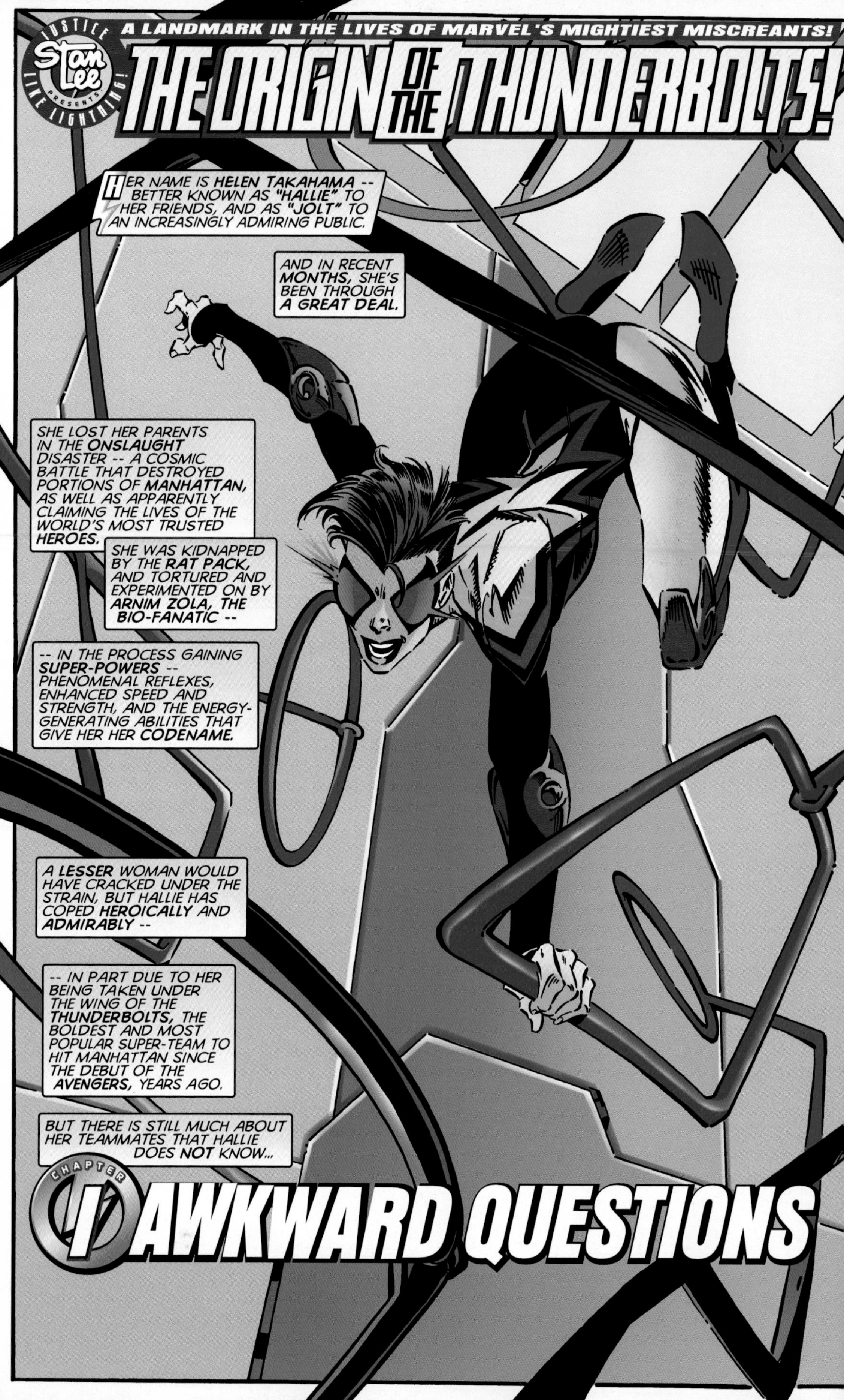
Stan Lee PRESENTS
JUSTICE LIKE LIGHTNING!
A LANDMARK IN THE LIVES OF MARVEL'S MIGHTIEST MISCREANTS!
THE ORIGIN OF THE THUNDERBOLTS!
HER NAME IS HELEN TAKAHAMA -- BETTER KNOWN AS "HALLIE" TO HER FRIENDS, AND AS "JOLT" TO AN INCREASINGLY ADMIRING PUBLIC.
AND IN RECENT MONTHS, SHE'S BEEN THROUGH A GREAT DEAL.
SHE LOST HER PARENTS IN THE ONSLAUGHT DISASTER -- A COSMIC BATTLE THAT DESTROYED PORTIONS OF MANHATTAN, AS WELL AS APPARENTLY CLAIMING THE LIVES OF THE WORLD'S MOST TRUSTED HEROES.
SHE WAS KIDNAPPED BY THE RAT PACK, AND TORTURED AND EXPERIMENTED ON BY ARNIM ZOLA, THE BIO-FANATIC --
-- IN THE PROCESS GAINING SUPER-POWERS -- PHENOMENAL REFLEXES, ENHANCED SPEED AND STRENGTH, AND THE ENERGY-GENERATING ABILITIES THAT GIVE HER HER CODENAME.
A LESSER WOMAN WOULD HAVE CRACKED UNDER THE STRAIN, BUT HALLIE HAS COPED HEROICALLY AND ADMIRABLY --
-- IN PART DUE TO HER BEING TAKEN UNDER THE WING OF THE THUNDERBOLTS, THE BOLDEST AND MOST POPULAR SUPER-TEAM TO HIT MANHATTAN SINCE THE DEBUT OF THE AVENGERS, YEARS AGO.
BUT THERE IS STILL MUCH ABOUT HER TEAMMATES THAT HALLIE DOES NOT KNOW...
CHAPTER 1
AWKWARD QUESTIONS

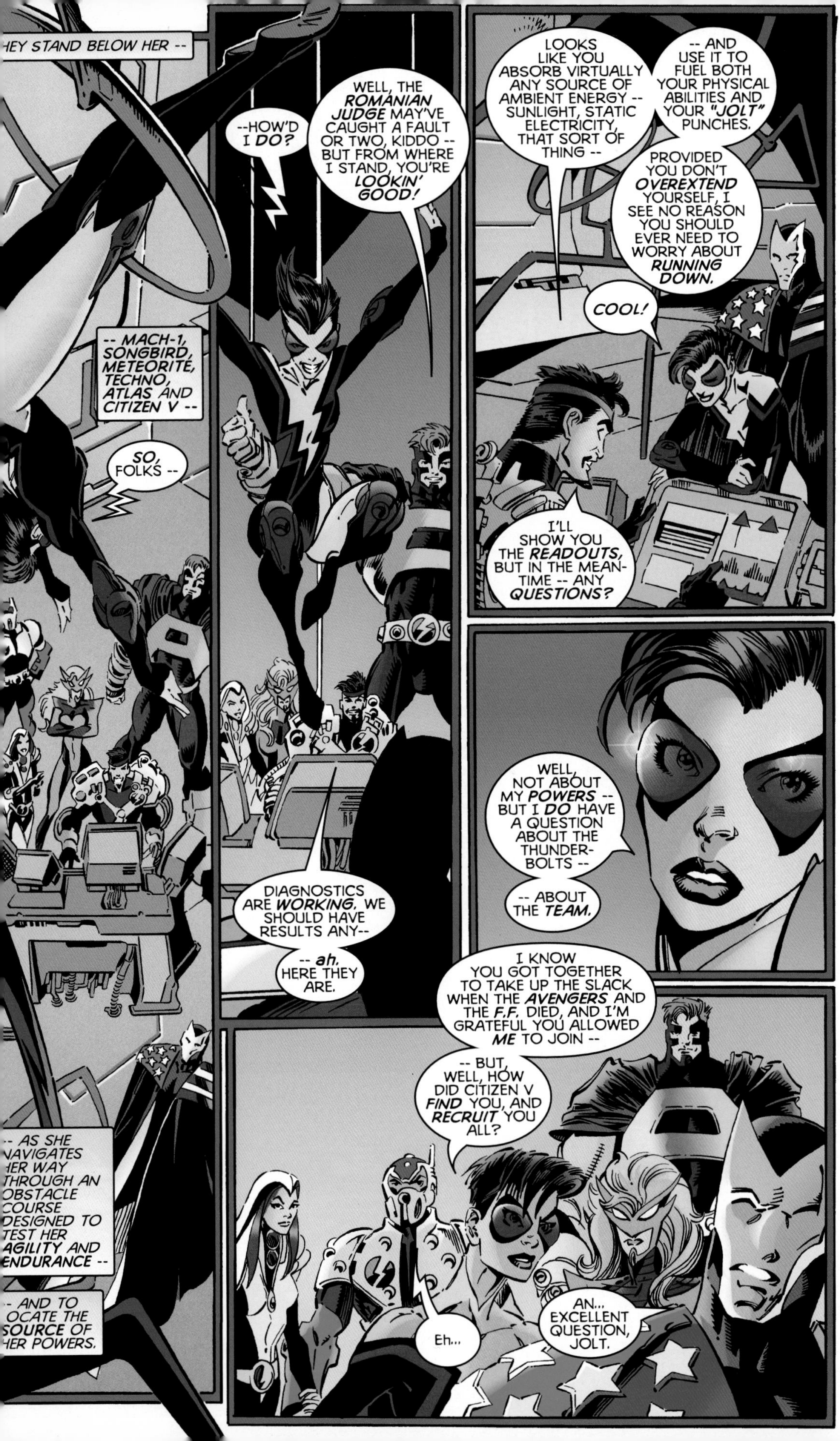
HEY STAND BELOW HER --
-- MACH-1, SONGBIRD, METEORITE, TECHNO, ATLAS AND CITIZEN V --
SO, FOLKS --
-- AS SHE NAVIGATES HER WAY THROUGH AN OBSTACLE COURSE DESIGNED TO TEST HER AGILITY AND ENDURANCE --
- AND TO OCATE THE SOURCE OF HER POWERS.
--HOW'D I DO?
WELL, THE ROMANIAN JUDGE MAY'VE CAUGHT A FAULT OR TWO, KIDDO -- BUT FROM WHERE I STAND, YOU'RE LOOKIN' GOOD!
DIAGNOSTICS ARE WORKING. WE SHOULD HAVE RESULTS ANY--
-- ah. HERE THEY ARE.
LOOKS LIKE YOU ABSORB VIRTUALLY ANY SOURCE OF AMBIENT ENERGY -- SUNLIGHT, STATIC ELECTRICITY, THAT SORT OF THING --
-- AND USE IT TO FUEL BOTH YOUR PHYSICAL ABILITIES AND YOUR "JOLT" PUNCHES.
PROVIDED YOU DON'T OVEREXTEND YOURSELF, I SEE NO REASON YOU SHOULD EVER NEED TO WORRY ABOUT RUNNING DOWN.
COOL!
I'LL SHOW YOU THE READOUTS, BUT IN THE MEAN-TIME -- ANY QUESTIONS?
WELL, NOT ABOUT MY POWERS -- BUT I DO HAVE A QUESTION ABOUT THE THUNDER-BOLTS --
-- ABOUT THE TEAM.
I KNOW YOU GOT TOGETHER TO TAKE UP THE SLACK WHEN THE AVENGERS AND THE F.F. DIED, AND I'M GRATEFUL YOU ALLOWED ME TO JOIN --
-- BUT, WELL, HOW DID CITIZEN V FIND YOU, AND RECRUIT YOU ALL?
Eh...
AN... EXCELLENT QUESTION, JOLT.

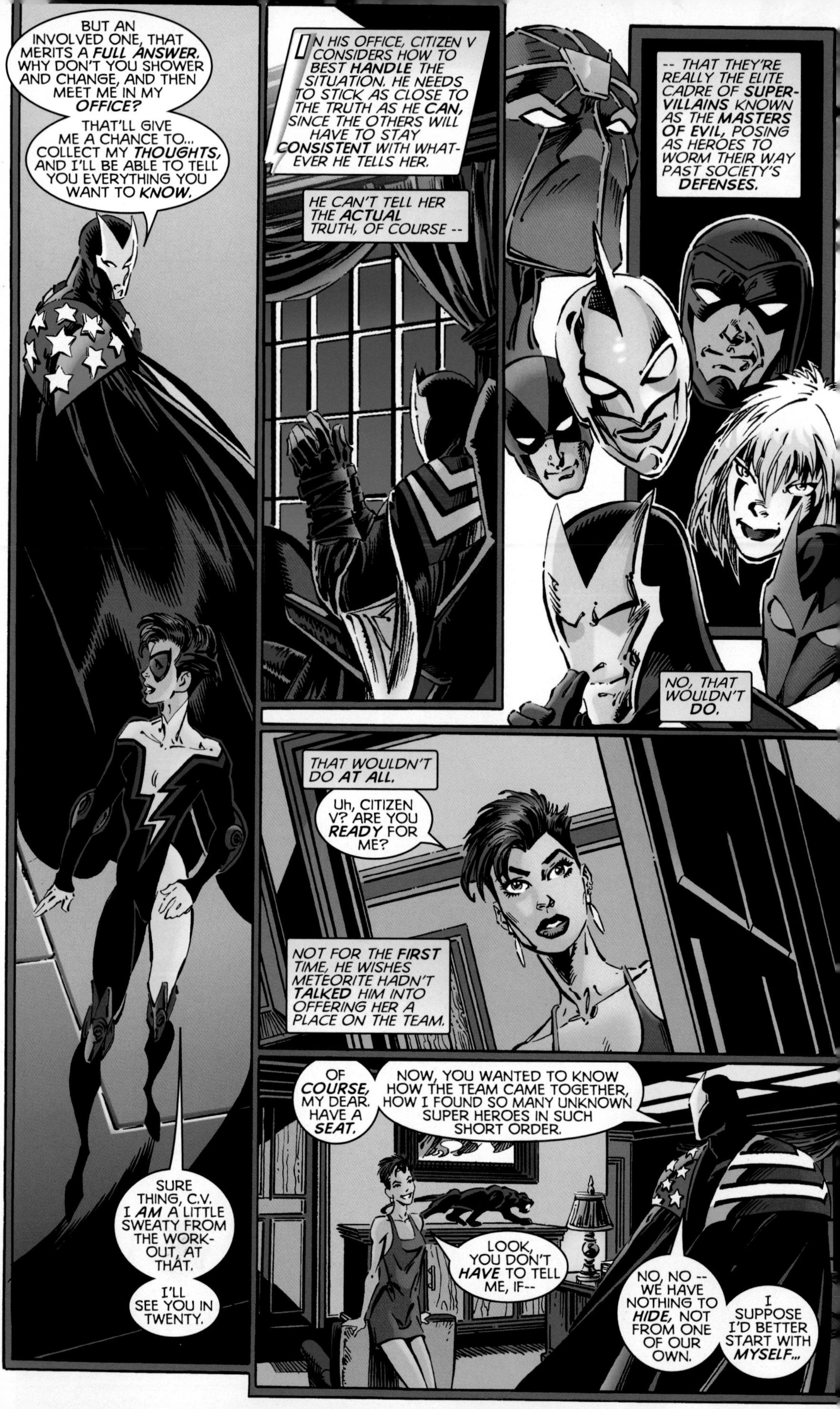
BUT AN INVOLVED ONE, THAT MERITS A FULL ANSWER. WHY DON'T YOU SHOWER AND CHANGE, AND THEN MEET ME IN MY OFFICE?
THAT'LL GIVE ME A CHANCE TO... COLLECT MY THOUGHTS, AND I'LL BE ABLE TO TELL YOU EVERYTHING YOU WANT TO KNOW.
SURE THING, C.V. I AM A LITTLE SWEATY FROM THE WORK-OUT, AT THAT.
I'LL SEE YOU IN TWENTY.
IN HIS OFFICE, CITIZEN V CONSIDERS HOW TO BEST HANDLE THE SITUATION. HE NEEDS TO STICK AS CLOSE TO THE TRUTH AS HE CAN, SINCE THE OTHERS WILL HAVE TO STAY CONSISTENT WITH WHAT-EVER HE TELLS HER.
HE CAN'T TELL HER THE ACTUAL TRUTH, OF COURSE --
-- THAT THEY'RE REALLY THE ELITE CADRE OF SUPER-VILLAINS KNOWN AS THE MASTERS OF EVIL, POSING AS HEROES TO WORM THEIR WAY PAST SOCIETY'S DEFENSES.
NO, THAT WOULDN'T DO.
THAT WOULDN'T DO AT ALL.
Uh, CITIZEN V? ARE YOU READY FOR ME?
NOT FOR THE FIRST TIME, HE WISHES METEORITE HADN'T TALKED HIM INTO OFFERING HER A PLACE ON THE TEAM.
OF COURSE, MY DEAR. HAVE A SEAT.
NOW, YOU WANTED TO KNOW HOW THE TEAM CAME TOGETHER, HOW I FOUND SO MANY UNKNOWN SUPER HEROES IN SUCH SHORT ORDER.
LOOK, YOU DON'T HAVE TO TELL ME, IF--
NO, NO -- WE HAVE NOTHING TO HIDE, NOT FROM ONE OF OUR OWN.
I SUPPOSE I'D BETTER START WITH MYSELF...

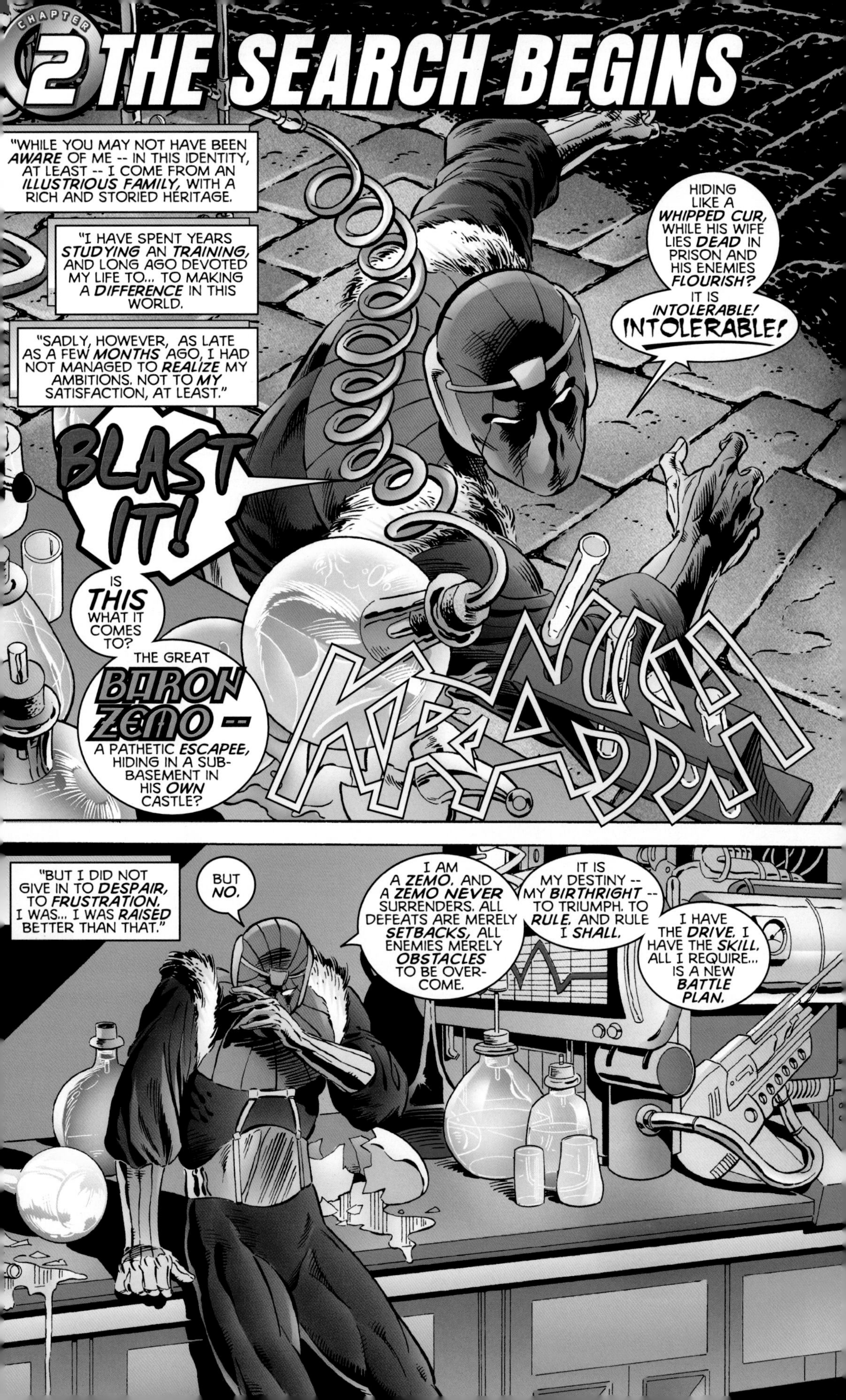
CHAPTER 2 THE SEARCH BEGINS
"WHILE YOU MAY NOT HAVE BEEN AWARE OF ME -- IN THIS IDENTITY, AT LEAST -- I COME FROM AN ILLUSTRIOUS FAMILY, WITH A RICH AND STORIED HERITAGE.
"I HAVE SPENT YEARS STUDYING AN TRAINING, AND LONG AGO DEVOTED MY LIFE TO... TO MAKING A DIFFERENCE IN THIS WORLD.
"SADLY, HOWEVER, AS LATE AS A FEW MONTHS AGO, I HAD NOT MANAGED TO REALIZE MY AMBITIONS. NOT TO MY SATISFACTION, AT LEAST."
BLAST IT!
IS THIS WHAT IT COMES TO? THE GREAT BARON ZEMO -- A PATHETIC ESCAPEE, HIDING IN A SUB-BASEMENT IN HIS OWN CASTLE?
HIDING LIKE A WHIPPED CUR, WHILE HIS WIFE LIES DEAD IN PRISON AND HIS ENEMIES FLOURISH? IT IS INTOLERABLE! INTOLERABLE!
KRASH
"BUT I DID NOT GIVE IN TO DESPAIR, TO FRUSTRATION. I WAS... I WAS RAISED BETTER THAN THAT."
BUT NO.
I AM A ZEMO. AND A ZEMO NEVER SURRENDERS. ALL DEFEATS ARE MERELY SETBACKS, ALL ENEMIES MERELY OBSTACLES TO BE OVERCOME.
IT IS MY DESTINY -- MY BIRTHRIGHT -- TO TRIUMPH. TO RULE, AND RULE I SHALL.
I HAVE THE DRIVE, I HAVE THE SKILL. ALL I REQUIRE... IS A NEW BATTLE PLAN.

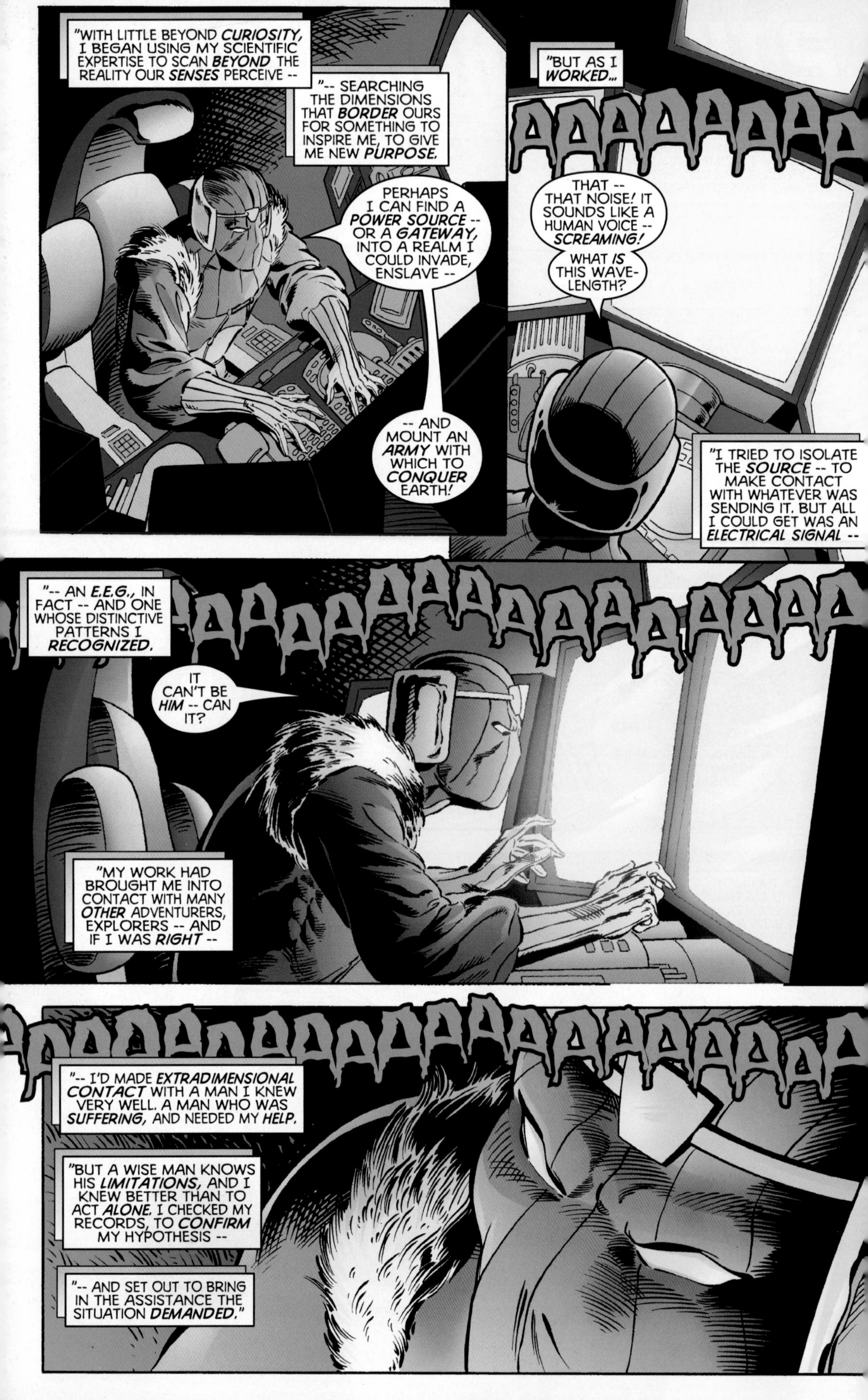
"WITH LITTLE BEYOND *CURIOSITY,* I BEGAN USING MY SCIENTIFIC EXPERTISE TO SCAN *BEYOND* THE REALITY OUR *SENSES* PERCEIVE --
"-- SEARCHING THE DIMENSIONS THAT *BORDER* OURS FOR SOMETHING TO INSPIRE ME, TO GIVE ME NEW *PURPOSE.*
PERHAPS I CAN FIND A *POWER SOURCE* -- OR A *GATEWAY,* INTO A REALM I COULD INVADE, ENSLAVE --
-- AND MOUNT AN *ARMY* WITH WHICH TO *CONQUER* EARTH!
"BUT AS I *WORKED...*
AAAAAAAA
THAT -- THAT NOISE! IT SOUNDS LIKE A HUMAN VOICE -- *SCREAMING!*
WHAT *IS* THIS WAVE-LENGTH?
"I TRIED TO ISOLATE THE *SOURCE* -- TO MAKE CONTACT WITH WHATEVER WAS SENDING IT. BUT ALL I COULD GET WAS AN *ELECTRICAL SIGNAL* --
"-- AN *E.E.G.,* IN FACT -- AND ONE WHOSE DISTINCTIVE PATTERNS I *RECOGNIZED.*
AAAAAAAAAAAAAAAA
IT CAN'T BE *HIM* -- CAN IT?
"MY WORK HAD BROUGHT ME INTO CONTACT WITH MANY *OTHER* ADVENTURERS, EXPLORERS -- AND IF I WAS *RIGHT* --
AAAAAAAAAAAAAAAAAAAA
"-- I'D MADE *EXTRADIMENSIONAL CONTACT* WITH A MAN I KNEW VERY WELL. A MAN WHO WAS *SUFFERING,* AND NEEDED MY *HELP.*
"BUT A WISE MAN KNOWS HIS *LIMITATIONS,* AND I KNEW BETTER THAN TO ACT *ALONE.* I CHECKED MY RECORDS, TO *CONFIRM* MY HYPOTHESIS --
"-- AND SET OUT TO BRING IN THE ASSISTANCE THE SITUATION *DEMANDED.*"

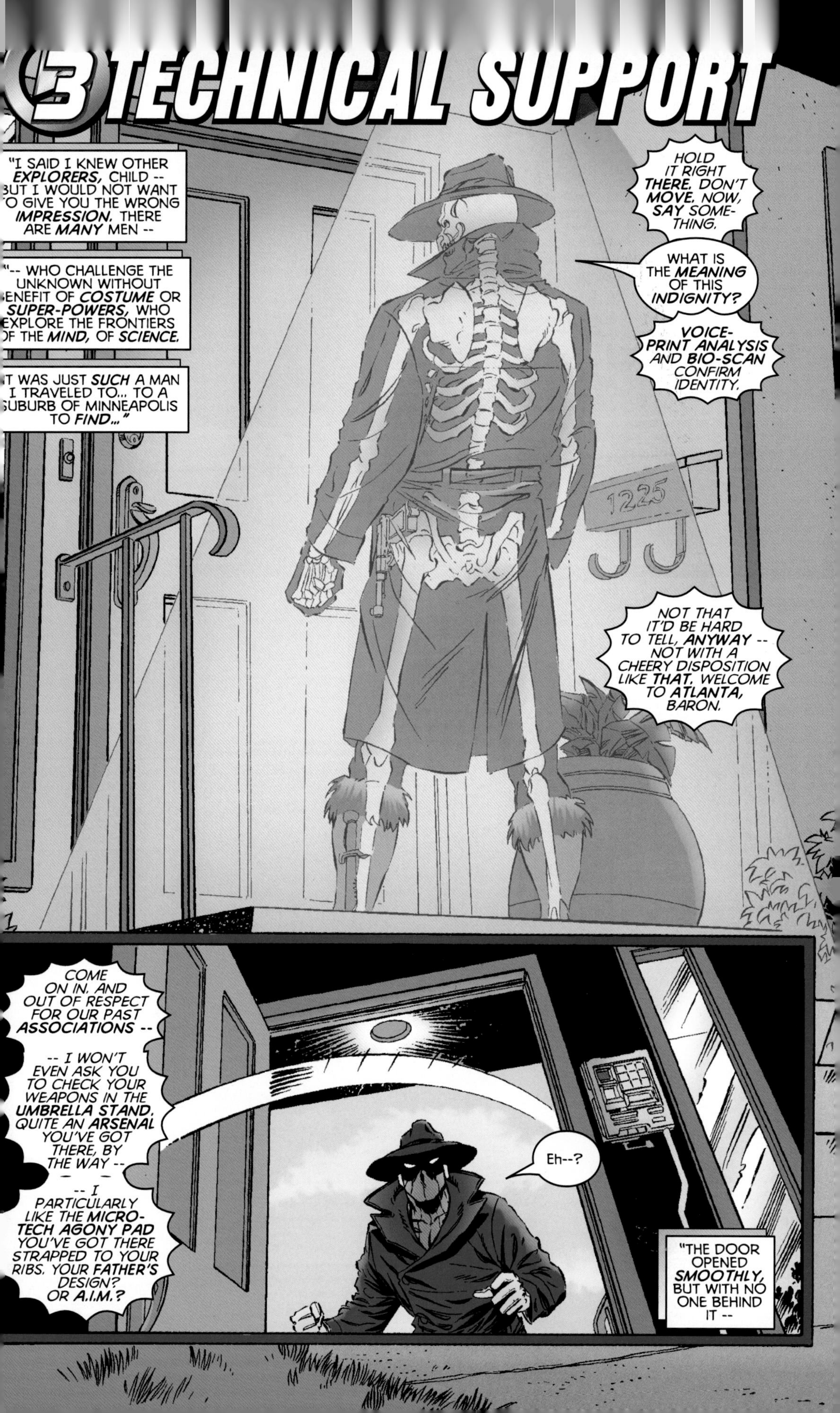
3 TECHNICAL SUPPORT
"I SAID I KNEW OTHER EXPLORERS, CHILD -- BUT I WOULD NOT WANT TO GIVE YOU THE WRONG IMPRESSION. THERE ARE MANY MEN --
"-- WHO CHALLENGE THE UNKNOWN WITHOUT BENEFIT OF COSTUME OR SUPER-POWERS, WHO EXPLORE THE FRONTIERS OF THE MIND, OF SCIENCE.
IT WAS JUST SUCH A MAN I TRAVELED TO... TO A SUBURB OF MINNEAPOLIS TO FIND..."
HOLD IT RIGHT THERE. DON'T MOVE. NOW, SAY SOMETHING.
WHAT IS THE MEANING OF THIS INDIGNITY?
VOICE-PRINT ANALYSIS AND BIO-SCAN CONFIRM IDENTITY.
1225
NOT THAT IT'D BE HARD TO TELL, ANYWAY -- NOT WITH A CHEERY DISPOSITION LIKE THAT. WELCOME TO ATLANTA, BARON.
COME ON IN. AND OUT OF RESPECT FOR OUR PAST ASSOCIATIONS --
-- I WON'T EVEN ASK YOU TO CHECK YOUR WEAPONS IN THE UMBRELLA STAND. QUITE AN ARSENAL YOU'VE GOT THERE, BY THE WAY --
-- I PARTICULARLY LIKE THE MICRO-TECH AGONY PAD YOU'VE GOT THERE STRAPPED TO YOUR RIBS. YOUR FATHER'S DESIGN? OR A.I.M.?
Eh--?
"THE DOOR OPENED SMOOTHLY, BUT WITH NO ONE BEHIND IT --

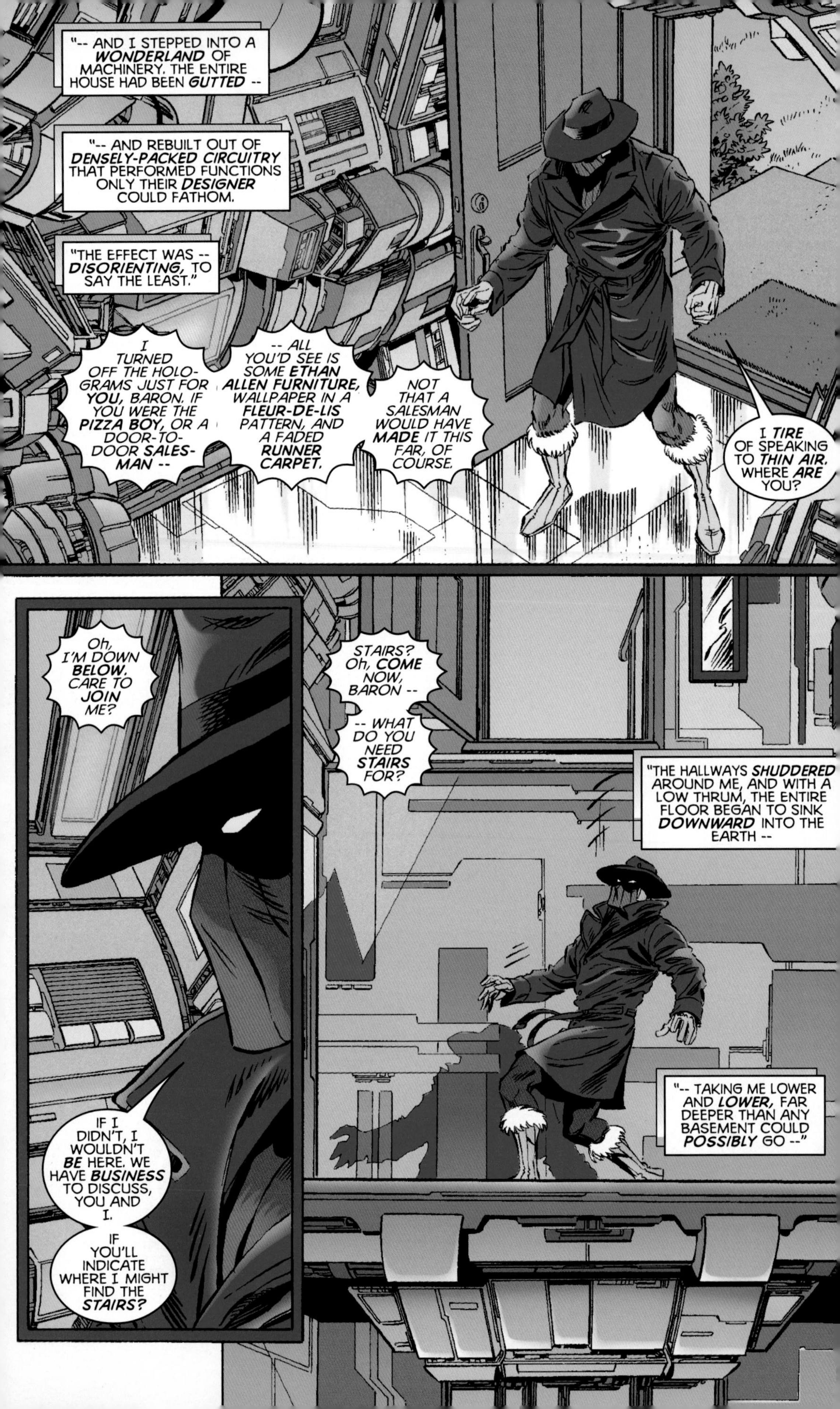
"-- AND I STEPPED INTO A WONDERLAND OF MACHINERY. THE ENTIRE HOUSE HAD BEEN GUTTED --
"-- AND REBUILT OUT OF DENSELY-PACKED CIRCUITRY THAT PERFORMED FUNCTIONS ONLY THEIR DESIGNER COULD FATHOM.
"THE EFFECT WAS -- DISORIENTING, TO SAY THE LEAST."
I TURNED OFF THE HOLO-GRAMS JUST FOR YOU, BARON. IF YOU WERE THE PIZZA BOY, OR A DOOR-TO-DOOR SALES-MAN --
-- ALL YOU'D SEE IS SOME ETHAN ALLEN FURNITURE, WALLPAPER IN A FLEUR-DE-LIS PATTERN, AND A FADED RUNNER CARPET.
NOT THAT A SALESMAN WOULD HAVE MADE IT THIS FAR, OF COURSE.
I TIRE OF SPEAKING TO THIN AIR. WHERE ARE YOU?
Oh, I'M DOWN BELOW. CARE TO JOIN ME?
IF I DIDN'T, I WOULDN'T BE HERE. WE HAVE BUSINESS TO DISCUSS, YOU AND I.
IF YOU'LL INDICATE WHERE I MIGHT FIND THE STAIRS?
STAIRS? Oh, COME NOW, BARON --
-- WHAT DO YOU NEED STAIRS FOR?
"THE HALLWAYS SHUDDERED AROUND ME, AND WITH A LOW THRUM, THE ENTIRE FLOOR BEGAN TO SINK DOWNWARD INTO THE EARTH --
"-- TAKING ME LOWER AND LOWER, FAR DEEPER THAN ANY BASEMENT COULD POSSIBLY GO --"

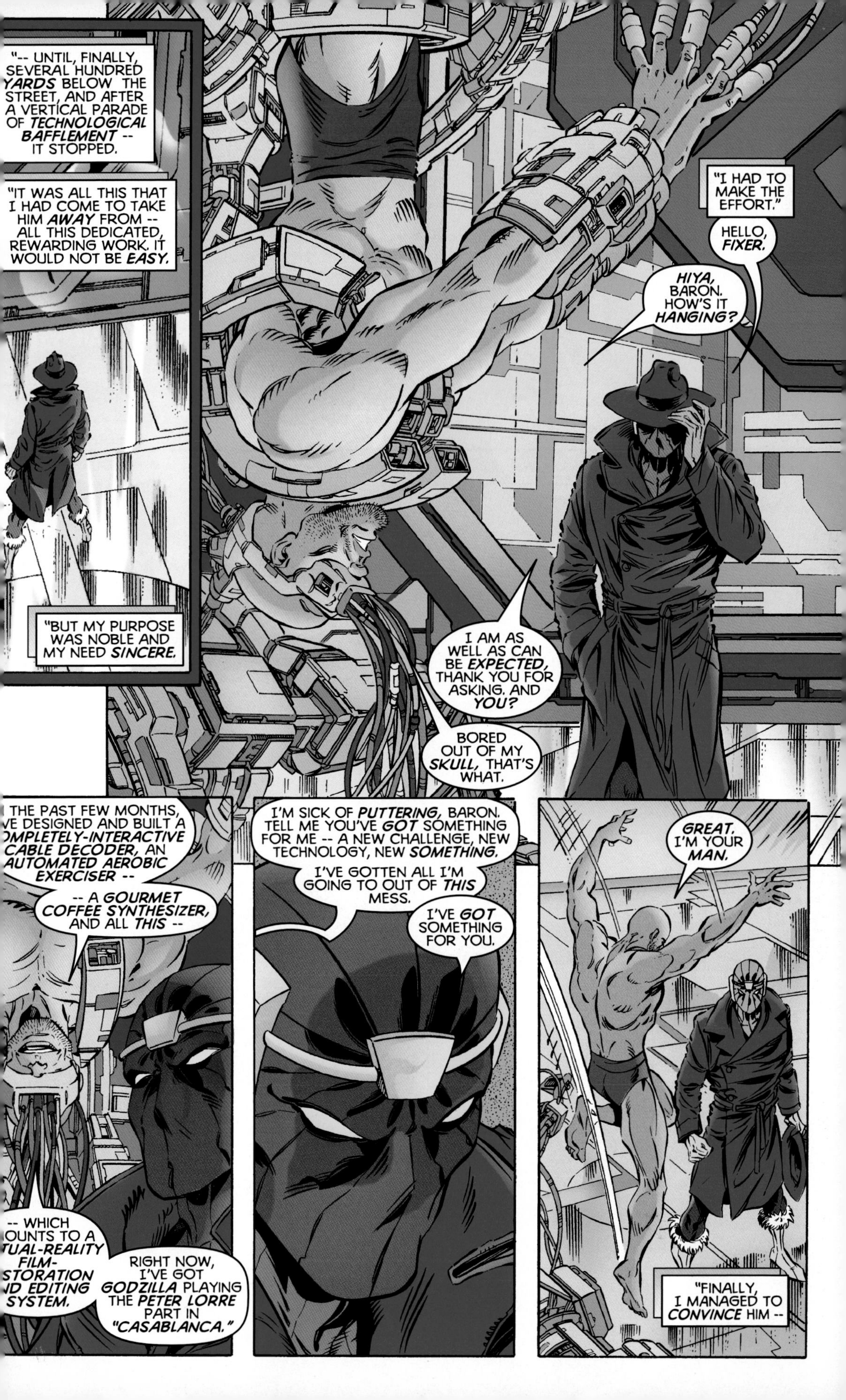
"-- UNTIL, FINALLY, SEVERAL HUNDRED YARDS BELOW THE STREET, AND AFTER A VERTICAL PARADE OF TECHNOLOGICAL BAFFLEMENT -- IT STOPPED.
"IT WAS ALL THIS THAT I HAD COME TO TAKE HIM AWAY FROM -- ALL THIS DEDICATED, REWARDING WORK. IT WOULD NOT BE EASY.
"BUT MY PURPOSE WAS NOBLE AND MY NEED SINCERE.
"I HAD TO MAKE THE EFFORT."
HELLO, FIXER.
HIYA, BARON. HOW'S IT HANGING?
I AM AS WELL AS CAN BE EXPECTED, THANK YOU FOR ASKING. AND YOU?
BORED OUT OF MY SKULL, THAT'S WHAT.
THE PAST FEW MONTHS, VE DESIGNED AND BUILT A OMPLETELY-INTERACTIVE CABLE DECODER, AN AUTOMATED AEROBIC EXERCISER --
-- A GOURMET COFFEE SYNTHESIZER, AND ALL THIS --
-- WHICH OUNTS TO A TUAL-REALITY FILM- STORATION ID EDITING SYSTEM.
RIGHT NOW, I'VE GOT GODZILLA PLAYING THE PETER LORRE PART IN "CASABLANCA."
I'M SICK OF PUTTERING, BARON. TELL ME YOU'VE GOT SOMETHING FOR ME -- A NEW CHALLENGE, NEW TECHNOLOGY, NEW SOMETHING.
I'VE GOTTEN ALL I'M GOING TO OUT OF THIS MESS.
I'VE GOT SOMETHING FOR YOU.
GREAT. I'M YOUR MAN.
"FINALLY, I MANAGED TO CONVINCE HIM --

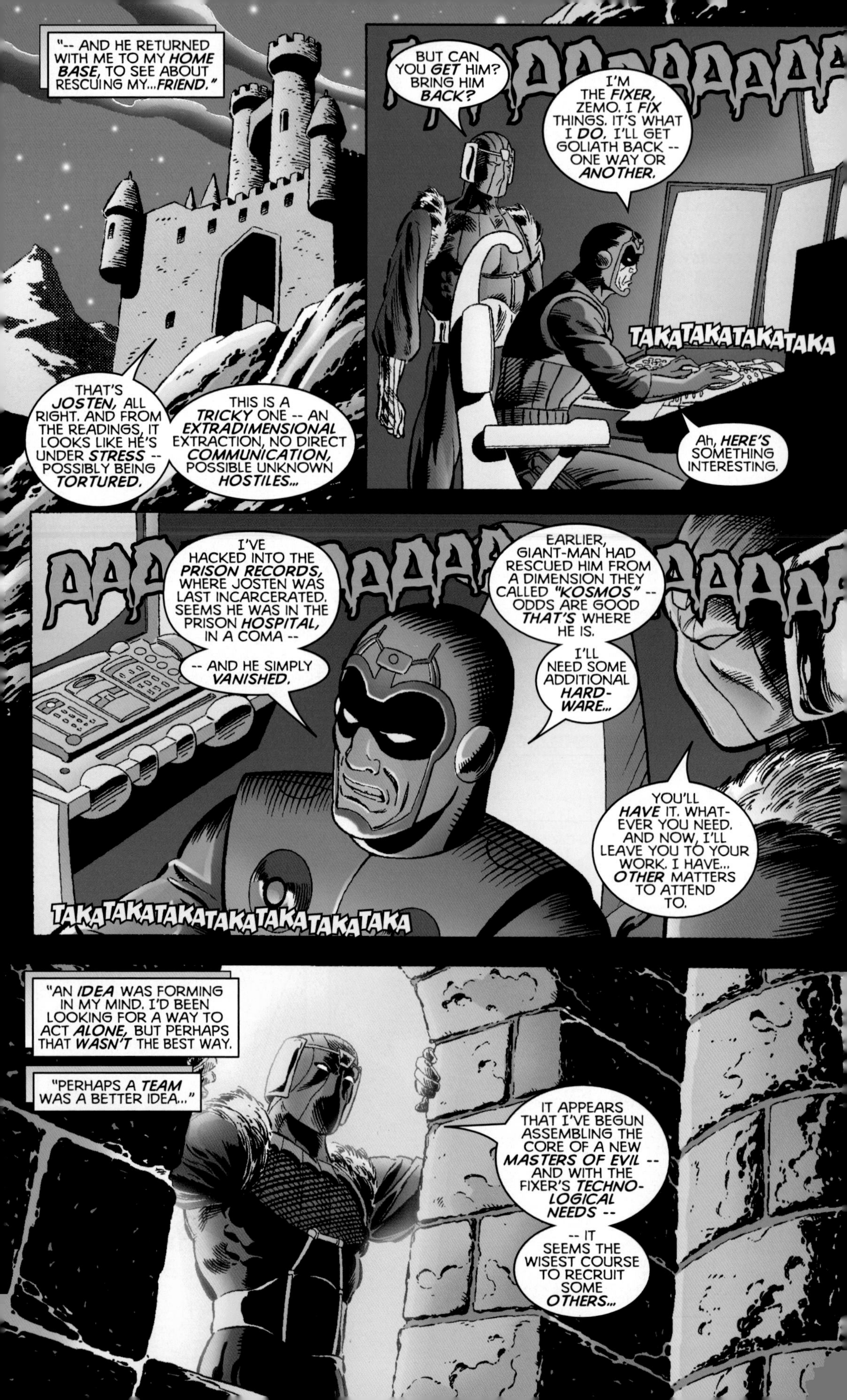
"-- AND HE RETURNED WITH ME TO MY HOME BASE, TO SEE ABOUT RESCUING MY... FRIEND."
THAT'S JOSTEN, ALL RIGHT. AND FROM THE READINGS, IT LOOKS LIKE HE'S UNDER STRESS -- POSSIBLY BEING TORTURED.
THIS IS A TRICKY ONE -- AN EXTRADIMENSIONAL EXTRACTION, NO DIRECT COMMUNICATION, POSSIBLE UNKNOWN HOSTILES...
BUT CAN YOU GET HIM? BRING HIM BACK?
I'M THE FIXER, ZEMO. I FIX THINGS. IT'S WHAT I DO. I'LL GET GOLIATH BACK -- ONE WAY OR ANOTHER.
TAKATAKATAKATAKA
Ah, HERE'S SOMETHING INTERESTING.
I'VE HACKED INTO THE PRISON RECORDS, WHERE JOSTEN WAS LAST INCARCERATED. SEEMS HE WAS IN THE PRISON HOSPITAL, IN A COMA --
-- AND HE SIMPLY VANISHED.
EARLIER, GIANT-MAN HAD RESCUED HIM FROM A DIMENSION THEY CALLED "KOSMOS" -- ODDS ARE GOOD THAT'S WHERE HE IS.
I'LL NEED SOME ADDITIONAL HARD-WARE...
TAKATAKATAKATAKATAKATAKATAKA
YOU'LL HAVE IT. WHAT-EVER YOU NEED. AND NOW, I'LL LEAVE YOU TO YOUR WORK. I HAVE... OTHER MATTERS TO ATTEND TO.
"AN IDEA WAS FORMING IN MY MIND. I'D BEEN LOOKING FOR A WAY TO ACT ALONE, BUT PERHAPS THAT WASN'T THE BEST WAY.
"PERHAPS A TEAM WAS A BETTER IDEA..."
IT APPEARS THAT I'VE BEGUN ASSEMBLING THE CORE OF A NEW MASTERS OF EVIL -- AND WITH THE FIXER'S TECHNO-LOGICAL NEEDS --
-- IT SEEMS THE WISEST COURSE TO RECRUIT SOME OTHERS...

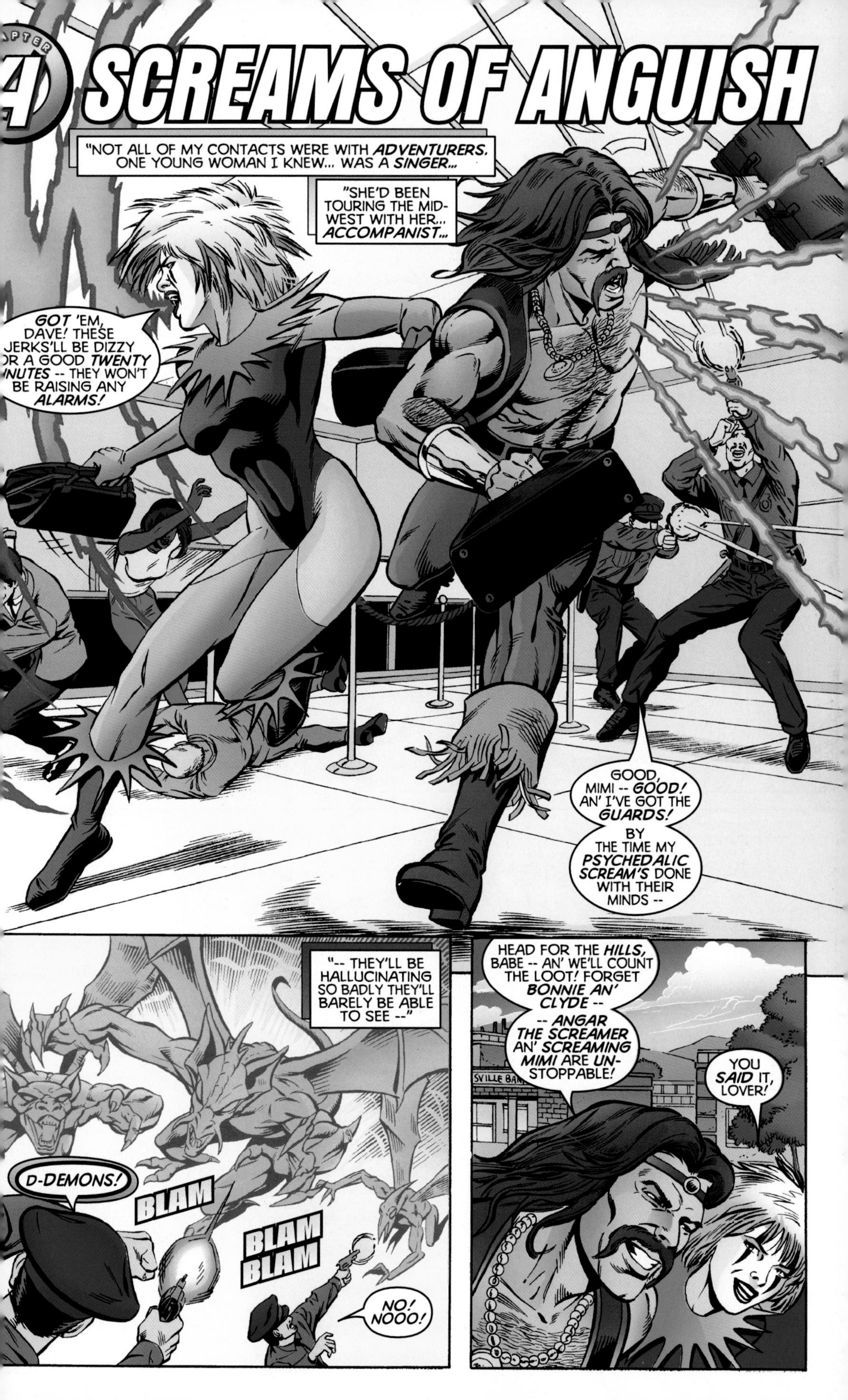

4 SCREAMS OF ANGUISH
"NOT ALL OF MY CONTACTS WERE WITH ADVENTURERS. ONE YOUNG WOMAN I KNEW... WAS A SINGER...
"SHE'D BEEN TOURING THE MID-WEST WITH HER... ACCOMPANIST...
GOT 'EM, DAVE! THESE JERKS'LL BE DIZZY OR A GOOD TWENTY INUTES -- THEY WON'T BE RAISING ANY ALARMS!
GOOD, MIMI -- GOOD! AN' I'VE GOT THE GUARDS!
BY THE TIME MY PSYCHEDALIC SCREAM'S DONE WITH THEIR MINDS --
"-- THEY'LL BE HALLUCINATING SO BADLY THEY'LL BARELY BE ABLE TO SEE --"
D-DEMONS!
BLAM
BLAM BLAM
NO! NOOO!
HEAD FOR THE HILLS, BABE -- AN' WE'LL COUNT THE LOOT! FORGET BONNIE AN' CLYDE --
-- ANGAR THE SCREAMER AN' SCREAMING MIMI ARE UN-STOPPABLE!
YOU SAID IT, LOVER!

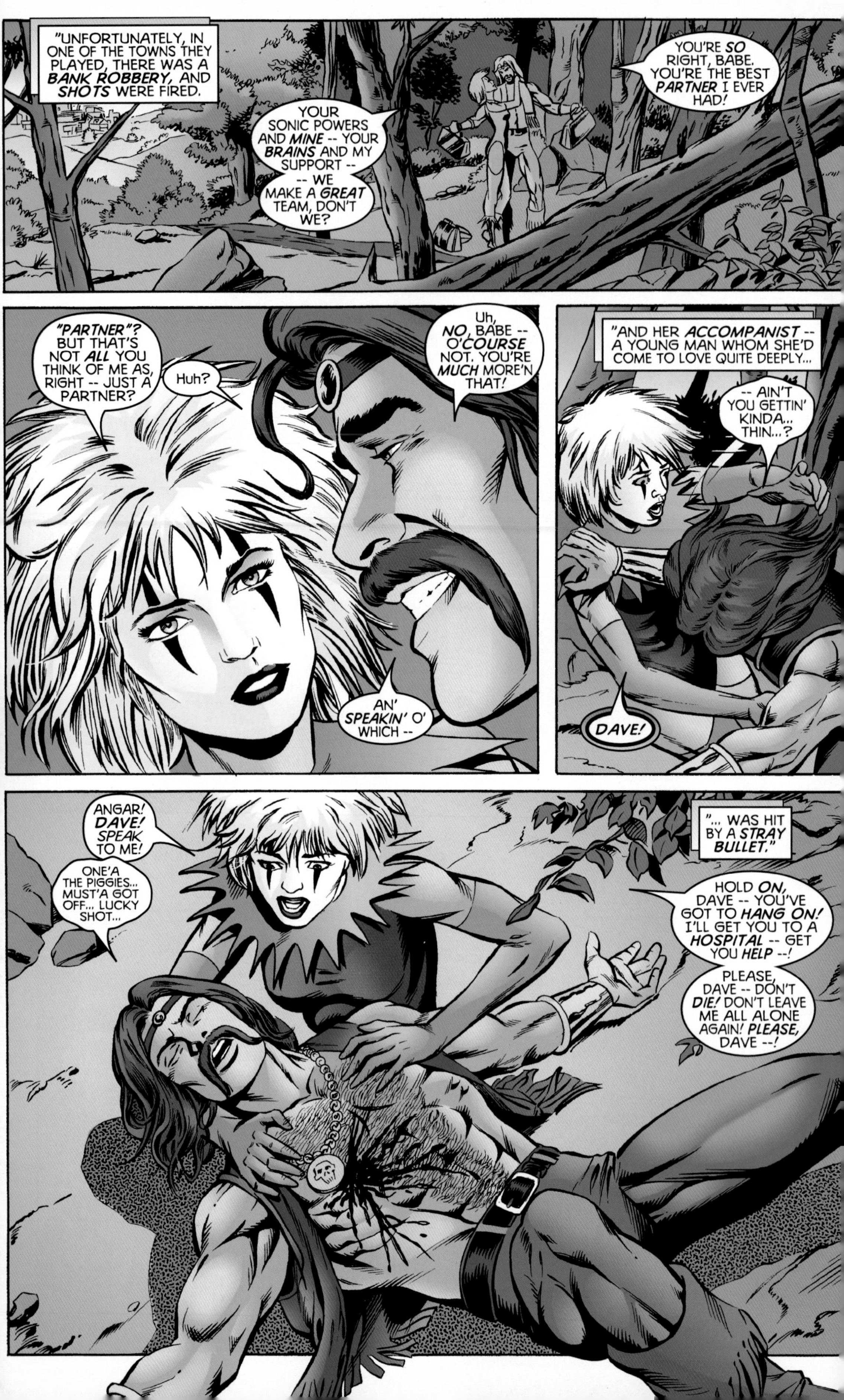
"UNFORTUNATELY, IN ONE OF THE TOWNS THEY PLAYED, THERE WAS A *BANK ROBBERY,* AND *SHOTS* WERE FIRED.
YOUR SONIC POWERS AND *MINE* -- YOUR *BRAINS* AND MY SUPPORT --
-- WE MAKE A *GREAT* TEAM, DON'T WE?
YOU'RE *SO* RIGHT, BABE. YOU'RE THE BEST *PARTNER* I EVER HAD!
"PARTNER"? BUT THAT'S NOT *ALL* YOU THINK OF ME AS, RIGHT -- JUST A PARTNER?
Huh?
Uh, *NO,* BABE -- O'*COURSE* NOT. YOU'RE *MUCH* MORE'N THAT!
AN' *SPEAKIN'* O' WHICH --
"AND HER *ACCOMPANIST* -- A YOUNG MAN WHOM SHE'D COME TO LOVE QUITE DEEPLY...
-- AIN'T YOU GETTIN' KINDA... THIN...?
DAVE!
ANGAR! *DAVE! SPEAK* TO ME!
ONE'A THE PIGGIES... MUST'A GOT OFF... LUCKY SHOT...
"... WAS HIT BY A *STRAY BULLET.*"
HOLD *ON,* DAVE -- YOU'VE GOT TO *HANG ON!* I'LL GET YOU TO A *HOSPITAL* -- GET YOU *HELP* --!
PLEASE, DAVE -- DON'T *DIE!* DON'T LEAVE ME ALL ALONE AGAIN! *PLEASE,* DAVE --!

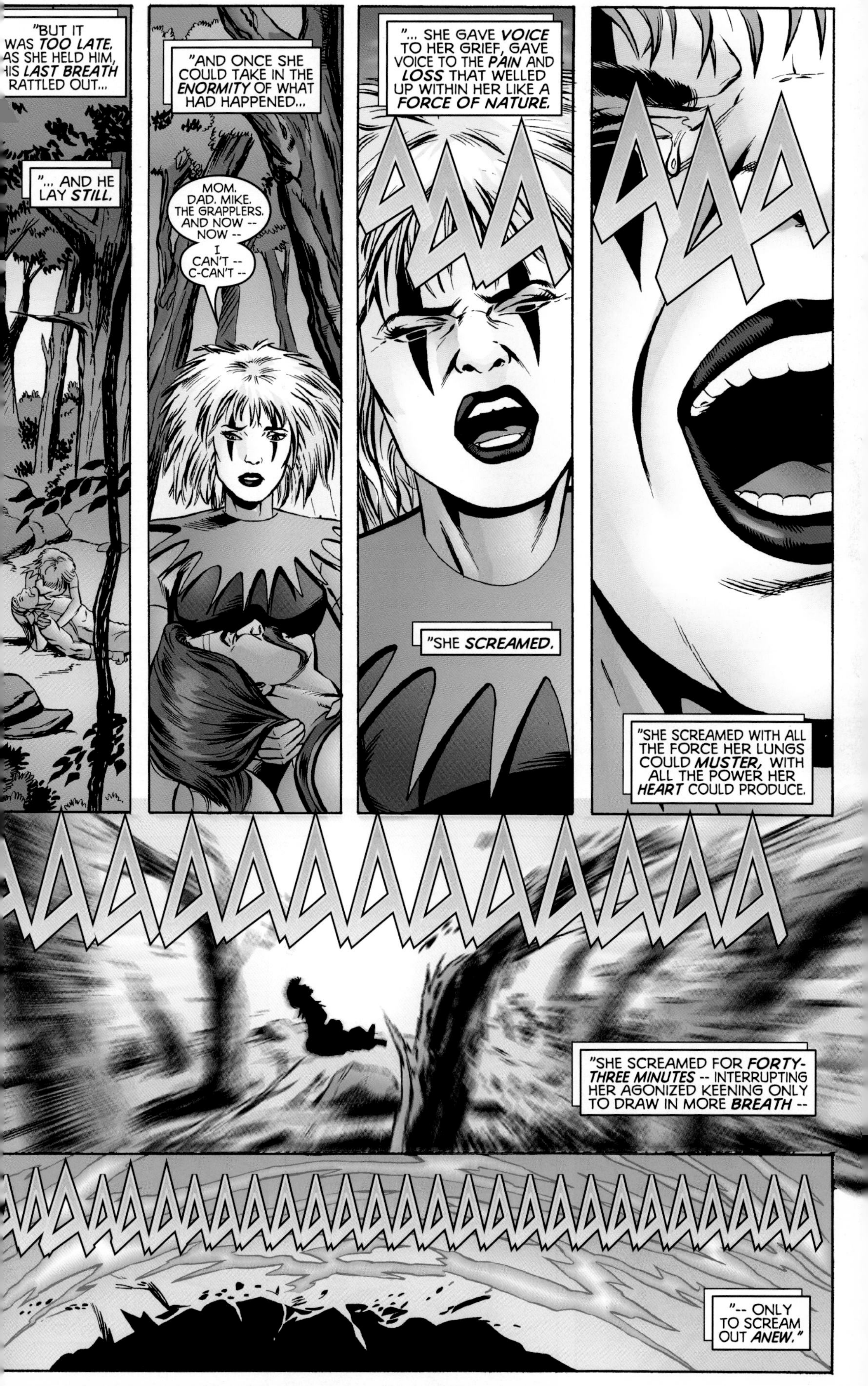
"BUT IT WAS TOO LATE. AS SHE HELD HIM, HIS LAST BREATH RATTLED OUT...
"... AND HE LAY STILL.
"AND ONCE SHE COULD TAKE IN THE ENORMITY OF WHAT HAD HAPPENED...
MOM. DAD. MIKE. THE GRAPPLERS. AND NOW -- NOW --
I CAN'T -- C-CAN'T --
"... SHE GAVE VOICE TO HER GRIEF, GAVE VOICE TO THE PAIN AND LOSS THAT WELLED UP WITHIN HER LIKE A FORCE OF NATURE.
AAAA
AAA
"SHE SCREAMED.
"SHE SCREAMED WITH ALL THE FORCE HER LUNGS COULD MUSTER, WITH ALL THE POWER HER HEART COULD PRODUCE.
AAAAAAAAAAAAAA
"SHE SCREAMED FOR FORTY-THREE MINUTES -- INTERRUPTING HER AGONIZED KEENING ONLY TO DRAW IN MORE BREATH --
AAAAAAAAAAAAAAAAAAAAAAAAAAAAAAAAAAAAAAA
"-- ONLY TO SCREAM OUT ANEW."

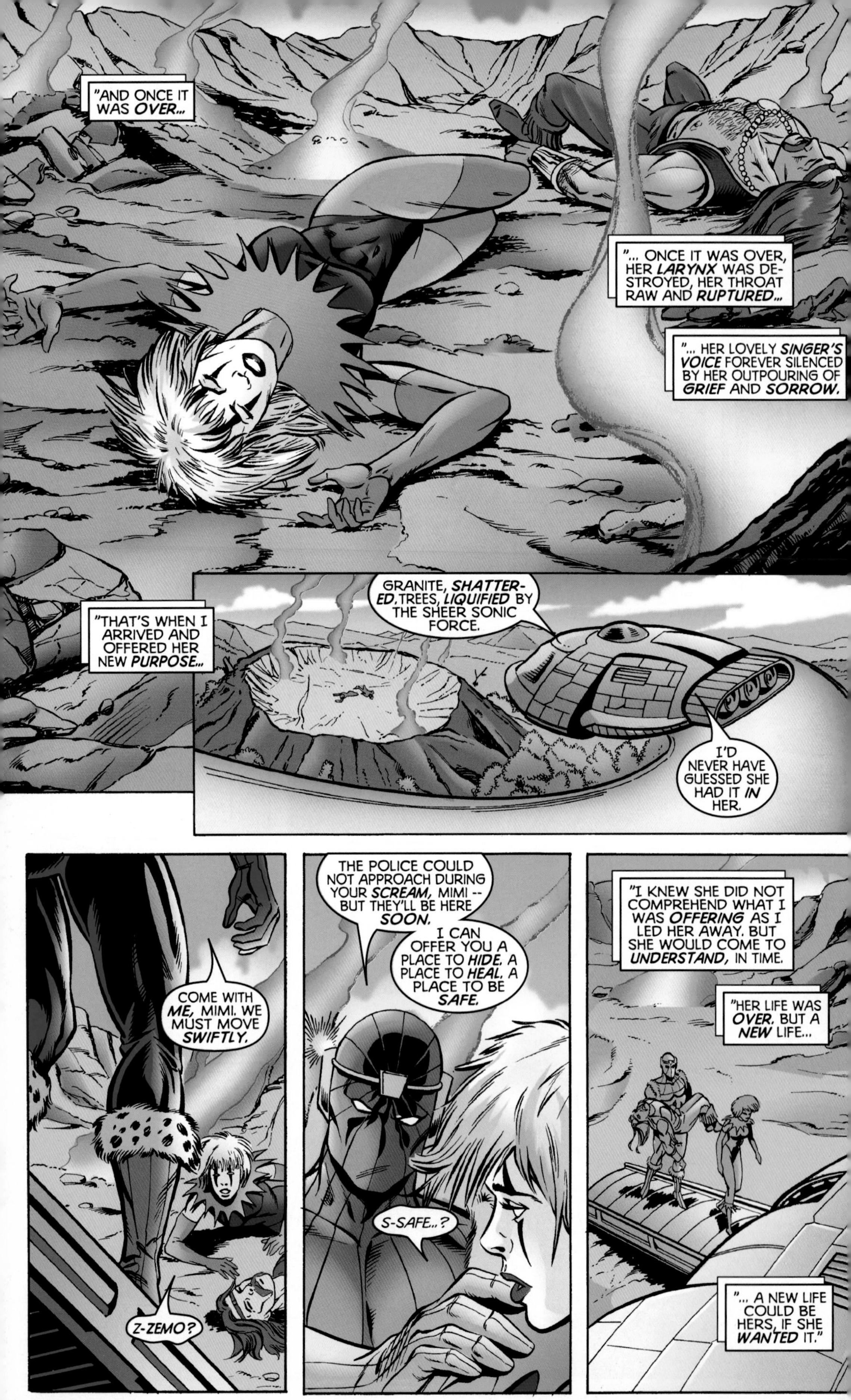
"AND ONCE IT WAS OVER...
"... ONCE IT WAS OVER, HER LARYNX WAS DESTROYED, HER THROAT RAW AND RUPTURED...
"... HER LOVELY SINGER'S VOICE FOREVER SILENCED BY HER OUTPOURING OF GRIEF AND SORROW.
"THAT'S WHEN I ARRIVED AND OFFERED HER NEW PURPOSE...
GRANITE, SHATTERED, TREES, LIQUIFIED BY THE SHEER SONIC FORCE.
I'D NEVER HAVE GUESSED SHE HAD IT IN HER.
COME WITH ME, MIMI. WE MUST MOVE SWIFTLY.
Z-ZEMO?
THE POLICE COULD NOT APPROACH DURING YOUR SCREAM, MIMI -- BUT THEY'LL BE HERE SOON.
I CAN OFFER YOU A PLACE TO HIDE, A PLACE TO HEAL, A PLACE TO BE SAFE.
S-SAFE...?
"I KNEW SHE DID NOT COMPREHEND WHAT I WAS OFFERING AS I LED HER AWAY. BUT SHE WOULD COME TO UNDERSTAND, IN TIME.
"HER LIFE WAS OVER, BUT A NEW LIFE...
"... A NEW LIFE COULD BE HERS, IF SHE WANTED IT."

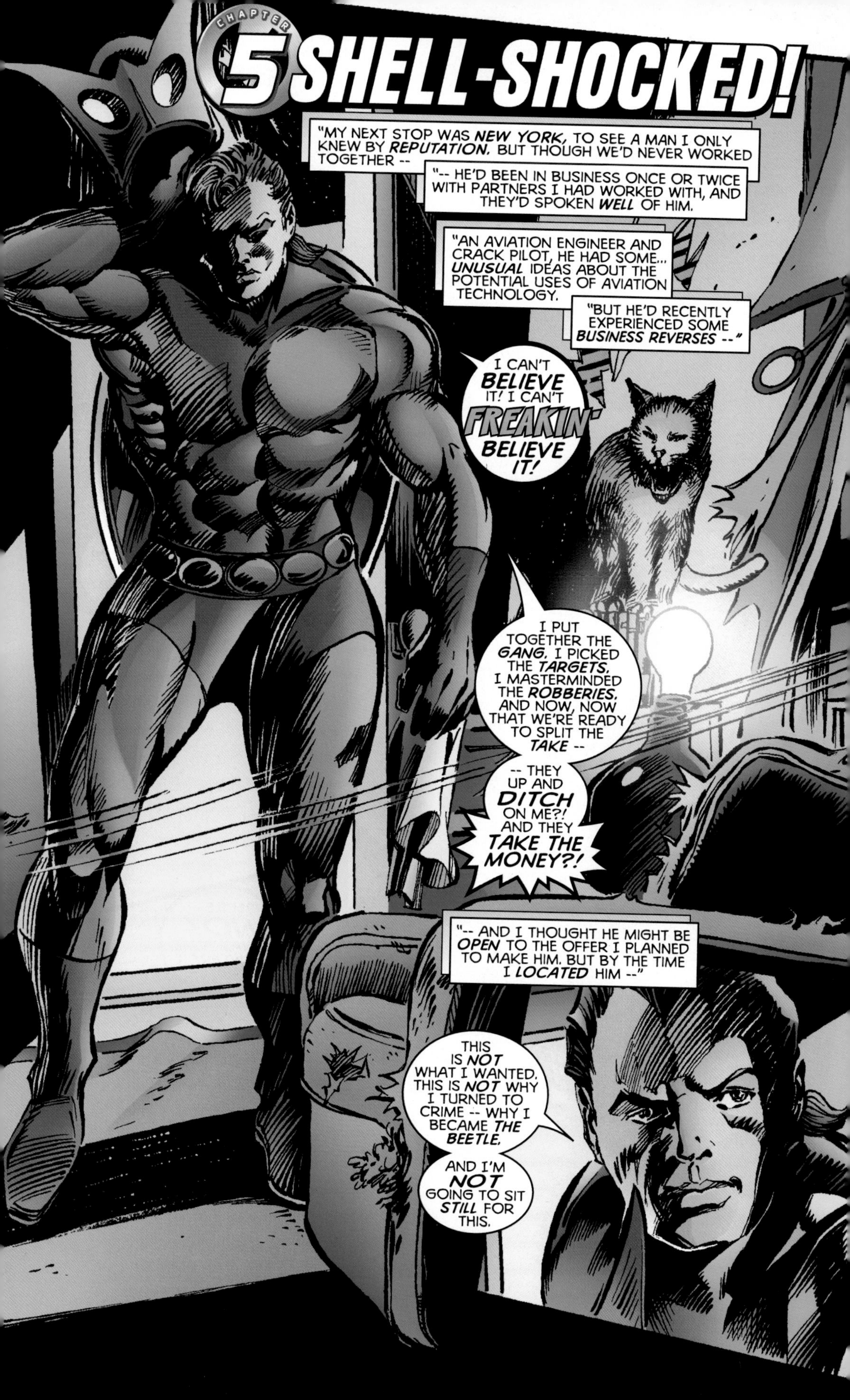

CHAPTER 5 SHELL-SHOCKED!
"MY NEXT STOP WAS NEW YORK, TO SEE A MAN I ONLY KNEW BY REPUTATION. BUT THOUGH WE'D NEVER WORKED TOGETHER --
"-- HE'D BEEN IN BUSINESS ONCE OR TWICE WITH PARTNERS I HAD WORKED WITH, AND THEY'D SPOKEN WELL OF HIM.
"AN AVIATION ENGINEER AND CRACK PILOT, HE HAD SOME... UNUSUAL IDEAS ABOUT THE POTENTIAL USES OF AVIATION TECHNOLOGY.
"BUT HE'D RECENTLY EXPERIENCED SOME BUSINESS REVERSES --"
I CAN'T BELIEVE IT! I CAN'T FREAKIN' BELIEVE IT!
I PUT TOGETHER THE GANG, I PICKED THE TARGETS, I MASTERMINDED THE ROBBERIES, AND NOW, NOW THAT WE'RE READY TO SPLIT THE TAKE --
-- THEY UP AND DITCH ON ME?! AND THEY TAKE THE MONEY?!
"-- AND I THOUGHT HE MIGHT BE OPEN TO THE OFFER I PLANNED TO MAKE HIM. BUT BY THE TIME I LOCATED HIM --"
THIS IS NOT WHAT I WANTED. THIS IS NOT WHY I TURNED TO CRIME -- WHY I BECAME THE BEETLE.
AND I'M NOT GOING TO SIT STILL FOR THIS.

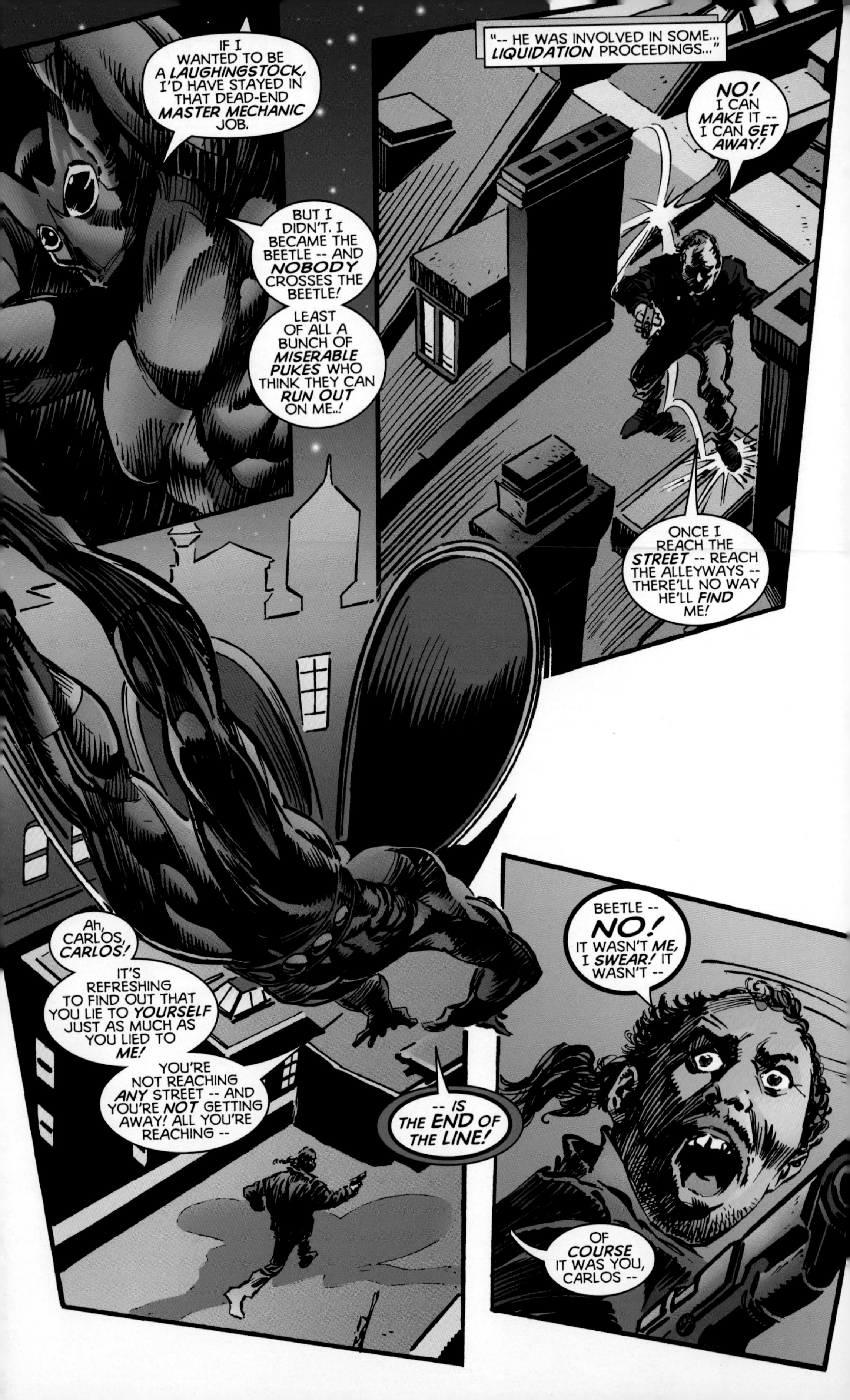
IF I WANTED TO BE A LAUGHINGSTOCK, I'D HAVE STAYED IN THAT DEAD-END MASTER MECHANIC JOB.
BUT I DIDN'T. I BECAME THE BEETLE -- AND NOBODY CROSSES THE BEETLE!
LEAST OF ALL A BUNCH OF MISERABLE PUKES WHO THINK THEY CAN RUN OUT ON ME..!
"-- HE WAS INVOLVED IN SOME... LIQUIDATION PROCEEDINGS..."
NO! I CAN MAKE IT -- I CAN GET AWAY!
ONCE I REACH THE STREET -- REACH THE ALLEYWAYS -- THERE'LL NO WAY HE'LL FIND ME!
Ah, CARLOS, CARLOS!
IT'S REFRESHING TO FIND OUT THAT YOU LIE TO YOURSELF JUST AS MUCH AS YOU LIED TO ME!
YOU'RE NOT REACHING ANY STREET -- AND YOU'RE NOT GETTING AWAY! ALL YOU'RE REACHING --
-- IS THE END OF THE LINE!
BEETLE -- NO! IT WASN'T ME, I SWEAR! IT WASN'T --
OF COURSE IT WAS YOU, CARLOS --

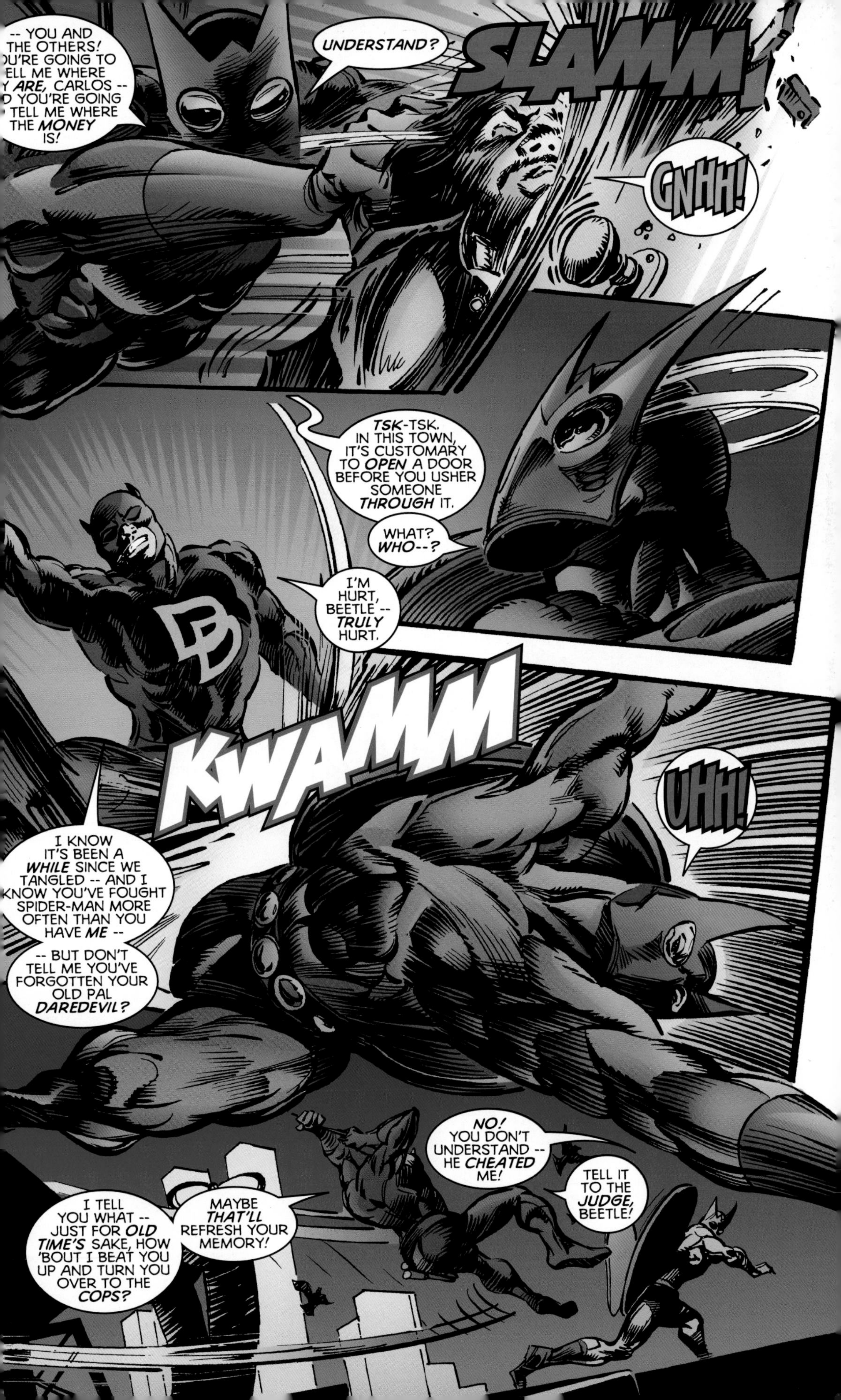
-- YOU AND THE OTHERS! OU'RE GOING TO ELL ME WHERE Y ARE, CARLOS -- D YOU'RE GOING TELL ME WHERE THE MONEY IS!
UNDERSTAND?
SLAMM!
GNHH!
TSK-TSK. IN THIS TOWN, IT'S CUSTOMARY TO OPEN A DOOR BEFORE YOU USHER SOMEONE THROUGH IT.
WHAT? WHO--?
I'M HURT, BEETLE -- TRULY HURT.
KWAMM
UHH!
I KNOW IT'S BEEN A WHILE SINCE WE TANGLED -- AND I KNOW YOU'VE FOUGHT SPIDER-MAN MORE OFTEN THAN YOU HAVE ME --
-- BUT DON'T TELL ME YOU'VE FORGOTTEN YOUR OLD PAL DAREDEVIL?
MAYBE THAT'LL REFRESH YOUR MEMORY!
NO! YOU DON'T UNDERSTAND -- HE CHEATED ME!
TELL IT TO THE JUDGE, BEETLE!
I TELL YOU WHAT -- JUST FOR OLD TIME'S SAKE, HOW 'BOUT I BEAT YOU UP AND TURN YOU OVER TO THE COPS?

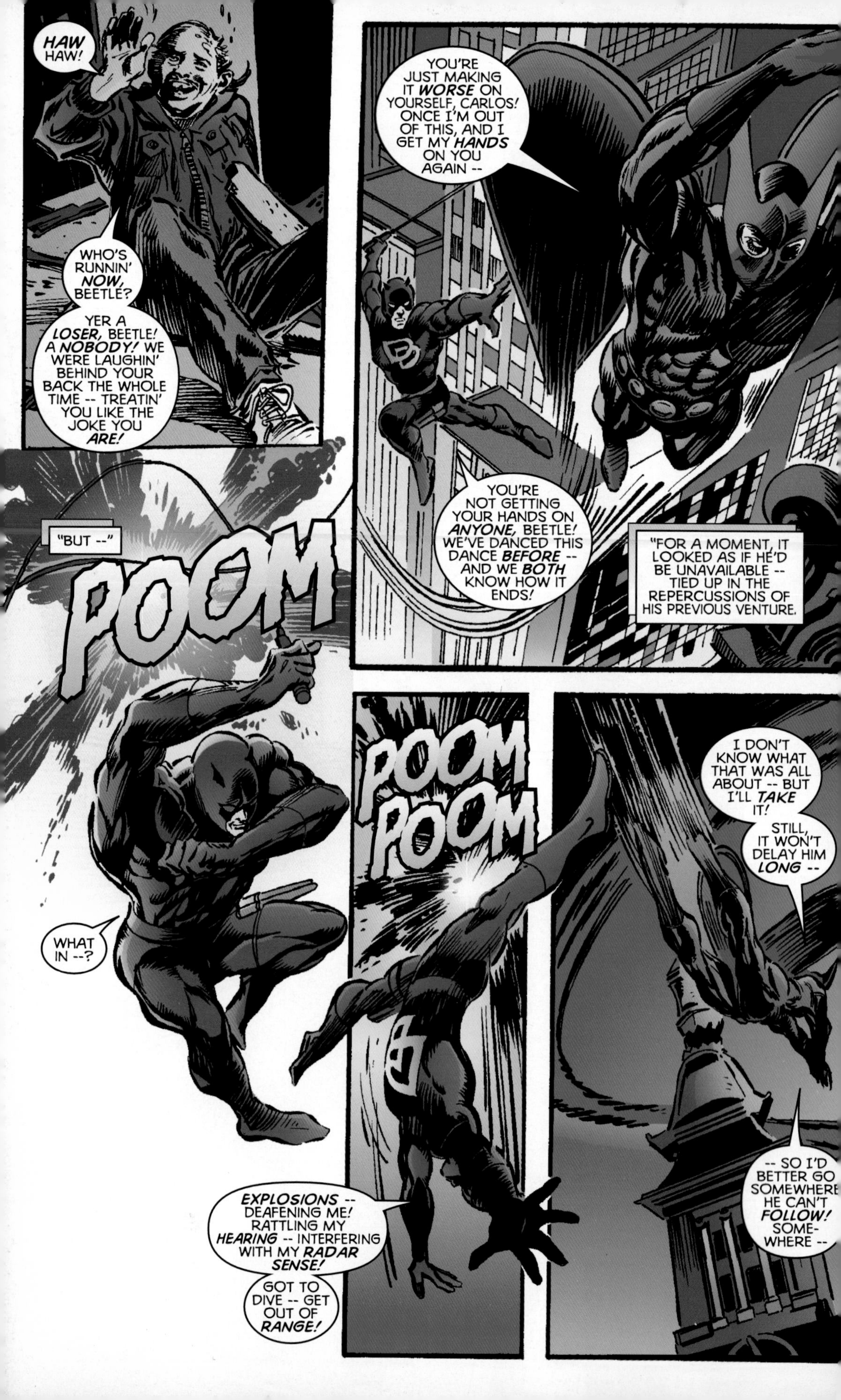
HAW HAW!
WHO'S RUNNIN' NOW, BEETLE?
YER A LOSER, BEETLE! A NOBODY! WE WERE LAUGHIN' BEHIND YOUR BACK THE WHOLE TIME -- TREATIN' YOU LIKE THE JOKE YOU ARE!
YOU'RE JUST MAKING IT WORSE ON YOURSELF, CARLOS! ONCE I'M OUT OF THIS, AND I GET MY HANDS ON YOU AGAIN --
YOU'RE NOT GETTING YOUR HANDS ON ANYONE, BEETLE! WE'VE DANCED THIS DANCE BEFORE -- AND WE BOTH KNOW HOW IT ENDS!
"FOR A MOMENT, IT LOOKED AS IF HE'D BE UNAVAILABLE -- TIED UP IN THE REPERCUSSIONS OF HIS PREVIOUS VENTURE.
"BUT --"
POOM
WHAT IN --?
POOM POOM
EXPLOSIONS -- DEAFENING ME! RATTLING MY HEARING -- INTERFERING WITH MY RADAR SENSE!
GOT TO DIVE -- GET OUT OF RANGE!
I DON'T KNOW WHAT THAT WAS ALL ABOUT -- BUT I'LL TAKE IT!
STILL, IT WON'T DELAY HIM LONG --
-- SO I'D BETTER GO SOMEWHERE HE CAN'T FOLLOW! SOME-WHERE --

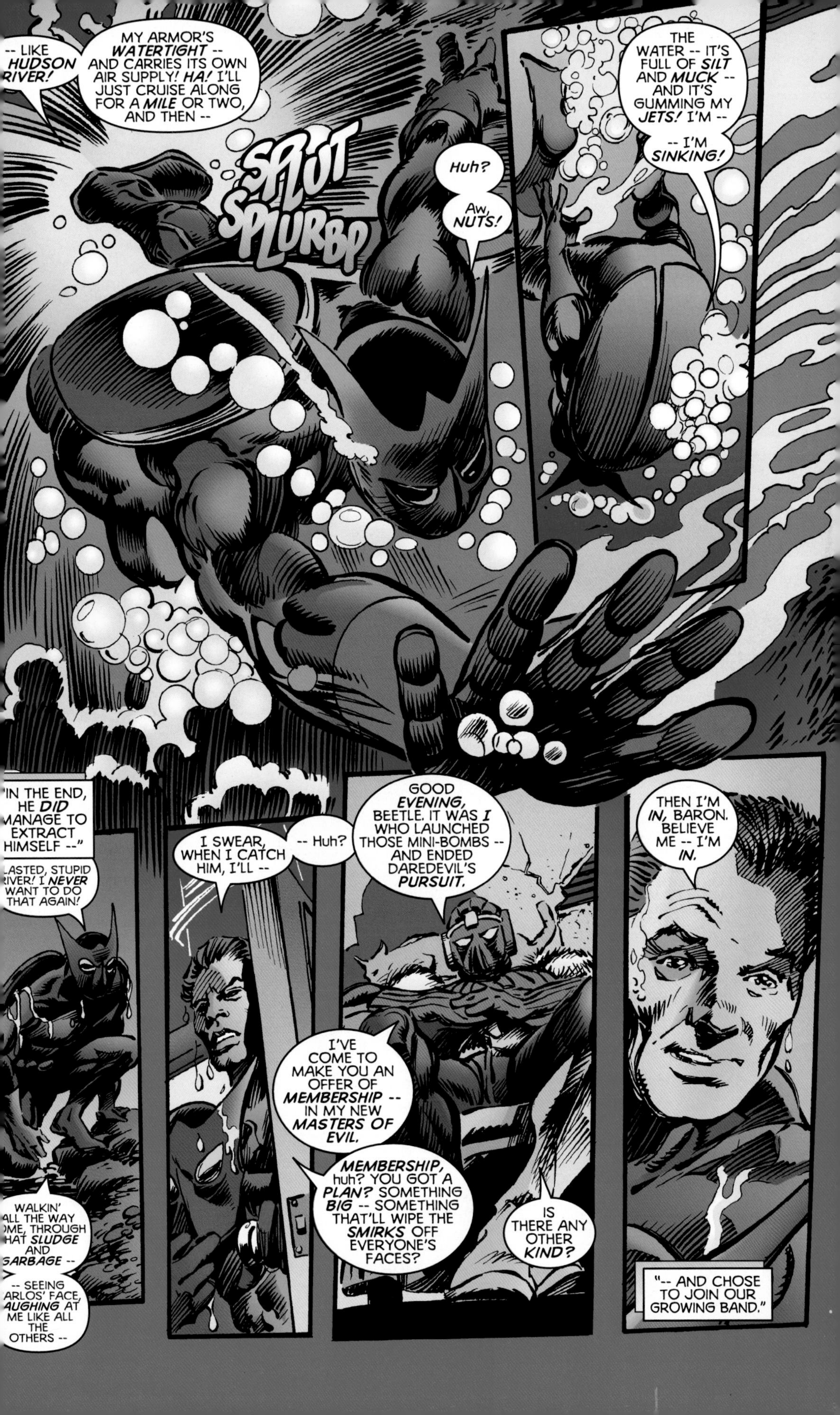
-- LIKE HUDSON RIVER!
MY ARMOR'S WATERTIGHT -- AND CARRIES ITS OWN AIR SUPPLY! HA! I'LL JUST CRUISE ALONG FOR A MILE OR TWO, AND THEN --
SPLUT SPLURBB
Huh?
Aw, NUTS!
THE WATER -- IT'S FULL OF SILT AND MUCK -- AND IT'S GUMMING MY JETS! I'M --
-- I'M SINKING!
"IN THE END, HE DID MANAGE TO EXTRACT HIMSELF --"
LASTED, STUPID RIVER! I NEVER WANT TO DO THAT AGAIN!
WALKIN' ALL THE WAY OME, THROUGH HAT SLUDGE AND GARBAGE --
-- SEEING ARLOS' FACE, AUGHING AT ME LIKE ALL THE OTHERS --
I SWEAR, WHEN I CATCH HIM, I'LL --
-- Huh?
GOOD EVENING, BEETLE. IT WAS I WHO LAUNCHED THOSE MINI-BOMBS -- AND ENDED DAREDEVIL'S PURSUIT.
I'VE COME TO MAKE YOU AN OFFER OF MEMBERSHIP -- IN MY NEW MASTERS OF EVIL.
MEMBERSHIP, huh? YOU GOT A PLAN? SOMETHING BIG -- SOMETHING THAT'LL WIPE THE SMIRKS OFF EVERYONE'S FACES?
IS THERE ANY OTHER KIND?
THEN I'M IN, BARON. BELIEVE ME -- I'M IN.
"-- AND CHOSE TO JOIN OUR GROWING BAND."

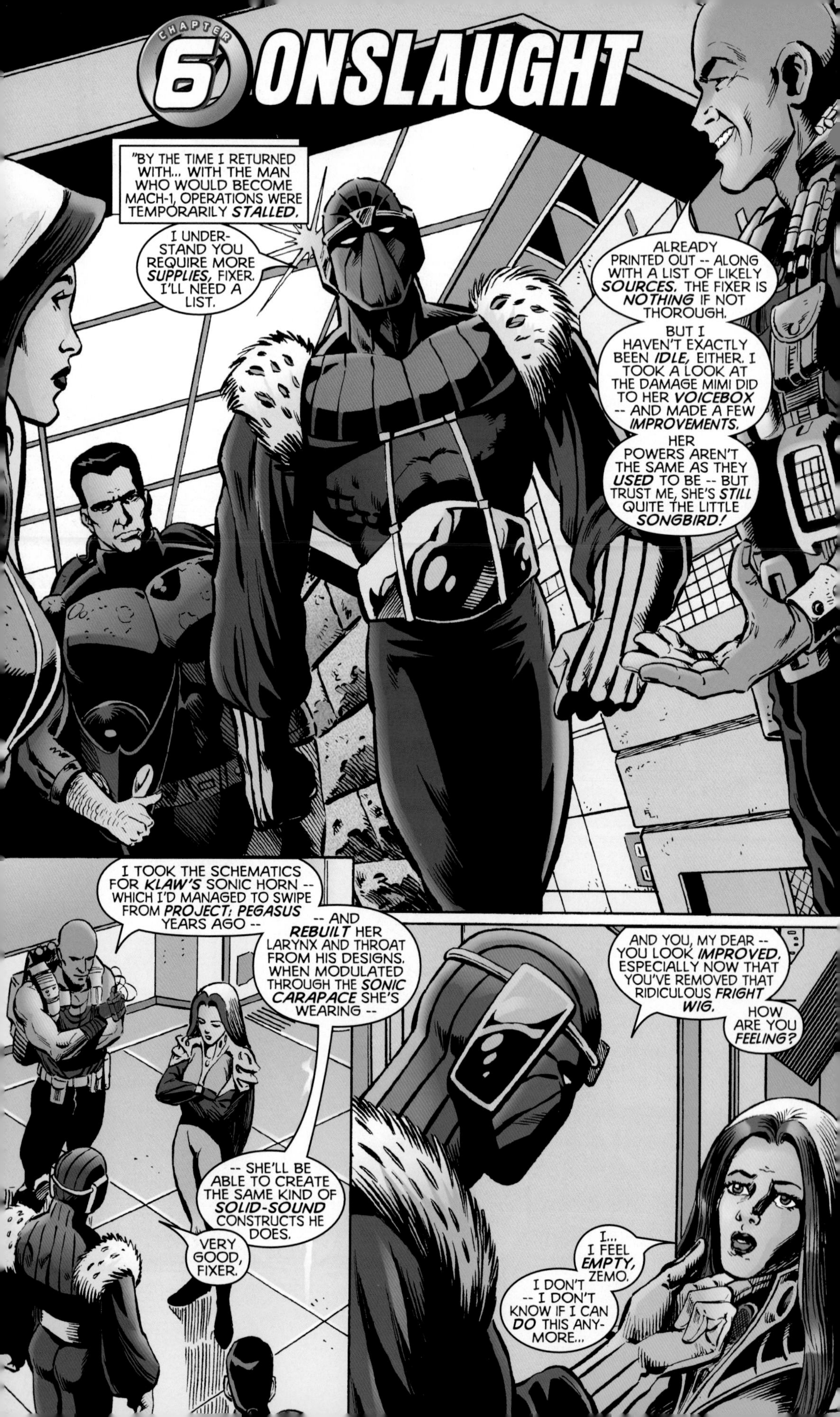
CHAPTER 6 ONSLAUGHT
"BY THE TIME I RETURNED WITH... WITH THE MAN WHO WOULD BECOME MACH-1, OPERATIONS WERE TEMPORARILY STALLED.
I UNDERSTAND YOU REQUIRE MORE SUPPLIES, FIXER. I'LL NEED A LIST.
ALREADY PRINTED OUT -- ALONG WITH A LIST OF LIKELY SOURCES. THE FIXER IS NOTHING IF NOT THOROUGH.
BUT I HAVEN'T EXACTLY BEEN IDLE, EITHER. I TOOK A LOOK AT THE DAMAGE MIMI DID TO HER VOICEBOX -- AND MADE A FEW IMPROVEMENTS.
HER POWERS AREN'T THE SAME AS THEY USED TO BE -- BUT TRUST ME, SHE'S STILL QUITE THE LITTLE SONGBIRD!
I TOOK THE SCHEMATICS FOR KLAW'S SONIC HORN -- WHICH I'D MANAGED TO SWIPE FROM PROJECT: PEGASUS YEARS AGO --
-- AND REBUILT HER LARYNX AND THROAT FROM HIS DESIGNS. WHEN MODULATED THROUGH THE SONIC CARAPACE SHE'S WEARING --
-- SHE'LL BE ABLE TO CREATE THE SAME KIND OF SOLID-SOUND CONSTRUCTS HE DOES.
VERY GOOD, FIXER.
AND YOU, MY DEAR -- YOU LOOK IMPROVED, ESPECIALLY NOW THAT YOU'VE REMOVED THAT RIDICULOUS FRIGHT WIG.
HOW ARE YOU FEELING?
I... I FEEL EMPTY, ZEMO.
I DON'T -- I DON'T KNOW IF I CAN DO THIS ANYMORE...

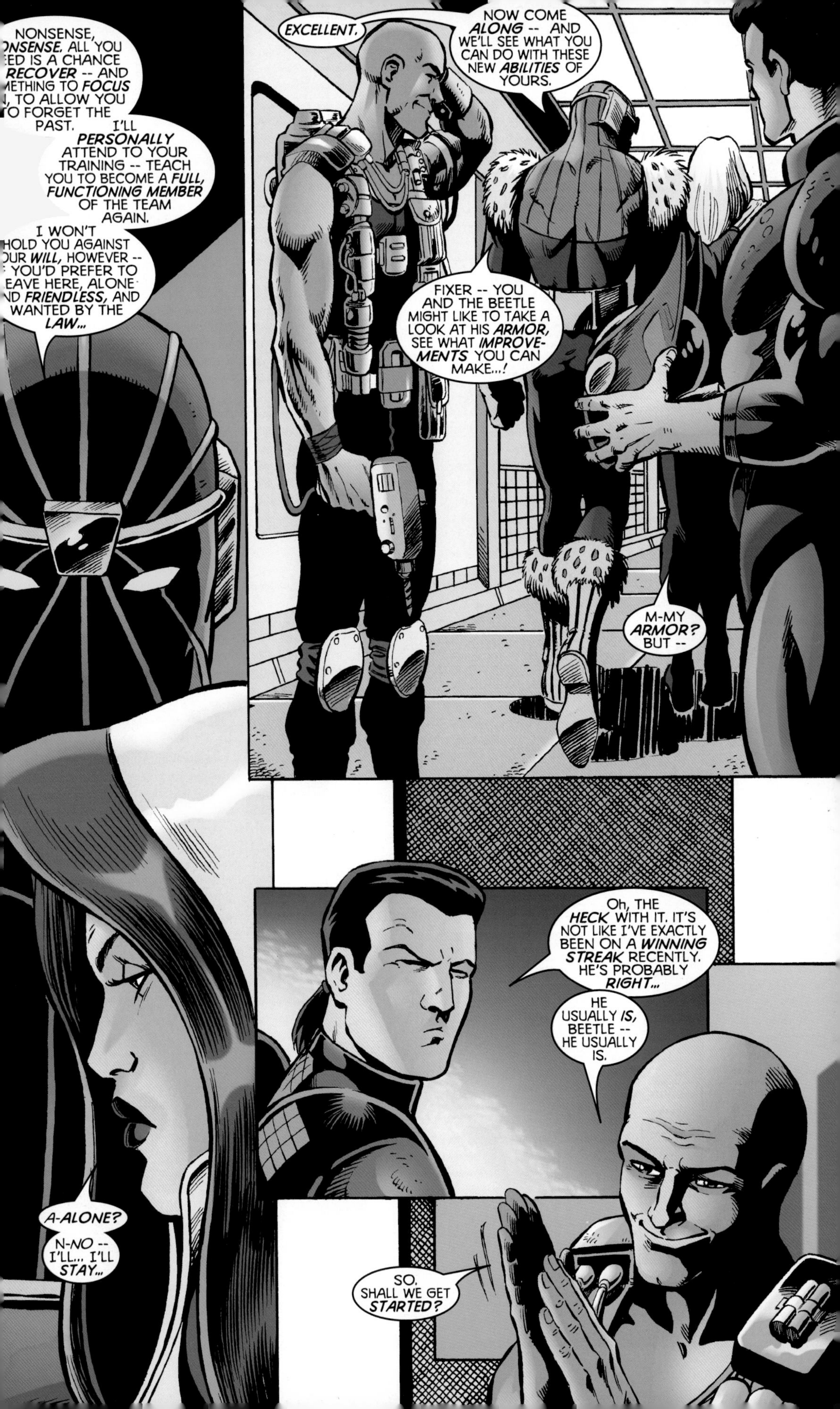
NONSENSE, NONSENSE. ALL YOU NEED IS A CHANCE TO RECOVER -- AND SOMETHING TO FOCUS ON, TO ALLOW YOU TO FORGET THE PAST.
I'LL PERSONALLY ATTEND TO YOUR TRAINING -- TEACH YOU TO BECOME A FULL, FUNCTIONING MEMBER OF THE TEAM AGAIN.
I WON'T HOLD YOU AGAINST YOUR WILL, HOWEVER -- IF YOU'D PREFER TO LEAVE HERE, ALONE AND FRIENDLESS, AND WANTED BY THE LAW...
A-ALONE?
N-NO -- I'LL... I'LL STAY...
EXCELLENT.
NOW COME ALONG -- AND WE'LL SEE WHAT YOU CAN DO WITH THESE NEW ABILITIES OF YOURS.
FIXER -- YOU AND THE BEETLE MIGHT LIKE TO TAKE A LOOK AT HIS ARMOR, SEE WHAT IMPROVEMENTS YOU CAN MAKE...!
M-MY ARMOR? BUT --
Oh, THE HECK WITH IT. IT'S NOT LIKE I'VE EXACTLY BEEN ON A WINNING STREAK RECENTLY. HE'S PROBABLY RIGHT...
HE USUALLY IS, BEETLE -- HE USUALLY IS.
SO, SHALL WE GET STARTED?

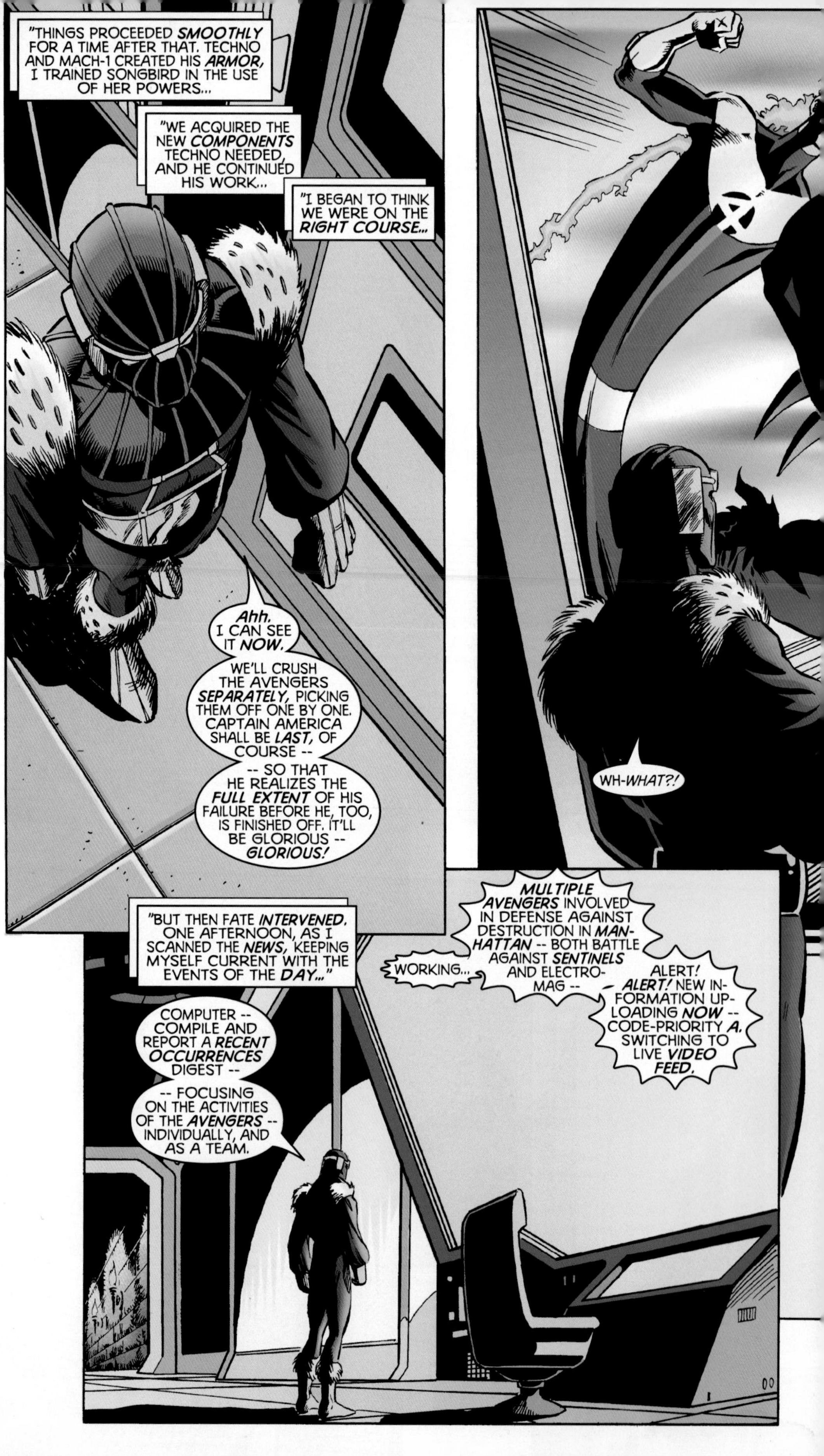
"THINGS PROCEEDED *SMOOTHLY* FOR A TIME AFTER THAT. TECHNO AND MACH-1 CREATED HIS *ARMOR,* I TRAINED SONGBIRD IN THE USE OF HER POWERS...
"WE ACQUIRED THE NEW *COMPONENTS* TECHNO NEEDED, AND HE CONTINUED HIS WORK...
"I BEGAN TO THINK WE WERE ON THE *RIGHT COURSE...*
Ahh. I CAN SEE IT *NOW.*
WE'LL CRUSH THE AVENGERS *SEPARATELY,* PICKING THEM OFF ONE BY ONE. CAPTAIN AMERICA SHALL BE *LAST,* OF COURSE --
-- SO THAT HE REALIZES THE *FULL EXTENT* OF HIS FAILURE BEFORE HE, TOO, IS FINISHED OFF. IT'LL BE GLORIOUS -- *GLORIOUS!*
WH-*WHAT?!*
"BUT THEN FATE *INTERVENED.* ONE AFTERNOON, AS I SCANNED THE *NEWS,* KEEPING MYSELF CURRENT WITH THE EVENTS OF THE *DAY...*"
COMPUTER -- COMPILE AND REPORT A *RECENT OCCURRENCES* DIGEST --
-- FOCUSING ON THE ACTIVITIES OF THE *AVENGERS* -- INDIVIDUALLY, AND AS A TEAM.
WORKING...
MULTIPLE AVENGERS INVOLVED IN DEFENSE AGAINST DESTRUCTION IN *MAN-HATTAN* -- BOTH BATTLE AGAINST *SENTINELS* AND ELECTRO-MAG --
ALERT! *ALERT!* NEW IN-FORMATION UP-LOADING *NOW* -- CODE-PRIORITY *A.* SWITCHING TO LIVE *VIDEO FEED.*

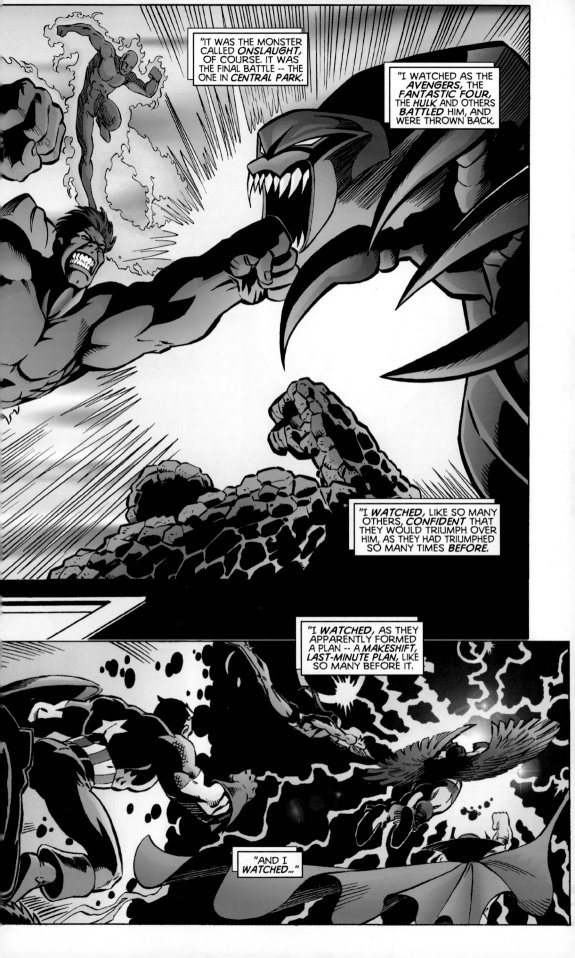

"IT WAS THE MONSTER CALLED *ONSLAUGHT*, OF COURSE. IT WAS THE FINAL BATTLE -- THE ONE IN *CENTRAL PARK.*

"I WATCHED AS THE *AVENGERS*, THE *FANTASTIC FOUR*, THE *HULK* AND OTHERS *BATTLED* HIM, AND WERE THROWN BACK.

"I *WATCHED*, LIKE SO MANY OTHERS, *CONFIDENT* THAT THEY WOULD TRIUMPH OVER HIM, AS THEY HAD TRIUMPHED SO MANY TIMES *BEFORE.*

"I *WATCHED*, AS THEY APPARENTLY FORMED A PLAN -- A *MAKESHIFT, LAST-MINUTE PLAN*, LIKE SO MANY BEFORE IT.

"AND I *WATCHED*..."

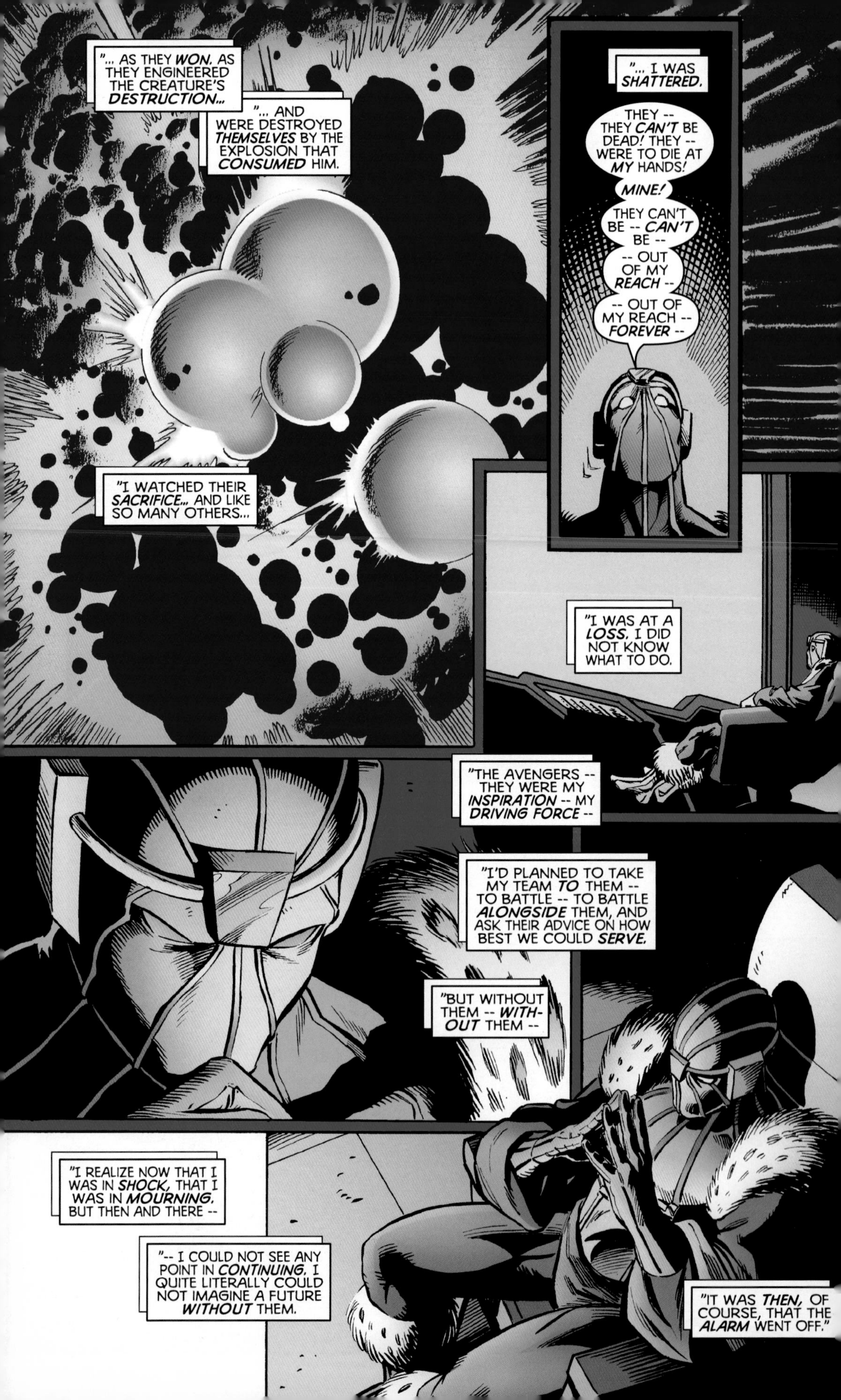
"... AS THEY WON, AS THEY ENGINEERED THE CREATURE'S DESTRUCTION...
"... AND WERE DESTROYED THEMSELVES BY THE EXPLOSION THAT CONSUMED HIM.
"I WATCHED THEIR SACRIFICE... AND LIKE SO MANY OTHERS...
"... I WAS SHATTERED.
THEY -- THEY CAN'T BE DEAD! THEY -- WERE TO DIE AT MY HANDS!
MINE!
THEY CAN'T BE -- CAN'T BE --
-- OUT OF MY REACH --
-- OUT OF MY REACH -- FOREVER --
"I WAS AT A LOSS. I DID NOT KNOW WHAT TO DO.
"THE AVENGERS -- THEY WERE MY INSPIRATION -- MY DRIVING FORCE --
"I'D PLANNED TO TAKE MY TEAM TO THEM -- TO BATTLE -- TO BATTLE ALONGSIDE THEM, AND ASK THEIR ADVICE ON HOW BEST WE COULD SERVE.
"BUT WITHOUT THEM -- WITH-OUT THEM --
"I REALIZE NOW THAT I WAS IN SHOCK, THAT I WAS IN MOURNING. BUT THEN AND THERE --
"-- I COULD NOT SEE ANY POINT IN CONTINUING. I QUITE LITERALLY COULD NOT IMAGINE A FUTURE WITHOUT THEM.
"IT WAS THEN, OF COURSE, THAT THE ALARM WENT OFF."

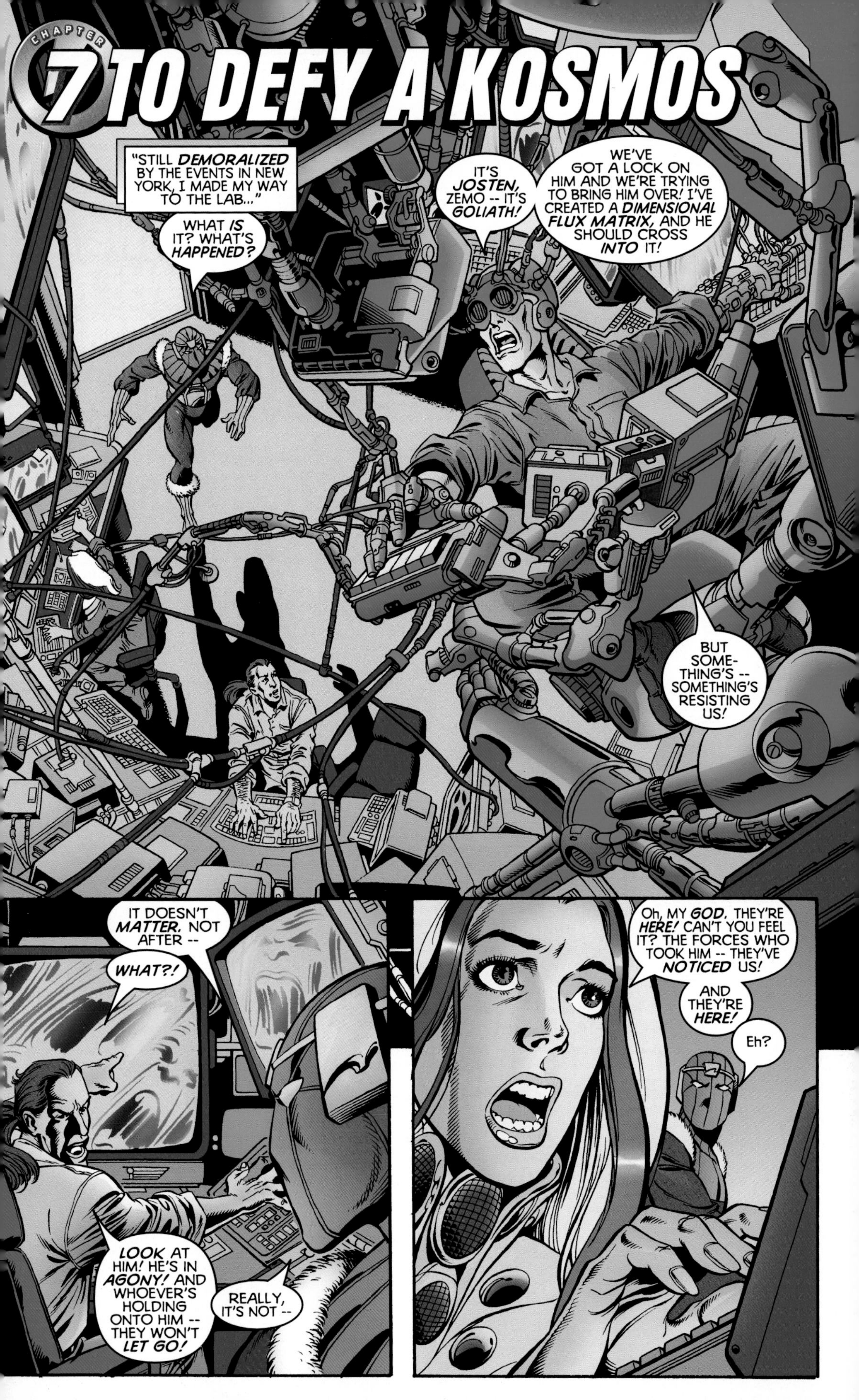
CHAPTER 7 TO DEFY A KOSMOS
"STILL DEMORALIZED BY THE EVENTS IN NEW YORK, I MADE MY WAY TO THE LAB..."
WHAT IS IT? WHAT'S HAPPENED?
IT'S JOSTEN, ZEMO -- IT'S GOLIATH!
WE'VE GOT A LOCK ON HIM AND WE'RE TRYING TO BRING HIM OVER! I'VE CREATED A DIMENSIONAL FLUX MATRIX, AND HE SHOULD CROSS INTO IT!
BUT SOME-THING'S -- SOMETHING'S RESISTING US!
IT DOESN'T MATTER. NOT AFTER --
WHAT?!
LOOK AT HIM! HE'S IN AGONY! AND WHOEVER'S HOLDING ONTO HIM -- THEY WON'T LET GO!
REALLY, IT'S NOT --
Oh, MY GOD. THEY'RE HERE! CAN'T YOU FEEL IT? THE FORCES WHO TOOK HIM -- THEY'VE NOTICED US!
AND THEY'RE HERE!
Eh?

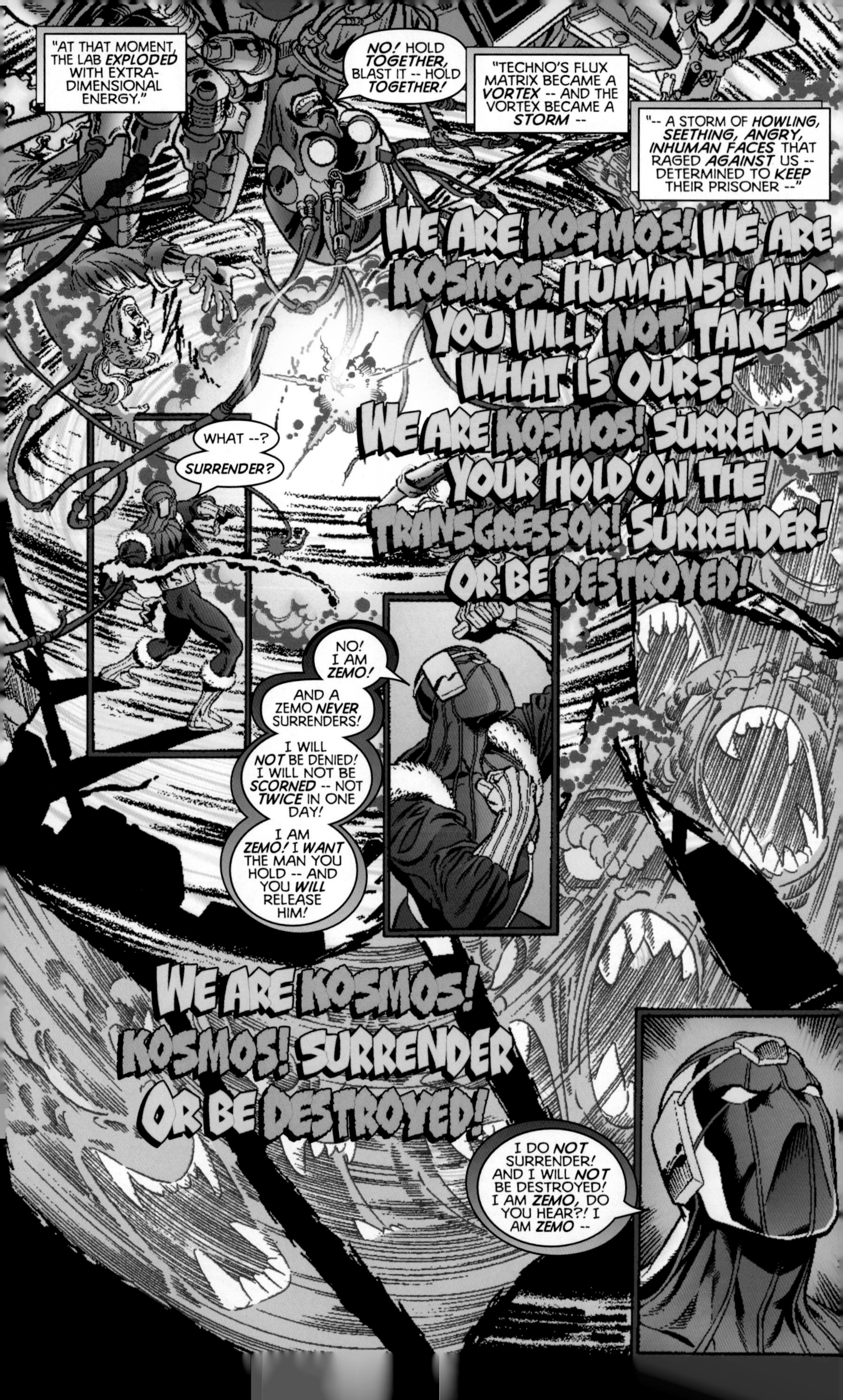
"AT THAT MOMENT, THE LAB EXPLODED WITH EXTRA-DIMENSIONAL ENERGY."
NO! HOLD TOGETHER, BLAST IT -- HOLD TOGETHER!
"TECHNO'S FLUX MATRIX BECAME A VORTEX -- AND THE VORTEX BECAME A STORM --
"-- A STORM OF HOWLING, SEETHING, ANGRY, INHUMAN FACES THAT RAGED AGAINST US -- DETERMINED TO KEEP THEIR PRISONER --"
WE ARE KOSMOS! WE ARE KOSMOS, HUMANS! AND YOU WILL NOT TAKE WHAT IS OURS!
WE ARE KOSMOS! SURRENDER YOUR HOLD ON THE TRANSGRESSOR! SURRENDER! OR BE DESTROYED!
WHAT --?
SURRENDER?
NO! I AM ZEMO!
AND A ZEMO NEVER SURRENDERS!
I WILL NOT BE DENIED! I WILL NOT BE SCORNED -- NOT TWICE IN ONE DAY!
I AM ZEMO! I WANT THE MAN YOU HOLD -- AND YOU WILL RELEASE HIM!
WE ARE KOSMOS! KOSMOS! SURRENDER OR BE DESTROYED!
I DO NOT SURRENDER! AND I WILL NOT BE DESTROYED! I AM ZEMO, DO YOU HEAR?! I AM ZEMO --

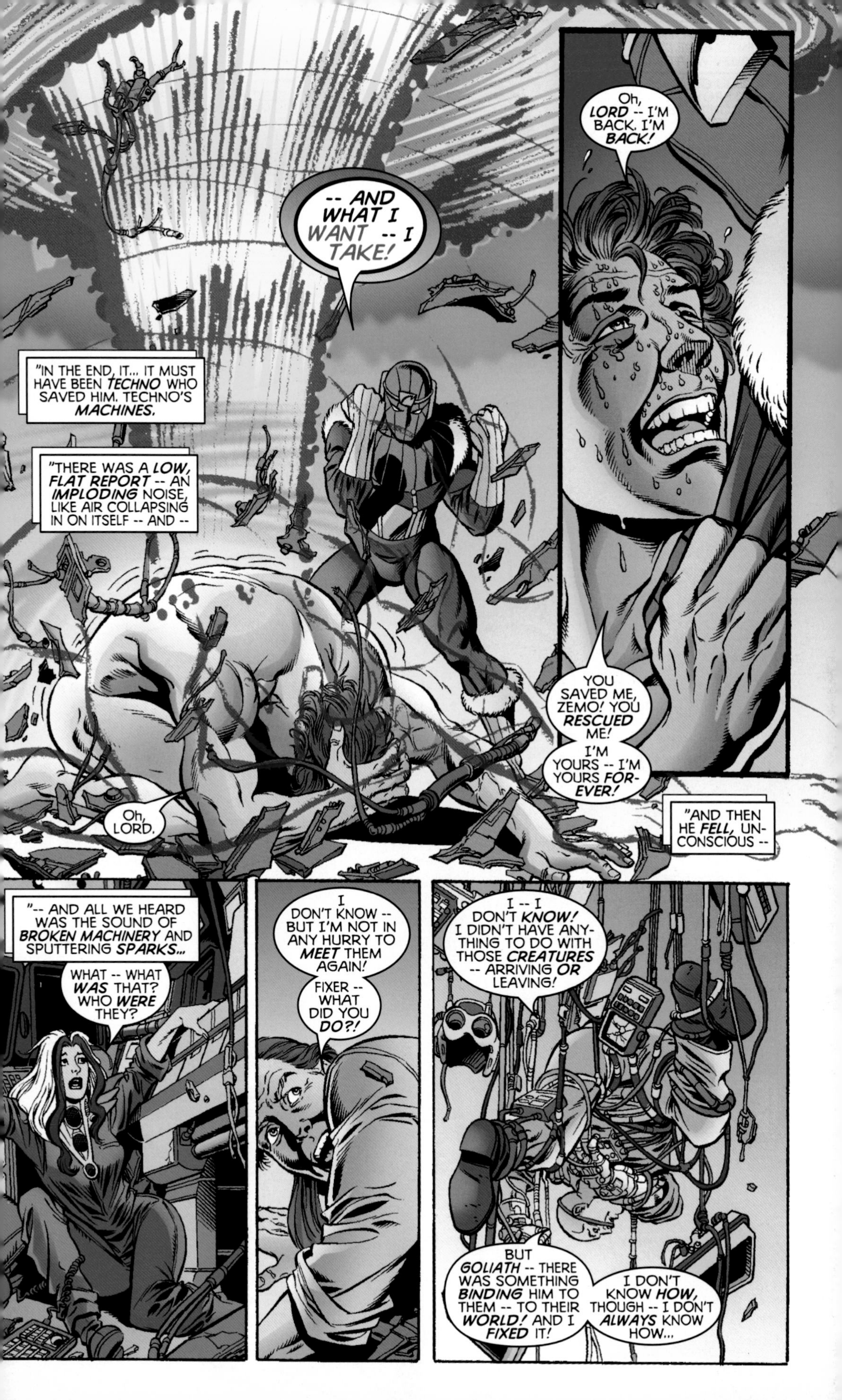
-- AND WHAT I WANT -- I TAKE!
Oh, LORD -- I'M BACK. I'M BACK!
"IN THE END, IT... IT MUST HAVE BEEN TECHNO WHO SAVED HIM. TECHNO'S MACHINES.
"THERE WAS A LOW, FLAT REPORT -- AN IMPLODING NOISE, LIKE AIR COLLAPSING IN ON ITSELF -- AND --
Oh, LORD.
YOU SAVED ME, ZEMO! YOU RESCUED ME!
I'M YOURS -- I'M YOURS FOREVER!
"AND THEN HE FELL, UNCONSCIOUS --
"-- AND ALL WE HEARD WAS THE SOUND OF BROKEN MACHINERY AND SPUTTERING SPARKS...
WHAT -- WHAT WAS THAT? WHO WERE THEY?
I DON'T KNOW -- BUT I'M NOT IN ANY HURRY TO MEET THEM AGAIN!
FIXER -- WHAT DID YOU DO?!
I -- I DON'T KNOW! I DIDN'T HAVE ANYTHING TO DO WITH THOSE CREATURES -- ARRIVING OR LEAVING!
BUT GOLIATH -- THERE WAS SOMETHING BINDING HIM TO THEM -- TO THEIR WORLD! AND I FIXED IT!
I DON'T KNOW HOW, THOUGH -- I DON'T ALWAYS KNOW HOW...

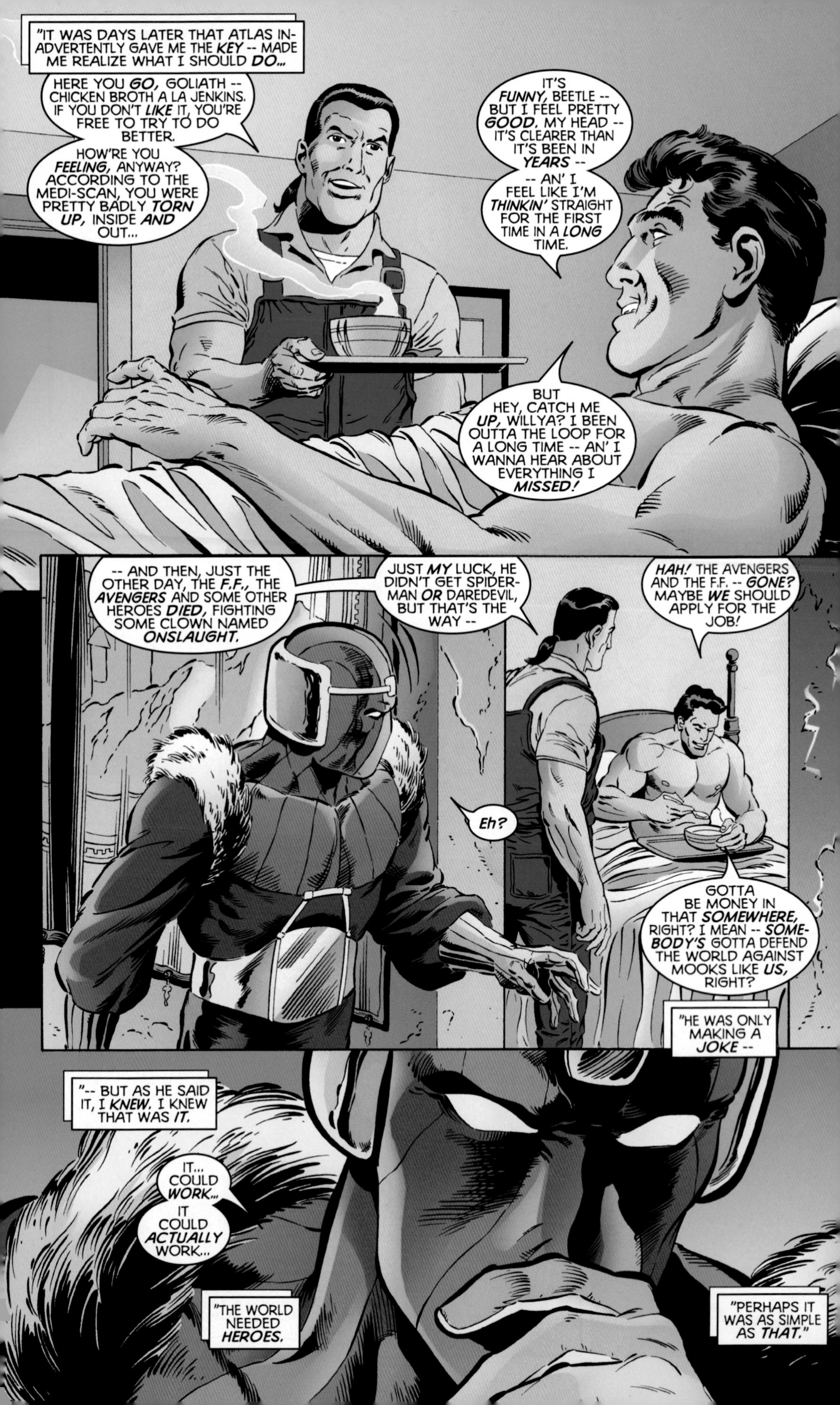
"IT WAS DAYS LATER THAT ATLAS INADVERTENTLY GAVE ME THE KEY -- MADE ME REALIZE WHAT I SHOULD DO...
HERE YOU GO, GOLIATH -- CHICKEN BROTH A LA JENKINS. IF YOU DON'T LIKE IT, YOU'RE FREE TO TRY TO DO BETTER.
HOW'RE YOU FEELING, ANYWAY? ACCORDING TO THE MEDI-SCAN, YOU WERE PRETTY BADLY TORN UP, INSIDE AND OUT...
IT'S FUNNY, BEETLE -- BUT I FEEL PRETTY GOOD. MY HEAD -- IT'S CLEARER THAN IT'S BEEN IN YEARS --
-- AN' I FEEL LIKE I'M THINKIN' STRAIGHT FOR THE FIRST TIME IN A LONG TIME.
BUT HEY, CATCH ME UP, WILLYA? I BEEN OUTTA THE LOOP FOR A LONG TIME -- AN' I WANNA HEAR ABOUT EVERYTHING I MISSED!
-- AND THEN, JUST THE OTHER DAY, THE F.F., THE AVENGERS AND SOME OTHER HEROES DIED, FIGHTING SOME CLOWN NAMED ONSLAUGHT.
JUST MY LUCK, HE DIDN'T GET SPIDER-MAN OR DAREDEVIL, BUT THAT'S THE WAY --
HAH! THE AVENGERS AND THE F.F. -- GONE? MAYBE WE SHOULD APPLY FOR THE JOB!
Eh?
GOTTA BE MONEY IN THAT SOMEWHERE, RIGHT? I MEAN -- SOMEBODY'S GOTTA DEFEND THE WORLD AGAINST MOOKS LIKE US, RIGHT?
"HE WAS ONLY MAKING A JOKE --
"-- BUT AS HE SAID IT, I KNEW. I KNEW THAT WAS IT.
IT... COULD WORK...
IT COULD ACTUALLY WORK...
"THE WORLD NEEDED HEROES.
"PERHAPS IT WAS AS SIMPLE AS THAT."

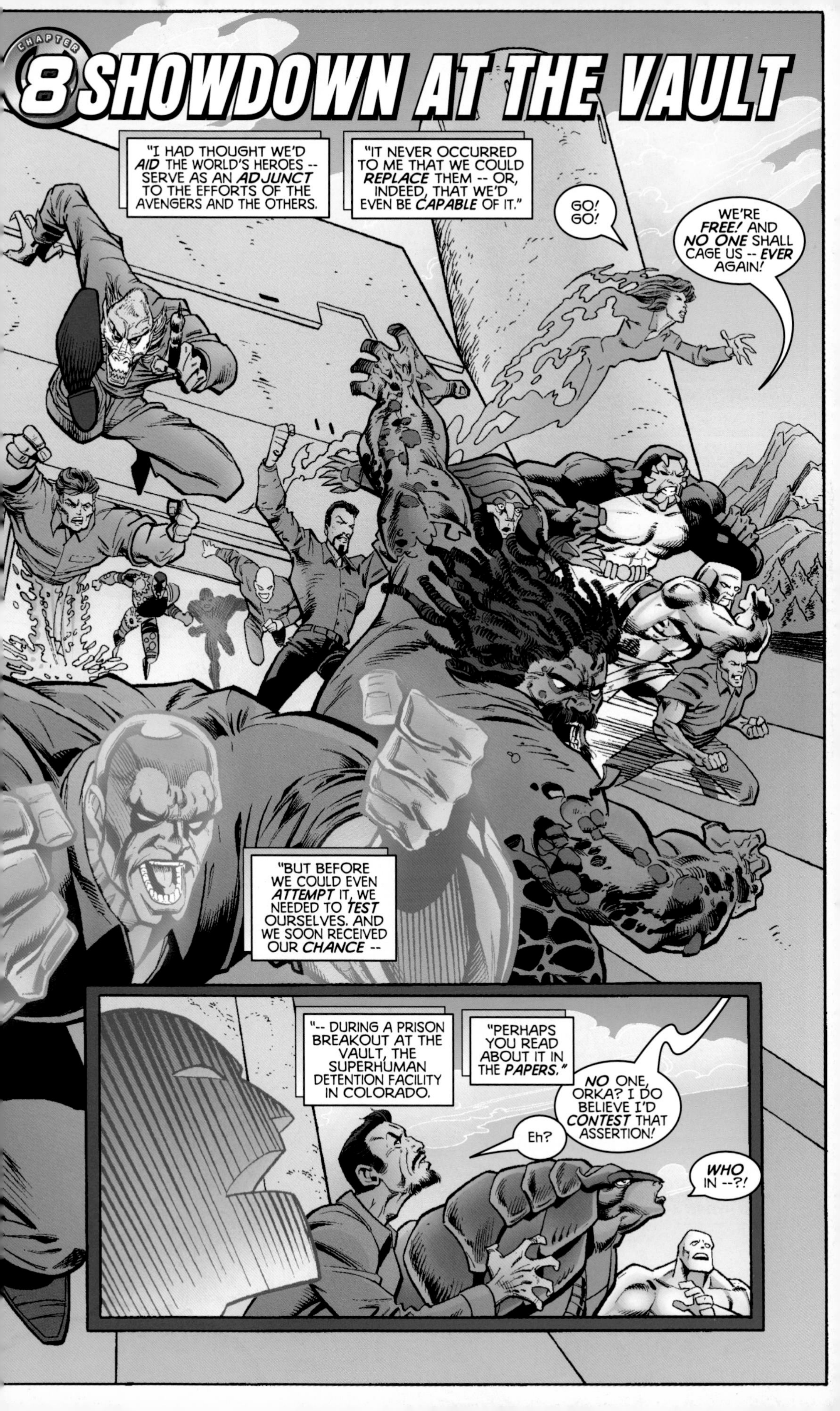
CHAPTER 8 SHOWDOWN AT THE VAULT
"I HAD THOUGHT WE'D AID THE WORLD'S HEROES -- SERVE AS AN ADJUNCT TO THE EFFORTS OF THE AVENGERS AND THE OTHERS.
"IT NEVER OCCURRED TO ME THAT WE COULD REPLACE THEM -- OR, INDEED, THAT WE'D EVEN BE CAPABLE OF IT."
GO! GO!
WE'RE FREE! AND NO ONE SHALL CAGE US -- EVER AGAIN!
"BUT BEFORE WE COULD EVEN ATTEMPT IT, WE NEEDED TO TEST OURSELVES. AND WE SOON RECEIVED OUR CHANCE --
"-- DURING A PRISON BREAKOUT AT THE VAULT, THE SUPERHUMAN DETENTION FACILITY IN COLORADO.
"PERHAPS YOU READ ABOUT IT IN THE PAPERS."
NO ONE, ORKA? I DO BELIEVE I'D CONTEST THAT ASSERTION!
Eh?
WHO IN --?!

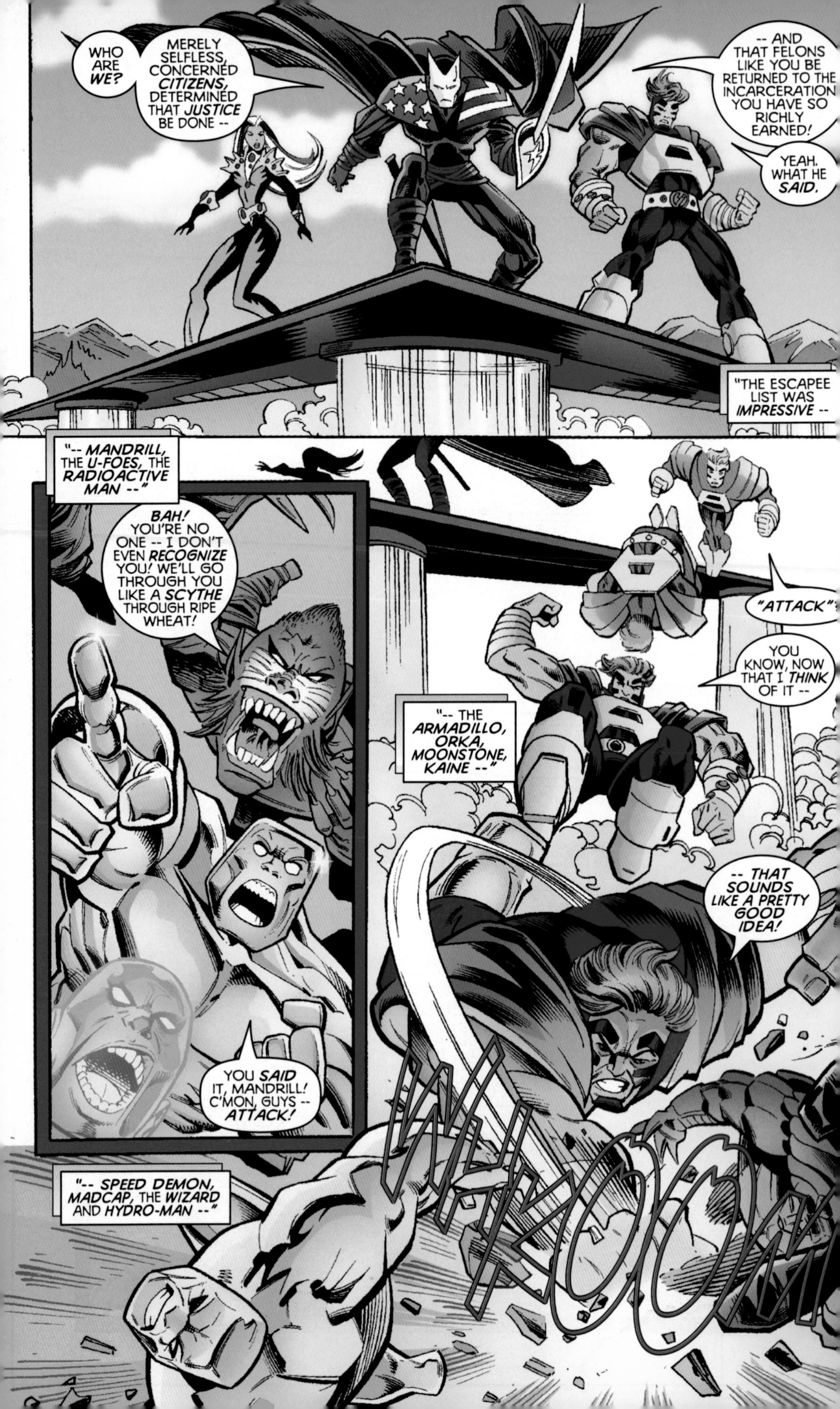
WHO ARE WE?
MERELY SELFLESS, CONCERNED CITIZENS, DETERMINED THAT JUSTICE BE DONE --
-- AND THAT FELONS LIKE YOU BE RETURNED TO THE INCARCERATION YOU HAVE SO RICHLY EARNED!
YEAH. WHAT HE SAID.
"THE ESCAPEE LIST WAS IMPRESSIVE --
"-- MANDRILL, THE U-FOES, THE RADIOACTIVE MAN --"
BAH! YOU'RE NO ONE -- I DON'T EVEN RECOGNIZE YOU! WE'LL GO THROUGH YOU LIKE A SCYTHE THROUGH RIPE WHEAT!
YOU SAID IT, MANDRILL! C'MON, GUYS -- ATTACK!
"ATTACK"?
YOU KNOW, NOW THAT I THINK OF IT --
"-- THE ARMADILLO, ORKA, MOONSTONE, KAINE --"
-- THAT SOUNDS LIKE A PRETTY GOOD IDEA!
"-- SPEED DEMON, MADCAP, THE WIZARD AND HYDRO-MAN --"
WHKOOM

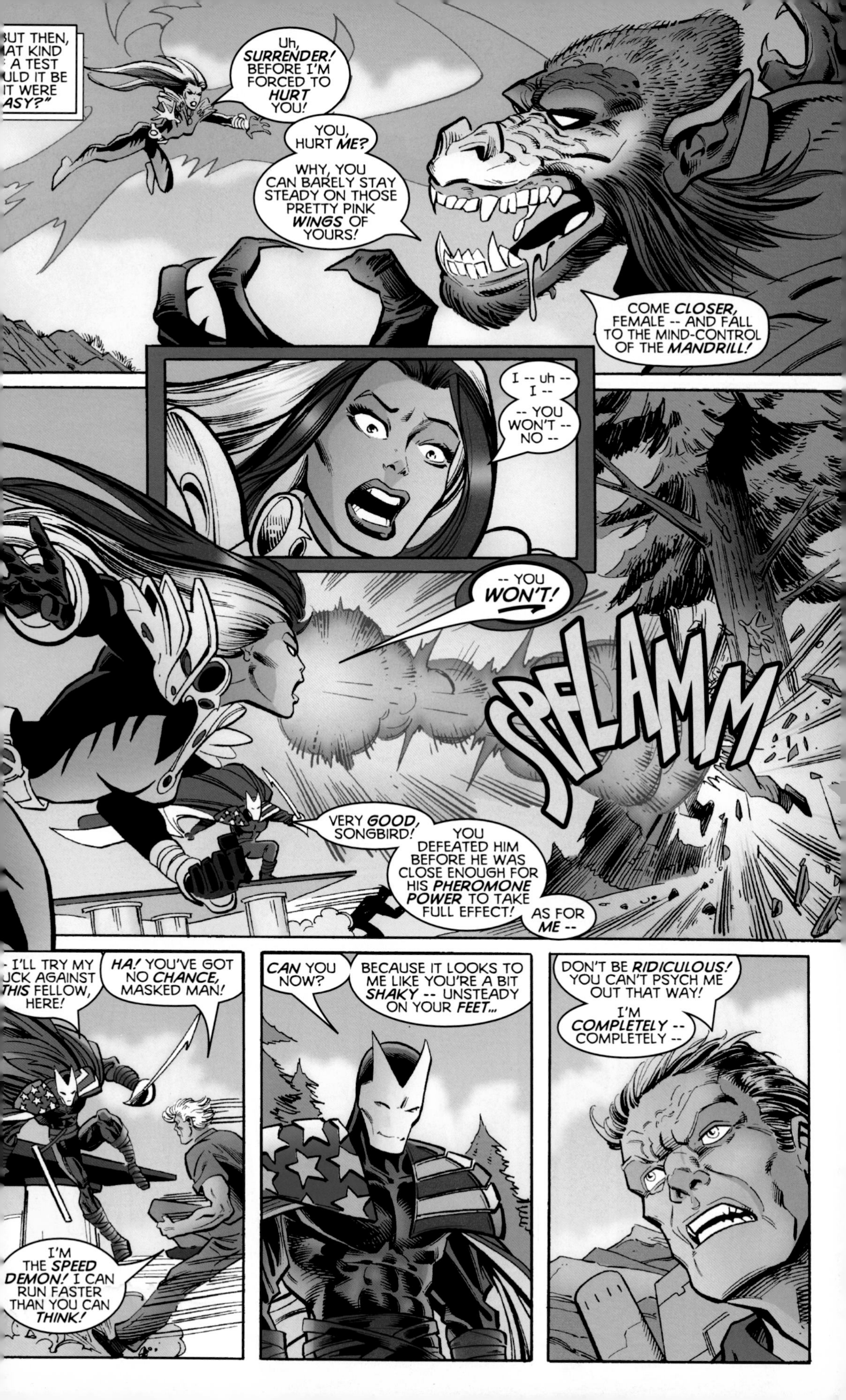

BUT THEN, WHAT KIND OF A TEST WOULD IT BE IF IT WERE EASY?"
Uh, SURRENDER! BEFORE I'M FORCED TO HURT YOU!
YOU, HURT ME?
WHY, YOU CAN BARELY STAY STEADY ON THOSE PRETTY PINK WINGS OF YOURS!
COME CLOSER, FEMALE -- AND FALL TO THE MIND-CONTROL OF THE MANDRILL!
I -- uh -- I --
-- YOU WON'T -- NO --
-- YOU WON'T!
SPFLAMM
VERY GOOD, SONGBIRD!
YOU DEFEATED HIM BEFORE HE WAS CLOSE ENOUGH FOR HIS PHEROMONE POWER TO TAKE FULL EFFECT!
AS FOR ME --
-- I'LL TRY MY LUCK AGAINST THIS FELLOW, HERE!
HA! YOU'VE GOT NO CHANCE, MASKED MAN!
I'M THE SPEED DEMON! I CAN RUN FASTER THAN YOU CAN THINK!
CAN YOU NOW?
BECAUSE IT LOOKS TO ME LIKE YOU'RE A BIT SHAKY -- UNSTEADY ON YOUR FEET...
DON'T BE RIDICULOUS! YOU CAN'T PSYCH ME OUT THAT WAY!
I'M COMPLETELY -- COMPLETELY --

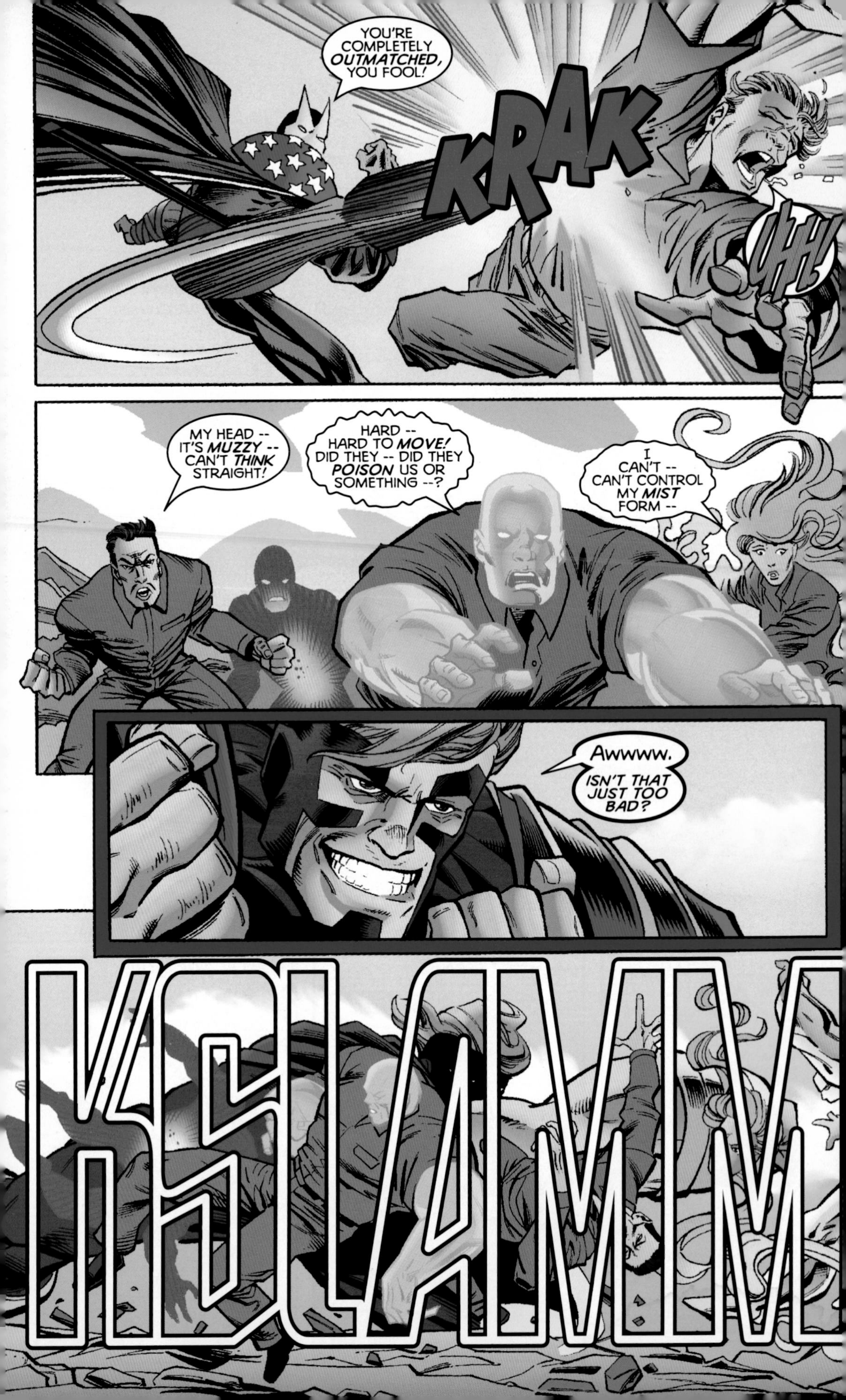
YOU'RE COMPLETELY OUTMATCHED, YOU FOOL!
KRAK
UHH!
MY HEAD -- IT'S MUZZY -- CAN'T THINK STRAIGHT!
HARD -- HARD TO MOVE! DID THEY -- DID THEY POISON US OR SOMETHING --?
I CAN'T -- CAN'T CONTROL MY MIST FORM --
Awwww. ISN'T THAT JUST TOO BAD?
KSLAMM

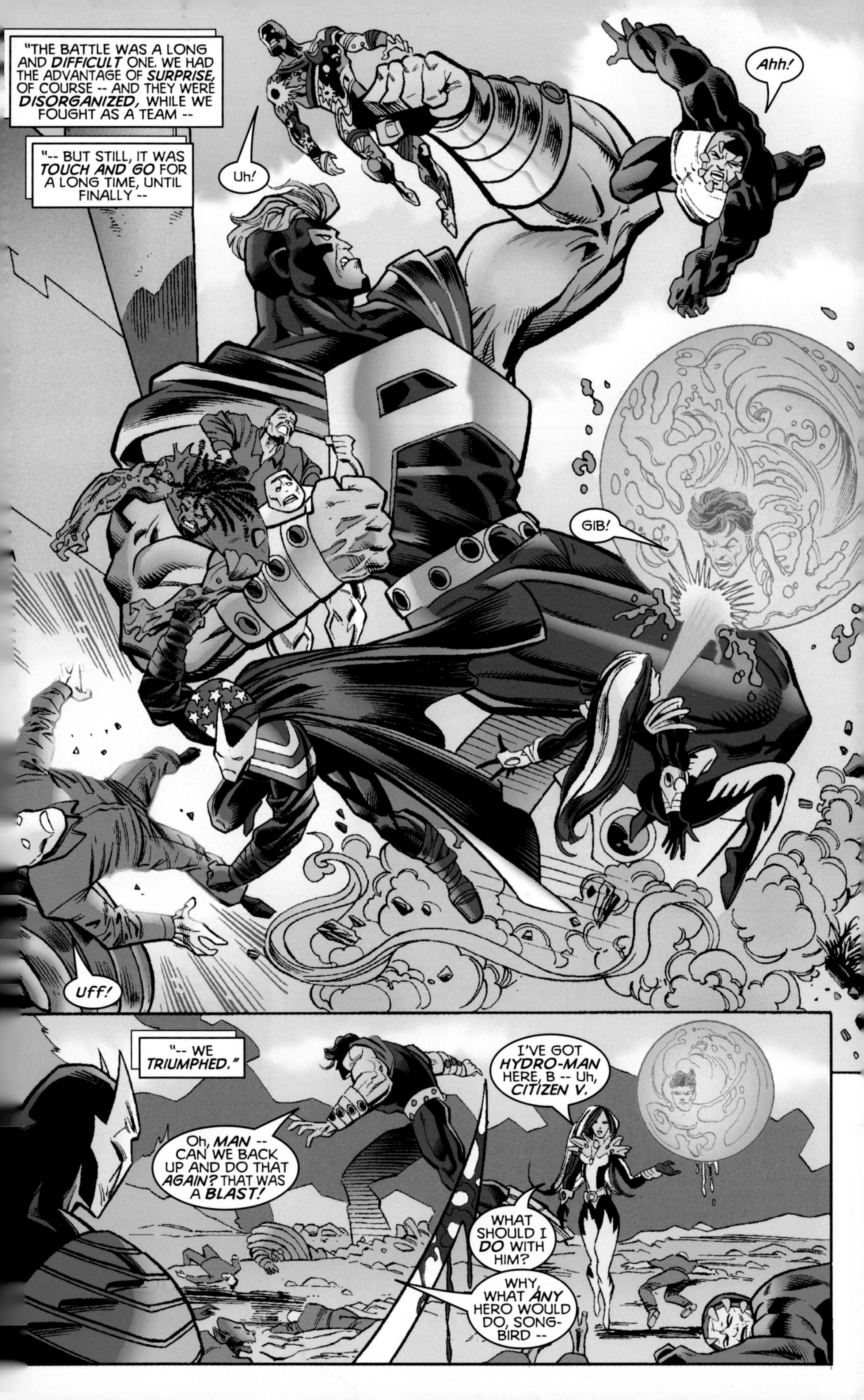
"THE BATTLE WAS A LONG AND DIFFICULT ONE. WE HAD THE ADVANTAGE OF SURPRISE, OF COURSE -- AND THEY WERE DISORGANIZED, WHILE WE FOUGHT AS A TEAM --
"-- BUT STILL, IT WAS TOUCH AND GO FOR A LONG TIME, UNTIL FINALLY --
Uh!
Ahh!
GIB!
Uff!
"-- WE TRIUMPHED."
Oh, MAN -- CAN WE BACK UP AND DO THAT AGAIN? THAT WAS A BLAST!
I'VE GOT HYDRO-MAN HERE, B -- Uh, CITIZEN V.
WHAT SHOULD I DO WITH HIM?
WHY, WHAT ANY HERO WOULD DO, SONG-BIRD --

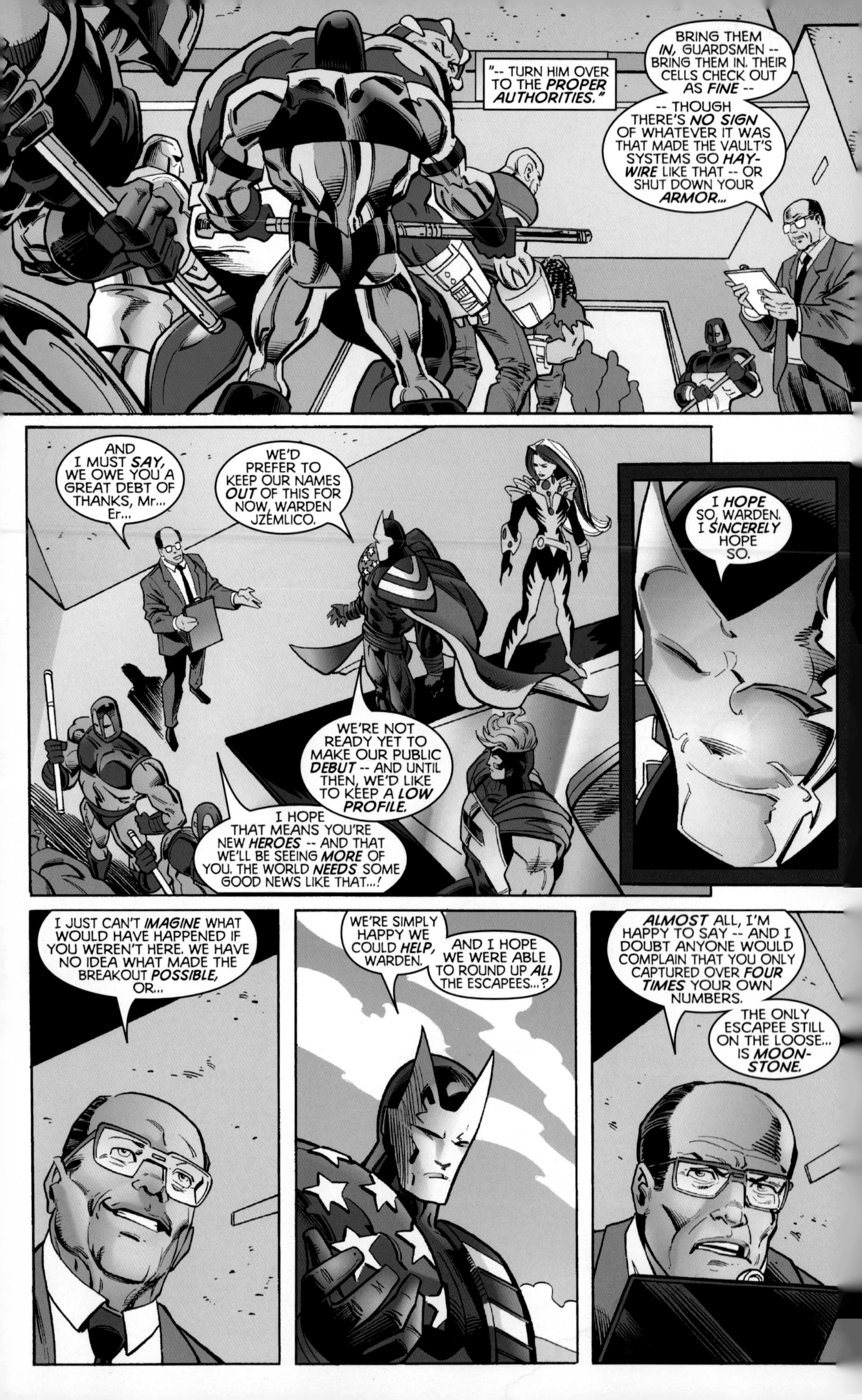
"-- TURN HIM OVER TO THE PROPER AUTHORITIES."
BRING THEM IN, GUARDSMEN -- BRING THEM IN. THEIR CELLS CHECK OUT AS FINE --
-- THOUGH THERE'S NO SIGN OF WHATEVER IT WAS THAT MADE THE VAULT'S SYSTEMS GO HAY-WIRE LIKE THAT -- OR SHUT DOWN YOUR ARMOR...
AND I MUST SAY, WE OWE YOU A GREAT DEBT OF THANKS, Mr... Er...
WE'D PREFER TO KEEP OUR NAMES OUT OF THIS FOR NOW, WARDEN JZEMLICO.
WE'RE NOT READY YET TO MAKE OUR PUBLIC DEBUT -- AND UNTIL THEN, WE'D LIKE TO KEEP A LOW PROFILE.
I HOPE THAT MEANS YOU'RE NEW HEROES -- AND THAT WE'LL BE SEEING MORE OF YOU. THE WORLD NEEDS SOME GOOD NEWS LIKE THAT...!
I HOPE SO, WARDEN. I SINCERELY HOPE SO.
I JUST CAN'T IMAGINE WHAT WOULD HAVE HAPPENED IF YOU WEREN'T HERE. WE HAVE NO IDEA WHAT MADE THE BREAKOUT POSSIBLE, OR...
WE'RE SIMPLY HAPPY WE COULD HELP, WARDEN.
AND I HOPE WE WERE ABLE TO ROUND UP ALL THE ESCAPEES...?
ALMOST ALL, I'M HAPPY TO SAY -- AND I DOUBT ANYONE WOULD COMPLAIN THAT YOU ONLY CAPTURED OVER FOUR TIMES YOUR OWN NUMBERS.
THE ONLY ESCAPEE STILL ON THE LOOSE... IS MOON-STONE.

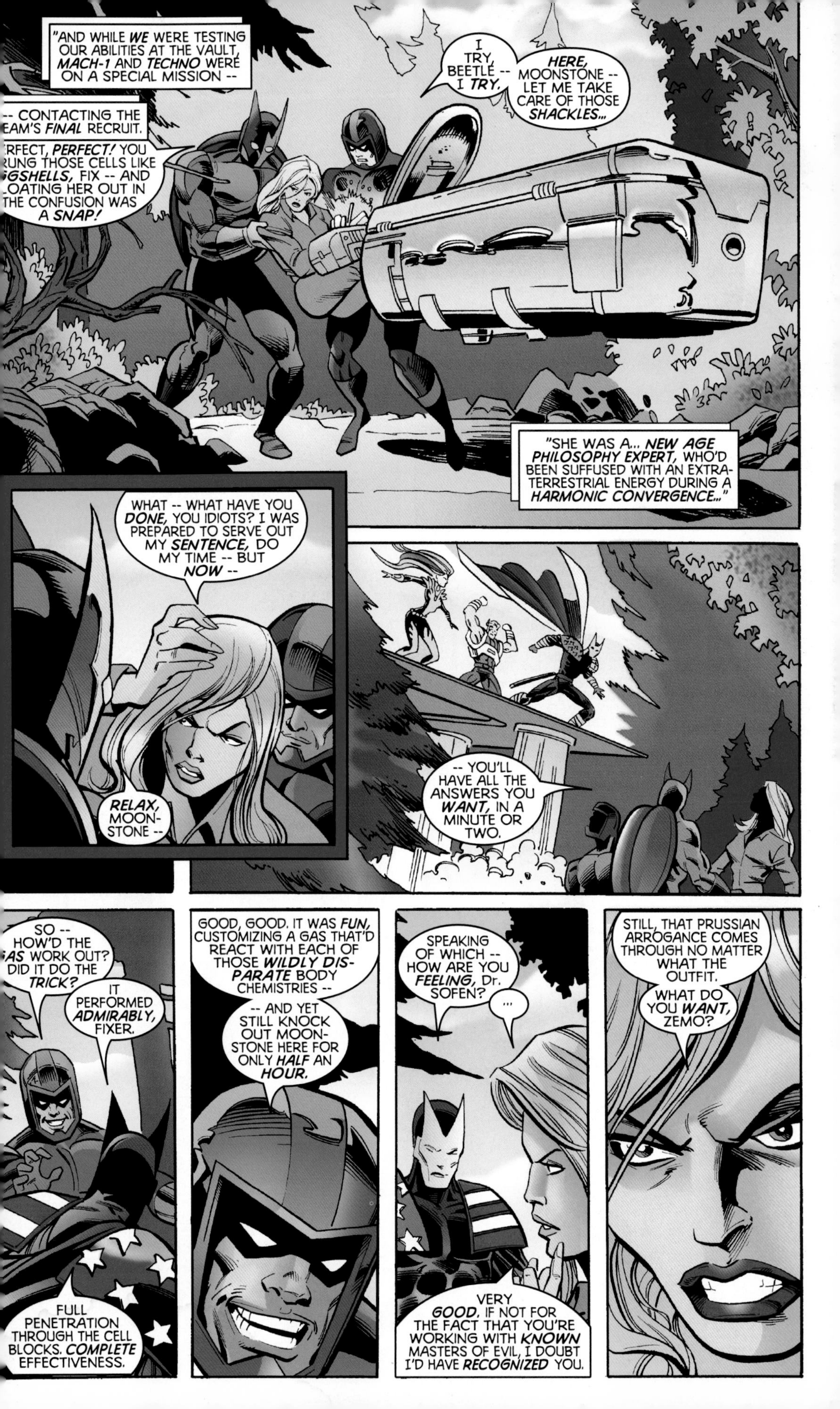
"AND WHILE WE WERE TESTING OUR ABILITIES AT THE VAULT, MACH-1 AND TECHNO WERE ON A SPECIAL MISSION --
-- CONTACTING THE EAM'S FINAL RECRUIT.
RFECT, PERFECT! YOU RUNG THOSE CELLS LIKE GSHELLS, FIX -- AND OATING HER OUT IN THE CONFUSION WAS A SNAP!
I TRY, BEETLE -- I TRY.
HERE, MOONSTONE -- LET ME TAKE CARE OF THOSE SHACKLES...
"SHE WAS A... NEW AGE PHILOSOPHY EXPERT, WHO'D BEEN SUFFUSED WITH AN EXTRA-TERRESTRIAL ENERGY DURING A HARMONIC CONVERGENCE..."
WHAT -- WHAT HAVE YOU DONE, YOU IDIOTS? I WAS PREPARED TO SERVE OUT MY SENTENCE, DO MY TIME -- BUT NOW --
RELAX, MOON-STONE --
-- YOU'LL HAVE ALL THE ANSWERS YOU WANT, IN A MINUTE OR TWO.
SO -- HOW'D THE GAS WORK OUT? DID IT DO THE TRICK?
IT PERFORMED ADMIRABLY, FIXER.
FULL PENETRATION THROUGH THE CELL BLOCKS. COMPLETE EFFECTIVENESS.
GOOD, GOOD. IT WAS FUN, CUSTOMIZING A GAS THAT'D REACT WITH EACH OF THOSE WILDLY DIS-PARATE BODY CHEMISTRIES --
-- AND YET STILL KNOCK OUT MOON-STONE HERE FOR ONLY HALF AN HOUR.
SPEAKING OF WHICH -- HOW ARE YOU FEELING, Dr. SOFEN?
...
VERY GOOD, IF NOT FOR THE FACT THAT YOU'RE WORKING WITH KNOWN MASTERS OF EVIL, I DOUBT I'D HAVE RECOGNIZED YOU.
STILL, THAT PRUSSIAN ARROGANCE COMES THROUGH NO MATTER WHAT THE OUTFIT.
WHAT DO YOU WANT, ZEMO?

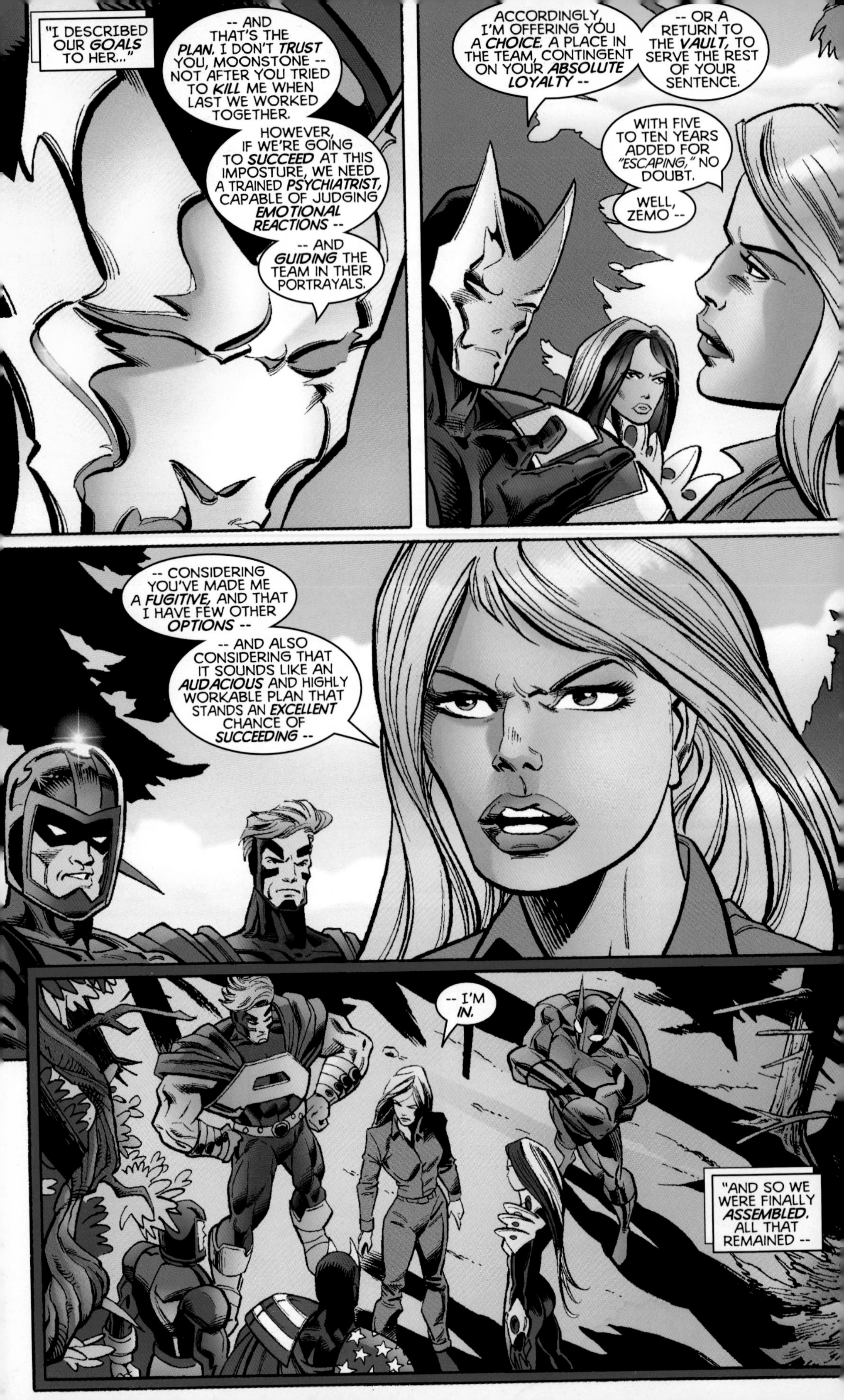
"I DESCRIBED OUR GOALS TO HER..."
-- AND THAT'S THE PLAN. I DON'T TRUST YOU, MOONSTONE -- NOT AFTER YOU TRIED TO KILL ME WHEN LAST WE WORKED TOGETHER.
HOWEVER, IF WE'RE GOING TO SUCCEED AT THIS IMPOSTURE, WE NEED A TRAINED PSYCHIATRIST, CAPABLE OF JUDGING EMOTIONAL REACTIONS --
-- AND GUIDING THE TEAM IN THEIR PORTRAYALS.
ACCORDINGLY, I'M OFFERING YOU A CHOICE. A PLACE IN THE TEAM, CONTINGENT ON YOUR ABSOLUTE LOYALTY --
-- OR A RETURN TO THE VAULT, TO SERVE THE REST OF YOUR SENTENCE.
WITH FIVE TO TEN YEARS ADDED FOR "ESCAPING," NO DOUBT.
WELL, ZEMO --
-- CONSIDERING YOU'VE MADE ME A FUGITIVE, AND THAT I HAVE FEW OTHER OPTIONS --
-- AND ALSO CONSIDERING THAT IT SOUNDS LIKE AN AUDACIOUS AND HIGHLY WORKABLE PLAN THAT STANDS AN EXCELLENT CHANCE OF SUCCEEDING --
-- I'M IN.
"AND SO WE WERE FINALLY ASSEMBLED. ALL THAT REMAINED --

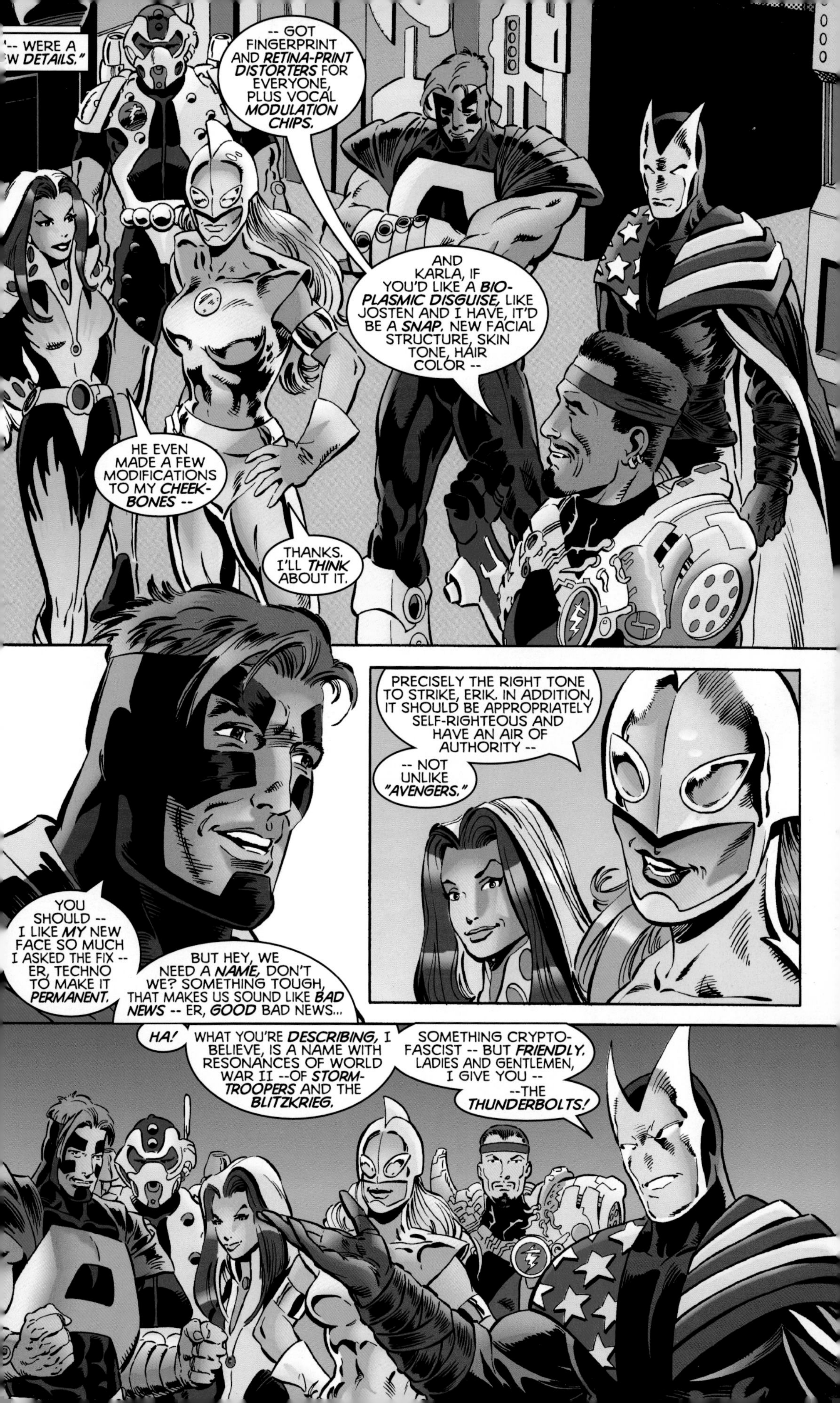

"-- WERE A FEW DETAILS."
-- GOT FINGERPRINT AND RETINA-PRINT DISTORTERS FOR EVERYONE, PLUS VOCAL MODULATION CHIPS.
AND KARLA, IF YOU'D LIKE A BIO-PLASMIC DISGUISE, LIKE JOSTEN AND I HAVE, IT'D BE A SNAP. NEW FACIAL STRUCTURE, SKIN TONE, HAIR COLOR --
HE EVEN MADE A FEW MODIFICATIONS TO MY CHEEK-BONES --
THANKS. I'LL THINK ABOUT IT.
YOU SHOULD -- I LIKE MY NEW FACE SO MUCH I ASKED THE FIX -- ER, TECHNO TO MAKE IT PERMANENT.
BUT HEY, WE NEED A NAME, DON'T WE? SOMETHING TOUGH, THAT MAKES US SOUND LIKE BAD NEWS -- ER, GOOD BAD NEWS...
PRECISELY THE RIGHT TONE TO STRIKE, ERIK. IN ADDITION, IT SHOULD BE APPROPRIATELY SELF-RIGHTEOUS AND HAVE AN AIR OF AUTHORITY --
-- NOT UNLIKE "AVENGERS."
HA!
WHAT YOU'RE DESCRIBING, I BELIEVE, IS A NAME WITH RESONANCES OF WORLD WAR II --OF STORM-TROOPERS AND THE BLITZKRIEG.
SOMETHING CRYPTO-FASCIST -- BUT FRIENDLY. LADIES AND GENTLEMEN, I GIVE YOU --
--THE THUNDERBOLTS!

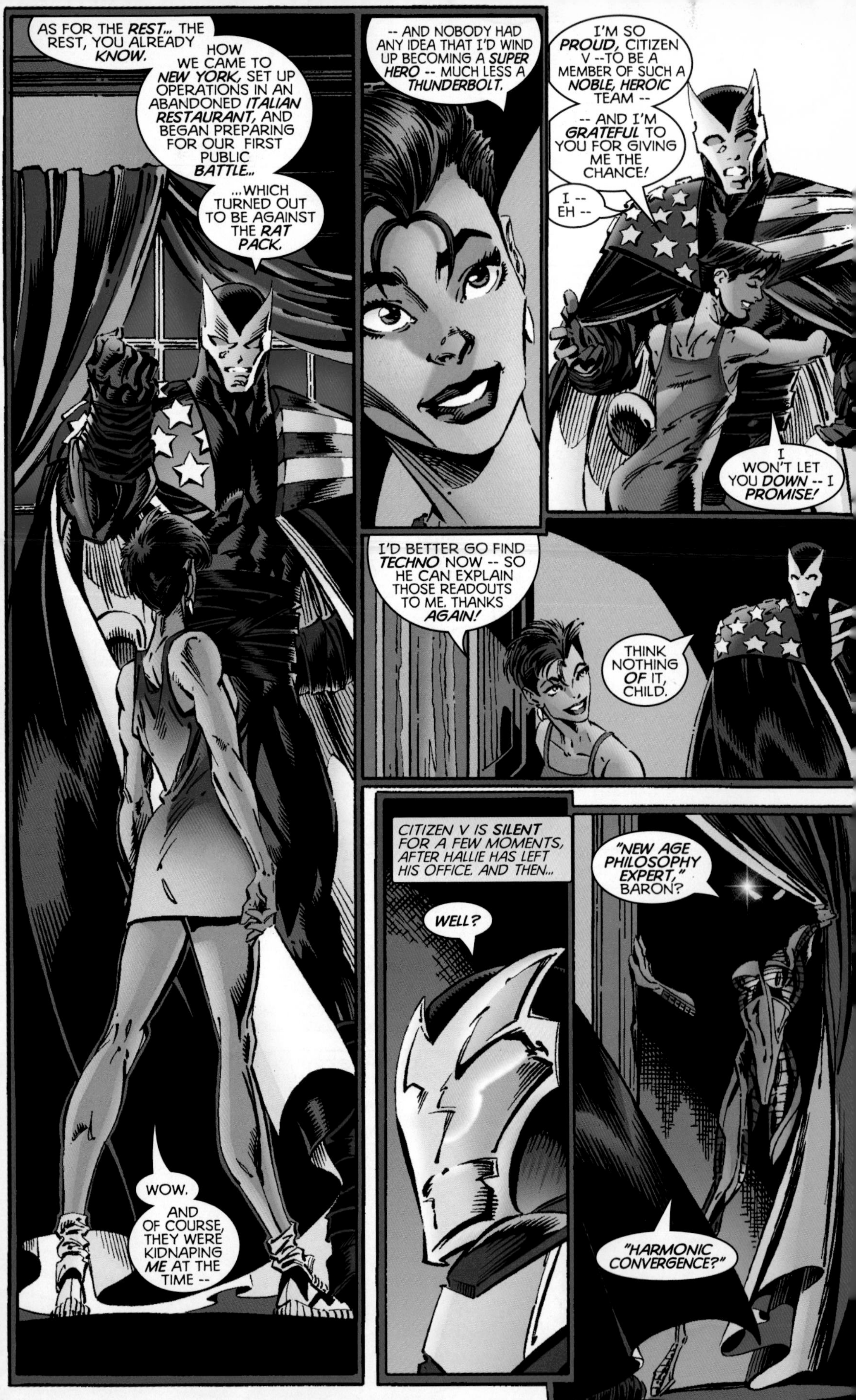
AS FOR THE REST... THE REST, YOU ALREADY KNOW.
HOW WE CAME TO NEW YORK, SET UP OPERATIONS IN AN ABANDONED ITALIAN RESTAURANT, AND BEGAN PREPARING FOR OUR FIRST PUBLIC BATTLE...
...WHICH TURNED OUT TO BE AGAINST THE RAT PACK.
WOW.
AND OF COURSE, THEY WERE KIDNAPING ME AT THE TIME --
-- AND NOBODY HAD ANY IDEA THAT I'D WIND UP BECOMING A SUPER HERO -- MUCH LESS A THUNDERBOLT.
I'M SO PROUD, CITIZEN V --TO BE A MEMBER OF SUCH A NOBLE, HEROIC TEAM --
-- AND I'M GRATEFUL TO YOU FOR GIVING ME THE CHANCE!
I -- EH --
I WON'T LET YOU DOWN -- I PROMISE!
I'D BETTER GO FIND TECHNO NOW -- SO HE CAN EXPLAIN THOSE READOUTS TO ME. THANKS AGAIN!
THINK NOTHING OF IT, CHILD.
CITIZEN V IS SILENT FOR A FEW MOMENTS, AFTER HALLIE HAS LEFT HIS OFFICE. AND THEN...
WELL?
"NEW AGE PHILOSOPHY EXPERT," BARON?
"HARMONIC CONVERGENCE?"

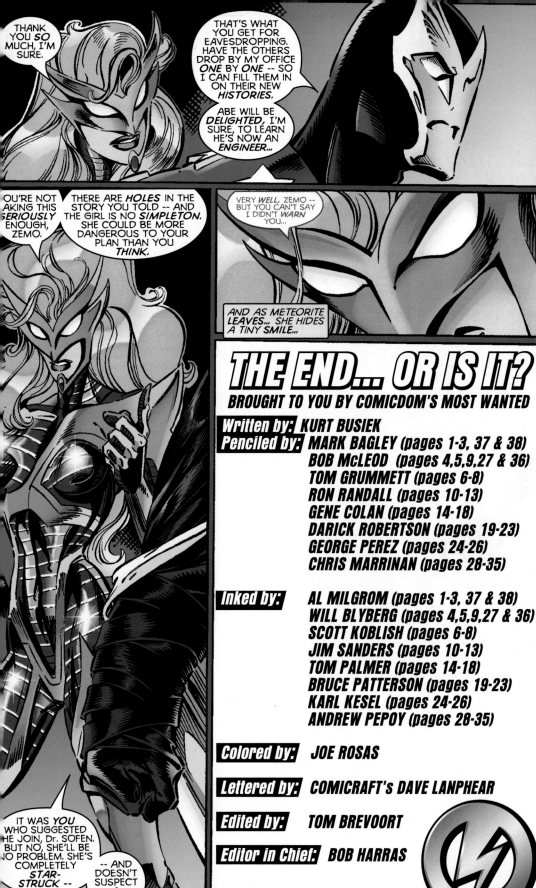

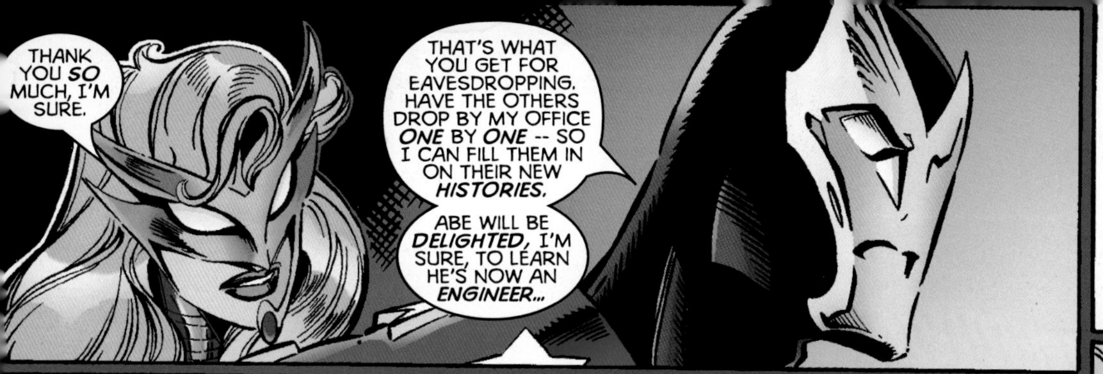
THANK YOU *SO* MUCH, I'M SURE.
THAT'S WHAT YOU GET FOR EAVESDROPPING. HAVE THE OTHERS DROP BY MY OFFICE *ONE* BY *ONE* -- SO I CAN FILL THEM IN ON THEIR NEW *HISTORIES.*
ABE WILL BE *DELIGHTED,* I'M SURE, TO LEARN HE'S NOW AN *ENGINEER...*

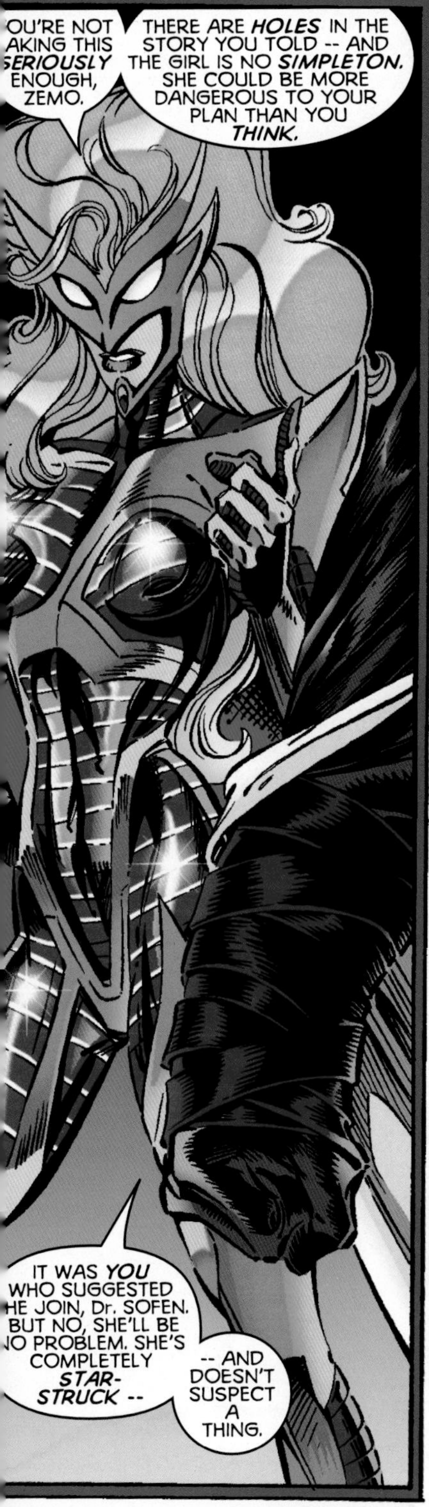
OU'RE NOT AKING THIS *ERIOUSLY* ENOUGH, ZEMO.
THERE ARE *HOLES* IN THE STORY YOU TOLD -- AND THE GIRL IS NO *SIMPLETON.* SHE COULD BE MORE DANGEROUS TO YOUR PLAN THAN YOU *THINK.*
IT WAS *YOU* WHO SUGGESTED HE JOIN, Dr. SOFEN. BUT NO, SHE'LL BE O PROBLEM. SHE'S COMPLETELY *STAR-STRUCK* --
-- AND DOESN'T SUSPECT A THING.

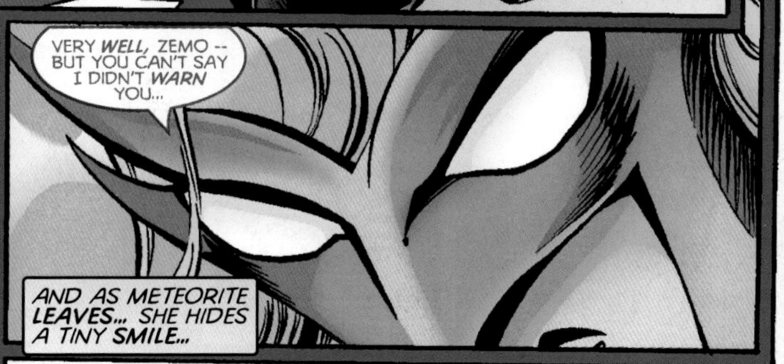
VERY *WELL,* ZEMO -- BUT YOU CAN'T SAY I DIDN'T *WARN* YOU...
AND AS METEORITE *LEAVES...* SHE HIDES A TINY *SMILE...*

THE END... OR IS IT?

BROUGHT TO YOU BY COMICDOM'S MOST WANTED

Written by: KURT BUSIEK

Penciled by: MARK BAGLEY (pages 1-3, 37 & 38)
BOB McLEOD (pages 4,5,9,27 & 36)
TOM GRUMMETT (pages 6-8)
RON RANDALL (pages 10-13)
GENE COLAN (pages 14-18)
DARICK ROBERTSON (pages 19-23)
GEORGE PEREZ (pages 24-26)
CHRIS MARRINAN (pages 28-35)

Inked by: AL MILGROM (pages 1-3, 37 & 38)
WILL BLYBERG (pages 4,5,9,27 & 36)
SCOTT KOBLISH (pages 6-8)
JIM SANDERS (pages 10-13)
TOM PALMER (pages 14-18)
BRUCE PATTERSON (pages 19-23)
KARL KESEL (pages 24-26)
ANDREW PEPOY (pages 28-35)

Colored by: JOE ROSAS

Lettered by: COMICRAFT's DAVE LANPHEAR

Edited by: TOM BREVOORT

Editor in Chief: BOB HARRAS

Also Available From

MARVEL®

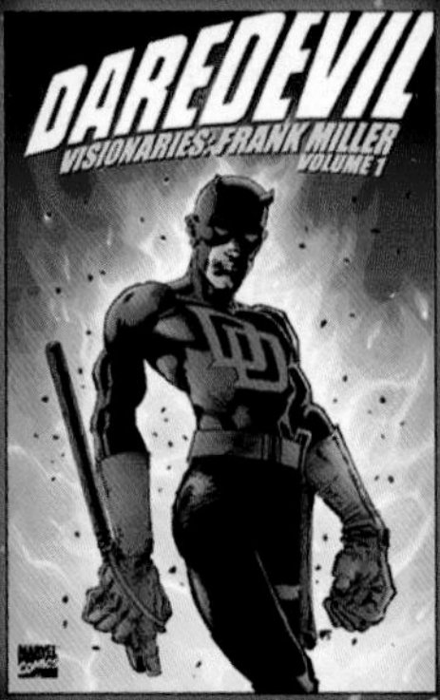
DAREDEVIL
VISIONARIES: FRANK MILLER
VOLUME 1

Daredevil Visionaries: Frank Miller Vol. 1
$17.95 US $27.50 CAN
ISBN # 07851-0757-6

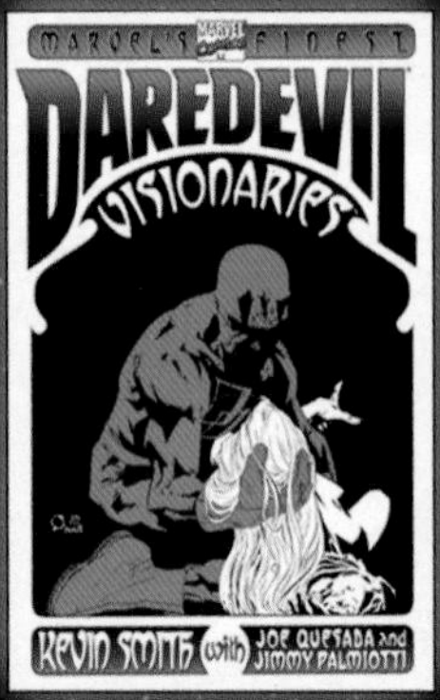
MARVEL'S FINEST
DAREDEVIL
VISIONARIES
KEVIN SMITH with JOE QUESADA and JIMMY PALMIOTTI

Daredevil Visionaries: Kevin Smith
$19.95 US $29.95 CAN
ISBN # 07851-0737-1

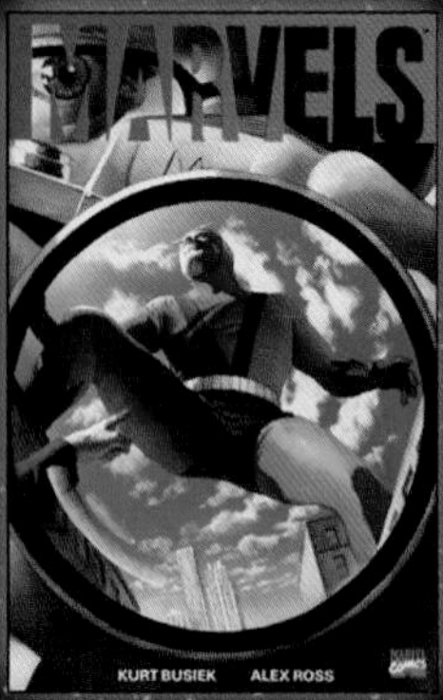
MARVELS
KURT BUSIEK
ALEX ROSS

Marvels
$19.95 US $29.95 CAN
ISBN # 07851-0049-0

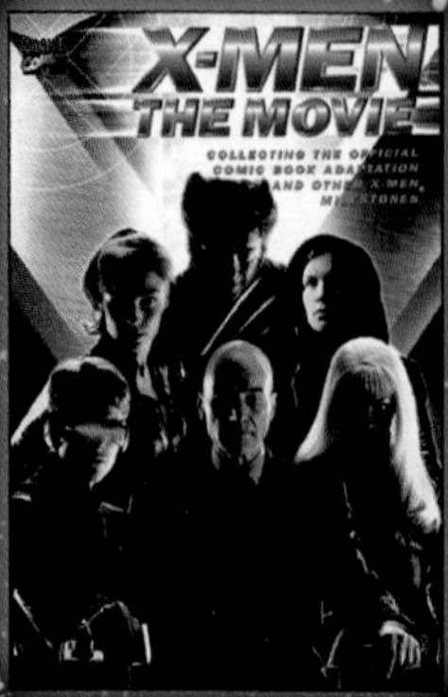
X-MEN
THE MOVIE

X-Men: The Movie
$14.95 US $21.95 CAN
ISBN # 07851-0749-5

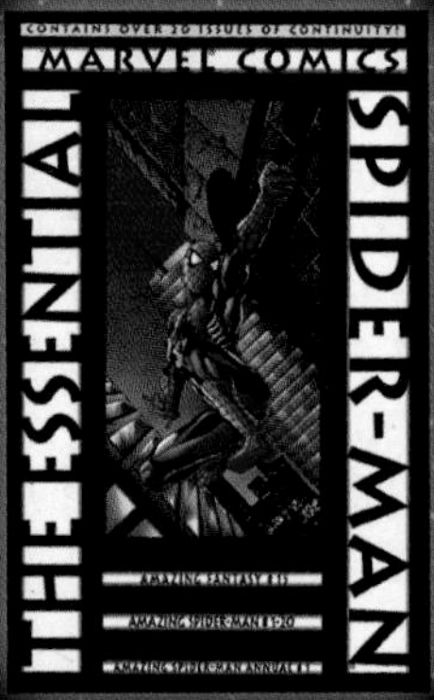
MARVEL COMICS
THE ESSENTIAL
SPIDER-MAN

The Essential Spider-Man Vol. 1
$14.95 US $21.95 CAN
ISBN # 07851-0658-8

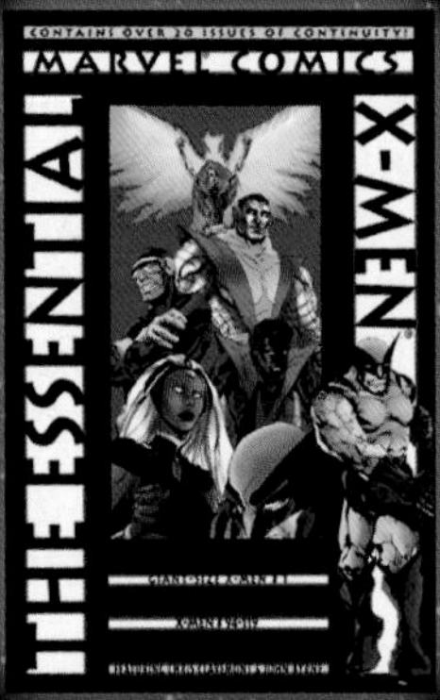
MARVEL COMICS
THE ESSENTIAL
X-MEN

The Essential X-Men Vol. 1
$14.95 US $21.95 CAN
ISBN # 07851-0256-6

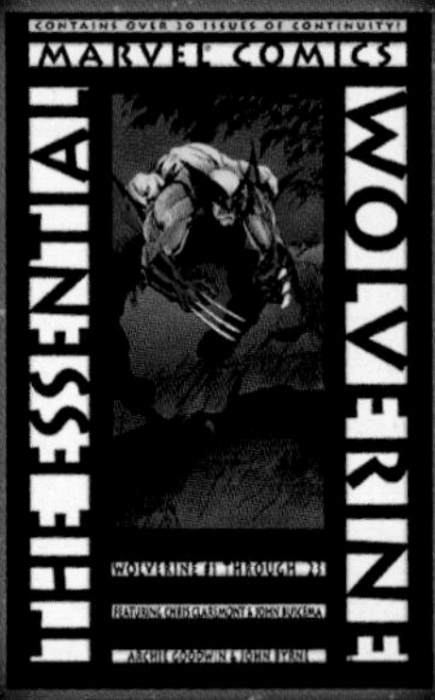
MARVEL COMICS
THE ESSENTIAL
WOLVERINE

The Essential Wolverine Vol. 1
$14.95 US $21.95 CAN
ISBN # 07851-0257-4

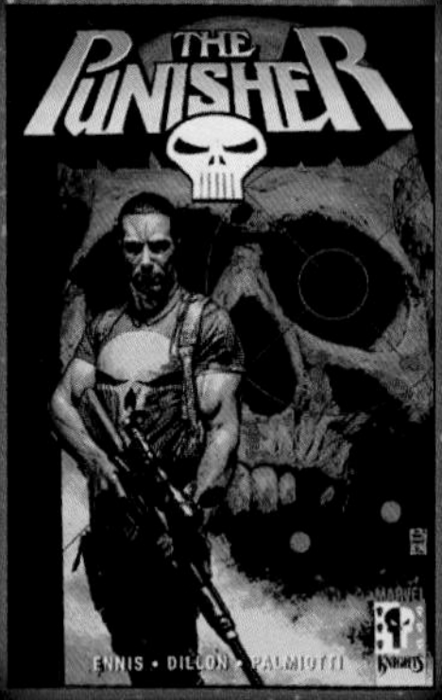
THE PUNISHER
ENNIS • DILLON • PALMIOTTI

The Punisher
$24.95 US $37.95 CAN
ISBN # 07851-0783-5

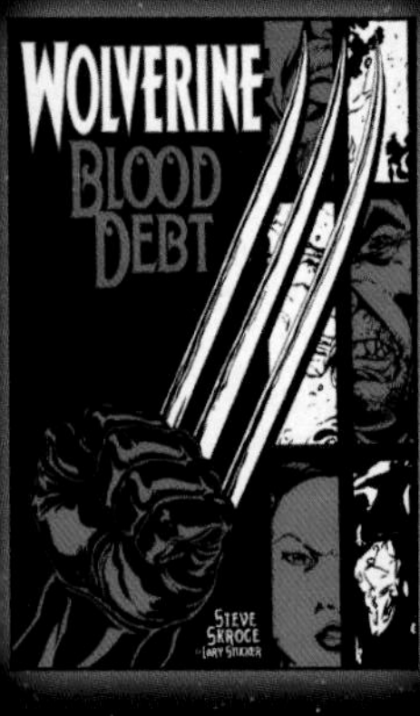
WOLVERINE
BLOOD
DEBT
STEVE SKROCE

Wolverine: Blood Debt
$12.95 US $19.95 CAN
ISBN # 07851-0785-1

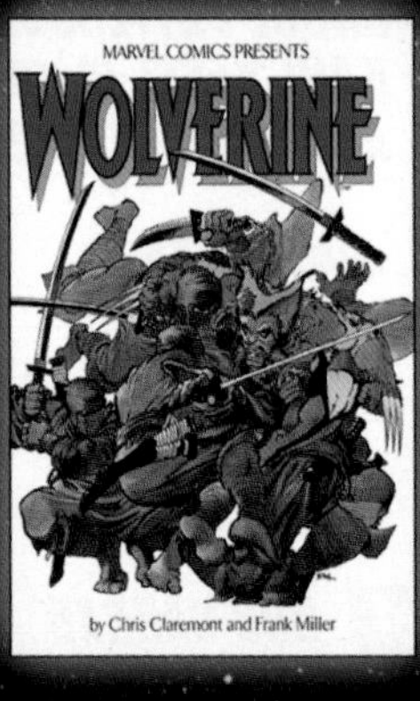
MARVEL COMICS PRESENTS
WOLVERINE
by Chris Claremont and Frank Miller

Wolverine
$12.95 US $19.95 CAN
ISBN # 087135277X

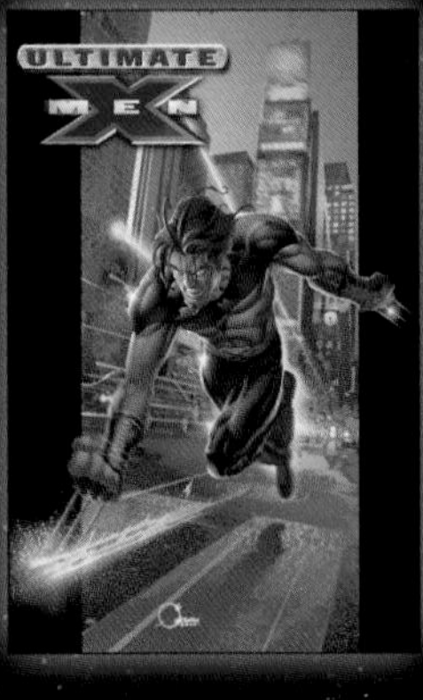
ULTIMATE
X-MEN

Ultimate X-Men
$14.95 US $21.95 CAN
ISBN # 07851-0788-6

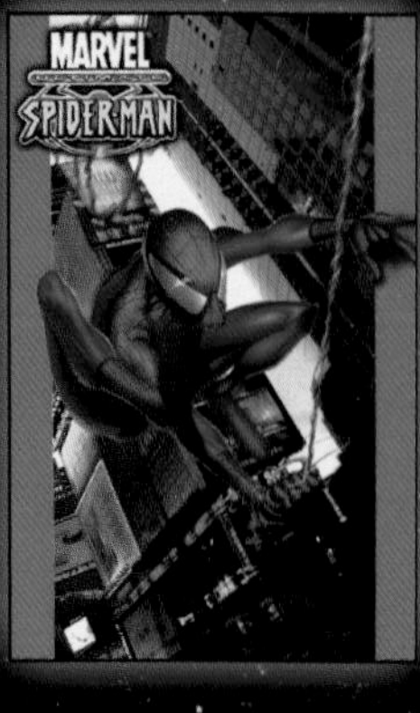
MARVEL
SPIDER-MAN

Ultimate Spider-Man
$14.95 US $21.95 CAN
ISBN # 07851-0774-6